D0461116

WITHDRAWN

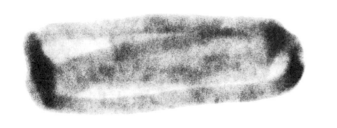

THE RELIGIOUS RIGHT

A Reference Handbook
Third Edition

THE RELIGIOUS RIGHT

A Reference Handbook
Third Edition

Glenn H. Utter and John W. Storey

Grey House
Publishing

PUBLISHER:	Leslie Mackenzie
EDITORIAL DIRECTOR:	Laura Mars-Proietti
MARKETING DIRECTOR:	Jessica Moody

AUTHORS:	Glenn H. Utter and John W. Storey
COPYEDITOR:	Elaine Alibrandi
COMPOSITION & DESIGN:	ATLIS Systems

Grey House Publishing, Inc.
185 Millerton Road
Millerton, NY 12546
518.789.8700
FAX 518.789.0545
www.greyhouse.com
e-mail: books @greyhouse.com

Publisher's Cataloging-In-Publication Data
(Prepared by The Donohue Group, Inc.)

Utter, Glenn H.

   The religious right : a reference handbook / Glenn H. Utter and John W. Storey. — 3rd ed.

   p. : ill. ; cm.

   Previous editions published: Santa Barbara, Calif. : ABC-CLIO.
   Includes bibliographical references and index.
   ISBN: 978-1-59237-113-6

1. Religious right—United States. 2. Christianity and politics—United States. 3. Religious right—United States—Bibliography. 4. Christianity and politics—United States—Bibliography. I. Storey, John W. (John Woodrow), 1939- II. Title.

BR526 .U88 2007
277.3/0825

Contents

6 Directory of Organizations

7 Suggested Readings

8 Selected Multimedia Resources

Introduction

This is the third edition of *The Religious Right: A Reference Handbook*. The two previous editions were published by ABC-CLIO, this is the first published by Grey House Publishing.

Features of the new edition:

- The authoritative experience of authors Glenn H. Utter and John W. Storey, presenting a balanced view of a most controversial and passionate topic
- Currency of data, with all elements verified and updated through 2006
- New articles, 12 new biographical profiles, and dozens of photographs
- Improvements to organization and accessibility of data, including an expanded Table of Contents, plus helpful introductory material for individual chapters
- A new section with 13 primary source documents

Chapter Summaries

1. The *Introduction,* a 30-page essay titled *The Religious Right in America* begins its discussion in 1919, with the adoption of the Eighteenth Amendment on Prohibition, continues through the 2004 Presidential election and ends by discussing recent judicial appointments and the increased intensity of the religious right's political activism.
2. A *Chronology* that ranges from 1835, marking publication of the controversial *The Life of Jesus* to 2006, when President Bush aligned with the religious right, rejecting congressional legislation that would ease federal funding for stem cell research. This edition includes 32 new chronological entries
3. *Biographical Profiles* now total 54 with 12 new profiles: David Barton; Ted Haggard; Richard Land; Joyce Meyer; Richard John Neuhaus; Rodney Lee Parsley; Paige Patterson; Tony Perkins; Paul

Pressler; Rick Santorum; Phyllis Schlafly; and Rick Warren. Many profiles are now accompanied by photographs.

4. *Analysis of Survey Data* has been updated with survey data from both the National Opinion Center and Baylor Institute for Studies of Religion. This chapter offers 16 tables on topics ranging from *Belief in God* to *Religious Preferences and Marital Status*. Survey results are analyzed in detail.

5. *Primary Documents & Quotations* is a new chapter that includes two main sections—*Religious Right Views* and *Commentary on the Religious Right*, each with several sub topics that range from *Culture and the Culture War* to the *Right to Bear Arms*. This chapter includes both quotations—39 new to this edition—and 13 articles—all new to this edition. These articles include work by prominent writers and journalists and discuss intelligent design, voting as Christians, and apocalypse.

6. *Directory of Organizations* includes 73 organizations both in support of (62), and critical of (11), the religious right. Each updated listing includes contact information, key contacts and publications, as well as a detailed description of the organization's history and activities.

7. *Suggested Readings* (previously called Print Resources) offers three distinct sections—works from the religious right, about the religious right, and organization periodicals. These are further broken down into *biographies, educational works* and *political works*. Each listing includes not only title, author and publisher, but also a thoughtful description. There are 36 new listings to this edition.

8. *Multimedia Resources* (previously called Non-Print Resources) includes 8 categories from *DVDs* to *Radio and Television*, including an article on TV Evangelists. Each listing includes length, price, source and a brief description. This edition includes 70 new multimedia resource listings.

The Religious Right: A Reference Handbook ends with a *Glossary* and *Index*.

Preface

In 1930 Ludwig Wittgenstein, an eminent philosopher, remarked in a foreword that he would like to say "This book is written to the glory of God." But he thought better of it, fearing that readers of the time would misunderstand the intent that he had written not out of pride and vanity but goodwill. A reference to the glory of God at one time would have been appropriate, perhaps even expected. That Wittgenstein thought the purpose of his expression would be lost on a large portion of the population of the 1930s attested to the trend toward secularization, a trend that haunts many Americans today, large majorities of who have consistently expressed a belief in God. In weighing the potential for success of the contemporary religious right, the ongoing effects of secularization must be kept in mind.

Terms such as *religious right* and *Christian right* are difficult to pin down largely because they encompass groups of considerable diversity, ranging from mainline and evangelical Protestants to conservative Jews and Catholics. "Religious Right" has generally been the expression of choice for the authors, as it is somewhat more inclusive than "Christian right." This latter phrase makes it awkward to include Jews, for instance, some of who have identified with Christian conservatives on various issues. Another problem arises with regard to the term *evangelical*. Specifically, who are the evangelicals, and are they all on the political right? To answer the second half of the question first — no. Evangelicals are to be found on both sides of the spectrum. The Sojourners offer a case in point. Theological conservatism notwithstanding, this group is on the left with regard to matters such as poverty and nuclear disarmament. It looks at issues from the vantage point of those at the bottom of society. African American evangelicals likewise often join the left in debates over civil rights and other concerns.

Evangelical is almost as elusive a term as *religious right*. Theologically, an evangelical is one who claims a personal relationship with Jesus based upon a "born-again" experience, accepts the authority of the Bible in matters of faith and practice, and spreads the gospel through evangelism. Since the early 1800s most American Protestants, save Episcopalians, have been evangelicals. Historically, the term is derived from the Greek *evangelion*, meaning "good news," and it was applied in the sixteenth century to Lutherans in Germany; in the eighteenth century to those Anglicans who introduced hymn singing, Sunday schools, and missionary societies; in the late nineteenth and early twentieth century to Pentecostals in America; and since the 1940s to conservative American Protestants who wish to be differentiated from fundamentalists. In this last sense, the difference is more a matter of temperament than theology. Jerry Falwell is a fundamentalist; Billy Graham is an evangelical. Although in this book we frequently use *evangelical* as a catchall for all conservative Protestants, we just as frequently distinguish between mainline bodies, such as Presbyterians, Methodists, Episcopalians, Disciples of Christ, and evangelical groups, such as Southern Baptists, Assemblies of God, Missouri Synod Lutherans, and Churches of Christ.

Individuals such as J. Gresham Machen and Cyrus Scofield have been included in this study because they provide continuity, showing that various facets of the contemporary religious right have roots in the nineteenth century. The premillennialism of Jerry Falwell can be seen in John Nelson Darby, for instance, and Francis Schaeffer's repudiation of secular humanism bears similarities to Machen's earlier condemnation of liberalism. Otherwise, this study deals only with individuals and organizations on the religious right that have endeavored since World War II to influence public policy through the political process. Thus, we treat the religious right as an essentially political movement that courts voters for "moral" candidates, lobbying Congress on everything from public school prayer to abortion, and joins religious conservatives in judicial proceedings involving home schooling, sex education, and textbooks. Accordingly, the focus is upon people such as Billy James Hargis, who fashioned the Christian Crusade, and Pat Robertson, founder of the Christian Coalition and more recently, D. James Kennedy, R.C. Sproul, and Marvin Olasky.

Alexis de Tocqueville, that observant Frenchman who traveled America during the presidency of Andrew Jackson, was impressed by this country's separation of church and state. Indeed, he noted that the American clergy prided itself on aloofness from politics. This stance was wise, he thought, for in nations such as his own, where the flag and the cross were allies, there was no way to criticize the state without rebuking the church. Americans, by contrast, could indulge in bitter political debates without trampling religious institutions. Of course, de Tocqueville was not altogether correct. The great political controversies in this country, from slavery to abortion, have always involved fundamental moral considerations. And the churches have readily joined the fray, fighting and dividing over these concerns. Still, de Tocqueville's observation seems basically sound. When religion identifies itself intimately with a political cause and then wraps that cause in the flag and anoints it with God, the opposition has little recourse but to attack both its political and religious adversaries. Over time, both the religious left and right have invoked God's blessing in behalf of political objectives and in so doing have at times shown a certain self-righteous arrogance; but the contemporary religious right has carried the identification of God and Caesar to a new level through its "moral" report cards which, on the basis of voting records, designate politicians as basically godly or ungodly. Most significantly, perhaps, these report cards disclose the intimacy between the current religious right and conservative Republicans. Among other things, this study helps to elucidate this development.

All aspects of this third edition have been updated and, in most cases, expanded. There are twelve new biographical entries, for example, and the chronology has been brought to December 2006. Moreover, the essay that follows this Preface discusses the heretofore-neglected relationship between the religious right, premillennial theology, and foreign policy. The fate of Israel, for instance, figures prominently in premillennial visions of the end of time, visions ardently embraced by many Christian conservatives on the religious right. This goes a long way toward explaining the fervent support of Israel by many religious conservatives in this country, such as Jerry Falwell and John Hagee. A testimony to the current popularity of premillennial expectations is witnessed in the astonishing success of the apocalyptic *Left Behind* thrillers of Tim LaHaye and Jerry Jenkins, novels that point toward Israel and a climactic battle between good and evil at Armageddon.

Once again, the authors would like to acknowledge the assistance of friends and colleagues, notably Professor Carol Atmar, a lecturer in the Lamar University history department who read much of the manuscript and offered useful suggestions, and Professor James True, the Jack Brooks Chair of Government and Public Service, and Thomas Sowers, assistant Professor of Political Science at Lamar University, both of whom provided valuable assistance in analyzing General Social Survey data.

Glenn H. Utter

John W. Storey

About the Authors

Glenn H. Utter, professor and chair of the Political Science Department at Lamar University, was educated at Binghamton University, the University of Buffalo, and the University of London. Utter specializes in modern political theory and American political thought. He wrote *Encyclopedia of Gun Control and Gun Rights* (2000); co-edited *American Political Scientists: A Dictionary* (1993, 2002); and co-wrote *Campaign and Election Reform* (1997), *Religion and Politics* (2002), and *Conservative Christians and Political Participation* (2004). He has written several articles for political science journals and other scholarly publications.

John W. Storey, educated at Lamar University, Baylor University, and the University of Kentucky is a specialist in southern religious history. His writings have appeared in numerous scholarly publications, and two of his previous studies, *Texas Baptist Leadership and Social Christianity, 1900–1980* (1986) and *Southern Baptists of Southeast Texas, 1888–1988* (1988), won the Texas Baptist Historical Society's Church History Award. He is currently professor and chair of the History Department at Lamar University.

1

The Religious Right in America

Impact in America

Thomas Jefferson's famous metaphor to the contrary notwithstanding, there has never been an absolute wall between church and state in American society. Ever since the Puritans came ashore in the early 1600s, religious leaders have often sought to influence public policy on a variety of social issues, and political leaders of all persuasions have just as readily appealed to the divine. A generation before the Civil War, for instance, the churches had already clashed and divided over slavery; in the late nineteenth and early twentieth centuries the social gospel inspired many churchgoers to pursue legislative remedies to urban, industrial ills; the adoption of the Eighteenth Amendment on prohibition in 1919 was a crowning achievement for the religious establishment; and today many religious bodies maintain lobbyists in the nation's capital to sway politicians on everything from prayer in public schools to world hunger.

To many religious leaders, political activism in no way violates the separation of church and state, for in their view religion has a responsibility to address vital issues. Likewise, public officials have often invoked the authority of religion, hinting that a divine force directed American history. Both Abraham Lincoln in his second inaugural and John F. Kennedy in his 1961 address, for instance, used a religious framework to explain national purpose. In 1949 Harry Truman described the Cold War as a contest between the powers of light and darkness; in 1953 'God's Float' led Dwight D. Eisenhower's inaugural parade; and since 2001 President George W. Bush, who as governor of Texas had appealed to many Christians by proclaiming June 10, 2000, "Jesus Day" in Texas, has frequently used the language of religion to justify domestic and foreign policies. Typical was his 2003 State of the Union address in which he spoke of the "power, wonder-working power, in the goodness and idealism and faith of the American people," an obvious reference to that evangelical hymn, "There is Power in the Blood." His 2005 inaugural address, called "God drenched" by one observer, was somewhat unique in that it moved from overtly Christian to more ecumenical rhetoric, as in the allusion to "the truths of Sinai, the Sermon on the Mount, the words of the Quran, and the varied faiths of our people." Small wonder many Americans easily blur the line between church and state and shroud their history in religious symbolism, with George Washington likened to Moses and July 4 and December 25 both serving as occasions for nationalistic and religious exaltation.

Despite the religious shallowness of many Americans, there is no denying the religiosity of the American public. This struck Alexis de Tocqueville, that discerning Frenchman who crisscrossed the nation from New York to New Orleans in 1831. There was 'no country in the world,' he observed, 'where the Christian religion retains a greater influence over the souls of men than in America.' De Tocqueville's observation has a contemporary ring, for surveys from 1947 to 2006 suggest America is the most religious of the modern western nations. And "nothing in the last half-century," wrote George Gallup, Jr., in June 2000, has "dislodged the conviction of Americans that there is a power in the universe . . . greater than ourselves–not wars; not the problem of evil and the obvious sufferings of innocent people; not the 'death of God' movement; not social upheavals nor the lures of the modern world." Indeed, current surveys show that 96 percent of all adult Americans believe in God, 84 percent contend God is actively involved in their lives, 85 percent insist God performs miracles today, 70 percent belong to a church or synagogue, 40 percent claim to attend church weekly, 59 percent believe religion is an important aspect of daily life, and 65 percent consider religion the answer to many of the nation's present ills. This augurs well for calls to political action rooted in religious principles, as shown only a generation or so ago by the 'religious left.' In pursuit of racial justice, for instance, the National Council of Churches pricked the nation's conscience in the 1950s and 1960s. This coalition of religious groups, along with Presidents Kennedy and Lyndon B. Johnson, challenged Americans to live up to the egalitarian ideals of their faith. Accordingly, the Council brought the power of religion to bear on the civil rights legislation of the 1960s.[1]

So in light of this country's long-standing interaction between religion and politics, why has the religious right attracted such attention since World War II? Why have Jerry Falwell and the Moral Majority and Pat Robertson and the Christian Coalition aroused such alarm in some quarters? What is so different about the religious right? In terms of fundamental theological concerns, there is nothing particularly new. Contemporary Christians on the right are no less disturbed by higher criticism of the Bible and Darwinian evolution than their conservative forebears of the late nineteenth and early twentieth centuries, as attested to by persistent efforts over the last decade or so to have 'creation science' or "intelligent design" accorded equal time with Darwinism in public school classrooms. Two developments in this ongoing tug-of-war have had an unsettling effect on much of the scientific community. In October 1999 Baylor University, a reputable Baptist institution in Waco, Texas, established the Michael Polanyi Center to study intelligent design, the idea that some life forms are too complex to have evolved by chance through a process of Darwinian natural selection. Proponents of this view, which has gained strength since the 1980s, believe mathematical models can prove that some intelligent agent outside the universe has been responsible for directing creation. To opponents, this kind of academic activity amounts to just another cloak for creationism, and the ultimate purpose of Baylor's new center, they insist, is to promote the teaching of intelligent design in the public schools. Disclosing the ambivalence, or perhaps pragmatism, of the American public on such issues, polls released in 2000 and 2005 showed that overwhelming majorities supported the teaching of both evolution and creationism in the public schools. The 2005 poll conducted by the Pew Forum on Religion and Public Life is especially significant in that it showed that both conservative Christians and majorities of secular respondents favored the teaching of both points of view. In August 2005 President Bush weighed in, announcing that both views should be taught in schools "so people can understand what the debate is about." And if a higher authority was needed, Pope Benedict XVI joined the chorus for intelligent design in November 2005. But to Nobel Laureate Steven Weinberg, a world renowned physicist, the current vogue for equal time, sounding so fair and innocent, did not bode well for science.[2]

Nowhere perhaps has the debate been more bitter and personal than in Kansas. In August 1999 the Kansas Board of Education, dominated by religious fundamentalists, made the teaching of evolution in the state's public schools optional and announced that questions dealing with evolution would no longer be included in state assessment tests. "Disgraceful" was the American Association for the Advancement of Science's description of the new Kansas standards, but Linda Holloway, the former chair of the board who had pushed adoption of the guidelines, blithely dismissed the national scientific organization. "Clearly," said she, the scientists "have an ax to grind about evolution." Holloway was subsequently voted out, and in 2001 the board reversed itself. But the battle resumed in 2004, and in November 2005 a bitterly split Kansas State Board of Education voted 6-4 to incorporate intelligent design into its science curriculum. To John West of the Discovery Institute, which promotes intelligent design, this gave Kansas "the best science standards in the nation," but to Eugenie Scott of the National Center for Science Education, which defends Darwinian evolution, the new standards were nothing more than creationism in disguise. If Kansas has become a laughing stock, as opponents of intelligent design assert, then Minnesota, New Mexico, Pennsylvania, Arkansas, and Texas deserve at least a chuckle.

Early Political Involvement: The Anti-Communism Movement

But it is not theology and concern about evolution so much as active involvement in the political process that separates the contemporary religious right from conservative religious forces of the pre–World War II era. Believing Armageddon to be nigh, conservative Christians, especially those of a fundamentalist and evangelical variety, have traditionally concentrated more on redeeming sinners and preparing themselves for the imminent return of Jesus than on active political involvement. The Joneses of South Carolina—Bob, Sr.,

Bob, Jr., and Bob III, leaders of the fundamentalist Bob Jones University in Greenville, South Carolina—still reflect this viewpoint, and so did Jerry Falwell until the 1970s. Agitated by the political activism of the religious left on behalf of civil rights reforms, the future leader of the Moral Majority informed his Lynchburg, Virginia, congregation in 1965 that God had given no command to engage 'in marches, demonstrations, or any other [political] actions.' Preachers, he added, were 'not called to be politicians but soul winners.' But Falwell underwent a dramatic metamorphosis. At a special bicentennial service on July 4, 1976, the Virginian fused a nationalistic love of country with an intense religious zeal. 'The idea that religion and politics don't mix was invented by the Devil to keep Christians from running their own country,' asserted Falwell. 'If [there is] any place in the world we need Christianity,' he continued, 'it's in Washington. And that's why preachers long since need to get over that intimidation forced upon us by liberals, that if we mention anything about politics, we are degrading our ministry.'[4]

Falwell's political awakening, as well as that of multitudes of other Americans on the religious right, can be understood only in terms of foreign and domestic developments since World War II. To people on the religious, as well as political, right, the years since 1945 have been fraught with peril. Abroad, the communists appeared to be winning the Cold War, as exemplified by the triumph of Mao Tse-Tung in China, the failure to achieve victory in Korea, the costly quagmire in Vietnam, the continuing presence of Fidel Castro, the 'giveaway' of the Panama Canal, and leftist successes in Central America. And at home 'socialist' governmental programs (the religious right tends to equate liberalism with socialism and socialism with communism), the teaching of evolution in the public schools, a soaring divorce rate, Supreme Court decisions banning organized prayer in the public schools, growing numbers of abortions, urban violence and crime, the Equal Rights Amendment (ERA), the assertiveness of the 'gay' community, 'smutty' television programs, the AIDS epidemic, and President Bill Clinton's misbehavior in the White House with Monica Lewinski confirmed the religious right's belief that cherished moral values were in decline.

Uniting the voices of the religious right in the late 1940s was an intense fear of communism. Indeed, a symbiotic tie swiftly emerged between the religious and political right. Politicians such as Senator Joseph McCarthy of Wisconsin drew support from the religious right, for instance, while otherwise obscure preachers such as Carl McIntire gained national prominence through close association with the political right. Thus, in defense of God and country, preachers and politicians of the right embraced in a righteous crusade to save America. McIntire was typical. This autocratic and self-righteous Presbyterian who lived into his 90s became an elder statesman of sorts for a certain segment of the religious right. Fiercely independent, he forged his own denomination in 1937, the Bible Presbyterian Church, and through the weekly columns of the *Christian Beacono* kept his followers advised on matters of God and Caesar. By the 1950s he had established a network of educational institutions, such as the Faith Theological Seminary in Philadelphia, and had begun to broadcast his messages for religious and political redemption on a regular program entitled *The Twentieth-Century Reformation Hour*. Basically, McIntire told Americans that national well-being hinged upon a return to the 'old-time' Christian values upon which the nation presumably had been founded. Accomplishing this would not be easy, however, because of the communist conspiracy. To McIntire, the major Protestant bodies all harbored communists, the National Council of Churches was nothing but a communist front, and the Revised Standard Version of the Bible was communist-inspired. At the height of his influence in the early 1960s, McIntire's call for national salvation, as heard daily on *The Twentieth-Century Reformation Hour*, was carried by at least 200 stations.[5]

By 1960 the religious right had become more cluttered, as additional crusaders joined the cause, notably the trio of Edgar C. Bundy, Frederick Schwarz, and Billy James Hargis. Bundy, an ordained Southern Baptist minister without a congregation, took charge of the Church League of America in 1956. This ultra-conservative agency, which Bundy moved from Chicago to Wheaton, Illinois, labored to awaken Protestant ministers to the reality of the communist conspiracy. Schwarz, an Australian physician and lay preacher who had come to the United States initially at the request of McIntire, launched the Christian Anti-Communism Crusade in 1952. His prominence was enhanced considerably by Billy Graham, who in 1957 arranged for him to address a group of congressmen on communism. Schwarz repeatedly told American audiences that the communist method of conquest was infiltration, a process he believed already far advanced in the halls of academe, the press corps, and the State Department. More zealous perhaps than the other two, Hargis, a Disciples of Christ minister, began in 1951 the Christian Echoes National Ministry, better known as the Christian Crusade. Although closely associated in the mid-1950s with McIntire's organizations, Hargis increasingly went his own way. From radio in the 1960s he moved to television in the early 1970s with smoothly packaged programs. At one stage, 146 stations telecast his messages. In 1973 he founded American Christian College.[6]

These ministers often enjoyed cordial ties to secular counterparts, thereby obscuring the line in the public's mind between the religious and secular right. Such was the case of Robert Welch, who founded the John Birch Society in 1958. Welch was a well-educated, widely traveled, and successful businessman who had become disillusioned with politics after running unsuccessfully for lieutenant-governor of Massachusetts and supporting the failed presidential candidacy of Senator Robert A. Taft, an Ohio Republican, in 1952. In 1956 he retired from business and became an anticommunist warrior. Welch was not a minister, but he named the John Birch Society for 'a young fundamentalist Baptist preacher from Macon, Georgia,' who allegedly had been murdered by Chinese communists after World War II. And ministers on the right certainly saw an ally in Welch and his organization. McIntire called the society 'a good patriotic American organization,' and Hargis referred to Welch as 'a great American patriot.' Such admiration was not surprising, for Welch and the preachers had much in common.[7]

The early ministers of the religious right, as well as Welch, were as one not only in their intense anticommunism, but also in their conspiratorial view of history. The 'paranoid style in American politics' was historian Richard Hofstadter's description of the tendency to see conspiracy as the causal force in American history, a tendency prompted by morbid suspicion. And men such as McIntire, Hargis, and Welch were nothing if not suspicious of those with whom they disagreed. They took for granted that their adversaries were pawns of Satan, and thus parties to a sinister conspiracy in which outward acts concealed darker intentions. Within this context, for instance, Supreme Court decisions regarding prayer in the public schools were just one aspect of a broader communist conspiracy to destroy the Christian moorings upon which the Founding Fathers supposedly had anchored the nation. More an article of faith than a product of empirical observation, such a view of history was unfazed by evidence. Consequently, the collapse of communism in central and eastern Europe fooled everyone but Hargis. He asserted in August 1994 that while the American news media 'looks the other way,' communism 'is making a dramatic, secret comeback.' Continued Hargis: 'There is a Red threat and it is alive and thriving.'[8] Time changed nothing for Hargis. The conspiracy was ongoing, protected by the reticence of the liberal media.

Emergence of the New Religious Right

Preachers such as McIntire and Hargis were eventually forced into the background by the easing of the anticommunist hysteria that spawned them in the 1950s. For all but the most devout true believers, it became difficult to sustain a belief in a communist conspiracy in light of the removal of the Berlin Wall, the unification of Germany, and the collapse of the Soviet Union. The resurgence of the new religious right in the 1970s was led by a group of electronic preachers—Pat Robertson, president of the Christian Broadcasting Network (CBN) and host of *The 700 Club*; James Robison, a Texas Southern Baptist; and Jerry Falwell, leader of the Moral Majority. Preachers such as these still employed apocalyptic imagery in discussing the global struggle—liberty against atheistic communism, light against darkness—but the constant emphasis upon conspiracy was absent. Instead of communism, 'secular humanism' unified these newer leaders of the religious right. Many religious conservatives sensed that secular humanists, who supposedly were entrenched in the courts, media, and schools, systematically undermined the supernaturalism of Judeo-Christianity. Robertson was typical. In 1986 he rebuked the 'small elite of lawyers, judges, and educators' who had 'taken the Holy Bible from our young and replaced it with the thoughts of Charles Darwin, Karl Marx, Sigmund Freud, and John Dewey.'[9] Like 'modernism' of an earlier era, secular humanism quickly became an evangelical catchall for every imaginable 'sin,' from violence in the streets to the lack of discipline in the public schools. And to combat these ills the more recent religious right was much readier to join the political fray than its counterpart of the 1950s. Whereas McIntire and Hargis often spoke to political issues and frequently endorsed specific bills, such as those seeking to 'restore' prayer in the public schools, Falwell and Robertson were far more inclined to instruct their followers on issues, conduct voter-registration drives, engage in legislative lobbying, and target specific politicians for defeat, as in the case of Senator John McCain during the 2000 presidential primary in South Carolina.

The religious right of the 1970s and beyond differed in yet another significant respect from that of the 1950s. The former has been more ecumenical. A mutual concern over such family-related issues as abortion, sex education in the schools, homosexuality, and the ERA enabled many Protestant fundamentalists and some conservative Jews, Mormons, and Catholics to rise above theological differences and join hands in the quest for 'family values.' Particularly illustrative here was Phyllis Schlafly. Stung by the ERA, which was approved by Congress in 1972 but never ratified by the required three-fourths of the state legislatures, and the Supreme Court's decision on abortion in 1973, Schlafly, a Roman Catholic, started the Eagle Forum in 1975. This organization spearheaded the drive to kill the ERA, and in so doing drew support from Falwell. If the Catholic Schlafly and the Baptist fundamentalist Falwell could set aside theological differences on behalf of common social values, so could other religious conservatives.

The ecumenism of the religious right, to be sure, has been more across denominational and religious than racial lines. While African-American Christians, for instance, especially those in the South, were as theologically conservative as Falwell, they never moved in sizeable numbers to the religious right. A possible explanation is that many religiously conservative whites have all too frequently opposed political and social initiatives beneficial to minorities. The close association between the religious right and former Senator Jesse Helms, the prominent North Carolina Republican, illustrates the problem. It was difficult for many African Americans to feel comfortable in a movement that welcomed a politician who had always objected to civil rights legislation and criticized federal programs to assist the poor. Making matters worse was a voter guide distributed across the South by the Christian Coalition in the 1996 presidential race. It used the image of a black man to represent issues the organization opposed and a white man for measures it favored. Claiming a printer error, Ralph Reed, then executive director of the Christian Coalition, apologized, but Julian Bond, a board member of the National Association for the Advancement of Colored People and a former Georgia congressman, was unimpressed. He all but accused Reed and the Christian Coalition of hypocrisy, suggesting the director's lofty preachments "about racial equality and Christian morality" were easily "tossed aside in favor of racial wedges and voter manipulation" at "election time."[10] Given such suspicion on the part of African Americans, the ecumenism of the religious right does not extend much beyond white Americans and their 'social' concerns.

By the mid-1970s the social issues that brought diverse but predominantly white groups together on the religious right generally fell into one of three categories—educational, family, or moral. As evidenced by the Supreme Court's 1962-1963 school prayer decisions, the growing trend toward secularization in the public schools not only alarmed many conservative Christians, but also prompted some of them to seek private schooling for their children. Just as many Catholics had insulated themselves within a system of parochial schools in the nineteenth century, some Protestant evangelicals sought to do the same in the twentieth century. Robertson voiced the mood when he wrote in 1980: 'Christians must educate their youth in new schools which teach biblical principles and a biblical life-style in which the Lordship of Jesus Christ is acknowledged in every facet of their lives.' More recently members of the nation's largest Protestant denomination, the fundamentalist-controlled Southern Baptist Convention, expressed the same opinion. In 2004 and 2006 the convention debated but did not pass resolutions urging Baptists to remove their children from public schools in favor of home schooling or Christian private schools. Defending this position, the cosponsor of the 2006 resolution, Bruce Shortt, a Houston, Texas, attorney and author of *The Harsh Truth About Public Schools*, cited opposition to intelligent design and approval of homosexuality in the public schools.[11] A logical consequence of the private school movement has been support for tuition tax credits and vouchers, and therein lay the possibility of cooperation between many Protestant evangelicals and Catholics.

Another area of likely agreement among people of differing faiths was the family. Of special concern were the ERA and the Supreme Court's 1973 decision on abortion. Paradoxically, many conservatives affirmed their support of women while simultaneously denouncing the ERA. Their opposition supposedly was not to equality of treatment for women, but rather to any fundamental restructuring of the family allegedly at odds with the Bible. Consequently, religious conservatives opposed the ERA, convinced it would alter scripturally rooted male-female roles and even legitimatize homosexuality. Robertson spoke for many others when he asserted that the proposed amendment would protect 'homosexuals, lesbians, sadomasochists, and … anyone else who engaged in any other sexual practice whether or not that practice was prohibited by the Bible, religious dogma, existing federal or state law.' The same fervency with which the religious right objected to the ERA metamorphosed in the 1990s and early twenty-first century into support for a constitutional amendment to "save" marriage from homosexuals. And the rhetoric in 2006 of James Dobson, head of Focus on the Family, strained credulity about as much as that of Robertson. Said Dobson: "For more than forty years, the homosexual activist movement has sought to implement a master plan that has had as its centerpiece the utter destruction of the family," and if it succeeds "the family as it has been known for more than five millennia will crumble, presaging the fall of Western civilization itself."[12] Just as disparate elements of the religious right of the 1950s had been as one in opposing communism, so now, as the remarks of Robertson and Dobson suggest, divergent strands were unified against homosexuality and same-sex unions. Or, to borrow Cal Thomas's words, "softness on gays" had "replaced COMMUNISTS as the Religious Right's No. 1 enemy."[13]

As for abortion, the position of many evangelical Protestants and the Catholic hierarchy was essentially the same—except when the mother's life was endangered, the rights of the unborn fetus were paramount to the mother's choice. The intensity of this debate was undiminished by the Food and Drug Administration's approval in fall 2000 of the French abortion pill, RU-486. Stubbornly resisted for years by the religious right, RU-486 was no more likely to ensure privacy for women and physicians than promised by *Roe v. Wade* in 1973. From different sides of the religious spectrum came immediate expressions of outrage over the FDA's decision. While Richard Land, head of the Southern Baptist Convention's Ethics and Religious Liberty Commission, labeled the pill "a dangerous drug that is fatal for unborn babies and hazardous to their mothers," Fran Maier, Chancellor of the Catholic Archdiocese of Denver, served notice: "RU-486 only streamlines the process of destroying a human life." More ominously, the director of Operation Save America, Flip Benham, threatened to uncover physicians who prescribed the pill and expose them "doctor by doctor." Those who administered RU-486, Benham warned, would "put their practice in jeopardy." With polls showing that 47 percent of Americans disapproved of the pill, RU-486 reenergized antiabortion forces and strengthened the sense of unity among people of diverse faiths on the religious right. But rather than attacking the 1973 *Roe* decision head-on, antiabortion groups have been reasonably successful chipping away at the edges, making abortions more difficult by requiring parental consent and other restrictions. In 2006 the South Dakota legislature altered the strategy, enacting legislation that prohibited abortion under any circumstances. While many religious and secular allies had no quarrel with the law's objective, some seriously questioned the wisdom of charting a course that almost certainly will lead to a Supreme Court showdown over *Roe* itself.[14]

The moral concerns of the religious right revolve around drug abuse, pornography, television programs, and movies. With its constant barrage of nudity, profanity, and violence, television has been a frequent target. Donald E. Wildmon, a Methodist minister from Tupelo, Mississippi, believed the industry undermined 'family' values, and in the mid-1970s he launched a movement to purify the air waves.[15] Adding weight to the claims of the religious right was a 2000 report by ten major health organizations, including the American Medical Association, which attributed much youthful violence to television, movies, videogames, music, and the Internet. Of the twenty-six wealthiest nations, the United States, according to the American Academy of Family Physicians, had the highest homicide and suicide rates among young people. The report concluded with a call to Hollywood to be more responsible.[16] This indicates that some of the moral concerns of the religious right are also the concerns of multitudes of other Americans. And politicians, ever mindful of the next election, have paid some attention. Hardly an election passes without all sides posturing over the "filth in Hollywood," and in 2005 President Bush signed into law the Family Entertainment and Copyright Act, which shielded from lawsuits one of a growing number of companies that market PG, PG-13, and R movies that have had "objectionable" material (profanity and sexually explicit scenes) deleted.

Political Buildup to the 1980 Election

The outcome of the 1976 presidential race brought hope to many religious conservatives, for Jimmy Carter was an acknowledged 'born again' Southern Baptist from the Deep South, a Georgian with whom many on the religious right could easily identify. Moreover, by focusing national attention on and enhancing the stature of conservative evangelicals, Carter's victory emboldened many on the religious right increasingly to measure public issues against biblical standards of morality. As a result, matters of moral concern to Christian conservatives became politicized, and in turn Christian conservatives increasingly entered the political fray not only to protect their way of life, but also to 'restore' the nation to its moral roots. Ironically, it was not long before President Carter himself incurred the wrath of his religious kinfolks. They were dismayed by his endorsement of the ERA, his failure to prevent federally subsidized abortions, his refusal to support voluntary prayer in the public schools, and the suggestion in 1978 of his commissioner to the Internal Revenue Service (IRS) that Christian schools should be taxed. Tim LaHaye's judgment was common. 'Between 1976 and 1980,' he wrote in 1981, 'I watched a professing Christian become president of the United States and then surround himself with a host of humanistic cabinet ministers' who 'nearly destroyed our nation.'[17]

LaHaye's frustration was matched by Falwell's. The articulate Virginia pastor had become by the late 1970s an institution of sorts. His Thomas Road Church, an independent Baptist congregation, numbered approximately 15,000; his Sunday services, *The Old-Time Gospel Hour*, entered millions of homes via radio and television; and his capacity for fundraising was already well-established. Coincident with the disenchantment of people such as LaHaye and Falwell with the Carter administration was the appearance of several conservative lobbyists, men who saw in disaffected religious conservatives a reservoir of potential voters for conservative political causes. The key figures were Howard Phillips, leader of the right-wing lobbying group Conservative Caucus, Edward E. McAteer, a marketing specialist from Colgate-Palmolive Company and a Southern Baptist layman, Robert Billings, head of the National Christian Action Coalition, Richard Viguerie, a direct-mail expert who began the *Conservative Digest*, and Paul Weyrich, a Catholic who had organized the Committee for the Survival of a Free Congress in 1974. Credit goes primarily to Billings and McAteer for bringing Falwell and Weyrich together, and thereby the wedding of secular and religious conservatives.[18]

Whether politically savvy secular conservatives such as Weyrich subsequently dominated and used religious conservatives such as Falwell is debatable. John Buchanan, the director of People for the American Way, a liberal lobby, insisted the political right actually created the religious right.[19] This is clearly inaccurate. The religious right had been around for a long time, and the relationship that evolved between it and the political right in the late 1970s was symbiotic. While Weyrich coined the term 'moral majority' and brought organizational talent to the movement, Falwell added righteous indignation and promised voters for the cause. Together, Weyrich, Falwell, and others forged the Moral Majority, Inc., in 1979 and set out to rescue America from secular humanism. And popular perception to the contrary notwithstanding, the Moral Majority was more than a Christian fundamentalist organization. From the outset it appealed to and drew at least some support from conservative Catholics, Jews, and Mormons. Indeed, Falwell's willingness to broaden the religious base of the Moral Majority sometimes offended his fundamentalist allies.

The Moral Majority was only one of three conservative religious agencies created in 1979. The other two were the Christian Voice and the Religious Roundtable. A California-based organization which by 1980 claimed the support of 37,000 pastors from forty-five denominations and a membership of 187,000,[20] the Christian Voice assumed the task of evaluating the morality of public officials. Toward that end it developed a morality scale based on fourteen key issues, and a politician whose position coincided with that of the Christian Voice was deemed 'moral.' Disturbed and angered by societal changes involving the family, women, sex, divorce, homosexuality, and television programming, the Christian Voice was against abortion, racial quotas, forced busing, the Department of Education, gay rights, SALT II, pornography, drugs, higher taxes, and sex education without parental consent. It was for the 'restoration' of prayer in the public schools, free enterprise, the defense of Taiwan, and a balanced federal budget. Republicans usually came closer to meeting the Christian Voice's standard of Christian morality than Democrats. However, when convicted Abscam defendants scored higher on the Christian Voice's morality scale than did congressional proponents of alleviating world hunger and poverty, it became glaringly obvious the moral report cards had more to do with 'correct' political behavior than morality.[21]

The Religious Roundtable, McAteer's principal organizational contribution to the religious right, attempted to connect prominent figures from the political and religious right. In August 1980 it sponsored the National Affairs Briefing in Dallas, Texas. Nonpartisan billing to the contrary, this was a Protestant fundamentalist and conservative Republican affair. Among those in attendance were the Southern Baptist patriarch W. A. Criswell, the longtime pastor of the First Baptist Church, Dallas, and a major figure in the successful fundamentalist effort during the 1980s to gain control of the Southern Baptist Convention, and Ronald Reagan, the only presidential candidate present. This meeting attracted national attention, not all of which was positive. The stridency of some of the speakers, along with hints of antisemitism, bothered many Americans.

Although the Moral Majority shared the field with other organizations on the religious right in 1979-1980, it soon became the primary focus of national attention. With the presidential race of 1980 looming, the Moral Majority hastily established local chapters in forty-seven states, conducted voter-registration drives and educational seminars for religious conservatives, and targeted several prominent politicians for defeat. While it claimed to be nonpartisan, in 1980 the Moral Majority invariably opposed liberal Democrats, such as Senators George McGovern of South Dakota, Frank Church of Idaho, Alan

Cranston of California, John Culver of Iowa, and Birch Bayh of Indiana. And Falwell's eagerness to discredit President Carter prompted the former, just weeks before the election, to fabricate an unflattering story about homosexuals on the president's staff. Although unapologetic, the minister later confessed his lie.[22] The Moral Majority, tending to equate morality with a narrow set of political options, was clearly more comfortable with conservative Republicans. Herein lies the seed that would grow into a pervasive sense by 2000, or certainly 2004, that the Republican party alone represents virtue, values, and God.

Fallout from the 1980 Election

The results of the 1980 elections thrilled the religious right, although analysts disagreed sharply over the causes for the defeat of incumbents Carter, McGovern, Church, and Bayh. To be sure, Falwell, as well as Weyrich, Phillips, McAteer, and Viguerie, claimed considerable responsibility. As Viguerie put it, 'the white followers of the TV evangelical preachers gave Ronald Reagan two-thirds of his ten-point margin in the election.' But other post-election observers were far more skeptical, suggesting Falwell and his followers merely *rode*, but did not *create*, the antiadministration sentiment so evident in the election. Bayh agreed, explaining his loss more in terms of high interest and unemployment rates than the religious right. By this analysis, President Reagan was not especially beholden to religious conservatives, and, noticeably, he did not appoint a representative of the Moral Majority to a major administration post and disregarded Falwell's objections to the appointment of Sandra Day O'Connor to the Supreme Court. On the other hand, Reagan, with an eye toward the midterm congressional elections, soothed the religious right by choosing Billings for an important post in the Department of Education, appointing C. Everett Koop, an evangelical opponent of abortion as surgeon general, taking a stronger stand against abortion, and endorsing a constitutional amendment allowing organized prayer in the public schools.[23]

While probably never as influential as either its followers or detractors supposed, the Moral Majority definitely ebbed as the 1980s progressed, assailed from within and without. Falwell and Weyrich had faced a dilemma from the beginning. How could the Moral Majority broaden its base by appealing to moderate religious conservatives without alienating its staunchly fundamentalist core? The difficulty of this situation was apparent by the early 1980s. As Falwell eased toward the evangelical center, territory long occupied by Billy Graham, he quickly aroused suspicion. By softening somewhat his opposition to abortion, allowing that it was permissible if the mother's life was endangered, endorsing equal rights for women once the ERA had become 'a dead issue,' and distancing himself from the virulently anti-Catholic Bob Jones, Jr., Falwell gained few converts from the evangelical mainstream and angered many on the fundamentalist right. Jones, for instance, called the Moral Majority the instrument of Satan and Falwell 'the most dangerous man in America as far as BIBLICAL Christianity is concerned.' Such outbursts supported the assessment of Graham, who doubted Falwell could move with his constituency into the evangelical mainstream.[24]

Many critics outside the religious fold were just as biting as Jones. To arouse Americans to the allegedly intolerant and dangerous views of the Moral Majority, several former senators who had been defeated in 1980 took to the stump in 1981-1982. McGovern organized Americans for Common Sense to counter Falwell's group. And Senator Barry Goldwater of Arizona, the elder statesman of Republican conservatism, castigated the Virginian for his ideological rigidity. Goldwater's rebuke had been sparked by Falwell's opposition to the Supreme Court nomination of O'Connor. Meanwhile, John Buchanan and People for the American Way loudly observed that the Christian Voice's 'morality report cards' consistently gave low marks to African-American, Jewish, and female lawmakers. Coincidentally, Buchanan had been one of the lawmakers the Moral Majority opposed in 1980. Although he was an ordained Southern Baptist minister and a Republican congressman from Alabama, his vote to extend the time allowed for passage of the ERA had angered Falwell. Buchanan lost in the GOP primary.[25]

One of the more discerning critiques of Falwell and the religious right came from the distinguished historian Henry Steele Commager. Addressing a Conference on Church and State at Baylor University in 1982, he charged that the likes of 'Oral Roberts and Jerry Falwell and their camp followers' concerned 'themselves not with public sin but with private vice, or what they conclude is vice—especially the sins of the flesh and of infidelity, which they interpret by their own standards.' While wringing their hands over 'personal sin,' in other words, they had little if anything to say of 'social sins.' Listen again to Commager: 'They have much to say about the wickedness of limiting posterity, whether by birth control or abortion, but have very little if anything to say about the kind of world children will be born into or about the systematic destruction of a rightful inheritance of natural resources.'[26]

As Falwell discovered, political activism by one side invariably generated counterattacks by the other side. After all, the religious right itself had been to some extent a response to the activism of the religious left in the 1950s and 1960s. The result for Falwell and the Moral Majority was a negative public perception. A Gallup Poll in late 1981 disclosed that over half the people who were aware of the Moral Majority viewed it unfavorably, and the response to Falwell personally was equally critical.[27] The consequence of Falwell's growing unpopularity was that many conservative politicians refused to be identified with the Moral Majority in the elections of 1982, 1984, and 1986. With his influence apparently waning, Falwell changed the name of the Moral Majority to Liberty Federation in January 1986, and thereafter lowered his political profile. 'I've redirected my priorities,' he later explained, 'and have no intention of working as hard in the political arena as I have in the past.'[28]

If Falwell had expected calm to accompany his political retreat, he was sorely disappointed. With glaring evidence of material excess and sexual misbehavior, the PTL and Jimmy Swaggart scandals unfolded in 1987-1988. Stunned, the faithful retaliated against all the major televangelists by withholding contributions and voicing disapproval. A Gallup Poll in 1987 showed that 62 percent of the American public now viewed Falwell unfavorably, a negative rating surpassed only by Oral Roberts (72 percent), and Jim Bakker (77 percent). Even 24 percent found fault with Graham. By mid-1988 the PTL was ruined, Swaggart was disgraced, Robertson's presidential foray was a shambles, and Falwell faced financial disaster.[29] In 1989 the Moral Majority was dissolved.

Although the Moral Majority collapsed, the religious right survived. Indeed, it became more aggressive, particularly at the local and state levels, under the leadership of Robertson and his Christian Coalition. Never close, the relationship between Falwell and Robertson sheds some light on the religious right itself. Contrary to popular assumption, the religious right has never been all that cohesive. While they usually shared the same social concerns, people on the religious right often followed different drummers. Robertson, for instance, after initially agreeing in 1979 to serve as a director of McAteer's Religious Roundtable, soon recoiled from active involvement in any of the new organizations of the religious right. His explanation was vintage evangelical conservatism. Christians were to concentrate on saving souls, not winning votes. Later, in fall 1980, he remarked that critics had found 'an easy target' in the religious right 'because the conservative EVANGELICALS involved in politics—Christian Voice, Moral Majority, and Religious Roundtable—have been, at times, unsophisticated, simplistic and inept.'[30] As for Falwell, his professed friendship for Robertson did not translate into support of the latter's bid for the presidency. 'I personally wish,' Falwell said in 1987, 'that no minister would ever run for ... political office.'[31] George H. W. Bush, not Robertson, was Falwell's choice to succeed President Reagan in 1988. As exemplified by Falwell and Robertson, the religious right was a union of kindred spirits in which there were many fissures.

Robertson's withdrawal from religious right organizations in 1980 in no way diminished his support of conservative social causes. On the contrary, he maintained close ties to prominent figures on the religious and secular right, such as Weyrich and Senator Jesse Helms of North Carolina, and gave conservative commentators easy access to *The 700 Club*. He also began building a political apparatus of his own. In 1981 Robertson founded the Freedom Council, an organization designed to educate Christians on political issues, followed in 1982 by the National Legal Foundation, which offered legal assistance to religious causes. And in 1985-1986 he presided over the Council on National Policy, a conservative group that was periodically briefed on issues by figures such as Senator Helms and Secretary of Education William Bennett. By 1987 the successful televangelist clearly had his sights set on the presidency, apparently convinced he could overcome an unfavorable Gallup Poll rating of 50 percent. But amid the lingering PTL and Swaggart scandals of 1987-1988, as well as serious reservations among many Americans about electing a charismatic preacher to the presidency, the effort foundered. Robertson's political ambition had exceeded his grasp.[32] Columnist William F. Buckley's assessment probably was correct. He wrote in 1987 that while Robertson said all the things conservatives wanted to hear, Americans nonetheless were overwhelmingly unprepared 'to believe that any minister is, ultimately, a serious candidate.'[33]

Reorganization of the Religious Right and the Contract with America

Following the presidential debacle, Robertson regrouped, forming in 1989 the Christian Coalition. This organization differed in at least one significant way from the Moral Majority. Whereas Falwell's group operated largely from the top down, seeking to achieve its ends by swaying politicians in the nation's capital, Robertson's Coalition was a grassroots effort to influence policies at the local and state levels. By 1994 the movement claimed almost 1.5 million members, and its effect on local school board and state races was apparent from coast to coast. Indeed, Christian conservatives had gained control of Republican party leadership in Texas, Virginia, Oregon, Washington, Iowa, South Carolina, and Minnesota, and comprised substantial voting blocs in New York, California, and practically all the southern states. One of the more closely watched races of 1994 was in Virginia, where Republican Oliver North, the darling of the religious right, eventually lost a bitterly fought contest to the Democratic incumbent, Senator Charles Robb. Among other things, this race disclosed the willingness of the religious right to overlook the 'sins' of the candidate who supported its political agenda, while assailing the other for his 'weakness of the flesh.'

As for school board elections, these traditionally attract only a small percentage of the electorate, thereby enhancing the chance of any well-organized and determined group to obtain control. And Christian conservatives, sharing with multitudes of other Americans the current frustration with the public schools over everything from low scores on achievement tests to controversial textbooks to violence in the hallways, have been quick to seize the opportunity. In 1993 it was estimated that of the nation's 95,000 school board members, 7,153 were conservative Christians.[34] Texas was one of the major battlefields in the 1994 fall elections. With 60,000 members and 136 chapters in the Lone Star State, the Christian Coalition had its eyes on the state's fifteen-member Board of Education. To avoid jeopardizing its nonprofit status, the Christian Coalition endorsed no candidate by name, but rather encouraged its membership to support 'conservatives.' This left no doubt as to the anointed candidate in six of the districts. Republicans subsequently won in three of those races, giving candidates beholden to the religious right an eight-to-seven majority on the Texas board.[35]

The religious right was especially active in the 1994 congressional elections. The Christian Coalition alone distributed about 33 million voter guides and manned a vast network of telephone banks shortly before the November balloting. And the effort paid off. Overall, the Republicans elected seventy-three freshmen to the House and gained control of both houses of Congress for the first time since 1954. An exhilarated Louis Sheldon, leader of the Traditional Values Coalition, bespoke the mood of many fellow religionists. 'The election of 1980 with Ronald Reagan was great,' said he, but the 1994 outcome was "like we've died and gone to heaven."[36] Whether the Republican landslide was due more to the failure of Democratic leadership, pervasive frustration within the general populace, or the political activism of the religious right is debatable. Nevertheless, the Christian Coalition's Ralph Reed promptly claimed considerable credit for the religious right in the high-profile Republican victories of Steven Stockman over House veteran Jack Brooks of Texas, Rick Santorum over incumbent Senator Harris Wofford of Pennsylvania, and George W. Bush over Governor Ann Richards of Texas. There were, of course, some setbacks for religious conservatives, most notably North in Virginia.[37]

With so many of the freshmen Republicans, such as Stockman, Randy Tate of Washington, Lindsey Graham of South Carolina, Helen Chenoweth of Idaho, Steve Largent of Oklahoma, Mark Souder of Indiana, and Van Hilleary of Tennessee, beholden to it, the religious right had cause for optimism in 1995. To the extent the 1994 elections had aligned Congress more closely with the country's conservative mood, they seemed to portend good things for many of the religious right's objectives. For instance, a constitutional amendment on prayer appeared close to reality. "We need a moral guidepost for our children," proclaimed Jay Sekulow, chief counsel for Robertson's American Center for Law and Justice, who saw momentum for prayer "coming from the soul of America." Sekulow's perception appeared well founded. Laws in Georgia, Virginia, Maryland, Mississippi, Tennessee, and Alabama already permitted a moment of silence, and similar legislation was pending in Florida, Oklahoma, Pennsylvania, and South Carolina.[38] And television, long the bête noire of the religious right, had begun to treat religious subjects more sympathetically, as seen in such programs as *Picket Fences*, *L.A. Law*, *Northern Exposure*, and *Christy*. A special commentator on religion even joined Peter Jennings on ABC's evening news. The chairman of the conservative Media Research Center, L. Brent Bozell, noticed these changes in programming and exclaimed "something's happening out there."[39]

Ironically, what subsequently happened out there was far from satisfactory to many religious conservatives. The freshmen Republicans in whom they had such high hopes soon alienated much of the American public, created doubt about the judgment of Republican leadership in the House, and reenergized the Clinton presidency. Youthful, brash, and outspoken, these novice Republicans stormed into town in 1995 like some gunslinging posse of frontier marshals bent upon routing evil and restoring virtue. They were going to trim the size of government by balancing the budget and cutting taxes, and they were going to dislodge career politicians by setting term limits. And all the while they would curb government interference in religion, put prayer and the Ten Commandments back in public schools, make federal money available to sectarian groups performing worthy social tasks, and allow certain students to attend private schools at public expense.

Apparently it never occurred to many of the freshmen that there would be opposition to some of these objectives, or that other points of view existed. They were confident to the point of arrogance, perhaps hubris. Knowing "they were right," they gave no heed to "anyone else's point of view." Compromise "was a four-letter word" to them. As one astute observer remarked, "they didn't know what they didn't know."[40] Although the so-called Contract With America, the platform on which the freshmen had run, sailed through the House in early 1995, it stalled in the Senate. For all the fanfare, not much had been accomplished by late 1995, at which time House Republicans shut down the government in a contest of wills with President Clinton over the budget. This was a public relations disaster, one the House Republicans unwisely repeated in 1996.[41] Instead of principled newcomers, as they had been seen in 1994, the Republican freshmen were now increasingly perceived as stubborn children who flew into a tantrum if they failed to have their way. Senator Bob Kerrey (D-NE) said it best: "What we are trying to do is compromise with a minority in the House of Representatives which is basically saying, 'We will hold our breath until we get our way. We do not care if our face turns blue. We do not care if the government shuts down!'"[42] The Nebraska Democrat obviously was not alone in this sentiment, for some public weariness with the religious right and the "revolution of '94 was soon evident. Although the Christian Coalition raised and spent over $26 million in the 1996 midterm elections,[43] twelve of the freshmen, along with six senior House Republicans, were defeated for reelection. The House Republicans had overreached themselves, and in so doing demonstrated qualities many Americans associated with the religious right—intellectual rigidity, intolerance of differing views, inability to compromise, and a determination to impose itself on an unwilling public.

Fall of the Christian Coalition

The failure of the 104th Congress to deliver on the social objectives of religious conservatives, along with the outcome of the 1996 elections, was not the only sign of trouble on the religious right. The Christian Coalition, the nation's largest organization of religious conservatives, soon encountered hard times. Announcing his pending resignation as executive director in April 1997, Ralph Reed, who had guided the Christian Coalition since its inception, forged his own political consulting firm, Century Strategies, and offered his talents to aspiring conservative politicians. Randy Tate took the helm in August. Somewhat like Reed, this Washington native was something of a whiz kid. Only 22 years old and not yet out of college, he was elected to the state legislature in 1988, the same year in which he endorsed the presidential candidacy of Pat Robertson. Six years later, in 1994, he was one of the freshmen Republicans elected to the U.S. House. A Christian conservative, Tate's congressional votes against abortion and for repealing the assault weapons ban and defunding the National Endowment for the Arts and Humanities earned him a 100 percent rating by the Christian Coalition and the National Rifle Association, but failed to gain him reelection by Washington's voters in 1996.[44] Even so, Tate was Pat Robertson's kind of conservative, and so he was a suitable successor to Reed.

Whereas Reed had presided over a steadily expanding and influential organization, one which exercised considerable power within Republican ranks, Tate inherited a Christian Coalition soon beleaguered by dwindling membership, sagging contributions, internal dissent, external competition, and trouble with the IRS. Some skepticism had always existed about the size of the Christian Coalition, with detractors arguing that the organization inflated its membership rolls. Nevertheless, the organization apparently peaked in late 1996, claiming some two million members and reporting contributions of $26.4 million. Following the 1996 elections, contributions fell sharply, slipping to $17 million in 1997, a drop of 36 percent in one year. This forced the Coalition to cut its staff from 110 to 90 and to cease publication of its flagship magazine, *Christian America*, which was replaced with a bimonthly newsletter. By 1999, after additional bad news for Republicans at the polls in 1998, the Coalition had lost at least 700,000 members, several key aides had resigned, and the organization had an outstanding debt estimated at $2.5 million. Symptomatic of the internal turmoil, in January 1998 Jeanne Delli-Carpini, a top financial officer, was given a suspended six-year prison sentence for embezzling $40,346 in 1996 and 1997. Compounding these problems, by 1999 other voices, such as the Family Research Council, had begun to challenge the Christian Coalition for the hearts of religious conservatives.[45] It appeared to many observers by 2000 that the Christian Coalition was headed the way of the Moral Majority. In April 2000 the organization's last lobbyist in Washington, D.C., resigned, and a former field director for the northeast pronounced the Coalition "a defunct organization."[46] As if it did not have troubles enough, the Christian Coalition also ran awry of the IRS.

Robertson's avowal of nonpartisanship had always been suspect, particularly given the Coalition's obvious preference for Republican candidates. With the approach of the 1998 midterm elections, for instance, the Christian Coalition released its Congressional Scorecard, ranking all members of Congress on the basis of votes on twelve specific issues. Republicans in the House and Senate received average scores of 89.8 and 80.3, respectively, whereas Democrats in the two chambers earned average marks of 13.1 and 6.1, respectively.[47] To critics, such statistics mocked the Coalition's assertion of evenhandedness, a conclusion already reached by the Federal Election Commission (FEC). At stake was the Coalition's tax-exempt status as a nonprofit religious organization.

In 1996 the FEC sued the Christian Coalition on grounds it was little more than an arm of the Republican party. As early as 1992, according to the commission, the Coalition had been working "hand in hand" with President George H. W. Bush's reelection campaign. Robertson fought back, claiming First Amendment rights to free speech, but in 1998 the IRS sided with the FEC and denied the Coalition tax-exempt status. Among other things, the IRS pointed to the Coalition's distribution of about 72 million sample-voter guides in 1998 which invariably supported Republicans. This decision was upheld in 1999, leaving the Christian Coalition owing the IRS between $300,000 and $400,000 in back taxes.[48] Barry Lynn, executive director of Americans United for the Separation of Church and State and a longtime foe of Robertson, applauded the outcome, asserting the Coalition was "a hardball political machine ... masquerading as a religious group." According to Lynn, "overwhelming" evidence proved Robertson's organization had "been operating as virtually an arm of the Republican party."[49]

The outcome of the IRS suit prompted a restructuring of the Coalition. In mid-1999 the organization split, creating the Christian Coalition of America and the Christian Coalition International. Since the Texas chapter, the Christian Coalition of Texas, retained its tax exemption, it was rechristened the Christian Coalition of America and charged with continuing the nonprofit practice of "voter education." Observed Robertson: "Christian Coalition of America will continue to be a force in American politics and will remain a prominent fixture on the political landscape as the nation's number one pro-family, pro-life organization." The Christian Coalition International would be a for-profit political action committee. As such, it would endorse candidates, contribute financially to political causes, and continue the distribution of voter guides before elections. Robertson hailed the reorganization as a way of keeping the Coalition active in American politics, but the ever-vigilant Barry Lynn called it a shabby ploy to evade the recent IRS ruling. "This is the kind of disgraceful shell-game you find in a second-rate carnival in the middle of nowhere," he declared. Americans United for the Separation of Church and State planned to file suit against the Coalition's restructured tax-exempt status.[50]

Although her decision had no effect on the IRS ruling, Federal District Judge Joyce Green handed Robertson a partial victory in August 1999. She dismissed FEC charges that the Christian Coalition, through its literature, telephone banks, and other means, had improperly assisted candidates, including Senator Jesse Helms of North Carolina and former President George H. W. Bush, but nevertheless imposed a civil penalty against the organization for supporting Newt Gingrich's bid to become House speaker in 1994. Green also ruled the Coalition had inappropriately shared its mailing list with senatorial candidate Oliver North in 1994. Nevertheless, Robertson was clearly pleased, declaring "this is a decisive victory for First Amendment Freedom for all groups that want to involve themselves in federal issues."[51]

Troubled Relationship with the Republican Party

In many ways, the problems of the Christian Coalition reflected an emerging disillusionment within the religious right at large. An overview of the past twenty years left many religious conservatives feeling frustrated, perhaps even betrayed by their secular allies in the Republican party. Long-sought objectives appeared no closer to reality in 2000 than in 1980, from obtaining a constitutional amendment on school prayer to repealing *Roe v. Wade*, improving the quality of television programming and Hollywood films, blunting the gay-rights movement, winning the war on drugs, and providing vouchers and tuition tax credits to public school children. The matter of school prayer was especially galling, for polls since the early 1960s showed that most Americans joined hands with religious conservatives on this issue. A Gallup Poll in June 2000 was typical. Some 70 percent favored "daily spoken prayers in the nation's classrooms," and 74 percent wanted the Ten Commandments displayed.[52] Yet, the Supreme Court, although dominated by Republican appointees, consistently thwarted such efforts. Thus, unable to make America once again a shining city upon a hill, a moral beacon to the rest of the world, many religious conservatives asked themselves if the time had come to forsake the political arena and to concentrate anew on spiritual concerns.

That question echoed through the religious right in the late 1990s. Perhaps no group had worked harder to raise money, compile mailing lists, recruit foot soldiers, and make telephone calls for Republican causes than religious conservatives. And Republicans had dominated the White House for twelve years under Ronald Reagan and George Bush, and the party had controlled both houses of Congress since 1995. But what did the religious right have to show for it all? Not very much, at least in the opinion of James Dobson, the popular psychologist whose radio and television programs reached approximately 28 million Americans every week. Originating from Colorado Springs, Colorado, his radio program, *Focus on the Family*, was heard by about five million every day. By mid-1998 Dobson was in open rebellion against Republican party leadership. He warned that if the social agenda of religious conservatives continued to be ignored there would be a price to pay in upcoming elections. Specifically, Dobson wanted Congress to eliminate the National Endowment for the Arts, defund Planned Parenthood, and require parental consent for abortions. And if the Republicans failed to deliver, the radio host vowed he would "try to beat them this fall."[53] Dobson's irritation disclosed a growing rift between grassroots religious conservatism and political conservatism in the capital, a conflict between idealism and pragmatism.

Despite the scandals swirling around President Clinton, the Democrats gained ground in the 1998 midterm elections, gains which forced Republican Newt Gingrich to relinquish the speakership and resign from the U.S. House. And of the original seventy-three freshmen from 1994, only fifty-one remained. If the Republican "revolution of '94 was not dead, it had certainly wilted, and so had the religious right. Two prominent voices spoke the mood of many in 1999. The time had come to leave the political arena. "Politics has failed," announced Paul Weyrich on February 16. Coming from a man who perhaps had done more than anyone else to wed religious and secular conservatives, one present at the creation of the Moral Majority and Christian Coalition, Weyrich's words reverberated widely. The way to improve American culture, he elaborated, was through non-political means, and he offered as an example the home-schooling movement. Had those "parents stayed in the [political] battle to reform the public schools, they would have lost," he argued. But by simply separating "themselves from the public schools," over "a million young people are growing up with decent values." Similar paths supposedly were open to other religious conservatives. To be sure, the separatism Weyrich proposed was not a complete withdrawal from society. "I'm not suggesting that we all become Amish or move to Idaho," he explained. Religious conservatives should remain engaged as voters, if for no other reason than to protect themselves from greater government hostility.[54]

While Cal Thomas and Edward Dobson in their book, *Blinded by Might: Can the Religious Right Save America?* (1999), shared Weyrich's assessment of politics, they offered a slightly different remedy. Instead of cultural separatism, they suggested Christian conservatives resume the spiritual task of redeeming individual sinners. Both formerly associated with Jerry Falwell and the Moral Majority, Thomas was now a nationally prominent columnist with the Los Angeles Times Syndicate; Dobson was now pastor of a fundamentalist congregation, Calvary Church, in Grand Rapids, Michigan. According to the authors, religious conservatives had been right on the issues but wrong on strategy. They would have been better served by preaching the gospel than organizing for political battle, for "real change must come from the bottom up or, better yet, from the inside out." Aggressive political activism by the religious right, the authors believed, had contaminated the message of Jesus rather than uplifted the moral fiber of society. Just as "too-close [an] association" with the Democratic party in the 1950s and 1960s had diminished the moral authority of the National Council of Churches, so too the contemporary religious right because of its association with the Republican party. This was unavoidable, the authors observed, because politics was "about a kingdom of compromise" and the advancement of an "agenda incrementally," whereas "the kingdom of God" was "about truth and no compromise." Moral revival, they concluded, was "not the job of politics or politicians," but rather "the unique work of the church."[55] Even Pat Robertson seemed somewhat in agreement with Thomas and Dobson. Although showing no signs of leaving the political playing field himself, he nevertheless acknowledged that evangelicals had "been thoroughly disabused of the notion that the kingdom of God will come through political influence." Thus, "missions, . . . getting people into the kingdom of God," Robertson insisted, was now "the main thrust" of his life. Perhaps so, but Robertson cannot seem to resist either politics or making outrageous remarks, as in his call in late 2005 for the assassination of Venezuelan President Hugo Chavez. This brought a sharp rebuke from Thomas, who declared that instead of apologizing Robertson should in fact "retire and . . . take his bombastic conservative and liberal colleagues with him."[56]

Weyrich, Thomas, and others not only raised significant issues, but also revealed some uncertainty of purpose among religious conservatives by 2000. To be sure, neither Weyrich nor Thomas spoke for all their religious kinfolks. Jerry Falwell was unhappy with his old colleagues, as was Jay Sekulow, head of the American Center for Law and Justice. Sekulow accused Thomas and Dobson of encouraging religious conservatives to "unilaterally disarm and withdraw from politics." That would be a mistake, for "a lot of good has come out of political activism by religious people." Yet others faulted Thomas and Dobson for failing to give convincing alternatives to religious conservatives.[57] In part because of such internal turmoil, the religious right did not play as prominent, certainly not as visible, a role in 2000 as it had in previous presidential campaigns.

President Bush, the Religious Right and the 2000 Election

Evidence that something was changing in the religious-political landscape was apparent as George W. Bush edged toward the Republican presidential nomination in 1999-2000. Although the favorite of such religious conservatives as Robertson and Falwell, the Texas governor, with an eye toward the political center, kept a respectful distance from the religious right. Indeed, since 1995 Bush had clashed with the religious and social conservatives, all Republicans, on Texas's fifteen-member State Board of Education. At issue was everything from vouchers and textbook selection to investment of educational funds and federal ties to local schools. To the governor, the religious conservatives were intractable unless they got their way; to the religious conservatives, the governor had failed to keep his 1994 campaign pledges. It was not until 1997, when the state legislature enacted a religious freedom statute and a parental notification law on abortion, that the Bush administration delivered on matters dear to the state's religious right. But this did not mean that Bush, while admittedly wanting to retain their support, had surrendered to religious conservatives. In 1999, for instance, Bush ignored the hard-right wing of the California Republican party; in June 2000 he skipped the Texas Republican party convention, an affair permeated by religious sentiments; the National Republican Convention in summer 2000 kept the Christian Coalition at bay; and Bush did not make the usual courtesy call on Pat Robertson at the Christian Coalition's annual gathering in September 2000. Neither Bush nor his vice presidential running mate, Richard Cheney, for instance, attended the Coalition's Washington, D.C., rally, although Bush did address the gathering via television from Texas.[58]

Instead of being angered by Bush's aloofness, many powerful figures on the religious right were curiously silent as the 2000 race gained momentum. It was as if both sides had come to an unspoken understanding. Bush subscribed to most of the values and objectives of the religious right, but made no binding, public profession of such as he courted moderates with talk of "compassionate conservatism," a term borrowed from conservative Republican guru Marvin Olasky. Meanwhile, on the religious right people like Robertson, Falwell, and Ralph Reed, apparently satisfied the governor's heart was in the right place, remained in the background and made few demands so as not to jeopardize Bush's prospects. For instance, regarding Bush's failure to appear in person at the Coalition's September rally, Robertson remarked: "I'm sophisticated enough to understand the strategy here, and it's a very deliberate and delicate strategy." In other words, the Virginia preacher understood the Texas politician's need to attract moderates.[59] Likewise, on abortion, a bedrock principle of evangelical conservatives, Robertson reflected a similar comprehension. When the Food and Drug Administration in fall 2000 finally approved RU-486, the televangelist refused to make it an issue. "It's a distraction," Robertson asserted, one cleverly designed to trap Bush just weeks before the November election. As the televangelist explained, if Bush "says he strongly opposes the pill ruling, the women will go against him. And if he says he's for the ruling, then the pro-life people will go against him." In Robertson's opinion, the governor had avoided the pitfall by playing it "very well so far."[60]

Such an attitude demonstrated that the religious right, at least many of its leaders, had matured politically. The movement had become more pragmatic, recognizing the need to give a little, to compromise a bit, to win at the polls. Some concessions for victory felt better than moral purity in defeat. And what did religious conservatives expect in return for giving Bush an easy ride in the 2000 campaign? Robertson again is illustrative. The next president would likely nominate two or more justices to the Supreme Court, and Robertson wanted to be sure Bush made those recommendations. Even though the Texas governor had made no promises, he was definitely more likely than Al Gore to consider only pro-life candidates.[61]

The Texas governor's stunning loss to Senator John McCain of Arizona in the New Hampshire Republican primary in early 2000 almost wrecked this delicate balancing act between the Bush campaign and the religious right. Now desperately needing a victory in the upcoming South Carolina Republican primary, the heretofore presumed frontrunner made a hard right turn politically in February 2000 and threw himself into the awaiting arms of religious conservatives. All of a sudden the Republican presidential race turned nasty, as Ralph Reed, operating largely behind the scene, and Robertson helped orchestrate a ferociously negative attack on McCain. By telephone, e-mail, and other means, South Carolinians were "informed" of the senator's first wife, alleged marital infidelities, usage of profane language, and "softness" on the gay issue. In a telephone message sent to thousands, Robertson even accused McCain of being allied with "vicious" anti-Christian bigots.[62] Bush handily won, but some observers wondered at what cost. To Cal Thomas, the South Carolina contest proved that "people who are supposed to serve a higher kingdom ... can get down and dirty with the best of the pagans." Likewise, to *Washington Post* columnist E. J. Dionne, Jr., it gave the lie to Bush's professed "compassionate conservatism," to the idea that "being Christian meant just not delivering votes to the ballot box but meals to the poor, mentoring to the young, comfort to the afflicted." And to William Kristol, a staunchly partisan Republican and publisher of *The Weekly Standard*, it signaled the "crackup" of the religious right. Reasoned Kristol: "The Christian Right ... is finished because of what Ralph Reed and Pat Robertson have done in South Carolina, because of the meanness of the assault."[63] Kristol was correct about the sordid nature of the South Carolina campaign, but mistaken about the anticipated demise of the religious right. People committed to a "higher calling" have often proven remarkably adept at rationalizing whatever means necessary to accomplish a desired end.

Once the South Carolina primary was over, Bush, though damaged in the eyes of some moderates, moved back toward the political center, and religious conservatives resumed a lower profile. To be sure, Jerry Falwell soon announced "People of Faith 2000," a plan to register at least 10 million voters, and in May and September, respectively, Robertson warned against McCain's selection for the vice presidency and cautioned that the Christian Coalition should not be taken for granted.[64] That the religious right was far from dead in 2000, however, came from the politicians themselves. The public square was anything but naked of religious sentiments during the presidential campaign, as candidates seemingly vied with one another for claims to the divine. Bush confided that Jesus was his favorite philosopher, while Gore countered that he always consulted Jesus before making any decision. And Joseph Lieberman,

Gore's running mate and an Orthodox Jew, the first to be nominated by a major party in a presidential race, intoned that America was "the most religious country in the world," that all Americans were the "children of the same awesome God," and that "there must be a place for faith in America's public life." Displaying some partisan jealousy, Cal Thomas called Lieberman an "itinerant Jewish evangelist" who used "God as a campaign surrogate to bless his and Al Gore's policies."[65] *New York Times* columnist Maureen Dowd, with her usual wit, put it all in perspective. "The main battleground state is the state of grace," she observed. "Democrats and Republicans are seeking a geographical advantage, but it is celestial. Both sides seem weirdly obsessed with snagging a divine endorsement."

George W. Bush's First Term

If Bush snagged a divine endorsement, he snared no heavenly mandate. Indeed, the election's outcome offered a lesson in biblical humility. Bush lost the popular count by over 500,000 votes, and he gained the necessary electoral margin only after a heated legal battle for Florida's twenty-five electors. It would seem that President-elect Bush owed more to Ralph Nader for taking votes away from Gore than to the religious right. Yet, the future president did have a debt to evangelicals for rescuing his faltering campaign in the South Carolina primary, and there was an early indication the religious right would be rewarded. By naming several women, two Hispanics, and two African Americans, Bush drew praise for the diversity of his cabinet nominees. But the recommendation of John Ashcroft set off an alarm among many moderates and liberals. Slain in his bid for reelection to the U.S. Senate from Missouri by a dead man, Mel Canaan, who was killed in a plane crash just three weeks before the November 2000 election, Ashcroft was resurrected as Bush's attorney general designate. A devoutly religious member of the Assemblies of God Church, Ashcroft did not drink, smoke, or dance; he opposed most abortions and affirmative action; and he favored charitable choice and the carrying of concealed handguns. Notably, the Missouri senator was Robertson's first choice for the presidency. "I'm interested in picking a winner, not a loser," commented the televangelist in 1998, "and among Christian conservatives John Ashcroft's certainly number one right now." In December 2000 another prominent minister on the religious right, Louis P. Sheldon, head of the Traditional Values Coalition, praised the nomination of Ashcroft, calling him "a committed Christian" who understood "that true justice" came "not from the laws of men, but from the ultimate lawgiver: God."[67]

If many moderate Americans were dismayed by the U. S. Senate's confirmation of Ashcroft as attorney general, a man many of them thought would be the religious right's Trojan Horse in the new administration, they were stunned by the hard-right direction of the Bush presidency. Given the controversial circumstances of the 2000 election, many observers assumed Bush would pursue a moderate course and govern from the political center. Instead he behaved as though he had won a mandate to lead from the right. There was growing dissatisfaction with the administration as 2001 progressed, and Democrats sensed an opportunity in the upcoming congressional elections of 2002. But the terrorist attack of September 11, 2001, that destroyed the World Trade Center's twin towers and killed almost 3,000 people completely altered the political dynamics. Believing God at his side, Bush quickly rallied the nation for a war on terrorism. According to Bob Woodward, within days of 9/11 Bush and his aides were talking as though God had "chosen" him to "lead at that moment." Said one administration insider to the Christian weekly *World*, "I think President Bush is God's man at this hour, and I say this with a great sense of humility." And following Bush's address to Congress on September 20, Michael Gerson, the president's speech writer, called and said, "Mr. President, when I saw you on television, I thought—God wanted you there." President Bush reportedly answered, "He wants us all here, Gerson." In Bush's mind, the events of 9/11 apparently provided a "great opportunity," "the moment history has given us to extend liberty to others around the world."[68]

From that point forward President Bush repeatedly linked 9/11, divine will, and whatever objective—domestic or foreign—the administration was in pursuit of at the moment. Afghanistan and Iraq aside, 9/11 supposedly justified the Patriot Act, increased airport security, the administration's energy policy, tax cuts, unemployment, federal deficits, and the weakening of environmental and workplace protections.[69] Adding to the litany in her inimitable style, columnist Maureen Dowd observed in early 2004 that "Mr. Bush irrationally arranges the facts to fit his initial assessment that 9/11 justified blowing off the UN and some close allies to invade Iraq."[70] In fact, by the time Dowd made her observation some Americans had begun to question not only the administration's quick usage of 9/11 to vindicate aims that seemed to have more to do with Republican politics than national security, but also the situation in Iraq itself. An ABC News poll in 2003 showed that support for the war had fallen from 70 percent in April to 54 percent in September. As one Texas oilman, an acquaintance of the president, put it, the matter in the Middle East was "a never-ending situation." Afghanistan was "already turning out to be a bleeder," he added, and Iraq would "be a bleeder too."[71]

If the growing doubts of others fazed President Bush, it was not evident from his public posture. Turning once more to religious rhetoric in his January 2003 State of the Union speech, he called upon the nation to trust in "Providence," to have faith in "the loving God behind all of life, and all of history." The "sacrifice" Americans were making in the Middle East would ensure "the liberty of strangers," which was not America's but "God's gift to humanity." Speaking a few weeks later to the Religious Broadcasters in Nashville, Bush again suggested that the American course in the Middle East was in harmony with God's will, declaring that the nation had been "called" to bring peace and liberty to the world. Skeptics could dismiss Bush's religiosity as a sham, the posturing of a cynical politician courting the righteous vote, but his language— "Providence," "called," "sacrifice," "loving God," "God's gift" —resonated with many evangelicals on the religious right who saw in the president a man of virtue, values, God. A religious broadcaster who had heard Bush in Nashville put it plainly. "It seems as if he is on an agenda from God.

The Scriptures say God is the one who appoints leaders," and if President Bush "truly knows God, that would give him a special anointing." Another broadcaster concurred. "At certain times, at certain hours in our history, God has had a certain man to hear His testimony."[72] The stage was set for another hard-fought presidential campaign, one in which values, morality, and religion would take center stage.

The 2004 Election

Early in 2004 there was already talk of a "religion gap," or as Cal Thomas preferred, a "God gap,"[73] the contention that regular churchgoers—godly people in other words—were far more likely to be Republicans than Democrats. Lending support to this belief were exit polls from the 2000 election which showed Bush winning 56 percent of the voters who said they attended church weekly, as opposed to only 41 percent for Gore. This was proof to many on the religious right that the Republican party was the party of God, the party of values, the party that would return prayer to the schools, stop abortions, prevent stem-cell research, and check the advancement of homosexuality. As for Pat Robertson, there was no need even to hold an election, for by January 2004 he had already received a heavenly message that it was going to be "a blowout election" that Bush would "win in a walk."[74]

Admittedly, evangelical Protestants who attended services weekly definitely preferred Bush in 2000, giving him 64 percent of their votes to Gore's 34 percent, but a more thorough analysis of the election results disclosed the complexity of the religious community. Voters who went to church a few times a month chose Gore over Bush, 55 percent to 40 percent. Catholics who attended Mass weekly gave Bush a 7 percent edge, but those who attended Mass a few times a month went for Gore by the same margin. For African-American evangelicals, Gore was the favorite. Overall, 91 percent of Bush's supporters in 2000 identified themselves as religious, 81 percent of Gore's. More specifically, the breakdown for Bush was 41 percent evangelical, 22 percent mainline Protestant, 21 percent Catholic, 11 percent seculars, and 5 percent Jewish and others; for Gore, 48 percent Protestant, 23 percent Catholic, 19 percent seculars, and 10 percent Jews and others.[75] Such figures show that neither party had a lock on the religious vote, and certainly neither could lay claim to being God's party. Even so, the Republicans had the advantage in the "bumper sticker" campaign. Weekly worshippers identified with the Republican party, and so the GOP had to be "God's Own Party."

Put on the defensive by Republican religiosity, Democratic hopefuls for the 2004 presidential nomination scrambled "to find religion," sometimes with comical results. The early frontrunner, Howard Dean, a Congregationalist who had previously been a Catholic, then an Episcopalian, assured an Iowa audience that he prayed daily, and in New Hampshire, demonstrating an ecumenical flare, he used the Muslim expression for "God willing," *inshallah*. And as he prepared to head into the evangelical South, Dean announced his intention to talk more about God and Jesus. This prompted a reporter to inquire of the candidate his favorite book of the New Testament. Dean answered Job, amusing the biblically literate who knew the book to be in the Old Testament. Ever ready to pounce on religious flimflam, especially from the left, Cal Thomas strongly implied that Dean's sudden religiosity was nothing more than political opportunism calculated "to bamboozle Southern religious Democrats."[76] When asked about his faith, Catholic John Kerry, the eventual Democratic nominee, revealed that he had been an altar boy, had once considered the priesthood, and had worn a rosary around his neck during his service in Vietnam. But, added the New Englander, his faith was "more personal," not something to "throw . . . at people".[77] That comment would have been befitting in 1960 of John Kennedy, whose Catholicism many Protestants across the nation feared would sway public policies. Indicative of how much the landscape had changed, evangelicals in 2004 wanted a man in the White House whose faith *would* guide politics.

If Kerry was hesitant to "throw" his religion at people, not so President Bush, whose own spiritual flipflopping (Episcopalian/Presbyterian/Methodist) was never scrutinized in the same fashion as Dean's. In June 2004 the Bush campaign announced a plan to enlist the direct support of the nation's churches that was not only unprecedented but also breathtaking in its audacity. Volunteers were asked to send church directories to the Bush campaign headquarters by July 31; they were to talk to various groups within the congregation about the president and recruit five more volunteers for the cause by August 15; they were to host at least two campaign-related potluck dinners with church members by September 17; and in October they were to call church members, distribute voter guides, and place notices in church bulletins about the necessity of Christians going to the polls in November. Defending this effort, a spokesperson for the administration asserted that "people of faith have as much right to participate in the political process as any other community." But liberal and some conservative groups were wary. The executive director of Americans United for Separation of Church and State, Barry Lynn, was astonished by so blatant an attempt "to meld a political party with a network of religious organizations." That Lynn considered the effort a violation of church-state separation is not surprising, but even Richard Land, director of the Ethics and Religious Liberty Commission of the Southern Baptist Convention, a body increasingly friendly toward Republicans since the early 1990s, was concerned. "If I were a pastor," said Land, "I would not be comfortable doing that." The Bush campaign was unmoved. "We strongly believe that our religious outreach program," responded a spokesperson, "is well within the framework of the law."[78]

While the November outcome of the presidential election pleased the religious right, the movement sustained numerous setbacks at the state and local levels. To be sure, Texans overwhelmingly approved an amendment prohibiting gay marriage, but Maine voters handily turned aside an attempt to repeal that state's new gay-rights law, which proscribed discrimination based on sexual orientation in employment and public accommodations. Californians defeated a proposition requiring parental notification by minor girls seeking an abortion, and in Dover, Pennsylvania, all eight Republican school board members who had attracted national attention earlier in the year by requiring the teaching of intelligent design in science classes were turned out. And the Virginia electorate rejected the gubernatorial candidacy of Republican Jerry Kilgore, heavily backed by the religious right, in favor of Tim Kaine, a Catholic who had argued that he could separate his personal opposition to abortion and the death penalty from his duty as governor to uphold the legality of both.[79]

As for the presidential contest itself, Bush probably owed as much to Roman Catholics as to Protestant evangelicals. Paradoxically, Kerry faced aggressive opposition from his own church's conservative hierarchy, including some bishops who threatened to refuse him communion or even excommunicate him. The effect was devastating. Kerry in 2004 received 5 percent fewer Catholic votes than had southern Baptist Gore in 2000, and this was crucial in several swing states. In Ohio, for instance, Bush carried 55 percent of the Catholic votes.[80] But it was evangelical voters, who had given Bush about a third of his margin of victory, who received most of the attention, and whose leaders were quick to take full credit for the Republican triumph. And why not? Just days after the election Karl Rove, the president's top political strategist, was on NBC's *Meet the Press* paying tribute to those regular churchgoers who had turned out in such heavy numbers to support Bush. And the press, as Mark Danner cleverly observed, seemed "happy to play along" with this assessment, creating through repetition "the appearance ... [of] reality".[81] Bob Jones III, who needed no encouragement from Rove or anyone else, took for granted that Bush was indebted to the religious right. As he saw it, the president was obligated to "pass legislation defined by BIBLICAL norms" and to "leave an imprint of righteousness upon this nation that brings with it the blessings of Almighty God." Toward that end Jones urged the president to purge moderates from his administration. "If you have weaklings around you who do not share your biblical values, shed yourself of them," he declared, adding: "You owe the liberals nothing. They despise you because they despise your Christ."[82] Focus on the Family's James Dobson, who for the first time had publicly endorsed a presidential candidate and had actively campaigned for several conservative Republican senatorial candidates, held a special program, "Moral Victory in America," to praise God for saving the nation from a Kerry presidency. Explaining his vigorous role in this campaign, Dobson stated, "I simply could not sit this one out. I just feel this year, I had to do everything I could to keep the loony left from capturing the United States Supreme Court and shaping its liberal decisions for the next 25 years."[83]

The Religious Right Today

Amid the post-election euphoria was a certain amount of wariness on the religious right. Evangelicals had labored in the political vineyards before only to be disappointed once their votes had been harvested. The attitude of Robert Knight, head of an affiliate of Concerned Women for America, a conservative Christian advocacy group, was widespread. "Business as usual isn't going to cut it," he noted, "where the GOP rides to victory by espousing traditional family values and then turns around and rewards the liberals in its ranks." Wasting no time savoring 2004, Jerry Falwell organized a few days after the election a refurbished version of the Moral Majority, the Faith and Values Coalition. The objective was not only to serve notice that evangelicals were watching closely to see if Republican deeds now matched their campaign rhetoric, but also to frustrate the future presidential ambitions of candidates supportive of abortion and gay rights. Falwell had former New York Mayor Rudolph Giuliani and Arizona Senator John McCain specifically in mind.[84]

The composition of the Supreme Court is a major concern of the religious right, for many social conservatives hold judges, more so than lawmakers, responsible for moving the nation away from traditional values. The school prayer decisions of the early 1960s, the abortion decision of the early 1970s, and just recently the gay marriage decision of Massachusetts' Supreme Court come to mind. This explains the instant outrage of James Dobson and Louis Sheldon, Chairman of the Traditional Values Coalition, to the prospect of Pennsylvania Senator Arlen Specter, a moderate Republican who considered it unlikely that antiabortion judges could gain Senate confirmation, becoming chairman of the powerful Senate Judiciary Committee. While Sheldon threatened political retaliation against Republicans who backed Specter, Dobson pressured the Senate Republican caucus to consider someone else, the Pennsylvanian's seniority notwithstanding.[85] The religious right failed to block Specter, but it succeeded against President Bush's first Supreme Court nominee, Harriet Miers of Texas, a moderate unacceptable to many social conservatives. The president's other two selections—John Roberts to replace the deceased William Rehnquist as chief justice and Samuel Alito to replace the retiring Sandra Day O'Connor—met the approval of religious conservatives and were confirmed over strong liberal opposition.

Whether these judicial appointments will produce the desired result for the religious right remains to be seen. The only thing certain so far is that the new justices have altered the court's ideological balance somewhat. Roberts, Alito, Antonin Scalia, and Clarence Thomas constitute a solid conservative counterpoise to liberals John Paul Stevens, David Souter, Ruth Bader Ginsburg, and Stephen Breyer. This leaves Justice Anthony Kennedy, who emerged during the court's 2005-2006 term as the new "swing vote," a position long occupied by O'Connor. This perhaps does not bode well for the religious right, for in the past Kennedy has voted with the liberals to uphold gay rights and abortion rights. This also means that if the president has an opportunity to nominate another Supreme Court justice, and if that nominee is of the same temperament as Roberts and Alito, the confirmation battle will be titanic. And Dobson, Falwell, Sheldon, Robertson, and others of their kind will certainly rally the religious faithful to ensure a more godly future for the nation.

The political activism of the religious right, which has grown more intense, sometimes even venomous, since the 1980s, raises the perennial issue of religion and politics. The righteous, whether of the left or right, have the right to engage in politics, and organized religion is entitled to bring pressure to bear on matters of public concern. That is exactly what the religious left did in the

1950s and 1960s, and so also the religious right since the late 1970s. The dispute arises over the arrogation of God by one side to support a specific set of political objectives, thereby implying the other side is ungodly and irreligious. And of this practice the religious right has been guilty. Admittedly a biased observer, John Buchanan nevertheless put it aptly. "The fatal flaw of the Religious Right," he said, "is to baptize the mentality of the John Birch Society."[86] This assurance of God's support perhaps accounts for the religious right's propensity for harsh, judgmental rhetoric. How else could one explain Robertson's outburst in Iowa in 1992? 'The feminist agenda is not about equal rights for women,' he asserted. 'It is about a socialist, anti-family political movement that encourages women to leave their husbands, kill their children, practice witchcraft, destroy capitalism and become lesbians.'[87] The religious right has all too often indulged in this kind of inflammatory speech, apparently convinced that its opponents on everything from the ERA and abortion to guns and homosexuality are Satan's minions.

Footnotes

1. See Sanford Kessler, *Tocqueville's Civil Religion, American Christianity and the Prospects for Freedom* (Albany: State University Press, 1994), p. 12; Alexis de Tocqueville, *Democracy in America*, vol. I (New York: Vintage, 1945, 12th ed.), p. 314; 'Emerging Trends,' Princeton Religious Research Center, December 1992, p. 1, April 1993, pp. 3–4, January 1994, pp. 1–3, March 1994, pp. 1–2, June 2000, pp. 1–2; James F. Findlay, Jr., *Church People in the Struggle* (New York: Oxford University Press, 1993), pp. 3–75; John W. Storey, 'Religious Fundamentalism and Politics of the Far Right,' in *conflict and Change, America 1939 to Present* (St. Louis: River City, 1983), pp. 65–76; *Newsweek*, March 10, 2003, p. 28; and *The New York Review*, Nov. 6, 2003, pp. 82–83; and George W. Bush, inaugural address, Jan. 20, 2005.

2. *Houston Chronicle*, March 11, 2000, p. 23A, Oct. 18, 2000, pp. 29–30A, Oct. 20, 2000, p. 31A, and Aug. 31, 2005, p. A6; and *Beaumont Enterprise*, Nov. 12, 2005, p. 11A

3. *Mother Jones*, Jan.-Feb. 2000, pp. 35–37, *Houston Chronicle*, Sept. 27, 2000, p. 14A, Nov. 9, 2005, p. A3; and *Chronicle of Higher Education*, Oct. 29, 1999, pp. 7–8B.

4. Richard V. Pierard, "Religion and the New Right in Contemporary American Politics," in *Religion and Politics* (Waco: Baylor University Press, 1983), p. 64.

5. See Storey, pp. 67–68.

6. *Ibid.*, pp. 68–72.

7. *Ibid.*, p. 72.

8. Richard Hofstadter, *The Paranoid Style in American Politics and Other Essays* (New York: Vintage Books, 1967), pp. 3–40; and Billy James Hargis, *Christian Crusade*, vol. 42, no. 8, August 1994, p. 1. More recent publication show no change in Hargis's worldview. See "Russia is arming the Red Chinese—just as before!," Newsletter, Oct. 1999.

9. See David Edwin Harrell, Jr., *Pat Robertson, A Personal, Religious and Political Portrait* (New York: Harper and Row, 1987, p. 212.

10. "Religious and Civil Rights Leaders Urge Christian Coalition to Repudiate Use of Race as a Wedge Issue by Candidates and Organizations," The Interfaith Alliance, Oct. 21, 1996, Internet; Harley Collins, "Christian Coalition Not Practicing What it Preaches," March 20, 1998, Internet.

11. See Harrell, p. 207; *Houston Chronicle*, June 15, 2006, p. A13.

12. See Harrell, p. 205; *The New Yorker*, June 19, 2006, p. 30.

13. *Beaumont Enterprise*, Feb. 23, 2000, p. 11A.

14. *Maranatha Christian Journal*, Nov. 21, 2000, pp. 1–2, http://www.mcjonline.com/news/oob/20000929a.htm; *Newsweek*, Oct. 9, 2000, p. 28, and *The New Yorker*, June 26, 2006, pp. 46–53.

15. See Storey, p. 75.

16. *Houston Chronicle*, Dec. 13, 2000, p. 4A.

17. See Harrell, pp. 184–95.

18. See *Newsweek*, Sept. 15, 1980, pp. 28–36.

19. See Harrell, p. 185.

20. *Houston Chronicle*, July 8, 1980, sec. 4, p. 28.

21. See Pierard, p. 63.

22. *Newsweek*, Sept. 15, 1980. p. 32.

23. See Pierard, pp. 67–68, 71.

24. Walter H. Capps, *The New Religious Right: Piety, Patriotism, and Politics* (Columbia: University of South Carolina Press, 1990), p. 99; and *Newsweek*, April 26, 1982, pp. 89–91.

25. *US New & World Report*, June 21, 1982, pp. 43–44. See also *Newsweek*, Sept. 15, 1980, p. 32.

26. Henry Steele Commager, "Religion and Politics in American History," in *Religion and Politics* (Waco: Baylor University Press, 1983), pp. 53–54.

27. *US News & World Report*, June 21, 1982; pp. 43–44; *Washington Post*, June 13, 1982, p. 2A, and Aug. 21, 1981, p. 143.

28. *Houston Chronicle*, April 5, 1987, sec. 1, p. 7.

29. *Newsweek*, July 13, 1987, p. 52, and July 11, 1988, pp. 26–28.

30. See Harrell, pp. 187–88.

31. *Houston Chronicle*, April 5, 1987, sec. 1, p. 7.

32. See Harrell, pp. 80–81, 188, 207, 124–15; and *Newsweek*, July 13, 1987, p. 52.

33. See Harrell, p. 226.

34. *Houston Chronicle*, Sept. 4, 1994, pp. 20–21A.

35. *Ibid*, p. 21A, See also Nov. 10, 1994, pp. 25, 27, 30A.

36. *Ibid.*, Nov. 10, 1994, p. 26A.

37. *Ibid.*

38. *Newsweek*, Oct. 3, 1994, p. 48.

39. *Houston Chronicle*, June 4, 1994, sec. E, p. 1.

40. Linda Killian, *The Freshmen, What Happened to the Republican Revolution?* (Boulder, Colorado: Westview Press, 1998), pp. 14–22.

41. *Ibid*, pp. 187–95, 254–59, 376, 406–407.

42. *Ibid*, p. 185.

43. *Houston Chronicle*, June 11, 1999, p. 4A.

44. See Killian, pp. 385–86.

45. *Beaumont Enterprise*, June 11, 1999, p. 8A; *Newsweek*, June 21, 1999, p. 39; and *Christianity Today*, March 2, 1998, vol. 42, No. 3, p. 74, ctedit@aol.com.

46. Freedom Writer, "End of the Road," Summer 2000, http://apocalypse.berkshire.net/~:fas/fn0006/coalition.html.

47. Steve Benen, "Christian Coalition Congressional Scorecard Flunks Democrats,' Americans United for Separation of Church and State, June 1998, pp. 1–2, Internet.

48. *Newsweek*, June 21, 1999, p. 39; *Beaumont Enterprise*, June 11, 1999, p. 8A.

49. *Beaumont Enterprise*, June 11, 1999, p. 8A.

50. *Ibid.*; and *Houston Chronicle*, June 11, 1999, p. 4A.

51. *Houston Chronicle*, Aug. 3, 1999, p. 3A.

52. *Emerging Trends*, Sept. 2000, p. 5.

53. *U.S. News & World Report*, May 4, 1998, pp. 20–21.

54. *Washington Post Weekly Edition*, March 8, 1999, p. 10; *Christianity Today.Com*, Sept. 6, 1999, p. 1, http://www.findarticles.com/cf_1/m1060/10_43/55820705/p1/article.jhtml.

55. *Beaumont Enterprise*, March 28, 1999, p. 3B, and April 23, 1000, p. 2D, *Houston Chronicle*, June 12, 1999, p. 1E.

56. *Newsweek*, Aug. 24, 2000, pp. 41–42, and *Beaumont Enterprise*, Sept. 2, 2005, p. 13A.

57. *The Christian Century*, May 19, 1999, pp. 1–2, http://www.findarticles.com/cf_1/m1058/16_116/54898666/p1/article.jhtml; *The American Enterprise Online*, April 2000, pp. 1–2, http://www.findarticles.com/cf_1m2185/3_11/61402621/p1/article.jhtml.

58. *Houston Chronicle*, Sept. 7, 1999, pp. 1, 16A, Sept. 27, 1999, p. 9A, June 18, 2000, p. 30A; Paul Burka, "The Disloyal Opposition," *Texas Monthly*, Dec. 1998, http://www.texasmonthly.com/mag/1998dec/schoolboard.1.2.3.4.html.

59. *Beaumont Enterprise*, Sept. 30, 2000, p.9A.

60. *Newsweek*, Oct. 9, 2000, p. 30; *The Inquirer*, Sept. 30, 2000, pp. 1–2, http://inq.philly.com/content/inquirer/2ooo/109/30/front_page/right30.htm.

61. *The Washington Post National Weekly Edition*, March 17, 2000, p. 14; *Beaumont Enterprise*, Sept. 30, 2000, p. 9A; *Newsweek*, April 24, 2000, p. 43.

62. *Houston Chronicle*, Feb. 29, 2000, pp. 1, 4, 5A.

63. *Beaumont Enterprise*, Feb. 19, 2000, p. 40A, Feb. 23, 2000, p. 11A; *The Washington Post National Weekly Edition*, Oct. 9, 2000, p. 21.

64. *Houston Chronicle*, May 8, 2000, p. 4A; *Beaumont Enterprise*, April 23, 2000, p. 2B, Sept. 30, 2000, p. 9A.

65. *Beaumont Enterprise*, Oct. 29, 2000, p. 2B.

66. *Ibid.*, Aug. 14, 2000, p. 10A.

67. *Ibid.*, Dec. 25, 2000, p. 16A; *Houston Chronicle*, Dec. 23, 2000, p. 18A, Dec. 24, 2000, pp.1, 20A, and Dec. 29, 2000, p. 45A.

68. *The New York Review of Books*, Nov. 6, 2003, pp. 84–85.

69. *Ibid.*, p. 85.

70. Maureen Dowd, *Bushworld, Enter At Your Own Risk* (New York: G.P. Putnam's Sons, 2004), p. 50.

71. *The New York Review of Books*, Nov. 6, 2003, p.86.

72. *Ibid.*

73. *Beaumont Enterprise*, Jan. 4, 2004, p. 2B.

74. *Ibid.*, Jan. 13, 2004, p. 18A.

75. *The American Prospect*, March 2004, pp. 38–40; and *Baptist Standard*, Feb. 9, 2004, p. 13.

76. *Beaumont Enterprise*, Jan. 4, 2004, p. 2B. See also *Houston Chronicle*, Jan. 11, 2004, p. 4C.

77. *Beaumont Enterprise*, Jan. 13, 2004, p. 18A.

78. 78 *Houston Chronicle*, June 6, 2004, p. 18A, July 2, 2004, p. 12A.

79. *Baptist Standard*, Nov. 14, 1005, p. 6.

80. *The New York Review of Books*, Jan. 13, 2005, p. 53.

81. *Ibid.* Also, *Houston Chronicle*, Nov. 10, 2004, p. A15.

82. *The New York Review of Books*, Jan 13, 2005, p. 53; and *Houston Chronicle*, Nov. 13, 2004, p. A4.

83. *Houston Chronicle*, Nov. 21, 2004, p. A17.

84. *Ibid.*, Nov. 13, 2004, p. A4.

85. *Ibid.*, Nov. 13, 2004, p. A4, Nov. 21, 2004, p. A17.

86. Harrell, p. 218.

87. *Houston Chronicle*, Nov. 10, 1994, p. 26A.

2

Chronology

Historically speaking, the religious right is a relatively recent development, but its roots extend far into the nineteenth century. Hence, the purpose of the chronology is to provide depth and context to the contemporary movement. Accordingly, 1835 is an appropriate starting point, inasmuch as a German publication that year symbolizes for many of today's Christian conservatives, including those on the religious right, the dangers of theological liberalism. By the same token, the 1843 entry on William Miller underscores the fact that end-time expectations, such as those popularized most recently by the *Left Behind* series, are hardly new to the American experience. And the 1859 reference to Charles Darwin's famous opus requires no explanation, for the debate over evolution is as heated today as it was in the 1920s. In essence, items in the chronology are intended to illuminate, either directly or indirectly, not only the present religious, political, and social concerns of the religious right, but also the origins of those concerns. In a sense, the current religious right is a manifestation of impulses that run deep in American history. The chronology accentuates that point.

1835–
1836

The Life of Jesus by the German theologian David Friedrich Strauss not only creates a sensation in Europe, but also comes to symbolize the kind of biblical scholarship that will appall American religious conservatives in the later nineteenth century. Relying upon the "myth theory," Strauss argues that Jesus represented not a divine intervention in history, but rather a psychological projection of the beliefs of people at a particular moment. This kind of "higher criticism" offends many religious conservatives.

1843

William Miller, a New York farmer and Baptist preacher, predicts that Jesus will return to earth on March 21. After Jesus fails to appear, Miller adjusts his calculations, which are based primarily on the prophecies of Daniel, and announces the return will occur on October 22, 1844.

1859   Charles Darwin's *Origin of Species* sets forth a theory of evolution based upon natural selection. To the religious community, the implications of Darwin are astonishing. In one fell swoop the British naturalist replaces purpose, direction, and spirit with a random, non-directed, and thoroughly materialistic explanation of existence. While many Christians seek to reconcile their faith with the new science, just as many recoil and prepare for battle against the new ideas.

1871   James Freeman Clarke's widely read *Ten Great Religions* disturbs many Christian conservatives, for it suggests that Christianity is just one of many important religions, and that many things thought to be unique to Judeo-Christianity, such as floods, crucifixions, resurrections, and virgin births, are actually common to other religions.

1874   Francis L. Patton of McCormick Theological Seminary, a Presbyterian institution in Chicago, charges the pastor of the Fourth Presbyterian Church in Chicago, David Swing, of heresy. Although acquitted by the local presbytery, Swing nonetheless resigns and establishes an independent congregation.

In *Outline of Cosmic Philosophy*, John Fiske, a popular philosopher and historian associated for a while with Harvard University, seeks to resolve the conflict between religion and Darwin by simply asserting that evolution is God's way of doing things.

1876   Religious conservatives led primarily by Presbyterians launch the Niagara Bible Conferences. Influenced greatly by John Nelson Darby (1800–1882), an Anglican minister who helped establish the Plymouth Brethren movement in Great Britain, these conferences, which will occur annually for about a quarter century, concentrate on biblical prophecy. Darby's sway is readily apparent in the widespread acceptance by many religionists who attend these meetings of dispensational premillennialism, the twofold belief that history is divided into seven distinct dispensations, and that Christ's return will inaugurate a thousand-year reign of earthly righteousness.

1878   Professor Alexander Winchell of Vanderbilt University is censured by the General Conference of the Southern Methodist Church for contradicting the Genesis account of creation. When the professor refuses to resign, the Methodist school eliminates his position.

1879   Southern Baptist Theological Seminary in Louisville, Kentucky, forces one of its professors, Crawford H. Toy, to resign for questioning the absolute authority of the Bible.

1882   Professor Ezra P. Gould is fired from Newton Theological Seminary, a Baptist school in Massachusetts, for heretical teachings.

1886   The uncle of Woodrow Wilson, Professor James Woodrow of Columbia Theological Seminary, a Presbyterian school in South Carolina, is fired as a result of an address in which he had argued that Darwinian evolution and religion were reconcilable.

To educate students in an institution untainted by modernist sentiments, the world-renowned evangelist Dwight L. Moody establishes the Moody Bible Institute in Chicago. Its curriculum is steeped in missions, evangelism, and Bible prophecy. The school becomes the prototype for countless other "Bible institutes" across the nation.

1891   Professor Charles A. Briggs of Union Theological Seminary (New York) faces heresy charges because of his rejection of the theory of "verbal inspiration" of the Bible. Although Union Seminary, a Presbyterian school, stands behind him, Briggs resolves the problem for the Presbyterians by becoming an Episcopalian.

1892   Professor Henry Preserved Smith of Lane Theological Seminary, a Presbyterian school in Cincinnati, Ohio, is convicted of heresy by the Presbytery of Cincinnati. Smith subsequently obtains a librarian's position at Union Seminary and becomes a Congregationalist.

1895   The Niagara Bible Conference enunciates the five "essentials" of Christianity, essentials which will guide fundamentalists from this point forward—the inerrancy of the Bible, the deity and virgin birth of Jesus; the substitutionary atonement; the bodily resurrection of Jesus; and the second coming.

1896   The founding president of Cornell University, Andrew Dickinson White, writes *A History of the Warfare of Science with Theology*. At sharp variance with the fundamentalists, who fear science, White argues that religion has retarded scientific thought.

1909   An annotated edition of the scriptures, *The Scofield Reference Bible*, perhaps the most influential source of dispensational premillennial ideas in the twentieth century, is prepared by Cyrus I. Scofield (1843–1912), a lawyer-turned-preacher who pastored the First Congregational Church, Dallas, Texas, from 1882–1895 and again from 1902–1907. Scofield's commentaries subsequently become "the Bible" for many fundamentalists.

1910–   *The Fundamentals: A Testimony to the Truth*, a set of twelve pamphlets
1915   each about 125 pages long, is published over a five-year period at the expense of two wealthy Presbyterian laymen from California. Distributed free to ministers, seminary professors, theology students, Sunday school directors, and YMCA leaders throughout the country, these booklets, each written by a prominent religious conservative,

not only reaffirm the "essentials" of the Niagara Bible Conference of 1895, but also denounce evolution, higher criticism, Catholicism, Mormonism, Jehovah's Witnesses, Christian Scientists, Spiritualism, and much more.

1919   In an effort to give direction to their crusade against modernism, some 6,000 like-minded believers, spurred on by William Bell Riley, pastor of the First Baptist Church, Minneapolis, from 1897–1942, gather in Philadelphia and create the World Christian Fundamentals Association. This organization, which includes the country's most prominent fundamentalists, leads the charge in favor of anti-evolution laws and against John T. Scopes for teaching evolution in Tennessee.

Ratification of the Eighteenth Amendment, which ushers in national prohibition, is viewed with justifiable pride by many church people, for they, working closely with the Anti-Saloon League and other agencies, contributed measurably to the amendment's success.

1920   Curtis Lee Laws, the editor of *The Watchman-Examiner*, a Northern Baptist paper, coins the term "fundamentalist," asserting that such a Christian is one willing to battle for the fundamentals of the faith.

1922   President Frank L. McVey of the University of Kentucky urges the people of his state to oppose the anti-evolution bill being debated by the state legislature. McVey's courageous stand contributes to the bill's subsequent defeat in Kentucky.

1923   The Oklahoma legislature passes the nation's first anti-evolution law, followed a short time later by Florida, the adopted home of William Jennings Bryan, who crusades tirelessly on behalf of anti-evolution laws.

1924   Reflecting liberal sentiment within Presbyterianism, the Auburn Affirmation rejects such basic fundamentals as inerrancy of the Bible, the virgin birth, substitutionary atonement, the bodily resurrection of Jesus, and the reality of biblical miracles. Appalled by this statement, J. Gresham Machen rallies the denomination's conservative forces.

1925   The Tennessee legislature enacts a measure making it illegal to teach evolution in the public schools. A few months later John Thomas Scopes, a young teacher in Dayton, is brought to trial for violating the new statute. The resulting "monkey affair" attracts national attention, for it pits two prominent figures against one another. The American Civil Liberties Union retains the famous Chicago criminal attorney Clarence Darrow for the defense, while the World Christian

Fundamentals Association brings in the former secretary of state and frequent presidential contender William Jennings Bryan for the prosecution. Inasmuch as Scopes is convicted and the anti-evolution law upheld, the fundamentalists prevail at Dayton. On the other hand, many Americans are appalled by the whole spectacle and wonder about the wisdom of state-mandated "solutions" to moral and religious questions. The World Christian Fundamentals Association declines rather abruptly after the trial.

Upon Bryan's death, which occurs just days after the conclusion of the Scopes trail, Paul W. Rood, a California evangelist, organizes the Bryan Bible League in Turlock, California. Fiercely opposed to the theory of biological evolution, Rood and the Bryan Bible League spearhead the failed attempt to enact an anti-evolution law on the west coast.

1926   The Mississippi legislature passes an anti-evolution law.

Bob Jones, Sr., founds his college in College Point, Florida. This fundamentalist school is unaffiliated with any religious denomination.

1928   Arkansas, which is the only state to do so by popular referendum, outlaws the teaching of evolution by a vote of almost two-to-one. Although this is the last of five southern states to pass such legislation, the same objective is achieved throughout the country, north and south, by applying pressure at the local level, notably on school boards.

1929   J. Gresham Machen abandons Princeton Theological Seminary because of its liberal teachings and founds his own Westminster Theological Seminary in Philadelphia.

1933   Thirty-four American humanists, including educator John Dewey, sign *The Humanist Manifesto*, which fundamentalists will later point to as "the Bible" of secular humanism.

1936   The liberal wing of the Presbyterian Church defrocks J. Gresham Machen, who promptly establishes the Presbyterian Church of America.

1941   To counter the Federal (later National) Council of Churches, Carl McIntire founds the American Council of Christian Churches. Made in the image of its creator, this fundamentalist organization is rigidly separatist, admitting to membership only those who share its narrow theology and who eschew association with nonbelievers.

Under the auspices of the Moody Bible Institute, five evangelical scientists journey to Chicago to discuss formation of a creationist society. The result is the American Scientific Affiliation, whose growing membership is dominated by Mennonites, Baptists, and Presbyterians in the middle Atlantic and Midwestern states. Tension soon emerges within the Affiliation between strict biblical literalists and evangelical scientists inclined toward a more metaphorical view of Genesis.

1942   The National Association of Evangelicals, which welcomes both individuals and denominations into its membership, is established as a fundamentalist alternative to the Federal Council of Churches. It soon becomes an alternative for many conservative Christians who are uncomfortable with the rigid dogmatism of fundamentalists such as Carl McIntire and Bob Jones.

1947   Radio evangelist Charles Fuller establishes Fuller Theological Seminary in Pasadena, California. This institution becomes identified with a more moderate, less separatist variety of fundamentalism. In the tradition of John Nelson Darby and C. I. Scofield, Fuller is a dispensationalist.

Bob Jones University moves to its present site in Greenville, South Carolina.

1951   With headquarters in Cincinnati, Ohio, Circuit Riders, Inc., is organized to combat socialism and/or communism and all other forms of alleged anti-American teachings in the Methodist Church. Actually, Myers Lowman, founder of this group, scrutinizes virtually all the major religious bodies in America and identifies sizeable numbers in each as either communist or procommunist. He considers approximately one-third of the scholars who collaborated on the Revised Standard Version of the Bible to be procommunist.

Another crusading anticommunist, Billy James Hargis, incorporates the Christian Echoes National Ministry, better known as the Christian Crusade.

1953   At the behest of Carl McIntire, Billy James Hargis takes charge of a Bible Balloons project to float portions of the Bible into eastern European communist countries in gas-filled balloons. On May 7 some 10,000 balloons are set aloft from West Germany.

1954   The phrase "under God" is added to the pledge of allegiance to the flag.

Bernard Ramm, a Baptist theologian and philosopher of science, publishes *The Christian View of Science and Scripture*, which provides theological support for a more progressive approach to creationism, an approach more in harmony with conventional geology regarding the age of Earth and humankind.

1956   "In God We Trust," which was inscribed on American currency the previous year, becomes the national motto. Coming at the height of Cold War tensions, this and other gestures of government support for religion appeal to many Americans.

1958   Named for "a young fundamentalist Baptist preacher from Macon, Georgia," who allegedly was murdered by Chinese communists after World War II, the John Birch Society is launched by Robert Welch. This organization and its leader enjoy cordial relations with such figures on the religious right as Carl McIntire and Billy James Hargis.

1960   Pat Robertson launches the Christian Broadcasting Network (CBN).

1962   In *Engel v. Vitale*, popularly known as the School Prayer decision, the Supreme Court declares it unconstitutional to recite a brief, nondenominational prayer which was composed by the New York State Board of Regents. The prayer seems inoffensive enough, declaring simply: "Almighty God, we acknowledge our dependence upon Thee, and we beg Thy blessing upon us, our parents, our teachers and our Country." But to the Supreme Court, this public encouragement of religion violates the establishment clause of the First Amendment. The decision ignites a furor.

Disturbed by the content of many public school textbooks, Mrs. Norma Gabler of Longview, Texas, makes her first trip to the state capital to protest to the Texas Education Agency. The teaching of evolution, as well as anything else contrary to Mrs. Gabler's religious and patriotic views, offends the Texas housewife.

1963   The Supreme Court's decision in *Abingdon v. Schempp* involves two cases of required Bible reading in the public schools of Pennsylvania and Maryland. Mindful of the public outcry against its decision of the previous year, the Court takes pains in this case to explain the government's position of neutrality in matters of religion. Taking into account both the establishment and free exercise clauses of the First Amendment, the justices declare that statutes which either advance or inhibit religious expression violate the Constitution. On this basis, the Court rules against the states of Pennsylvania and Maryland. The Maryland case is all the more appalling to many religious conservatives since it has been brought by atheist Madalyn Murray.

Although the public reaction in 1963 is somewhat more restrained than it was to the decision of the previous year, many Americans are nonetheless angered. Hence, almost immediately several congressmen and senators seek to amend the Constitution, notably Representative Frank J. Becker of New York and Senator Everett Dirkson of Illinois. These efforts are unsuccessful.

Henry M. Morris, a Southern Baptist engineer known primarily for efforts to reconcile science and biblical literalism, joins several like-minded creationists in founding the Creation Research Society in Midland, Michigan. Although the Society initially is dominated by Missouri Synod Lutherans and Baptists, it also draws some support from Seventh-Day Adventists, Reformed Presbyterians, Reformed Christians, and Brethren. Morris and his group object vigorously to the "creeping evolutionism" of the older and more "liberal" creationist society, the American Scientific Affiliation.

1965   Rousas John Rushdoony, a California evangelist, founds the Chalcedon ministries and initiates an effort to "reconstruct" society in accordance with God's laws, a society comparable to that of the seventeenth century Puritans. Although these reconstructionists discard premillennial and dispensational eschatology, they stand with religious fundamentalists against "secular humanism," abortion, higher taxes, and bigger government. Evangelist Pat Robertson has spoken highly of Rushdoony. While opposed to abortion, the reconstructionists have not supported the militant tactics of Operation Rescue.

1969   Conservatives and fundamentalists among the Missouri Synod Lutherans elect J. A. O. Preus as president and embark upon a campaign to purify both the Synod and Concordia Seminary in Saint Louis. Committed to biblical inerrancy, conservative Lutherans rail against the "evils" of Darwin, Marx, and Freud.

1970   Tim LaHaye and Henry Morris establish the Christian Heritage College in San Diego, California. Their objective is to offer a liberal arts education in full accord with the Bible. The advancement of scientific creationism is a special concern, and so Morris launches the Institute for Creation Research, which in turn spearheads several efforts to find the remains of Noah's ark.

With funds from the National Science Foundation, Jerome Bruner of Harvard University develops a new social science curriculum for the nation's fifth- and sixth-graders. Titled *Man: A Course of Study*, the new textbooks arouse the ire of many religious conservatives because of their emphasis upon cultural relativity and de-emphasis of religion. The resulting controversy not only shelves the books and threatens the National Science Foundation itself, but also shows the ability of the religious right to mobilize its forces for a national campaign.

1971   In *Lemon v. Kurtzman* the Supreme Court sets forth a three-pronged test for determining whether a statute runs afoul of either the free exercise or establishment clauses of the First Amendment. The Court establishes three criteria for the appropriateness of a statute: (1) it must have a secular legislative purpose; (2) its principal effect must neither promote nor retard religion; and (3) it must avoid excessive government entanglements with religion. Laws transgressing any part of the test are unconstitutional.

1973   By a margin of seven to two, the Supreme Court in *Roe v. Wade* holds that laws restricting abortion during the first six months of pregnancy are unconstitutional. No decision of the Supreme Court since the prayer cases of the early 1960s so angers the religious right. Along with "restoring" prayer in the public schools, organizations on the religious right are as one in their resolve to restrict abortions. Indeed, opposition to abortion enables many religious and political, Protestant and Catholic conservatives to overlook their differences and cooperate on behalf of a common objective.

Mel Gabler takes early retirement from Exxon Pipeline and joins his wife Norma in a full-time crusade to purge public school textbooks in Texas of unsatisfactory material. To accomplish this objective, they found Educational Research Analysts. The Gablers believe that too many textbooks undermine both Judeo-Christian values and pride in America.

1976   Jimmy Carter, a "born again" Southern Baptist layman, is elected president. Because of Carter's religious persuasion, the media suddenly show considerable interest in evangelicals and fundamentalists. Ironically, many on the religious right, initially hopeful because of Carter's victory, are soon disappointed.

1977   The National Federation for Decency, better known as the Coalition for Better Television, is organized by Donald Wildmon of Tupelo, Mississippi. Working closely with other religious right groups, particularly the Moral Majority, the Coalition endeavors to make the air waves "safe" for family viewing.

1978   Jerome Kurtz, President Jimmy Carter's Internal Revenue Commissioner, announces plans to withdraw tax exemptions from private, including church, schools that were established presumably to avoid court-ordered public school desegregation. This decision infuriates many figures on the religious right who see it as another example of government hostility toward religion.

1979   With the help of Paul Weyrich, a conservative political strategist who coins the term "moral majority," Howard Phillips, leader of the Conservative Caucus, and Edward McAteer, a marketing specialist for Colgate-Palmolive Company, Jerry Falwell establishes the Moral Majority, Inc. The purpose is to give political expression to Americans on the religious right, Americans who feel their sentiments have been ignored too long. With the 1980 presidential race on the horizon, the Moral Majority embarks upon a crusade to destroy "secular humanism" and to restore the nation's religious heritage.

The Religious Roundtable is organized under the leadership of Edward McAteer. This organization labors to bring the religious and political right together.

Headquartered in Pasadena, California, the Christian Voice identifies fourteen specific issues by which the Christian morality of politicians supposedly can be assessed. Like many other organizations on the religious right, the Christian Voice is more "anti" than "pro." It opposes higher taxes, sex education without parental consent, forced busing, abortion, racial quotas, homosexual rights, the Department of Education, the Salt II arms agreement with the Soviet Union, drugs, and pornography. It favors free enterprise, prayer in the public schools, and a balanced federal budget.

Led by Texans Paul Pressler of Houston and Paige Patterson of Dallas, Southern Baptist fundamentalists elect one of their own president of the Southern Baptist Convention and set out to purge the denomination's schools and agencies of "liberals." By controlling the presidency, and the vast appointive power that goes with that office, the fundamentalists hope to gain control of the denomination's numerous committees and boards.

1980   Sponsored by Edward McAteer's Religious Roundtable, the National Affairs Briefing at the Reunion Arena in Dallas brings together prominent figures from the religious and political right. Presidential candidate Ronald Reagan attends.

In *Stone v. Graham* the Supreme Court declares unconstitutional a Kentucky law requiring the posting of the Ten Commandments in each public elementary and secondary classroom. In the eyes of the court, the purpose of the statute is clearly religious, for the first five commandments prescribe religious, not secular, duties.

Jerry Falwell's pamphlet, "Armageddon and the Coming War with Russia," voices the belief, so typical of many figures on the religious right, that a Russian invasion of Israel will precipitate a nuclear war, the battle of Armageddon, in which the world will be destroyed.

Echoing the same sentiment, Pat Robertson, in his *700 Club News-letter*, goes so far as to suggest that the titanic battle will occur by fall 1982.

Ronald Reagan is elected president with the strong support of religious right organizations such as Jerry Falwell's Moral Majority.

1981   Jerry Falwell advises "every good Christian" to oppose President Reagan's nomination of Sandra Day O'Conner to the Supreme Court because of the abortion issue. This prompts the Republican party's elder statesman, Barry Goldwater of Arizona, to retort that "every good Christian" should give the Virginia pastor a kick in the pants.

1982   President Ronald Reagan, in obvious deference to the religious right, becomes the first incumbent president to endorse a school prayer amendment. President Reagan informs Congress that the time has come to "allow prayer back in our schools."

Louis Sheldon founds the Traditional Values Coalition, a California-based organization, and aggressively seeks the defeat of politicians at odds with his "traditional values."

An antiabortion amendment fails to receive congressional approval after serious consideration.

1983   In *Bob Jones University v. United States* the Supreme Court strips the fundamentalist school of its tax-exempt status because of its racial practices. Convinced that the Bible prohibits interracial dating and marriage, Bob Jones University had excluded African Americans until 1971, at which time blacks who were married within their race were admitted. Applications from unmarried blacks were not accepted until 1975, at which time the university prohibited interracial dating and marriage among its students. This rule led eventually to the loss of the school's tax-exempt status.

1984   On March 5 Senate Majority Leader Howard H. Baker, Jr., opens the debate on President Reagan's proposed school prayer amendment. For two weeks the Senate grapples with the proposal. Senator Jesse Helms, a Republican from North Carolina, favors the proposal, while Senators Lowell Weicker and John Danforth, also Republicans, lead the opposition. When the vote is taken on March 20, a majority, 56 to 44, supports the amendment. However, the amendment does not receive the required two-thirds majority, and so the president's amendment fails. A defiant Senator Helms vows that the fight has only begun.

During the course of debate, several senators on each side of the issue indicate support for "equal access" legislation, a measure guaranteeing equal access to public school facilities for voluntary religious activities. In August Congress passes the Equal Access Act.

The Evangelical Voter, an analysis by Stuart Rothenberg and Frank Newport, challenges the assumption that evangelicals constitute a monolithic bloc of Christian voters. According to this study, income, race, education, and occupation seem to influence voting patterns more than religious beliefs. Moreover, evangelicals are more likely to be Democrats than Republicans, and they embrace diverse viewpoints. This report raises questions about the efficacy of mobilizing Christian conservatives for political purposes.

1985   In *Wallace v. Jaffree* the Supreme Court strikes down a 1981 Alabama law which allows school children a moment of silence "for meditation or voluntary prayer." The justices rule that Alabama lawmakers had violated the establishment clause of the First Amendment.

1987   In *Edwards v. Aguillard* the Supreme Court rules against Louisiana's Balanced Treatment for Creation-Science and Evolution-Science in Public School Instruction Act. This measure made it illegal to teach Darwinian evolution in Louisiana's public schools unless allowance has been made for the teaching of "creation science." According to the court, the Louisiana law promotes neither academic freedom nor scientific knowledge.

On March 4 Judge W. Brevard Hand of the United States District Court of the Southern District of Alabama in Mobile bans 31 textbooks from the public schools of Alabama on the basis that they illegally teach the "religion of secular humanism," thus violating the establishment clause of the First Amendment. Agreeing that secular humanism is a religion, many conservative Christians hail Judge Hand's ruling, which will be reversed by the 11th U.S. Circuit Court of Appeals in August.

Televangelist Jim Bakker, founder of the PTL ("Praise the Lord" or "People That Love") Club, is accused of adultery and financial wrongdoing. Jerry Falwell, momentarily given control of Bakker's empire, soon becomes embroiled in a nasty struggle to retain the PTL.

The Southern Baptist Convention faces another battle between the fundamentalist forces and the more moderate wing of the organization. Despite the efforts of a Peace Committee to resolve the conflict, the conservatives score another victory, electing inerrantist Adrian Rogers to the presidency of the Convention. However, later in the year the conservatives lose the fight for control of Mercer University and several state governing boards.

Reflecting growing conservative control, the Southern Baptist Convention's Public Affairs Committee votes by a narrow seven-to-five margin to support the U.S. Supreme Court nomination of Judge Robert Bark, whose positions on pornography, homosexuality, and the role of religion in American history strike a responsive chord within the convention.

In the case of *Mozert v. Hawkins County Board of Education*, Tennessee, a three-judge appeals court panel unanimously overturns an earlier ruling of U.S. District Court Judge Thomas G. Hull, who had allowed the children of Christian fundamentalists to take reading classes at home rather than read public school textbooks offensive to their beliefs. The books in question supposedly contained passages on witchcraft, astrology, pacifism, and feminism. To many conservative Christians, this decision is just another example of discrimination against fundamentalists.

1988   Although ultimately unsuccessful, Pat Robertson mounts a campaign for the presidency and early in the year outpolls Vice President George Bush in the Iowa caucuses. Fissures on the religious right soon surface, as many of the other right-wing evangelists support alternative candidates.

Jimmy Swaggart, the enormously successful Baton Rouge, Louisiana, Pentecostal, is engulfed in a sex scandal that undermines his ministry. This scandal, along with the PTL disgrace, has a damaging impact on televangelism in general. Donations fall sharply, forcing severe cutbacks in numerous ministries. For instance, Swaggart's college collapses and Falwell's faces bankruptcy.

Operation Rescue, one of the more aggressive antiabortion groups, emerges into national prominence by the usage of civil disobedience against abortion clinics. This group not only pickets, but also attempts to block women from entering clinics. As a result of protests at the Democratic National Convention, demonstrators from Operation Rescue clog Atlanta's jails. While religious fundamentalists applaud the objective, not all support the group's militant tactics.

The release of Martin Scorsese's film, *The Last Temptation of Christ*, angers the religious right. Pat Robertson denounces the movie, for instance, while Donald Wildmon runs counter-advertisements on 700 Christian radio stations and mails out over two million letters. Conservative columnist Pat Buchanan gives encouragement to the attack.

1989   The Christian Coalition, with headquarters in Chesapeake, Virginia, is organized in the wake of Pat Robertson's failed presidential bid in 1988. Describing itself as pro-family, this organization opposes abortion, pornography, condom distribution, waiting periods for handgun purchases, and tax and welfare programs that allegedly discriminate against mothers who stay home with their children. By keeping a "scorecard" on each member of Congress, this organization keeps local constituents informed on how their representatives or senators vote on "family" and "moral" issues.

1990   In *Board of Education of Westside Community School District v. Mergens*, the Supreme Court upholds the Equal Access Act, thereby ensuring religious groups the same access as secular groups to public school facilities.

              In *Oregon v. Smith* Justice Antonin Scalia, writing for the majority, holds that government need show only a "reasonable interest" as opposed to a "compelling interest" in order to limit the free exercise of religion. According to Scalia, the compelling interest doctrine, enunciated in *Sherbert v. Verner* (1963) and *Wisconsin v. Yoder* (1972), is a "luxury we can no longer afford." This prompts many in the religious community, including some on the right, to urge Congress to enact legislation "correcting" the High Court's decision.

1991   Paul Weyrich's National Empowerment Television (NET) hits the air waves. The purpose is not only to make the public aware of what is wrong with the government, but also to offer prescriptions for change. Viewer call-ins consume much of the new network's air time.

1992   The growing influence of the religious right within the Republican Party is evident at the national convention in Houston, Texas. The party's platform embraces the "pro-family" positions of the Christian right.

1993   In November Congress passes the Religious Freedom Restoration Act and President Bill Clinton applauds the measure. Its purpose is to restore the compelling interest test previously set aside in *Oregon v. Smith*.

1994   Dr. Jacob A. O. (Jack) Preus, former president of the Lutheran Church-Missouri Synod, who has led the attack against the denomination's liberals, dies in August in Burnsville, Minnesota.

              Condemning President Bill Clinton's "liberal agenda," Pat Robertson's Christian Coalition mounts a vigorous attack on the president and the Democratic Party. The objective is to "reclaim America" by defeating liberal Democrats in the November congressional elections.

Former Marine Lieutenant-Colonel Oliver North, who attracts national attention because of his role in the Iran-Contra scandal, wins the Republican Party's nomination for the U.S. Senate from Virginia. A born-again Christian who appeals openly to the religious right, North has the endorsement of Pat Robertson. North eventually loses the bitterly fought race to the Democratic incumbent, Charles Robb.

The growing political influence of the religious right at the state level is apparent not only in Virginia, but also in Texas, Oklahoma, and Kentucky.

The Anti-Defamation League releases a report entitled "The Religious Right: The Assault on Tolerance and Pluralism in America," which accuses evangelical and fundamentalist Christian leaders of playing upon fear and hatred in pursuit of political power. The report singles out the Christian Coalition, calling it exclusionist, a threat to American democracy, pluralism, and religious freedom, and hostile toward Jews. Pat Robertson replies that the report is filled with half-truths and fabrications "reminiscent of the political style practiced by Joseph McCarthy in the 1950s." This war of words illustrates conservative Jews and Christians in the quest for certain objectives of the religious right.

L. Brent Bozell, chairman of the conservative Media Research Center, notes that such television programs as *Picket Fences*, *L.A. Law*, *Northern Exposure*, and *Christy* have begun to treat religious figures and subjects with more sensitivity.

Several prominent Roman Catholics and evangelical Protestants issue Evangelicals and Catholics Together: The Christian Mission in the Third Millennium. This cautious statement of cooperation between groups that in the past have quarreled bitterly over matters of doctrine dismays many evangelical Christians. So while conservative Protestants and Catholics often share common positions on abortion and school prayer, ancient theological differences continue to hamper political cooperation.

Candidates beholden to the religious right score major victories in the November elections, as the Republicans obtain a majority in the House of Representatives for the first time in forty years, and also regain control of the Senate.

1995   More than thirty Jewish and conservative Christian leaders hold a five-hour meeting in Washington in an effort to stem the angry rhetoric prompted by last year's Anti-Defamation League report on the Christian right. In essence, the two sides agree to disagree without rancor. Jerry Falwell describes the gathering as positive, and Ralph Reed hopes to avoid such hostility in the future, but Abraham Foxman of the Anti-Defamation League declares that "the report stands." Foxman acknowledges that the report has caused Christian conservatives "pain," but hastily adds that Jews are also pained by the seeming antisemitism of some of Pat Robertson's remarks and the religious right's constant reference to the United States as a "Christian" nation.

Encouraged by the recent national elections, leaders of eight conservative and evangelical Christian groups prepare a constitutional amendment that would allow student-led prayers in public schools. Asked about school prayer on *This Week With David Brinkley*, a weekly ABC television program, House Speaker Newt Gingrich, R-Georgia, replies that a religious freedom bill of some sort, one that would go beyond merely school prayer, probably would come before the House after the Easter recess.

Speaking to the Conservative Political Action Conference, Ralph Reed warns that the Christian Coalition will not support the Republican party in 1996 unless the party's presidential and vice presidential candidates oppose abortion. This is a departure from Reed's effort to expand the base of the Christian Coalition by toning down the harsh rhetoric on moral issues.

Two prominent Southern Baptist leaders, Larry Lewis, president of the Southern Baptist Home Mission Board, and Richard Land, executive director of the convention's Christian Life Commission, come under attack for signing Evangelicals and Catholics Together. Critics contend the document is heretical, making too many concessions to Catholic doctrine, while defenders counter that theological differences should not deter evangelicals and Catholics from working together on such issues as abortion and school prayer.

Speaking from convention headquarters in Nashville, Tennessee, Jim Henry, president of the Southern Baptist Convention, and Richard Land, head of the convention's Christian Life Commission, declare their opposition to the nomination of Henry Foster as U.S. surgeon general. The two Baptist leaders object to Foster's stand on abortion. This brings a stern rebuke on NBC Nightly News from journalist and fellow Baptist Bill Moyers, who asserts that the Southern Baptist Convention has been "captured by a political posse allied with the Republican Party." Concludes Moyers: "The irony is that Henry Foster, MD, himself a Baptist, has been a lifelong crusader against teenage pregnancy and probably more successful at preaching abstinence than a dozen doctors of theology. But when God becomes partisan, religion becomes unforgiving and all subtlety excommunicated."

September

1996   The Christian Coalition is accused of racism for mailing out sample-voter guides which use a black man to portray issues the organization opposes and a white man to represent matters it supports. Ralph Reed apologizes, claiming a printer error, but Julian Bond, a board member of the National Association for the Advancement of Colored People, hints at hypocrisy, suggesting Reed's lofty preachments "about racial equality and Christian morality" are "tossed aside in favor of racial wedges and voter manipulation" at "election time."

November

1996   Over the opposition of the religious right, Bill Clinton defeats Republican challenger Bob Dole of Kansas. At the same time, twelve of the seventy-three Republican freshmen elected in 1994 are defeated for reelection, suggesting some public weariness with the Newt Gingrich-led "Republican Revolution of '94."

April

1997   Ralph Reed announces that he will step down as executive secretary of the Christian Coalition on September 1 to organize a political consulting firm, Century Strategies. He plans to work for the election of conservative politicians in upcoming elections. The U.S. Supreme Court declares the Religious Freedom Restoration Act unconstitutional, but leaves the door open to such legislation from the states. Split 6–3, the Court rules in *City of Boerne, Texas, v. Flores* (June 25) that Congress had exceeded its authority in the Religious Freedom Restoration Act, for that law "is not a proper exercise of Congress' ... enforcement power because it contradicts vital principles necessary to maintain separation of powers and the federal-state balance."

August

1997   Randy Tate, a staunchly conservative Republican elected to the U.S. House in 1994 from Washington's ninth congressional district, but defeated for reelection in 1996, assumes leadership of the Christian Coalition.

1998   Efforts to impeach President Bill Clinton gain momentum when it becomes apparent that his unequivocal denial on national television of a sexual relationship with a White House intern, Monica Lewinsky, is false. For many on the religious right, the president's misbehavior is symptomatic of the nation's moral decline.

June

1998   With congressional elections looming, the Christian Coalition releases its Congressional Scorecard, ranking all members of Congress on the basis of votes on twelve specific issues. Republicans in the House and Senate receive average scores of 89.8 and 80.3, respectively, whereas Democrats in the two chambers earn average marks of 13.1 and 6.1, respectively. To critics, such one-sided statistics mock the Christian Coalition's claim of nonpartisanship.

    Reflecting the reservations of some Americans about such legislation, Governor Pete Wilson, R-California, vetoes the California Religious Freedom Protection Act.

October

1998   As the midterm elections approach, Ralph Reed, now an independent political consultant, advises Republicans to tone down their rhetoric. It makes Republicans look mean-spirited, he observes, when they accuse others of "having the wrong values."

November

1998   Republicans suffer serious setbacks in the midterm elections, as Democrats gain five seats in the House and hold their own in the Senate. Democrats interpret their success as a signal from the American public to end the impeachment investigation of the president.

    Criticized for his party's poor performance in the midterm elections, House Speaker Newt Gingrich announces he will resign from the House and not seek the speakership in the forthcoming congressional term.

December

1998   Ralph Reed's first outing as an independent political strategist produces mixed results. While many of his candidates win, Reed loses a high-profile contest in Alabama, where Fob James, the Republican incumbent, is defeated.

Randy Tate of the Christian Coalition praises the House for its vote in favor of impeachment and calls on President Clinton to resign—this in the face of national polls showing continuing public support for the beleaguered president.

January

1999   Jerry Falwell arouses controversy when he asserts the Antichrist is a Jewish man who probably is alive now. In the face of protest, Falwell backtracks: "I apologize to my Jewish friends here and around the world, and I apologize to the Christians here for having created any kind of rift. I apologize not for what I believe, but for my lack of tact and judgment in making a statement that served no purpose whatsoever."

With the public showing little support for impeachment, Pat Robertson announces that Republicans should call off the effort to remove President Clinton. Polls in late December 1998 and January 1999 show that most Americans disapprove of the House's vote to impeach and object to the Senate's effort to remove Clinton. Indeed, 72 percent of Americans support the president's handling of his office.

Pat Robertson's announcement on impeachment bewilders many of his followers. One of the kinder responses comes from Andrea Sheldon, executive director of the Family Values Coalition, who remarks simply that friends sometimes disagree.

The Senate fails to convict the president.

As the state's legislative session begins, Texas Governor George W. Bush sides with social and religious conservatives on a parental notification law on abortion, a pilot program to test vouchers in private schools, and passage of the Religious Freedom Restoration Act. Even so, hardliners on the religious right, suspicious of the governor's commitment to their agenda, dub him "Conservative Lite."

Reflecting growing disenchantment within the political right, two former aides to Jerry Falwell and the Moral Majority—Cal Thomas, now a nationally syndicated newspaper columnist, and Ed Dodson, now a Michigan pastor—conclude in a new book, *Blinded by Might*, that "religious conservatives are best served by preaching the Christian gospel—not by preaching organized political involvement." Religious people should certainly continue to vote and run for office, assert the authors, but the "ordained clergy, left and right, from Jesse Jackson to Jerry Falwell should withdraw from partisan politics." This advice, coming from two of their own, does not set well with many on the religious right.

To the bemusement of some and the ire of others, Jerry Falwell announces that Tinky Winky, the oldest and biggest of television's psychedelic quartet of Teletubby children's characters, is a symbol of gay pride.

April

1999   While acknowledging "there is no easy solution to the violence and depravity that has swept America's schools," Randy Tate offers "the timeless values of faith and morality" as a potential remedy. Predictably, Tate supports school prayer, asserting: "When kids come together to pray, they more than likely will not come together to fight."

May

1999   Prone to intemperate remarks, Pat Robertson, on his television program, *The 700 Club*, criticizes Scotland for its tolerance of homosexuals, declaring "you can't believe how strong homosexuals are" in that "dark land." This prompts the Bank of Scotland to cancel a planned business venture with the televangelist.

After acknowledging that she believes in God, 17-year-old Cassie Bernall is slain along with eleven other Columbine High School classmates, thus becoming a martyr to many evangelical Christians. The attack at Columbine High in Littleton, Colorado, sparks renewed interest in religion in public schools, such as school prayer and posting of the Ten Commandments.

Former House Speaker Newt Gingrich tells a Republican Women Leaders Forum that teachers' unions bear responsibility for the Littleton shootings. "We have had a 35-year experiment in a unionized, bureaucratic, secular assault on the core values of this country .... God has been driven out of the classroom. We have seen the result in a secular, atheistic system in which God is not allowed to exist."

June

1999   Rep. Robert Aderhalt, R-Alabama, tacks the Ten Commandments to a juvenile crime bill designed to decrease school violence. Aderhalt believes the commandments will promote "the right values" in children and calm violence.

Governor Jeb Bush of Florida, brother of Gov. George W. Bush of Texas, signs legislation creating the nation's first statewide education voucher program. The law permits students in poor-performing public schools to attend private schools, including sectarian ones, of their choice at taxpayer expense. Fifty-eight students promptly enroll in the program, thereby receiving what Governor Jeb Bush calls "opportunity scholarships" of $3,389 from the state.

Craig Scott, 16-year-old brother of Rachel Scott, one of the twelve Columbine shooting victims, tells the Southern Baptist Convention: "I definitely think if we had prayers in school, this would never have happened."

Rep. Bob Barr, R-Georgia, in a House debate, suggests the Littleton shootings would not have occurred if the Ten Commandments had been posted in the school.

The U.S. House votes to allow the posting of the Ten Commandments in schools and other public buildings. Tom Flynn, a former Roman Catholic and the current director of the First Amendment Task Force for the Council of Secular Humanism, calls the vote not only an insult to millions of Americans, but also "a piece of legislative grandstanding that will almost certainly be ruled unconstitutional."

Jerry Falwell's newspaper, *National Liberty Journal*, asserts that the all-female Lilith Fair concert tour is named for a demon. According to ancient Jewish literature, Lilith was created by God as Adam's first wife, but she left Eden and dwelled with demons after refusing to be submissive to Adam.

Governor George W. Bush signs the Texas Religious Freedom Restoration Act, which forces the state to show a compelling interest, such as the protection of public health or safety, before restricting the free exercise of religion. Says Bush: "Texas will not stand for government interference with the free exercise of religion."

Pat Robertson's Christian Coalition loses its tax-exempt status, concluding a suit begun in 1996 when the Federal Election Commission sued the Coalition, claiming it was little more than an arm of the Republican party.

July

1999   The 11th U.S. Circuit Court of Appeals in Atlanta unanimously agrees that public school students in Alabama may pray on the public address system and at graduation exercises so long as they do not proselytize and so long as school personnel has no direct role in such activity. To prohibit students from engaging in any kind of prayer at school, reasons the appellate court, would be to foster atheism. "Permitting students to speak religiously signifies neither state approval nor disapproval of that speech," the judges declare.

August

1999   Federal District Judge Joyce Green dismisses the charges brought by the Federal Election Committee in 1996 that the Christian Coalition, through its literature, telephone banks, and other means, had worked for the reelection of Senator Jesse Helms, R-North Carolina, and President George Bush. Pat Robertson calls the decision a "decisive victory for First Amendment freedom."

By a 6–4 vote the Kansas Board of Education stuns the scientific community, making the teaching of evolution optional in the public schools and deleting questions about evolution from state assessment tests.

Some Kansas critics believe the decision on evolution makes the state look backward, a sentiment confirmed when a subsequent study commissioned by the Thomas B. Fordham Foundation and released in September 2000 ranks Kansas dead last with regard to the teaching of science.

Pat Robertson endorses political assassinations, reasoning that it makes more sense "to take out" someone like Yugoslav President Slobodan Milosevic or Iraqi President Saddam Hussein than to spend "billions of dollars on a war that harms innocent civilians." Sarcastically, Washington, D.C., columnist Marianne Means wonders if political assassination is Robertson's idea of "a good family value."

September

1999   A Gallup Poll discloses that 68 percent of Americans favor the teaching of creationism alongside evolution. This is not surprising, given that 44 to 50 percent of Americans since the late 1970s have consistently affirmed the belief that God created humans in their present form no more than 10,000 years ago.

Whether aware of such statistics or not, presidential aspirants for 2000 are careful not to offend the religious right on evolution. Vice President Al Gore says "localities should be free to teach creationism as well" as evolution; Governor George W. Bush believes youngsters "ought to be exposed to different theories about how the world started"; Steve Forbes dismisses evolution as "a massive fraud"; and Gary Bauer categorically rejects the notion that humans descended "from apes."

October

1999   Quietly following the lead of Kansas, the Kentucky Education Department substitutes the phrase "change over time" for the word "evolution" in its new science guidelines. This concerns many science teachers, given the periodic efforts in Kentucky to teach creationism.

Republican leaders in the U.S. House introduce a voucher bill, the Academic Emergency Act, allowing students in failing public schools to attend private schools at state expense.

Pat Robertson offers his assessment of potential presidential candidates for 2000. He dismisses Gary Bauer, with whom he agrees on numerous issues, as a "lost cause"; Elizabeth Dole is just "a Southern Belle"; and Jesse Ventura, the Reform party governor of Minnesota, is "off his rocker." Perhaps chastened by recent Republican setbacks, a more pragmatic Robertson supports George W. Bush, believing the Texas governor has the best chance of winning in 2000.

November

1999   Responding to a ruling by the 5th U.S. Circuit Court of Appeals which went against the Santa Fe Independent School District, near Galveston, Texas, the U.S. House approves a resolution urging the Supreme Court to approve prayer before high school football games.

December

1999   A federal judge in Ohio declares Cleveland's voucher program illegal.

President Bill Clinton encourages public schools to invite churches and faith-based organizations to assist in programs during and after school designed to advance student literacy, improve discipline, and enhance school safety. "I have never believed the Constitution required our schools to be religion-free zones," declares the president, "or that our children must check their faith at the schoolhouse door."

February

2000   Senator John McCain easily defeats presumed frontrunner Governor George W. Bush in the New Hampshire Republican primary. This suddenly makes the approaching South Carolina primary crucial to the Bush campaign.

Gary Bauer abandons the presidential race after a poor showing in New Hampshire and endorses Senator John McCain just prior to the hotly contested South Carolina primary. With the Republican contest heating up, Governor George W. Bush delivers an address at Bob Jones University, a staunchly fundamentalist and anti-Catholic institution in South Carolina. The McCain campaign exploits this, hinting in Michigan, a state with a large Catholic populace and the next Republican battleground, that Bush is anti-Catholic.

The Texas governor subsequently apologizes to Catholics for his Bob Jones appearance, explaining: "On reflection, I should have been more clear in disassociating myself from anti-Catholic sentiments and racial prejudice."

Governor George W. Bush remarks that Jesus is his "favorite political philosopher."

With the religious right taking the initiative, an all-out smear campaign is begun against Senator John McCain in South Carolina. By telephone, e-mail, and other means, voters are "informed" about the senator's first wife, alleged marital infidelities, usage of profane language, and "softness" on the gay issue. Pat Robertson, in a recorded telephone message sent to thousands, accuses McCain of being allied with "vicious" anti-Christian bigots.

The Bush campaign at first denies any knowledge of efforts to tarnish McCain in South Carolina, but later admits to funding some of Robertson's calls.

Campaigning in Virginia, Senator John McCain levels a stinging attack on Pat Robertson and Jerry Falwell. Declares McCain: "Neither party should be defined by pandering to the outer reaches of American politics and the agents of intolerance, whether they be Louis Farrakhan or Al Sharpton on the left or Pat Robertson and Jerry Falwell on the right." It is unfortunate, McCain suggests, that Governor George W. Bush has linked himself to those who practice the "political tactics of division and slander."

Governor George W. Bush handily wins the Republican primaries in South Carolina and Virginia. "But at what cost?" asks columnist Cal

Thomas, who concludes that the South Carolina contest shows that "people who are supposed to serve a higher kingdom . . . can get down and dirty with the best of the pagans."

March

2000   Although Cal Thomas concedes that when preachers "get down and dirty with . . . politicians they can expect to be treated as . . . politicians," he nevertheless believes Senator John McCain "has gone too far in denouncing Pat Robertson and Jerry Falwell as 'agents of intolerance.'"

Judge L. Ralph Smith, Jr., of the Circuit Court of Florida, rules that the use of tax money for private-school education is a violation of the state constitution. This derails Florida's new voucher program, but Governor Jeb Bush vows "this is the first inning of a long, drawn-out legal battle."

The Republican party primary in Texas allows voters to express their position on student-initiated prayers at school sporting events. Statewide, 94 percent of Republican voters approve the proposition. Since the resolution is nonbinding, critics accuse Texas Republicans of grandstanding.

April

2000   Jerry Falwell introduces "People of Faith 2000," a plan to register at least 10 million voters with the help of local pastors. Falwell's claim of nonpartisanship to the contrary, critics insist the Virginia preacher's real intention is to advance the presidential fortunes of Governor George W. Bush.

Cal Thomas chides Jerry Falwell for his "People of Faith 2000," claiming his friend "has again succumbed to the temptation of politics and its illusion of power." Asserts Thomas: "'People of Faith 2000' will raise some money and make noise, but it will change little."

By a 2–1 margin, the 6th U.S. Circuit Court of Appeals strikes down Ohio's state motto, "With God, all things are possible." Adopted in 1959 and inscribed on state stationery, reports, and tax returns, the motto, according to the Court, amounts to a government endorsement of Christianity. Taken from Matthew 19:26, the motto presumably expresses a sentiment not shared by Muslims and Jews. This prompts the dissenting judge to wonder about the inscription on U.S. coins, "In God We Trust," which has been upheld by federal appeals courts.

May

2000   House Majority Whip Tom DeLay contends that if George W. Bush wins the presidency there will be "a very aggressive counterattack on the anti-religious crusade of the news media and the entertainment industry."

On NBC-TV's *Meet the Press*, Pat Robertson warns Governor George W. Bush not to pick Senator John McCain as his vice presidential running mate. Robertson accuses McCain of intemperance.

June

2000   Emerging as something of a celebrity to the religious right, Marran Ward, the Santa Fe Independent School District student who challenged the restriction on prayer before football games, gives the invocation at the Texas Republican party's convention in Houston.

Divided 6–3, the Supreme Court upholds the 5th U.S. Circuit Court of Appeals regarding the Santa Fe Independent School District and prayer before sporting events. Says Justice John Paul Stevens, such prayer "has the improper effect of coercing those present to participate in an act of religious worship." Taking place on government property at a school-sponsored event, pre-game prayer, Stevens continues, gives the impression of having the state's "seal of approval."

Governor George W. Bush attacks the Santa Fe decision for preventing devout students from expressing their faith, but Cal Thomas, while disagreeing with the Court's majority, concludes pre-game prayer actually "trivializes the act of prayer." Conservative Christians, he asserts, are "fooling themselves" if they think such prayers signify that "all must be right with the world," improve "the quality of the game," or contribute to "fewer injuries."

August

2000   Linda Holloway, who chaired the Kansas Board of Education and supported the new standards on evolution, is defeated for reelection.

Maureen Dowd, *New York Times* columnist, captures the increasingly religious mood of the presidential race, writing: "The main battleground state is the state of grace. Democrats and Republicans are seeking a geographical advantage, but it is celestial. Both sides seem weirdly obsessed with snagging a divine endorsement."

Al Gore picks Connecticut Senator Joseph Lieberman, an Orthodox Jew, as his vice presidential running mate, the first Jew put forth in a presidential campaign by a major party. By selecting a man of such devout faith, the vice president blunts the ability of the Republican party to use the Clinton scandals in the upcoming presidential campaign.

Joseph Lieberman talks openly about religion on the campaign trail. Invoking the authority of George Washington, he tells audiences in Chicago, Detroit, and South Bend, Indiana, that religion reinforces morality. "There must be a place for faith in America's public life," he declares, and he hopes his nomination will encourage people "to feel more free to talk about their faith." On another occasion Lieberman hails America as "the most religious country in the world" and proclaims all Americans the "children of the same awesome God."

Disclosing divergent attitudes within the American Jewish community, Abraham H. Foxman, national director of the Anti-Defamation League, urges Senator Lieberman to stop making "overt expressions" of religious belief on the campaign trail. Foxman believes such religious emphasis in the political arena "becomes inappropriate and even unsettling in a religiously diverse society such as ours."

As appeals to the divine become more frequent, Governor George W. Bush tells a B'nai B'rith convention in Washington of his support for Israel and admiration of faith-based social programs. Adds Bush: "Our nation is chosen by God and commissioned by history to be a model to the world of justice and inclusion and diversity without division. Jews and Christians and Muslims speak as one in their commitment to a kind, just, tolerant society."

September

2000   Not to be outdone, Vice President Al Gore, a Southern Baptist, reveals that before making any decision he asks, "What would Jesus do?"

The Food and Drug Administration's approval of the abortion pill, RU-486, draws sharp criticism from many on the religious right. Rev. Flip Benham, director of Operation Save America (formerly Operation Rescue), warns that any doctor who "thinks he can prescribe this and have any degree of anonymity . . . is mistaken." He adds that if doctors "want to put their practice in jeopardy, they can start prescribing this pill."

Governor George W. Bush criticizes the Food and Drug Administration, calling the decision mistaken, but gives no pledge to ban RU-486 if elected president. Vice President Al Gore favors the decision.

Putting pragmatism above morality, Pat Robertson remains noticeably silent about RU-486, explaining he does not want to put Governor George W. Bush on the spot with the presidential election so near.

For Pat Robertson, Senator Lieberman poses a dilemma. While admiring the senator for his high moral values, the televangelist worries lest he pull voters away from Bush.

Although aware of Bush's need to court moderate and swing voters, Pat Robertson warns that the Christian Coalition should not be taken for granted.

October

2000   Describing Joseph Lieberman as an "itinerant Jewish evangelist," Cal Thomas accuses the Democratic vice presidential hopeful of "using God as a campaign surrogate to bless his and Al Gore's policies."

November

2000   In a document titled "The U.S. Supreme Court and the Culture of Death," some 300 U.S. Catholic bishops accuse the High Court of bringing "our legal system to the brink of endorsing infanticide." In unusually strident language, the bishops blame the Court for helping "to create an abortion climate, in which many Americans turn to the destruction of innocent life as an answer to social and personal problems." Particularly upsetting to the bishops is a recent Supreme Court ruling overturning Nebraska's ban on so-called partial-birth abortions.

With the presidential race dragging on without resolution, some on the religious right suspect the Democrats of trying to steal the election. The Christian Coalition warns of "an unfolding miscarriage of justice," while Jerry Falwell contends Vice President Al Gore's efforts are "now being viewed by grassroots people everywhere as an attempt to steal the White House."

December

2000   Cincinnati's 6th U.S. Circuit Court of Appeals declares Cleveland's school voucher program unconstitutional, explaining: "This scheme involves the grant of state aid directly and predominantly to the coffers of the private, religious schools."

July

2001   Alabama Chief Justice Roy Moore places a huge 5,300-pound Ten Commandments monument in the lobby of the state judicial building. Civil rights groups file a lawsuit on behalf of three Alabama attorneys who see the monument as an infringement on their First Amendment rights.

August

2001   Televangelist Pat Robertson warns Disney World in Orlando, Florida, that it should stop celebrating Gay Pride Month lest it incur God's wrath. "I would warn Orlando that you're right in the way of some serious hurricanes," Robertson says, and "It'll bring about terrorist bombs. It'll bring earthquakes, tornadoes, and possibly a meteor."

September

2001   On September 11, 2001, nineteen Islamic terrorists hijack four American commercial airliners and crash two of them into the World Trade Center, reducing New York City's twin towers to rubble and killing approximately 3,000 people; a third plane crashes into the Pentagon, killing nearly 200 more; and the fourth plunges into the Pennsylvania countryside, brought down as a result of an attempt by passengers to regain control of the aircraft. All aboard are killed. President Bush proclaims, "We're at war," and he vows: "The people who knocked these buildings down will hear from us all soon."

Two days after 9/11 the Rev. Jerry Falwell appears on Pat Robertson's *The 700 Club* and blames "the pagans and the abortionists and the feminists and the gays" for the attack. Robertson agrees. Both men later apologize, but a few days later Robertson returns to the same theme. "We have insulted God at the highest level of our government," he says. "Then we say, 'why does this happen?' It is happening because God Almighty is lifting his protection from us."

November

2001   Franklin Graham, son of evangelist Billy Graham and head of Samaritan's Purse, tells an NBC-TV interviewer that Islam is "a very evil and wicked religion." In subsequent statements Graham asserts that "the God of Islam is not the God of the Christian faith," for "the two are different as lightness and darkness."

The Arkansas Baptist Convention, reflecting the view of many evangelical Christians, declares the Harry Potter books by J. K. Rowling "anti-Christian," charging that they promote occult practices.

March

2002   U.S. Attorney General John Ashcroft tells the National Religious Broadcasters meeting at Opryland in Nashville, Tennessee, that God is on America's side. Echoing a theme frequently made by President Bush since the 9/11 attack, Ashcroft tells the broadcasters that "we know God is not neutral in the battle of good and evil."

June

2002   Via satellite President Bush addresses the Southern Baptist Convention meeting in St. Louis. The president praises the body, declaring that Baptists "have been guardians of separation of church and state, preserving the integrity of both. Yet you never have believed in separating religious faith from political life." According to the president, the SBC and his administration have much in common, such as a "culture of life" and the "sacred institutions" of marriage and family.

Illustrative of the extreme remarks coming from some on the religious right after 9/11, the Rev. Jerry Vines, pastor of the First Baptist Church, Jacksonville, Florida, attracts national attention with the assertion that "Islam is not as good as Christianity. Christianity was founded by the virgin-born Jesus Christ. Islam was founded by Mohammed, a demon-possessed pedophile who had twelve wives, and his last one was a nine-year-old girl." Vines adds that Jehovah, unlike Allah, does not "turn anyone into a terrorist that will try to bomb people and take the lives of thousands."

Islamic leaders in the United States are shocked by Vines's remarks, calling them "hate-filled and bigoted" and "medieval."

Indicative of the close tie between some on the religious right and Israel, Richard Land, head of the Southern Baptist Ethics and Religious Liberty Commission, announces that support of Israel is a "matter of being obedient to God." This comes as part of a Stand for Israel campaign, an effort to mobilize 100,000 churches and one million American Christians to support Israel. Other speakers at the gathering are Oliver North and Jerry Falwell, both of whom join Land in asserting that support for Israel is important to America's future. According to Land, God has blessed America because America has "blessed the Jews."

Politicians from the president on down waste no time voicing disagreement with the decision of a three-judge panel of the 9th U.S. Circuit Court of Appeals in California that the Pledge of Allegiance is unconstitutional. "Ridiculous" declares President Bush; "nuts" adds Senate Majority Leader Tom Daschle. The court's ruling comes as a result of a case filed by a parent who objected to the phrase "under God," considering it an establishment of religion.

In a 5–4 decision the Supreme Court upholds the constitutionality of Cleveland, Ohio's, school voucher program, even though over 95 percent of the vouchers are used to subsidize religious schooling. While Chief Justice William Rehnquist says the Cleveland program is "entirely neutral with respect to religion," Justice John Paul Stevens considers the ruling "profoundly misguided." President Bush and his secretary of education, Rod Paige, applaud the decision. In fact, the president regards it as historic as the 1954 *Brown* desegregation case, and he vows to push other cities to adopt programs similar to Cleveland's.

July

2002   On the first July 4 celebration since 9/11, President Bush travels to Ripley, West Virginia, for a highly charged religious, patriotic experience. The president declares that "the wisdom and the blessing of Divine Providence have guided the nation for 226 years." The crowd shouts the Pledge of Allegiance, accentuating "under God" in defiance of the recent ruling by the appellate court panel. In response President Bush asserts, "No authority of government can ever prevent an American from pledging allegiance to this one nation under God."

August

2002   A state circuit judge in Florida declares that state's 1999 voucher program unconstitutional, citing a provision in the Florida constitution which explicitly prohibits the usage of tax money for religious purposes. Governor Jeb Bush disagrees with the decision and vows to appeal.

The results of an Associated Press poll disclose mixed feelings among Americans toward vouchers. By a margin of 51 to 40 percent they *favor* vouchers to send children to private schools. But when informed that such a program would take funds away from public schools, they *oppose* vouchers by a 2-to-1 margin. Whether Republican, Democrat, or independent, support for vouchers drops significantly when the prospect of diverting money from public schools is raised.

Unable to secure congressional approval for his faith-based initiative proposal, President Bush defiantly issues a sweeping executive order instructing federal agencies to consider religious groups for federal funding, even those that take religion into account for purposes of hiring. Five cabinet-level agencies promptly respond, including the Department of Health and Human Services, which announces that churches, synagogues, and mosques will be allowed to use federal money not only for programs infused with religion, but also to consider religion in the hiring and firing of workers. Robert Polito, director of Health and Human Services' Center for Faith-Based and Community Initiatives, sees no problem with this, but Barry Lynn, director of Americans United for Separation of Church and State, describes the initiative as a "giant faith-based slush fund." As for the lack of congressional support, "It would be great to have legislation," Polito cavalierly declares, "but there's a ton of stuff I can do without it." Philosophical and religious differences aside, the manner in which the White House sidesteps Congress arouses considerable resentment.

October

2002   Appearing on CBS's *60 Minutes*, Jerry Falwell says he believes the prophet Mohammad "was a terrorist," and "a violent man, a man of war." Shi'a Muslim clerics in Lebanon and Iran react angrily, one declaring "the death of that man [Falwell] is a religious duty."

December

2002   Former President Jimmy Carter, a lifelong Baptist, is the second U.S. Baptist ever to be awarded the Nobel Peace Prize. While many secular and religious leaders around the country applaud the former president, the fundamentalist leaders of the Southern Baptist Convention are conspicuous by their silence. This prompts one observer to compare the silence accorded Carter to the silence that greeted the other American Baptist to receive the award, Martin Luther King, Jr., in 1964.

January

2003   President George W. Bush proclaims January 19, 2003, National Sanctity of Human Life Day, underscoring his administration's "compassionate alternative" to abortion.

March

2003   The Southern Baptist Convention and Franklin Graham's Samaritan's Purse report that they have teams of workers poised to enter

Iraq as soon as it is safe to do so. The two organizations, which have close ties to President Bush, plan to minister to the spiritual and physical needs of the Iraqis. In light of the harsh comments of Graham and some prominent Southern Baptists about Islam and the prophet Mohammad, this announcement attracts considerable interest.

April

2003   Colorado becomes the first state since the Supreme Court upheld the constitutionality of public school vouchers to implement such a program. Opponents plan to challenge the program, asserting that the state constitution prohibits the usage of tax money for religious schools. According to the Education Commission of the States in Denver, twenty-four states studied voucher programs in 2002, but none implemented one.

Secretary of Education Rod Paige arouses the concern of some Americans with his assertion that he "would prefer to have a child in a school that has a strong appreciation for the values of the Christian community, where a child is taught to have a strong faith." To the Rev. Barry Lynn, executive director of Americans United for Separation of Church and State, Paige's remark shows "an astonishing mix of disrespect for both America's religious diversity and the public schools."

May

2003   The Rev. Ted Haggard, president of the National Association of Evangelicals, which represents about 43,000 congregations, and Paul Marshall, senior fellow at the Center for Religious Freedom, a human rights group, issue a public rebuke to fellow evangelicals such as Franklin Graham who have made derogatory remarks about Islam. Such comments, assert the duo, endanger missionaries in the Middle East and achieve nothing aside from "boosting the ego" of those who say such things.

Speaking to about 800 people at a prayer breakfast at the Israeli embassy in Washington, D.C., Richard Land repeats remarks made in mid-2002 about the need for the U.S. to support Israel. Echoing Land is the prominent San Antonio, Texas, televangelist John Hagee, who declares: "As Christians, we believe that Jerusalem is now and forever shall be the eternal and undivided capital of the state of Israel. Jerusalem is not up for negotiation with anyone for any reason at any time in the future." This kind of support for Israel explains in large measure why Jews and evangelicals have drawn closer together in recent years.

June

2003   Showing frustration with President Bush's "faith-based initiative," Ron Sider, president of Evangelicals for Social Action, declares: "I am within a hair's breadth of concluding that the faith-based initiative is a cynical cover for ignoring the poor." This comes in the midst of debates over administration tax proposals that would harm the poor. Jim Wallis, head of a mainline Protestant and Catholic coalition known as Call to Renewal, echoes Sider's assertion.

July

2003   President Bush renews his push for voucher programs, endorsing legislation that would give District of Columbia children private school tuition grants in the amount of $7,500 a year. Bush calls the proposal an attempt to achieve fairness for low-income children, but Senator Ted Kennedy of Massachusetts is "amazed that in the midst of unprecedented school budget cuts and teacher layoffs this president is proposing $75 million for private schools in Washington, D.C., under the guise of giving students 'school choice.'"

A federal appeals court orders Alabama Chief Justice Roy Moore to remove his Ten Commandments monument from the state judicial building. Conservative Christians rally to Moore's defense, seeing the judge as a stalwart man of God persecuted by a hostile government. Moore refuses to obey the order and is suspended from the bench. He vows to take the matter to the Supreme Court and appeals to conservative Christians for support.

November

2003   The Supreme Court subsequently refuses to hear Moore's appeal. The Alabama judge remains defiant, telling Fox News Channel, "We've got to understand where our morality comes from. It comes from God." Barry Lynn, director of Americans United for Separation of Church and State, applauds the Supreme Court, declaring: "It is time for Moore to face facts: he's on the wrong side of the Constitution."

A study by the Rockefeller Institute of Government discloses little enthusiasm at the state level for the federal government's faith-based initiatives. Only fifteen states thus far have sought to involve faith-based groups in providing social services. The reason, perhaps, is that about half of the states already have long-standing arrangements with groups such as Catholic Charities and Lutheran Social Services and see no need to forge direct ties with specific congregations. According to the director of the Rockefeller Institute, "While the spotlight on the faith-based initiative has been very bright in Washington, it tends to get much dimmer once you get outside the Beltway." Jim Towey, head of the White House Office of Faith-Based and Community Initiatives, disputes the study, claiming there has been an "explosion" of interest from the states in recent months.

January

2004   Although the Ten Commandments monument has been removed from the state judicial building in Montgomery, Alabama, tourists continue to visit the rotunda where it previously rested. Typical of the attitude of many conservative evangelicals, one visitor from Tulsa, Oklahoma, remarks: "It's like visiting a graveyard, a graveyard of the moral absolute this country once stood for."

   Congress approves the nation's first federally funded school voucher program, allocating $14 million a year in private school tuition grants to District of Columbia school children. This is not only a major election-year victory for President Bush, who has championed the program, but also a stimulant to the national movement for vouchers.

May

2004   Tim LaHaye and Jerry Jenkins complete the twelfth volume of their bestselling *Left Behind* series, a thrilling account based upon a conservative Christian interpretation of such matters as the Rapture, Armageddon, and the Second Coming. To at least one critic, the LaHaye-Jenkins series is clever and effective propaganda for the worldview of the religious right.

October

2004   After twenty-five years of silence on the issue, the Supreme Court announces that it will decide whether displays of the Ten Commandments in courthouses, town halls, and other government property are constitutional. Displays in Kentucky and Texas prompt the court's decision, reactions to which vary sharply, depending upon whether one supports or objects to such displays.

   The Dover, Pennsylvania, school board instructs biology teachers to discuss intelligent design as an alternative to Darwinist evolution. This decision sharply splits the community.

December

2004   The Bush administration's top Supreme Court lawyer, Paul Clement, urges that displays of the Ten Commandments be allowed on government property. Such displays are common around the nation, he asserts, and they are important in educating people "about the nation's history and celebrating its heritage."

March

2005   President Bush throws his weight behind a federal, faith-based grant to the Salvation Army of Janesville, Wisconsin, even though the Army's project includes Bible study. Said the president: "The city had no right to tell the Salvation Army that the price of running a center was giving up its prayers." The president also threatens to promote his faith-based program with more executive orders if Congress fails to act.

The case of Terri Schiavo, a Florida woman determined by physicians to be brain dead but kept alive in a vegetative state on a life-support system, draws national attention when the federal government and the state of Florida intervene to prevent the woman's husband from ending life-support. While the intrusion of state and federal authorities is generally praised by religious conservatives who see this as a pro-life issue, polls show that two-thirds of Americans disagree with President Bush, his brother Governor Jeb Bush of Florida, Senate Majority Leader Bill Frist, and Congressman Tom DeLay.

April

2005   Billed as "Justice Sunday," the Family Research Council, a conservative Christian organization, plans an April 24 telecast to mobilize opposition to Democratic filibusters against President Bush's judicial nominees. Advertisements for the telecast compare the plight of Christians on behalf of the president's nominees to the struggle of racial minorities for equality in the 1960s. Senate Majority Leader Bill Frist of Tennessee plans to appear on the program, prompting a rebuke from Democratic Senate Minority Leader Harry Reid of Nevada. "What is going on ... is not Republican mainstream politics," says Reid, "it is radical Republican politics." Other critics suspect that Frist's alignment with Christian conservatives is motivated by presidential ambition. "He seems to be going out of his way to pander to the radical religions right leaders," declares Ralph Neas, president of the liberal People for the American Way, who frankly sees a tie between Frist's new-found religiosity and "his aspirations to be president of the United States."

May

2005   On ABC's *This Week* Pat Robertson asserts that liberal judges "are destroying the fabric that holds our nation together" and present a greater threat than "a few bearded terrorists who fly into buildings." Such remarks reflect the importance many on the religious right attach to the appointment by President Bush of conservatives to the Supreme Court.

June

2005   President Bush addresses the Southern Baptist Convention, praising Baptists for being "soldiers in the army of compassion." He then touches on four issues dear to all conservative evangelicals: a "family amendment" to prevent gay marriage; legislation to curb abortion; the appointment of more conservative judges; and government support for faith-based initiatives.

         The Supreme Court renders a split verdict on displays of the Ten Commandments on government property.

August

2005   Televangelist Pat Robertson's call for the assassination of Venezuelan President Hugo Chavez shocks some fellow Christians. "Pat Robertson does not advance the Christian faith by announcing on television his own preferences about who around the world he wants killed," remarks Phil Strickland of the Baptist General Convention of Texas. Others note the difficulty of condemning Muslim terrorism when Christians such as Robertson advocate violence. As he has done many times before, Robertson later apologizes, attributing his comment to "frustration" over the failure of the U.S. government to deal with a man who has "found common course with terrorists."

         On "Justice Sunday: II" in Nashville, Tennessee, an event planned for the purpose of enlisting conservative Christian support for the appointment of conservative federal judges, many of the speakers voice an opinion common to the religious right—namely, that conservative Christians are a persecuted majority hounded by "secular fundamentalists" and maligned in "the media, public schools, universities, and Hollywood." Typical is the view of the Rev. Franklin Graham. "There is an attempt by secularists," he asserts, "to take Jesus Christ and to take God out of every aspect of our society." Senate Majority Leader Bill Frist, a speaker at the first "Justice Sunday" in April, is not invited to this one in his home state because of his recent decision to support an expansion of embryonic stem-cell research.

Former President Jimmy Carter delivers a speech to the Baptist World Centenary Congress in Birmingham, England, in which he characterizes fundamentalism as rigid in doctrine, male-dominated, and restrictive in its membership. Instead of uniting, it divides Christians, with fundamentalists assuming that their way is the only way to salvation.

The National Council on Bible Curriculum in Public Schools, located in Greensboro, North Carolina, claims that its course, "The Bible in History and Literature," is being taught as an elective in thirty states by 312 school districts. Many Americans see no harm in teaching the Bible in public schools as literature, but critics of the National Council's program insist it is sectarian in purpose and not at all vigorous academically. The National Council's tie to the religious right is evident in its website, which asserts: "The Bible was the foundation and blueprint for our Constitution, Declaration of Independence, our educational system and our entire history until the last 20 to 30 years."

September

2005   U.S. District Court Judge Lawrence K. Karlton of Sacramento, California, reopens the Pledge of Allegiance controversy, announcing that he is bound by the 2002 ruling of the 9th U.S. Circuit Court of Appeals that the words "under God" render the pledge unconstitutional. Governor Arnold Schwarzenegger immediately denounces the decision, and religious conservatives argue that the ruling underscores the need to gain Senate confirmation of President Bush's conservative nominees to the High Court.

November

2005   Former President Jimmy Carter contends that Democrats need to reach out to religious voters if they hope to regain the presidency. According to Carter, the Republicans are vulnerable on human rights, the war in Iraq, and cutting the taxes of the rich instead of caring for the poor. To Carter, these are all moral, value-laden issues.

December

2005   Sponsored by Baylor University in Waco, Texas, and Temple University in Philadelphia, the prestigious Jewish Theological Seminary hosts the first-ever meeting of conservative Jews and Protestant evangelicals. The dialogue is respectful, but some tension surfaces.

Both sides agree on support of Israel, but differences emerge on domestic matters. According to Abraham Foxman, director of the Anti-Defamation League, "the key domestic challenge" confronting Jews is the arrogant "Christian Right" campaign to "Christianize all aspects of American life."

January

2006   The Florida Supreme Court strikes down a statewide voucher system that allows children to attend private schools at taxpayer expense. In its 5–2 ruling the Court explains that the voucher program undermines the public schools and violates Florida's constitution. This is a severe disappointment to Governor Jeb Bush, who vows to search for ways to continue the program.

Pat Robertson apologizes for a remark made a few days earlier on his *The 700 Club* implying that Prime Minister Ariel Sharon's stroke was God's punishment for the Israeli leader's decision to withdraw from Gaza. This "was dividing God's land," Robertson had said, "and I would say woe unto any prime minister of Israel who takes a similar course."

Under legal pressure, the El Tejon School District in rural California drops plans to teach a philosophy class on intelligent design. "This sends a strong signal to school districts across the country that they cannot promote creationism or intelligent design as an alternative to evolution, whether they do so in a science class or a humanities class," declares a spokesperson for Americans United for the Separation of Church and State.

A new NBC television program, *Book of Daniel*, draws fire from the conservative American Family Association for its unflattering portrayal of Christianity. It features an Episcopal priest, Father Daniel, a pill popper whose daughter sells pot, whose sons are (the eldest) gay and (the youngest) having sex, and whose father, also a priest, is having an illicit affair.

Indicative of their intention to appeal to religious voters, Democrats in the U.S. House set up a Faith Working Group, while Senator Harry Reid, the minority leader, creates a website called "Word to the Faithful."

February

2006   Some eighteen states consider legislation that will protect health care workers who refuse to provide care that conflicts with their religious beliefs, such as filling prescriptions for birth control and morning-after pills on the grounds the drugs cause abortions. Such proposals are alarming to advocates of abortion rights, family planning, AIDS prevention, gay civil rights, and assisted suicide. Religious conservatives support the effort.

March

2006   Embattled U.S. Congressman Tom DeLay of Texas delivers a speech to a D.C. audience of about 300 entitled "The War on Christians and the Value-Voter in 2006." DeLay is introduced by the Rev. Rick Scarborough, who hails the congressman as a man appointed by God "to represent righteousness in government." The once powerful but now disgraced lawmaker sees himself as a persecuted defender of Christianity by a culture that allows "abortion on demand," the killing of "millions of innocent children," the degradation of "the institution of marriage," and the treatment of "Christianity like some second-rate superstition." The Rev. Barry Lynn of Americans United for Separation of Church and State dismisses the gathering, insisting there is no war on Christianity. But there are, he adds, a lot of "second-tier preachers" out for publicity.

The Georgia legislature passes a bill funding elective Bible courses in public schools.

May

2006   Proving the old saying that politics makes for strange bedfellows, Senator John McCain of Arizona, who in the 2000 presidential primaries called Pat Robertson and Jerry Falwell "evil" and "agents of intolerance," delivers the commencement address at Falwell's Liberty University. Neither McCain nor Falwell mention past differences as they continue a rapprochement begun several months earlier when the televangelist visited the politician in D.C. McCain obviously hopes his new friendship with Falwell will help him mend fences with the religious right as the 2008 presidential race draws near.

June

2006   Senate Majority Leader Bill Frist brings the Federal Marriage Amendment before the Senate again. Since it is not expected to pass in either the Senate or House, many skeptics see politics rather than morality as the driving force. President Bush, who heretofore has not had much to say about gay marriage, joins the cause for the amendment. "Activist courts," he asserts, "have left our nation with no other choice." This is an issue that many on the religious right feel strongly about. According to Richard Land, for instance, gay marriage is "the one issue ... that eclipses even ... abortion ... among Southern Baptists." And James Dobson warns Republican leaders that if they "forget us" on this issue, "we'll forget you."

Senator Barack Obama of Illinois criticizes fellow Democrats for failing to "acknowledge the power of faith in the lives of the American people," and he urges the party to compete for the support of evangelicals and other churchgoers. "Not every mention of God in public is a breach to the wall of separation," he says, adding that children reciting the Pledge of Allegiance surely do not "feel oppressed or brainwashed as a consequence of muttering the phrase 'under God.'" Obama concludes that unless Democrats reach out to religious Americans and "tell them what we stand for, Jerry Falwells and Pat Robertsons will continue to hold sway."

Kevin Phillips, once a member of the Richard Nixon administration, warns of the danger of religious fundamentalism in his new book, *American Theocracy*. According to Phillips, the Republican party draws much of its support from evangelicals who take the Bible literally and who insist upon the teaching of intelligent design, object to stem-cell research, refuse to accept scientific findings on global warming, and support a host of "pro-life" causes. To Phillips, the Republican party, by pandering to religious fundamentalists, has become a religious party that too often puts the interest of religious extremists ahead of the national interest.

July

2006   Ralph Reed, the former "boy wonder" of the Christian Coalition, strikes out in his bid to win the Republican primary for lieutenant governor of Georgia. A religious-right platform notwithstanding, Reed's ties to scandal-ridden lobbyist Jack Abramoff prove to be his undoing.

In the first veto of his administration, President Bush sides with the religious right, rejecting congressional legislation easing federal funding for embryonic stem-cell research. "This bill would support the taking of innocent human life in the hope of finding medical benefits for others," explains the president. "It crosses a moral boundary that our decent society needs to respect." Polls show that most Americans disagree with Bush, and there is speculation that Republicans will pay a price for the president's veto in the November elections. Moreover, five states—California, Connecticut, Illinois, Maryland, and New Jersey—push ahead with stem-cell research without federal money.

Twenty-six Republicans join most Democrats to kill the proposed constitutional amendment banning gay marriage. Since the Senate had already rejected the proposal a few weeks earlier, the House vote is purely symbolic, prompting speculation that the real intent was to put congressmen on record before the upcoming November elections. Seeing this as an issue that energizes religious conservatives, many Republicans vow to continue the fight to "save" marriage. Declares House Speaker Dennis Hastert, "Be assured that this issue is not over."

While many Americans have reservations about electing a Mormon or a Muslim president, a Los Angeles Times/Bloomberg poll discloses that anti-Catholicism and antisemitism are fading in American politics. This partially explains the increasing ability of conservative Protestants, Catholics, and Jews to cooperate on a range of religious right issues.

3

Biographical Profiles

Most of the individuals profiled here have risen to prominence since World War II. Intellectually and theologically, however, much of the contemporary religious right, as shown in the chronology, is rooted in the nineteenth and early twentieth centuries. To provide some sense of continuity, therefore, several figures from an earlier era, such as John Nelson Darby, J. Gresham Machen, and Francis Schaeffer, have been included. Other individuals, such as Robert Welch, Paul Weyrich and Phyllis Schlafly, more political conservatives than fundamentalist Christians, have been included because their goals have much in common with those of the religious right. Although women have certainly contributed to the religious right, very few have occupied prominent positions of leadership. One must keep in mind that the religious right nourishes the conservative view that a woman's place is in home nurturing children and supporting her husband, an attitude inhospitable to women pursuing careers beyond family and hearth. Thus, with only a few exceptions, almost all the profiles are of men, highlighting the male dominance of the religious right. Since as people on the religious right are often associated with organizations, and in fact organizations often have been built around particular personalities, readers should consult Chapter 6 along with these profiles.

David Barton (1954–)

David Barton's efforts to present a perspective on U.S. history that highlights the role the Christian religion played in the development of the nation has brought high praise from evangelical and fundamentalist Christian groups, but much criticism from historians and groups critical of the religious right. Barton, founder and president of Wallbuilders, a religious organization headquartered in Aledo, Texas, was born in Austin and received a bachelor of arts degree in religious education from Oral Roberts University. From 1974 to 1975 he served as youth director at Aledo Christian Center, and from 1975 to 1977 as youth director for churches in Oklahoma. He returned to Aledo in 1977 as Christian education director. In 1987 he established Wallbuilders and began exploring U.S. history with the goal of casting doubt on the claim that prominent early Americans, including the framers of the U.S. Constitution, intended a strict separation of state and church and affirming the commitment of prominent early Americans to Christianity.

In 1989 Barton published *The Myth of Separation*, in which he presented numerous quotations attributed to such historical figures as Patrick Henry, George Washington, James Madison, Benjamin Franklin, and Thomas Jefferson that expressed support for the idea that the United States was founded on the Christian religion. For instance, according to Barton, George Washington had stated that "It is impossible to rightly govern the world without God and the Bible," and Thomas Jefferson had proclaimed that "I have always said and always will say that the studious perusal of the Sacred Volume will make us better citizens." Critics quickly challenged many of the quotations, claiming that no original source could be found for them. They questioned Barton's authority as a historian, noting that he had no extensive formal training in historical research. Barton responded to the criticisms, admitting that several of the quotations he used could not be verified by original documents. Subsequently, he published *Original Intent: The Courts, the Constitution and Religion* (third edition, 2004), in which quotations were checked more meticulously. However, critics remained unsatisfied because the earlier unsubstantiated quotes continued to appear in the media. The major concern of those who supported strict separation of church and state appeared to be that, by detailing the so-called "censored" religious history of the nation, Barton was arguing not only that the United States possessed a Christian heritage, but also that the nation should continue to be guided by Christian principles, including prayer in the public schools. In *America: To Pray? Or Not to Pray?* (fifth edition, 2002) Barton presented data to support his contention that the decline in moral values and the increase in premarital sex, rapes, and murders occurred after the 1962 U.S. Supreme Court decision in *Engel v. Vitale* that ruled unconstitutional officially sanctioned prayer in the public schools.

Barton has been active in partisan politics, following a general trend in the religious right of supporting the Republican party. He served as the deputy chairman of the Texas Republican party, and in 2004 the Republican National Committee provided him with financial support to travel around the nation encouraging voter turnout in the November election. Barton devotes his greatest energies to producing educational materials. A curriculum resource produced by the National Council on Bible Curriculum in Public Schools titled *The Bible in History and Literature* frequently cites Barton's books. Barton's challenges to the notion of strict separation of church and state have provided the religious right with resources to challenge a more secular interpretation of American society.

Gary L. Bauer (1946–)

Gary Bauer was undoubtedly the more conservative of the Republican presidential aspirants in 2000, but his campaign experience represents the often complex and personally risky combination of religion and politics. For many years Bauer worked for conservative Christian causes, serving as a congressional lobbyist for James Dobson's organization, Focus on the Family (FF). Until 2000 Bauer headed the Family Research Council (FRC), an offshoot of FF formed in 1988. Before leaving the organization to campaign for the presidency, he had raised the annual budget to $14 million and established a mailing list of 400,000 people. The organization became not only a conduit for fund-raising, but also a source of committed volunteers to work in campaigns and loyal voters to go to the polls on election day. In 1997 Bauer created the Campaign for Working Families, a political action committee that raised over $2 million from 90,000 donors, a group to which he turned to raise funds for his bid for the presidency.

Raised in Newport, Kentucky, Bauer received a B.A. in 1968 from Georgetown College in Kentucky and a J.D. in 1973 from Georgetown University. After working for a trade association, he joined Ronald Reagan's presidential campaign in 1980 as a senior policy analyst and served the Reagan administration in various capacities, including deputy undersecretary for planning, budget and evaluation; chairman of the president's Special Working Group on School Discipline; assistant to the president for policy development; and undersecretary in the Department of Education. In 1988 and 1996 Bauer expressed displeasure with the Republican presidential candidates—George Bush and Robert Dole, respectively—concluding their credentials were insufficiently conservative. This dissatisfaction undoubtedly influenced his decision to seek the Republican nomination in 2000 despite advice to the contrary from fellow religious right leaders Pat Robertson and James Dobson.

During his brief campaign for the Republican nomination, Bauer advocated policy positions supportive of conservative Christian values. He avidly opposed legalized abortion and objected to the push for a "right to die," which, he warned, would result in a "duty to die." Bauer advocated additional reforms of the welfare system, arguing for an end to cash entitlements which he claimed encouraged irresponsibility. Any assistance should be tied to changing the behavior of recipients. He called for tax cuts for families rather than increased spending on government programs. Bauer opposed any special legislative action to protect "gay rights." He promised to tie any foreign policy actions to the willingness of foreign governments to recognize their citizens' freedom of religion. These orthodox conservative positions notwithstanding, Bauer raised eyebrows among those on the religious right by advocating positions, such as a patients' bill of rights and campaign finance reform, more conducive to a moderate or liberal candidate. Bauer's accidental fall from a New Hampshire stage while flipping pancakes foreshadowed his disappointing showing in that state's primary.

After dropping out of the race, he endorsed Senator John McCain for the nomination, thus gaining the further disapproval of many on the religious right. An even greater heresy was Bauer's presence when McCain publicly denounced Pat Robertson and Jerry Falwell as "agents of intolerance." His own Family Research Council and his long-time ally, James Dobson, publicly criticized his support for McCain. Although the religious right's disaffection with Bauer may be interpreted as a reaction to someone moderating his conservative views in order to broaden political support, the source of Bauer's difficulties with former allies may be due in part to his idealism. For instance, Bauer was critical of Pat Robertson for supporting trade with China and not mentioning his own broadcast interests in that country.

Although Bauer no longer has ties to the Family Research Council, he still operates his political action committee. He plans to continue an active public life, writing speeches and expressing his opinions in the media, and will perhaps write a book about his campaign experiences. Bauer may also work for reform in the Republican party, which he believes is too closely tied to corporate interests.

Robert J. Billings (1926–1995)

A major supporter of Christian schools, Robert Billings was a member of the Department of Education during President Ronald Reagan's administration. He graduated from Bob Jones University and served as a high school principal, but left that position because of what he considered excessive government interference and the dominance of humanist values in public education. He and his wife began establishing Christian schools across the nation. He also served as president of Hyles-Anderson College. In 1976 he ran an unsuccessful campaign for Congress. Billings founded the National Christian Action Coalition in 1978, a successor to Christian School Action. One of the Coalition's major goals was to oppose government involvement in Christian schools. Consequently, Billings directed the effort against the Internal Revenue Service when that agency in 1978 sought to deny tax exemption to Christian schools for alleged racial discrimination. In 1979 he helped to persuade Jerry Falwell to form Moral Majority and assisted in rallying support for Falwell among influential people in the religious right. He became the organization's first executive director.

Billings left Moral Majority in 1980 to serve as a religious adviser in Ronald Reagan's campaign for the presidency. After Reagan became president, Billings was named the director of regional offices in the Department of Education. In this post he played a major role in fending off Internal Revenue Service proposals to tax religious schools. Even so, in 1983 the Supreme Court reversed the Reagan administration's decision to grant tax-exempt status to Billings's alma mater, Bob Jones University. Like other leaders of the religious right in 1988, Billings supported a Republican candidate for president, backing Senator Robert Dole's unsuccessful attempt to gain the nomination. Billings has been quoted as saying that people do not wish to think for themselves, but desire leadership and want to be told what to think by those who are more closely involved with politics.

Bill Bright (1921–2003)

Founder and leader of Campus Crusade for Christ for nearly fifty years, Bill Bright has patterned a conservative Christian message intended to appeal to contemporary Americans. Still attached to fundamentalist beliefs such as bib-

Bill Bright. Photo courtesy of Campus Crusade for Christ.
Used by permission.

lical inerrancy and the blood atonement of Christ, Bright nonetheless introduced alternative techniques for "selling" Christianity conducive with modern
consumer culture and the hope for financial success, using athletes and popular music stars to attract young people on college campuses. In the late 1960s,
during youth protests against the war in Vietnam, Bright stated his support for
student radicals, using such phrases as "revolution now" and commenting
that dissent was an important ingredient in society. However, Bright remained
committed to a conservative agenda, including preservation of family values,
personal initiative, and the capitalist system.

Bright, who was born in Coweta, Oklahoma, had a conversion experience
at age sixteen. His participation in the Hollywood Presbyterian Church, which
had a relaxed atmosphere, mixing evangelizing with social interaction, undoubtedly had a later influence on Bright's choice of professions. In 1946 he
entered Princeton Seminary, but transferred after a year to the more conservative Fuller Seminary in Pasadena, California. In his final year at the seminary
the idea of the Campus Crusade came to him, and so he left the school and
rented a house near the University of California at Los Angeles and began his
campaign for religious conversion. Billy Graham, who in 1955 recommended a
more friendly approach to spreading the Gospel message, confirmed Bright's
belief that personal religious commitment, especially among youth, was necessary to combat the trend toward secularism in the United States and the advance of communism around the world. Thus, Bright's approach emphasized

the need of personal conversion but never unequivocally condemned American materialist culture.

Bright combined entrepreneurial skills with a pragmatic approach to the Christian faith, claiming that spiritual laws governed people's relationship with God and treating biblical accounts as rationally founded and empirically verifiable. He presented a simple message to potential converts: although God loves each person, sin separates that person from God. Therefore, since Jesus Christ was the only path to God, each person must individually accept Christ as savior. Bright developed straightforward methods which are used by Crusade participants for approaching students. Training seminars were offered at Crusade headquarters at Arrowhead Springs, California. In the 1960s Bright formed Athletes in Action (AIA), an adjunct to Campus Crusade. The AIA basketball team played exhibition games with college teams, taking the opportunity to "witness" to the audience during halftime.

In 1972 Bright initiated EXPLO events, public rallies intended to motivate high school and college students to use Campus Crusade methods to create converts in their homes, churches, and schools. At EXPLO '74, held in South Korea, Bright's political naivete became evident when he announced his support for President Park Chung Hee's regime. Billy Graham, who had worked with Bright's Campus Crusade, disapproved of Bright's support for the repressive regime. Of concern to others has been Bright's tight organizational control and seeming intolerance of differing opinions and criticism. Others have indicated their concern for his ties to wealthy donors such as Nelson Bunker Hunt. Some critics expressed concern for Bright's acceptance of contemporary American economic values, fearing his movement would be compromised by the very secular world he hopes to transform.

These reservations notwithstanding, in the 1990s Bright's campus ministries continued to expand. In 1996 Bright won the Templeton Prize in Religion for advancing the understanding of God and spirituality, which included an award of over $1 million. Bright's Campus Crusade organization had expanded to nearly 13,000 full-time workers and over 101,000 volunteers in 165 countries. Among his projects was an attempt to mobilize millions of Christians around the world to fast and pray for spiritual revival. Bright hoped to extend his conservative Christian message worldwide, expressing the intention of converting one billion people and establishing one million churches by the year 2000.

William Jennings Bryan (1860–1925)

William Jennings Bryan's influence on the development of the religious right stems largely from his participation as a prosecutor in the 1925 Scopes trial in which John T. Scopes was charged with violating a state law forbidding the teaching of evolution in the public schools of Tennessee. At issue in this trial was the conflict between a literal interpretation of the Bible and scientific explanations of natural events, a conflict in which fundamentalists disclosed deep suspicions toward a modern society seemingly at odds with their religious beliefs. Despite his association with fundamentalist opposition to evolu-

Williams Jennings Bryan, head-and-shoulders portrait, facing right. Copyright 1907.
Prints and Photographs Division, Library of Congress.

tion theory, Bryan's political life involved the pursuit of objectives that cannot readily be associated with a religious right ideology, then or now.

Bryan, a native of southern Illinois, graduated as class valedictorian from Illinois College in 1881. He entered Union Law School in Chicago and received his law degree in 1883. He moved to Lincoln, Nebraska, in 1887, immediately became active in politics, and was elected to the U.S. House of Representatives in 1890. In 1896 he captured the Democratic party's nomination for the presidency. The American people rejected him at the polls in 1896, again in 1900, and yet again in 1908, giving Bryan the dubious distinction of having been defeated in three presidential elections. After Woodrow Wilson was elected president in 1912, he chose Bryan as his secretary of state. Bryan attempted to maintain a basically pacifist stance and opposed American involvement in

World War I. Wilson's policy of "neutrality," which in fact favored Great Britain and France, led Bryan to resign his position in the Wilson cabinet.

Unlike many fundamentalists, Bryan did not find premillennialism an attractive doctrine. He supported many progressive policies and causes: women's suffrage, direct popular election of the president, a national minimum wage, direct election of U.S. senators, a graduated income tax, and the use of government to control the power of corporations. On other issues, such as prohibition and Sabbatarianism, Bryan took more conservative positions closer to the hearts of fundamentalists.

Bryan opposed the teaching of evolution, an issue to which he devoted increasing attention as his influence in politics faltered. He argued that state legislatures had the right to restrict the teaching of evolution, at least to the extent that such instruction must label evolution as a mere hypothesis or "guess" as to the origin of humankind. Evolution was not only a poorly founded conjecture, but also represented a serious threat to society. Acceptance of the social Darwinian view of the survival of the fittest, which to Bryan was the essence of evolution, would weaken God's presence in people's lives. He regarded the teaching of evolution to be an issue best decided democratically: the people have the right to control their own schools and can do so through the institutions of representative democracy. This view gained new popularity in some state legislatures in the 1980s.

Bryan was ill equipped to criticize the theory of evolution and a scientific method about which he knew virtually nothing. He had generally limited his reading to the Bible and such other sources as the classics and the writings of Thomas Jefferson. Except for the daily newspaper, he inquired little into developments of the modern world. Although the World Christian Fundamentals Association had asked him to prosecute Scopes, prominent fundamentalists deserted him to face the crafty Clarence Darrow, Scopes's defense attorney, alone. Bryan and Darrow confronted each other directly at the 1925 trial. When he unwisely agreed to be cross-examined by Darrow, Bryan's ignorance of the theory he so strongly criticized became apparent. Due to Bryan's nationally reported humiliation, the jury's guilty verdict against Scopes was a pyrrhic victory. Bryan died within a week of the trial's conclusion.

Edgar C. Bundy (1915–)

During the 1950s and 1960s Edgar Bundy, executive director of the Church League of America, played a leading role in the anticommunist movement. After receiving a B.A. from Wheaton College in 1938, he enlisted in the army in 1941 and served for six years, ultimately reaching the rank of major. In 1942 he became an ordained Southern Baptist minister. After World War II Bundy served as chief of research and analysis in the Intelligence Section of the Alaskan Air Command. He left the military in 1948 to become the city editor of the Wheaton, Illinois, *Daily Journal*. The following year the Senate Appropriations Committee invited him to testify on the communist threat in the Far East. Numerous invitations to speak at meetings of various political and patriotic groups soon followed, and for a time he worked with Carl McIntire in public relations and as a researcher.

Bundy became active in the Illinois American Legion, playing a role in condemning the *Girl Scout Handbook* for containing "un-American" material and writing a resolution for the Legion's 1955 national convention declaring the United Nations Educational, Scientific, and Cultural Organization subversive. In 1956 the Church League of America named him its executive director. He edited the League's *News and Views*, which became an important source of information on anticommunism for the religious right. Bundy recorded lectures with titles such as "The Perils of the Social Gospel" and "The Perversion of the Bible" for usage by the League's counter-subversion seminars. His book, *Collectivism in the Churches* (1958) described the way in which various elements in American society, including those supporting the social gospel, were subverting American liberty.

Charles E. Coughlin (1891–1979)

The controversial "radio priest" of the 1930s and precursor of contemporary televangelism, Charles Coughlin had an estimated radio audience of 40 million listeners during the height of his fame. If not a major player, he was a considerable irritant in American politics of the 1930s. Coughlin studied theology at St. Michael's College at the University of Toronto and, after teaching at Assumption College in Windsor, Ontario, for six years, entered the diocese of Detroit in 1923. Possessing a rich baritone voice, Coughlin early on made occasional radio broadcasts. In 1925 he was appointed priest in a parish in Royal Oak, a suburb of Detroit. Coughlin began a radio program in order to raise funds to remedy the financial problems of the parish. By 1930 broadcasts from his church, the Shrine of the Little Flower, were carried over several Columbia Broadcasting System stations. After CBS dropped his program, Coughlin established his own network that ultimately included twenty-six independent stations. With the start of the Great Depression, he focused on the international monetary crisis and assailed those groups, particularly the big banks, allegedly responsible for America's economic plight. Although initially a Roosevelt supporter, Coughlin soon became a severe critic of New Deal policies and a fierce opponent of communism.

In the mid-1930s Coughlin entered more directly into politics. In 1935 persistent rumors circulated that he and Governor Huey Long of Louisiana were gravitating toward one another, and in 1936 he supported third-party candidate William Lemke for the presidency. That same year Coughlin founded the National Union for Social Justice and the magazine *Social Justice*. The magazine became controversial for publishing such writings as the discredited *Protocols of the Elders of Zion*, which prompted charges of antisemitism. Partially due to his opposition to American involvement in World War II, Coughlin came under federal grand jury investigation. In 1942 he ceased publication of his magazine and ended his radio program after it came increasingly under review by church authorities. Although Coughlin occasionally wrote about political issues, he remained out of the public limelight, devoting his energies to priestly duties in his Detroit parish until his retirement in 1966.

John Nelson Darby (1800–1882)

This Anglican minister, who left the Church of Ireland to become a leader of the Plymouth Brethren, found in post-Civil War America fertile soil for his dispensational premillennial beliefs. Between 1859 and 1877 he toured the United States at least six times, winning numerous converts to his views, particularly among Baptists and Presbyterians. Through the likes of James Brooks, Cyrus Scofield, and J. Frank Norris, Darby's influence on American fundamentalism has been substantial. Born in London, Darby was educated at Trinity College, opened a law practice in Ireland, became a minister upon conversion to Christianity, soon declared Anglicanism bankrupt, and joined the Brethren in 1828 because of their simple ways, congregational autonomy, and adherence to scripture. When the Brethren split in the 1840s, Darby became the leader of the more rigid faction, called the Darbyites.

For the most part, Darby's dispensational premillennialism was rather conventional. He divided history into distinct epochs, or dispensations, each of which differed with regard to God's plan of redemption. The crucifixion and the Jewish rejection of Jesus marked the end of one dispensation and opened another, the church age. This era in turn would end with the Rapture, followed swiftly by the seven-year reign of the Antichrist, a period of Tribulation during which Jews would be horribly persecuted. The eventual defeat of the Antichrist at the Battle of Armageddon and the triumphal return of Christ would initiate the millennium. The most distinctive aspect of Darby's thought centered on the reestablishment of a Jewish nation. Indeed, Darby's end-of-time scenario was tied closely to the fate of the Jews, a surviving remnant of whom supposedly would come to recognize Jesus as the long-awaited Messiah.

Several factors account for the acceptance of Darbyism in this country. First, Darby vigorously defended and zealously promoted his variant of dispensational premillennialism. Second, in an age when Darwinism and liberal theology undermined confidence in the scriptures, Darby's emphasis upon biblical authority and literalism appealed to many conservatives. And, third, the Niagara Bible Conferences initiated by James Brooks, the success of the Scofield Reference Bible, and the prominence of J. Frank Norris among fundamentalists ensured a wide audience.

James C. Dobson (1936–)

A psychologist and former professor of pediatrics at the University of Southern California School of Medicine, James Dobson heads Focus on the Family, an organization concerned with social issues affecting the "traditional" family structure. His popular thirty-minute weekday radio program, *Focus on the Family,* has a daily audience of four million. By radio and television combined, he reaches approximately 28 million people every week, giving him larger reach than either Jerry Falwell or Pat Robertson at their height. While Dobson gives advice about problems people face in contemporary family life and emphasizes traditional Christian values, he does not present the explicitly Christian message of other radio evangelists and seldom refers directly to biblical texts. His book on child rearing, *Dare to Discipline* (1970), became a popular evangelical alternative on the subject. To date, his books have sold over 16 million copies, and his tracts and pamphlets have sold additional millions. He has a large staff of some 1,300, including several licensed family counselors who deal with emergency situations and other trained staff members who deal with less urgent cases.

Dobson's involvement in national politics has come as a result of his concern for the family. He was selected to attend a White House Conference on the Family during President Jimmy Carter's administration, and he served on six government panels during President Ronald Reagan's administration, the most notable of which was the Commission on Pornography headed by Attorney General Edwin Meese. Believing his views, as well as those of his followers, were not receiving enough attention in Washington, Dobson created the Family Research Council, an advocacy group headed until recently by Gary Bauer. The son, grandson, and great-grandson of Nazarene preachers, Dobson has been a moralist in the political arena, a visionary who expects the process to yield swift, transforming results. This made Dobson quick to rebuke his more pragmatic political and spiritual kinfolks, people who share his objectives but understand more clearly the necessity of compromise. Thus, in 1996 Dobson faulted Ralph Reed for not attacking more aggressively Colin Powell's position on abortion, and in 1998 he threatened to wreak havoc on Republicans unless the party delivered on the issues of importance to religious and social conservatives. Dobson illustrates the dilemma faced by the Republican party. If it meets the demands of the popular and influential radio and television host, it runs the risk of alienating Americans of more moderate persuasion.

Dobson assumed a lower profile after the 2000 presidential race, explaining that he did not want to politicize Focus on the Family. But in May 2003, while continuing to chair the board of directors, he turned over daily operations of his organization to Don Hodel, a former member of Ronald Reagan's cabinet and an executive of the Christian Coalition. This freed Dobson to devote more attention to an issue of vital importance to him, the institution of marriage, which he believed to be in grave danger. In 2004, as a private citizen, he publicly endorsed a presidential candidate for the first time and vigorously campaigned for about twenty-five Republican candidates. One of Dobson's more prominent targets was Senate Minority Leader Tom Daschle of South Dakota, who was defeated by John Thune. With several Supreme Court nominations hanging in the balance, Dobson remarked that he could not sit out the 2004 election. He had to do all that he could "to keep the loony left from capturing the United States Supreme Court."

Colonel V. Doner (1949–)

Colonel Doner, presently CEO of Children's Hunger Relief Fund, was one of the co-founders of Christian Voice, a religious right organization that became active in national politics in the 1980s. Doner and his colleagues in Christian Voice claimed that, through their campaign activities, they were responsible for defeating President Jimmy Carter and thirty incumbent congressmen in the 1980 election. Christian Voice published moral report cards on congressional Democrats and ran controversial campaign ads, including one that identified President Carter with the homosexual rights movement. Doner was noted for his combative style in his appearances on such television programs as *60 Minutes* and *Phil Donohue*.

In his book, *The Samaritan Strategy* (1989), Doner pondered the political activities of the religious right movement of the 1980s. He described the movement's association with the Republican party and revealed the extent of Republican financial support in 1984 in co-founding (with Tim LaHaye) the American Coalition for Traditional Values. Doner claimed that by 1986 Republican leaders had begun to fear the expanding influence of the Christian right and therefore halted financial assistance. Doner left Washington in 1986, having decided that the religious right had failed to achieve its objectives. After leaving Washington, Doner, reflecting on past political involvement, concluded that the religious right neglected to demonstrate sufficient concern for those in need, such as abused children and the homeless. Altering strategy, Doner began to seek contacts with more liberal evangelical Christians to try to work together in achieving common service goals. He claimed that Christians will merit the opportunity for leadership in their communities by caring for those in need.

Colonel V Doner. Photo courtesy of Colonel V. Doner.
Used by permission.

Jerry Falwell (1932–)

The religious right's most prominent spokesman by the early 1980s, Jerry Falwell demonstrated that fundamentalist Christians could be effectively involved in the political process. Raised among rowdy bootleggers in the hill country of central Virginia, his formative years gave no hint of later religious stature. After becoming a Christian in 1952, he attended Bible Baptist College in Missouri. Four years later he returned home to Lynchburg, established an independent Baptist church in a vacant bottling plant, promptly took to the air waves with a thirty-minute radio program, and within six months aired his first telecast. The smoothly articulate pastor quickly became an institution. From only thirty-five members in 1956, his Thomas Road congregation numbered almost 20,000 by the early 1980s and his Sunday service, *The Old-Time Gospel Hour*, was carried to an estimated 21 million faithful listeners via 681 radio and television stations. Falwell's fundraising capacity was impressive. By 1980 he was generating about $1 million per week, enough to sustain a college, Liberty Baptist, with approximately 3,000 students, a home for alcoholics, a children's day school, a seminary, sixty-two assistant pastors, and 1,300 employees.

As noteworthy as these church-related achievements were, Falwell was becoming better known to the American public because of his venture into politics. Assisted by such conservative political strategists as Paul Weyrich, Howard Phillips, and Edward E. McAteer, the popular preacher launched Moral Majority, Inc., in 1979. The purpose was to give political voice to a growing tide of disenchanted Christian fundamentalists, religionists, who, like Falwell himself, had traditionally abstained from the political process. By the late 1970s Falwell was convinced that America's moral decline, as presumably exemplified by Supreme Court decisions on prayer in the public schools and abortion, the pervasiveness of "smutty" television, the assertiveness of the gay community, and the push for the Equal Rights Amendment, could be reversed only by vigorous political activism from the religious right. Ironically, it was disappointment with another "born again" Christian, President Jimmy Carter, a Southern Baptist layman, that prompted Falwell to political action.

The extent to which Moral Majority contributed to the success of conservative Republicans in the 1980s is open to debate, but there is no denying the organization's efforts. It hastily established local chapters in all the states, conducted voter registration campaigns and educational seminars, and targeted liberal Democrats for defeat. Claims of nonpartisanship notwithstanding, Moral Majority clearly was more at ease with a conservative Republican agenda. The organization was never very successful in attracting non-fundamentalists, and so in an effort to broaden its support, Falwell renamed it Liberty Foundation in 1987. That same year Falwell's ministries, like those of many other televangelists, suffered serious economic losses in the wake of the PTL scandal. A Gallup Poll disclosed that 62 percent of the American public viewed the preacher unfavorably. Consequently, in 1989 he dissolved Moral Majority, devoted more attention to his local congregation and college, and assumed a lower profile.

Falwell has continued to receive strident criticism, especially regarding his statements about Islam and sexual deviancy after the attack of September 11, 2001. He blamed the assault on America's moral decline, as exemplified by abortion, homosexuality, and lesbianism, and he labeled the prophet Mohammad a "terrorist." Most mainline Christians and some conservative evangelicals took exception, prompting Falwell to apologize. Said he on *60 Minutes* on September 30, "I intended no disrespect to any sincere, law-abiding Muslim." That Falwell's influence has waned is certainly true, but it is much too premature to count the televangelist out. Witness the emerging coziness between Senator John McCain of Arizona and Falwell as the former maneuvers toward a possible run for the presidency again in 2008.

William ("Billy") Franklin Graham (1918–)

Although less active politically than other key figures in the religious right, Billy Graham can be credited with practicing a biblically based and passionate style of evangelism that set the standard for many others. He helped to make evangelical Christianity acceptable once again to the general American public. Graham attended Bob Jones University in 1936 and Florida Bible Institute from 1937 to 1940, where he was ordained a Southern Baptist minister in 1939, and graduated from Wheaton College in 1943. He assumed the duties of pastor at the First Baptist Church in Western Springs, Illinois, in 1943 and the following year became a preacher for the Youth for Christ organization. From 1947 to 1952 Graham served as president of Northwestern Schools in Minneapolis, Minnesota. During the early postwar years he began holding highly successful crusades and in 1950 formed the Billy Graham Evangelistic Association to help coordinate his activities. In 1952 Graham resigned from Northwestern Schools and moved to Montreat, North Carolina. In 1955, believing that the journal *Christian Century* was too liberal, he assisted in establishing the more conservative *Christianity Today.*

In 1952 President-elect Dwight Eisenhower asked for Graham's advice about an inaugural prayer, and thus began the evangelist's long association with national political figures. He gave the opening prayer at President Lyndon Johnson's 1965 inauguration and led President Richard Nixon's Sunday worship services at the White House. Not surprisingly, Graham became known as the "friend to presidents." After Nixon's resignation under the shadow of the Watergate scandal, Graham showed less enthusiasm for such political associations.

In the 1950s and 1960s Graham, in accord with other religious right leaders, was a strong anticommunist. During the American involvement in Vietnam, he was an uncritical supporter of government policy. On other public policy issues, Graham took conservative stands, such as opposing the school prayer ban and criticizing the Supreme Court for being too lenient with criminals. Although he emphasizes a decidedly conservative theology and focuses primarily on the need for personal conversion, Graham has been willing to express his concern for social justice. This willingness first became apparent in the early 1950s when he ended segregated seating at his crusades.

William Franklin Graham. Photo courtesy of Billy Graham Evangelistic Association. Used by permission, all rights reserved.

In the 1980s he unexpectedly began to raise questions about the dangers of the arms race. Although some elements of the religious right have criticized Graham's more moderate, essentially nonpolitical evangelism, attitude surveys over the years indicate he has consistently remained one of the more esteemed Americans.

Robert Grant (1936–)

One of the leading figures in the religious right during the 1980s, Grant was one of the founders of Christian Voice in 1978 and of the American Freedom Coalition (AFC) in 1987. He remains president of the AFC. He graduated from Wheaton College and Fuller Theological Seminary and was the founding dean of the California Graduate School of Theology. In 1975 he established American Christian Cause, a California organization that opposed gay rights and pornography. Christian Voice, originally named Citizens United in 1976 and

Robert Grant. Photo courtesy of Robert Grant.
Used by permission.

briefly called American Christians United, became well-known for constructing moral report cards that rated congressional and presidential candidates on a variety of issues, including foreign policy. For instance, Grant and his organization considered support for the Reagan administration's Strategic Defense Initiative, known as "Star Wars," to be pro-biblical. He also agreed with Reagan administration attempts to provide aid to the Nicaraguan Contras.

After a poor showing of his candidates in the 1986 congressional elections, Grant decided that Christians must cooperate with other groups, including non-Christians, to achieve common objectives. The religious right had become fragmented, having failed to build an effective coalition. Grant became one of the founders of the American Freedom Coalition and assumed the title of president. In establishing the new organization, he reportedly accepted financial assistance from Sun Myung Moon's Unification Church. In addition, a number of administrative officers were said to be members of the Unification Church. Grant stated that he did not agree with the Unification Church's theology and claimed that no one religious group dominated the AFC. In order to achieve a just cause, Grant concluded, sometimes money had to be accepted from those who have it and are willing to contribute.

John Hagee (1940–)

Over the last twenty-five years John Hagee, senior pastor at Cornerstone Church in San Antonio, Texas, and president of Global Evangelism Television, has developed a nationwide broadcast ministry. In addition to his daily and weekly television and radio programs, Hagee sells audio- and videotapes of his sermons and has published several popular books. He has consistently supported the religious right agenda, preaching on social and political topics such as abortion, environmentalism, feminism, the homosexual movement, and American foreign policy in the Middle East. During President Bill Clinton's administration, Hagee's sermons often contained humor critical of the president.

Born in Baytown, Texas, Hagee attended Trinity University on a football scholarship and received a bachelor's degree in 1964. He continued his studies at North Texas State University, earning a master's degree in 1966, and at Southwestern Bible Institute near Dallas, obtaining theological training. Subsequently, he was granted an honorary doctorate from Oral Roberts University. The son of a Baptist minister, Hagee began his career as an evangelist in 1958. In 1966 he became the founding pastor of what would ultimately become Trinity Church, a charismatic congregation in San Antonio. In the mid-1970s Hagee divorced his wife and married a member of the congregation. He left Trinity in 1975 to become pastor of the twenty-five-member Church of Castle Hill in San Antonio, and within two years built a new sanctuary seating 1,600 people. In 1987 the church, renamed Cornerstone, dedicated another sanctuary with a seating capacity of 5,000.

Hagee's influence among evangelicals has increased with the dissemination of his fundamentalist message through the electronic media. His church services are broadcast on 110 individual television stations as well as the Trinity Broadcasting Network (TBN) and the Inspirational Network. In Canada, Hagee's program is carried by the Vision Network. His speaking style is highly appealing to many fundamentalist Christians. Although rotund, he is very animated, presents his scriptural interpretations in a highly confident and uncompromising manner, and offers applications of scripture for listeners' daily lives. Hagee is a bestselling author, having written books on the end times and the millennium (*Beginning of the End* and *Final Dawn Over Jerusalem*), and alleged conspiracies in American government and society (*Day of Deception*). In addition, the Cornerstone pastor distributes a bimonthly magazine, *John Hagee Ministries*, to which he contributes articles. Hagee sells videotapes of his talks, such as *Take America Back*, a three-tape series including the subjects "Back to the Bible," "Back to Basics," and "Back to the Future" and "America Under Judgment," a tape in the *Curses: Their Cause and Cure* series.

Hagee's support for the religious right notwithstanding, he has been criticized by many evangelical Christians for claiming Jews have a separate covenant with God from that of Christians and therefore need not be converted to Christianity to achieve salvation. Contrary to a common stereotype of fundamentalist Christians, Hagee is an avid opponent of antisemitism. He has received accolades from Jewish organizations for his support of the Jewish people and the Israeli nation, having raised over $1 million to assist Soviet Jews wishing to resettle in Israel. In response to criticisms of his apparent adherence to a "dual covenant" theory of salvation, Hagee has charged those who challenge him on this theological point with encouraging antisemitism. Some fundamentalists have also expressed concern about Hagee's attachment to the Faith movement, including adherence to the prosperity doctrine—the claim that wealth can be achieved through obedience to God's laws and through giving to the church—and positive confession—the belief that Christians can speak certain states of affairs into reality if they have enough faith.

Ted Haggard (1956–)

Founder and pastor of the 14,000-member New Life Church in Colorado Springs, Colorado, Ted Haggard became one of the more influential leaders in the religious right, rivaling the prominence of such figures as James Dobson, head of Focus on the Family and a close friend. However, in October 2006 a former male prostitute in Denver announced that he had had a three-year sexual relationship with Haggard. Haggard ultimately admitted that he had purchased crystal meth, but claimed he never used the drug. He quickly resigned as president of the influential National Association of Evangelicals (NEA), an organization of 52 denominations and 45,000 churches representing 30 million church members that had chosen him as its leader in 2003. After reviewing the accusations made against him, the board of overseers at New Life Church decided that Haggard was guilty of "sexually immoral conduct" and removed him as the church's pastor.

A graduate of Oral Roberts University in 1978, Haggard became an associate pastor of a large church in Baton Rouge, Louisiana. In 1984, while traveling in Colorado, a friend riding with him claimed to have a vision of Haggard founding a church in that state. Haggard took the vision seriously and established New Life Church, meeting initially in the basement of his home and then in a succession of storefront buildings. By 2005 New Life was located in a new church building north of the city that seated more than 7,000 people. In addition to being president of the NEA, Haggard had established the Association of Life-Giving Churches, a network of churches allied with New Life Church and dedicated to assisting and energizing pastors and congregations.

On most issues, Haggard backed President George W. Bush. Reportedly, he took part in weekly conference calls with members of the president's staff or the president himself. During the 2004 election campaign, Haggard encouraged evangelicals to register and vote. He spoke out against abortion and homosexuality and supported amending the U.S. Constitution to define marriage as a union between one man and one woman. During the 2006 election campaign, Haggard championed the passage of a proposed amendment to the Colorado constitution banning gay marriage. However, Haggard supported the U.S. Supreme Court decision in *Lawrence v. Texas* (2003) that found unconstitutional a Texas anti-sodomy law. Haggard stated that although the church should speak against immoral behavior, the state should not be engaged in regulating what consenting adults do in their bedrooms. At times he disagreed with other religious right figures, for instance, criticizing Pat Robertson for suggesting that the United States government assassinate Venezuelan president Hugo Chavez. In 2004 the NAE, under Haggard's leadership, issued "For the Health of the Nation: An Evangelical Call to Civic Responsibility," which called for action on such traditional evangelical issues as abortion and gay marriage, but also included statements on poverty, education, and welfare.

Many in the mainline denominations as well as some evangelicals questioned Haggard's advocacy of free-market economics and the application of those principles to churches. He supported the Bush administration's decision not to submit the Kyoto Protocol to the U.S. Senate for ratification. Haggard held that solutions to environmental problems should result from free-market processes, and that the protocol would jeopardize U.S. sovereignty. Critics questioned the biblical relevance of market principles to church life, arguing that, unlike Jesus, who chased the money changers from the temple, supporters of free-market economics have welcomed them back in.

Ironically, in the second edition of his book, *Your Primary Purpose: How to Reach Your Community and World for Christ*, published in February 2006, Haggard commented that Christians were capable of living sinless lives. Some speculated that Haggard's shocking fall from a top leadership position in the religious right just before the November 2006 election, when combined with a host of other reported misdeeds of Republicans, contributed to that party's defeat in many close election races that year.

Hank Hanegraaff (1950–)

President of the Christian Research Institute (CRI), Hank Hanegraaff is both highly revered and avidly attacked by those in the evangelical Christian community. Hanegraaff has taken stands strongly opposing abortion and supporting creationism, positions which correspond closely to the religious right. However, he has attacked certain individuals and movements in the evangelical community which he claims depart from orthodox Christian beliefs. On his nationally broadcast daily radio program, *The Bible Answer Man*, Hanegraaff responds to the questions of callers, which often deal with movements that Hanegraaff severely criticizes. He also travels the country as a guest speaker at church conferences and gatherings. The CRI's major objective is to expose cults which allegedly distort the Christian message. Examples of movements the CRI brands as cults are the Mormon church, the Jehovah's Witnesses, and the Masons. However, the Trinity Broadcasting Network and its owner Paul Crouch, as well as various personalities who appear on the network, such as Benny Hinn and Kenneth Copeland, come under attack for their presumed departure from the true faith and descent into cultic behavior.

Raised as an adherent of the Christian Reformed Church, Hanegraaff states that he became a true Christian after investigating scientific evidence for creation, the resurrection of Jesus, and the inspiration of the Bible. He served as a staff member in D. James Kennedy's Evangelism Explosion and participated in other church programs. Hanegraaff later associated with Walter Martin, then head of the CRI. When Martin died, Hanegraaff assumed the presidency of the organization.

Hanegraaff has written several books dealing with topics relevant to contemporary Christianity in the United States. Two books which have raised controversy among evangelicals are *Christianity in Crisis* and *Counterfeit Revival*. In *Christianity in Crisis* Hanegraaff attacks various televangelists who present what he considers unbiblical messages, such as adherents of the so-called "Faith movement" and "health and wealth gospel," the belief that God rewards people who demonstrate adequate faith. In *Counterfeit Revival* he investigates evangelists who encourage emotional displays at public meetings, claiming such behavior is a sign of God's presence. A case in point is Rodney Howard Brown, originally from South Africa, whose preaching of "holy laughter" rouses audiences into uncontrollable bouts of laughter and strange behavior. Hanegraaff objects to the recent trends of the health and wealth gospel and holy laughter not only because he considers them unbiblical, but also because they defy rationality and calm consideration of the facts. Similarly, in his most recent publication, *The Face that Demonstrates the Farce of Evolution*, Hanegraaff does not pit science against religious belief, but instead accuses supporters of evolution theory of being unscientific, dishonest, and unwilling to admit that a conscious designer is at work in the universe. An instructor who teaches methods of improving the memory, Hanegraaff often uses acronyms. The "FACE" in the title of this anti-evolution book means Fossil follies; Ape-men fiction, frauds, and fantasy; Chance; and Empirical science. The "Farce" in the title stands for "Fossil record: an embarrassment for evolutionists"; "Ape-men are fraud, fiction, and fantasy"; "Recapitulation— the theory that the human fetus repeats, or recapitulates, stages in human evolution, has been discredited"; "Chance renders evolution not just improbable, but impossible"; and "Empirical science supports intelligent design and the creation of fully formed, complex organisms." During the period of widespread speculation prior to January 1, 2000, about a computer-related disaster, Hanegraaff published *The Millennium Bug Debugged*, in which he criticized the sensational journalism surrounding Y2K. His latest work, *Resurrection*, offers what Hanegraaff considers definite proof that Jesus rose from the dead.

Billy James Hargis (1925–2004)

In the depths of the Cold War in the 1950s, Billy James Hargis represented the propensity of evangelists of the religious right to combine a fundamentalist Christian message with extreme patriotism and anticommunism. In 1943 Hargis began his studies for the ministry at Ozark Bible College in Bentonville, Arkansas, but remained there only a year. He ultimately received a bachelor of arts degree from Pikes Peak Bible Seminary in 1957 and a bachelor of theology degree from Burton College in Colorado Springs, Colorado, in 1958. He was awarded an honorary doctor of laws degree from Bob Jones University in 1961. Hargis founded the Christian Crusade organization to save America from communism. To this day each issue of his *Christian Crusade Newspaper* contains the quote, "All I want to do is preach Jesus and save America." He gained notoriety in 1953 by participating with Carl McIntire in the Bible Balloon project, a plan to float balloons carrying Bible messages to Iron Curtain countries. In the early 1960s Hargis became more actively involved in politics, urging his followers to work for conservatives in election campaigns. During the tumultuous times of the late 1960s and early 1970s, Hargis identified campus radicals, antiwar protesters, and advocates of black power with communism and a general decline of moral values in America.

In 1974 Hargis announced that, due to health problems, he was giving up much of his work in the Christian Crusade and was resigning as president of the American Christian College in Tulsa, which had been founded just five years earlier. He also intended to stop his tours around the country and cease his weekly syndicated television programs. A strong opponent of sexual transgressions, Hargis in 1976 found himself accused of sexual misconduct by one female and three male students at his college. He emphatically denied the charges. The accusations came on the heels of Hargis's final separation from the American Christian College. Since that time, Hargis has maintained his Christian Crusade ministry in Neosho, Missouri, and conducts yearly Bible conferences that include a good deal of political commentary. More recent issues of *Christian Crusade Newspaper* continue to warn against the dangers of communism and celebrate conservative Republican victories in congressional elections. However, Hargis has never regained his earlier fame and influence.

Gary Jarmin (1949–)

As one of the religious right's most active leaders during the 1980s, Gary Jarmin played a key role as a legislative lobbyist. By the late 1980s he was instrumental in refocusing part of the movement away from explicitly Christian lobbying efforts in Washington and toward a more secular, grassroots orientation. Jarmin was the legislative director of Christian Voice and the administrator of the organization's Moral Government Fund, a political action committee that made donations to congressional campaigns in the 1980s. Christian Voice began the controversial practice of issuing moral ratings of congressional and state officials. The organization grew out of anti-gay rights and anti-pornography campaigns in California in the late 1970s. Jarmin became field director for American Coalition for Traditional Values in 1984 and also became the political director for American Freedom Coalition when the new organization was established in 1987. A major objective for AFC, Jarmin believed, was the building of local organizations, called precinct councils, to concentrate on local issues. Among the reasons for the new emphasis were an in-

Gary Jarmin. Photo courtesy of Gary Jarmin.
Used by permission.

creasing awareness of social needs and the desire to avoid theological divisions, along with the emerging realization that increased religious tolerance was necessary in order to build alliances with other organizations that shared the AFC's goals.

The general ineffectiveness of the religious right in the 1986 congressional elections convinced Jarmin and others that Christians by themselves could not alter the political mood of the country. Others in the religious right were troubled with Jarmin's apparent willingness to accept support from, and work with, representatives of Reverend Sun Myung Moon's Unification Church. In the mid-1980s Jarmin characterized the Republican party as an instrument to be used to achieve the objectives of the Christian right. As Reagan's presidency drew to a close, Jarmin noted that the Christian right had not achieved all that it had sought, but that involvement with the administration had provided valuable experience in government and politics.

Bob Jones, Sr. (1883–1968)

Perhaps no family has been more vigorous in the battle against modernism than that of Bob Jones, Sr. And perhaps there has been no family trio more alike in fundamentalist temperament and theology than Jones, Sr., Bob Jones Jr. (1911–), and Bob Jones III (1939–). An Alabama native, Jones, Sr., was converted in a Methodist church at age 11, preached his first revival at 12, had a brush-arbor church with fifty-four members at 13, was a licensed minister at 15, became a circuit rider at 16, and was orphaned at 17. Although an eager student, Jones enjoyed limited opportunities for schooling. In December 1900 he enrolled at Southern University in Greensboro, Alabama, but left after two years to become a full-time evangelist. An effective pulpiteer, he was compared by many observers to Billy Sunday. Although best known in the South, he preached in much of the North, from Illinois to New York.

Jones, Sr., accepted the Bible literally, as do his son and grandson, and any deviation from this narrow approach was heresy. Accordingly, he abandoned Methodism, convinced the denomination had embraced modernism, and devoted himself to fundamentalist causes. He was active in the World Christian Fundamentals Association, founded in 1919; he served on the Moody Bible Institute's continuing education faculty; and in 1926 established his own college, Bob Jones University, which has been located in Greenville, South Carolina, since 1947. The presidency of the school has passed from father to son to grandson.

Despite many common interests with other religious fundamentalists, the Joneses represent a separatist variety of fundamentalism. They will therefore have nothing to do with either unbelievers or those who associate with unbelievers. In the 1950s and 1960s, for instance, they denounced Billy Graham for allowing non-fundamentalists to participate in his local crusades and for not directing converts to fundamentalist congregations. Likewise, in the 1980s they scorned Jerry Falwell for allowing Catholics and other "infidels" into Moral Majority. Carl McIntire was the kind of fundamentalist most admired by the Joneses, and like McIntire, the Joneses have been unwilling to play down theological differences for the sake of political cooperation.

D. James Kennedy (1938–)

D. James Kennedy's sermon messages of spiritual and cultural renewal are televised nationwide from the 9,500-member Coral Ridge Presbyterian Church in Fort Lauderdale, Florida. Kennedy was born in Augusta, Georgia, and was raised in Chicago. While in high school, he moved with his family to Florida. He earned his B.A. from the University of Tampa and his master's of divinity degree from Columbia Theological Seminary. He has also received a master's of theology degree from Chicago Graduate School of Theology and a Ph.D. from New York University. Among Kennedy's many publications are *Evangelism Explosion, Character and Destiny: A Nation In Search of Its Soul*, and *The Gates of Hell Shall Not Prevail*.

In 1962 Kennedy founded Evangelism Explosion International, a training program for lay people. This program now operates worldwide to increase the membership of church congregations. In 1989 Kennedy began the Knox Theological Seminary, which trains pastors dedicated to the Reformed tradition. The seminary is committed to a belief in the inerrancy of the Bible. In addition to his weekly television program (*The Coral Ridge Hour*), a daily half-hour radio program (*Truths That Transform*), and a daily sixty-second radio commentary (*Reclaiming America*), Kennedy's Coral Ridge Ministries also include the Center for Christian Statesmanship, which attempts to minister to people in government and political positions in Washington, D.C. The Center for Reclaiming America, another segment of the Coral Ridge Ministries, strives to inform Americans about issues considered crucial to the Christian faith and to motivate them to support biblical principles on which Kennedy claims the nation was founded. The Center is geared to help citizens "reclaim their communities for Christ." In 1971 Kennedy founded the Westminster Academy, a Christian school in Fort Lauderdale which provides instruction from kindergarten through the twelfth grade.

Beverly LaHaye (1930–)

Wife of religious right leader Tim LaHaye, Beverly LaHaye has played a major role in organizing conservative Christian women in support of the religious right's political agenda. LaHaye, whose father died when she was young, grew up in Missouri and Michigan during the Great Depression. With her husband, she first gained national attention in the 1970s by offering seminars that advocated greater sexual gratification for Christian married couples. She and her husband Tim published *The Act of Marriage: The Beauty of Sexual Love*, which within a few years had sold more than one million copies. The book is essentially a sex manual for Christians. She began her own ministry in the late 1970s, publishing such books as *The Spirit-Controlled Woman* (1976) and *How to Develop Your Child's Temperament* (1977). Although LaHaye regards women as individuals in their own right who should engage actively in politics, she

*Beverly LaHaye. Photo courtesy of Concerned Women for America.
Used by permission.*

advises them to remain subordinate to their husbands and to household duties.

In 1979 she formed Concerned Women for America (CWA) with only nine members. By 1987 she claimed a membership of more than 500,000 women organized into 1,800 local chapters. In 1985 LaHaye moved with her husband to Washington, D.C., where she established the new national office of CWA. In 1987 she was given life tenure as president of the organization. LaHaye has gained a well-deserved reputation for effective political advocacy on behalf of conservative Christian causes. In September 1987 she testified in favor of Robert Bork, President Ronald Reagan's unsuccessful nominee to be the next chief justice of the Supreme Court. LaHaye has concentrated efforts as much on local as on national issues. For instance, CWA was given credit in 1986 for the defeat of an Equal Rights Amendment to the Vermont state constitution. LaHaye hosts *Beverly LaHaye Today,* a daily radio program, and, following her husband's lead, has published two novels—*Seasons Under Heaven* (1999) and *Showers in Season* (2000)—having conservative Christian themes.

Tim LaHaye (1926–)

Tim LaHaye first gained national prominence for his Family Life Seminars and workshops on Christian marriage, which he conducted with his wife, Beverly. The LaHayes co-authored *The Act of Marriage: The Beauty of Sexual Love,* in which they claimed Christians can experience great sexual enjoyment. LaHaye attended Western Conservative Baptist Seminary and in 1956 moved to San Diego, California, to become the pastor of Scott Memorial Baptist Church. His book *The Battle for the Mind* (1980) focused on "secular humanism" as a major threat to Christianity. He defined humanism as a religion that places sole confidence in human beings and acknowledges no need for God. In *The Coming Peace in the Middle East* (1984), LaHaye identified philosophies and philosophers he considered harmful to humankind.

One of the founders of Moral Majority, he started a branch of that organization, Californians for Biblical Morality, in 1980. That same year he created the Council for National Policy, a coalition of religious right leaders. In 1983 LaHaye established the American Coalition for Traditional Values (ACTV), which conducted a voter registration campaign for the 1984 election. After the election, LaHaye announced that the organization had registered two million voters, although other sources claimed a much lower number. One of LaHaye's objectives was to acquire more government appointments for born-again Christians in President Ronald Reagan's second administration. LaHaye moved ACTV headquarters to Washington, D.C., in 1985, and in January 1986, reports surfaced that he had received financial support for ACTV from a representative of Sun Myung Moon's Unification Church. The following year LaHaye became an honorary national co-chairman of U.S. Representative Jack Kemp's campaign for the presidency, but resigned from that position when news reports disclosed statements in his published works critical of Roman Catholics and Jews. In the 1994 elections, he was actively involved in a nationwide voter drive to get conservative Christians to the polls. LaHaye, along with Jerry Jenkins, began to publish the bestselling series, *Left Behind*, in 1996, and they completed the twelve volumes in 2004, selling to date about 62 million copies.

Richard Land (1948–)

As leader of the Southern Baptist Convention's Ethics and Religious Liberty Commission (ERLC) since 1988, Dr. Richard Land has represented Baptist causes in Congress and in the company of United States presidents. He first arrived in Washington in 1987 with credentials that more than qualified him as a public spokesman. Passionate and authoritative on social, ethical, and public issues, he envisions the United States committed to the common good of humanity and liberated from the cult of self.

Born in Houston, Texas, and educated at Princeton and Oxford, Land is sixth generation in the Lone Star State. Ordained in 1969, the Southern Baptist minister has pastored churches in Texas, Louisiana, and England and has become nationally known through appearances on such programs as NBC's *Meet the Press*. In February 2005 *Time* magazine chose Land as one of the "Twenty-five Most Influential Evangelicals in America," calling him "God's Lobbyist" and "the Southern Baptist Convention's main man in Washington." Land told *Time* that the Reagan White House returned his calls promptly, Bush, Sr., not so quickly, and President Clinton's staff, eventually, not at all. The current administration (President George W. Bush and Land are longtime friends) arranges for a weekly teleconference.

From Target stores to television to Texas border patrol, Land's advocacy for family values ranks first among his priorities. *For Faith and Family*, one of his nationally syndicated programs, appeals to 1.5 million listeners weekly on more than 600 U.S. radio stations and worldwide on the Internet. His three-hour caller-friendly *Richard Land Live!* is a syndicated weekend broadcast on Salem Radio Network. In December 2005 Land and twenty-four signers representing Baptist conventions wrote six letters to Target, Sears, and Home Depot, urging them to reverse their refusal to use the word "Christmas" in their advertisements and in in-store promotions. Land advised those companies to reconsider "before Christians take their business to stores more supportive of their values." The letter to Target CEO Robert Ulrich informed him that 85 percent of the American public professes or sympathizes with Christianity. Land declared, "We think a time will come when Target and other businesses will regret their part in destroying the true meaning of Christmas." When the same message went to Sears CEO Alwyn Lewis and Home Depot head Bob Naradelli, "Merry Christmas" soon reappeared on store fronts and Internet sites.

According to Land, the current immigration crisis has been precipitated by the government's failure to enforce U.S. border laws. Effective border patrol can only be realized when biblical mandates are applied. He proposes criminal background checks and mandatory English, supporting a "guest-worker" program as "a fair and practical way to deal with the over twelve million illegal immigrants." Land's efforts to advance the sanctity of human life and rights and to protect marriage rose to the top of the Southern Baptist ERLC agenda for 2006. In a statement released in March 2006, Land and Barret Duke, ERLC vice president for public policy, announced promotions for the following measures: the Unborn Child Pain Awareness Act, the Child Custody Protection Act, a ban on human cloning for research and reproductive purposes, the Marriage Protection Amendment (a constitutional amendment to protect marriage as the union of a man and a woman), the ADVANCE Democracy Act (to help end dictatorship and to promote democracy in other countries without military intervention), and the Workplace Religious Freedom Act. Considering that ERLC-backed measures, such as the provision of federal funds for the collection, testing, and storage of stem cells from umbilical-cord blood, became law in the first half of the 109th Congress in 2005, Land and Duke expect to effect the passage of more Southern Baptist conviction-based legislation in 2006.

At the Southern Baptist Convention, June 13, 2006, in Greensboro, North Carolina, Land's report confirmed that the nation's future looked bleak but not without hope. He pointed to strides already made: congressional passage of the Born-Alive Infant Protection Act, Unborn Victims of Violence Act, North Korea Human Rights Act of 2004, the Sudan Peace Act, Trafficking Victims Protection Act, and legislation creating a cord-blood, stem-cell bank, among other measures. Land urged listeners to encourage government to protect traditional marriage and oppose same-sex marriage. Land stresses the need to obey the Great Commission's call to evangelism, to carry the word into every American home via the media and in partnership with the second Bush presidency. George W. Bush is "overtly evangelical," according to Land, expressing his faith in religious language in speeches, including references to divine providence in America's mission after 9/11. Land has dealt with every White House since Ronald Reagan, but in the case of President Bush, Land recalled the newly inaugurated president's comment, "I believe God wants me to be president." Evidently, both God and Richard Land have had their way.

Hal Lindsey (1930–)

The most successful spinner in recent years of apocalyptic scenarios, Hal Lindsey has fueled the Christian right's belief that Armageddon is nigh. The Houston, Texas, native attended the University of Houston for two years, but dropped out, served a stint in the Coast Guard, and later worked as a tugboat captain on the Mississippi River. An avowed agnostic, he was converted as a result of reading a Gideon New Testament, and soon thereafter was absorbed by the biblical prophecies of Ezekiel and Revelation. From 1958 to 1962 he attended Dallas Theological Seminary, earning a master's degree in theology. The next ten years he spent with the Campus Crusade for Christ, speaking to audiences throughout the United States and in Mexico and Canada.

In 1970 Lindsey published *The Late Great Planet Earth*. The astonishing success of this work, which reportedly sold 20 million copies in fifty-two languages worldwide and was made into a movie in 1978, demonstrated the appetite for the visionary genre, and Lindsey capitalized on the hunger. He churned out in rapid succession a string of apocalyptic thrillers, such as *Satan Is Alive and Well* (1972), *The Terminal Generation* (1976), and *The 1980s: Countdown to Armageddon* (1980). Typical of this kind of literature, which tends to flourish during eras of national and international stress, Lindsey's works saw in current events a fulfillment of biblical prophecies about the end of time. The restoration of Israel in 1948, along with Israel's control of Jerusalem in 1967, convinced Lindsey that the "terminal generation" was at hand, although he wisely avoided precise dates. And until the 1980s, when he espoused a strong military to resist communism abroad and endorsed capitalist values to counter socialist tendencies at home, he had also generally avoided identification with a specific political agenda. Lindsey obviously was at ease with the religious right, and figures on the religious right, such as Pat Robertson and Jerry Falwell, were just as happy with his vision of doom, evidence of which they, too, saw in American society. Lindsey continues to present his interpretations of biblical prophecy in published works and in the broadcast media. He has become a regular on Trinity Broadcasting Network.

J. Gresham Machen (1881–1937)

This strong-willed and querulous Presbyterian professor who was schooled at Johns Hopkins University, Princeton Theological Seminary, and in Germany could be regarded as the theological and ideological grandfather of contemporary fundamentalists. As a teacher at Princeton Seminary from 1906 to 1929, he raised issues that still excite the religious right, from biblical inerrancy to open hostility toward all forms of liberalism. Typical of his unbridled attack upon modernism was *Christianity and Liberalism* (1923), a work in which he asserted that it was impossible to be a Christian and a liberal at the same time.

*J. Gresham Machen. Photo courtesy of PCA Historical Center, St. Louis, MO.
Used by permission.*

Increasingly intolerant of the more liberal sentiments of other denominational and seminary leaders, a disgruntled Machen left Princeton and founded
Westminster Theological Seminary in Philadelphia in 1929. Continuing his
attack, Machen now accused the denomination's missionaries of doctrinal infidelity. Eventually defrocked in 1936 over this dispute, he promptly established
the rival Presbyterian Church of America. Even this new group was soon torn
by schism, giving substance to the claim that if Machen had lived long enough,
he ultimately would have been the denomination's only member. Machen's
student, Carl McIntire, would go on to influence the direction of the religious
right in post-World War II America.

Clarence E. Manion (1896–1979)

After leaving a twenty-five-year career in academics, Clarence Manion established the *Manion Forum of the Air*, a popular political broadcast in the 1950s
and 1960s. A Roman Catholic, Manion received a B.A. in 1915 from St. Mary's
College in St. Mary, Kentucky. He attended Catholic University of America,
receiving his M.A. in 1916 and M.Ph. in 1917. He went on to the University of
Notre Dame, where he received his J.D. in 1922. In 1925 Manion was appointed professor of constitutional law at Notre Dame, and in 1941 he began
serving as dean of the College of Law, a position he held until 1952. The following year he became head of President Eisenhower's Inter-Governmental
Relations Commission.

Soon becoming dissatisfied with the Eisenhower administration, Manion
resigned his position after one year to found the *Manion Forum*, a weekly radio
series consisting of conservative commentary. First broadcast over sixteen
radio stations, by 1965 the *Manion Forum* was being carried by more than 300
radio and television stations. The program included Manion's own commentaries as well as interviews with political, educational, business, and military
personalities. In the late 1950s Manion joined the John Birch Society, becoming

one of its original directors. Although he supposedly did not always agree with the organization—for example, he did not support its claim that President Dwight Eisenhower was an agent of the Communist party—he refused to resign from the society. Known for his often extreme public statements, Manion demonstrated cordiality and personal warmth in his private life. He published several books, including *Let's Face It* (1956), *The Conservative American* (1964), and *Cancer in the Constitution* (1972). In addition to his own publications, Manion inspired and published Barry Goldwater's *Conscience of a Conservative* (1960), the book that helped launch Goldwater's successful bid for the Republican presidential nomination in 1964.

Edward E. McAteer (1927–2004)

Along with Paul Weyrich and Howard Phillips, Edward McAteer has worked tirelessly to involve the religious right in the political process. A marketing specialist from the Colgate-Palmolive Company, he was an active Southern Baptist layman whose pastor in Memphis, Tennessee, contributed significantly to the fundamentalist takeover of the Southern Baptist Convention. The Religious Roundtable, established in 1979 with a council of 56, the same number that signed the Declaration of Independence, was McAteer's primary organizational contribution to the religious right. And just as Weyrich worked to enlist Falwell for Moral Majority, McAteer sought just as diligently to bring James Robison to the Roundtable. Indeed, in 1979 McAteer recruited a quintet of notable fundamentalists—Robison, Falwell, Pat Robertson, James Kennedy, and Charles Stanley—to serve on the board of this new organization.

Bringing people from the religious and political right together, McAteer's group sponsored the National Affairs Briefing (NAB) in Dallas, Texas, in August 1980. Nonpartisan billing notwithstanding, this was a fundamentalist and conservative Republican affair. Of the 1980 presidential candidates, Ronald Reagan was the only one to attend the gathering. The national attention this meeting attracted was not altogether beneficial for either McAteer or the Christian right. The stridency of some of the speakers, along with hints of antisemitism, disturbed many Americans. And following McAteer's unsuccessful race for the U.S. Senate in 1984, the Roundtable's influence declined sharply. Although his support of conservative causes remained as fervent as ever, McAteer did not support Weyrich's effort to recast the Christian right's social objectives in terms of a secular "cultural revolution." He was too much of a Baptist fundamentalist to embrace a political strategy that deliberately omitted the God of Judeo-Christianity, however desirable the ends.

Carl McIntire (1906–2002)

A virulent anticommunist crusader, Carl McIntire reached the height of his influence during the Cold War era of the 1950s. As a student at Princeton Theological Seminary in the 1920s, he had come under the sway of fundamentalist J. Gresham Machen. Accordingly, when Machen left Princeton and founded Westminster Theological Seminary in 1929, McIntire followed. Upon graduation in 1931, the intelligent and energetic young Presbyterian became the pastor of a major fundamentalist congregation, the Collingswood, New Jersey, Presbyterian Church. Proving to be rigidly doctrinaire, autocratic, self-righteous, and intolerant of opposing views, McIntire subsequently disrupted almost every religious agency he touched. Continuing as pastor of the New Jersey church into his late 80s, McIntire further divided the congregation by refusing to step down.

In 1936 McIntire, along with Machen, was expelled from the Presbyterian Church (USA), and for a brief time thereafter he was affiliated with Machen's Presbyterian Church of America. But the mixture of these two strong-willed Calvinists was volatile at best, and an eruption was not long in coming. In

Carl McIntire. Photo courtesy of PCA Historical Center, St. Louis, MO. Used by permission.

1937 McIntire forged his own denomination, the Bible Presbyterian Church, and upon this foundation erected his own religious empire. He kept the faithful informed through the columns of the *Christian Beacon*, begun in 1936, and *The Twentieth Century Reformation Hour*, a thirty-minute radio broadcast begun in 1955, and he trained loyal disciples at his Faith Theological Seminary in Philadelphia and at colleges in Cape Canaveral, Florida, and Pasadena, California.

Unfortunately, McIntire's ability to create was matched by a proclivity for disruptive controversy. His autocratic methods and dogmatic beliefs invariably spawned dissent. In 1956 he was unceremoniously expelled from the American Council of Christian Churches, a body which he had founded in 1941, and in 1971 a bitter schism occurred at Faith Theological Seminary. The school's president, most faculty members, and approximately half the students left in protest of McIntire's high-handed leadership and outspoken support of complete military victory in Vietnam.

Both prone to conspiratorial thinking, McIntire and Senator Joe McCarthy of Wisconsin easily gravitated together. The association was symbiotic. The cleric gave the politician a touch of divinity, whereas the politician enhanced the quarrelsome Presbyterian's national stature. McCarthy paid attention to McIntire, and therefore the preacher's charges of religious and political apostasy in high places received more extensive press coverage. A young minister whose own career as an anticommunist crusader received a boost from McIntire was Dr. Billy James Hargis.

Joyce Meyer (1943–)

Televangelist Joyce Meyer has been called the nation's most popular woman minister. Her television program *Life in the Word*, based in St. Louis, Missouri, appears on stations in forty-three states as well as in South America, Europe, Africa, India, and Asia. Meyer has published more than fifty books on various topics, including self-help books as well as more theologically oriented writing. In her talks and writings, she has been very forthcoming about her past, revealing that she was a victim of child abuse and that her first marriage ended in divorce. Meyer has been involved in public issues. In 2002 she gave the keynote speech at the Christian Coalition's Road to Victory tour. Her organization, Joyce Meyer Ministries, encourages political participation by evangelicals, asking listeners and viewers to remain informed and pray about current events and issues, and to take action. Through her initiative, Stand Up and Be Counted, Meyer encourages supporters to take a stand "for righteousness" and "against immorality." The organization website (www.joycemeyer.org) provides information about U.S. representatives and senators and upcoming elections, offers advice to those who wish to write public officials, and guides people through the process of registering to vote. The site presents legislative proposals that the organization supports, such as the Houses of Worship Free Speech Restoration Act (a measure intended to allow church ministers to take political stands without losing tax-exempt status), a Pledge of Allegiance Protection Act, and a Human Cloning Prohibition Act.

Critics of Meyer have questioned the financial practices of Joyce Meyer Ministries. Articles in the *St. Louis Post-Dispatch* in 2003 revealed that the ministry paid $2 million for a home for Meyer and her husband, bought a private jet for $10 million, and provided housing for their children at a cost of $2 million. Reportedly, Meyer purchased a vacation home for $500,000. Subsequently, the board of directors, which is composed in part of family members, decided to reduce Meyer's salary and allow her to use more of the income from her books. In 2003 Wall Watchers, an organization that monitors the financial affairs of Christian ministries, asked the U.S. Internal Revenue Service to investigate seven groups, including Joyce Meyer Ministries.

Meyer has received criticism from other conservative Christian groups that question her theology. For instance, the Christian Research Institute (CRI), an organization that investigates religious cults, has challenged Meyer's theological stands, considering them unbiblical. The CRI faults Meyer for sharing the so-called "word of faith" and prosperity ministries of televangelists like Kenneth Copeland, Benny Hinn, and T. D. Jakes. Among the beliefs the CRI finds objectionable are those that ascribe specific demons for particular sins and personal difficulties and consider certain spirits capable of maintaining an individual in a constant condition of unbelief. Nonetheless, Meyer remains popular with faithful followers and her ministry receives an estimated $8 million in donations each month.

Dwight Lyman Moody (1837–1899)

A noted nineteenth-century revivalist, Dwight L Moody established the standard for highly organized evangelism campaigns in twentieth-century America. Born in Northfield, Massachusetts, Moody moved to Boston while still a teenager to become a boot and shoe salesman. While in Boston, Moody became active in the Young Men's Christian Association (YMCA) and the Congregational Church. He moved to Chicago in 1856 to continue his successful business ventures and there renewed his association with the YMCA. In 1860 he began to work exclusively for that religious organization and during the Civil War was involved in efforts to evangelize wounded soldiers.

In 1872 Moody traveled to Great Britain and began a popular revivalist campaign in Scotland, Ireland, and England, ending with a four-month stay in London in 1875. Returning to the United States, he conducted well-organized revival meetings in such large cities as Philadelphia, New York, and Boston. The popularity of these evangelistic efforts can be attributed to Moody's uncomplicated presentation of a loving and merciful God. Along with fellow evangelist Ira Sankey, Moody produced collections of gospel hymns that added to the enthusiasm of audiences at revival meetings. After another tour of Great Britain from 1881 to 1884, Moody began organizing an annual student Bible conference. He founded three schools: the Northfield Academy for Young Women in 1879, the Mount Hermon School for Young Men in 1881, and the Chicago Bible Institute for Home and Foreign Missions (now the Moody

Bible Institute) in 1889. The two latter schools served as a training ground for urban evangelists and as the source of inexpensive religious publications.

Moody's major accomplishment was to tailor traditional evangelical Protestantism for urban residents in a newly emerging industrial America. As a conservative evangelical, however, Moody found it difficult to deal with the conflicts beginning to arise between liberal and conservative wings of American Protestantism.

Richard John Neuhaus (1936–)

Recognized as a major voice of the neoconservative political and social movement, Father Richard John Neuhaus has traveled a circuitous route in becoming what some might view as an oxymoron: a fundamentalist intellectual. Born in Pembroke, Ontario, the son of a Missouri Synod Lutheran, he has come far from his Depression-era childhood. The author of six books and numerous articles, he currently oversees the production and publication of a monthly journal, *First Things*, promoting the neoconservative agenda. But his arrival at this post was hardly direct. He was expelled from a Lutheran high school in Nebraska, and at age 16 he ran a gas station/grocery store in Cisco, Texas. Without completing high school, he graduated from a church college, the Concordia Seminary in St. Louis, and later Washington University and Wayne State University.

In a survey of national leadership, *U.S. News and World Report* named Neuhaus one of the thirty-two most "influential intellectuals in America." In *Time* magazine's February 2005 issue, he was included as one of "The 25 Most Influential Evangelicals in America." Calling Neuhaus's influence "Bushism Made Catholic," *Time* recounted President George W. Bush's meeting with

Richard John Neuhaus. Photo courtesy of Richard John Neuhaus. Used by permission.

journalists from religious publications in 2004. The authority Bush most often cited was not a fellow evangelical, but "Father Richard."

Using the combined strengths of his education and religious upbringing, Neuhaus began his public life in the manner of a fighting liberal pastor, serving a mostly minority Lutheran congregation in Brooklyn, which grew under his leadership from twenty-four members in 1961 to 600 in 1975. Neuhaus promoted a liberal-progressive, socially conscious agenda, opposing the Vietnam War, supporting the civil rights movement, and working to relieve the plight of America's poor. Through these efforts he first rose to national prominence, forming Clergy and Laymen Concerned about Vietnam with Brooklyn College sociology professor Peter Berger. Both advocated revolution.

Neuhaus began to find his revolution tainted, however, when he failed to convince fellow revolutionaries to support his pro-life and anticommunism ideology. Believing both to be supported by the Christian Gospel and the leftist tradition of supporting the weak, Neuhaus changed his revolutionary tone and became a spokesman for the neoconservatives, promoting democratic capitalism and associating himself with the American Enterprise Institute, a conservative think tank. Promoting faith-based government initiatives, he has supported a return to traditional Judeo-Christian values and opposed abortion, stem-cell research, cloning, same-sex marriage, and judicial activism, joining his voice to Robert H. Bork, Charles W. Colson, and Robert P. George.

His own union with the Lutheran Church ended when, after thirty years as a Lutheran pastor, he could no longer find convincing reasons not to be a Roman Catholic. Neuhaus joined the Roman Catholic Church in 1990 and received ordination as a priest from the Archdiocese of New York in 1991. In addition to his priestly duties, Neuhaus serves on the board of the Institute on Religion and Democracy, Ethics and Public Policy Center, and Foundation for Community and Faith-Centered Enterprise, as well as the right-wing World Youth Alliance and the Becket Fund Advisory Board. He has served the Carter, Reagan, and Bush administrations. Although not an evangelical, Neuhaus has helped articulate religious bases for President Bush's public policies. Neuhaus exerts considerable influence and has labored diligently and successfully to deliver for Bush the support and votes of conservative Catholics, a bloc that contributed significantly to the president's 2004 victory.

Cardinal John O'Connor (1920–2000)

Cardinal John O'Connor, the outspoken Roman Catholic Archbishop of New York for sixteen years, took vocal stands on such issues as abortion, contraception, and homosexuality, and was highly criticized for politicizing his church office. O'Connor used the pulpit as well as a regular newspaper column to publicize controversial positions on a variety of issues. Although often labeled a conservative, O'Connor might better be called a communitarian, for his concerns included the welfare of the less well-to-do and the moral values of the entire community. He was outspoken on many subjects, strongly believing the church should be a guide in everyday life. In 1990 O'Connor declared that

Catholic politicians who took a pro-choice position on the issue of abortion risked excommunication from the church. In 1998 the Cardinal announced his boycott of professional baseball because the Yankees and the Mets played games on Good Friday.

O'Connor was born in Philadelphia to a working class family. He attended public schools until his junior year in high school, when the Christian Brothers at West Catholic High School sparked his ambition to become a missionary. After his ordination as a priest in 1945, O'Connor worked with disabled children and pursued degrees in ethics, clinical psychology, and political science. He served as a chaplain during the Korean War, beginning a twenty-seven-year career as a chaplain in the Navy and Marine Corps. In 1965 O'Connor served in Vietnam, receiving the Legion of Merit Award. He wrote a book defending American involvement in Vietnam, a work he later came to regret. He ultimately became chaplain at Annapolis and Chief of Navy Chaplains. In 1979 O'Connor left military service with the rank of rear admiral, became bishop in Scranton, Pennsylvania, in 1983, and was appointed archbishop in New York in 1984. In 1985 Pope John Paul II made him a cardinal. His close relationship with John Paul increased O'Connor's influence within the church hierarchy.

O'Connor was most often considered politically conservative, largely due to his vocal opinions on such social issues as abortion and homosexuality. He became a major advocate for the pro-life forces, heading the bishops' Committee on Pro-Life Activities in the early 1990s. To O'Connor, gay and lesbian lifestyles were equivalent to biblical sin, and he objected to gay Catholics marching in New York's St. Patrick's Day parade. Believing that "good morality is good medicine," he criticized health care professionals for what he considered a failure to deal with the moral aspects of AIDS, including "sexual aberrations" and drug abuse. However, O'Connor served on the President's Commission on AIDS, initiated several programs for AIDS victims, and worked personally to assist those afflicted with the disease. Despite fervent opposition to abortion rights, he strongly opposed the bombing of abortion clinics. Responding to such bombings in 1995, the archbishop offered himself as the target to anyone who wished to kill someone at an abortion clinic.

Although O'Connor was closely associated with many conservative Christian causes, he worked to improve the condition of workers and the poor, supporting the causes of organized labor and advocating improved health care. In the early 1990s he intervened in the labor-management controversy in the New York newspaper industry, meeting with labor leaders in an effort to end strikes. He opposed the death penalty, a position consistent with his antiabortion stand in support of the preservation of human life. In the 1980s O'Connor criticized the Reagan administration's support for counter-revolutionary guerrillas in Central America and the proposal to build a missile defense system.

Marvin Olasky (1950–)

To some observers Marvin Olasky is "the godfather of 'compassionate conservatism'"; to others, "a leading thinker and propagandist of the Christian

Marvin Olasky. Photo by Marsha Miller. Used by permission.

right," or, more harshly, an overly zealous Presbyterian fundamentalist whose "historical judgments are so crude and pinched" they will most likely "buttress the stereotypes of those who are prejudiced against religious conservatives." One thing for certain, Olasky has the ear of President George W. Bush, who said of the University of Texas-Austin journalism professor: "Marvin offers not just a blueprint for government, but also an inspiring picture of the great resources of decency, caring, and commitment to one another that Americans share." One detects in this remark the nebulous outlines of the president's compassionate conservatism. So, who is Olasky?

An intellectual vagabond, Olasky has embraced at different times sharply divergent philosophical and religious expressions. His search for a worldview governed by explicit and discernable laws led him from Judaism to atheism to Marxism-Leninism to Christian fundamentalism. Born in Massachusetts of second-generation Russian Jewish immigrants, Olasky, as he put it, "was bar mitzvahed at thirteen and an atheist at fourteen." Entering the American Studies program at Yale in 1968, coincidentally just as Bush was leaving, he was soon immersed in left wing politics, protesting the war in Vietnam and championing the causes of labor. He graduated from Yale in 1971, and from that point to late 1973 his life veered radically from one direction to another. He married his first wife, took a job as a reporter in Oregon, joined the Communist party, and made a pilgrimage to Russia. By the end of 1973 he had divorced his wife, abandoned communism, and entered the graduate program at the University of Michigan in American Culture. Not long afterward he met Susan Northway, an undergraduate at Michigan, who would become his second wife in 1976. From 1973 to 1976 Olasky moved to the political and religious right. Since his doctoral dissertation, "Clean Pictures with Red Blood? American Popular Film and the Adversary Intention," dealt with politics and American films, he studied the classic westerns and was impressed by their strong sense of right and wrong. He prepared a course on early American literature, reading numerous Puritan sermons in the process. And he studied the Christian existentialists. In 1976 Olasky became a Christian. John Wayne and Jonathan Edwards had displaced Marx and Lenin.

A one-year stint as a lecturer at San Diego State in 1976–1977 was followed by five and a half years in public relations for DuPont Corporation in Delaware. By 1983, when Olasky arrived at the University of Texas as an assistant professor of journalism, he had matured as a Calvinist, a Presbyterian fundamentalist, and an outspoken critic of abortion and welfare. A prolific writer, authoring some 200 articles and numerous books, Olasky perhaps would have remained an obscure journalism professor and right wing polemicist but for the opportune publication of *The Tragedy of American Compassion*. Released in 1992 on the cusp of the "Republican revolution of '94," this work expressed the sentiment of many conservatives. Specifically, Olasky offered a rationale for slashing welfare and downsizing government, and doing it all in the name of family values and compassion. Instead of the "false compassion" of the existing welfare state, which doled out material aid without providing spiritual guidance or imposing discipline on the poor, true compassion nourished the soul as well as the body. And "faith-based" institutions, presumably having proven their superiority to secular governmental agencies, should receive tax support to advance programs for the needy.

Former Secretary of Education William Bennett pronounced *The Tragedy of American Compassion* the "most important book on welfare and social policy in a decade" and sent a copy to Republican Newt Gingrich, the new speaker of the House. Addressing the nation as speaker for the first time in 1995, Gingrich proclaimed: "Our models are Alexis de Tocqueville and Marvin Olasky. We are going to redefine compassion and take it back." That was a heady moment, and all of a sudden Olasky was a celebrity to the religious and political right, a frequent guest on television talk shows, and a favorite of newspaper reporters. Of course, critics—and there were many—argued that it would be impossible for private, religious-based charities to meet all the needs of destitute Americans. After all, government programs to help the poor had emerged earlier in the century in part because of the inability of private charity to meet such vast needs. Critics therefore believed Olasky's ideas were being used by cynical conservative politicians primarily to dismantle various social programs. If such censure bothered him, it was not apparent in Olasky's most recent book, *Compassionate Conservatism* (2000), for which Bush wrote the foreword. Although Olasky is much more intensely evangelistic than Bush, always seizing the opportunity to proselytize, the two men hold comparable views on welfare and the relative importance of religion and government in helping the poor. That alone ensures Olasky's continued prominence for the near future.

Rodney Lee (Rod) Parsley (1957-)

As leaders who have dominated the religious right movement for many years advance in age, younger luminaries such as Rod Parsley, senior pastor at World Harvest Church in Columbus, Ohio, have arisen. Parsley's 12,000-member megachurch, which began in the late 1970s with a small group of followers, today consists of a 5,000-seat sanctuary, a staff of 400, and a television ministry—*Breakthrough*—that appears regularly on the Trinity Broadcasting Network and more than 1,400 other stations and cable outlets. Parsley founded and serves as president of the Center for Moral Clarity, a political organization closely associated with his church that is dedicated to championing the values of conservative Christians and effecting moral change in American society. In *Silent No More* (2005), Parsley presents his view of the present moral condition of the United States, discusses issues of concern to conservative Christians, and encourages those sympathetic to the religious right agenda to become active politically. Parsley has questioned the doctrine of separation of church and state, campaigned for a ban on late-term abortions, strongly supported Israel, and expressed criticism of Islam. He has supported congressional passage of the Houses of Worship Free Speech Restoration Act, which would ease Internal Revenue Service restrictions on pastors, thus allowing them to speak from the pulpit in support of specific candidates without their churches losing tax exemption status.

In 2004 Parsley supported a measure on the Ohio ballot to ban gay marriage. Although as a religious leader Parsley could not campaign for specific candidates without jeopardizing the tax-exempt status of his church, commentators suggested that his campaign efforts in favor of the anti-gay marriage measure, which passed, brought to the polls voters more likely to support George W. Bush. Ohio proved to be a crucial state for President Bush's successful re-election bid. Despite Parsley's claim to be neither a Democrat nor a Republican, but a "Christocrat," he tends to support political positions more favorable to the Republican agenda. Various Republican leaders have courted his support, including U.S. Senator Bill Frist and Texas Governor Rick Perry.

Parsley supported President George W. Bush's nomination of John Roberts as chief justice of the U.S. Supreme Court, and was included in a conference call that the president held shortly after announcing the nomination. In 2005 Parsley formed Reformation Ohio, an initiative geared to bring "moral renewal" to the state of Ohio. Among its four-year goals, the program is intended to reach more than one million people, convert 100,000 of them, and add at least 400,000 to the state's voter registration rolls. A significant part of this effort is reaching out to teenagers.

With a congregation estimated to be 40 percent African American, Parsley holds out the promise of attracting African Americans to the largely white religious right movement. In December 2004 James Dobson of Focus on the Family invited Parsley to a meeting of white and African-American religious leaders to discuss plans for bridging the gap between white and black evangelical churches. Parsley's strong conservative Christian positions on such issues as gay marriage and abortion are the basis for appealing to more conservative African-American evangelicals. He worked with Ohio Secretary of State John Kenneth Blackwell, an African American, in the campaign for the state gay-marriage ban. Parsley has declared his opposition to racism, criticizing the income gap between blacks and whites. However, he does not look to government to initiate programs to ameliorate the situation. Rather, Parsley advocates less government interference in people's lives so that they may succeed individually. This economic position coincides with Parsley's Pentecostal-related doctrine that prosperity may be achieved by demonstrating faith through "sowing a seed": money given to the church will be returned to the donor many times over.

Parsley's church operations have been criticized by other Christian groups, some of them evangelical. Ministry Watch, a conservative Christian association that tracks the financial practices of religious organizations, has denounced Parsley for failing to join the Evangelical Council for Financial Accountability, an alliance that requires its members to make public the financial statements of their religious enterprises. Others have found fault with Parsley's Word of Faith theology, which associates religious belief with economic prosperity. Some have expressed concern with the selling of such items as prayer cloths through the *Breakthrough* television program that supposedly bring health and wealth.

Paige Patterson (1942–)

Born in Forth Worth, Texas, and educated at Hardin-Simmons University in Abilene, Texas, and New Orleans Baptist Theological Seminary, Paige Patterson now serves as the eighth president of Southwestern Baptist Theological Seminary in Forth Worth. Ordained at 16, Patterson pastored numerous churches in Texas, Louisiana, and Arkansas before becoming president of Criswell College in Dallas in 1975, a post he held until 1992. He took the helm of Southeastern Baptist Theological Seminary in 1992 and remained there until he left for Southwestern in 2003.

Concerned about the course of his denomination, Patterson joined Paul Pressler in 1979 in a well-planned effort to gain control of the Southern Baptist Convention (SBC) and thereby "restore" it to its biblical roots. Patterson rallied the faithful by charging that many leaders of Baptist institutions and major churches no longer believed the "inerrant" Bible, a phrase that meant to Patterson and other fundamentalists that the original manuscripts of the Bible contained no errors and were literally correct in matters of history and science. Demonstrating a tendency for hyperbole, Patterson told a Baptist congregation in St. Louis that accepting the Bible as inerrant was the only route to true revival and the only way to "stave off" World War III.

Redirection and salvation required drastic alteration. A new emphasis on pastoral authority marks a departure from the traditional Baptist teaching on the priesthood of every believer. The Patterson-Pressler duo insisted that the pastor was the unquestionable ruler of the church. In Baptist seminaries students traditionally had been exposed to various theological viewpoints. That ended with the fundamentalist takeover. Patterson insisted upon a faculty hired to indoctrinate their charges. Adrian Rogers, the first SBC president elected by the fundamentalists in 1979, clarified the lesson. "If we say pickles have souls, they (the professors) better teach that pickles have souls."

A far-reaching change guided by Patterson and his fundamentalist allies has been the promotion of specific religious agendas through the political process. Instead of shaping public morality strictly through the witness of the church, the denomination would effect change through the power of the state. The religious right belonged not only behind the pulpit, but also on the Senate floor, in the Supreme Court chambers, and, certainly, in the Oval Office.

Finally, objecting to certain advancements made by women in church life, Patterson, joined by Pressler, supported an SBC resolution in 1984 that excluded women from becoming deacons or pastors. In 1998 the duo insisted that women "graciously submit" to men and return to the Garden, reminding them that the first sin was woman's. In 2000 changes in the Baptist Faith and Message statement confirmed that women could not serve as pastors. According to Patterson's interpretation, the "proper" place for women was as teachers of Christian education and church music, particularly if they were teaching women and children. In the face of sharp criticism as a misogynist, Patterson was forced to concede that all persons have "gifts," but they differ for men and women. As Terri Stoval, women's program director at Southwestern, put it, Baptist women are prepared for "leadership roles" as lay readers, church staff members, denominational employees, or missionaries. Patterson's wife, Dorothy, defends her husband's view on submission, asserting that a woman should take "part in the ministry with her husband" and derive pride and pleasure in the roles of "homemaker and helper."

During the SBC's Pastors' Conference in Greensboro, North Carolina, on June 12, 2006, seminary presidents Albert Mohler and Paige Patterson engaged in a friendly debate, particularly over the doctrine of election. Demonstrating a sense of humor, Patterson quipped: "The calling of God is made to all men, and then men must decide whether they will respond to the calling or not . . . .

The real question we are here to discuss today is whether or not you are here of your own free will." Turning serious, Patterson closed with a challenge. "My fervent prayer is that whatever your beliefs are about the sovereignty of God, you will join me in taking the Gospel to the ends of the earth." Whatever else one may say about Patterson, he has certainly avoided what he sees as a significant flaw in "good classroom teachers," namely that "it is a sin to be boring."

Tony Perkins (1963–)

Since 2003, when he became president of the Family Research Council, a conservative Christian organization associated with James Dobson's Focus on the Family, Tony Perkins has been an enthusiastic advocate of the religious right agenda, including limited government and family values. He has campaigned for the legal recognition of marriage as a union between one man and one

Tony Perkins. Photo courtesy of Family Research Council. Used by permission.

woman and worked for passage of the Unborn Victims of Violence Act, which opponents consider a step in the direction of prohibiting abortion. Among other issues, Perkins has asked supporters of the Family Research Council to back passage of legislation that would increase monetary penalties for radio and television stations that broadcast sexually explicit programs. Along with other religious right leaders, Perkins has strongly supported the appointment of judges who support judicial restraint. In 2005 he took part in "Justice Sunday," a rally held to urge the U.S. Senate to consent to President George W. Bush's judicial nominees. In 2006, noting that President Bush's greatest legacy could be the transformation of the federal courts, Perkins urged the president to make appropriate nominations.

After graduating from Liberty University, Perkins entered the U.S. Marine Corps. When he left military service, he became a law enforcement officer, joining the Baton Rouge, Louisiana, police department. From 1996 to 2004 Perkins served in the Louisiana state house of representatives, winning election as a Republican from a suburban Baton Rouge district. Among his legislative initiatives, Perkins introduced measures to require public schools to use Internet filtering software on computers and to mandate that the public schools observe a time of silent prayer each day. He authored a Covenant Marriage Act, a law permitting couples seeking to marry to sign a marriage license that states their intention to remain married for life. The law narrowed the grounds for divorce for those couples married under its provisions. Perkins also initiated the American History Preservation Act, legislation intended to prohibit censorship of "America's Christian heritage" in the state's public schools. In 2002 Perkins ran an unsuccessful campaign for the U.S. Senate.

In 2005, during the controversy over the court-ordered removal of the feeding tube from Terri Schiavo, the Florida woman in a vegetative state, Perkins appeared frequently in the media to call for Congress and the federal courts to maintain Schiavo's life. A strong supporter of the Republican party and President George W. Bush, Perkins nonetheless has criticized administration policies when he thought they contradicted conservative Christian values. For instance, he expressed concern over the religious policies of the Iraq and Afghanistan government that the United States government accepted. He noted that, although the Bush administration gave assurances that the new Iraqi constitution would allow religious liberty, the document prohibits passage of any law deemed inconsistent with Islam. He was concerned that Christians would be prohibited from professing their faith freely in these countries. Nonetheless, Perkins remains a strong Bush supporter.

Paul Pressler (1930–)

Paul Pressler is a lifelong Baptist descended from a long line of Texas Baptists. Educated at Princeton, he wrote his thesis on politics, centering around his grandfather, Judge E. E. Townes, from whom he had learned the ins-and-outs of Texas politics. Pressler began his political career in the Texas legislature in 1957. He practiced law with the firm of Vinson and Elkins for twelve years, and then, in 1970, became a judge in the 133rd District Court. In 1978 Pressler was appointed to the Texas Court of Appeals, where he served until his retirement in 1993.

In 1979 fundamentalists launched an effort to gain control of the Southern Baptist Convention (SBC), the largest Protestant body in the nation, and Paul Pressler was a chief architect of the drive. For Pressler, the desire to "save" his denomination began in 1961 when he and his wife were dismissed as Sunday school teachers at the Second Baptist Church, Houston, Texas, as a result of a dispute over the proper interpretation of Genesis. His resolve was strengthened a few years later when several young people from Second Baptist who had gone to Baylor University in Waco, Texas, reported to him during their freshman year that religion professors at the Baptist school allegedly did not believe the Genesis account of creation. Convinced now more than ever that the SBC was rife with liberals who rejected the inerrant Word of God, Pressler set out to gain control of the SBC and restore it to its historic, biblical roots. Thus began an acrimonious, decade-long battle between Baptist fundamentalists and moderates for control of the SBC. Pressler and his allies eventually won, and they did in fact set the SBC on a "rightward" course, one that was in close accord with the Republican party.

Pressler's main ally was Paige Patterson, then president of Criswell College in Dallas, Texas. In 1980 Pressler delivered a speech entitled "Going for the Jugular," which was essentially a fundamentalist blueprint for taking over the SBC. Pressler and Patterson had researched and understood the SBC's presidential election process, and they knew that if they could win ten successive annual elections, they could control the SBC. This was because the SBC president has extensive appointive powers over convention boards and institutions, and to control that office for at least a decade would enable fundamentalists to fill these appointive positions with their people. The trick was to get enough like-minded Baptists to attend the annual conventions and to vote for the "anointed" candidate. To accomplish this, Pressler and Patterson tirelessly crisscrossed the South, planting seeds of doubt among the faithful about the fidelity of many Baptist preachers and teachers. Pressler recalled later that he often gave six or seven talks a day, and the watchword always was *inerrant*. Pressler and Patterson both charged that many fellow Baptists doubted the inerrancy of the Bible. Normally no more than 2,000 to 4,000 would attend a convention, but at the height of the contest between the fundamentalists and moderates, 20,000 was not unusual.

By 1990 it was over. Fundamentalists, better organized than their moderate opponents and highly motivated, controlled the SBC. In the process they had also wisely cultivated the support of Billy Graham and Ronald Reagan. In 1987, by which time victory was virtually in hand, Pressler reflected on the struggle with reconstructionist Gary North. "What we did was spiritually motivated, theologically motivated," said Pressler, "and we were concerned for the theological well-being of not only our denomination but those to whom we should be witnessing."

SBC decisions made throughout the 1990s reflect the body's move to the right. In 1992 two churches were disfellowshipped from the SBC, one for approving the ordination of a gay man, the other for blessing the union of two gay people. In 1997 the fundamentalists generated more conflict by boycotting the Walt Disney Company, accusing Disney of being anti-family and anti-Christian. The theme park's transgression was the introduction of "Gay Days," appointed for homosexuals to attend and openly celebrate their lifestyle choice. When, in the late 1990s, the Baptists selected Salt Lake City as their convention site, the outcome was predictable. Their aggressive proselytizing among the local Mormons brought outcries of agitated disapproval.

Texas Baptist Bill Moyers, as well as other critics, sees Pressler as a self-appointed savior with grandiose notions. He has orchestrated not only a sacred victory, but also achieved a strong voice, even leadership, in the GOP. Moyers believes that the Pressler zeal for the straight and narrow controls the Republican party and threatens to make of the United States a theocracy. Speaking at the Union Theological Seminary in September 2005, Moyers dubbed the group "fundamentalist radicals" and renamed the Republican membership "God's Own Party," its ranks made up of "God's Own People 'marching as to war.'" Pressler revealed his theocratic tendencies further at the Conference on Religious Liberty at Southwestern Seminary, where he stated that "The Bill of Rights did not prohibit a state or municipality from establishing a religion."

Ralph Reed (1961–)

Ralph Reed was born in Portsmouth, Virginia, only a short distance from Pat Robertson's first broadcast studio. His early years were interrupted by frequent moves. His father was a navy doctor, and by the time Reed entered high school, the family had lived in seven towns in five states. Upon graduation from high school in Toccoa, Georgia, he entered the University of Georgia. In summer 1991 a U.S. Senate internship took him to Washington, D.C., where he remained through the fall working with the National College Republicans. He returned to the University of Georgia in spring 1982, completed his degree, then resumed his efforts in the nation's capital with the National College Republicans. With the approach of the 1984 senatorial race in North Carolina between Jim Hunt and Jesse Helms, the outspoken Republican incumbent whose political and religious conservatism made him a favorite of the religious right, Reed left Washington for Raleigh. He promptly founded Students for America and joined the fray in behalf of the North Carolina senator. Reed unquestionably loved politics; even so, he entered the graduate program at Emory University on a scholarship, obtained a Ph.D. in history in 1986, and anticipated a career in academia. Three years later he was the executive secretary of Robertson's new Christian Coalition.

Reed's fondness for conservative politics and causes was long-standing. As a child he read biographies of the presidents, as well as William L. Shirer's *The Rise and Fall of the Third Reich*, which impressed upon him the power of politics. At the University of Georgia he was a College Republican, debater, and columnist for the school paper, *Red and Black*. Reed eventually lost this journalistic position because he plagiarized a story. Always on the political right of every issue, Reed was a leader among campus conservatives by 1982. Shortly thereafter he discovered religion. This nominal Methodist smoked and drank until the early 1980s, whereupon he promptly put away cigarettes and John Barleycorn and became a born-again, charismatic Christian. God and Caesar now became allies, as Reed discovered the "true" meaning of politics. "I now realize," said the new convert, "that politics is a noble calling to serve God and my fellow man." Appropriately, his dissertation at Emory, which focused on the early history of church-related colleges, criticized some sectarian schools for sacrificing their religious heritage for endowments.

Although Reed supported Jack Kemp over Robertson in the 1988 presidential primaries, the Virginia televangelist admired the young man's organizational talent and religious commitment. When Robertson formed the Christian Coalition in 1989, Reed became its executive secretary. Despite his affable nature and disarming good looks, Reed is a shrewd political strategist. One admirer aptly described him as "the Christian Lee Atwater." He always wanted to win, but he also recognized the road to victory took many turns. Accordingly, Reed sought to broaden the Christian Coalition to make it more ecumenical. He therefore occasionally downplayed such issues as abortion, homosexuality, and prayer in the schools, emphasizing instead taxes, crime, and education. This kind of flexibility, foes acknowledged, made Reed a formidable opponent. Still, this was a risky strategy, and it was difficult for the Christian Coalition to attract moderate conservatives without offending its hardcore base. In summer 1997, following Republican setbacks in the 1998 elections, Reed left the Christian Coalition to found his own political consulting firm, Century Strategies. He has since offered his talents to conservative Republican candidates, and he played a significant, albeit behind-the-scenes, role in George W. Bush's victory in the bitter Republican presidential primary in South Carolina in winter 2000.

In 2006 Reed ran in the Republican primary for lieutenant governor of Georgia, his first bid for elective office. Running on a thoroughly religious-right platform, it appeared early on that the former Christian Coalition whiz would have no difficulty. However, the unfolding Jack Abramoff scandal eventually overwhelmed him. Opponent State Senator Casey Cagle repeatedly emphasized Reed's connections to the disgraced lobbyist, even hinting that Reed could face criminal charges for accepting $5.3 million from two Indian tribes.

Marion Gordon "Pat" Robertson (1930–)

Perhaps the religious right's most successful television entrepreneur, Pat Robertson was born and reared in Lexington, Virginia. The son of a prominent politician, Senator A. Willis Robertson, and a devoutly religious mother, the intelligent and charming Robertson seemed marked for success. A Phi Beta Kappa graduate of Washington and Lee University, he subsequently studied at the University of London, served as a non-combatant with the Marines in Korea (1951–1952), and enrolled in Yale Law School, graduating in 1955. Although reared a Baptist, the youthful Robertson was not particularly religious, as evidenced by a fondness for women, whiskey, and poker. In 1956, this all changed.

Following a religious experience that was helped along by a staunch fundamentalist whom his mother respected, Robertson promptly entered The Biblical Seminary, later rechristened the New York Theological Seminary, in New York City. And it was here at this conservative enclave from 1956 to 1959 that he became a charismatic evangelical. In 1959 Robertson returned to Virginia, purchased a television station in Portsmouth, and launched the Christian Broadcasting Network (CBN) in January 1960. Three years later, wishing to raise funds to cover monthly costs of $7,000, he sought to enlist 700 listeners who would pay $10 per month. From this emerged The 700 Club and later *The 700 Club Program*, which deliberately copied the format of *The Johnny Carson Show*. Jim Bakker, a religious fundraiser par excellence who later established the PTL complex at Charlotte, North Carolina, joined CBN in 1965. Bakker deserves considerable credit for the success of Robertson's telethons. By 1975 CBN had an estimated 110 million viewers, and in 1979 Robertson opened an impressive International Headquarters Building and CBN University at Virginia Beach. By 1987 his empire sprawled over 380 acres and employed over 4,000 people.

Robertson's social concerns were virtually identical to those of other figures on the religious right. He opposed abortion, homosexuality, pornography, and the Equal Rights Amendment, and he encouraged prayer in the public schools and tuition tax credits for private schooling. Failing miserably in the 1988 presidential campaign to translate television celebrity status into political success, Robertson quickly regrouped. In 1989 he founded the Christian Coalition, heir to Jerry Falwell's Moral Majority, and thereby institutionalized his pro-family, "values oriented" politics. Quickly becoming the most powerful political body of religious conservatives, the Coalition pursued an aggressive grassroots campaign to defeat politicians, from school board elections on up, whose values were not sufficiently pro-family. Although the organization continues to wield considerable influence, it reached its climax about 1996–1997, declining significantly thereafter. In spring 2000 Robertson, who had dropped the title "Reverend" just prior to his 1988 presidential run, reaffirmed his ordination vows, attached the title once again to his name, and announced his "heart" was "on missions" and "getting people into the kingdom of God." This did not mean, however, that the televangelist was leaving the political playing field. Indeed, he has continued to keep one foot planted squarely in Caesar's world, the other in God's. As with James Dobson, Robertson has been much concerned about judicial appointments, and he looked favorably upon President Bush's two Supreme Court nominees.

James Robison (1943–)

Often billed as "God's Angry Man" because of a belligerent pulpit style and rigid dogmatism, James Robison was second in prominence only to Jerry Falwell in calling America to repentance for its "wicked" ways. Destitute and abandoned by her alcoholic husband, Robison's mother advertised him at

James Robison. Photo by David Edmonson. Used by permission.

birth in a Houston, Texas, newspaper and subsequently gave him to a Baptist minister and his wife in Pasadena, a Houston suburb. When Robison was five, his mother reclaimed him, headed to Austin, Texas, and over the next decade went through a series of marriages and divorces. At age 15 Robison returned to his foster parents in Pasadena, experienced conversion, and at age 18 resolved to become an evangelist.

Robison attended East Texas Baptist College and San Jacinto Junior College, but he dropped out and embarked upon full-time evangelism in late 1963. At 6′3″ and over 200 pounds, he was a commanding presence in the pulpit. In 1965 he established the James Robison Evangelistic Association and five years later aired his first thirty-minute television program. By 1980, with headquarters near Fort Worth, Texas, he employed 150 full-time staff members, and his television show, *James Robison, A Man With A Message*, was carried by 100 stations in twenty-eight states. Many observers saw the young evangelist as an eventual successor to Billy Graham.

Casting himself as pro-life, pro-moral, pro-family, and pro-America, Robison quickly became a major voice on the religious right. He denounced abortion, homosexuality, premarital sex, the Equal Rights Amendment, and "secular humanism" with as much passion as and much more stridency than Falwell, with whom he was closely associated in the 1980s. Along with Edward E. McAteer, he helped organize the Religious Roundtable in 1979, and in August the following year the Roundtable's National Affairs Briefing (NAB) at the Reunion Arena in Dallas brought him to the attention of a national audience. Despite its nonpartisan billing, the NAB turned into a love fest for presidential candidate Ronald Reagan. Typical of so many on the religious right in the 1980s, Robison found in Reagan a knight to carry the banner for God and country.

In the 1990s Robison changed the name of his organization from the James Robison Evangelistic Association to Life Outreach International. This organization was established to provide humanitarian assistance to the needy in the United States and around the world. Two of its ministries are Mission Feeding and Water for Life. In addition, the organization trains new believers to spread the Gospel. Robison also changed the format of his television program, now called *Life Today*, introducing a talk-show setting in which he and his wife Betty interview guests from all walks of life and give viewers an opportunity to call for prayer.

Hugh Ross (1945–)

Hugh Ross is president of Reasons To Believe, a California-based organization which attempts to provide Christians with scientifically valid reasons for their religious faith. Ross's defense of Christian belief coalesces well with a conservative perspective that Christian beliefs are compatible with a modern scientific understanding of the world and that events described in the Bible can be scientifically verified. Ross hosts the weekly television program *Reasons to Believe*, on which he discusses various scientific subjects in the context of Christian faith. Although he admits that the universe is billions of years old, thus disagreeing with the "young earth" theologians, he contends there is clear evidence of design in the universe. Ross elicits mixed reactions from fundamentalist Christians who agreed with his claim for design, but are uncomfortable with his conclusions about the age of the universe. Nonetheless, when referring to the early chapters of the book of Genesis, Ross sometimes speaks as though he takes literally the stories of Adam and Eve, the Garden of Eden, and the fall into sin as the cause of human death.

A native of Canada, Ross received a bachelor of science in physics from the University of British Columbia in 1967, and M.S. and Ph.D. degrees in astronomy from the University of Toronto. He received a grant from the Canadian National Research Council for postdoctoral study at the California Institute of Technology, where he investigated distant quasi-stellar objects, called quasars. Ross claims scientific studies and historical examination of scripture convinced him the Bible was the true word of God. He argues that believers should check the evidence for their beliefs, evidence which he contends consistently confirms the existence of the Christian God.

From 1973 to 1978 Ross served as research fellow in radio astronomy at the California Institute of Technology. It was during this period that he became ac-

Hugh Ross. Photo © Jeff Miku. Used by permission.

tively involved in Christian ministry, becoming minister of evangelism at the Sierra Madre Congregational Church, a position he held from 1976 to 1987. He continues to serve that church as minister of apologetics. In 1986 he established Reasons To Believe. In 1997 he became a lecturer in the Simon Greenleaf Institute of Apologetics at Trinity Law School in Santa Ana, California.

Ross has published several books on science and the Christian faith, including *The Fingerprint of God: Recent Scientific Discoveries Reveal the Unmistakable Identity of the Creator* (1991), *Creation and Time: A Biblical and Scientific Perspective on the Creation-Date Controversy* (1994), *Beyond the Cosmos: What Recent Discoveries in Astronomy and Physics Reveal About the Nature of God* (1996), and *The Genesis Question: Scientific Advances and the Accuracy of Genesis* (1998). In addition, Ross has produced several videotapes on science and religious belief which are available through his organization.

Rick Santorum. Image provided by the U.S. Senate Historical Office.

Rick Santorum (1958–)

Entering the U.S. Senate in 1995 representing Pennsylvania, Rick Santorum championed various conservative causes. A Roman Catholic, he is considered a staunch ally of the religious right. He has supported limitations on abortion and has spoken against homosexuality, describing homosexual acts as deviant sexual behavior contrary to the traditional family. Santorum supports passage of a constitutional amendment defining marriage as a union between one man and one woman. In 2004, during the Senate debate on the Federal Marriage Amendment, he claimed that the defense of marriage was a crucial aspect of homeland security.

Born in Winchester, Virginia, and raised in Butler County, Pennsylvania, Santorum received a BA degree from Pennsylvania State University in 1980 and a master of business administration degree from the University of Pittsburgh in 1981. He worked for Republican state Senator J. Doyle Corman, directing the Pennsylvania state senate local government committee from 1981 to 1984, and the transportation committee from 1984 to 1986. In 1986 he received a law degree from Dickinson School of Law and began a law practice in Pittsburgh. In 1990 Santorum won election to the U.S. House of Representatives, serving two terms before running successfully for the U.S. Senate in 1994. He was reelected in 2000.

In 2001 Santorum attempted unsuccessfully to include an amendment in the No Child Left Behind bill that would have required the public schools to include in science classes so-called scientific controversies. The amendment mentioned the theory of evolution as an example, thus mandating the presentation of intelligent design as an alternative theory of the origin of human beings. In March 2005 he strongly supported legislation mandating that the federal courts hear appeals from the Florida state court system, which had consistently ruled that the husband of Terri Schiavo, a woman who had been in a vegetative state for many years, could have his wife's feeding tube removed. The federal courts ultimately refused to intervene. Responding to charges that the Schiavo legislation violated the right to privacy, Santorum responded that he did not believe the U.S. Constitution protected any such right. He has criticized the U.S. Supreme Court decision in *Griswold v. Connecticut* (1965), in which the Court ruled in favor of those challenging a state law prohibiting the sale of contraceptives, basing the decision on a right to privacy.

In 2005 Santorum published *It Takes a Family: Conservatism and the Common Good,* in which he criticized the nation's public school system and referred to the practice of mothers working outside the home as resulting from radical feminism. In 2006 he faced a difficult reelection campaign. With an approval rating in May of less than 40 percent, Santorum faced Democratic opponent Bob Casey Jr., Pennsylvania state treasurer, who led the senator consistently in the polls. Santorum was considered the Republican senator most likely to be defeated. His political future rested on his political skills as well as support from his conservative base, including the religious right. Nonetheless, Santorum became a victim of the electoral shift to the Democratic party, losing the senatorial election to Casey.

Francis Schaeffer (1912–1984)

If J. Gresham Machen was the intellectual grandfather of contemporary fundamentalism, Francis Schaeffer certainly was the father. These spiritual kinsmen both believed America had drifted far from its Christian moorings. For Machen, the "villain" was liberalism in the nation's churches; for Schaeffer, it was secular humanism in western culture. In 1929 Machen, certain that Princeton Theological Seminary had succumbed irretrievably to liberalism, left the Presbyterian school and established Westminster School of Theology in Philadelphia. Even this conservative haven soon proved too liberal for one of Machen's strong-willed disciples, Carl McIntire, who subsequently founded Faith Theological Seminary in Wilmington, Delaware, in 1937. Amid the controversy between these two doctrinaire Presbyterians, Schaeffer's theological pilgrimage began. He entered Machen's school in 1935, but finished with McIntire in 1937.

Schaeffer was born in Philadelphia. His working class parents were nominal Lutherans. Set on a career in engineering, he went to Drexel Institute, but soon switched to Hampden-Sydney College, a Presbyterian institution in Virginia. From this liberal arts school he journeyed to Westminster Seminary, where Machen and McIntire already were feuding over matters of eschatology, Christian liberty, and denominational sectarianism. For a decade, 1937 to 1947, Schaeffer pastored in St. Louis, ministering primarily to blue collar workers and children. Sponsored by the Independent Board of Presbyterian Missions, Schaeffer was sent to Europe in 1947, and over the next few years he traveled and preached extensively across the continent. In 1954 he bought a chalet in Huénoz, Switzerland, named it L'Abri, The Shelter, and became a guru of sorts to his neighbors, students, and spiritual travelers of all types. Joining an anti-McIntire group in founding Covenant College and Seminary and the Evangelical Presbyterian Church, he severed ties with his old mentor in 1956. Diagnosed with cancer in 1978, Schaeffer returned to the United States, where his attention turned increasingly to the debate on abortion.

Schaeffer's evangelistic endeavors had made him well-known by the early 1960s. A torrent of well-received tapes, films, and books made him a household name in much of the English-speaking Christian world by the 1970s. In many of his 25 books Schaeffer gave the positions of the religious right a scholarly gloss. His *No Final Conflict* (1975) was a defense of biblical literalism. To question the historicity of Genesis, he argued, was to raise doubts about the reliability of all scripture. Originally conceived as a Christian response to *Civilization*, a popular PBS series by Kenneth Clark and Jacob Bronowski, Schaeffer's most sweeping assessment, *How Should We Then Live? The Rise and Decline of Western Thought and Culture* (1976), dealt with the bête noire of the religious right, secular humanism. From the Greeks and Romans to the Renaissance to the Enlightenment, Schaeffer contrasted the "weaknesses" of human-centered cultures to the "strengths" of Christianity, which was rooted in God's absolute truth. The result of humanism could be seen in the ovens of Auschwitz and the abortion clinics of the United States. Tim LaHaye's popular work, *The Battle for the Mind* (1980), owes much to Schaeffer's treatise. Written with C. Everett Koop, *Whatever Happened to the Human Race?* (1979) was an unsparing indictment of abortion. This cheapening of life Schaeffer attributed to the erosion of the Christian view of humanity. Intended as a guide for Christian activism, *A Christian Manifesto* (1981) called the righteous to battle. Schaeffer applauded Jerry Falwell's Moral Majority, for it had boldly entered the political arena in behalf of divine law. Other Christians should not only follow suit, but also, as a last resort, engage in civil disobedience. To Schaeffer, the use of state funds for abortion certainly justified such resistance. Significantly, Randall Terry, leader of Operation Rescue, one of the more militant antiabortion groups, readily acknowledges his debt to Schaeffer. Indeed, in Schaeffer all of the religious right had found a spokesman of intellectual vigor and sophistication.

Phyllis Schlafly (1924–)

Phyllis Schlafly has been a nationally prominent leader of the pro-family movement since founding Eagle Forum in 1972 and mounting a successful drive to kill the Equal Rights Amendment (ERA). By the time she joined the fight, thirty of the necessary thirty-eight states had already ratified the proposed amendment, and the ultimate success of this long-sought feminist objective appeared imminent. But with dire predictions of women being drafted into the military, same-sex marriages, publicly funded abortions, and a significant expansion of federal power, Schlafly turned the tide against the ERA and earned the gratitude of many Christian conservatives, Protestants as well as

Phyllis Schlafly. Photo courtesy of Eagle Forum Archives. Used by permission.

Catholics. By June 30, 1982, the deadline for ratification, the amendment had fallen three states short. This was perhaps Schlafly's most notable foray into political waters, but it was not her first and would not be her last.

The Great Depression had considerable impact on Schlafly's family. Her father lost his job and was not gainfully employed again until World War II. Financial responsibility thus shifted to the mother, who not only kept the family solvent but also supported Phyllis's education in a prestigious Catholic school for girls. Obviously bright, Schlafly subsequently worked her way through Washington University in St. Louis, graduating Phi Beta Kappa in 1944. A master's degree in government from Radcliffe followed in 1945 and, eventually, a law degree from Washington University Law School in 1978. With marriage in 1949 to John Fred Schlafly, scion of a prominent St. Louis family, came financial security. She and her husband had six children, and in 1972 Schlafly was named Illinois Mother of the Year, befitting recognition for one so devoted to family causes.

If the family was her first concern, politics was a close second. But instead of the moderately liberal New Deal and its social programs, programs implemented during her formative years, it was Republican conservatism and its aversion to big government that inspired Schlafly. In 1946 she successfully managed the congressional campaign of a fellow St. Louis Republican, but six years later lost her own bid to become a member of Congress. Nevertheless, she has attended and taken on an active part in every Republican national convention since 1952. Particularly memorable was the 1964 gathering, for her book, *A Choice, Not an Echo*, attracted national attention that year. It was a stinging attack on the liberalism and alleged corruption of the northeastern Republican establishment exemplified by Nelson Rockefeller of New York. Conservative Barry Goldwater of Arizona was the *choice* Schlafly recommended. In 1967 Schlafly launched her own political newsletter, *The Phyllis Schlafly Report*, which is still in circulation, and three years later made another unsuccessful run for Congress from Illinois.

Schlafly has written extensively over the years on a wide range of subjects, but mostly on matters of interest to social and political conservatives. On the family there is *The Power of the Positive Woman* (1977) and *The Power of the Christian Woman* (1981); on childcare, *Who Will Rock the Cradle?* (1990); on feminism, *Feminist Fantasies* (2003); on the judiciary, *Judicial Tyranny: The New Kings of America?* (2005) and *The Supremacists: The Tyranny of Judges and How to Stop It* (2004); and on education, *Child Abuse in the Classroom* (1984). Begun in 1976 and continuing into the present, her weekly syndicated column currently appears in 100 newspapers. And lest people fear that Schlafly has mellowed with time, a 2006 interview in *The New York Times* will ease their minds. That the status of women has improved considerably in the later twentieth century Schlafly readily concedes. But none of the credit goes to the feminist movement. Rather, women can thank labor-saving devices, such as washing machines, clothes dryers, and paper diapers.

Strictly speaking, Schlafly is not a member of the religious right. Her Roman Catholicism notwithstanding, she more properly belongs to the secular political right. President Ronald Reagan implied as much in a 1984 tribute that acknowledged her work in the political, not religious, sphere. Said he: "Eagle Forum has set a high standard of volunteer participation in the political and legislative process." The issues she addressed, however, especially regarding women, abortion, and the family, found a receptive audience in the religious right and enabled her to cooperate in the 1980s with religious fundamentalists like Jerry Falwell. And the pursuit of common objectives by the likes of Schlafly and Falwell sheds some light on the nature of the religious right. Although dominated by Protestant evangelicals, the movement since the early 1980s has always involved other religious conservatives, such as Catholics, Jews, and Mormons.

Frederick Charles Schwarz (1913–)

A fervent anticommunist crusader, Fred Schwarz came to the United States from Australia in the early 1950s at the invitation of Carl McIntire and the American Council of Christian Churches. Schwarz received a medical degree from the University of Queensland and practiced as a psychiatrist in Sydney until 1953, when he came to the United States. He joined W. E. Pietsch, a radio evangelist, in Waterloo, Iowa, where he became one of the founders of the Christian Anti-Communism Crusade. Although initially tied to McIntire's American and International Councils of Christian Churches, Schwarz placed less emphasis on spreading a Christian message than on disseminating a doctrine of anticommunism. In 1958 Schwarz moved his organization to Long Beach, California. He ultimately de-emphasized association with McIntire's two councils, did not appeal directly to Christian fundamentalists for their support, and showed little concern for such fundamentalist positions as the premillennial return of Christ. Although he presented no clear theological position, Schwarz nonetheless saw conservative Christianity as the only possible alternative to communism.

In the 1950s Schwarz used the air waves to disseminate his message, but increasingly thereafter he traveled the nation, offering "schools" on anticommunism. His presentations stressed the nature of the world as divided into good and evil forces. In 1957 Schwarz received increased attention when he appeared before the House Un-American Activities Committee to testify as an expert on communism. His book *You Can Trust the Communists (To Be Communists)* portrayed communists as well-organized and exceptionally intelligent individuals whose behavior was predictable once people understood their very logical, but ultimately insane, thought. He also characterized as mental illness the belief that negotiations with communists could bring peace. In the 1970s Schwarz and his organization were active in presenting an anticommunist message in many countries, including El Salvador and the Philippines. Now in his eighties, Schwarz has retired and returned to Australia. The Christian Anti-Communism Crusade, meanwhile, continues under new leadership and distributes a newsletter renamed *The Schwarz Report*.

Cyrus Ingerson Scofield (1843–1921)

Cyrus Scofield is considered one of the more important figures to influence the character of premillennialist thought in the twentieth century. Born in Tennessee, he fought on the Confederate side in the Civil War and subsequently set up a law practice in Kansas. Accused of stealing political contributions from a candidate for public office, he left Kansas in 1877, abandoning his wife and two children. She divorced him in 1883. Scofield moved on to St. Louis, Missouri, where he was arrested and imprisoned on charges of forgery. While in prison Scofield was converted to Christianity and in 1882 became pastor of the First Congregational Church in Dallas, Texas. He edited *The Believer*, a monthly publication, and directed a Bible correspondence course.

Cyrus Ingerson Scofield.

In 1895 Scofield moved to Massachusetts to become a faculty member at Dwight L. Moody's Northfield Bible School and began work on a project to provide notes for the King James version of the Bible. The result was the *Scofield Reference Bible*, considered by many observers to be one of the more important popularizations of premillennial dispensationalism. The non-technical presentation gained wide popularity among laypersons. Scofield believed that anyone could interpret biblical prophecy. Formal learning and theological training were unnecessary. Sales of the reference Bible from its first publication in 1909 to 1967 are estimated at between five and 10 million copies, and a revised edition in 1967 so far has sold nearly three million copies. Some authorities have argued that the special format of Scofield's Bible, in which notes are presented on the same page with scriptural text, caused many readers to accord as much authority to the annotations as to the scriptures. In any event, many twentieth-century Bible students have embraced Scofield's scriptural notes unaware perhaps of the author's specific interpretation.

Scofield divided history into distinguishable time periods, indicating that God's relationship with human beings is progressing from one age to the next. Beginning with Innocence, the world proceeds to the ages of Conscience, Human Government, Promise, Law, and Grace, the time period from Christ to the present. The final stage, called the Kingdom Age, would occur after the prophesied Battle of Armageddon. Christ would govern the world as a theocracy for 1,000 years, followed by the final judgment and the end of all ages. Scofield, like subsequent premillennialists, doubted the prospects for peace and human improvement before Christ's direct intervention. At the end of World War I Scofield claimed that any attempt to establish a world order would only hasten the coming of the Antichrist. Asserting that Christ and the Apostles were not reformers, Scofield argued that the church should prepare for the end of time rather than become involved in social reform. Only in the millennial age would humans turn away from their corrupted natures. Christ's rule would lead to the defeat of selfishness and the elimination of inequalities in worldly goods.

Contemporary writers such as Hal Lindsey reflect Scofield's influence. Scofield emphasized the importance of Israel as a nation, for instance, and claimed in 1916 that Russia would invade the Holy Land in the end time. Although his contemporaries tended to hold the same view, Scofield put special emphasis on such an invasion in his Bible and elsewhere.

Jay Alan Sekulow (1956–)

As chief council for the American Center for Law and Justice (ACLJ), Jay Sekulow has proven an articulate advocate for the right of Christians to proselytize to the general public. He has presented his case on such television programs as *Good Morning America, Nightline, CNN Crossfire,* and *Larry King Live.* Sekulow appears regularly on Pat Robertson's *The 700 Club.* One of his primary areas of activity is defending parents and students who challenge local school districts' interpretations of Supreme Court rulings on school prayer.

Jay Alan Sekulow. Photo by Jeff Stanger. Used by permission.

Sekulow earned his B.A. and J.D. degrees from Mercer University. In 1990 he established the ACLJ in Virginia Beach, Virginia. He has published several books that provide advice for Christians concerned about expressing their beliefs in the public realm. In *And Nothing But the Truth* (1996), Sekulow and coauthor Keith Fournier relate their experiences fighting legal battles on church-state issues. The authors describe situations which proved to their satisfaction that religious expression is being suppressed in the public realm and Judeo-Christian values are being displaced as a vital ingredient of our society. In *Knowing Your Rights* (1993), Sekulow explains the rights, especially freedom of speech, that Christians have and the framework within which they can exercise those rights. In *From Intimidation to Victory*, he deals with several issues involving the right of Christians to freedom of speech, including the rights of parents to speak out against such evils as abortion and to employ the strategy of civil disobedience. In *Christian Rights in the Workplace*, he emphasizes that the law does not prohibit religious employees or employers from speaking about their faith in the workplace.

Sekulow has served as lead counsel and presented oral arguments before the Supreme Court in several cases. In *Board of Airport Commissioners v. Jews for Jesus* (482 U.S. 569, 1987), the Court invalidated an airport regulation restricting the distribution of religious literature in airport terminals. In *Board of Education of Westside Community Schools v. Mergens* (496 U.S. 226, L.Ed. 2d 191, 1990), the Court ruled that the Equal Access Act was constitutional, thus providing high school students with the right to establish Bible and prayer clubs. In *Lamb's Chapel v. Center Moriches School District* (113 S. Ct. 2141, 1993), the

Court ruled that a school district inappropriately prohibited the showing of the James Dobson film, *Turn Your Heart Toward Home,* in a school facility.

R.C. Sproul (1938–)

R. C. Sproul is best known in Christian circles as the founder of Ligonier Ministries, described as a teaching fellowship to educate Christians about their faith. Sproul is the principal teacher, having written over forty-five books and produced dozens of video- and audiotaped lectures dealing with such biblical and theological themes as predestination and election, the providence of God, biblical inerrancy, the Holy Spirit, church creeds, and the doctrine of justification by faith. He has produced longer lecture series, including *Dust to Glory,* fifty-seven presentations on the Bible; *The Consequences of Ideas,* a series on Western philosophy, including treatments of such philosophers as Plato, Aristotle, Augustine, Hume, Kant, and Nietzsche; and most recently *Foundations: An Overview of Systematic Theology,* which includes sixty presentations on such topics as angels and demons, the creation of human beings, the nature of sin, election and reprobation, and the end of the age and the return of Christ. These presentations, as well as a half-hour daily radio program, *Renewing Your Mind,* and regular appearances at weekend seminars around the country, have attracted a devoted following to Sproul's fundamentalist theology.

Sproul is the editor of *Tabletalk,* a monthly magazine that serves as a daily devotional. Each issue has a theme, which, although not explicitly political, often deals with a social issue, such as homosexuality or marital fidelity. For instance, the March 1997 issue, titled "Homosexuality: Unnatural Selection," contained articles condemning homosexuality; the August 2000 issue was

R.C. Sproul Photo. © Ligonier Ministries. All rights reserved. Used by permission.

titled "Liberalism: Spiritual Adultery," claiming the term "liberal Christian" was an oxymoron; and the September 2000 issue dealt with "Defiling the Body," sexual infidelity among clergy and laypeople. Issues also have theological themes such as preserving the fundamental beliefs of the Christian faith in the contemporary church against advocates of secularism.

After earning his Ph.D. from the Free University of Amsterdam at the age of 25, Sproul began teaching theology and philosophy at various colleges and seminaries. He is a Presbyterian and holds to the Calvinist roots of the denomination. Presently he is a professor of theology and apologetics at Knox Theological Seminary in Fort Lauderdale, Florida, and also conducts seminars at Westminster Theological Seminary. However, Sproul's primary interest for thirty years has been lay teaching, a task for which his organization is geared.

Sproul is the intellectual descendant of such conservative American theologians as J. Gresham Machen and Francis Schaeffer. He has continued their strong objections to the liberal trends in Christian theology begun in the late nineteenth century and their reaffirmation of traditional Christian beliefs such as the inerrancy of scripture, some form of creationism as opposed to evolution, and the historicity of Christ's birth, death, and resurrection. Like Schaeffer, Sproul believes that secular humanism represents a major threat to the Christian roots of western culture. Among Sproul's concerns is an alleged "anything goes" attitude in mainstream churches. Although Sproul's preference for conservatism might be interpreted as a political stand, he tends to remain aloof from any explicit statement of political preferences. Nonetheless, his social conservatism and preference for a fundamentalist theology coincide with the religious right's more overtly political stands.

Randy Tate (1965–)

Critics once described Randy Tate, an intensely religious political conservative and successor to Ralph Reed as executive director of the Christian Coalition, as the "the poster boy of the radical right," a perception seemingly bolstered by the ratings of several special-interest groups. Whereas Tate's congressional voting record earned a zero from the Sierra Club and League of Conservation Voters, it scored a 100 from the Christian Coalition and National Rifle Association. Born in Puyallup, Washington, Tate attended Tacoma Community College and in 1988 obtained a baccalaureate from Western Washington University. Something of a political junkie, he was elected to the state legislature while in his senior year at the university, and in 1988 he supported the presidential bid of televangelist Pat Robertson. After three terms in the state legislature, where he became the Republican caucus chairman, Tate was elected to the U.S. House, swept into office by the so-called "Republican revolution of '94."

Tate only narrowly defeated his Democratic opponent in 1994, but he acted as though he had won by an overwhelming majority and thus had the whole-hearted support of his district to pursue the objectives of religious and social conservatives. He was a true believer who quickly caught the eye of House Majority Whip Tom Delay (R-TX), as well as Speaker Newt Gingrich. He

Randy Tate. Photo courtesy of Congressional Pictorial Directory, 104th.

worked to restrict abortion rights, eliminate the National Endowment for the Humanities and the Corporation for Public Broadcasting, repeal the assault weapons ban, prevent any increase in the minimum wage, establish English as the nation's official tongue, prohibit flag burning by a constitutional amendment, provide vouchers for students to attend private schools, and weaken environmental restrictions. Tate made the mistake of attempting to impose a narrow agenda which lacked broad public support. Most Americans, whether Republicans or Democrats, did not want a woman's right to an abortion eliminated, or environmental regulations rolled back, or the ban on assault weapons repealed. Opposed by labor unions and environmental groups, Tate, despite strong backing from the Christian Coalition and other conservative organizations, was defeated in 1996. The assessment of Tate's Democratic opponent was discerning: "Randy Tate will do a very good job of representing the Republican Party in the Ninth District. I'll do a good job of representing everybody in the district."

In August 1997 Tate, prematurely bald and looking older than his 31 years, took the helm of the Christian Coalition. Another run for Congress was an option, Tate explained, but "after much prayer" he concluded "this position affords an even greater opportunity to shape the future of America." Making family issues a top priority, the Coalition under Tate has opposed late-term abortions, sought the repeal of the marriage tax penalty, objected to legislation according "special rights based on sexual behavior," urged the defeat of state gay-adoption laws, and supported efforts to allow inner-city parents to send their children to the best school of their choice. In 1998 Tate praised the U.S. House for its vote to impeach President Bill Clinton, then urged the president to spare the country more turmoil by resigning. Polls in late 1998, as well as the outcome of the midterm elections, showed that most Americans did not share Tate's opinion on impeachment and resignation.

Cal Thomas (1940–)

Cal Thomas is the best known evangelical Christian journalist on the contemporary scene, one whose conservative judgments emanate from a deeply rooted Judeo-Christian moral code. A native of Washington, D.C., the lanky 6'7" Thomas played basketball for his alma mater, American University. Interested in broadcast journalism at an early age, he became a disc jockey and news reader at 16, and two years later joined NBC News in Washington, D.C., as a copy boy. Rising through the ranks, he worked as a radio and television reporter for the network in the 1960s. Thomas has also been associated with PBS television and, while in the army, Armed Forces Radio and Television in New York City. His column with the Los Angeles Times Syndicate began in 1984 and today is carried by over 500 newspapers, making Thomas one of the nation's more widely read commentators.

A religious conservative, Thomas was influenced by Richard Halverson, former chaplain of the U.S. Senate, and Francis Schaeffer, the prestigious philosopher-theologian of the religious right. As with many other religious conservatives, he was dismayed by the feminist and gay rights movements, as well as the increased rates of abortions and divorces, developments seen by people of Thomas's persuasion as the ill-favored results of liberalism. Consequently, Thomas joined Jerry Falwell and served as a vice president of Moral Majority in the early 1980s. Through the political process he and his spiritual kinfolk intended to stem the nation's perceived moral and cultural decline. Given such active involvement in the religious right, Thomas's recent "awakening" was highly significant. The religious right, according to Thomas in *Blinded by Might* (1999), written in collaboration with Edward Dobson, had little to show for twenty years of political activism. Indeed, Thomas believed "the moral landscape of America" had gotten worse and concluded: "Two decades after conservative Christians charged into the political arena, bringing new voters and millions of dollars with them in hopes of transforming the culture through political power, it must be acknowledged that we have failed."

Although religious conservatives should remain active as voters, they should no longer expect politics to transform the moral climate of America. Virtue, or morality, cannot be imposed from above by government, but rather must be chosen from below by the people themselves. Thomas thus argued the time had come to return to the traditional evangelical pursuit of saving individual sinners. The strength of religious conservatives lay in the transforming power of the Gospel, not the coercive power of the state. As an example of how religious conservatives could effect constructive change, Thomas cited the establishment of crisis pregnancy centers across the nation. More than anything in the political arena, this, thought Thomas, had contributed to a reduction in abortions.

While still in agreement with their objectives, Thomas, true to the sentiments expressed in *Blinded by Might*, frequently took issue with religious conservatives during the 2000 presidential campaign. The nastiness of the South Carolina Republican primary, for instance, proved that people supposedly committed to a higher calling could "get down and dirty with the best of the pagans." As for the excuse, "The left does it," Thomas retorted: "I wasn't aware that the pagan left had replaced biblical principles in setting the agenda for the Christian church." Thomas also chided Falwell, whose "People of Faith 2000" was supposed to register 10 million new voters. The effort, said Thomas, would "raise some money and make noise," but would "change little." And at times there was humor, as in his characterization of Joseph Lieberman as an "itinerant Jewish evangelist." This last remark suggests that while Thomas faults his religious brethren for their continuing faith in politics, he nonetheless remains a partisan. He opposed Al Gore and Lieberman during the 2000 presidential campaign, and he takes issue now with those who consider George W. Bush too dumb and inexperienced to be president. Thomas is convinced Bush has the wisdom, a virtue apparently paramount to knowledge, to surround himself with able people.

Most recently Thomas took a swipe at the Rev. Richard Cizik, the vice president of governmental affairs for the National Association of Evangelicals. Cizik, a Reagan-era conservative and supporter of Moral Majority, is solidly planted on the religious right. He opposes abortion, gay marriage, and embryonic stem-cell research. But he also has another cause—global warming. "This is not a Red State issue or a Blue State issue or a green issue," asserts Cizik. "It's a spiritual issue." Cizik believes the Book of Genesis calls upon Christians to be stewards of the Earth, environmentalists, if you will. And for this he drew Thomas's ridicule. "What is it with evangelical Christians that so many of them need a cause beyond the [great] commission they've been given?" asks Thomas. If Christians want to clean up the planet, he contends, they should clean up "the hearts of men and women" and prepare them "for the world to come."

Rick Warren (1954-)

That Rick Warren is a conservative Christian is undisputed, but he is no carbon copy of other preachers generally associated with the religious right, such as Jerry Falwell or Pat Robertson. Warren represents a younger generation of evangelicals, one not easily categorized. Large of girth, goateed, casually attired, usually jeans and Hawaiian shirts, he does not fit the stereotypical image of a minister. And his large megachurch, 20,000 or so strong, Saddleback Church in Lake Forest, California, mirrors the pastor's easygoing personality. Instead of traditional hymns, contemporary music prevails; instead of pews, stained glass, and lofty towers, the church sanctuary and surrounding buildings bring to mind a sprawling college campus; instead of coats and ties, T-shirts and sandals predominate; and instead of sermons heavy on theology (Warren readily admits that he is no theologian), members are treated to folksy conversations on the practical application of the Gospel, what people and churches can do to make life better for others. And as is true of all megachurches today, loudspeakers and television screens are everywhere, ensuring that the pastor's visage and words are seen and heard by all.

So, who is Rick Warren? He was born in San Jose, California, the son of a Baptist preacher who had founded seven churches in northern California and who was carpenter enough to construct quite a few more. Warren wanted to be like his father, to build a congregation from the ground up, but first was the matter of education. After high school Warren obtained a B.A. from California Baptist University, then a master of divinity degree from Southwestern Baptist Theological Seminary in 1979. That December Warren, loading his belongings in a U-Haul trailer, left Texas with wife Kay and their four-month-old child headed for Saddleback Valley in Orange County. Three months later, Easter 1980, he stood before 204 curious seekers for the first public service of Saddleback Valley Community Church. For the next thirteen years the congregation assembled wherever it could find a place to meet, seventy-nine different locations in all; today its permanent campus occupies 120 acres.

The remarkable numerical growth of Saddleback Church makes Warren a major figure in the "church growth movement," a phenomenon that sharply divides much of the Christian community. Advocates of church-growth strategies look upon numbers as evidence of God's blessing, an indication that a church is fulfilling its divine mission. Therefore, they have no qualms about using techniques normally associated with the world of business. Opponents counter that it is unseemly and perhaps unscriptural to employ the gimmicks of advertising to "sell religion" in much the same way an auto dealer peddles his vehicles. This usually entails the watering down of theology for the sake of expanding enrollments.

Warren is a proponent of church growth, and he has conducted hundreds of seminars on the subject around the globe. Written in 1995, his *The Purpose-Driven Church* was basically a how-to recipe for church builders, stressing worship, fellowship, discipleship, ministry, and evangelism. It is also worth noting that Warren frequently cites his good friend, management guru Peter Drucker. Warren is best known, of course, for *The Purpose-Driven Life* (2002), which has sold over 30 million copies in English alone, making him a wealthy man, so much so that he now tithes 90 percent of his income. The book has also given Warren national and world prominence, which in turn has gained him access to national and world leaders. Without losing sight of the need to grow churches, Warren has used his prominence to draw attention to global concerns such as poverty, homelessness, and AIDS.

Herein emerges fissures on the religious right. Warren is in step with the religious right on such matters as abortion and embryonic stem cell research, but he parts company on issues such as global poverty, the use of torture, homelessness, and AIDS. As one observer noted of Warren, it is difficult to peg a man who stands with the religious right on some concerns and with liberal Catholicism on others. Motivated by the basic Christian ethic of people helping people, members of Warren's church make missionary trips to Africa, resolve to feed the poor and hungry, and confront the AIDS pandemic. On this last matter, an international conference held at Saddleback Church in late 2006 drew considerable criticism from many fellow Christian conservatives. Whereas some objected because of the religious right's longstanding association of AIDS to homosexuality and promiscuity, others resented the presence of Illinois Senator Barack Obama, whose views on abortion were offensive.

Warren answered that the time had come for "people . . . who normally won't even speak to each other" to get together—in other words, evangelical Christians and gays. Warren had the same advice when his trip to Syria in November 2006 brought swift criticism from many evangelicals and Jews. "I believe it is a mistake to not talk to nations considered hostile," he asserted, adding that "isolation and silence has never solved conflict anywhere, whether between spouses or between nations." Genocide in Rwanda has been another concern of Warren and Saddleback Church, and Rwandan President Paul Kagame has welcomed the American pastor in hopes of making Rwanda "the first purpose driven nation."

Perhaps Warren represents the "new face" of the religious right, a fervently evangelistic Christian concerned about the social application of the Good News, about people helping people, individually and through their churches. In a sense, Warren is actually more akin to those northern evangelicals of the 1840s and 1850s whose religion motivated them to pursue numerous social reforms, including ending slavery, than he is to many of his contemporaries on the religious right.

Robert H. W. Welch, Jr. (1899–1985)

Founder of the John Birch Society and its leader for twenty-five years, Robert Welch dedicated himself to fighting what he saw as a communist conspiracy to capture American government and society. He received a degree from the University of North Carolina and attended the U.S. Naval Academy and Harvard University Law School, but failed to graduate from either. In 1921 he started a successful candy business. He left the company in 1956 and devoted himself thereafter to fighting the communist conspiracy that he fervently believed was enveloping America.

In 1958 Welch met with eleven other businessmen to form the John Birch Society, named for a Baptist missionary to China who had been killed by Chinese communists at the end of World War II. Welch considered Birch to be the first casualty of World War III. The transcript of Welch's lengthy presentation at that meeting was published as *The Blue Book*. Representing the basic philosophy and objectives of the society, this book called for three things: "less government, more individual responsibility, and a better world." In *The Politician*, a biographical manuscript first published in 1958, Welch stated that communists had infiltrated the highest levels of American government. He believed Dwight Eisenhower had not only become president through communist maneuverings, but was also a knowing agent of the communist conspiracy. Welch charged other noted Americans, including Presidents Franklin Roosevelt and Harry Truman, Secretary of State John Foster Dulles, and General George C. Marshall, with varying levels of complicity in the communist plot to gain control of American government.

Although he came from a fundamentalist Baptist background, Welch did not maintain formal ties to that tradition. His beliefs have been described as universalistic; he selected no particular brand of Christianity as the one true faith. His writings demonstrated a belief in the individualistic liberalism of the

Robert H. W. Welch Jr. Photo courtesy of the John Birch Society. Used by permission.

nineteenth century as well as a suspicion of democracy, which he described as demagoguery and a fraud. After the mid-1960s Welch's fame declined. Maintaining his strong anticommunist stance, he once referred to President Ronald Reagan as a "lackey" of communist conspirators. Welch stepped down as president of the John Birch Society in 1983.

Paul Weyrich (1942–)

Sometimes described as the religious right's point man, Paul Weyrich not only enunciated conservative positions in the 1970s and 1980s in an extreme way, but also labored diligently to politicize the religious right. Behind his cherubic exterior lurked a pugnacious temperament. A Roman Catholic of blue collar origins, he was born in Racine, Wisconsin. Strictly speaking, Weyrich was not a member of the religious right, but rather a shrewd political strategist who saw Protestant fundamentalists as an untapped pool of voters for conservative causes. The trick was to bring them into the political process and to unite them with conservative Roman Catholics. Weyrich saw in certain "social" issues an opportunity to achieve precisely this goal. There was little if any difference, he believed, between many Protestant fundamentalists and Catholics on such matters as abortion, prayer in the public schools, and anticommunism. Jerry Falwell and Pope John Paul II merely represented different sides of the same coin.

Out of headquarters in Washington, D.C., Weyrich operated the Committee for the Survival of a Free Congress, basically a training school for conservative political candidates. Along with Edward E. McAteer and Howard Phillips, he not only courted Falwell but also coined the phrase "Moral Majority." As conceived by Weyrich, Moral Majority was to bring religious fundamentalists of whatever stripe together for common political ends. Meanwhile, the Religious Roundtable, headed by McAteer, was seen by Weyrich as an umbrella organization designed to coordinate the political efforts of several religious right groups, including Moral Majority and Christian Voice. Weyrich even attempted to unite religious and secular conservatives in the cause of "cultural conservatism," meaning basically political objectives that Christians, Jews, and even atheists could pursue without abandoning their respective theological positions. Given his continued association with the Free Congress Research and Education Foundation and prominence on the religious and secular right for such a long time, it came as a shock when Weyrich in February 1999 declared "the culture war" lost and "politics" a failure. A disillusioned

Paul Weyrich. Chairman and CEO of Free Congress Foundation. Photo used by permission.

Weyrich believed the time had come for religious and social conservatives to pursue their objective by means other than politics.

Donald Ellis Wildmon (1938–)

Television programming has been the primary concern of this mild-mannered but determined Methodist minister from Tupelo, Mississippi. In the belief that most television programs undermined "traditional" family values, he encouraged his congregation one Sunday in December 1976 to turn off the tube for a week. Convinced by resulting coverage in the national press that he had hit upon an idea whose time had come, Wildmon promptly organized the National Federation for Decency in 1977, renamed the American Family Association in 1987. Headquartered initially in Wildmon's family dining room, the new organization boldly set out to purify the air waves. By 1992 the American Family Association operated out of a new building, had a staff of thirty-five, claimed to have 450,000 members in 640 chapters nationwide, and conducted state-of-the-art direct-mailing operations that raised over $6 million annually.

Wildmon's strategy was twofold: first, to monitor network shows for sexual content, profanity, and violence; and, second, to threaten with boycotts the corporate sponsors of offensive programs. In this way he would punish not only the networks, but also the businesses that funded unacceptable shows. Accordingly, Pepsi, Dr. Pepper, Wendy's, Domino's Pizza, Ralston Purina, General Mills, Honda, Mazda, AT&T, and others have all incurred the preacher's wrath. The extent to which such pressure tactics have succeeded is

Donald Ellis Wildmon. Photo courtesy of Donald Wildmon. Used by permission.

debatable. If AT&T, as Wildmon believed, discontinued its advertisements on *Saturday Night Live* because of his threats, Holiday Inn, Johnson and Johnson, Waldenbooks, and others have ignored the television censor with apparent impunity. During the 1980s Wildmon, a member of Moral Majority, worked closely with Jerry Falwell to make the air waves "safe" for family viewing.

In 2005 Wildmon announced a boycott of Ford Motor Company because of its advertisements in gay publications. The company denied caving in to Wildmon's pressure, but it nevertheless dropped the gay publications, eliciting the concern of several gay groups. As for Wildmon, he took credit for his American Family Association, adding: "While we still have a few differences with Ford, we feel that our concerns are being addressed in good faith and will continue to be addressed in the future."

4

Analysis of Survey Data

This study focuses primarily on the "elite" of the religious right—organizations and their leaders. If the religious right ended there, it would be of little consequence to the social and political fabric of the United States. Millions of ordinary Americans, however, agree with the religious right's conservative interpretation of American society and politics. This agreement not only adds significantly to the perceived moral force of the movement, but also accounts for the generous financial support of many conservative Christians. Multitudes of evangelical Christians, awakened by charismatic leaders and mobilized by grassroots organizations, have become a force to be reckoned with on election day.

Religion and the American Population

To illuminate some of the religious attitudes of Americans, attitudes that help in understanding the appeal of the religious right, this chapter relies primarily on a data analysis of the National Opinion Research Center's General Social Survey (GSS) data. Table 4.1 summarizes the results of the 1998 and 2000 General Social Survey, in which respondents were asked to select the category, ranging from "I don't believe in God" to "I know God really exists and I have no doubts about it," that best expresses their belief about God. The results in the two years indicate a basic stability among Americans regarding a belief in God. If the four categories indicating some level of belief are combined, roughly 90 percent of those surveyed express belief in God or a "higher power" (91.8 percent in 1998 and 89.5 percent in 2000).

Table 4.2, derived from the 2006 Baylor Institute for Studies of Religion survey, provides additional insight into the religious beliefs of Americans.

These survey results indicate that a greater proportion of evangelical Protestants express adherence to traditional Christian beliefs than do mainline Protestants, although a significant majority of both groups stated that they had no doubts about God's existence and that Jesus is the son of God. A negligible proportion of each group expressed extreme doubt about the existence of God and the nature of Jesus. Larger proportions of evangelicals and mainline Protestants were willing to question the claim that the Bible presents the literal truth.

Table 4.1
Belief in God (Percentage)

Don't believe	3.3
Don't know, no way to find out	4.9
Believe in higher power	9.5
Believe sometimes	4.7
Believe with doubts	14.7
Believe without doubts	62.8
Don't know	0.1

Source: 1998 General Social Survey, N = 1,165.

Table 4.2
Religious Beliefs of Evangelicals and Mainline Protestants (Percentage)

	Evangelical Protestant	*Mainline Protestant*
Belief about God		
No doubts that God exists	86.5	63.6
Don't believe in anything beyond the physical world	0.4	0.7
Belief about Jesus		
Jesus is the son of God	94.4	72.2
Jesus is a fictional character	0.0	0.9
Belief about the Bible		
Literally true	47.8	11.2
Ancient book of history and Legends	6.5	22.0

Source: 2006 Baylor Institute for Studies of Religion Survey—American Piety in the 21st Century. (p. 14).

The Baylor survey categorized respondents according to their denominational affiliation as either black Protestant, evangelical Protestant, mainline Protestant, Catholic, Jewish, "other," or unaffiliated. Table 4.3 presents the proportion of the sample categorized as mainline or evangelical Protestant. While evangelicals composed just over 33 percent of the total sample, they represented approximately 50 percent of those interviewed in the South but only 13 percent of the interviewees in the East. Evangelicals are slightly more female than the overall sample, and are overrepresented in the household income category of less than $35,000 and underrepresented in the category of more than $100,000. Evangelicals between 18 and 30 years of age are overrepresented, perhaps reflecting in part the appeal of more fundamentalist churches, whether denominational or nondenominational, to younger families.

In our analysis of General Social Survey data, we divide respondents' church affiliation into two categories: "evangelical Protestant" and "mainline Protestant." For example, respondents indicating their church affiliation as Missouri Synod Lutheran, Wisconsin Synod Lutheran, Southern Baptist, Churches of Christ, or Assemblies of God were categorized as "evangelical Protestant." Respondents stating their church membership as Congregationalist, Methodist, Episcopalian, Presbyterian, Disciples of Christ, Evangelical Lutheran Church in America, or American Baptist were categorized as "mainline Protestant." For a more thorough categorization of evangelical and Protestant churches, Table 4.4 includes those denominations listed in each category

Table 4.3
Evangelical and Mainline Protestants (Percentage)

	Evangelical Protestants	*Mainline Protestants*
Gender		
Male	30.0	22.1
Female	36.7	22.1
Race		
White	35.4	24.1
African American	9.5	7.7
Age		
18-30	39.0	20.1
31-44	34.9	17.6
45-64	31.3	22.5
65+	33.1	28.1
Education		
High school or less	18.0	22.0
College or more	23.5	29.0
Household income		
$35,000 or less	39.3	20.3
More than $100,000	26.9	22.0
Region		
East	13.1	26.0
South	50.3	19.3
Midwest	33.7	26.0
West	31.7	17.7
Total sample	33.6	22.1

Source: 2006 Baylor Institute for Studies of Religion Survey—American Piety in the 21st Century (p. 11).

in the Baylor Religion Survey and the number of adherents in each (including children and regular participants in addition to church membership).

The following tables, drawn from General Social Surveys, compare the views of evangelical and mainline Protestants. Table 4.5 presents the regional distribution of those respondents indicating an evangelical Protestant church affiliation in contrast to those who state an affiliation with non-evangelical, or mainline, churches.

More than one-third (37.9 percent) of evangelical respondents reside in the South Atlantic region. When the South Atlantic, East South Central, and West South Central regions are combined, approximately 66 percent of evangelicals reside in these areas, reinforcing the view that more conservative Christians tend to prevail in the southern states. In contrast, mainline Protestant adherents tend to be more evenly distributed throughout the nation, but with nearly one-quarter situated in the South Atlantic region. Politically, the larger proportion of evangelicals in the population helps to explain the increasing success of conservative candidates in southern states.

Political Preferences

Recent campaigns and elections suggest a close relationship between the religious right and the Republican party. The religious right provides campaign resources and voters for the Republicans, while the party supports evangelicals on issues such as abortion, pornography, prayer in the schools, and

Table 4.4
Evangelical and Mainline Protestant Church Adherents

	Number	Percent
Evangelical Protestant		
Assemblies of God	2,561,998	8.3
Christian and Missionary Alliance	331,106	1.1
Christian Reformed	248,938	0.8
Church of God (Cleveland, Tenn.)	974,198	3.2
Church of the Nazarene	907,331	2.9
Churches of Christ	1,645,584	5.3
Free Methodist	96,237	0.3
Mennonite Church	156,345	0.5
Lutheran–Missouri Synod	2,521,062	8.1
Presbyterian Church in America	315,293	1.0
Seventh-Day Adventist	923,046	3.0
Southern Baptist Convention	19,881,467	64.2
Wisconsin Evangelical Lutheran	405,078	1.3
Total	30,967,683	100.0
Mainline Protestant		
Congregationalist	84,380	0.3
Disciples of Christ	1,017,784	4.0
Episcopal	2,314,756	9.0
Presbyterian Church (USA)	3,141,566	12.2
Evangelical Lutheran Church in America	5,113,418	19.8
American Baptist	1,767,462	6.9
Unitarian	182,698	0.7
United Methodist	10,350,629	40.1
Friends (Quakers)	113,086	0.4
United Church of Christ	1,698,918	6.6
Total	25,784,697	100.0

Source: Jones, Dale E., Sherri Doty, Clifford Grammich, James E. Horsch, Richard Houseal, Mac Lynn, John P. Marcum, Kenneth M. Sanchagrin, and Richard H. Taylor. 2002. *Religious Congregations and Membership in the United States 2000.* Nashville, TN: Glenmary Research Center.

Table 4.5
Religious Preference by Region (Percentage)

Region	Evangelical Protestant	Mainline Protestant
New England	0.4	1.3
Middle Atlantic	5.2	13.4
East North Central	12.6	19.8
West North Central	6.0	10.6
South Atlantic	37.9	23.7
East South Central	11.7	6.8
West South Central	16.8	10.1
Mountain	3.6	5.8
Pacific	5.8	8.6
Total	100.0	100.0

Source: 2004 General Social Survey, N = 927.

"family values." Therefore, we expect a larger proportion of evangelicals to support the Republican party than do mainline Protestants. Table 4.6 presents a cross-tabulation of religious preference by political party identification derived from 1998 and 2004 GSS data.

A larger proportion of evangelical than mainline respondents in 1998 and 2004 expressed a preference for the Democratic party. However, party identifi-

Table 4.6
Religious Preference and Party Affiliation, 1998 and 2004

	1998		2004	
	Evangelical Protestant	Mainline Protestant	Evangelical Protestant	Mainline Protestant
Republican	27.6	35.8	33.1	35.3
Democrat	41.6	32.0	39.4	29.9
Independent	30.8	32.2	27.5	34.8
Total	100.0	100.0	100.0	100.0

Source: 1998 and 2004 General Social Survey, N = 1,098 (1998); 919 (2004).

Table 4.7
Voter Preference for President, 1996, 2000, and 2004

	Evangelical Protestant	Mainline Protestant
1996		
Robert Dole	37.8	43.2
Bill Clinton	51.4	46.9
Ross Perot	10.8	9.9
Total	100.0	100.0
2000		
George W. Bush	53.8	57.5
Albert Gore	45.6	41.0
Ralph Nader	0.6	1.5
Total	100.0	100.0
2004		
George W. Bush	78.0	50.0
John Kerry	22.0	50.0
Total	100.0	100.0

Sources: 1998 and 2002 General Social Surveys (for 1996 and 2002), N = 751 (1998); 656 (2004); Fourth National Survey of Religion and Politics, Post-Election Sample, University of Akron (for 2006), N = 2,730 (http://pewforum.org/docs/print.php?DocID=64),

cation in the United States, while a good indicator of voter preference, can be an unreliable predictor. Many evangelical Protestants, while identifying with the Democratic party, may vote for Republican candidates more consistent with their religious preferences. Voter preferences in the 1996, 2000, and 2004 presidential elections, presented in Table 4.7, show steadily increasing voter support for the Republican party candidate among evangelical Protestants. Although both groups questioned in these surveys reported greater support for the Democratic than the Republican party, a larger proportion of evangelical Protestants supported the Republican candidate than did mainline Protestants. In the 2004 survey more than three-fourths of evangelical respondents reported voting for Republican George W. Bush.

Of special note, Table 4.6 indicates that approximately one-third of both evangelical and mainline Protestants claim to be independents. Therefore, neither the Republican nor the Democratic party has an especially strong hold on either religious group. Support can shift rather swiftly depending on the dominant issues in a particular campaign.

Perhaps ideological preference rather than party identification is the factor that distinguishes evangelicals from mainline Protestants. Table 4.8 furnishes some support for this alternative expectation. Larger proportions of evangel-

Table 4.8
Voter Preference for President, 2004 (Percentage)

Ideology	Evangelical Protestant		Mainline Protestant	
	1998	2004	1998	2004
Liberal	21.1	16.5	24.8	25.3
Conservative	36.0	42.9	35.3	37.8
Moderate	38.0	37.8	37.8	35.3
Don't Know	4.9	2.8	2.1	1.6
Total	100.0	100.0	100.0	100.0

Source: 1998 and 2004 General Social Survey, N = 1,111 (1998); 444 (2004),

ical and mainline respondents categorize themselves as conservative than as liberal. In 2004 more than twice as many evangelical respondents stated a conservative than a liberal preference. When conservative and moderate categories for 2004 are combined, approximately 73 percent of both evangelical and mainline respondents are in that combined group.

To the extent that evangelical Protestants become more politically active, one would expect conservative candidates of either party to fare better than liberal candidates. Exit polling supported by the Pew Forum on Religion and Public Life for the 2006 congressional election indicated that white evangelical Christians continued to support Republican candidates. Despite various charges of corruption lodged against Republican lawmakers, 72 percent of this group supported Republican candidates for the U.S. House of Representatives. In contrast, white mainline Protestants divided fairly evenly between the two major parties, with 47 percent supporting Democratic candidates and 51 percent opting for Republican candidates. Those not affiliated with any religious group preferred Democratic over Republican candidates by a margin of 74 percent to 22 percent (http://pewform.org/docs/index.php?DocID=174).

Policy Preferences

Opinions about specific policy issues can be as informative as partisan or ideological self-identification in determining political preferences. For instance, the General Social Survey asked whether too little money, about the right amount, or too much money was being spent in various policy areas. Table 4.9 indicates the percentage of evangelical and mainline Protestants who thought "too little" money was being devoted to these areas. Overall, on socioeconomic issues, there is little difference between evangelical and mainline Christians. Only slight differences were found, and in some categories the proportion of evangelical Protestants exceeded that of mainline Protestants responding "too little." Spending for big cities and for welfare are the two categories in which a majority of both evangelicals and mainline Protestants did not say that too little money is being spent. With regard to the cities, we speculate that responses reflect fiscal conservatism and place of residence rather than religious viewpoints.

Table 4.9
Religious Preference and the Support of Public Spending

| Issue | Evangelical Protestant | | Mainline Protestant | |
	1998	2004	1998	2004
Improving and protecting nation's health	68.9	82.1	62.2	78.7
Improving nation's education system	69.3	74.4	69.8	71.6
Solving problems of big cities	47.2	37.7	43.1	36.3
Improving and protecting the environment	54.0	58.2	58.2	62.7
Welfare	15.0	26.0	14.7	22.9

Source: 1998 and 2004 General Social Survey, N = 576 (1998); 426 (2004).

Table 4.10
Religious Preference and Attitude toward Legalizing Marijuana

| | Evangelical Protestant | | Mainline Protestant | |
	1998	2004	1998	2004
Legalize	18.7	22.1	24.3	34.3
Don't legalize	76.3	67.5	68.3	59.4
Don't know	5.0	10.4	7.4	6.3
Total	100.0	100.0	100.0	100.0

Source: 1998 and 2004 General Social Survey, N = 747 (1998); 291 (2004).

Social and Moral Issues

Social and moral issues that leaders of the religious right have often used in their criticisms of contemporary American society were also examined. GSS respondents were asked, for instance, if they thought marijuana should be made legal. The results are summarized in Table 4.10. The distribution is in the expected direction. Both groups oppose legalization by large margins, but a larger percentage of evangelicals (67.5 versus 59.4 percent) in 2004 were in opposition.

Respondents were asked their opinion of a married person who has sex with someone other than his or her marriage partner. Table 4.11 provides a summary of the results. Although large proportions of both evangelicals and mainline Protestants objected to extramarital sex, a larger proportion of evangelicals expressed disapproval, with the difference larger in 2004 than in 1998. Combining the alternatives that such behavior is "always wrong" and "almost always wrong" in the 2004 results, there is no significant difference between evangelical Protestants (93.7 percent) and mainline Protestants (95.2 percent).

Another issue of great concern to the religious right is homosexuality, particularly the assertiveness of the gay community in pursuit of civil rights. Table 4.12 reports the results of a General Social Survey question asking respondents their attitude toward homosexual relationships. A large difference in attitudes is expressed on this issue, with approximately 80 percent of evangelical Protestant respondents in 2004 stating that homosexuality is always wrong, and about 46 percent of mainline Protestants holding this position. The

Table 4.11
Religious Preference and Attitude toward Extramarital Sex

	Evangelical Protestant		Mainline Protestant	
	1998	2004	1998	2004
Always wrong	82.8	89.1	81.7	79.2
Almost always wrong	10.2	4.6	10.9	16.0
Sometimes wrong	3.4	2.9	4.4	3.2
Not wrong at all	2.4	2.8	1.5	0.8
Don't know	1.2	0.6	1.5	0.8
Total	100.0	100.0	100.0	100.0

Source: 1998 and 2004 General Social Survey, N = 750 (1998); 300 (2004).

Table 4.12
Religious Preference and Attitude toward Homosexuality

	Evangelical Protestant		Mainline Protestant	
	1998	2004	1998	2004
Always wrong	72.6	79.8	51.3	46.4
Almost always wrong	5.3	1.7	5.6	6.4
Sometimes wrong	3.6	2.3	7.7	11.2
Not wrong at all	14.1	15.0	27.4	32.8
Don't know	4.4	1.2	8.0	3.2
Total	100.0	100.0	100.0	100.0

Source: 1998 and 2004 General Social Survey, N = 749 (1998); 298 (2004).

proportion of evangelical respondents between 1998 and 2004 responding "Always wrong" increased, while the proportion of mainstream respondents decreased, suggesting greater polarization on this issue. Responses to a question in the 1994 General Social Survey coincide with these findings. Respondents were asked whether they regarded homosexuality as a choice or something that cannot be changed. Although 63 percent of evangelical Protestants responded that homosexuality is a choice, just 37 percent of mainline Protestants held this position. Religious right groups tend to regard sexual preference as something that can be changed and have recommended religious therapies that allegedly convert "gays" into "straights." These findings regarding attitudes toward extramarital sex and homosexuality help explain the trend in many states in recent years to pass constitutional amendments defining marriage as a union between one man and one woman.

In addition to homosexuality, religious right leaders express strong opposition to pornography. Table 4.13 indicates the opinions of respondents regarding the legal status of pornography. Although more than one-half of evangelical respondents in 2004 expressed a preference for laws making pornography illegal for all, 43 percent of mainline respondents supported that option. Fifty-four percent of mainline Protestants, but just 41 percent of evangelical Protestants, were willing to restrict the prohibition against pornography to those under eighteen years of age, while having no restrictions on the access to pornography of those over eighteen. A very small proportion in both groups was willing to accept no limitations on pornography at all.

Table 4.13
Attitudes about the Legality of Pornography

	Evangelical Protestant		Mainline Protestant	
	1998	2004	1998	2004
Illegal to all	46.0	53.4	43.0	43.0
Illegal to those under 18	50.3	41.1	52.8	53.9
Legal	3.0	4.9	3.9	3.1
Don't know	0.7	0.6	0.3	–
Total	100.0	100.0	100.0	100.0

Source: 1998 and 2004 General Social Survey, N = 748 (1998); 291 (2004).

Religious right organizations have emphasized their strong opposition to both homosexuality and pornography; therefore, it is not surprising to discover that the opinions of evangelical Protestants coincide with this opposition.

Abortion is perhaps the most important issue unifying religious right groups that, due to doctrinal differences, would otherwise likely have little to do with one another. A number of questions in the General Social Survey deal with the issue of abortion and the circumstances under which respondents would not object to the procedure. These circumstances include ones in which the baby may have a serious defect, the woman is married and does not want any more children, the woman's health is seriously endangered by the pregnancy, the woman cannot afford any more children, the pregnancy resulted from rape, the woman is not married and does not want to marry the man, and the woman wants an abortion for any reason at all. Table 4.14 reports respondents' opinions about the permissibility of abortion in these circumstances.

In each circumstance, evangelicals are less likely than mainline Protestants to approve of the legal right to an abortion. The greater willingness of mainline Protestants to give weight to nonreligious factors when considering an abortion would be viewed by many on the religious right as a "humanist" perspective. In some circumstances, however, a large majority of evangelicals are willing to support this legal right. These conditions include the strong chance of a birth defect, the health of the pregnant woman is seriously endangered, and the pregnancy resulted from rape.

If these survey results truly reflect the attitudes of evangelicals, the more militant antiabortion groups do not represent accurately the opinions of evangelical Americans, a large majority of whom is willing to accept legal abortion in some of the above-mentioned circumstances. Both religious groups, however, are much less willing to sanction legal abortions under other conditions. Less than 50 percent of both religious groups are willing to approve of abortions if the mother does not want or cannot afford any more children or if the mother is not married. The complexity of opinions on this question leads to the conclusion that there is no clear-cut solution to the abortion issue.

Religious right groups have made prayer in public schools one of their major causes and advocate a constitutional amendment to allow for at least voluntary prayer. Table 4.15 summarizes the results of a question that asked

Table 4.14
Religious Preference and Conditions under Which an Abortion Should Be Legal (Percentage)

| | Evangelical Protestant | | | | Mainline Protestant | | | |
	Yes	No	Don't Know	Total	Yes	No	Don't Know	Total
Birth defect								
1998	69.5	25.2	5.3	100.0	83.8	12.1	4.1	100.0
2004	69.6	28.1	2.3	100.0	81.6	15.2	3.2	100.0
Unwanted								
1998	27.6	67.8	4.6	100.0	46.6	47.8	5.6	100.0
2004	32.6	62.7	4.7	100.0	48.0	49.6	2.4	100.0
Health of the Woman								
1998	81.4	14.0	4.6	100.0	89.7	5.6	4.7	100.0
2004	80.2	16.9	2.9	100.0	92.8	4.8	2.4	100.0
Can't afford								
1998	29.9	64.0	6.1	100.0	47.2	46.9	5.9	100.0
2004	29.8	65.5	4.7	100.0	46.4	51.2	2.4	100.0
Rape								
1998	70.7	24.0	5.3	100.0	86.1	11.2	2.7	100.0
2004	70.3	24.5	5.2	100.0	82.3	15.3	2.4	100.0
Not married								
1998	27.1	68.1	4.8	100.0	46.6	48.1	5.3	100.0
2004	29.7	67.4	2.9	100.0	46.4	50.4	3.2	100.0
Any reason								
1998	27.8	67.1	5.1	100.0	43.8	50.6	5.6	100.0
2004	26.0	70.0	4.0	100.0	50.8	46.8	2.4	100.0

Source: 1998 and 2004 General Social Survey, N = 752 (1998); 297 (2004).

Table 4.15
Supreme Court Decision on Lord's Prayer and Bible Reading

| | Evangelical Protestant | | Mainline Protestant | |
	1998	2004	1998	2004
Approve	29.7	13.4	41.5	41.2
Disapprove	68.1	84.3	54.1	55.6
Don't know	2.2	2.3	4.4	3.2
Total	100.0	100.0	100.0	100.0

Source: 1998 and 2004 General Social Survey, N = 727 (1998); 298 (2004).

respondents their opinion of the U.S. Supreme Court's ruling that no state or local government may require the reading of the Lord's Prayer or Bible verses in public schools. The responses suggest that conservative Christian leadership has strong backing from evangelical Protestants, over two-thirds of whom registered disapproval. In addition, more than 50 percent of mainline Protestant respondents also disagreed with the Court's decision. Religious groups' public objections to more recent Supreme Court decisions, such as the *Santa Fe Independent School District v. Doe* (2000) ruling prohibiting organized prayer at public school sporting events, may help to explain the increased disapproval of the Supreme Court on the school prayer issue.

Holding an opinion on an issue does not necessarily spur action in support of that opinion. One of the main objectives of religious right organizations has been to activate evangelical Protestants politically. Accordingly, General Social Survey reports were examined to determine the extent to which evangelicals

Table 4.16
Religious Preference and Marital Status (Percentage)

	Evangelical Protestant		Mainline Protestant	
	1998	2004	1998	2004
Married	48.3	53.0	50.6	56.6
Widowed	11.0	10.2	15.7	9.1
Divorced	17.2	13.4	15.9	14.1
Separated	3.3	4.7	1.7	2.3
Never married	20.2	18.7	16.1	17.9
Total	100.0	100.0	100.0	100.0

Source: 1998 and 2004 General Social Survey, N = 1,113 (1998); 927 (2004).

participate in the electoral process. Given sampling error and assuming that overreporting of voter turnout applies equally to each group, evangelical voting levels (63 percent voting) compare favorably with mainline Protestants (69 percent voting) for the 2004 presidential election (http://pewforum.org/docs/index.php?DocID=64). Inasmuch as evangelical Protestants traditionally have tended to remain aloof from the political arena, recent findings on voter turnout suggest that the efforts of religious right organizations have been successful in getting growing numbers of the faithful to the polls.

Potential for Success

Survey results indicate that Americans hold religion to be an important part of their lives. For more than forty years the Gallup organization has asked Americans, "How important would you say religion is in your own life—very important, fairly important, or not very important?" The percentage of those interviewed who responded that religion is either "very" or "fairly" important remains consistently high, falling in the 84–88 percent range from 1992 through 2006 (http://www.galluppoll.com/content/?ci=16908&pg=1). The preceding discussion suggests that, with a few exceptions, large proportions of evangelical Protestants hold conservative views on many social and moral issues consistent with the religious right.

Although these findings bode well for the religious right, disclosing the possibility of directing American politics away from perceived secular trends, one should be wary of hasty conclusions. Many students of the religious right have serious doubts about the movement's ability to impose its influence more widely on what they perceive to be an essentially secularized American society. Some limited evidence for this reservation can be found in survey results on marital status, as found in Table 4.16. Evangelical Protestants appear to be as susceptible to the pressures of contemporary life as are mainline Protestants. In a fundamental area of moral life and "family values," no significant differences are evident between evangelical and mainline Protestants with regard to the percentage in each group reporting being divorced. The moral failings of such religious right leaders as Jim Bakker and Jimmy Swaggart, and more recently Ted Haggard, add to the perception that contemporary American culture presents temptations that are not always easily resisted.

Responses to questions dealing with abortion, summarized in Table 4.14, indicate the willingness of both evangelical and mainline Protestants to acknowledge situations in which abortion appears to be a reasonable alternative, despite efforts of religious right organizations to invoke biblical mandates against the practice.

These observations suggest that contemporary social conditions may be deeply at odds with certain of the goals of the religious right. Social changes resulting from the improving economic status of women and advancing technology (such as the RU-486 abortion pill and the "morning after" pill) make possible what previously would have been unthinkable. And such changes, when combined with the presupposed value of individual choice that underpins classical liberal ideology, permit a freedom often at odds with the "traditional values" that the religious right advocates. To attempt to limit such developments can be compared with trying to put the proverbial genie back in the bottle. Nonetheless, we recognize the genuine concern of those evangelical Christians who wish to achieve what they perceive to be a better world for themselves and their children. Therefore, we expect the religious right to remain active, but not necessarily to consistently achieve major victories in the American political arena. Although religious belief can inform political activity, religion and politics are inherently different forms of activity that, when commingled, can each have a detrimental effect on the other.

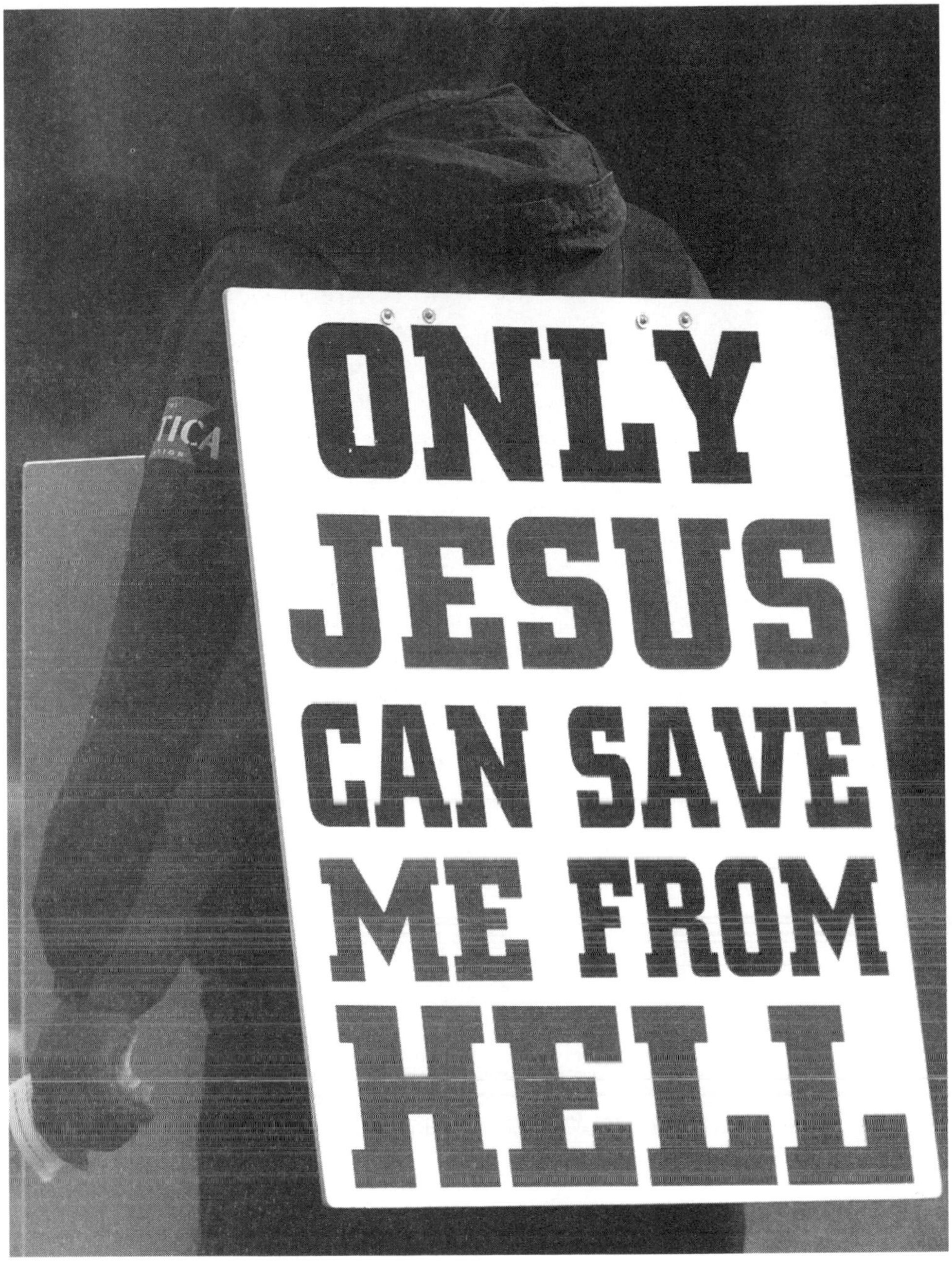
ONLY
JESUS
CAN SAVE
ME FROM
HELL

5

Primary Documents & Quotations

Religious Right Views

Commentary on the Religious Right

Two criteria were used to select the following primary documents and quotations. First, selections are included dealing with issues that throughout the twentieth century and into the twenty-first have drawn the attention of conservative Christians. Such issues as abortion, restricting prayer in the public schools, the teaching of the theory of evolution, and the call for same-gender marriage have appalled many fundamentalist Christians and energized them to political action. This first section—**Religious Right Views**—begins below.

Second, we have included selections from many prominent leaders in the religious right, including Jerry Falwell, James Dobson, and Tim LaHaye, who have expressed these concerns publicly in order to mobilize their constituency and gain the attention of the general public. In addition to expressing outrage at political and cultural trends, religious right spokespersons have advocated various measures, including permitting the teaching of 'intelligent design' in the public schools as an alternative to the theory of evolution, imposing greater restrictions on abortion, and ratifying constitutional amendments at the state and national levels defining marriage as a union between one man and one woman. Characteristic of interest group politics in a pluralistic society, the religious right has not gone unchallenged. Therefore, in addition to documents representative of religious right positions, we have included responses from those providing analyses of, and critical commentary on, religious right beliefs, activities, and leaders. This second section—**Commentary on the Religious Right**—begins on page 202.

Both sections include various categories, from *Antiabortion* to *Foreign Policy*; see Table of Contents on previous page. Within each category, quotations appear first, followed by articles. No quotation is necessarily representative of all religious right leaders or of religious commentators and critics of the religious right.

I.   Religious Right Views

America's Christian Heritage

The Constitution, as far as we're concerned, is a Christian document.

> —Gary Jarmin, *Christian Century* (April 16, 1980)

You find that anytime America was on its knees, both our economy and our security and our spiritual temperature rose at the same time, and whenever we got off our knees all three have deteriorated.

> —Robert J. Billings, *Christian Century* (October 8, 1980)

The critical issue of our day is the relationship of Christ and His Word to our political and legal system in the United States. Who has jurisdiction over every aspect of American society, Jesus Christ or the State? Is this to be a Christian nation or a humanistic nation? The only faithful answer that a Bible-believing Christian can give is this: "Blessed is the nation whose God is the LORD"

(Psalm 33:12). "For the LORD is our judge, the LORD is our lawgiver, the LORD is our king; He will save us" (Isaiah 33:22).

—Gary DeMar, *God and Government: A Biblical and Historical Study* (1982)

Today my belief in the dream that is America is stronger than it has ever been. But I am also convinced that the American dream is at risk. It is at risk for families who must spend more and more hours working just to make ends meet. It is at risk for children who grow up without fathers. It is at risk for a generation of young people trapped in a system of public education that neither challenges their minds nor sharpens their character. It is at risk for the unborn, the aged, and the infirm. And it is at risk for millions of Americans trapped in poverty unable to find hope, uncertain about finding opportunity.

—Randy Tate, Statement on becoming executive director of the Christian Coalition (August 1997)

I believe our nation was chosen by God and commissioned by history to be a model of justice and inclusion and diversity without division.

—Governor George W. Bush, speaking to the Simon Wiesenthal Center Museum for Tolerance (March 2000)

The Founders . . . knew the nation would grow ever more diverse; in Virginia, Thomas Jefferson's bill for religious freedom was "meant to comprehend, within the mantle of its protection, the Jew and the Gentile, the Christian and the Mahometan, the Hindoo and infidel of every denomination." And thank God—or, if you choose, thank the Founders—that it did indeed.

—Jon Meacham, *American Gospel* (2006)

HOLDING THE LINE

By Dr. D. G. Hart

American Protestantism split in two during the 1920s and has not been the same since. In denominational controversies, especially among Presbyterians and Baptists, and in courtroom debates over teaching evolution in public schools, the once unified front of mainline Protestantism, a constituency that included Congregationalists, Presbyterians, Episcopalians, Baptists, Methodists, Disciples, with some Lutherans on the fringes, divided into evangelical and liberal halves. Not until the 1940s, with the formation of the National Association of Evangelicals, would the more conservative side achieve the institutional coherence that characterized the mainline through the Federal Council of Churches (which in 1951 became the National Council of Churches). Still, ever since the 1920s the shorthand way of distinguishing evangelical from mainline Protestants has been the standard way of making sense of American Protestantism. For that reason it is possible to say that the fundamentalist-modernist controversy has not ended.

Yet, as important as the division in American Protestantism was and still is, the so-called "two-party" paradigm of evangelical vs. mainline Protestants is also misleading. The debates that divided Protestants during the 1920s were real and built upon developments within the Protestant denominations extending back to the decade just after the Civil War. But the tendency to lump conservatives and liberals into competing camps since the 1920s also obscures as much as it clarifies. A more accurate assessment is to recognize at least four different Protestant groups: denominational conservatives, conservative evangelicals, moderate evangelicals, and liberal Protestants.

These different voices drew upon different conceptions of the church and its chief tasks, as well as diverse estimates of the role Christianity should play in American public life.

American Protestantism United

In most histories of American Protestantism, the fundamentalist-modernist controversy stemmed from a constellation of intellectual novelties that arose in the second half of the nineteenth century, beginning with Charles Darwin's *Origin of Species* (1859). Not only did Darwin's understanding of natural selection undermine God's role in creation and providence, but new approaches to the study of ancient texts also raised doubts about the divine character of the Bible. If Darwin's study of the various mechanisms of nature that might account for the variety of species seemed to make God unnecessary for the beginning and preservation of the natural world, so too did the examination of the Bible's literary and historical qualities tend to play down the necessity of

D.G. Hart, the author of many books on religious studies, is director of honors programs and faculty development at the Intercollegiate Studies Institute in Wilmington, Delaware.

This article is reprinted with permission from *Tabletalk Magazine*, March 2006.

divine inspiration for the composition of Scripture. In both cases, the problems raised by evolutionary theory and by higher criticism, which emphasized the natural, or human, aspects of human and biblical origins, meant that the divine contribution either to creation or the inspiration of the Bible became marginal or even doubtful. Instead of God creating man and woman by divine fiat, and instead of the Holy Spirit inspiring the prophets and apostles to write the canonical texts, the new scholarship in biology and biblical studies taught that science could explain the uniqueness of man or the Bible on grounds that were observable or quantifiable—as any good science did.

These intellectual challenges, aided and abetted by new academic institutions such as the research university and graduate programs that generated specialized scholarship, were important factors that would eventually pull Protestants into rival camps. On the one side, the modernists attempted to accommodate the new science so that the churches would not look like obstacles to progress and the advance of knowledge. As cowardly as this motive might seem, it also sprang genuinely from a desire to defend Christian truth. The way modernists embraced the new ideas was to downplay the supernatural and miraculous aspects of Christianity as matters that were peripheral to the faith's ethical and spiritual core. In effect, modernists attempted to naturalize Christianity so that it would not conflict with the new science and the social progress it appeared to beckon. On the other side, fundamentalists dug in their heels (rightly so) on the supernatural and miraculous character of Christianity and especially the person and work of Christ. Practically any list of the so-called fundamentals, the list of essential doctrines from which fundamentalists took their name, featured the virgin birth, miraculous deeds, vicarious death, and resurrection of Christ, along with affirmations of the inerrancy of the Bible because of its divine authorship, as well as the miraculous nature of regeneration or the new birth. It is not an overstatement to say that the new science drove Protestants into natural and supernatural camps, with only a few such as Princeton Seminary's Benjamin B. Warfield trying to hold on to the importance of both the human and the divine components of the Bible, as well as the divine and natural qualities of creation. For most Protestants, the human-divine continuum was a zero-sum game with either the one or the other side taking all winnings.

Still, despite the obvious theological disagreements that the new scholarship provoked, the fundamentalist-modernist controversy did not occur in the 1870s or 1880s but had to wait almost another half-century until the 1920s. The timing of the conflict, consequently, requires any historical explanation to take into account factors other than the ideas and doctrines that would divide liberal and conservative Protestants. Here the rise of Protestant ecumenism is key, as a dynamic that postponed the most heated disagreements and eventually polarized Protestants into even bolder antagonism.

Soon after the Civil War, a number of Protestant leaders created and promoted organizations that were designed to draw the denominations into greater cooperation and unanimity. One was the Evangelical Alliance, an agency founded in London in 1846 and that gained in 1867 an American branch. Within a decade, Presbyterians had created the Presbyterian Alliance, an organization started in 1877 to include those Reformed denominations that balked at the theological inclusiveness of the Evangelical Alliance. The latter and broader agency enlisted Reformed, Arminian, and Baptist denominations and individuals into a cooperative venture designed to unite Protestants against the multitude of "isms" that were threatening the Christian character of the United States—namely, materialism, atheism, Roman Catholicism, the violation of the Christian Sabbath, the consumption of alcoholic beverages, and various other social ills that posed dangers to the Christian family. A reiteration of Roman Catholic vigor, first in the pope's Syllabus of Errors (1864) and second in the First Vatican Council (1869–1870), which asserted papal infallibility, and then with the increasing number of Roman Catholic immigrants in America's cities, alarmed Protestants into feeling that the religious influences that had contributed to the United States' political institutions and stable culture were under siege. Denominational leaders especially hoped that forming a united Protestant front against the apparent unity of Rome was crucial to protecting America's Christian way of life. The Presbyterian Alliance was designed to involve in this show of Protestant strength those Reformed denominations with second thoughts about joining an association like the Evangelical Alliance that consisted of denominations that were neither Calvinistic in doctrine nor Presbyterian in church government.

The motivation that led American Protestants to create and join these cooperative ventures helped to minimize the intellectual disagreements that were becoming increasingly apparent as the new scholarship dominated colleges, universities, and seminaries. The most notable achievement of Protestant ecumenism between the Civil War and World War I was the Federal Council of Churches, founded in 1908 as a federation of the largest Protestant denominations with the mission of building ties that would insure Protestants were working together rather than at cross purposes. The Federal Council, however, was not the end of these ecumenical impulses. Just after World War I, a time in which the denominations cooperated extensively to provide spiritual and physical assistance to the soldiers in Europe and to rally support for the war among church members at home, Protestant leaders unveiled plans for an "organic" union of those same denominations who were members of the Federal Council. Although the plan failed, its design was a "united" Protestant Church in the United States that would join all of its member denominations under a larger and more generic Protestant umbrella to carry on the work of the church and to promote the goal of Christianizing the nation. From 1870 to 1920, then, at the same time that Darwinism and higher criticism were dividing Protestants into competing theological camps, a drive for Protestant unity was also at work to keep those rivalries together within the same denominations and interdenominational agencies.

The Tie That Divides

During the 1920s both the ecumenical and intellectual dynamics of American Protestants teamed up not to cancel each other out, as they had for almost a half century, but to make the differences between liberal and conservative Protestants even more glaring. The modernist-fundamentalist controversy proceeded along two fronts, first in denominational skirmishes and second along cultural antagonisms. Many of the Protestant denominations experienced these conflicts in varying degrees, from Episcopalians to Methodists. For the sake of greater specificity the case of northern Presbyterians, the Presbyterian Church U.S.A., will help to illuminate how these developments in American Protestantism played out in the life of one denomination.

The theological controversy within the Presbyterian Church went through three phases. The first ran from roughly 1922 to 1925 and involved conservatives opposing the bold expressions of liberal Protestantism. In 1922, Harry Emerson Fosdick preached what was in effect the opening shot in the controversy with his provocative sermon, "Shall the Fundamentalists Win?" The liberal Baptist, who was stated supply at New York's First Presbyterian Church, accused fundamentalists of intolerance and called their essential doctrines, such as inerrancy and premillennialism, minor matters in the scope of world events. The Presbytery in New York also added to the conservative alarm when it ordained two men who would not affirm the virgin birth. Conservatives believed that these were ample signs of liberalism infecting the church, and they tried to discipline the Presbyterians in New York. But in several successive General Assemblies, the denomination showed no willingness to be divisive and chose instead administrative solutions that were designed to lessen the tensions. One of these measures involved a study committee whose report blamed conservatives for the contentiousness in the church, and it called for all sides, especially conservatives, to stop their public criticisms of liberals. The drive for unity had supplanted a concern for correct doctrine.

Administrative solutions to the controversy also characterized the second phase of the Presbyterian controversy. Here the warning to conservatives that they should cease their opposition played out directly at Princeton Seminary, the school where the leading conservatives, such as J. Gresham Machen, taught. Between 1927 and 1929 the General Assembly appointed a committee whose task it was to explore the nature of antagonisms at Princeton. The committee eventually recommended a reorganization of the school that took the conservative majority on the board and turned it into a minority. At that point, Machen left Princeton to found Westminster Theological Seminary in Philadelphia because he believed the school had been forced to toe the party line of church unity, which in turn meant the avoidance of any significant disagreement.

The last phase of the Presbyterian controversy was unexpected and again involved an administrative effort to preserve unity at the expense of theological clarity. In 1932, an interdenominational report on foreign missions, called "Re-Thinking Missions," exposed a serious weakness in the witness of the Presbyterian Board of Foreign Missions, which was one of the agencies sponsoring the study. The report found that the old motive for missions, namely, salvation from sin and death, was gone, and that a new rationale needed to be found, one that involved cooperation with other religions in the civilization of non-Western nations and peoples. Again, conservatives tried to apply some discipline to the officials in charge but also failed. In response, Machen established an independent agency for foreign missions. The Presbyterian hierarchy ruled that this independent institution was unconstitutional and ordered that Machen's presbytery bring him to trial. In 1935 he and several other board members of the independent missions agency were convicted, and in 1936 they lost their appeal, which led them to form a new Presbyterian denomination, the Orthodox Presbyterian Church.

What stands out in the denominational part of the fundamentalist controversy is that the ecumenical drive that had dominated Protestant agencies since 1870 had cultivated an organizational ethos that made theological disagreement anathema. In effect, Protestants, as the Presbyterian example makes clear, never had a real chance to hear or debate the new ideas that were being taught or critiqued in the seminaries because of the need to avoid problems that might divide the churches organizationally. Some conservatives were able to make their concerns known, and did so in response to outright provocation by liberals. But when conservatives did criticize, they were branded as divisive and unloving, if not deceitful. The slogan of the era fittingly was "doctrine divides, ministry unites." With that mindset, the answer to Fosdick's question, "Shall the fundamentalists win?," was virtually inevitable. It was emphatically, "NO!"

The other front in the fundamentalist-modernist controversy was cultural, and its chief exhibit was the Scopes Trial, a highly orchestrated event in Dayton, Tennessee, that did little to reveal the Bible's teaching about creation, Darwin's understanding of evolution, or the way American democracy might legitimately handle different points of view in public institutions. As much as William Jennings Bryan, the best-known Presbyterian layman of the era, saw the trial as an opportunity to vindicate the Bible and the people's belief in the good book, folks in Dayton saw it as a chance to put a small struggling town on the map, while the leaders of the American Civil Liberties Union saw the trial as the moment to expose the backwardness of fundamentalist beliefs. Although John T. Scopes, the biology teacher charged with violating state law, was convicted and fined $100, the real loser at Dayton was Bryan who within a few days of the trial died, thus adding ignominy to the humiliation of being ridiculed in court and by the press.

Why Two Parties Won't Work

The Scopes Trial was actually several steps removed from the Presbyterian controversy, even though Bryan was a Presbyterian and even though he invited Machen to testify in Dayton (which he declined). Because the churches and school boards and legislatures were fighting over religion at the same time, observers then, and academics since, have lumped the two conflicts together to comprise the fundamentalist-modernist controversy. But in fact, closer inspection of the Scopes Trial and church disputes like the Presbyterian controversy reveal that the issues were actually different and that the opposition to liberalism, whether theological or cultural, reflected a diverse set of convictions.

Bryan and Machen, for instance, though opposed to liberalism, did so for different reasons. For Bryan, liberalism was threatening Christian civilization in the United States, hence the need to expurgate evolution from the public schools. But Bryan gave little support to the efforts that Machen initiated in the Presbyterian Church. As Machen explained in his most popular book, *Christianity and Liberalism* (1923), the real cause for alarm in the church was not how God created or in what way Christ would return, as important as these teachings might be. Something far more basic was at stake, namely, the doctrines of sin and grace. As compelling as Machen's argument was, it not only failed to persuade fundamentalists like Bryan but it alienated evangelicals like Machen's colleague at Princeton Charles Erdman who was a professor of practical theology, devotee of Dwight L. Moody, and a premillennialist. Although an evangelical, Erdman did believe that liberals should be tolerated in the church as part of an expression of Christian unity and charity. For this reason, merely to call the disputes of the 1920s a "fundamentalist-modernist" controversy, as if there were clearly one modernist outlook and one fundamentalist outlook, is to miss the substantial disagreements among conservatives, the real issues at stake in the contest, and even why the churches avoided grappling with those issues.

Still, the point here is more than simply a call for greater historical accuracy. Instead, it is to try to learn from the past and understand the threat that liberalism posed to the church and why her response was inadequate. Liberalism was a valiant but misguided effort to preserve the influence of Christianity within American culture at a time when science and new scholarship threatened to render the Christian faith implausible. But to maintain Christianity's intellectual respectability, liberals also gutted the faith of what was both most offensive and most essential, namely, the person and work of Christ. Some conservatives tried to hold on to their positions within the mainline churches in order to continue to use those institutional resources on behalf of the Gospel. Others hoped to establish rival institutions to the mainline churches that would retain both the essential teachings of Christianity and the historic influence of Protestantism on the American nation. Still, others recognized that a choice needed to be made between the Gospel and the culture because of the inherent tension between the folly of the cross and the wisdom of the world.

What was at stake in the fundamentalist-modernist controversy was not the secularization of America but the secularization of the church. During the 1920s and 1930s, Protestants faced a choice between retaining either the status of the church or the message of the Gospel. This is a decision that has confronted the church in every age. But in the particular instance of the fundamentalist-modernist controversy, the choices made continue to affect America's Protestants.

Antiabortion

Beliefs have no credibility when unaccompanied by sacrifice. We must stubbornly refuse to remain silent in the face of the holocaust of God's unborn children. Not all of us in the church will be called upon by our Lord to do the same thing in the same way. All of us can, however, be supportive of sacrificial intervention that gives credibility to our words. This must involve much more than peaceful civil disobedience at abortion clinics to save the lives of unborn children. But surely it can include it.

—Randy C. Alcorn, Is *Rescuing Right?* (1990)

What we must change is not our message, but our behavior. Babies are dying whose lives could be saved if pro-life advocates were equipped to argue their case persuasively. We can win if we force abortion advocates to defend killing babies. The battle over partial-birth abortion indicates this.

—Scott Klusendorf, "The Vanishing Pro-Life Apologist: Putting the 'Life' Back into the Abortion Debate," *Christian Research Journal* (vol. 22, no. 1, 1999)

Each of us, exquisitely knitted together, is an irreplaceable gift made in the image of God. We are called to see Christ in the faces of other human beings, including those the "common sense" of our society does not see as human, or as completely human. Seeing Christ in the faces of others as they stand smiling before us is easy, but we need to see him, as Mother Teresa did, in an Untouchable covered in filth and flies and in a handful of undifferentiated human cells. Even when a person cannot recognize his own humanity he suffers from a mental illness or is in a comatose state, the image of God remains for us to see.

—C. T. Maier, "Killing for Kindness," *Touchstone* (October 2005)

Anticommunism

For not only is this loss of reinforcing faith in the cement of our morals a weakness in itself of immense significance, but like all of our weaknesses it has been pounced upon by the Communists, and used and made worse by them with great skill and determination for their own purposes. . . . The Communists are able to use this lack of moral stamina among their enemies in a thousand ways to make their own progress easier and the conquest of those enemies more rapid.

—Robert Welch, *The Blue Book of the John Birch Society* (1961)

Make no mistake about it. The Communists are winning. Hitler died; Nazism died with him. Mussolini died; Fascism died with him. Tojo died; Japanese militarism died with him. Stalin is dead; COMMUNISM LIVES ON. Lenin is dead; COMMUNISM LIVES ON. Why? Because Communism is a satanic weapon more powerful than the atom bomb, hydrogen bomb, cobalt bomb, or all of them combined, to bring about the seven-year Tribulation Period in which the whole world will worship Satan and his son, the anti-Christ, who will be the leader of a godless world government, and his religious counter-part, the "false prophet," the false Messiah.

—Billy James Hargis, *Communist America: Must It Be?* (1986)

Emerging from its lair of godless materialism, dressed in garments of science, Communism seduces the young and utilizes their perverted religious enthusiasm to conquer the world. Building on the doctrines of godless materialism, Communism has completely reversed the meaning of our basic moral terms. When we, in our ignorance of this fact, insist on interpreting their phraseology as if they believed the Christian philosophy from which we have derived our basic concepts, we aid and abet them in their program for our conquest and destruction.

—Fred C. Schwarz, "Love: Communist Style," *The Schwarz Report* (December 1999)

Biblical Inerrancy

No one, as far as I know, holds that the English translation of the Bible is absolutely infallible and inerrant. The doctrine held by many is that the Scriptures *as originally given* were absolutely infallible and inerrant, and that our English translation is a *substantially accurate* rendering of the Scriptures as originally given. We do not possess the original manuscripts of the Bible. These original manuscripts were copied many times with great care and exactness, but naturally some errors crept into the copies that were made. We now possess so many good copies that by comparing one with another, we can tell with great precision just what the original text was. Indeed, for all practical purposes the original text is now settled. There is not one important doctrine that hangs upon any doubtful reading of the text.

—Reuben A. Torrey, *Difficulties and Alleged Errors and Contradictions in the Bible* (1907)

If Paul is wrong in this factual statement about Eve's coming from Adam [1 Cor. 11:8], there is no reason to have certainty in the authority of any New Testament factual statement, including the factual statement that Christ rose physically from the dead.

—Francis A. Schaeffer, *No Final Conflict: The Bible without Error in All That It Affirms* (1975)

Being wholly and verbally God-given, Scripture is without error or fault in all its teaching, no less in what it states about God's acts in creation, about the events of world history, and about its own literary origins under God, than in its witness to God's saving grace in individual lives. . . . This authority of Scripture is inescapably impaired if this total divine inerrancy is in any way limited or disregarded, or made relative to a view of truth contrary to the Bible's own; and such lapses bring serious loss to both the individual and the Church.

—Chicago Statement on Biblical Inerrancy, Norman L. Geisler, ed., *Inerrancy* (1979)

I'm an inerrantist. I believe in the word of God. I'm just not mad about it.

—Frank Page, South Carolina pastor elected president of the Southern Baptist Convention over the hand-picked candidates of the fundamentalists, *Baptist Standard* (June 26, 2006)

Compassionate Conservatism

I've described myself as a compassionate conservative, because I am convinced a conservative philosophy is a compassionate philosophy that frees individuals to achieve their highest potential. It is conservative to cut taxes and compassionate to give people more money to spend. It is conservative to insist upon local control of schools and high standards and results; it is compassionate to make sure every child learns to read and no one is left behind. It is conservative to reform the welfare system by insisting on work; it is compassionate to free people from dependency on government. It is conservative to reform the juvenile justice code to insist on consequences for bad behavior; it is compassionate to recognize that discipline and love go hand in hand.

—Texas Governor George W. Bush, in an address at the Austin Convention Center (March 7, 1999)

Compassionate conservatism is neither an easy slogan nor one immune from vehement attack. It is a full-fledged program with a carefully considered philosophy. It will face in the twenty-first century not easy acceptance but dug-in opposition. It will have to cross a river of suspicion concerning the role of religion in American society. It will have to get past numerous ideological machine-gun nests. Only political courage will enable compassionate conservatism to carry the day and transform America.

—Marvin Olasky, *Compassionate Conservatism* (2000

The "compassionate conservative" candidate for public office wants you to see him as a person who wants to cut your taxes while at the same time raising your benefits. "Compassion" speaks to the benefits, "conservative" to the taxes, and in all the confusion we forget that we're talking about only one pile of money. Place your bets on "compassion" not on "conservative," and remember, they're compassionate with your money.

—R. C. Sproul, Foreword to James R. White, *The Potter's Freedom* (2000)

Culture and the Culture War

If you look at the cultural war that's going on, most of what those who disagree with us represent leads to death—abortion, euthanasia, promiscuity in heterosexuality, promiscuity in homosexuality, legalization of drugs. There are only two choices. It really is that clear. It's either God's way, or it is the way of social disintegration.

—James Dobson, *U.S. News & World Report* (May 4, 1998)

Liberalism agrees with Satan.... The God of the Bible does not have good intentions for us, Satan said, and liberals agree. The God of the Bible is against premarital sex, against homosexual behavior, against the lust for money, against the things human beings want to do. The God of the Bible, they say, is a bad God, a false God. This is what all the "mainstream churches" today teach. It is the viewpoint of most social and political liberals, who hate the so-called "Christian Right" because they hate the teaching of the Bible. For them, the God of the Bible is an evil god.

—James B. Jordan, "Hath God Said?" *Tabletalk* (August 2000)

Liberalism has ... become a rival faith to traditional religion, because contemporary liberalism cannot tolerate any view of life more ultimate than its own, or any wisdom that might call into question the wisdom of the liberal state. Indeed, as some liberals forthrightly admit, religion's claims to ultimacy are precisely what make it dangerous, since citizens should not be "distracted" from their political tasks. Although quick to condemn what it regards as immoral, liberalism does not sit easily with a belief in sin, since positing a deeply flawed human nature calls into question the very possibility of social engineering, of the achievement of any kind of earthly utopia.

—James Hitchcock, "Political Orphans," *Touchstone* (April 2003)

The courts say no creationism, no prayer in public schools. Humanism and evolution can be taught, but everything I believe is disallowed.

—Roger Moran, Southern Baptist advocate of home schooling, quoted in the *Beaumont Enterprise* (September 3, 2006)

I am a deceiver and a liar. There's a part of my life that is so repulsive and dark that I have been warring against it for all of my adult life.... The accusations that have been leveled against me are not all true, but enough of them are true that I have been appropriately and lovingly removed from the ministry.

—Ted Haggard, president of the National Association of Evangelicals. Letter of resignation to his Colorado Springs, Colorado, congregation (2006)

The culture war is not of our choosing. We did not seek it or declare it. We really only wanted to be left alone to live by our patrimony in the normal human way. Many of us are even reluctant to admit that it is a concerted aggression and not just a series of accidental collisions. So we have been retreating steadily, and many of our troops have been routed or gone over to the enemy.

Perhaps we should remind ourselves of what we ought to be defending: a culture, which is the sum of the life of a community and which contains all that is human. Its most important parts are the most intangible. What is threatened with destruction is the American form (however attenuated) of the substantive and positive side of what was once called Western civilization.

—George Garrett, "Hollywood Blues," *Touchstone* (July 2006)

Economics and Capitalism

When men are taught that the capitalist system is rigged against them, that they have a legal and moral right to welfare payments, and that those who live well as a result of their own labor, effort, and forecasting skills are immoral and owe the bulk of their wealth to the poor, we must recognize the source of these teachings: the pits of hell.

—Gary North, *The Sinai Strategy: Economics and the Ten Commandments* (1986)

The Bible promotes free enterprise. The book of Proverbs and the parables of our Lord clearly promote private property ownership and the principles of capitalism. We therefore are strong free-enterprisers.

—Jerry Falwell, *Houston Chronicle* (April 5, 1987)

Work is the heart and soul, the cornerstone of Biblical charity. In fact, much of the outworking of Biblical charity is little more than a subfunction of the doctrine of work. Its operating resources are the fruit of work: the tithe, hospitality, private initiative, and voluntary relief. Its basic methodologies are rooted in the work-ethic: gleaning, training, lending, and facilitating. Its primary objectives revolve around a comprehension of the goodness of work: productivity, rehabilitation, and entrepreneurial effort.

—George Grant, *Bringing in the Sheaves: Transforming Poverty into Productivity* (1988)

Education

When a student reads in a math book that there are no absolutes, every value he's been taught is destroyed. And the next thing you know, the student turns to crime and drugs. . . .

Crime, violence, immorality and illiteracy . . . the seeds of decadence are being taught universally in schools.

—Mel and Norma Gabler, *Texas Monthly* (November 1982)

It's not surprising that Harry [Potter] has suddenly soared to the peaks of popularity in schools across the country. His story fits right into the international program for multicultural education. . . . The envisioned global community calls for a common set of values that excludes traditional beliefs as intolerant and narrow—just as the Harry Potter books show. . . .

The biblical God simply doesn't fit into his world of wizards, witches, and other gods.

—Billy James Hargis, "Bestseller Harry Potter Teaches Wrong Lessons," *Christian Crusade Newsletter* (January 2001)

The popularity of Harry Potter is evidence that our dull, materialistic educational system is starving children's imaginations. The main problem with the Potter series is its positive spin on "witchcraft," though the series also retains elements of good fantasy.... The best antidote for Christian families to the negative effects of fantasy is to ground their children in positive literature and, above all, in the wonders of the Word of God.

—Gene Edward Veith, "Good Fantasy and Bad Fantasy," *Christian Research Journal* (vol. 23, no. 1, 2001)

The infusion of an atheistic, amoral, evolutionary, socialistic, one-world, anti-American system of education in our public schools has indeed become such that if it had been done by an enemy, it would be considered an act of war.

—D. James Kennedy, pastor of the Coral Ridge Presbyterian Church, Fort Lauderdale, Florida, quoted in the *Beaumont Enterprise* (September 3, 2006)

End Times

I'm going to tell you with zeal and enthusiasm and passion Jesus is coming on the clouds of glory to call us home.... Now, ladies and gentlemen, I want you to know, if you've read the "Left Behind" books, [but] more importantly, if you've read the Bible, you know ... that Christ is coming, and we believe that that day is very, very near.

—Gary Frazier, founder of the Texas-based Discovery Ministries, Inc., quoted in *Vanity Fair* (December 2005)

Environmentalism

We really need to address the burning of fossil fuels. If we are contributing to the destruction of the planet, we need to do [something] about it.

—Pat Robertson, *700 Club* (2006)

Here we go again! A "core group" of "influential" evangelical leaders is about to try to address "global warming" using political weapons.

Like previous efforts—Prohibition in the 1920s and the Moral Majority with which I was associated in the 1980s—this one is doomed because it distracts and dilutes the primary calling of evangelicals.

Do evangelicals have time on their hands because they've finished the mission to "go and make disciples of all nations"? Is this not a great enough commission that "global warming" and a host of other "issues" must be added to make evangelicals contemporary and relevant?

—Cal Thomas, opposing the new environmental thrust of some evangelicals, "Evangelical Distraction," *Beaumont Enterprise* (March 20, 2005)

If evangelicals make the environment another cause, they likely will be as frustrated and disappointed as when they exercised misplaced faith in politics to cure other social evils.

—Cal Thomas (2006)

Evolution, Creationism, and Intelligent Design

Perhaps the most difficult doctrine which evolution has yet to reconcile to religion is the position that man, by the supposition that he evolved into a higher organism from a man-like ape (or ape-like man), is no more than a specialized primate. The implication, of course, is that all physical, intellectual and social traits in man can be observed in a rudimental state in apes. While there are some who speak of the social behavior of apes; the human-like mannerisms of dogs; the intelligence of chimpanzees, dolphins, or whales; true religion teaches that man is a unique being in all creation.

—Dean R. Zimmerman, *Evolution: A Golden Calf* (1976)

Darwinism is a theory of empirical science only at the level of microevolution, where it provides a framework for explaining phenomena such as the diversity that arises when small populations become reproductively isolated from the main body of the species. As a general theory of biological creation Darwinism is not empirical at all. Rather, it is a necessary implication of a philosophical doctrine called scientific naturalism, which is based on the nonscientific assumption that God was always absent from the realm of nature. Evolution in the Darwinian sense is inherently antithetical to theism, although evolution in some entirely different and nonnaturalistic sense could conceivably (if not demonstrably) have been God's chosen method of creation.

—Phillip E. Johnson, "What Is Darwinism?" *Christian Research Journal* (July–August 1997)

Perhaps the principal way the Discovery Institute contributes to the ID [Intelligent Design] community is to support research and writing at pressure points in a variety of natural sciences: those places in nature where the evidence for design is strongest and the case for materialism is weakest. Why must such research be supported by a private organization? Because of the unfortunate hangover from nineteenth-century materialism, much of the scientific establishment rejects out of hand proposals that seek to consider the viability of intelligent design.

—Jay W. Richards, "Reality and Reluctant Science," *Touchstone* (July/August 2004)

If anxiety over the challenge from Intelligent Design motivates Harvard's scientists to recognize the flaws in their arguments and thus to support their position by making genuine discoveries rather than by relying upon intimidation and *a priori* assumptions, we should get credit for a major contribution to science.

—Phillip E. Johnson, "From Soup to Science," *Touchstone* (April 2006)

A PREMILLENNIAL PORTRAIT OF MODERN AMERICA

By Paul Boyer

For an American to plow through the hundreds of popular prophecy books published since 1945 is an unsettling experience. From these works emerges a picture of a nation mired in wickedness and trembling on the brink of chaos— a nation whose destiny is as grim as it is certain.

While some writers found specific biblical allusions to the United States, most relied on general scriptural discussions of the end times, such as Jesus' preview of mankind's final stage, recorded in the Gospel of Luke:

> As it was in the days of Noe, so shall it be also in the days of the Son of
> man.
> They did eat, they drank, they married wives, they were given in marriage,
> until the day that Noe entered into the ark, and the flood came, and de-
> stroyed them all.
> Likewise also as it was in the days of Lot; they did eat, they drank, they
> bought, and they sold, they planted, they builded;
> But the same day that Lot went out of Sodom it rained fire and brim stone
> from heaven, and destroyed them all.
> Even thus shall it be in the day when the Son of man is revealed.

In the version of this sermon in the Gospel of Matthew, Jesus explicitly instructs believers to observe social trends carefully for signs of the end and concludes somberly: "Therefore be ye also ready: for in such an hour as ye think not the Son of man cometh."[15] Passages such as these sent prophecy writers back to the accounts in Genesis of Noah's Flood and the destruction of Sodom and Gomorrah—periods of wickedness, impiety, sensual indulgence, and sexual immorality distressingly similar, they contended, to conditions in contemporary America.

Wilbur Smith in 1949 found a mirror of postwar American society in the catalog of end-time evils set forth in II Timothy:

> In the last days perilous times shall come.
> For men shall be lovers of their own selves, covetous, boasters, proud, blas-
> phemers, disobedient to parents, unthankful, unholy.
> Without natural affection, trucebreakers, false accusers, incontinent, fierce,
> despisers of those that are good,
> Traitors, heady, highminded, lovers of pleasures more than lovers of God;
> Having a form of godliness, but denying the power thereof: from such turn
> away.

Paul Boyer, a U.S. cultural and intellectual historian, specializing in American religious history, prophetic and apocalyptic belief, and First Amendment issues, is Merle Curti Professor of History Emeritus at the University of Wisconsin-Madison.

> For of this sort are they which creep into houses, and lead captive silly
> women laden with sins, led away with divers lusts,
> Ever learning, and never able to come to the knowledge of the truth.[16]

In their comments on the United States, prophecy writers also invoked the destruction of wicked Babylon foretold in Revelation and elsewhere in the Bible. A 1979 prophecy work drew a detailed comparison between modern America and Babylon: like the ancient kingdom on the Euphrates, the United States too possessed great military power, boasted of its "technical, scientific" achievements, sheltered an "apostate world church movement" (the World Council of Churches), and encouraged "loose morals and defiance of God's laws" worldwide through its movies and TV programs. Clearly, the authors concluded, America would have "a prominent role in preparing the world for the last Babylonian system."[17] Building on these and other biblical descriptions of end-time wickedness, writers constructed their profile of a nation far gone in evil and debauchery.

Doleful recitals of human sinfulness as evidence of the last days have, of course, long been a staple of prophecy writing. In 250 A.D., Cyprian, Tertullian's successor as bishop of Carthage, wrote:

> Who cannot see that the world is already in its decline, and no longer has the strength and vigor of former times? There is no need to invoke Scripture authority to prove it. The world tells its own tale and in its general decadence bears adequate witness that it is approaching its end... There is less innocence in the courts, less justice in the judges, less concord between friends, less artistic sincerity, less moral strictness.[18]

Martin Luther preached that conditions in early-sixteenth-century Germany (including the "commercial operations" that were "encircling and swallowing up the world") precisely matched Jesus' description of the end times, and concluded that "the day of judgment is not far off." In 1756, concluding a series of sermons on the end-time signs (including earthquakes), Jonathan Mayhew of Massachusetts wrote, "There has probably been no age or period of the world, wherein events have more nearly corresponded to this prophetic description, than the present."[19] Despite the formulaic nature of prophecy writers' jeremiads, the particular themes emphasized in different time periods can be instructive. In making their case for the imminence of the Rapture, post-World War II premillennialists singled out those features of contemporary American life they found especially unsettling.

The rising tide of sexual immorality rolled across many, many pages. Arno Gaebelein in the 1930s had noted the alarming increase in condom sales, and postwar prophecy writers endlessly deplored similar evidence of rampant sexuality. Tim LaHaye warned in 1972 of "an avalanche of pornographic filth." Wrote Jack Van Impe in 1979: "Swingers are the rage of the day. They get together for a supper bash and end up exchanging their mates for a night of glorified orgies. How low can humans go?" Sex magazines and X-rated movies are everywhere, he went on; "savages are roaming the streets raping and sodomizing victims"—a reminder that "earth's goriest, blood-soaked hour" would soon strike.[20]

Abortion figured prominently among the end-time signs in prophecy writing of the 1970s and 1980s. "In addition to the killing of people on our streets," observed a 1988 author, "we now tolerate the most terrible of all crimes—the murder of the unborn ... The blood of innocent children is on the hands of an unrepentant generation. Can judgment be far behind?" Venereal disease, genital herpes, and AIDS made their successive appearance as evidences of sexual decay.[21]

Warnings of moral collapse led naturally to discussions of popular music. In *The Days of Noah*, a 1963 prophecy work, M. R. DeHaan found jazz, swing, and "tin-pan tabulations which defy all effort at description" so full of "squeaks and squawks and empty groans and baby talk and monkey moans [that] we read of people going almost completely crazy under [their] spell." The rise of rock and roll provided a rich field for such criticism. Backward masking, the process by which rock groups allegedly recorded lewd and blasphemous messages and then inserted them backward in their songs, particularly fascinated prophecy writers, relating as it did not only to their concerns about raging immorality, but also to [an] obsession with conspiracies.[22]

The changing status of women offered further evidence of social disintegration. Muted in the domestic 1950s, this theme surfaced frequently thereafter as women sought careers and a revived feminist movement captured public attention. DeHaan linked the rising divorce rate and other signs of moral breakdown to "women leaving their homes and children to enter factories and shops and offices." A 1981 writer blamed TV's portrayal of "weak fathers [and] dominant mothers" for the spread of secular humanism. The proposed Equal Rights Amendment, he went on, reflected the false belief "that mere men and women can decide what is good and evil without regard to divine directives." Mourned the pentecostal prophecy speaker Roy Hicks, "Homes and marriages are no longer considered sacred ... women take to the streets to strike for equality with men, even if it means going to war and fighting to show their equality." The true aim of the women's movement, agreed Dave Hunt, was not equality but matriarchy—a demonic inversion of the God-ordained social order. James McKeever's *End-Times News Digest* in 1990 described the environmental movement and radical feminism as a twin-pronged plot to revive witchcraft and displace Father God with Mother Nature.[23]

The so-called New Age movement, with its interest in meditation, Eastern religions, and a vaguely pantheistic harmony with nature, preoccupied post-1970 prophecy writers as well. Dave Hunt devoted an entire book to *The New Age Movement in Prophecy*. He speculated that this movement in its many guises—the Montessori system, Waldorf schools, Freudianism, Indian gurus, the human potential movement, secular humanism, biofeedback, radical feminism, planetary consciousness—could be "part of a cosmic conspiracy to install the Antichrist." When the end comes, he said, "millions of New Agers in thousands of network groups around the world will be sincerely implementing Antichrist's programs in the name of peace, brotherhood, and love." Prophecy writers cited a 1972 *Time* cover story on Satanism, astrology, and other occult fads as confirmation that the last days were at hand.[24]

Quoting scriptures that foretell an end-time upsurge in "unnatural affections," prophecy writers reacted vehemently to the greater openness of homosexuality in post-1970 U.S. culture. Citing the rising tide of "sodomy, homosexuality and Lesbianism," Boston evangelical leader Harold John Ockenga declared at the 1971 Jerusalem prophecy conference: "Between 1965 and 1970 the moral dam gave way and. .. the resulting flood has played havoc with civilization. . . Certain groups could hardly go any lower; they meet every day one of the many details predicted for the last days of this age." The reason God destroyed Sodom, Wilbur Smith reminded the same gathering, "was nothing else but homosexuality." Many writers cited a cryptic phrase in the Book of Daniel describing the coming Evil One ("Neither shall he regard ... the desire of women") to argue that Antichrist himself will be homosexual.[25]

The most gripping images of America as Sodom appeared in the much-reprinted prophecy books of the Assemblies of God evangelist David Wilkerson. In contrast to most prophecy interpreters, Wilkerson in *The Vision* reported verbatim communications from God foretelling a coming "moral landslide" of "nudity, perversion, and a flood of filth." Television networks will show barebreasted women; churches will feature nude dancing; "wild, roving mobs of homosexual men" will attack unsuspecting victims openly on the streets.[26] Wilkerson, now speaking in his own voice, returned to the fray in *Set the Trumpet to Thy Mouth* (1985) with a long recital of all-pervasive wickedness

> God is going to judge America for its violence, its crimes, its backslidings, its murdering of millions of babies, its flaunting of homosexuality and sadomasochism, its corruption, its drunkenness and drug abuse, its form of godliness without power, its lukewarmness toward Christ, its rampant divorce and adultery, its lewd pornography, its child molestation, its cheatings, its robbings, its dirty movies, and its occult practices ... America today is one great holocaust party, with millions drunk, high, shaking their fist at God, daring him to send the bombs.[27]

While early-nineteenth-century commentators had viewed America's prosperity as confirmation of God's favor, post-1945 premillennialists saw the nation's wealth and consumer abundance as yet another ominous end-time sign. The same America fighting godless communism abroad "denies God and glories in materialism" at home, declared a speaker at a 1961 prophecy conference. Rich America was concerned about cars, college, cottages, and crabgrass, not about conversion," proclaimed an alliterative writer in 1970. The nation's "comfortable, affluent, high standard of living," he went on, enabled Satan "to lull people into spiritual insensitivity." Tim LaHaye in *The Beginning of the End* (1972) saw the rise of "monumental fortunes" and the proliferation of "the pleasure-seeking rich" as evidence of America's approaching doom.[28]

The more favorable the economic indicators, prophecy writers suggested, the more ominous the eschatological meaning. Indeed, although most popularizers foresaw an economic collapse just before Antichrist's rise, a few anticipated an end-time economic boom. "A careful examination of the Biblical description of the 'last days,'" concluded a 1983 writer, revealed that an interval of "unprecedented peace and prosperity" would lead directly to the final holocaust. The last days would see unparalleled affluence and "a mad round of materialism and pleasure seeking," agreed the authors of *Prosperity in the End Time*. Sodom, they noted, basked in great wealth just before its incineration. The computer boom, the knowledge explosion, and military spending fueled by the prophesied end-time wars would all contribute to the feverish prosperity of America's final days. Rising income and a surging Gross National Product all too easily diverted attention from the truly important: "Hypnotized by affluence, the world continues its binge of eating and drinking, buying and selling, planting and building, as it did in the days of Noah and Lot ... But God's prophetic clock keeps ticking."[29]

While nineteenth-century writers of a postmillennial bent had praised *education* as a counterweight to immorality and apostasy, postWorld War II expositors typically treated the schools as part of the problem, not part of the solution. Wilbur Smith in 1949 saw America's "Godless, Bibleless, Christless secular education" as clearing the path for Antichrist, and similar fears eddied through scores of subsequent prophecy works. Many writers, quoting a prophecy in Daniel that "knowledge shall be increased" in the last days, treated educational advances as simply another end-time portent.[30]

On this point, the prophecy popularizers reinforced fundamentalism's broader indictment of contemporary education. Salem Kirban's prophecy novel *666* included the following Tribulation-era exchange between a young woman and her father:

> "Dad, when did religion start falling apart? I mean, when did people start turning away from Christ and developing their own theology?"
>
> "That's a hard question to answer, Faye," George replied. "Some say it started in the late 1800s and in the early 1900s. Perhaps the most marked change occurred way back in 1968–69 almost coinciding with the then-famous campus revolts."[31]

Tim LaHaye, prophecy writer, TV evangelist, and later head of the Washington-based American Coalition for Traditional Values, offered a particularly alarming survey of U.S. education. The younger generation—"the confused 'Age of Aquarius'"—he wrote, was falling prey to the "scoffers" and sophisticated unbelievers "on the faculties of tax-supported colleges." He went on, "The most intellectually trained members of our culture," in propagating "Darwinism and evolution, Marxism and socialism, Freudianism and liberalism," had spawned "the most lawless generation of young people in all of history." When divine judgment falls on Russia, LaHaye declared, the consuming fire would also seek out Moscow's U.S. sympathizers, including "the

Communists on the university campus." In ferreting out subversives in the classroom and elsewhere, he declared, "the F.B.I. may someday get help from an unexpected source—Almighty God."[32]

America's vaunted scientific accomplishments further deepened prophecy expositors' sense of spreading apostasy. Ray Stedman offered a typical formulation of the premillennialist view: "The day is coming, Jesus says, when the triumph of the scientific method, as we know it today, will bring man to confirm himself in the deadly delusion that he is his own god, and does not need any other." Advocates of solving society's problems through "the scientific methods of observation, experiment, and logic," he said, were peddling the same false message of human self-sufficiency. And Stedman's reading of prophecy told him that the problem would only worsen: "Doubtless a mad science, like the Sorcerer's Apprentice, will go blithely on, mixing evil potions and conjuring up still more fearful forces of uncontrollable, murderous power."[33]

Prophecy writers saw in modern science mankind's most recent effort to become as gods—the boast of Antichrist. With advances in fields from nuclear weaponry to gene control, wrote Roy Hicks, soon "there will be nothing that man cannot do unless God stops him." Confronted with "surging human brilliance . . . , God [will] have to take action."[34]

Prophecy popularizers subjected America's technological prowess to the same scathing analysis. While employing every technological means available to disseminate their message, from videocassettes to communications satellites to computerized high-speed printing presses, they saw technology's prophetic significance as wholly ominous. Television, predictably, they portrayed as corrosive of morality and a prelude to Antichrist's global thought control. David Wilkerson's apocalyptic discussion of TV—"that speaking idol"—offered in intensified form a theme common to scores of prophecy works: "Satan has taken full possession of secular television . . . Demonic principalities and powers are now in full control . . . , including the horrible erotic commercials . . . Television . . . is the mouth of hell, swallowing multitudes of our precious children."[35]

Supersonic air travel, the interstate highway system, and other transportation advances simply confirmed Daniel's prophecy that in the last days "many shall run to and fro." The space program reminded Jack Van Impe of Jeremiah's prophecy that "though Babylon should mount up to heaven," its destruction was sure. The planting of a U.S. flag on the moon, he added, fullfilled Jesus' words that the last days would see "signs in the sun, and in the moon." M. R. DeHaan, discussing *Coming Events in Prophecy* in 1962 as the National Aeronautics and Space Administration rushed to put an American on the moon, dismissed the space race as "open defiance of God's plan" as plainly conveyed in Psalm 115: "The heaven, even the heavens, are the Lord's: but the earth hath he given to the children of men." Generalizing from this example, DeHaan drove home the familiar premillennial argument:

After centuries and millenniums of our flaunted civilization, and boasting of human progress, with its advance in education and reform, [and] scientific evolution, the heart of man has not been improved one bit ... The more educated a sinner is, the more dangerous he becomes ... Nowhere in the entire Bible is there a single verse to support the contention that this world will become better and better until at last by the efforts of man in the field of education, science, and the preaching of a watered-down, social "gospel," man will finally learn his lesson and the age will climax in a great worldwide revival, and then wars will be abolished, and the nations live in peace. *No! No!* My friend, the Bible knows nothing of such a program! Instead the Bible teaches without exception that the world will grow worse and worse.[36]

Such themes, of course, had preoccupied evangelical writers for centuries. New England's Puritan ministers had perfected the jeremiad, with its stylized lamentations about the spread of immorality and irreligion. But for these late-twentieth-century prophecy writers, the nation's wickedness and apostasy functioned as signs of the endtime moral collapse foretold in Scripture. Events and trends rich in prophetic meaning abounded; one had only to identify and interpret them. As Ray Stedman put it, "If we could learn to read life rightly, almost everything is a sign." No hint of moral declension escaped the notice of these devout semiologists. A 1947 writer discussed that year's New York City newspaper strike as one of the "Unmistakable Signs of Our Times." A 1982 author cited the rise in overdue library books as one of many evidences of the approaching end.[37]

These authors described America's apostasy regretfully, conceding that things had once been very different. In some early postwar prophecy writings, the longing for the soaring civic millennialism that had nearly vanished from cultural discourse the sense of the magnitude of the nation's betrayal of its once-bright promise-became almost palpable.[38] John Walvoord, discussing "America in Prophecy" at the height of the Vietnam War, offered a somber view of the nation's past, present, and future:

History has many records of great nations which have risen to unusual power and influence only to decline because of internal corruption or international complications. It may well be that the United States of America is today at the zenith of its power much as Babylon was in the sixth century B. C. prior to its sudden downfall at the hands of the Medes and Persians ... God has offered unusual benefits to the United States both in a material and religious way, but they have been used with such profligacy that ultimate divine judgment may be expected.[39]

During the troubled 1970s, as Watergate, the Vietnam War's bitter finale, and successive energy crises jolted the nation, a sense of divine displeasure obsessed prophecy writers. The United States had "fallen away into a quagmire of wickedness and lasciviousness, immorality and debauchery, deceitfulness and false religions," observed Charles Taylor in *The Destiny of America*, and for this it must suffer. "Perhaps no nation in history has had a greater opportunity than America to realize a social and political utopia, if such were attainable," wrote Merrill Unger in 1973. Lyndon Johnson's early years as president had propelled this lofty effort to "a grand crescendo," Unger added, but despite Johnson's attempts to achieve a Great Society, human wickedness had reasserted itself, as the Bible said it would. Another 1970s popularizer made the point aphoristically: "America has ceased to be good—she will cease to be great."[40]

Despite their political activism in the 1980s, prophecy writers felt a deepened sense of national decline in these years. America faced a "clear and imminent danger," Hal Lindsey warned in 1981: "THE CRISIS OF INTERNAL DECAY." Although its "foundations and roots were anchored in God and the Bible," agreed Jack Van Impe in 1983, "America ... is on the decline, and may soon suffer horrendous judgment."[41]

This cosmic drama of a once-favored but now-apostate people hurtling to ruin became almost hypnotic in its repetition. "God ... set [America] in a good land and blessed its founding fathers," wrote David Wilkerson in 1985; "but evil has become so great, disobedience so widespread, God has declared, 'I will pluck it up, pull it down, destroy it, as it seemeth good to me.'" John Walvoord, reflecting in 1989 on America's prophetic role, reiterated the views he had taught for decades: the nation had once figured importantly in God's plan as a sponsor of missionary endeavor and friend of the Jews; indeed, this role explained its years of power, prosperity, and well-being. But the century's end saw conditions growing steadily worse; after the Rapture, with all Christian influence removed, the United States will "go down like a stone."[42]

Pat Robertson grappled throughout the 1980s with the issue of America's prophetic destiny. *The Secret Kingdom* (1982), ostensibly a work of postmillennial optimism proclaiming the right of believers to assert "dominion" over the earth, opened with a brief chapter that encapsulated the bleaker premillennialist view of American history. Robertson described an evening when he had stood near Cape Henry, where the James River and Chesapeake Bay join the Atlantic, reflecting on the piety of Virginia's first English colonists, who had planted a cross in the sand and dedicated the land to God. From these beginnings "grew the most prosperous nation in humanity's history. Unparalleled freedom and creativity burst upon the earth." But then Robertson's reverie, like that of Nick Carraway at the end of F. Scott Fitzgerald's *Great Gatsby*, darkened:

> As I surveyed that historical site and looked eastward at the Atlantic beneath that dazzling moon, I was gripped by the renewed realization that a dread disease had fastened itself upon the lands sending forth our forefathers. As I turned westward toward my car, my mind's eye swept across the huge country that lay before me. And I mourned more deeply because the same sickness was fastening itself upon my land, the new world so sincerely dedicated to God three hundred and seventy-five years ago.[43]

Robertson elaborated this interpretive schema—pious beginnings followed by a long decline—in two documents of 1986: his book *America's Dates with*

Destiny and the manifesto that launched his 1988 presidential campaign, "A New Vision for America." As Stephen O'Leary and M. W. McFarland have observed, Robertson in these works offered a *Heilsgeschichte*, or salvation-history, of America, in which discovery and settlement, Declaration of Independence, Revolution, and Constitution all function as sacred events and texts.[44]

But, as in the Puritan jeremiads on which these works are patterned, Robertson balanced his vision of America's divine origins with a recital of its fall. Offering a familiar catalog of sins, from drug addiction to sexual immorality, he pinpointed one source of the infection—the public schools:

> We have permitted during the past twenty-five years an assault on our faith and values that would have been unthinkable to past generations of Americans. We have taken virtually all mention of God from our classrooms and textbooks ... We have taken the Holy Bible from our young and replaced it with the thoughts of Charles Darwin, Karl Marx, Sigmund Freud, and John Dewey.[45]

As one might expect of a prophecy expounder turned presidential candidate, particularly one with a basically hopeful and activist temperament, Robertson ended his *Heilsgeschichte* on an upbeat note. If Americans would only once again choose virtuous leaders—himself, for example the downward spiral could be reversed and divine favor regained.[46] But few prophecy popularizers embraced Robertson's politicized postmillennialism. They shared his sense of America's decline into apostasy and wickedness, but not his hope of restoration this side of the Second Coming.

Expressions such as those we have quoted from Graham, Van Impe, LaHaye, and Walvoord—as well as Robertson in his darker moods—could be multiplied many times over from the works of contemporary popularizers. Their verdict on late-twentieth-century America, though full of sorrow and regret, was harsh: the nation had fallen into apostasy and grievous sin, and the situation was worsening with every passing hour. The judgment was all the more implacable because postwar America stood in such tragic contrast to the spiritual promise and millennial hope it had once embodied. As Walvoord observed in 1967, "The question no longer is whether America deserves judgment, but rather why divine judgment has been so long withheld from a nation which has enjoyed so much of God's bounty."[47]

References

15. Luke 17:26–30; Matt. 24:44.

16. Wilbur M. Smith, "The Cruelty of Modern Man," *Sunday School Times*, 91 (Feb. 5, 1949), 107–108; II Tim. 3:1–7.

17. David Webber and Noah Hutchings, *Is This the Last Century?* (Nashville, Thomas Nelson Publishers, 1979), pp. 115–118; Rev. 18 (quoted passage Rev. 18:2). See also Jack Van Impe, *11: 59 and Counting* (Royal Oak, Mich., Jack Van Impe Ministries, 1983), p. 161 (America as the "political Babylon"); David Wilkerson, *Set the Trumpet to Thy Mouth* (Lindale, Tex., World Challenge, 1985), p. 3.

18. Cyprian quoted in Jacques Lacarriere, *Men Possessed by God: The Story of the Desert Monks of Ancient Christendom*, tr. Roy Monkcom (Garden City, N.Y., Doubleday and Co., 1964); excerpt reprinted in William Griffin, ed., *Endtime: The Doomsday Catalog* (New York, Collier Books, 1979), p. 54.

19. Martin Luther quoted in Wilbur M. Smith, "Signs of the Second Advent of Christ," in Carl F. H. Henry, ed., *Prophecy in the Making* (Carol Stream, Ill., Creation House, 1971), pp. 190–191; Jonathan Mayhew, *Practical Discourses Delivered on Occasion of the Earthquakes in November 1755* (Boston, 1760), pp. 369–370, quoted in Ruth H. Block, *Visionary Republic: Millennial Themes in American Thought, 1756–1800* (Cambridge, Cambridge University Press, 1985), p. 35.

20. Gaebelein, *As It Was So It Shall Be*, p. 152; Tim LaHaye, *The Beginning of the End* (Wheaton, Ill., Tyndale House Publishers, 1972), p. 128; Jack Van Impe, *Signs of the Times* (Royal Oak, Mich., Jack Van Impe Ministries, 1979), pp. 30, 31, 32.

21. David Hocking, *The Coming World Leader: Understanding the Book of Revelation* (Portland, Oreg., Multnomah Press, 1988), p. 167.

22. M. R. DeHaan, *The Days of Noah* (Grand Rapids, Zondervan Publishing Co., 1963), pp. 46–47; Van Impe, *11: 59 and Counting*, pp. 42–44 (backward masking); Jacob Aranza, *Backward Masking Unveiled*, advertised in David Webber and Noah Hutchings, *Computers and the Beast of Revelation* (Shreveport, La., Huntington House, 1986), back page.

23. DeHaan, *Days of Noah*, p. 43; William R. Goetz, *Apocalypse Next: Updated* (Cathedral City, Calif., Horizon House Publishers, 1981), p. 279; Roy Hicks, *Another Look at the Rapture* (Tulsa, Harrison House, 1982), pp. 18–19; Dave Hunt, *Peace, Prosperity, and the Coming Holocaust: The New Age Movement in Prophecy* (Eugene, Oreg., Harvest House Publishers, 1983), p. 69; James McKeever, "Father God and Mother Nature," *End-Times News Digest* (Omega Ministries, Medford, Oreg.), June 1990, p. 7.

24. *Hunt, Peace, Prosperity, and the Coming Holocaust*, pp. 35 (quoted passage), 52, 68, 80, 108, 122, 145, 180, 198, 232 (quoted passage); James Montgomery Boice, *The Last and Future World* (Grand Rapids, Zondervan Publishing Co., 1974), p. 77; *Time*, June 19, 1972.

25. Harold John Ockenga, "Fulfilled and Unfulfilled Prophecies," in Henry, *Prophecy in the Making*, pp. 305, 306; Boice, *Last and Future World*, p. 54; Dan. 11:37. See also Smith, "Signs of the Second Advent of Christ," p. 200.

26. David Wilkerson, *The Vision* (New York, Pyramid Books, 1974), pp. 43, 44, 50, 79.

27. Idem, *Set the Trumpet to Thy Mouth* (Lindale, Tex., World Challenge, 1985), pp. 1–2, 20–21. Wilkerson gained fame in evangelical and pentecostal circles with *The Cross and the Switchblade* (1963) on his work with New York City street gangs. By the 1970s, says David Edwin Harrell, Jr., "no man's voice carried more authority in the charismatic revival" Harrell, *All Things Are Possible: The Healing and Charismatic Revivals in Modern America* (Bloomington, Indiana University Press, 1975), pp. 186–187.

28. J. Vernon McGee, "The Crisis of This Present Hour," in *The Prophetic Word in Crisis Days* (Findlay, Ohio, Dunham Publishing Co., 1961), p. 39; Robert Glenn Gromacki, *Are These the Last Days?* (Schaumburg, Ill., Regular Baptist Press, 1970), pp. 64, 65; LaHaye, *Beginning of the End*, p. 89. See also Hal Lindsey, *The 1980s: Countdown to Armageddon* (New York, Bantam Books, 1981), p. 142.

29. Hunt, *Peace, Prosperity, and the Coming Holocaust*, p. 18, Roger Campbell and David Campbell, *Prosperity in the End Time* (Fort Washington, Pa., Christian Literature Crusade, 1983), p. 67 (quoted passage), 70, 73, 81, 94 (quoted passage).

30. Wilbur M. Smith, "The Exclusion of God and the Exaltation of Man in Education," *Sunday School Times*, 91 (Jan. 15, 1949), 43; Dan. 12:4. See also Campbell and Campbell, *Prosperity in the End Time*, p. 79; Goetz, *Apocalypse Next: Updated*, p. 263; M. R. DeHaan, *Coming Events in Prophecy* (Grand Rapids, Zondervan Publishing Co., 1962), p. 101.

31. Salem Kirban, *666* (Wheaton, Ill., Tyndale House Publishing Co., 1970), p. 248. See also Van Impe, *11:59 and Counting*, p. 150; Carl G. Johnson, *Prophecy Made Plain for Times like These* (Chicago, Moody Press, 1972), p. 47.

32. LaHaye, *Beginning of the End*, pp. 77, 107, 118, 136.

33. Ray C. Stedman, *What's This World Coming To?* (Ventura, Calif., Regal Books, 1986; orig. publ. 1970 as *What on Earth's Going to Happen?*), pp. 41, 42, 65.

34. Hicks, *Another Look at the Rapture*, pp. 16, 18. See also J. Barton Payne, *The Imminent Appearing of Christ* (Grand Rapids, Wm. B. Eerdman's Publishing Co., 1962), p. 160.

35. Wilkerson, *Set the Trumpet to Thy Mouth*, pp. 53, 55, 65.

36. Campbell and Campbell, *Prosperity in the End Time*, p. 79 ("many shall run to and fro"); Van Impe, *11:59 and Counting*, p. 165; Van Impe, *Signs of the Times*, p. 24; M. R. DeHaan, *Coming Events in Prophecy* (Grand Rapids, Zondervan Publishing Co., 1962), pp. 101, 108, 113 (quoted passages pp. 108, 113). The biblical passages quoted in this paragraph are from Dan. 12:4, Jer. 51:53, Luke 21:25, and Ps. 115:16.

37. Ray Stedman, *What on Earth's Going to Happen?* (Glendale, Calif., Regal Books, 1970), p. 44; William Ward Ayer, *What Goes On Here?* (Grand Rapids, Zondervan Publishing Co., 1947), p. 34; Paul Lee Tan, *Jesus Is Coming* (Rockville, Md., Assurance Publishers, 1982), p. 40. Cf. Mike Evans, *The Return* (Nashville, Thomas Nelson Publishing Co., 1986), p. 41: "Like enormous billboards beside the freeway, the dramatic prophecies of the Bible . . . cry out to us declaring that the days in which we live are the beginning of the end."

38. See, for example, Charles O. Benham, *101 Roadsigns to Our Next Pearl Harbor and to Armageddon* (Washington, D.C., National Forecast Magazine, 1945), p. 107; Ayer, *What Goes On Here?* pp. 68, 149.

39. John F. Walvoord, *The Nations in Prophecy* (Grand Rapids, Zondervan Publishing Co., 1967), reprinted in Walvoord, *The Nations, Israel, and the Church in Prophecy* (Grand Rapids, Zondervan Publishing Co., 1988), p. 174. See also Billy Graham, *World Aflame* (New York, Penguin Books, 1967; orig. publ. 1965), pp. 169, 192.

40. Charles R. Taylor, *The Destiny of America* (Van Nuys, Calif., TimeLight Books, 1972), p. 72; Merrill F. Unger, *Beyond the Crystal Ball* (Chicago, Moody Press, 1973), pp. 139–140; Carl Johnson, *Prophecy Made Plain for Times like These*, p. 39.

41. Lindsey, *The 1980s*, pp. 133, 141; Van Impe, *11:59 and Counting*, pp. 159–160. See also Hicks, *Another Look at the Rapture*, p. 18.

42. Wilkerson, *Set the Trumpet to Thy Mouth*, p. 18; author interview with John F. Walvoord, Aug. 8, 1989.

43. Pat Robertson, *The Secret Kingdom* (New York, Bantam Books, 1984; orig. publ. 1982), p. 14.

44. Idem, *America's Dates with Destiny* (Nashville, Thomas Nelson Publishers, 1986); idem, "A New Vision for America," Washington, D.C., address, Sept. 17, 1986; Stephen O'Leary and M. W. McFarland, "The Political Use of Mythic Discourse: Prophetic Interpretation in Pat Robertson's Presidential Campaign," *Quarterly Journal of Speech*, 75 (Nov. 1989), 433–452, esp. 438–449.

45. Robertson, *America's Dates with Destiny*, p. 444 (quoting "A New Vision for America").

46. Ibid., pp. 445–446.

47. Walvoord, *The Nations in Prophecy*, p. 174.

Foreign Policy

Southern Baptists overwhelmingly support Israel's right to live at peace with her neighbors within secure borders and they pray for the peace of Jerusalem to prevail in the Middle East.

> —Richard Land of the Southern Baptist Convention regarding Israel's invasion of Lebanon, quoted in the *Beaumont Enterprise* (August 12, 2006)

THE CHRISTIAN ZIONIST THREAT TO PEACE: Spend Your Vacation Fighting for Israel

By Aaron D. Wolf

In assessing the political conditions necessary to establish a lasting peace in Israel-Palestine, Americans are confronted with a theological question: Does the Bible insist that Christians take a certain view regarding the treatment of the Jewish people in particular, their presence in the Holy Land, or the placement of the borders of Israel?

One particular subset of American Christianity answers that question in the affirmative. Yes, they believe, the Bible does mandate that we treat the Jews—specifically, the Jews of Israel—not merely as another ethnic group of fallen (sinful) people, made in the image of God and in need of the Gospel, but as one that holds God's unique favor and is deserving of our full, unconditional support. This subset is made up largely of American evangelicals who are committed to something called dispensationalism. "The essence of Dispensationalism," according to Charles Ryrie, a dispensationalist theologian, "is the distinction between Israel and the Church. This grows out of [our] consistent employment of normal or plain interpretation, and it reflects an understanding of the basic purpose of God in all His dealings with mankind as that of glorifying Himself through salvation and other purposes as well."

The fruits of this "normal or plain interpretation" of the Bible have raised any number of red flags for conservative theologians of all Christian denominations. Of greater concern to us here, however, is the way in which many popular and powerful dispensationalist leaders apply their apocalyptic understanding of the place of the modern state of Israel on the stage of world history—the "other purposes" by which God must be glorified—in the form of "Christian Zionism."

When President Bush, himself an evangelical, proposed statehood for Palestine in his 2002 "Road Map," several key evangelical leaders denounced the plan, hinting that they would withdraw support for him if he failed to reconsider. According to their Christian Zionist understanding of dispensation-

Aaron D. Wolf, a church historian, is the associate editor of *Chronicles: A Magazine of American Culture*.

This article first appeared in the May 2005 issue of *Chronicles*. Reprinted with permission from the May 2005 issue of *Chronicles: A Magazine of American Culture*, a publication of The Rockford Institute in Rockford, Illinois.

alism, there simply cannot be a Palestinian state, because God has promised all of Eretz Israel to the Jews—forever. The borders of the state of Israel must extend, literally, to biblical proportions, including all of the land that is now in dispute—the West Bank, Gaza, the Golan Heights, and all of Jerusalem—and we must do everything in our power to make it so.

Addressing this way of thinking is essential to the success of any peace plan for the Middle East that involves the United States, because the sheer size of the umbrella group that we call evangelical—there are an estimated 65 million evangelicals in the United States—means that, in a democracy, their deeply held beliefs matter. (President Bush won the White House in November 2004 with fewer than 61 million votes.) Although, obviously, all 65 million evangelicals are not militant Christian Zionists, many are beholden to leaders who are unflinching supporters of the state of Israel and actively hostile toward the Palestinians. Paul Charles Merkley, author of Christian Attitudes Towards the State of Israel, conservatively estimates that Christian Zionists number in the "tens of millions."

The greatest source of Christian Zionist influence is found in the Christian media. Evangelical Christians are fed a steady diet of dispensationalist/Zionist interpretations of the news every day through the radio and television programs of Pat Robertson (CBN News, The 700 Club); Jerry Falwell (the Liberty Channel, which broadcasts, among other things, Zola Levitt Presents); John Hagee; Benny Hinn (This Is Your Day!); Kerby Anderson (Point of View); Jack Van Impe (Jack Van Impe Presents); and countless others, with audiences in the millions. Megachurches, which are virtual media centers, hold prophecy conferences all across America and invite rabbis to come and speak to Christians on Israeli history and politics. Perhaps most influential have been the best-selling books of the Left Behind series, by Timothy LaHaye and Jerry B. Jenkins. The 12-book series, offering a fictional account of the playing-out of dispensationalist interpretations of biblical prophecy, has enjoyed sales of over 62 million units, eclipsing Hal Lindsey's dispensationalist fantasy novel, The Late Great Planet Earth, the best-selling book of the 1970's.

The net effect of this constant barrage of media attention focused on Israel as the center of God's plan for the world is that Christians who may not be experts on the "70th Week of Daniel" or the "Four Horsemen of the Apocalypse" are nonetheless prone to accept any negative interpretation of the Palestinians and are favorable toward the fulminations of politicians and journalists who reject any right of return for Palestinians and the very idea of Palestinian statehood. It means that the neoconservatives and members of Likud who are eager to increase their own power and sphere of influence can easily find an audience willing to listen and organize at the grassroots level in support of their candidacies and policies. And it means that Israel-first politicians, Jewish resettlement groups (which bring tens of thousands of Jews from around the world to populate settlements in such hot zones as the West Bank), and far-right Israeli Zionist groups have an American cash cow eager to fund their efforts—efforts that war against any final-status settlement for peace.

Evangelicals are encouraged to lavish money on various pro-Israel groups, such as John Hagee's Exodus II, which has given over $3.7 million to finance the immigration of over 6,000 Russian Jews to Israel; or Rabbi Yechiel Eckstein's HaKeren Leyedidut, which has raised $100 million over the past eight years; or Pat Robertson's Bless Israel, in which Christians are asked to "show your support for Israel by blessing their [sic] economy." In addition, they are prodded to attend such spectacles as the Christian Coalition's "Christian Solidarity for Israel Rally" in Washington (2002) to hear speeches by Dick Armey, J.C. Watts, Tom DeLay, and Jerusalem Mayor Ehud Olmert and to sign pledges of total support for Ariel Sharon and his use of whatever means are necessary to defeat "terrorists."

Oftentimes, more moderate, mainstream evangelical groups give money and support to more radical Christian Zionist efforts. One group that enjoys the support of the Christian Coalition is the Battalion of Deborah, which conducted its "2005 Solidarity With Israel Tour" from February 20 to March 3. On February 23 to 24, paying guests enjoyed being "assigned to work at one of the Barak Brigade army bases." According to the promotional literature,

> The Barak Brigade is a tank unit in the Golan that serves along the Syrian border. Each participant will be issued an army uniform and assigned to work as a volunteer in tasks ranging from painting to oiling equipment and other important things in between ... but most of all loving and encouraging the young soldiers defending Israel.

Christian Zionist leaders are not shy about using a little muscle when it comes to playing hardball politics and have sometimes interfered in the peace process. In January 1998, for example, Israeli Prime Minister Benjamin Netanyahu embarked on a diplomatic mission to the United States to visit President Bill Clinton and Secretary of State Madeleine Albright. The Clinton administration intended to press Netanyahu to pursue a "credible withdrawal" of Israeli Defense Forces from the West Bank, to offer the Palestinian Authority some degree of limited autonomy, and to make greater efforts to comply with the Oslo accords. After Netanyahu's initial meeting with Albright, despite her statement to the media that the meeting went "extremely well," it was clear that Netanyahu would not budge on any of these issues. Yet President Clinton's frustration turned to outrage when, before meeting with him, Netanyahu attended a rally in Washington on Monday, January 19, of the Christian Zionist group Voices United for Israel, then held a private meeting with Jerry Falwell, Morris Chapman and Richard Lee (of the Southern Baptist Convention), and John Hagee (a San Antonio megachurch pastor). The purpose of both the rally and the closed-door meeting was, according to a New York Times report, to encourage Netanyahu to "oppose steps to give up any more land to the Palestinians." Falwell (who was, at the time, disseminating a video implicating President Clinton in the death of Vince Foster) made it clear to the prime minister that he could mobilize a substantial Republican voting bloc, the Christian Zionists, to counter any political fallout that might occur as a result of Netanyahu's refusal to negotiate. "There are about 200,000 evangelical pastors in America," said Falwell, "and we're asking them all through e-mail, faxes, letters, telephone, to go into their pulpits and use their influence in support of the state of Israel and the prime minister." The rally, cosponsored by Pat Robertson's and Ralph Reed's Christian Coalition and the National Religious Broadcasters, circumvented the peace process and sent a clear message to American evangelicals that only "liberals" (such as Bill Clinton) think that Israel should make land concessions in the quest for peace. Adding to this, President Clinton, after concluding his failed talks with Netanyahu, went on The Newshour With Jim Lehrer that very evening, as the Monica Lewinsky scandal was breaking, to deny that "there is a sexual relationship" and to describe his time with Netanyahu as "difficult."

The Republican Party, so heavily influenced by the neoconservatives, is happy to cultivate the dispensationalist evangelicals, both through promises of promoting their "moral values" and through tough talk about "terrorists"—where terrorist is often a synonym for Palestinian. A strange and perverse symbiosis exists between many politicians, who promise the moon to evangelicals, and popular evangelical leaders, who are so eager for access to the corridors of power that they are willing to compromise again and again on those "moral values" issues ("gay marriage," abortion, euthanasia) in order to stay in the loop.

America's evangelicals are, by and large, sincere in their commitment to what they believe the Bible teaches and think that those who deny their interpretation of Israel's place in the world and the land to which she is entitled are simply theological liberals who do not take the Bible seriously. In these troubled times, the last thing that Christians need to do is to stop taking the Bible seriously. However, in the absence of historic Christian teachings on the Last Days and biblical prophecy (so rarely confessed and taught by the traditional Christian denominations in America—Lutheran, Episcopalian, Roman Catholic, etc.), these Christians have come to believe that there is but one "literal" interpretation of the Bible when it comes to the land of Israel.

Some conservative evangelical intellectuals are bristling at the embarrassment that the efforts of the Christian Zionists provide them, opting for "progressive dispensationalism," which seeks to tone down the extreme obsession with Israel that characterizes Christian Zionism. Others are going a step further and renouncing dispensationalism altogether—while retaining a commitment to what is now called "historic premillennialism." Historic premillennialists do not radically divide Israel and the Church but emphasize continuity between the two Testaments, Old and New. Still others are embracing "covenant theology," a modern incarnation of the historic Christian eschatology embraced by some American Calvinists. Progressive dispensationalists, historic premillennialists, and covenant theologians engage in friendly debate and dialogue, reflecting their more balanced and academic approach to questions of biblical eschatology. This dialogue, however, seems to occur primarily among theologians and pastors and has not yet trickled down to the evangelical laity, who remain under the powerful influence of the Christian media.

If we are to remove the obstacle of Christian Zionism, we must encourage and support the efforts of those evangelical theologians who are earnestly seeking to reform evangelical eschatology in favor of a view that both takes the Bible seriously and places emphasis on the crucified and risen Christ (Who will, indeed, come again), not on the state of Israel. Furthermore, we must make every effort to expose the relationships among the Likud, the neoconservatives, and the Christian Zionist leadership and the cynical ways in which they seek to manipulate faithful evangelicals into supporting their secularist goals—goals that have nothing to do with the Gospel of Jesus Christ, from which evangelicals derive their name. Evangelicals must be brought to the conclusion that it is through the Church and the Gospel, not through the Republican Party, that God's purposes on earth are furthered. Today, with Christian Zionism exerting so significant an influence on 65 million Americans—and on politics and foreign affairs—such efforts are essential if we are to see a lasting peace in Israel-Palestine, something all Christians of good will should desire.

Homosexuality

Unless homosexuality be understood fundamentally as a transgression of God's Law, no further deliverance and recovery can be made. And not only must the Law of God be pressed upon the conscience, but God's forgiveness must also be offered. The repenting homosexual's only hope—his eternal security—is in the uncompromised message of the Scriptures.

—Charles McIlhenny, "Pointing the Way Home: A Pastor's Perspective," *Tabletalk* (March 1997)

The gay and lesbian agenda is gaining a head of steam across the nation. California and other states are in the process of establishing homosexuals as a bona fide minority, with all the privileges pertaining thereto. Minority status for homosexuals will guarantee them an equal place at the table with women, Hispanics and African-Americans in matters like affirmative action, job quotas, financial benefits for same-sex partners and much more. For the first time in American history, it appears we will soon be rewarding persons for their misbehavior. For Christian schools, churches and other ministries, tax-exempt status could eventually be denied to those who do not hire a quota of gays and lesbians as teachers, pastors and workers.

—Jerry Falwell, "My Open Letter to Mel White" (July 1999)

In our post-modern world if a word still carries the scent of goodness, all the baddies will claim it for their own. Thus the homosexual crowd lobbies for gay marriage, even though marriage has always been defined as a union between a man and a woman.

—R. C. Sproul, Foreword to James R. White, *The Potter's Freedom* (2000)

The notion that a same-sex marriage can carry out the function of procreation or replenishing the human race defies not only human logic but barnyard logic.

—Ken Blackwell, African American and Ohio Republican, *The New Yorker* (July 31, 2006)

Patriotism

We are not a perfect nation, but we are still a free nation because we have the blessings of God upon us. We must continue to follow in a path that will ensure that blessing. We must not forget that it is God Almighty who has made and preserved us as a nation.

—Jerry Falwell, *Listen, America!* (1980)

It's sad to think of the school children of the past who cringed at the thought of their flag touching the ground while being removed from the school flagpole. It's grim to remember the price paid for her raising at Iwo Jima. It's distressing to think of tears shed by wives and mothers who have seen her draped over the coffin of a loved one. But it's a marvel that no one has figured out why she can now be publicly burned. What further sign does God need give us as proof we have been conquered?

> —Pastor Pete Peters, *America Conquered* (1991)

Keep in mind that you have a Declaration of Independence that refers to God or the Creator four different times. You have sessions of Congress each day that begin with prayer. And, of course, if you look on our currency, it says "In God We Trust." So we believe the Pledge of Allegiance is an important right that ought to be upheld by the Supreme Court.

> —Scott McClellan, White House spokesman (quoted in the *Houston Chronicle*, October 15, 2003)

The reference to a "Nation under God" in the Pledge of Allegiance is an official and patriotic acknowledgment of what all students—Jewish, Christian, Muslim or atheist—may properly be taught in the public schools.

> —Solicitor General Theodore Olson in a brief filed on behalf of the federal government, quoted in the *Baptist Standard* (February 9, 2004)

Political Activism and Strategy

I realize that it is "popular" to be a born-again Christian. But for some strange reason it is "unpopular" to stand up and fight against the sins of our nation. Will you take a stand and help me Clean Up America? How would you answer these questions: Do you approve of pornographic and obscene classroom textbooks being used under the guise of sex education? Do you approve of the present laws legalizing abortion-on-demand that resulted in the murder of more than one million babies last year? Do you approve of the growing trend toward sex and violence replacing family-oriented programs on television? . . . If you are against these sins, then you are exactly the person I want on my team. I have put together a Clean Up America campaign that is going to shake this nation like it has never been shaken before. I cannot do it alone. Together we must awaken the moral conscience of our nation. The battle has just begun.

> —Jerry Falwell, quoted in Gerald Strober and Ruth Tomczak, *Aflame for God* (1979)

I had never actively solicited candidates for political office. Then, in the providence of God, I was subjected to a painful educational experience, when the church attempted to get a zoning variance passed by the city council. After three years of effort, we lost, 6 to 2. For the first time, I realized that men and women largely hostile to the church controlled our city.

> —Tim LaHaye, quoted in Kathleen C. Boone, *The Bible Tells Them So: The Discourse of Protestant Fundamentalism* (1980)

Friends, we are in real trouble right now, and it is time to take a stand and tell the authorities: "We can not and will not obey you when it means to surrender the lordship of Christ." Then we should be ready to defend ourselves in court and go to jail if necessary for our convictions. After all, we would be in pretty good company since much of the New Testament was penned in prison!

—Don Boys, *Christian Resistance: An Idea Whose Time Has Come—Again* (1985)

If the religious right is ever to accomplish its stated goal of returning our nation to moral sanity and spiritual stability, it must humbly but determinedly set its own course according to the wind of the Spirit of God. It must no longer be the pawn of powers and principalities, of godless men and institutions be they left or right. In short, the religious right must not compromise.

—George Grant, *The Changing of the Guard: Biblical Blueprints for Political Action* (1987)

Everyone wants to be in the "big time" politically. Everyone wants to run for governor. Let them. Meanwhile, we take over where today's politicians think that nothing important is happening. We should get our initial experience in ruling on a local level. We must prepare ourselves for a long-term political battle. We start out as privates and corporals, not colonels and generals. We do it God's way.

—Gary North, *Inherit the Earth: Biblical Blueprints for Economics* (1987)

You wait until the Sunday before the election and you distribute [moral report cards] all in one day. The election is held on Tuesday. Now why do we distribute them the Sunday before? It needs to be fresh in the voter's mind. Voters do not have a particularly long retention period. Number two, it does not give the liberal candidate that we're opposing time to go run back to all the churches screaming that he's not really that way, which is what they try to do if you give them a chance. Thirdly, when that liberal National Council of Churches minister stands in front of the pulpit and denounces the report card in the church service, it's too late because you've distributed it on Sunday, the election was held on Tuesday, and the minister denounces it the next Sunday, you see.

—Colonel Doner, quoted in Sara Diamond, *Spiritual Warfare: The Politics of the Christian Right* (1989)

The most urgent challenge for pro-family conservatives is to develop a broader issues agenda. The pro-family movement has limited its effectiveness by concentrating disproportionately on issues such as abortion and homosexuality. These are vital moral issues, and must remain an important part of the message. To win at the ballot box and in the court of public opinion, however, the pro-family movement must speak to the concerns of average voters in the areas of taxes, crime, government waste, health care, and financial security.

—Ralph Reed, "Casting a Wider Net," *Policy Review* (Summer 1993)

I guess it irritates me when people who know what is right put self-preservation and power ahead of moral principle. That is more offensive to me, in some ways, than what Bill Clinton does with interns at the White House.

—James Dobson, *U.S. News and World Report* (May 4, 1998), on his refusal to compromise for political gain.

You know, I had a drinking problem. Right now I should be in a bar in Texas, not the Oval Office. There is only one reason that I am in the Oval Office and not in a bar. I found faith. I found God. I am here because of the power of prayer.

—President George W. Bush, speaking to a group of clergymen visiting the White House shortly after his 2001 inauguration, quoted in *The New York Review* (November 6, 2003)

You can't find a values leader out there that is not disappointed, discouraged.

—Richard Viguerie, expressing the sentiment of many current Christian conservatives (2006)

Having witnessed the damage to the church's fundamental message of redemption from a too-close association with the 'kingdom of this world'—first in the liberal National Council of Churches ... and more recently with various conservative religious political movements—some evangelicals have decided to give it another go.

This time, the issue isn't abortion, gay rights or cleaning up offensive TV programs. They want to clean up the planet.

—Cal Thomas (2006)

I think there are lots and lots of young people, in their 20s to 40s, who are very impatient with older models of social engagement like those used by the religious right. They understand the importance of life issues and the family issues, but they know the concern for justice has to be broader and global. At least a good portion of the evangelical movement is looking for leaders who have a broader conception of social justice.

—Michael Gerson, former speech writer for President George W. Bush (2006)

There's a lot of discontentment [with the Republican party]. But unfortunately for most conservative evangelicals, there's no alternative.

—Marvin Olasky, quoted in the *Beaumont Enterprise* (October 30, 2006)

Republicans will find it increasingly difficult to appeal to the new evangelicals with tired symbols liked school prayer or the posting of the Ten Commandments.... These activists will expect serious proposals on an expanded moral agenda.... And they will not respond to a crude libertarianism that elevates the severe pleasures of cutting food stamps or foreign aid over the pursuit of the common good.

—Michael Gerson, *Newsweek* (November 13, 2006)

The White House showed the heartlessness of politics in Ted Haggard's fall. Haggard had once been welcomed at the White House, relied on to rally other evangelicals and invited to pray with the president.

Yet his downfall provoked only this reaction from a low-level White House spokesman: "He had been on a couple of calls, but was not a weekly participant in those calls. I believe he's been to the White House one or two times." To evangelicals who know that this statement was misleading, it was a revealing moment about the unchristian behavior politics inspires.

—David Kuo, author of *Tempting Faith, Houston Chronicle* (November 19, 2006)

Conservative Christians (like me) were promised that having an evangelical like Bush in office was a dream come true. Well, it wasn't. Not by a long shot. The administration accomplished little that evangelicals really cared about.

Nowhere was this clearer than on the issue of abortion. Despite strong Republican majorities, and his own pro-life stands, Bush settled for the largely symbolic partial-birth abortion restriction rather than pursuing more substantive change. Then there were the forgotten commitments to give faith-based charities the resources they needed to care for the poor. Evangelicals are not likely to fall for such promises in the future.

—David Kuo, *Houston Chronicle* (November 19, 2006)

VOTING AS CHRISTIANS

By Leon J. Podles

If a person is married, believes in God, goes to church, reads the Bible, and prays, chances are he will vote Republican—and he is a core member of the dreaded Religious Right. If a person is unmarried, never goes to church, never reads the Bible, and never prays, he will likely vote Democratic—and he belongs to the not-so-dreaded Secular Left. Certainly there are religious Democrats and irreligious Republicans, but according to the research of social scientists Louis Bolce and Gerald De Maio ("Our Secularist Democratic Party," *Public Interest*, Fall 2002), the Democratic Party has become the political home of unbelievers. (See Rod Dreher's article in this issue.)

Moreover, anti-Christian policies are far more entrenched in the Democratic Party than Christian policies are in the Republican. Republicans sometimes want to ignore abortion; Democrats want to promote it, and make it a litmus test. Despite their deep differences on other issues, all of the current Democratic presidential hopefuls made a pilgrimage to NARAL Pro-Choice America's "celebration" of the thirtieth anniversary of *Roe v. Wade* to testify to their commitment to abortion. The Democrats have reinstituted the constitutionally banned religious test for federal positions. If a judge is a faithful Catholic or Evangelical, the Democrats will likely try to block his appointment as a federal judge, for fear that it would reduce the accessibility of abortion.

Pro-abortion forces have a strong, probably unshakeable grip on the Democratic Party; pro-life forces have a weaker grip on the Republican Party. Voting Republican might or might not advance the protection of the unborn; voting Democratic will inevitably lead to the further entrenchment of abortion in American society, even if the Democrat is a pro-lifer who survived the abortionists' inquisitions.

Although the Democrats sometimes use libertarian language and claim they want to make abortion simply a matter between a women and her doctor, this is a lie. They want the government to fund abortion, to force insurers to cover abortion, to force Catholic hospitals to perform abortions, to prevent pro-life people from protesting abortion. The libertarian language cloaks a determination to use the government to forcibly "liberate" people from "oppressive and discriminatory" traditions, such as protecting the life of the unborn.

Marriage and religion are closely connected; procreation and a belief and trust in a Creator are closely allied. Those who reject the meaning that marriage, family, and traditional religion give to life suffer a void, which they try to fill by seeking meaning in politics. This was the curse of Europe in the twentieth century, as the false religions of Nazism and Communism captured state

Leon J. Podles, senior editor of *Touchstone: A Journal of Mere Christianity*, is the author of *The Church Impotent: The Feminization of Christianity* (Spence) and is at work on a new book, *Sinning Priests, Weak Bishops, and the Future of the Roman Catholic Church* (Spence).

after state. The new religion of liberation has its totalitarian aspect: It seeks to free man from his inherited prejudices (marriage, family, Christianity) through an activist state. This state, having created the void, then makes everyone dependent upon itself for meaning, at least for the only meaning it sees that life can hold: a perpetual liberation, a society that transgresses all boundaries.

Abortion has now destroyed more human life than Hitler and Stalin did—45 million in the United States, and tens of millions more in countries that have legalized abortion, some under pressure from the United States.

In a democratic society, legitimacy depends upon the voters. Voters have ultimate control of the system and can change the government if they really want to. Voting fraud and stolen elections can slow down but not stop a determined public; the judiciary and the bureaucracy in the end have to follow a determined and long-term public mood. A Christian voter performs a moral act when he votes. The morality of a government and the morality of an individual Christian are not the same thing—because God has instituted governments to enforce earthly justice, and a Christian has a destiny and a goal beyond this earth—but both governments and individual men are subject to moral laws.

Governments are ordained to protect the innocent from evildoers, from enemies foreign and domestic, and those who would destroy a child in the womb are evildoers. The US Supreme Court has declared a class of human beings outside the protection of the law, and the American government therefore does not carry out one of the purposes for which God has ordained it.

In a recent statement, the Vatican reiterated what has been the constant teaching of Christianity:

> Those who are directly involved in lawmaking bodies have a "grave and clear obligation to oppose" any law that attacks human life. For them and for every Catholic, it is impossible to promote such laws or to vote for them. . . . In this context, it must be noted also that a well-formed Christian conscience does not permit one to vote for a political program or an individual law which contradicts the fundamental contents of faith and morals.

This is common moral sense, which applies to anyone, Christian or non-Christian, believer or non-believer. We should not abandon our moral principles in the voting booth.

A vote for a Democrat today is almost always a vote for abortion and a vote to violate the consciences of those of us who oppose abortion. The effect of various fiscal polices on the poor are uncertain; the effect of abortion on human life is certain. Whatever can be said for or against Democratic economic policies from a Christian point of view, nothing can be said in favor of their abortion policy. They have favored abortion at every stage and at every opportunity; they see no problem with forcing Christians to pay for abortion through taxes and compulsory insurance coverage; they will force Christian institutions to accept abortion; they will silence those who protest abortion. When Democrats do not do these things, it is only because they are weak. When they are strong, what will restrain them?

Is it a sin to vote Democratic? Usually yes, because a vote for a Democrat is a vote for a supporter of abortion or a vote that strengthens a party whose only sacred tenet is the right to unrestricted abortion. A vote for a pro-abortion Republican is usually also wrong, because a vote for any pro-abortion candidate is counted by politicians as support for abortion.

We have been solemnly warned that we will be judged on how we use what has been entrusted to us on this earth, and a vote in our society has value—it is a "talent" that we have been given. If we will be judged severely for failing to use the talents God has entrusted to us, how much more severely will we be judged for misusing them? If we have not merely failed to do good, but have by our vote for a pro-abortion candidate contributed to evil, and enabled the million-fold and easily avoidable slaughter of the unborn to continue, what words will we hear from the Judge?

Prayer in the Schools

Supporters of prayer in school seek to restore traditional values. They call for a constitutional amendment to reaffirm and re-establish the original intent of the religious freedom clause of the First Amendment, that which has been stolen, twisted, and used against them. The issue, they insist, is the guaranteed preservation of religious liberty.

—Rus Walton, *Biblical Solutions to Contemporary Problems: A Handbook* (1988)

We cannot allow an out-of-control, activist judiciary to sacrifice our freedoms at the altar of politically correct, modern-day liberalism.

—Susan Weddington, chair of the Texas Republican party, expressing anger at the U.S. 5th Circuit Court of Appeals for disallowing prayer at school-sanctioned sporting events (January 2000).

Opponents of prayer ... contend that if it is allowed to take place openly, such as at a football game, someone who doesn't share the same faith will have to decide between not going to the game or feeling uncomfortable. But the government's primary responsibility should be to protect the freedoms of all the students rather than force a national practice of atheism so that some might be spared having to hear something they don't agree with.

—Sean R. Tuffnell, *Houston Chronicle* (January 2000)

Reconstructionism

God has a plan for the conquest of all things by His covenant people. That plan is His law. It leaves no area of life and activity untouched, and it predestines victory. To deny the law is to deny God and His plan for victory.

—Rousas John Rushdoony, *God's Plan for Victory* (1977)

Christianity has given birth to the greatest prosperity, stability, and liberty known in history. To the extent that the Christian view is also the biblical view (contrary to liberalism, which attempts to separate the two), we may expect God's objective blessings upon that people whose God is the Lord, as evidenced in their law code.

—Kenneth L. Gentry Jr., *God's Law in the Modern World: The Continuing Relevance of Old Testament Law* (1993)

Right to Bear Arms

The right to defend one's life, family, liberty and property is a God-given right, supported by Scripture and illustrated in God's Law as seen in Nature. Any person, group or government which would attempt to deprive one of this right, or attempt to persecute, prosecute or punish one for exercising this right, violates God's Law and is an enemy of God's people. Weapons are essential for self-defense and Jesus admonished His followers to purchase a sword. A firearm is the modern equivalent of a sword, thus gun control in any form or manner is in opposition to God's Law.

—*Remnant Resolves* (1988)

Secular Humanism

If the atheistic, amoral, one-world humanists succeed in enslaving our country, that missionary outlet [America] will eventually be terminated. As a Christian and as a pastor, I am deeply concerned that this ministry be extended. The eternal souls of millions of people depend on us to supply them with the good news. In addition, I am concerned that the 50 million children who will grow up in America during the next generation will have access to the truth, rather than the heresies of humanism.

—Tim LaHaye, *The Battle for the Mind* (1980)

A humanist is a humanist is a humanist! That is, he believes as a humanist, thinks as a humanist, acts as a humanist, and makes decisions as a humanist. Whether he is a politician, government official, or educator, he does not think like a pro-moral American, but like a humanist. Consequently, he is not fit to govern us or to train our young.

—Tim LaHaye, *The Battle for the Mind* (1980)

The humanistic ideas of moral relativity and individual divinity are destructive in and of themselves. But, when combined, this philosophical mixture has proven disastrous to the American culture: when everything is relative, pleasing yourself becomes the most important thing. When right and wrong do not exist, good and evil are viewed as concepts. As such, neither is based on truth, but on individual perception. If every individual is his own god, there is no Judge, so each is free to do what he pleases, no reward will be gained for good works, and no consequences paid for evil.

—Lynn Stanley, *The Blame Game: Why Society Persecutes Christians* (1996)

Taxation

Communism is a system of private property confiscation and control. Any means of property control and confiscation used in the U.S.A. today against the consent of the individual is a communist practice.... The graduated income tax is one of the strongest planks of the Communist Manifesto. Every Christian should be opposing it with all his strength.... But, lo, most Christians and pastors criticize those brave persons who are participating in Godly resistance. In fact, many pastors and Christians preach against sodomy and abortion; but at the same time they are supporting the practice of those very sins through the graduated income tax.

—Everett Sileven, *The Christian and the Income Tax* (1986)

Should we pay taxes to the government of the United States of America? Christ did not say to pay what Caesar demanded, nor did He say that God demanded anything. The individual must decide who he wishes to serve. If Caesar has a return due him for services rendered, then that which is Caesar's should be paid. But what about your God and His just dues? Did Caesar bring the sun and rain and the growth of crops and livestock? What does your government do with the tax money which you pay? Are they not paying for the murder of the unborn in abortion clinics? Are they not teaching the diabolical, satanic lie called humanism in the schools with your taxes paying the bills? Have you been taking that which is God's and paying for evil and wicked government? Did not our government lie to us about Pearl Harbor, Korea, Viet Nam, Watergate, energy shortage and social security? Your government is a liar and Satan is the father of lies and our churches are teaching that you must render unto our wicked government whatever they demand.

—M. J. "Red" Beckman, *Born Again Republic* (1988)

By the use of various methods of taxation, we have been deprived of the right to property contrary to God's Law against theft. Therefore, we, God's Covenant People, call for a repentance by our Government of all unscriptural methods of taxation as outlined in His Law.

—*Remnant Resolves* (1988)

It is conservative to cut taxes and compassionate to give people more money to spend.

—Governor George W. Bush, *The Texas Observer* (May 1999)

II. COMMENTARY ON THE RELIGIOUS RIGHT, SCHOLARLY AND POLEMICAL

Culture and the Culture War

In the eighties, America has given birth to a new form of terror, a campaign of fear and intimidation aimed at the hearts of millions. It is in two great American arenas—religion and politics—that this new terror has raised its head. In the past few years, a small group of preachers and political strategists has begun to use religion and all that Americans hold sacred to seize power across a broad spectrum of our lives. They are exploiting this cherished and protected institution—our most intimate values and individual beliefs—along with our civil religion—our love of country—in a concerted effort to transform our culture into one altogether different from the one we have known. It is an adventurous thrust: with cross and flag to pierce the heart of America without bloodshed. And it is already well under way.

—Flo Conway and Jim Siegelman, *Holy Terror: The Fundamentalist War on America's Freedoms in Religion, Politics and Our Private Lives* (1984)

In attempting to discover if the majority of Americans actually subscribe to the New Christian Right definition of public morality, scholars have conducted a multitude of opinion surveys based on local, state, and national samples. With an unusual degree of accord, these surveys have challenged the most enthusiastic claims about the extent of broad public support for the profamily agenda. In fact, support for the core items making up the "profamily" agenda has been limited to a minority of the population and apparently has declined over the course of the 1970s and 1980s. . . . In the face of New Right efforts to the contrary, the public apparently has become more liberal on issues like abortion, tolerance for homosexuality, and women's rights.

—Kenneth D. Wald, *Religion and Politics in the United States* (1987)

It should be recalled that conservative Christianity began to flourish at the very moment when the more sedate and rational branches of Protestantism were floundering. In the 1970s the United Presbyterian Church lost 21 percent of its members. The Episcopal Church lost 15 percent. The United Church of Christ and the United Methodists both lost 10 percent. As these moderate and liberal denominations, which recognized the complexities of modern life and resisted biblical simplification, declined, many of their former members defected . . . to conservative, born-again Christianity. They filled the thousands of new conservative churches and schools that were founded as the revival spread to every corner of the country and eventually claimed 60 million adherents. The revival became so successful that by 1980, despite the complaints of mainline Protestants and Catholics, the very word "Christian" had come to mean a born-again conservative.

—Michael D'Antonio, *Fall from Grace: The Failed Crusade of the Christian Right* (1989)

At times it has seemed that if evangelicals were to wake up as citizens of an African or Asian nation, their identity as followers of Christ would be profoundly shaken. Why? Not simply be cause of the differences in language, food, and culture, but because many American evangelicals have been truly more American than Christian, more dependent on historical myths than spiritual realities, more shaped by the flag than the cross. . . . These tendencies came to a climax in the eighties with the rise of the religious Right. What began as an appreciation of the contribution faith made in our nation turned into a false reliance on evangelicals' social standing in America. The evangelical identity shifted from being grounded in the source of blessing to being grounded in the blessing itself. Their status as pilgrims in search of the heavenly kingdom was less important than being citizens of a "Christian America." Following the pattern of most idolatry, something to be appreciated became a point of overattachment, a source of reliance, and finally an idol that led to public pride and self-deception.

—John Seel, "Nostalgia for the Lost Empire," in Os Guinness and John Steel, eds., *No God but God* (1992)

Conservative think tanks like the Heritage Foundation want to roll back the New Deal. [Tim] LaHaye wants to roll back the Enlightenment.

—Chip Berlet, *Right-Wing Populism in America: Too Close for Comfort* (2000)

This [the posting of the Ten Commandments in public schools] is all driven by looking for some kind of magic fix to school violence. If the mere presence of religious material stopped sin, the presence of Gideons [sic] Bible in hotel rooms would have stopped adultery long ago.

> —Barry Lynn, executive director of Americans United for the Separation of Church and State, *Houston Chronicle* (February 20, 2000)

By a series of recent initiatives, Republicans have transformed our party into the political arm of conservative Christians. The elements of this transformation have included advocacy of a constitutional amendment to ban gay marriage, opposition to stem cell research involving both frozen embryos and human cells in Petri dishes, and the extraordinary effort to keep Terri Schiavo hooked up to a feeding tube.

> —John C. Danforth, former U.S. senator (R-MO) and an Episcopal priest, *Houston Chronicle* (April 3, 2005)

In the '60s, how you felt about the Beatles and Rolling Stones, marijuana and LSD, and civil rights and the Vietnam War told people whose side of American society you were on. Likewise, Jerry Falwell and Tim LaHaye, the pro-life movement and marriage protection amendment, and the book of Revelation and George Bush are equally reliable gauges through which evangelical Christians today can distinguish friend from foe.

> —Craig Unger, "American Rapture," *Vanity Fair* (December 2005)

The religious right has gone too far. They've lost their focus on the spirit of Jesus and have separated the world into black and white, when the world is much more gray. I can't see Jesus standing with signs at an anti-gay rally. It's hard to picture.

> —Adam Hamilton, evangelical pastor, Leawood, Kansas (2006)

However dominant in terms of numbers, Christianity is only a thread in the American tapestry—it is not the whole tapestry. The God who is spoken of and called on and prayed to in the public sphere is an essential character in the American drama, but He is not specifically God the Father or the God of Abraham. The [religious] right's contention that we are a "Christian nation" that has fallen from pure origins and can achieve redemption by some kind of return to Christian values in based on wishful thinking, not convincing historical argument.

> —John Meacham, *American Gospel* (2006)

A new generation of evangelical believers is pressing beyond the religious right of Jerry Falwell and Pat Robertson, trying to broaden the movement's focus from the familiar wars about sex to include issues of social and economic justice.

> —Lisa Miller, *Newsweek* (November 13, 2006)

[Ted] Haggard seemed like a kinder, gentler and greener evangelical than many on the religious right. Yet he once equated Gay Pride Day with Murderer's Pride Day and looked to the Bible for the last word in science as well as religion. This was not just a man split between his walk and his talk. This was a man repulsed by himself.

—Ellen Goodman, nationally syndicated columnist, *Houston Chronicle* (November 19, 2006)

End Times

Why care about the earth when the droughts, floods, famine, and pestilence brought by ecological collapse are signs of the apocalypse foretold in the Bible? Why care about global climate change when you and yours will be rescued in the Rapture? Why bother to convert to alternative sources of energy and reduce dependence on oil from the volatile Middle East?

—Bill Moyers, "Welcome to Doomsday," *The New York Review* (March 24, 2005)

APOCALYPSE NOW

By Michael Ennis

Dallas, the state's mecca of materialism, is the global epicenter of doomsday theology? The end may be nearer than we think.

The public-relations firm that Dallas recently hired to come up with a catchy new slogan for the city probably won't pick "Athens of the Apocalypse." Even so, the only thing that sets Dallas apart from other American cities similarly replete with designer museums, five-star restaurants, and edgy little theatrical troupes is its unique end-of-the-world industry.

The city's eschatological infrastructure is perhaps most evident in its great faith factories, like the Prestonwood Baptist megachurch, in the northern suburb of Plano, where the authors of the best-selling Left Behind series, the Reverend Tim LaHaye and Jerry Jenkins, were recently taped by 60 Minutes II flogging their latest book beneath the live-action big screens in the arena-like sanctuary. But megachurches where millions anticipate the Rapture—the instant snatching-up of true believers to meet Jesus in the air—are familiar landmarks across a nation where Armageddon has become as American as baseball and apple pie. What distinguishes Dallas is that the end-times culture so avidly consumed there was also created there: The city that gave us America's team holds almost exclusive intellectual property rights to a distinctly American-style apocalypse. What might be called the Parousia Prairie ("Parousia" is Greek for "Second Coming") in and around Dallas is dotted with last-days think tanks, from Mal Couch's Tyndale Biblical Institute, in Fort Worth, to Thomas Ice's LaHaye-financed Pre-Trib Research Center, in Arlington, to the Dallas-based ministry of eschatological televangelist Zola Levitt.

These are only theological upstarts, however, compared with a nineteen-building campus in the heart of Dallas, minutes from downtown's postmodern office towers. Founded in 1924, Dallas Theological Seminary is the Yale of conservative Christianity: DTS graduates preside over dozens of the nation's top Bible institutes, and thousands more DTS alums head prominent churches. The house doctrine at DTS is a precise end-of-the-world formula known as dispensational premillennialism (because it divides all history into divinely determined ages, or dispensations, and predicts that the Second Coming will precede the Christian millennium, the thousand-year rule of Christ on earth). Almost miraculously, DTS faculty and graduates have transformed this arcane ism into a staple of American life and letters. Decades before the Left Behind series debuted, DTS graduates were selling last-days lit in numbers that presaged the advent of Harry Potter. The list is headed by Hal Lindsey's The Late Great Planet Earth (one of the best-selling books of the late twentieth century) and the 1974 multimillion-seller Armageddon, Oil and the Middle East Crisis, by the late John F. Walvoord, DTS's longtime president.

Michael Ennis, a novelist and critic, is a writer-at-large for *TEXAS MONTHLY* magazine.

This article is reprinted with permission from the July 2004 issue of *TEXAS MONTHLY.*

But DTS wasn't the beginning of the end in Dallas. The story actually starts with the father of the American Apocalypse, a complicated and evidently conflicted man who came to the city in 1882, when the population had just passed 10,000 and a few of the muddy streets had just been paved with bois d'arc planks. Thirty-nine years old when he took over as probational pastor of Dallas's tiny First Congregational Church, Cyrus Ingerson Scofield carried hefty baggage: Cashiered after a brief term as attorney general of Kansas amid rumors of influence-peddling, he began a downward spiral that included heavy drinking, allegations of forgery, and the abandonment of his wife and two young daughters. According to his as-told-to hagiography, in 1879 Scofield was challenged to accept Christ as his personal savior by a visitor to his St. Louis law office. Giving the matter "a moment's thought," Scofield fell to his knees and was born again—much like the warp-speed conversion of 747 captain Rayford Steele, the hero of the Left Behind series, who accepts Christ immediately after viewing a videotape explaining the instantaneous disappearance of millions throughout the world (it's the Rapture, stupid).

Cyrus I. Scofield would have recognized the rest of the basic plot behind the twelve-volume series, because the story elements had been formalized much earlier in the nineteenth century by a disaffected Anglo-Irish cleric named John Nelson Darby. Alarmed by various historic assaults on the authority of the church and Scripture (including the American Revolution, which had eschewed a state church), Darby determined to prove that the Bible was not only a literal history of the world but that its apocalyptic books, Daniel and Revelation, were an accurate history of the future. Beginning with the Rapture, Darby detailed a mathematically exact countdown to the end of time.

Scofield, who had come under the influence of Darby's theories in St. Louis, was an entrepreneurial sort, the kind of innovative merchandiser Dallas has always nurtured. Within a decade of arriving there, he had started his own nationwide Bible correspondence course and had welcomed into his burgeoning congregation many of the city's most familiar names, including Dallas Morning News publisher George Dealey. But Scofield's singular work of merchandising genius was a new package for Darby's theories. Published by the august Oxford University Press in 1909, the Scofield Reference Bible has no real rival as the most influential book ever conceived in Texas. Of course Scofield didn't write all of it, but the footnotes and commentaries he embroidered throughout the venerable King James text revolutionized the reading—and the marketing—of the world's best-selling book.

Scofield wasn't the first to annotate the Bible, but he was the first to do it in a splashy, graphically sophisticated (for the times) fashion, with Internet-like "chained" references that allowed readers to follow a theme or prophecy as it hopscotched from chapter to chapter and testament to testament. Paying particular attention to Darby's prophetic timeline, Scofield stitched together thousands of scattered verses into what we would now call a "virtual" narrative: The Rapture, followed by seven years of catastrophic Tribulation, when the Antichrist will rule the earth and billions will die; the Second Coming and the victory over Satan's minions at Armageddon, which will inaugurate the thousand-year reign of Christ on earth; the final defeat of Satan; and the Day of Judgment. While turn-of-the-century "modernists" insisted that the Bible was a meandering collection of stories, part history and part allegory, Scofield presented the carefully plotted work of a single divine author, dictated to 44 amanuenses over twenty centuries—a taut theological thriller conceived entirely in the mind of God.

The Scofield Reference Bible changed the course of American faith. Armed with Scofield's study aids, premillennialists headed an alliance of conservative Presbyterians and Baptists intent on defending the inerrancy of Scripture against the modernists. Though by the early twenties their movement had been labeled Fundamentalism, they were at heart Scofieldians, their bible the Scofield Reference Bible, whose total sales are now in the tens of millions. Scofield, who died in 1921, didn't live to see Fundamentalism flourish, much less become a political steamroller later in the century. But after his death, his closest disciple, Lewis S. Chafer, founded Dallas Theological Seminary and dedicated it to his mentor's end-of-the-world view.

Scofield also left a potent political legacy. The first to say that ancient ciphers like Gog and Magog actually refer to modern powers like Russia, he also insisted that the as-yet-unfulfilled promises God had made to Israel—including restoring its biblical borders—amounted to unpaid cosmic debts that God would have to settle before he could bring history to its conclusion. The birth of modern Israel, in 1948, began a mutually cynical dalliance between premillennialists and the Jewish state: If Scofield's biblical prophecy unfolds, after dutifully doing the spadework for Christ's millennial reign (he will rule from the rebuilt Jerusalem Temple), millions of Jews will die horribly in the Tribulation, with a fractional "remnant" spared to convert and witness the Second Coming. Most recently, suspicions that the Bush administration's faith-based Mideast policies have unduly submitted to premill pressures—principally in favoring the Israeli right, which is adverse to trading biblical lands for peace—have been aired in sources as friendly as the Dallas Morning News. But perhaps more telling of premill political clout are our president's less-public supplications; one of the first things candidate Bush did after announcing in 1999 was to submit his born-again bona fides to the low-profile but high-impact Council for National Policy. Co-founded by the finger-in-every-pie LaHaye (who also co-founded the Moral Majority with Jerry Falwell), the CNP is a who's who of the religious right, where premill theologians can confab with like-minded politicos such as House majority leader Tom DeLay (Attorney General John Ashcroft, a premill Pentecostal, and Health and Human Services Secretary Tommy Thompson resigned their memberships before joining the president's Cabinet).

A runaway winner in both the marketplace and the marketplace of ideas, Scofield's American Apocalypse combines a New Agey, Lord of the Rings mythological sprawl with an admirable logical consistency: For Americans who believe that the Bible is the literal word of God—that would be a third of us—Scofield's often tortuous last-days chronology brilliantly reconciles all the sweeping promises and often feverish predictions that God and his anointed spokespersons make throughout the Bible. Scofield's theology also "solves" evil, in that the biblical prophecies prove that God won't allow an evil world to go on much longer; from the very beginning, he's had an exit strategy.

But when you really crunch the numbers, the moral calculus of our American Apocalypse doesn't add up. Forget the thousands of devout Jews, Muslims, Buddhists, and just plain secularists who will die as driverless cars career across freeways and planes with raptured flight crews plunge from the sky; billions more nonbelievers are prophesied to die in the Tribulation. Compassionately, the premills explain that everyone will have the option to convert and be saved and that only the wicked will turn away from Christ when his truth is so visibly manifest. But in the end, the freedom of religious expression that our founding fathers guaranteed us will narrow to just two choices: Accept Christ as your personal savior or spend eternity in a lake of fire. For the tens of millions of Americans who believe the world will end the way the Bible says, this last-days holocaust isn't religious mythology; it's the inescapable truth. For the millions of children who are being raised with these beliefs (or are reading the series Left Behind: The Kids), it's their idea of the future. We are duly horrified by the convert-or-die edicts of Islamic militants, but evidently no one dares call it religious extremism—or just political hypocrisy—when the leaders of our war against terror pander to the proselytes of a similarly draconian final solution.

So we cheerfully wait for the end, living large on the edge of time, absorbing the cult of the last things into our culture of things. Cyrus I. Scofield was the paradigm in that respect as well; while finishing up the last Bible we'll ever really need, the Dallas pastor was apparently contemplating his royalties, confessing in a letter his expectations of owning three homes—in New York City, New Hampshire, and Sorrento, Italy. A worldly man who sailed frequently to Europe, he probably appreciated the irony of his own success.

He may even have glimpsed the real irony of his magnum opus. While apocalyptic visions are among the most venerable literary traditions in Judeo-Christian culture, these revelations of God's plan were always written by and for history's losers, tiny bands of powerless and persecuted Jews and Christians praying only for justice in the end. And because they could inspire a reckless conviction of divine empowerment, such prophecies were traditionally sealed, to be read only by the wisest elders. When Scofield began to mass-market the end of the world in Dallas a century ago, he actually created a rip in the fabric of civilization: an apocalypse unsealed in the malls and megachurches of history's most prosperous and powerful winners, with consequences we are powerless to foresee.

AMERICAN RAPTURE

Best-selling author and evangelical leader Tim LaHaye has contacts that extend to the White House. That could spell trouble, since his theology espouses a bloody apocalypse in Israel.

By Craig Unger

On a scorching afternoon in May, Tim LaHaye, the 79-year-old co-author of the "Left Behind" series of apocalyptic thrillers, leads several dozen of his acolytes up a long, winding path to a hilltop in the ancient fortress city of Megiddo, Israel. LaHaye is not a household name in the secular world, but in the parallel universe of evangelical Christians he is the ultimate cultural icon. The author or co-author of more than 75 books, LaHaye in 2001 was named the most influential American evangelical leader of the past 25 years by the Institute for the Study of American Evangelicals. With more than 63 million copies of his "Left Behind" novels sold, he is one of the best-selling authors in all of American history. Here, a group of about 90 evangelical Christians who embrace the astonishing theology he espouses have joined him in the Holy Land for the "Walking Where Jesus Walked" tour.

Megiddo, the site of about 20 different civilizations over the last 10,000 years, is among the first stops on our pilgrimage, and, given that LaHaye's specialty is the apocalypse, it is also one of the most important. Alexander the Great, Saladin, Napoleon, and other renowned warriors all fought great battles here. But if Megiddo is to go down in history as the greatest battlefield on earth, its real test is yet to come. According to the book of Revelation, the hill of Megiddo—better known as Armageddon—will be the site of a cataclysmic battle between the forces of Christ and the Antichrist.

To get a good look at the battlefields of the apocalypse, we take shelter under a makeshift lean-to at the top of the hill. Wearing a floppy hat to protect him from the blazing Israeli sun, LaHaye yields to his colleague Gary Frazier, the tour organizer and founder of the Texas-based Discovery Ministries, Inc., to explain what will happen during the Final Days.

"How many of you have read the 'Left Behind' prophecy novels?" asks Frazier.

Almost everyone raises a hand. "The thing that you must know," Frazier tells them, "is that the next event on God's prophetic plan, we believe, is the catching away of the saints in the presence of the Lord. We call it 'the Rapture.'"

Frazier is referring to a key biblical passage, in the first book of Thessalonians, that says the Lord will "descend from heaven with a shout.... The dead

---

Craig Unger, an American journalist and writer, served as deputy editor of the *New York Observer* and editor-in-chief of *Boston Magazine*. He has written about George H. W. Bush and George W. Bush for the *New Yorker*, *Esquire Magazine* and *Vanity Fair*, and his work is featured in Michael Moore's *Fahrenheit 9/11*. He is currently working on a book based on his article 'American Rapture.'

in Christ shall rise first. Then we which are alive and remain shall be caught up together with them in the clouds, to meet the Lord in the air."

The words "caught up" are sometimes translated as "raptured." As a result, adherents cite this as the essential scriptural depiction of the Rapture. "Christ is going to appear," Frazier continues. "He is going to call all of his saved, all of his children, home to be with him."

In other words, "in the twinkling of an eye," as the Rapturists often say, millions of born-again Evangelicals will suddenly vanish from the earth—just as they do in LaHaye's "Left Behind" books. They will leave behind their clothes, their material possessions, and all their friends and family members who have not accepted Christ—and they will join Christ in the Kingdom of God.

Frazier continues. "Jesus taught his disciples that he was going to go away to his father's house, but that he was not going to abandon them, because while he was gone he was going to prepare for them a suitable dwelling place.... And when the time was right, he would come back to claim his own.... Jesus is going to come and get his bride, which comprises all of us who are born again. "I have no question that right now, as we stand here, Jesus the son is saying to the father, I want to be with my bride.... In the same way that we wanted to be with our mates ... he wants to be with us. He wants us to be with him."

Frazier is a fiery preacher, and as his voice rises and falls, his listeners respond with cries of "Amen" and "That's right." "I'm going to tell you with zeal and enthusiasm and passion Jesus is coming on the clouds of glory to call us home.... Now, ladies and gentlemen, I want you to know, if you've read the 'Left Behind' books, [but] more importantly, if you've read the Bible, you know ... that Christ is coming, and we believe that that day is very, very near."

For miles around in all directions the fertile Jezreel Valley, known as the breadbasket of Israel, is spread out before us, an endless vista of lush vineyards and orchards growing grapes, oranges, kumquats, peaches, and pears. It is difficult to imagine a more beautiful pastoral panorama.

The sight LaHaye's followers hope to see here in the near future, however, is anything but bucolic. Their vision is fueled by the book of Revelation, the dark and foreboding messianic prophecy that foresees a gruesome and bloody confrontation between Christ and the armies of the Antichrist at Armageddon.

Addressing the group from the very spot where the conflict is to take place, Frazier turns to Revelation 19, which describes Christ going into battle. "It thrills my heart every time that I read these words," he says, then begins to read: "'And I saw heaven standing open.... And there before me was a white horse, whose rider is called Faithful and True. With justice he judges and makes war. His eyes are like blazing fire.'"

Frazier pauses to explain the text. "This doesn't sound like compassionate Jesus," he says. "This doesn't sound like the suffering servant of Isaiah 53. This is the Warrior King. He judges and makes war."

Frazier returns to the Scripture: "He has a name written on him that no one but he himself knows. He is dressed in a robe that is dipped in blood and his name is the word of God."

This is the moment the Rapturists eagerly await. The magnitude of death and destruction will make the Holocaust seem trivial. The battle finally begins.

Those who remain on earth are the unsaved, the left behind—many of them dissolute followers of the Antichrist, who is massing his army against Christ. Accompanying Christ into battle are the armies of heaven, riding white horses and dressed in fine linen. "This is all of us," Frazier says.

Frazier points out that Christ does not need high-tech weaponry for this conflict. "'Out of his mouth comes a sharp sword,' not a bunch of missiles and rockets," he says.

Once Christ joins the battle, both the Antichrist and the False Prophet are quickly captured and cast alive into a lake of fire burning with brimstone. Huge numbers of the Antichrist's supporters are slain.

Meanwhile, an angel exhorts Christ, "Thrust in thy sickle, and reap." And so, Christ, sickle in hand, gathers "the vine of the earth."

Then, according to Revelation, "the earth was reaped." These four simple words signify the end of the world as we know it.

Grapes that are "fully ripe"—billions of people who have reached maturity but still reject the grace of God—are now cast "into the great winepress of the wrath of God." Here we have the origin of the phrase "the grapes of wrath." In an extraordinarily merciless and brutal act of justice, Christ crushes the so-called grapes of wrath, killing them. Then, Revelation says, blood flows out "of the winepress, even unto the horse bridles, by the space of a thousand and six hundred furlongs."

With its highly figurative language, Revelation is subject to profoundly differing interpretations. Nevertheless, LaHaye's followers insist on its literal truth and accuracy, and they have gone to great lengths to calculate exactly what this passage of Revelation means.

As we walk down from the top of the hill of Megiddo, one of them looks out over the Jezreel Valley. "Can you imagine this entire valley filled with blood?" he asks. "That would be a 200-mile-long river of blood, four and a half feet deep. We've done the math. That's the blood of as many as two and a half billion people."

When this will happen is another question, and the Bible says that "of that day and hour knoweth no man." Nevertheless, LaHaye's disciples are certain these events—the End of Days—are imminent. In fact, one of them has especially strong ideas about when they will take place. "Not soon enough," she says. "Not soon enough."

If such views sound extraordinary, the people who hold them are decidedly not. For the most part, the people on the tour could pass for a random selection culled from almost any shopping mall in America. There are warm and loving middle-aged couples who hold hands. There is a well-coiffed Texas matron with an Hermès scarf. There's a ducktailed septuagenarian and a host of post-teen mall rats. There are young singles. One couple even chose this trip for their honeymoon. A big-haired platinum blonde with a white sequined cowboy hat adds a touch of Dallas glamour. There is a computer-security expert, a legal assistant, and a real-estate broker; a construction executive, a retired pastor, a caregiver for the elderly, and a graduate student from Jerry Falwell's Liberty University. They hail from Peoria, Illinois, and Longview, Texas, as well as San Diego and San Antonio. Most are fans of the "Left Behind" books. Some have attended the Left Behind Prophecy Conference on one of its tours of the U.S.

And while their beliefs may seem astounding to secular Americans, they are not unusual. According to a *Time*/CNN poll from 2002, 59 percent of Americans believe the events in the book of Revelation will take place. There are as many as 70 million Evangelicals in the U.S.—about 25 percent of the population—attending more than 200,000 evangelical churches. Most of these churches are run by pastors who belong to conservative political organizations that make sure their flocks vote as a hard-right Republican bloc.

A fascination with Revelation, the Rapture, and Christian Zionism has always been a potent, if often unseen, component of the American consciousness. More than three centuries ago, Puritans from John Winthrop to Cotton Mather saw America as a millennial kingdom linked to both the apocalypse and ancient Israel in a divine way that prefigured the Second Coming of Christ. America was to be the New Jerusalem, the Redeemer Nation, a people blessed with divine guidance.

Imagery from the book of Revelation has inspired poets and writers from William Blake and William Butler Yeats to Joan Didion and Bob Dylan. "The Battle Hymn of the Republic" draws references from Revelation. Elements of the book of Revelation—secularized or otherwise—turn up in movies starring Gary Cooper (*High Noon*), Gregory Peck (*The Omen*), Clint Eastwood (*Pale Rider*), and Mimi Rogers (*The Rapture*), as well as in NBC's *Revelations*. Already, there have been two "Left Behind" movies—available mostly on video—and a third is in production. LaHaye's "Left Behind" series of books, co-authored with Jerry Jenkins, has brought in $650 million to Tyndale House, its now affluent Christian publisher.

On the Internet, raptureready.com put its Rapture Index at 161 in the wake of Hurricane Katrina; anything over 145 means "fasten your seat belts." A number of Christian Web sites sell clothing emblazoned with Rapture logos. There was even a team of NASCAR drivers, Randy MacDonald and Jimmy Hensley, whose souped-up Chevy proudly displayed "Left Behind" insignia—not the most propitious message for a driver vying for pole position.

For all that, the new wave of Rapturemania is more than just another multi-billion-dollar addition to America's cultural junk heap. In the 60s, how you felt about the Beatles and Rolling Stones, marijuana and LSD, and civil rights and the Vietnam War told people whose side of American society you were on. Likewise, Jerry Falwell and Tim LaHaye, the pro-life movement and marriage-protection amendment, and the book of Revelation and George W. Bush are equally reliable gauges through which evangelical Christians today can distinguish friend from foe.

As befits the manifesto of a counterculture, the "Left Behind" series is a revenge fantasy, in which right-wing Christians win out over the rational, scientific, modern, post-Enlightenment world. The books represent the apotheosis of a culture that is waging war against liberals, gays, Muslims, Arabs, the U.N., and "militant secularists" of all stripes—whom it accuses of destroying Christian America, murdering millions of unborn children, assaulting the Christian family by promoting promiscuity and homosexuality, and driving Christ out of the public square.

It's a counterculture that sees Jews as key players in a Christian messianic drama, a premise that has led to a remarkable alliance between Christian Evangelicals and the Israeli right. As a result, political views drawn from an apocalyptic vision—once dismissed as extremist and delusional—have not merely swept mass culture but have shaped the political discourse all the way to Jerusalem and the White House. And if they are taken too seriously, the geopolitical consequences could be catastrophic.

The city of Jerusalem has a profound significance in the traditions of Judaism, Christianity, and Islam. And to all three religions no place in Jerusalem is more full of apocalyptic and messianic meaning than the Temple Mount—the massive, 144,000-square-meter platform, 32 meters high, built by King Herod as a base for the biggest and most grandiose religious monument in the world, the shining white stone Temple of the Jews.

To Jews, the Temple Mount marks the holy of holies, the sacred core of the Temple, where Jews worshipped for centuries. Beneath it, Orthodox Jews believe, is the foundation stone of the entire world. The Mount is the disputed piece of land over which Cain slew Abel. It is where Abraham took his son, Isaac, when God asked him to sacrifice the boy. At its outer perimeter is the Western Wall, or Wailing Wall, where Jews worship today. And messianic Jews believe the Mount is where the Temple must be rebuilt for the coming Messiah.

To Christians, the Temple is where Jesus threw out the money changers. Its destruction by the Romans in 70 A.D. came to symbolize the birth of Christianity, when a new Temple of Jesus, eternal and divine, replaced the earthly Temple made and destroyed by men.

And to Muslims the Temple Mount's Dome of the Rock is where Muhammad ascended to heaven nearly 1,400 years ago, making it the third-holiest site in Islam, behind Mecca and Medina.

After its victory over Arab forces in the Six-Day War, in June 1967, Israel briefly seized the Temple Mount, thereby realizing the dream of restoring Judaism's holiest place to the Jewish people. But Moshe Dayan, the venerated Israeli defense minister who won the battle, soon voluntarily relinquished control of it to the *Waqf*, a Muslim administrative body.

Over the next generation, some 250,000 mostly Orthodox Jews, citing God's promise to Abraham in Genesis—"all the land which thou seest, to thee will I give it, and to thy seed for ever"—moved into West Bank territories occupied by Israel after the 1967 war, and vowed to keep the government from giving the land back to the Palestinians.

Since Dayan's historic decision, Muslim authorities have usually allowed non-Muslims to come to the Temple Mount, as long as they don't move their lips in ways that suggest they are praying. As a result, the Temple Mount is one of the most explosive tinderboxes on earth. A visit to the site in September 2000 by Ariel Sharon inflamed tensions that soon erupted into the second intifada.

To evangelical Christians, the Mount is an elemental part of messianic theology, because a complete restoration of the nation of Israel, including the rebuilding of the Temple and the reclaiming of Judea and Samaria, is a prerequisite to the Second Coming of Christ. Likewise, to Orthodox Jews, nothing is more important to their messianic vision than reclaiming the Temple Mount and rebuilding the Temple—yet no single event is more likely to provoke a catastrophe.

No one knows this better than Yitshak Fhantich, an independent security, protection, and intelligence consultant who spent 28 years in Israeli intelligence, many as head of the Jewish Department of Shin Bet. From 1992 to 1995, he was the man in charge of investigating right-wing extremists, many of them strongly religious, who posed a threat to the Temple Mount. "The vast majority of settlers in the West Bank are positive people with sincere religious beliefs," says Fhantich. "But when you combine religious beliefs with right-wing political views, you have a bomb. The hard core among them will go to any extreme. They are ready to do anything—from killing Yitzhak Rabin to blowing up the mosques at the Temple Mount."

Indeed, in 1984, Fhantich and his team of 25 Shin Bet members assisted in the arrest of 26 Jewish terrorists for planning to blow up the mosques on the Temple Mount in an attempt to disrupt the peace process with Egypt, and in hopes that the Jews would then rebuild the Temple so that the Messiah would come.

And in 1995, Fhantich personally warned Prime Minister Yitzhak Rabin about the danger he faced from militant groups outraged by his agreement, as part of the 1993 Oslo accords, to relinquish the West Bank and Gaza territories to the Palestinians. "I told him, on the hit list, you're No. 1," Fhantich says. On November 4, 1995, Rabin was assassinated by a young Orthodox law student named Yigal Amir, whose activities Fhantich had been monitoring for more than a year.

In the 90s, Fhantich says, Israeli intelligence began watching Christian Evangelicals. "As the millennium approached, you had many people waiting for the appearance of Jesus Christ.... And Jerusalem, of course, is the home of the Jerusalem syndrome," he says, referring to the phenomenon whereby obsessive religious ideas can trigger violent behavior. "If someone believes God told him to do something, you cannot stop him. "The mosques on the Temple Mount are like the red flag for the bull. You have to be prepared minute by minute. These Christians, they believe what they are doing is sacred. Some of them are so naïve they can be taken advantage of. If something happens to the Temple Mount, I think these American Evangelicals will welcome such an act. After all, religion is the most powerful gun in the world."

Moreover, a potential attack on the Temple Mount, as disastrous as it would be, pales in comparison to the long-term geopolitical goals of some right-wing religious groups. Orthodox Jews, Christian Evangelicals, and the heroes of the "Left Behind" series share a belief that the land bordered by the Nile and Euphrates Rivers and the Mediterranean Sea and the wilderness of Jordan has been covenanted to Israel by God. Taken to its literal extreme, this belief obliges Israel not only to retain control of Gaza and the West Bank but also to annex all or parts of Egypt, Lebanon, Iraq, and Syria. Such a campaign of conquest would be certain to provoke a spectacular conflict.

The Carter Glass Mansion, in Lynchburg, Virginia, is a handsome manor house that serves as an administrative office for Liberty University and offers a magnificent view of the Blue Ridge Mountains. Inside is the office of Jerry Falwell, chancellor of the university, founding father of the Christian right, and longtime friend and colleague of Tim LaHaye, one of Liberty's most generous donors.

Recently recovered from a respiratory illness, Falwell, 72, is as serene and self-confident as ever, answering questions with the disarming candor that has enabled him to build personal friendships with even his fiercest ideological foes, from the Reverend Jesse Jackson to pornographer Larry Flynt. Behind his desk is a mounted page from the *Palestine Post*, dated May 16, 1948, headlined STATE OF ISRAEL IS BORN.

Explaining his affinity for Israel, Falwell says, "Long before I became a political activist, I'd been taught that the Abrahamic Covenant—Genesis 12 and Genesis 15—is still binding, where God told Abraham, 'I will bless them that bless you and curse them that curse you.' "It was obvious to me, beginning with the birth of the Israeli state, in 1948, and the Six-Day War, in 1967, that God was bringing his people back home. So I came to believe that it was in America's best interest to be a friend of Israel.... If America blessed the Jew, Israel in particular, God would bless America."

The special political relationship between the Israeli right and Evangelicals dates back to 1977, when, after three decades of Labor rule in Israel, Menachem Begin became the first prime minister from the conservative Likud Party. A romantic nationalist and serious biblical scholar, Begin pointedly referred to the lands of the West Bank by their biblical names of Judea and Samaria, and he reached out to American Evangelicals at a time when they were just coming out of a political hibernation that dated back to the Scopes trial of 1925 and Prohibition. "The prime minister said a person who has got the Bible in his home and reads it and believes it cannot be a bad person," recalls Yechiel Kadishai, a longtime personal aide to Begin. "He said the Evangelicals have to know that we are rooted in this piece of land. There should be an understanding between us and them." One of the first people Begin sought out was Jerry Falwell, who was achieving national recognition through his growing television ministry.

In 1980, Begin presented Falwell with the prestigious Jabotinsky Award, gave his ministry a private jet, and shared vital state secrets with the televangelist. Begin even called him before bombing Iraq's Osirak nuclear reactor, in

June 1981. "He said, 'Tomorrow you're going to read some strong things about what we are going to do. But our safety is at stake,'" Falwell recalls. "He said, 'I wanted you, my good friend, to know what we are going to do.' And, sure enough, they put one down the chimney."

In the early days of his ministry, Falwell, like other Evangelicals, had made a policy of not mixing religion and politics at all—much less on a global scale. "I had been taught in the seminary that religion and politics don't mix," he says. "Conservative theologians were absolutely convinced that the pulpit should be devoted to prayer, preaching, and exclusively to spiritual ministry. "But in the 60s the U.S. Supreme Court had decided to remove God from the public square, beginning with the school-prayer issue. Then, in 1973, the Supreme Court had ruled 7-to-2 in favor of abortion on demand. And I wondered, 'What can I do?'"

Several years later, Falwell got a call from Francis Schaeffer. An electrifying Presbyterian evangelist and author, Schaeffer is probably the most important religious figure that secular America has never heard of. Widely regarded by Evangelicals as one of their leading theologians of the 20th century, Schaeffer, who died in 1984, was to the Christian right what Marx was to Marxism, what Freud was to psychoanalysis. "There is no question in my mind that without Francis Schaeffer the religious right would not exist today," says Falwell. "He was the prophet of the modern-day faith-and-values movement."

A powerful influence on Falwell, LaHaye, Pat Robertson, and many others, Schaeffer asserted in the wake of *Roe* v. *Wade* that Evangelicalism could no longer passively accommodate itself to the decadent values of the secular-humanist world, now that it had sanctioned the murder of unborn babies. Almost single-handedly, he prodded Evangelicals out of the pulpit and into a full-scale cultural war with the secular world. "I was in search of a scriptural way that I, as pastor of a very large church, could address the moral and social issues facing American culture," Falwell says. "Dr. Schaeffer shattered that world of isolation for me, telling me that, while I was preaching a very clear gospel message, I was avoiding 50 percent of my ministry.... He began teaching me that I had a responsibility to confront the culture where it was failing morally and socially."

In 1979, Falwell was still "looking for a plan to mobilize people of faith in this country" when Tim LaHaye, then a pastor in San Diego, called him. LaHaye had just founded Californians for Biblical Morality, a coalition of right-wing pastors who fought against gay rights and even sought to ban the fantasy game Dungeons & Dragons in a Glendora community college on the grounds that it was an "occult" game.

When he visited San Diego, Falwell was impressed with how LaHaye had organized the pastors to confront the state government on moral and social issues. "When he told me how he did it, I wondered why we couldn't do it on a national basis," says Falwell.

And so, in 1979, Falwell launched the Moral Majority with LaHaye and other leading fundamentalist strategists to lobby for prayer and the teaching of creationism in public schools and against gay rights, abortion, and the Equal Rights Amendment. LaHaye's wife, Beverly, also entered the fray that year by founding Concerned Women for America, to "bring biblical principles into all levels of public policy" and oppose the "anti-marriage, anti-family, anti-children, anti-man" feminism put forth by the National Organization for Women.

Courtly, genteel, and soft-spoken, LaHaye hardly looks the part of a ferocious right-wing culture warrior. In public or in private, LaHaye is understated, the antithesis of the fire-and-brimstone preacher one might expect to deliver prophecies of the apocalypse and Armageddon. Yet even Falwell has said that LaHaye has done more than anyone to set the agenda for Evangelicalism in the U.S.

LaHaye's belief in the Rapture dates back to his father's funeral, in Detroit, when he was just nine years old. "The minister at the funeral said these words: 'This is not the end of Frank LaHaye,'" he told *The Christian Science Monitor*. "'Because he accepted Jesus, the day will come when the Lord will shout from heaven and descend, and the dead in Christ will rise first and then we'll be caught up together to meet him in the air.'"

Then the pastor pointed to the sky and the sun unexpectedly came out. "All of a sudden, there was hope in my heart I'd see my father again," LaHaye said.

From then on, LaHaye was entranced with Rapturist theology, which was popularized in the U.S. in the 19th century by a renegade Irish Anglican preacher named John Nelson Darby. A proponent of a prophetic branch of theology known as premillennial dispensationalism, Darby asserted that a series of signs—including wars, immorality, and the return of the Jews to Israel—signal the End of Days. Once the end is nigh, all true believers will be raptured to meet Christ. After that, Darby taught, the world will enter a horrifying seven-year period of Tribulation, during which a charismatic Antichrist will seize power. But in the end, he prophesied, the Antichrist will be vanquished by Christ at Armageddon, and Christ's 1,000-year reign of peace and justice will begin. This, in brief, is the theology taught by evangelists such as Jerry Falwell, John Hagee, and many others—including Tim LaHaye.

After graduating from the ultra-conservative Bob Jones University, in Greenville, South Carolina, LaHaye began preaching in nearby Pumpkintown at a salary of $15 a week. For 25 years, he served as pastor at Scott Memorial Baptist Church, in San Diego, transforming it from a congregation of 275 into one with 3,000 members.

Along the way, LaHaye avidly read Francis Schaeffer. "Schaeffer taught me the difference between the Renaissance and the Reformation," he says during the tour of Israel. "And you know what the difference is? The Renaissance was all about the centrality of man. The Reformation was all about clearing up the ways the [Catholic] Church had mucked up Christianity—and getting back to the centrality of God."

In *The Battle for the Mind*, his 1980 homage to Schaeffer, LaHaye lays out his worldview far more forcefully than he does in person, depicting America as a Bible-based country under siege by an elite group of secular humanists conspiring to destroy the nuclear family, Christianity itself, and even "the entire world." There are no shades of gray in this Manichaean tract, which asserts that secular humanism is "not only the world's greatest evil but, until recently, the most deceptive of all religious philosophies."

Life, LaHaye argues, has always been a battle between good and evil. "The good way has always been called 'God's way,'" he writes, and evil has been the way of man—specifically, the post-Renaissance, post-Enlightenment world of art, science, and reason. And, in his view, nothing man has come up with is worse than secular humanism, which he defines as "a Godless, man-centered philosophy" that rejects traditional values and that has "a particular hatred toward Christianity." "LaHaye writes as if there's a humanist brain trust sitting around reading [American philosopher and educational reformer] John Dewey, trying to figure out ways to destroy Christianity," says Chip Berlet, a senior analyst with Political Research Associates and the co-author of *Right-Wing Populism in America: Too Close for Comfort.*

In truth, while tens of millions of Americans might accurately be called secular humanists, very few characterize themselves as members of a humanist movement. But to LaHaye that only proves the deviousness of the humanist project. Instead of openly advocating their point of view, he writes, humanists have used the mass media and Hollywood, the government, academia, and organizations such as the A.C.L.U. and NOW to indoctrinate unsuspecting Christians.

As a result, LaHaye argues, good Evangelicals should no longer think of humanists as harmless citizens who happen not to attend church. In *The Battle for the Mind*, he spells out his political goals: "We must remove all humanists from public office and replace them with pro-moral political leaders." "In LaHaye's world, there are the godly people who are on their way to the Rapture," says Berlet. "And the rest of the world is either complicit with the Antichrist or, worse, actively assisting him. If you really believe in End Times, you are constantly looking for agents of Satan.... [And if] political conflicts are rooted in the idea that your opponent is an agent of the Devil, there is no compromise possible. What decent person would compromise with evil? So that removes it from the democratic process. "Conservative think tanks like the Heritage Foundation want to roll back the New Deal. LaHaye wants to roll back the Enlightenment."

Like Schaeffer's writings, LaHaye's book went largely unnoticed by the secular world, but the Christian right heartily embraced its declaration of war against secularism. Presbyterian televangelist D. James Kennedy hailed *The Battle for the Mind* as "one of the most important books of our time." Falwell wrote that all Christians must follow its tenets if America is to be saved from becoming "another Sodom and Gomorrah."

In 1981, LaHaye took up the challenge, resigning his pastorship to devote himself full-time to building the Christian right. He began by meeting with moneyed ultra-conservatives including Nelson Bunker Hunt, the right-wing oil billionaire from Dallas, and T. Cullen Davis, another wealthy Texas oilman who became a born-again Christian after being acquitted of charges of murdering his wife's lover and his stepdaughter.

Though still in its infancy, the Moral Majority had more than seven million people on its mailing list and had already played a key role in electing Ronald Reagan president. Beverly LaHaye's Concerned Women for America was on its way to building a membership of 500,000 people, making her "the most powerful woman in the new religious right," according to the *Houston Chronicle*. She and her husband also co-authored a best-selling marriage manual for Christians, *The Act of Marriage,* full of clinical advice such as the following: "Cunnilingus and fellatio have in recent years been given unwarranted publicity [but] the majority of couples do not regularly use it as a substitute for the beautiful and conventional interaction designed by our Creator to be an intimate expression of love." And in the mid-80s, LaHaye created the American Coalition for Traditional Values, which played an important role in re-electing Ronald Reagan, in 1984. He later became co-chairman of Jack Kemp's 1988 presidential campaign but was forced to resign when anti-Catholic statements he had written came to light.

With right-wing groups expanding at such a dizzying pace, LaHaye helped to found the Council for National Policy (C.N.P.) as a low-profile but powerful coalition of billionaire industrialists, fundamentalist preachers, and right-wing tacticians. Funded by Hunt and Davis, among others, the organization set out to create a coherent and disciplined strategy for the New Right.

Though its membership is secret, the rolls have reportedly included Falwell and Pat Robertson; top right-wing political strategists Richard Viguerie, Ralph Reed, and Paul Weyrich; Republican senators Jesse Helms and Lauch Faircloth (both of North Carolina), Don Nickles (Oklahoma), and Trent Lott (Mississippi); and Republican representatives Dick Armey and Tom DeLay (both of Texas). The late Rousas John Rushdoony, the right-wing theologian who hoped to reconfigure the American legal system in accordance with biblical law, was said to be a member, as was John Whitehead of the Rutherford Institute, who was co-counsel to Paula Jones in her lawsuit against Bill Clinton. "Ronald Reagan, both George Bushes, senators and Cabinet members—you name it. There's nobody who hasn't been here at least once," says Falwell, who confirms that he is a member. "It is a group of four or five hundred of the biggest conservative guns in the country."

The C.N.P. has access to the highest powers in the land. In 1999, George W. Bush courted evangelical support for his presidential candidacy by giving a speech before the council, the transcript of which remains a highly guarded secret. And since the start of his presidency, Falwell says, the C.N.P. has enjoyed regular access to the Oval Office. "Within the council is a smaller group called the Arlington Group," says Falwell. "We talk to each other daily and meet in Washington probably twice a month. We often call the White House and talk to Karl Rove while we are meeting. Everyone takes our calls." According to *The Wall Street Journal,* two high-ranking Texas judges who spoke to the Arlington Group in October at the suggestion of Karl Rove allegedly assured its members that Supreme Court nominee Harriet Miers would vote to overturn *Roe* v. *Wade*.

Sometime in the mid-80s, Tim LaHaye was on an airplane when he noticed that the pilot, who happened to be wearing a wedding ring, was flirting with an attractive flight attendant, who was not. LaHaye asked himself what would happen to the poor unsaved man if the long-awaited Rapture were to transpire at that precise moment.

Soon, LaHaye's agent dug up Jerry Jenkins, a writer-at-large for the Moody Bible Institute and the author of more than 150 books, many on sports and religion. In exchange for shared billing, Jenkins signed on to do the actual writing of the "Left Behind" series—a multi-volume apocalyptic fantasy thriller composed in the breezy, fast-paced style of airport bodice rippers but based on biblical prophecy.

The first volume, *Left Behind,* begins with a variation of what LaHaye observed in real life. While piloting his 747 to London's Heathrow Airport, Captain Rayford Steele decides he's had just about enough of his wife's infuriating religiosity. Thanks to Christian influences, she now believes in the Rapture. He puts the plane on autopilot and leaves the cockpit to flirt with a "drop-dead gorgeous" flight attendant named Hattie Durham.

But Hattie advises him that dozens of passengers have suddenly and mysteriously vanished. They have left behind their clothes, eyeglasses, jewelry, even their hearing aids.

The Rapture has come. Millions of Christians who have accepted Christ as their savior—including Rayford Steele's wife and young son—have been caught up into heaven to meet Him. Left behind are the vast armies of the Antichrist—those ungodly, evolutionist, pro-abortion secular humanists—and a smaller group of people like Steele, who are just beginning to see that Christ is the answer.

So begin the seven years of Tribulation forecast in the book of Revelation. Rayford Steele and his band of Tribulation warriors are mostly ordinary folks right out of the heartland—not unlike the participants in LaHaye and Frazier's tour of Israel. Doubters no more, they begin to form the Tribulation Force, to take on the armies of the Antichrist and win redemption.

Soon, the Force learns that the Antichrist is none other than Nicolae Carpathia, the dazzlingly charming secretary-general of the United Nations and *People* magazine's "Sexiest Man Alive." Carpathia turns the U.N. into a one-world government with one global currency and one religious order. Try as they might, the Force can't stop him from killing billions by bombing New York, Los Angeles, London, Washington, D.C., and several other cities, or from establishing himself as dictator and implanting biochips that scar millions of people with the number of the beast.

In fact, Carpathia and his Unity Army seem all but unstoppable until *Glorious Appearing*, the last volume in the series, when it becomes clear that God has another plan—the Second Coming of Jesus. The battles between the forces of Christ and of the Antichrist begin in Jordan, with Carpathia urging his troops to attack, only to be confronted with the ultimate deus ex machina:

"Heaven opened and there, on a white horse, sat Jesus, the Christ, the Son of the living God. . . . Jesus' eyes shone with conviction like a flame of fire, and He held His majestic head high. . . . On His robe at the thigh a name was written: KING OF KINGS AND LORD OF LORDS."

LaHaye is not the first author to cash in on the apocalypse. Hal Lindsey's 1970 Christian End Times book, *The Late Great Planet Earth*, which predicted that the world would come to an end around 1988, was the No. 1 nonfiction best-seller of the 70s. Nevertheless, LaHaye, Jenkins, and their aptly named literary agent, Rick Christian, had a tough time interesting publishers in their concept. Finally, LaHaye's nonfiction publishing company, Tyndale House, put up $50,000, boasting that it could market the book well enough to sell half a million copies.

Kicking off the series in 1995, as the millennium clock ran down, provided a convenient marketing device. According to *The Washington Post*, by 2001, 27 million copies of "Left Behind" books had been sold, along with 10 million related products such as postcards and wallpaper. Thanks to the astounding growth of Evangelicalism in America, even the uneventful passing of the millennium failed to dampen sales, which increased so greatly—to a pace of 1.5 million copies a month—that the series, originally planned to be 7 books, was extended to 12. By now, according to *BusinessWeek*, the "Left Behind" series has brought in more than $650 million to the Illinois-based Tyndale House, the largest privately owned Christian publisher in the country. Not surprisingly, LaHaye has sought to extend his brand with children's versions, a prequel (*The Rising*) written with Jenkins, and a new series, "Babylon Rising," about an Indiana Jones–like hero who uncovers the secrets of biblical prophecies.

When Jerry Falwell reflects on the past 25 years, even he is astounded at how far the Christian right has come. "I was not at all sure in 1979 when I started Moral Majority that we really could make a difference. But I knew we had to try," he says. "A quarter of a century later, I'm amazed at how a huge nation like America could be so affected and even turned around by the New Testament Church. "We're gaining ground every time the sun shines. I don't think this phenomenon is cresting, because there is a spiritual awakening in America right now."

When he started out, Falwell recalls, he was thrilled if 35 people came to church and left more than $100 on his offering plate. Today, revenue at his Thomas Road Baptist Church tops $200 million a year—and is likely to exceed $400 million in the near future.

The evangelical market is so big now that mainstream corporate America doesn't dare ignore it. *The Purpose-Driven Life*, by California pastor Rick Warren, published in 2002, has already sold 23 million copies, making it the fastest-selling nonfiction book of all time. Now religion is the hottest category in publishing, bringing in more than $3 billion a year. Time Warner, Random House, and HarperCollins have all put together religious imprints. There are more than 2,000 Christian radio stations. Christian music now outsells all classical and jazz releases combined. The EMI Group and Sony BMG Music Entertainment have acquired religious labels.

And the peak is nowhere in sight. "This is just the beginning," says Tim LaHaye. "Now we have media like we've never had before—alternative media, the Internet, and Fox News."

Throughout America, especially the South, a massive, fully developed subculture has emerged. In Greenville, South Carolina, more than 700 churches serve just 56,000 people. On a highway not far from town, a billboard reads, LET'S MEET ON SUNDAY AT MY HOUSE BEFORE THE GAME. —GOD.

And it's not about just going to church. There are movie nights for Christians, summer camps for Christian kids, Christian "poker runs," Christian marriage-counseling sessions, Christian Caribbean vacations, Christian specialty stores, and Christian ministries for singles, seniors, and the divorced. "It plays exactly the same role in shaping your beliefs that the counterculture of the 60s did for the left," says a former Evangelical. "Politically, you end up voting for that which reinforces your belief system. How you will appear in the eyes of the God you believe in—that's your anchor."

It is an insular world that is almost completely segregated from the secular world, including the mainstream media. "No one in our family read newspapers," says another former Evangelical, who left her church in Yuba City, California, and eventually moved to New York. "Growing up, our only source of information in my life was the pastor. We believed in what God had told him to say because we were children, and he was our shepherd, and he had been chosen by God."

A crucial part of that theology dictates a love for Israel, an affection based on faith more than on information. "When I grew up, I did not know Jews walked the face of the earth," she says. "I thought they lived only in biblical times. They were my brothers and sisters in the Lord, but I didn't know they still existed."

That love of Israel is sometimes accompanied by racist hatred of Arabs. On several occasions, an Israeli guide on LaHaye and Frazier's tour told the group that Arabs "breed like fleas" and would soon be forced into the desert. LaHaye's followers responded with warm laughter and applause.

From Israel's point of view, there are many reasons to welcome American Evangelicals, regardless of how well-informed they may be. Tourism is one. Last year, 400,000 Christian tourists visited Israel, where they spent more than $1.4 billion. "During the intifada, loyal Christians still came as tourists. We have to go to the grass roots. It is so important to make them lovers of Israel," says Benny Elon, Orthodox leader of the right-wing National Union, former tourism minister, and a frequent guest of the Christian Coalition's in the U.S.

And given that there are more than 10 times as many Evangelicals in America as Jews, it is understandable that Israel might seek their political support. "Israel's relationship with America can't be built only on the AIPAC [American Israel Public Affairs Committee] and the 2.5 percent of the population in America who are Jews," says Elon. "When Israel enjoys support because it is the land of the Bible, why should we reject that?" adds Uzi Arad, who served as foreign-policy adviser to former prime minister Benjamin Netanyahu and now heads the Institute for Policy and Strategy, a think tank in

Herzliya, Israel. "Whether it is because of expediency or because on some level we may be soulmates, each side offers the other something they want. And the Christian right is a political force to be reckoned with in America."

But Evangelicals have also played a role in disrupting the peace process. "I was ambassador for four years of the peace process, and the Christian fundamentalists were vehemently opposed to the peace process," says Itamar Rabinovich, who served as Israeli ambassador to the U.S. between 1993 and 1996, under the Labor governments of Rabin and Shimon Peres. "They believed that the land belonged to Israel as a matter of divine right. So they immediately became part of a campaign by the Israeli right to undermine the peace process."

No one played that card more forcefully than Benjamin "Bibi" Netanyahu, who as prime minister used the Christian right to fend off pressure from the Clinton administration to proceed with the peace process.

On a visit to Washington, D.C., in 1998, Netanyahu hooked up with Jerry Falwell at the Mayflower Hotel the night before his scheduled meeting with Clinton. "I put together 1,000 people or so to meet with Bibi and he spoke to us that night," recalls Falwell. "It was all planned by Netanyahu as an affront to Mr. Clinton."

That evening, Falwell promised Netanyahu that he would mobilize pastors all over the country to resist the return of parts of the occupied West Bank territory to the Palestinians. Televangelist John Hagee, who gave $1 million to the United Jewish Appeal the following month, told the crowd that the Jewish return to the Holy Land signaled the "rapidly approaching . . . final moments of history," then brought them to a frenzy chanting, "Not one inch!"—a reference to how much of the West Bank should be transferred to Palestinian control.

The next day, Netanyahu met with Clinton at the White House. "Bibi told me later," Falwell recalls, "that the next morning Bill Clinton said, 'I know where you were last night.' The pressure was really on Netanyahu to give away the farm in Israel. It was during the Monica Lewinsky scandal. . . . Clinton had to save himself, so he terminated the demands [to relinquish West Bank territory] that would have been forthcoming during that meeting, and would have been very bad for Israel."

In the end, no one played a bigger role in thwarting the prospect for peace than the Palestinian leader, Yasser Arafat, who rejected a deal with Netanyahu's successor, Ehud Barak, in 2000. In general, the Christian right has not gone to the mat to fight a two-state solution to the Israeli-Palestinian conflict. But when the peace process finally resumed during the Bush administration, the Christian right made certain its theology was not ignored. In March 2004, according to *The Village Voice*, a delegation from the Apostolic Congress, a religious group that believes in the Rapture, met with Elliott Abrams, then the National Security Council's senior director for Near East and North African affairs, to discuss its concern that Israel's disengagement from Gaza would violate God's covenant with Israel. As it happens, Netanyahu, for non-theological reasons, shared the Christian right's concern about the Gaza pullout to such an extent that he resigned from Sharon's cabinet last summer and has vowed to challenge him for the prime minister's post.

But this intrusion of End Times theology is of deep concern to Israelis who are not as hawkish as Netanyahu. "This is incredibly dangerous to Israel," says Gershom Gorenberg, a Jerusalem-based journalist and the author of *The End of Days*, a chronicle of messianic Christians and Jews and their struggle with Muslim fundamentalists over the Temple Mount. "They're not interested in the survival of the State of Israel. They are interested in the Rapture, in bringing to fruition a cosmic myth of the End Times, proving that they are right with one big bang. We are merely actors in their dreams. LaHaye's vision is that Jews will convert or die and go to hell. If you read his books, he is looking forward to war. He is not an ally in the safety of Israel."

Far from being a Prince of Peace, the Christ depicted in the "Left Behind" series is a vengeful Messiah—so vengeful that the death and destruction he causes to unconverted Jews, to secularists, to anyone who is not born again, is far, far greater than the crimes committed by the most brutal dictators in human history. When He arrives on the scene in *Glorious Appearing*, Christ merely has to speak and "men and women, soldiers and horses, seemed to explode where they stood. It was as if the very words of the Lord had superheated their blood, causing it to burst through their veins and skin." Soon, LaHaye and Jenkins write, tens of thousands of foot soldiers for the Antichrist are dying in the goriest manner imaginable, their internal organs oozing out, "their blood pooling and rising in the unforgiving brightness of the glory of Christ."

After the initial bloodletting, Nicolae Carpathia gathers his still-vast army, covering hundreds of square miles, and prepares for the conflict at Megiddo. As the battle for Armageddon is about to start, Rayford Steele climbs atop his Hummer to watch Christ harvest the grapes of wrath. Steele looks at the hordes of soldiers assembled by the Antichrist, and "tens of thousands burst open at the words of Jesus." They scream in pain and die before hitting the ground, their blood pouring forth. Soon, a massive river of blood is flowing throughout the Holy Land. Carpathia and the False Prophet are cast into the eternal lake of fire.

According to LaHaye and Jenkins, it is God's intent "that the millennium start with a clean slate." Committing mass murder hundreds of times greater than the Holocaust, the Lord—not the Antichrist, mind you—makes sure that "*all* unbelievers would soon die."

One of Steele's colleagues decides he'll have to talk to God about what to do next. After all, now that the secular humanists are gone and only believers remain, America is a very, very sparsely populated country. But if enough people are left, he wonders, isn't this the perfect opportunity "to start rebuilding the country as, finally for real, a Christian nation?"

Evolution, Creationism, and Intelligent Design

Let's be clear. "Intelligent Design" may be interesting as theology, but as science it is a fraud. It is a self-enclosed, tautological "theory" whose only holding is that when there are gaps in some area of scientific knowledge—in this case, evolution—they are to be filled by God.

> —Charles Krauthammer, syndicated columnist, "Face It: 'Intelligent Design' Is More Fraud than Science,' *Houston Chronicle* (November 28, 2005)

To be sure, Darwin's theory of evolution is imperfect. However, the fact that a scientific theory cannot yet render an explanation on every point should not be used as a pretext to thrust an untestable alternative hypothesis grounded in religion into the science classroom or to misrepresent well-established scientific propositions.

> —Federal judge John E. Jones, in his ruling against the Dover, Pennsylvania, school board, which had required the teaching of intelligent design as an alternative to evolution, quoted in the *Houston Chronicle* (December 21, 2005)

NATURAL 'KNOWLEDGE' AND NATURAL 'DESIGN'

By Richard Dawkins

Richard Dawkins, FRS, is the Charles Simonyi Professor of the Public Understanding of Science at Oxford University. An abbreviated version of this article was published in the special World Economic Forum Edition of Newsweek magazine. His latest book is The Ancestor's Tale.

As conscious animals, we think of knowledge as something that we consciously know. A zoologist might see knowledge as facts that are useful for survival and reproduction, whether or not they are known to a mind. An orb spider's survival tool is its web, and it behaves as if it "knows" how to build it. Each cell in an embryo lioness "knows" how to participate, with millions of other cells, in a virtuoso performance of orchestrated origami whose end product is an adult hunter: a carnivorous machine with limbs to run, eyes to see, claws to subdue, teeth and enzymes to dismember and dissolve, guts to digest, and two uteruses to make new embryos that will preserve that genetically encoded "knowledge."

A spider doesn't know how to make a web as a fisherman knows how to make a net. Spider genes are a recipe for legs, muscles, and spinnerets, together with a brain whose wiring diagram causes it to manipulate muscles in such a way that a web automatically results. The spider—presumably—knows nothing of webs or flies, any more than you knew how to build yourself during your nine months of unconscious gestation. Genes literally don't know anything; but, in a powerful sense, they store knowledge about environments from an ancestral past.

Beaver genes, "knowing" about an external world of rivers, trees, and dams, program bodies to exploit it. Like all mammal genes, beaver genes also "know" about the internal world of mammal biochemistries and mammal bodies, and they build cells that transact the first and construct the second. Genes "know" about their environment in the special, limited sense that a key "knows" the lock that it uniquely fits.

Where do genes gain their knowledge? All knowledge of the future must come from the past. Gene pools store knowledge of ancestral environments and program future bodies to use it. To the extent that the future resembles the past, bodies reproduce and pass on the same genes. Sometimes, bodies die, along with the genes inside them. In extreme cases, whole species go extinct.

But how is the information read out of the environment and into the genes? This is the indispensable role of natural selection, the stunningly simple yet powerful engine of evolution first discovered by Charles Darwin, although he expressed it differently. Neo-Darwinians speak of the nonrandom survival

Richard Dawkins, a best-selling author, is the Charles Simonyi Professor of the Public Understanding of Science at Oxford University. His books include *The Ancestor's Tale, The Selfish Gene, The Blind Watchmaker, Climbing Mount Improbable, Unweaving the Rainbow, A Devil's Chaplain* and *The God Delusion*.

of genes in gene pools. The gene pool of a species is the set of genes that is available, through sexual shuffling, for making individuals of that species. With the exception of clones or identical twins, every individual is unique. But genes are things you can count. As generations pass, good genes become more frequent in the gene pool; bad genes disappear. "Good" means the genes are good at building bodies that survive to reproduce in the environment of the species: woodland, sea, soil, coral reef, etc. Regardless of external environments, good genes are good at cooperating inside cells with other genes that have become frequent in the same gene pool and are, therefore, by definition, also good.

As a sculptor shapes a statue by subtraction of marble, so natural selection chisels the gene pool towards perfection as generations go by. It isn't only subtraction. New variation is added to the gene pool by mutation—random mistakes that occasionally turn out to be superior. The randomness of mutation is partly responsible for the widespread, ludicrous misconception that natural selection itself is a random process.

Nonrandom natural selection, automatically and without awareness or deliberation, funnels information about environments into the DNA of a species. This coded information fosters the illusion that organisms were designed precisely for their environments. Think of the uncanny resemblance of camouflaged insects to the background on which they sit. Think of the vertebrate eye, with its high-resolution trichromat retina, variable-focus lens, and light-metered fine adjustment of the pupil. But think, too, of the strange fact that the vertebrate retina (though not that of the independently evolved octopus) is arranged back-to-front. Light has to pass through a forest of connecting wires before hitting the photocells: exactly the kind of historical "mistake" you would expect of an evolved, as opposed to designed, instrument.

Several factors conspire to make the natural illusion of design persuasive, complex, and often beautiful. "Arms races" between predators and prey, or parasites and hosts, drive the perfection of evolutionary adaptation to spectacular heights. Perfection is enhanced by large numbers of genes, each of small effect, cooperating with each other in cartels of long standing. The evolution of beauty is abetted by the principle that Darwin called sexual selection. The gorgeous colors of a male bird of paradise certainly don't help it to survive as an individual. They do help the survival of genes that make it attractive to females.

Above all, the illusion of design depends upon the gradual accumulation of small improvements, escalating to levels of complexity and elegance that could not conceivably be achieved in a single lucky step. We are rightly incredulous of any suggestion that biological complexity could spring suddenly from primordial simplicity in one generation. But it is easy if each step of a gradual progression is derived from its immediate predecessor, which it closely resembles. That, in a sentence, is why evolution can so brilliantly explain life, where neither chance nor design can.

Intelligent Design works as a short-term proximal explanation of cameras and cars, prize roses and poodles. But it is fatally flawed as an ultimate explanation for anything, because it miserably fails to answer the $64,000 question: Who designed the designer? That is not a frivolous debating point. It looms menacingly and fatally over the case—such as it is—for Intelligent Design. And, by the way, there is nothing new about "Intelligent Design Theory." It boasts a slick, adman-crafted name, but (aside from an irrelevant shift into cellular biochemistry) it offers no new arguments beyond those that Darwin himself demolished in his magnanimous chapter on "Difficulties."

The central (and virtually only) argument offered in favor of Intelligent Design is the Argument from Improbability. Some biological feature—an eye or feather, biochemical pathway or bacterial flagellum—is claimed to be too statistically improbable (irreducibly complex, information-rich, etc.) to have evolved by natural selection (naïve, old-style creationists say "chance"). Therefore, by default, it must have been "designed." Positive evidence for design is never even considered: only alleged failures of the alternative.

It is hard to imagine a more lamentably weak argument. In every case that has been examined in detail, a complex biological feature always turns out to have a gradual, ascending path leading to it. In any case, no attempt is ever made to show that the so-called alternative theory of Intelligent Design fares any better at explaining the feature. Ultimately, however statistically improbable, however irreducibly complex an eye or flagellum or anything else might one day prove to be, any intelligent being capable of designing it would have to be even more statistically improbable and complex.

Disingenuously, Intelligent Design advocates try to disguise their religious motives by claiming that the designer's identity is left open. Not necessarily Yahweh, it could be an alien from space. Scientists would not object to that in principle, because the stellar alien, who might indeed be godlike from our humble viewpoint, presumably evolved by a gradual, cumulative process. You can roll the regress back if you wish, to a designer of the designer. But sooner or later you are going to have to foreswear what the philosopher Daniel Dennett calls "skyhooks" and employ a solidly founded "crane." The only natural crane we know is natural selection, and I have no doubt that, if life exists elsewhere in the universe, it will turn out to be, in the broad sense, Darwinian.

To the extent that creationists rely on the Argument from Improbability, they cannot get away with postulating an unevolved designer—who would have to be even more improbable. To the extent that they allow their unevolved supernatural designer to have sprung into existence ab initio, they should allow natural agents the same dubious privilege. Intelligent Design is not only bad science; it is bad logic, bad philosophy, and even—as my theologian friends point out—bad theology.

The United States is, by any standards, the leading scientific nation in the history of the world. Yet this unprecedented powerhouse of scientific achievement is being dragged down in derision, in the eyes of the entire educated world, by the aggressive ignorance and philistinism of its influential boondocks, occasionally redeemed by the likes of the splendid Judge John Jones in Pennsylvania. A second-rate mathematician, a mediocre biochemist, a born-again retired lawyer, and a Moonie have somehow succeeded in elevating themselves, in the eyes of influential but ignorant politicians, rich benefactors, and duped laymen, to near parity with the entire National Academy of Sciences. How has it been allowed to happen? When will this great country come to its senses and rejoin the civilized world?

INTELLIGENT DESIGN AND ATHEIST COURTS

By R. Cort Kirkwood

INTELLIGENT DESIGN had its day in court in Dover, Pennsylvania, and the result was sadly predictable. So was the reaction to it.

The evolutionist and atheist left ballyhooed the decision as another victory for science over superstition, and for the separation of Church and state. The intelligent-design crowd vowed to continue fighting, and talk radio unlimbered its voice. "Who should get a lump of coal for Christmas?" Sean Hannity's guest host asked. "The judge in the case about intelligent design!" answered one irate caller.

Yet no one with any sense, least of all serious Christians, is surprised or even disheartened by the decision, for one simple reason: The atheist left runs the courts and the schools, and sober Christians know they will never change that. They don't care what the public schools teach because their children do not attend them.

Intelligent design is the claim that some biological processes and structures are so complex that God, not evolution, must have created them. The trouble in Dover began when the school board said teachers must read a short statement about intelligent design in the ninth-grade biology class. The disclaimer said evolution is merely a theory, and that the "theory is not a fact. Gaps in the theory exist for which there is no evidence. . . . Intelligent design is an explanation of the origin of life that differs from Darwin's." The statement goes on from there, but you get the idea.

Using such phrases as "breathtaking inanity," the judge zapped the school board's statement with a judicial lightning bolt. He concluded that the proponents of intelligent design wanted to smuggle religion into the science classroom, a mortal sin against the leftist ideology of public schools.

The upshot was that the proponents of intelligent design put their chips on a vague, four-paragraph statement that said, essentially, nothing. The statement, the court case—all the hot air was a waste.

The decision was based on the palpably absurd and well-worn notion that teaching something, anything, about religion in a public school is "unconstitutional" and violates the "wall of separation between Church and State." Of course, it isn't the Constitution or the First Amendment that prohibits teaching religion in schools. The real prohibitive agent in these cases is the steamer trunk of erroneous case law cited by the judge and hoked up by anti-Christian, leftist courts that would have no power if the locals refused to abide them.

It is easy to sympathize with the parents of Dover who favor the teaching of intelligent design. They are rightly concerned about the anti-Christian gospel that schools pump into the minds of their children.

R. Cort Kirkwood, an award-winning journalist, is managing editor of the *Daily News-Record* in Harrisonburg, Virginia. He has been writing about American politics and culture for more than twenty years.

This article first appeared in the February 2006 issue of *Chronicles*. Reprinted with permission from the February 2006 issue of *Chronicles: A Magazine of American Culture*, a publication of The Rockford Institute in Rockford, Illinois.

Yet whatever the merits of intelligent design, it is only the proximate legal reason why the good folks in Dover lost. Ultimately, they lost because public schools are officially atheist and anti-Christian; and leftist courts, controlled by leftist litigants, lawyers, and judges, will smite anyone promoting any doctrine that threatens their godless creed.

If the courts have one commandment, it is that Christians may not question curricula. So the court case in Delaware was not really a legal refutation of intelligent design; it was another slap at religion. Years ago, the cause was prayer at the morning bell. Now, it's "abstinence education" and intelligent design. For the unions and leftist lawyers and judges who run the schools, religion is the enemy. They fought to extirpate it, and they won. The battle is over. Yet even if these regnant powers could be dislodged, what would it matter? Public schools are uniformly atrocious. They are blighted educationally and noxious morally. Repeated surveys show that some teachers are illiterate. Forget about the honor rolls and kids who graduate with a "4.5." Taking control of public schools, particularly given the constant litigation such control would invite, would be a pyrrhic victory.

The evangelicals and supporters of intelligent design must give up this fight and every other one as well, from contraceptives and school prayer to dress codes and homosexuals at the prom. The only intelligent course is to pull their kids out of the public schools. Private Christian academies are everywhere. Parochial schools abound. Better yet, there is homeschooling. Indeed, any serious Christian knows that putting a child in public school is a grave sin, given the crippling, lowbrow academics and anti-Christian cultural toxins to which such children are exposed.

Until Christian parents learn that their future lies outside the public schools, they will only strengthen the anti-Christian leftists they want to dethrone. To defeat them, parents must deprive schools of the malleable minds required to propagate their anti-American, anti-Christian ideology.

That would be an intelligent design.

DEVOLUTION: Why Intelligent design isn't

By H. Allen Orr

If you are in ninth grade and live in Dover, Pennsylvania, you are learning things in your biology class that differ considerably from what your peers just a few miles away are learning. In particular, you are learning that Darwin's theory of evolution provides just one possible explanation of life, and that another is provided by something called intelligent design. You are being taught this not because of a recent breakthrough in some scientist's laboratory but because the Dover Area School District's board mandates it. In October, 2004, the board decreed that "students will be made aware of gaps/problems in Darwin's theory and of other theories of evolution including, but not limited to, intelligent design."

While the events in Dover have received a good deal of attention as a sign of the political times, there has been surprisingly little discussion of the science that's said to underlie the theory of intelligent design, often called I.D. Many scientists avoid discussing I.D. for strategic reasons. If a scientific claim can be loosely defined as one that scientists take seriously enough to debate, then engaging the intelligent-design movement on scientific grounds, they worry, cedes what it most desires: recognition that its claims are legitimate scientific ones.

Meanwhile, proposals hostile to evolution are being considered in more than twenty states, earlier this month, a bill was introduced into the New York State Assembly calling for instruction in intelligent design for all public-school students. The Kansas State Board of Education is weighing new standards, drafted by supporters of intelligent design, that would encourage schoolteachers to challenge Darwinism. Senator Rick Santorum, a Pennsylvania Republican, has argued that "intelligent design is a legitimate scientific theory that should be taught in science classes." An I.D.-friendly amendment that he sponsored to the No Child Left Behind Act—requiring public schools to help students understand why evolution "generates so much continuing controversy"—was overwhelmingly approved in the Senate. (The amendment was not included in the version of the bill that was signed into law, but similar language did appear in a conference report that accompanied it.) In the past few years, college students across the country have formed Intelligent Design and Evolution Awareness chapters. Clearly, a policy of limited scientific engagement has failed. So just what is this movement?

First of all, intelligent design is not what people often assume it is. For one thing, I.D. is not Biblical literalism. Unlike earlier generations of creationists—the so-called Young Earthers and scientific creationists—proponents of intelligent design do not believe that the universe was created in six days, that Earth

H. Allen Orr, an evolutionary geneticist, is a professor at the University of Rochester, Department of Biology.

This article was originally published in *The New Yorker*, May 30, 2005. It is reprinted with permission from H. Allen Orr.

is ten thousand years old, or that the fossil record was deposited during Noah's flood. (Indeed, they shun the label "creationism" altogether.) Nor does I.D. flatly reject evolution: adherents freely admit that some evolutionary change occurred during the history of life on Earth. Although the movement is loosely allied with, and heavily funded by, various conservative Christian groups—and although I.D. plainly maintains that life was created—it is generally silent about the identity of the creator.

The movement's main positive claim is that there are things in the world, most notably life, that cannot be accounted for by known natural causes and show features that, in any other context, we would attribute to intelligence. Living organisms are too complex to be explained by any natural—or, more precisely, by any mindless—process. Instead, the design inherent in organisms can be accounted for only by invoking a designer, and one who is very, very smart.

All of which puts I.D. squarely at odds with Darwin. Darwin's theory of evolution was meant to show how the fantastically complex features of organisms—eyes, beaks, brains—could arise without the intervention of a designing mind. According to Darwinism, evolution largely reflects the combined action of random mutation and natural selection. A random mutation in an organism, like a random change in any finely tuned machine, is almost always bad. That's why you don't, screwdriver in hand, make arbitrary changes to the insides of your television. But, once in a great while, a random mutation in the DNA that makes up an organism's genes slightly improves the function of some organ and thus the survival of the organism. In a species whose eye amounts to nothing more than a primitive patch of light-sensitive cells, a mutation that causes this patch to fold into a cup shape might have a survival advantage. While the old type of organism can tell only if the lights are on, the new type can detect the direction of any source of light or shadow. Since shadows sometimes mean predators, that can be valuable information. The new, improved type of organism will, therefore, be more common in the next generation. That's natural selection. Repeated over billions of years, this process of incremental improvement should allow for the gradual emergence of organisms that are exquisitely adapted to their environments and that look for all the world as though they were designed. By 1870, about a decade after "The Origin of Species" was published, nearly all biologists agreed that life had evolved, and by 1940 or so most agreed that natural selection was a key force driving this evolution.

Advocates of intelligent design point to two developments that in their view undermine Darwinism. The first is the molecular revolution in biology. Beginning in the nineteen-fifties, molecular biologists revealed a staggering and unsuspected degree of complexity within the cells that make up all life. This complexity, I.D.'s defenders argue, lies beyond the abilities of Darwinism to explain. Second, they claim that new mathematical findings cast doubt on the power of natural selection. Selection may play a role in evolution, but it cannot accomplish what biologists suppose it can.

These claims have been championed by a tireless group of writers, most of them associated with the Center for Science and Culture at the Discovery Institute, a Seattle-based think tank that sponsors projects in science, religion, and national defense, among other areas. The center's fellows and advisers—including the emeritus law professor Phillip E. Johnson, the philosopher Stephen C. Meyer, and the biologist Jonathan Wells—have published an astonishing number of articles and books that decry the ostensibly sad state of Darwinism and extoll the virtues of the design alternative. But Johnson, Meyer, and Wells, while highly visible, are mainly strategists and popularizers. The scientific leaders of the design movement are two scholars, one a biochemist and the other a mathematician. To assess intelligent design is to assess their arguments.

Michael J. Behe, a professor of biological sciences at Lehigh University (and a senior fellow at the Discovery Institute), is a biochemist who writes technical papers on the structure of DNA. He is the most prominent of the small circle of scientists working on intelligent design, and his arguments are by far the best known. His book "Darwin's Black Box" (1996) was a surprise best-seller and was named by National Review as one of the hundred best nonfiction books of the twentieth century. (A little calibration may be useful here; "The Starr Report" also made the list.)

Not surprisingly, Behe's doubts about Darwinism begin with biochemistry. Fifty years ago, he says, any biologist could tell stories like the one about the eye's evolution. But such stories, Behe notes, invariably began with cells, whose own evolutionary origins were essentially left unexplained. This was harmless enough as long as cells weren't qualitatively more complex than the larger, more visible aspects of the eye. Yet when biochemists began to dissect the inner workings of the cell, what they found floored them. A cell is packed full of exceedingly complex structures—hundreds of microscopic machines, each performing a specific job. The "Give me a cell and I'll give you an eye" story told by Darwinists, he says, began to seem suspect: starting with a cell was starting ninety per cent of the way to the finish line.

Behe's main claim is that cells are complex not just in degree but in kind. Cells contain structures that are "irreducibly complex." This means that if you remove any single part from such a structure, the structure no longer functions. Behe offers a simple, nonbiological example of an irreducibly complex object: the mousetrap. A mousetrap has several parts—platform, spring, catch, hammer, and hold-down bar—and all of them have to be in place for the trap to work. If you remove the spring from a mousetrap, it isn't slightly worse at killing mice; it doesn't kill them at all. So, too, with the bacterial flagellum, Behe argues. This flagellum is a tiny propeller attached to the back of some bacteria. Spinning at more than twenty thousand r.p.m.s, it motors the bacterium through its aquatic world. The flagellum comprises roughly thirty different proteins, all precisely arranged, and if any one of them is removed the flagellum stops spinning.

In "Darwin's Black Box," Behe maintained that irreducible complexity presents Darwinism with "unbridgeable chasms." How, after all, could a gradual process of incremental improvement build something like a flagellum, which needs all its parts in order to work? Scientists, he argued, must face up to the fact that "many biochemical systems cannot be built by natural selection working on mutations." In the end, Behe concluded that irreducibly complex cells arise the same way as irreducibly complex mousetraps—someone designs them. As he put it in a recent Times Op-Ed piece: "If it looks, walks, and quacks like a duck, then, absent compelling evidence to the contrary, we have warrant to conclude it's a duck. Design should not be overlooked simply because it's so obvious." In "Darwin's Black Box," Behe speculated that the designer might have assembled the first cell, essentially solving the problem of irreducible complexity, after which evolution might well have proceeded by more or less conventional means. Under Behe's brand of creationism, you might still be an ape that evolved on the African savanna; it's just that your cells harbor micro-machines engineered by an unnamed intelligence some four billion years ago.

But Behe's principal argument soon ran into trouble. As biologists pointed out, there are several different ways that Darwinian evolution can build irreducibly complex systems. In one, elaborate structures may evolve for one reason and then get co-opted for some entirely different, irreducibly complex function. Who says those thirty flagellar proteins weren't present in bacteria long before bacteria sported flagella? They may have been performing other jobs in the cell and only later got drafted into flagellum-building. Indeed, there's now strong evidence that several flagellar proteins once played roles in a type of molecular pump found in the membranes of bacterial cells.

Behe doesn't consider this sort of "indirect" path to irreducible complexity—in which parts perform one function and then switch to another—terribly plausible. And he essentially rules out the alternative possibility of a direct Darwinian path: a path, that is, in which Darwinism builds an irreducibly complex structure while selecting all along for the same biological function. But biologists have shown that direct paths to irreducible complexity are possible, too. Suppose a part gets added to a system merely because the part improves the system's performance; the part is not, at this stage, essential for function. But, because subsequent evolution builds on this addition, a part that was at first just advantageous might become essential. As this process is repeated through evolutionary time, more and more parts that were once merely beneficial become necessary. This idea was first set forth by H. J. Muller, the Nobel Prize-winning geneticist, in 1939, but it's a familiar process in the development of human technologies. We add new parts like global-positioning systems to cars not because they're necessary but because they're nice. But no one would be surprised if, in fifty years, computers that rely on G.P.S. actually drove our cars. At that point, G.P.S. would no longer be an attractive option; it would be an essential piece of automotive technology. It's important to see that this process is thoroughly Darwinian: each change might well be small and each represents an improvement.

Design theorists have made some concessions to these criticisms. Behe has confessed to "sloppy prose" and said he hadn't meant to imply that irreducibly complex systems "by definition" cannot evolve gradually. "I quite agree that my argument against Darwinism does not add up to a logical proof," he says—though he continues to believe that Darwinian paths to irreducible complexity are exceedingly unlikely. Behe and his followers now emphasize that, while irreducibly complex systems can in principle evolve, biologists can't reconstruct in convincing detail just how any such system did evolve.

What counts as a sufficiently detailed historical narrative, though, is altogether subjective. Biologists actually know a great deal about the evolution of biochemical systems, irreducibly complex or not. It's significant, for instance, that the proteins that typically make up the parts of these systems are often similar to one another. (Blood clotting—another of Behe's examples of irreducible complexity—involves at least twenty proteins, several of which are similar, and all of which are needed to make clots, to localize or remove clots, or to prevent the runaway clotting of all blood.) And biologists understand why these proteins are so similar. Each gene in an organism's genome encodes a particular protein. Occasionally, the stretch of DNA that makes up a particular gene will get accidentally copied, yielding a genome that includes two versions of the gene. Over many generations, one version of the gene will often keep its original function while the other one slowly changes by mutation and natural selection, picking up a new, though usually related, function. This process of "gene duplication" has given rise to entire families of proteins that have similar functions; they often act in the same biochemical pathway or sit in the same cellular structure. There's no doubt that gene duplication plays an extremely important role in the evolution of biological complexity.

It's true that when you confront biologists with a particular complex structure like the flagellum they sometimes have a hard time saying which part appeared before which other parts. But then it can be hard, with any complex historical process, to reconstruct the exact order in which events occurred, especially when, as in evolution, the addition of new parts encourages the modification of old ones. When you're looking at a bustling urban street, for example, you probably can't tell which shop went into business first. This is partly because many businesses now depend on each other and partly because new shops trigger changes in old ones (the new sushi place draws twenty-somethings who demand wireless Internet at the café next door). But it would be a little rash to conclude that all the shops must have begun business on the same day or that some Unseen Urban Planner had carefully determined just which business went where.

The other leading theorist of the new creationism, William A. Dembski, holds a Ph.D. in mathematics, another in philosophy, and a master of divinity in theology. He has been a research professor in the conceptual foundations of science at Baylor University, and was recently appointed to the new Center for Science and Theology at Southern Baptist Theological Seminary. (He is a long-time senior fellow at the Discovery Institute as well.) Dembski publishes at a staggering pace. His books—including "The Design Inference," "Intelligent Design," "No Free Lunch," and "The Design Revolution"—are generally well written and packed with provocative ideas.

According to Dembski, a complex object must be the result of intelligence if it was the product neither of chance nor of necessity. The novel "Moby Dick," for example, didn't arise by chance (Melville didn't scribble random letters), and it wasn't the necessary consequence of a physical law (unlike, say, the fall of an apple). It was, instead, the result of Melville's intelligence. Dembski argues that there is a reliable way to recognize such products of intelligence in the natural world. We can conclude that an object was intelligently designed, he says, if it shows "specified complexity"—complexity that matches an "independently given pattern." The sequence of letters "jkxvcju-doplvm" is certainly complex: if you randomly type thirteen letters, you are very unlikely to arrive at this particular sequence. But it isn't specified: it doesn't match any independently given sequence of letters. If, on the other hand, I ask you for the first sentence of "Moby Dick" and you type the letters "callmeishmael," you have produced something that is both complex and specified. The sequence you typed is unlikely to arise by chance alone, and it matches an independent target sequence (the one written by Melville). Dembski argues that specified complexity, when expressed mathematically, provides an unmistakable signature of intelligence. Things like "callmeishmael," he points out, just don't arise in the real world without acts of intelligence. If organisms show specified complexity, therefore, we can conclude that they are the handiwork of an intelligent agent.

For Dembski, it's telling that the sophisticated machines we find in organisms match up in astonishingly precise ways with recognizable human technologies. The eye, for example, has a familiar, cameralike design, with recognizable parts—a pinhole opening for light, a lens, and a surface on which to project an image—all arranged just as a human engineer would arrange them. And the flagellum has a motor design, one that features recognizable O-rings, a rotor, and a drive shaft. Specified complexity, he says, is there for all to see.

Dembski's second major claim is that certain mathematical results cast doubt on Darwinism at the most basic conceptual level. In 2002, he focussed on so-called No Free Lunch, or N.F.L., theorems, which were derived in the late nineties by the physicists David H. Wolpert and William G. Macready. These theorems relate to the efficiency of different "search algorithms." Consider a search for high ground on some unfamiliar, hilly terrain. You're on foot and it's a moonless night; you've got two hours to reach the highest place you can. How to proceed? One sensible search algorithm might say, "Walk uphill in the steepest possible direction; if no direction uphill is available, take a couple of steps to the left and try again." This algorithm insures that you're generally moving upward. Another search algorithm—a so-called blind search algorithm—might say, "Walk in a random direction." This would sometimes take you uphill but sometimes down. Roughly, the N.F.L. theorems prove the surprising fact that, averaged over all possible terrains, no search algorithm is better than any other. In some landscapes, moving uphill gets you to higher ground in the allotted time, while in other landscapes moving randomly does, but on average neither outperforms the other.

Now, Darwinism can be thought of as a search algorithm. Given a problem—adapting to a new disease, for instance—a population uses the Darwinian algorithm of random mutation plus natural selection to search for a solution (in this case, disease resistance). But, according to Dembski, the N.F.L. theorems prove that this Darwinian algorithm is no better than any other when confronting all possible problems. It follows that, over all, Darwinism is no better than blind search, a process of utterly random change unaided by any guiding force like natural selection. Since we don't expect blind change to build elaborate machines showing an exquisite coördination of parts, we have no right to expect Darwinism to do so, either. Attempts to sidestep this problem by, say, carefully constraining the class of challenges faced by organisms inevitably involve sneaking in the very kind of order that we're trying to explain—something Dembski calls the displacement problem. In the end, he argues, the N.F.L. theorems and the displacement problem mean that there's only one plausible source for the design we find in organisms: intelligence. Although Dembski is somewhat noncommittal, he seems to favor a design theory in which an intelligent agent programmed design into early life, or even into the early universe. This design then unfolded through the long course of evolutionary time, as microbes slowly morphed into man.

Dembski's arguments have been met with tremendous enthusiasm in the I.D. movement. In part, that's because an innumerate public is easily impressed by a bit of mathematics. Also, when Dembski is wielding his equations, he gets to play the part of the hard scientist busily correcting the errors of those soft-headed biologists. (Evolutionary biology actually features an extraordinarily sophisticated body of mathematical theory, a fact not widely known because neither of evolution's great popularizers—Richard Dawkins and the late Stephen Jay Gould—did much math.) Despite all the attention, Dembski's mathematical claims about design and Darwin are almost entirely beside the point.

The most serious problem in Dembski's account involves specified complexity. Organisms aren't trying to match any "independently given pattern": evolution has no goal, and the history of life isn't trying to get anywhere. If building a sophisticated structure like an eye increases the number of children produced, evolution may well build an eye. But if destroying a sophisticated structure like the eye increases the number of children produced, evolution will just as happily destroy the eye. Species of fish and crustaceans that have moved into the total darkness of caves, where eyes are both unnecessary and costly, often have degenerate eyes, or eyes that begin to form only to be covered by skin—crazy contraptions that no intelligent agent would design. Despite all the loose talk about design and machines, organisms aren't striving to realize some engineer's blueprint; they're striving (if they can be said to strive at all) only to have more offspring than the next fellow.

Another problem with Dembski's arguments concerns the N.F.L. theorems. Recent work shows that these theorems don't hold in the case of co-evolution, when two or more species evolve in response to one another. And most evolution is surely co-evolution. Organisms do not spend most of their time adapting to rocks; they are perpetually challenged by, and adapting to, a rapidly changing suite of viruses, parasites, predators, and prey. A theorem that doesn't apply to these situations is a theorem whose relevance to biology is unclear. As it happens, David Wolpert, one of the authors of the N.F.L. theorems, recently denounced Dembski's use of those theorems as "fatally informal and imprecise." Dembski's apparent response has been a tactical retreat. In 2002, Dembski triumphantly proclaimed, "The No Free Lunch theorems dash any hope of generating specified complexity via evolutionary algorithms." Now he says, "I certainly never argued that the N.F.L. theorems provide a direct refutation of Darwinism."

Those of us who have argued with I.D. in the past are used to such shifts of emphasis. But it's striking that Dembski's views on the history of life contradict Behe's. Dembski believes that Darwinism is incapable of building anything interesting; Behe seems to believe that, given a cell, Darwinism might well have built you and me. Although proponents of I.D. routinely inflate the significance of minor squabbles among evolutionary biologists (did the peppered moth evolve dark color as a defense against birds or for other reasons?), they seldom acknowledge their own, often major differences of opinion. In the end, it's hard to view intelligent design as a coherent movement in any but a political sense.

It's also hard to view it as a real research program. Though people often picture science as a collection of clever theories, scientists are generally staunch pragmatists: to scientists, a good theory is one that inspires new experiments and provides unexpected insights into familiar phenomena. By this standard, Darwinism is one of the best theories in the history of science: it has produced countless important experiments (let's re-create a natural species in the lab—yes, that's been done) and sudden insight into once puzzling patterns (that's why there are no native land mammals on oceanic islands). In the nearly ten years since the publication of Behe's book, by contrast, I.D. has inspired no nontrivial experiments and has provided no surprising insights into biology. As the years pass, intelligent design looks less and less like the science it claimed to be and more and more like an extended exercise in polemics.

In 1999, a document from the Discovery Institute was posted, anonymously, on the Internet. This Wedge Document, as it came to be called, described not only the institute's long-term goals but its strategies for accomplishing them. The document begins by labelling the idea that human beings are created in the image of God "one of the bedrock principles on which Western civilization was built." It goes on to decry the catastrophic legacy of Darwin, Marx, and Freud—the alleged fathers of a "materialistic conception of reality" that eventually "infected virtually every area of our culture." The mission of the Discovery Institute's scientific wing is then spelled out: "nothing less than the overthrow of materialism and its cultural legacies." It seems fair to conclude that the Discovery Institute has set its sights a bit higher than, say, reconstructing the origins of the bacterial flagellum.

The intelligent-design community is usually far more circumspect in its pronouncements. This is not to say that it eschews discussion of religion;

indeed, the intelligent-design literature regularly insists that Darwinism represents a thinly veiled attempt to foist a secular religion—godless materialism—on Western culture. As it happens, the idea that Darwinism is yoked to atheism, though popular, is also wrong. Of the five founding fathers of twentieth-century evolutionary biology—Ronald Fisher, Sewall Wright, J. B. S. Haldane, Ernst Mayr, and Theodosius Dobzhansky—one was a devout Anglican who preached sermons and published articles in church magazines, one a practicing Unitarian, one a dabbler in Eastern mysticism, one an apparent atheist, and one a member of the Russian Orthodox Church and the author of a book on religion and science. Pope John Paul II himself acknowledged, in a 1996 address to the Pontifical Academy of Sciences, that new research "leads to the recognition of the theory of evolution as more than a hypothesis." Whatever larger conclusions one thinks should follow from Darwinism, the historical fact is that evolution and religion have often coexisted. As the philosopher Michael Ruse observes, "It is simply not the case that people take up evolution in the morning, and become atheists as an encore in the afternoon."

Biologists aren't alarmed by intelligent design's arrival in Dover and elsewhere because they have all sworn allegiance to atheistic materialism; they're alarmed because intelligent design is junk science. Meanwhile, more than eighty per cent of Americans say that God either created human beings in their present form or guided their development. As a succession of intelligent-design proponents appeared before the Kansas State Board of Education earlier this month, it was possible to wonder whether the movement's scientific coherence was beside the point. Intelligent design has come this far by faith.

Foreign Policy

Stunningly, there's been a transformation form evangelicals' once common-place anti-Semitism to a Semitophilicism of an extraordinary sort. In their reading of Revelation, for example, evangelical "premillenarians" have taken the creation of modern Israel as a sign from God that Christ's Second Coming—and with it, the Final Judgment—are now imminent.... What this has produced is an unholy alliance of convenience, in which Ariel Sharon and Benjamin Netanyahu have embraced the likes of Pat Robertson and Jerry Falwell as a means to win support for their policies, while for conservative evangelicals, a strong Israel is crucial to Revelation-inspired dreams. And for GOP strategists such as Ralph Reed and Karl Rove, it has meant the opportunity to coax Jewish support away from the Democrats—or at least toward support for a much more conservative Democratic Party less resistant to the GOP's agenda.

—Richard Parker, lecturer at John F. Kennedy School of Government, *The American Prospect* (March 2004)

GOD'S COUNTRY?

By Walter Russell Mead

Summary: Religion has always been a major force in U.S. politics, but the recent surge in the number and the power of evangelicals is recasting the country's political scene—with dramatic implications for foreign policy. This should not be cause for panic: evangelicals are passionately devoted to justice and improving the world, and eager to reach out across sectarian lines.

Evangelicals and Foreign Policy

Religion has always been a major force in U.S. politics, policy, identity, and culture. Religion shapes the nation's character, helps form Americans' ideas about the world, and influences the ways Americans respond to events beyond their borders. Religion explains both Americans' sense of themselves as a chosen people and their belief that they have a duty to spread their values throughout the world. Of course, not all Americans believe such things—and those who do often bitterly disagree over exactly what they mean. But enough believe them that the ideas exercise profound influence over the country's behavior abroad and at home.

In one sense, religion is so important to life in the United States that it disappears into the mix. Partisans on all sides of important questions regularly appeal to religious principles to support their views, and the country is so religiously diverse that support for almost any conceivable foreign policy can be found somewhere.

Yet the balance of power among the different religious strands shifts over time; in the last generation, this balance has shifted significantly, and with dramatic consequences. The more conservative strains within American Protestantism have gained adherents, and the liberal Protestantism that dominated the country during the middle years of the twentieth century has weakened. This shift has already changed U.S. foreign policy in profound ways.

These changes have yet to be widely understood, however, in part because most students of foreign policy in the United States and abroad are relatively unfamiliar with conservative U.S. Protestantism. That the views of the evangelical Reverend Billy Graham lead to quite different approaches to foreign relations than, say, those popular at the fundamentalist Bob Jones University is not generally appreciated. But subtle theological and cultural differences can and do have important political consequences. Interpreting the impact of religious changes in the United States on U.S. foreign policy therefore requires a closer look into the big revival tent of American Protestantism.

Why focus exclusively on Protestantism? The answer is, in part, that Protestantism has shaped much of the country's identity and remains today the

Walter Russell Mead is a Henry A. Kissinger Senior Fellow for U.S. Foreign Policy at the Council on Foreign Relations.

majority faith in the United States (although only just). Moreover, the changes in Catholicism (the second-largest faith and the largest single religious denomination in the country) present a more mixed picture with fewer foreign policy implications. And finally, the remaining religious groups in the United States are significantly less influential when it comes to the country's politics.

A Question of Fundamentals

To make sense of how contemporary changes in Protestantism are starting to affect U.S. foreign policy, it helps to understand the role that religion has historically played in the country's public life. The U.S. religious tradition, which grew out of the sixteenth-century Reformations of England and Scotland, has included many divergent ideologies and worldviews over time. Three strains, however, have been most influential: a strict tradition that can be called fundamentalist, a progressive and ethical tradition known as liberal Christianity, and a broader evangelical tradition. (Pentecostals have theological differences with non-Pentecostal evangelicals and fundamentalists, but Pentecostalism is an offshoot of evangelical theology, and thus the majority of American Pentecostals can be counted with evangelicals here.)

It would be wrong to read too much precision into these labels. Most American Christians mix and match theological and social ideas from these and other strands of Protestant and Christian thought with little concern for consistency. Yet describing the chief features of each strand and their implications for the United States' role in the world will nevertheless make it easier to appreciate the way changes in the religious balance are shaping the country's behavior.

Fundamentalists, liberal Christians, and evangelicals are all part of the historical mainstream of American Protestantism, and as such all were profoundly affected by the fundamentalist-modernist controversy of the early twentieth century. For much of the 1800s, most Protestants believed that science confirmed biblical teaching. When Darwinian biology and scholarly "higher criticism" began to cast increasing doubt on traditional views of the Bible's authorship and veracity, however, the American Protestant movement broke apart. Modernists argued that the best way to defend Christianity in an enlightened age was to incorporate the new scholarship into theology, and mainline Protestant denominations followed this logic. The fundamentalists believed that churches should remain loyal to the "fundamentals" of Protestant faith, such as the literal truth of the Bible.

The fundamentalists themselves were divided into two strands, originally distinguished as much by culture and temperament as by theology. The "separatists" argued that true believers should abandon churches that compromised with or tolerated modernism in any form. As U.S. society and culture became more secular and pluralistic, the separatists increasingly withdrew from both politics and culture. The other strand of the original fundamentalist movement sought continual engagement with the rest of the world. This strand was originally called neo-evangelical. Today, the separatists proudly retain the label of fundamentalist, while the neo-evangelicals have dropped the prefix and are now simply known as evangelicals.

The three contemporary streams of American Protestantism (fundamentalist, liberal, and evangelical) lead to very different ideas about what the country's role in the world should be. In this context, the most important differences have to do with the degree to which each promotes optimism about the possibilities for a stable, peaceful, and enlightened international order and the importance each places on the difference between believers and nonbelievers. In a nutshell, fundamentalists are deeply pessimistic about the prospects for world order and see an unbridgeable divide between believers and nonbelievers. Liberals are optimistic about the prospects for world order and see little difference between Christians and nonbelievers. And evangelicals stand somewhere in between these extremes.

Self-described fundamentalists are a diverse group, partly because there are many competing definitions of the term "fundamentalist" and, in keeping with the decentralized and sectarian character of American Protestantism, there is no generally accepted authoritative body to define what fundamentalists are or believe. As used here, the term "fundamentalist" involves three characteristics: a high view of biblical authority and inspiration; a strong determination to defend the historical Protestant faith against Roman Catholic and modernist, secular, and non-Christian influence; and the conviction that believers should separate themselves from the non-Christian world. Fundamentalists can be found throughout conservative Protestant Christianity, and some denominations more properly considered evangelical (such as the Southern Baptists and the Missouri Synod Lutherans) have vocal minorities that could legitimately be called fundamentalist. Fundamentalist denominations, such as the ultra-Calvinist Orthodox Presbyterian Church, tend to be smaller than liberal and evangelical ones. This is partly because fundamentalists prefer small, pure, and doctrinally rigorous organizations to larger, more diverse ones. It is also because many fundamentalist congregations prefer to remain independent of any denominational structure.

Many outsiders think of fundamentalism as an anti-intellectual and emotional movement. And it is true that most conservative American Protestants attach great importance to emotional and personal spiritual experience. But the difference between fundamentalists and evangelicals is not that fundamentalists are more emotional in their beliefs; it is that fundamentalists insist more fully on following their ideas to their logical conclusion. Fundamentalists are more interested than evangelicals in developing a consistent and all-embracing "Christian worldview" and then in systematically applying it to the world. It is one thing to reject (as many evangelicals do) Darwinian evolution because personal experience leads one to consider the Bible an infallible guide. It is something else entirely to develop (as some fundamentalists do) an alternative paradigm of "scientific creationism," write textbooks about it, and seek to force schools to teach it or withdraw one's children from those schools that will not. Fundamentalist-dominated institutions, such as the Independent Baptist movement and Bob Jones University, are not hotbeds of snake-handling revivalist Holy Rollers but host intense, if often unconventional, scholarship.

Devastated by a string of intellectual and political defeats in the 1920s and 1930s, fundamentalists retreated into an isolation and a pessimism that were foreign to the optimistic orientation of nineteenth-century American Protestantism. The effect of this retreat was to give fundamentalists a defensive and alienated outlook that bore a marked resemblance to the Puritan Calvinism of early New England. Like the Puritans, many fundamentalists hold the bleak view that there is an absolute gap between those few souls God has chosen to redeem and the many he has predestined to end up in hell. Calvinists once labored to establish theocratic commonwealths—in Scotland by the Covenanters and the Kirk Party, in England during Oliver Cromwell's ascendancy, and in New England, all during the seventeenth century. But in the last three centuries, theocratic state building has become both less attractive to and less feasible for hard-line fundamentalists. It is not only that demographic changes have made it difficult to imagine circumstances in which fundamentalists would constitute a majority. The experience of past commonwealths also shows that successor generations usually lack the founders' fervor. Sadder and wiser from these experiences, contemporary American fundamentalists generally believe that human efforts to build a better world can have only very limited success. They agree with the nineteenth-century American preacher Dwight Moody, who, when urged to focus on political action, replied, "I look upon this world as a wrecked vessel. God has given me a lifeboat and said, 'Moody, save all you can.'"

If fundamentalists tend to be pessimistic about the prospects for social reform inside the United States, they are downright hostile to the idea of a world order based on secular morality and on global institutions such as the United Nations. More familiar than many Americans with the stories of persecuted Christians abroad, fundamentalists see nothing moral about cooperating with governments that oppress churches, forbid Christian proselytizing, or punish conversions to Christianity under Islamic law. To institutions such as the UN that treat these governments as legitimate, they apply the words of the prophet Isaiah: "We have made a covenant with death, and with hell we are at agreement." It is no coincidence that the popular Left Behind novels, which depict the end of the world from a fundamentalist perspective, show the Antichrist rising to power as the secretary-general of the UN.

Fundamentalists, finally, are committed to an apocalyptic vision of the end of the world and the Last Judgment. As biblical literalists, they believe that the dark prophecies in both the Hebrew and the Greek Scriptures, notably those of the book of Revelation, foretell the great and terrible events that will ring down the curtain on human history. Satan and his human allies will stage a final revolt against God and the elect; believers will undergo terrible persecution, but Christ will put down his enemies and reign over a new heaven and a new earth. This vision is not particularly hospitable to the idea of gradual progress toward a secular utopia driven by technological advances and the cooperation of intelligent people of all religious traditions.

Liberal Thinking

Liberal Christianity finds the core of Christianity in its ethical teachings rather than in its classic doctrines. As far back as the seventeenth century, this current of Christian thinking has worked to demythologize the religion: to separate the kernel of moral inspiration from the shell of legend that has, presumably, accreted around it. Liberal Christians are skeptical about the complex doctrines concerning the nature of Jesus and the Trinity that were developed in the early centuries of the church's history. They are reluctant to accept various biblical episodes—such as the creation of the world in seven days, the Garden of Eden, and Noah's flood—as literal narrative. And their skepticism often also extends to the physical resurrection of Jesus and the various miracles attributed to him. Rather than believing that Jesus was a supernatural being, liberal Christians see him as a sublime moral teacher whose example they seek to follow through a lifetime of service—often directed primarily at the poor. The Unitarian Church, introduced to the United States in 1794 by the English scientist and theologian Joseph Priestly, is a denomination organized around these core ideas. Priestly was a friend of Benjamin Franklin and a significant theological influence on Thomas Jefferson, although both Franklin and Jefferson attended Episcopalian services when they went to church. As Darwinism and biblical criticism led others to question the literal accuracy of many biblical stories, liberalism spread widely through the mainline Protestant denominations—including the Methodist, Presbyterian, American Baptist, Congregational, Episcopal, and Lutheran churches—to which the United States' social, intellectual, and economic elites have generally belonged.

Although more doctrinally conservative Christians often consider progressives to be outside the Christian mainstream, liberal Christians claim to represent the essence of Protestantism. The Reformation, in their view, was the first stage of reclaiming the valuable core of Christianity. The original reformers purged the church of the sale of indulgences and ideas such as purgatory, papal infallibility, and transubstantiation. In attacking such established Christian doctrines as the Trinity, original sin, and the existence of hell, liberal Christians today believe they are simply following the "Protestant principle."

Liberal Christianity has a much lower estimate of the difference between Christians and non-Christians than do the other major forms of American Protestantism. Liberal Christians believe that ethics are the same all over the world. Buddhists, Christians, Hindus, Jews, Muslims, and even nonreligious people can agree on what is right and what is wrong; every religion has a kernel of ethical truth. The idea of the church as a supernatural society whose members enjoy special grace plays very little role in liberal Christianity.

Because most liberal Christians (with the important exception of "Christian realists" such as the theologian Reinhold Niebuhr) discard the doctrine of original sin, liberal Christianity leads to optimism both about the prospects for a peaceful world order and about international organizations such as the UN. Indeed, liberal Christians have often seen the fight to establish the kingdom of God as a call to support progressive political causes at home and abroad. They argue that the dark prophecies of Revelation point to the difficulty of establishing a just social order on earth—but that this order will nonetheless come to pass if everyone works together to build it.

Liberal Protestantism dominated the worldview of the U.S. political class during World War II and the Cold War. Leaders such as Franklin Roosevelt, Harry Truman, Dean Acheson, Dwight Eisenhower, and John Foster Dulles were, like most American elites at the time, steeped in this tradition. The liberal Christian approach also opened the door to cooperation with Roman Catholics and Jews, who were then becoming much more influential in the United States. Some of the optimism with which many liberal Christians today approach the problems of world order and cooperation across ethnic and religious lines reflects their earlier success at forming a domestic consensus.

In recent years, however, liberal Christianity has been confronted with several challenges. First, liberal Protestantism tends to evanesce into secularism: members follow the "Protestant principle" right out the door of the church. As a result, liberal, mainline denominations are now shrinking—quickly. Second, liberal Christians are often only tepidly engaged with "religious" issues and causes. Liberal Christians may be environmentalists involved with the Sierra Club or human rights activists involved with Amnesty International, but those activities take place in the secular world. Third, alienated from the Catholic hierarchy by their position on issues such as abortion and gay rights, and from Jews by their decreasing support for Israel, liberal Christians are losing their traditional role as the conveners of an interfaith community. Finally, the mainline denominations themselves are increasingly polarized over issues such as gay rights. Consumed by internal battles, they are less able to influence U.S. society as a whole.

Evangelicals and The Middle Path

Evangelicals, the third of the leading strands in American Protestantism, straddle the divide between fundamentalists and liberals. Their core beliefs share common roots with fundamentalism, but their ideas about the world have been heavily influenced by the optimism endemic to U.S. society. Although there is considerable theological diversity within this group, in general it is informed by the "soft Calvinism" of the sixteenth-century Dutch theologian Jacobus Arminius, the thinking of English evangelists such as John Wesley (who carried on the tradition of German Pietism), and, in the United States, the experience of the eighteenth-century Great Awakening and subsequent religious revivals.

The leading evangelical denomination in the United States is the Southern Baptist Convention, which, with more than 16.3 million members, is the largest Protestant denomination in the country. The next-largest evangelical denominations are the African American churches, including the National Baptist Convention, U.S.A., and the National Baptist Convention of America (each of which reports having about 5 million members). The predominately African American Church of God in Christ, with 5.5 million members, is the largest Pentecostal denomination in the country, and the rapidly growing Assemblies of God, which has 2.7 million members, is the largest Pentecostal denomination that is not predominately black. The Lutheran Church∫Missouri Synod, which has 2.5 million members, is the second-largest predominately white evangelical denomination. Like fundamentalists, white evangelicals are often found in independent congregations and small denominations. So-called parachurch organizations, such as the Campus Crusade for Christ, the Promise Keepers, and the Wycliffe Bible Translators, often replace or supplement traditional denominational structures among evangelicals.

Evangelicals resemble fundamentalists in several respects. Like fundamentalists, evangelicals attach a great deal of importance to the doctrinal tenets of Christianity, not just to its ethical teachings. For evangelicals and fundamentalists, liberals' emphasis on ethics translates into a belief that good works and the fulfillment of moral law are the road to God—a betrayal of Christ's message, in their view. Because of original sin, they argue, humanity is utterly incapable of fulfilling any moral law whatever. The fundamental message of Christianity is that human efforts to please God by observing high ethical standards must fail; only Christ's crucifixion and resurrection can redeem man. Admitting one's sinful nature and accepting Christ's sacrifice are what both evangelicals and fundamentalists mean by being "born again." When liberal Christians put ethics at the heart of their theology, fundamentalists and evangelicals question whether these liberals know what Christianity really means.

Evangelicals also attach great importance to the difference between those who are "saved" and those who are not. Like fundamentalists, they believe that human beings who die without accepting Christ are doomed to everlasting separation from God. They also agree with fundamentalists that "natural" people—those who have not been "saved"—are unable to do any good works on their own.

Finally, most (although not all) evangelicals share the fundamentalist approach to the end of the world. Virtually all evangelicals believe that the biblical prophecies will be fulfilled, and a majority agree with fundamentalists on the position known as premillennialism: the belief that Christ's return will precede the establishment of the prophesied thousand-year reign of peace. Ultimately, all human efforts to build a peaceful world will fail.

Given these similarities, it is not surprising that many observers tend to confuse evangelicals and fundamentalists, thinking that the former are simply a watered down version of the latter. Yet there are important differences between the fundamentalist and the evangelical worldviews. Although the theological positions on these issues can be very technical and nuanced, evangelicals tend to act under the influence of a cheerier form of Calvinism. The strict position is that Christ's sacrifice on the cross was only intended for the small number of souls God intended to save; the others have no chance for salvation. Psychologically and doctrinally, American evangelicals generally have a less bleak outlook. They believe that the benefits of salvation are potentially available to everyone, and that God gives everyone just enough grace to be able to choose salvation if he wishes. Strict Calvinist doctrine divides humanity into two camps with little in common. In the predominant evangelical view, God loves each soul, is unutterably grieved when any are lost, and urgently seeks to save them all.

All Christians, whether fundamentalist, liberal, or evangelical, acknowledge at least formally the responsibility to show love and compassion to everyone, Christian or not. For evangelicals, this demand has extra urgency. Billions of perishing souls can still be saved for Christ, they believe. The example Christians set in their daily lives, the help they give the needy, and the effectiveness of their proclamation of the gospel—these can bring lost souls to Christ and help fulfill the divine plan. Evangelicals constantly reinforce the message of Christian responsibility to the world. Partly as a result, evangelicals are often open to, and even eager for, social action and cooperation with nonbelievers in projects to improve human welfare, even though they continue to believe that those who reject Christ cannot be united with God after death.

Evangelicals can be hard to predict. Shocked by recent polls showing that a substantial majority of Americans reject the theory of evolution, intellectuals and journalists in the United States and abroad have braced themselves for an all-out assault on Darwinian science. But no such onslaught has been forthcoming. U.S. public opinion has long rejected Darwinism, yet even in states such as Alabama, Mississippi, and South Carolina, which have large actively Christian populations, state universities go on teaching astronomy, genetics, geology, and paleontology with no concern for religious cosmology, and the United States continues to support the world's most successful scientific community. Most evangelicals find nothing odd about this seeming contradiction. Nor do they wish to change it—unlike the fundamentalists. The pragmatism of U.S. culture combines with the somewhat anti-intellectual cast of evangelical religion to create a very broad public tolerance for what, to some, might seem an intolerable level of cognitive dissonance. In the seventeenth century, Puritan Harvard opposed Copernican cosmology, but today evangelical America is largely content to let discrepancies between biblical chronology and the fossil record stand unresolved. What evangelicals do not like is what some call "scientism": the attempt to teach evolution or any other subject in such a way as to rule out the possibility of the existence and activity of God.

Evangelicals are more optimistic than fundamentalists about the prospects for moral progress. The postmillennial minority among them (which holds that Christ will return after a thousand years of world peace, not before) believes that this process can continue until human society reaches a state of holiness: that the religious progress of individuals and societies can culminate in the establishment of a peaceable kingdom through a process of gradual improvement. This is a view of history very compatible with the optimism of liberal Christians, and evangelicals and liberal Christians have in fact joined in many common efforts at both domestic and international moral improvement throughout U.S. history. Although the premillennial majority is less optimistic about the ultimate success of such efforts, American evangelicals are often optimistic about the short-term prospects for human betterment.

In his 2005 book *Imagine! A God-Blessed America: How It Could Happen and What It Would Look Like*, the conservative evangelical Richard Land describes and justifies this evangelical optimism: "I believe that there could be yet another Great Awakening in our country, a nationwide revival.... Scripture tells us that none of us can know with certainty the day or hour of the Lord's return. Thus, we have no right to abandon the world to its own misery. Nowhere in Scripture are we called to huddle pessimistically in Christian ghettoes, snatching converts out of the world."

The Balance of Power

Recent decades have witnessed momentous changes in the balance of religious power in the United States. The membership of the liberal, historically dominant mainline Protestant churches mostly peaked in the 1960s. Since then, while the number of American Christians has grown, membership in the mainline denominations has sharply dropped. According to Christianity Today, between 1960 and 2003, membership in mainline denominations fell by more than 24 percent, from 29 million to 22 million. The drop in market share was even more dramatic. In 1960, more than 25 percent of all members of religious groups in the United States belonged to the seven leading mainline Protestant denominations; by 2003, this figure had dropped to 15 percent. The Pew Research Center reports that 59 percent of American Protestants identified themselves as mainline Protestants in 1988; by 2002-3, that percentage had fallen to 46 percent. In the same period, the percentage of Protestants who identified themselves as evangelical rose from 41 percent to 54 percent.

In 1965, there were 3.6 million Episcopalians in the United States—1.9 percent of the total population. By 2005, there were only 2.3 million Episcopalians—0.8 percent of the population. Membership in the United Methodist Church fell from 11 million in 1965 to 8.2 million in 2005. In the same period, that in the Presbyterian Church (U.S.A.) fell from 3.2 million to 2.4 million, and the United Church of Christ saw its membership decline by almost 50 percent.

Meanwhile, despite some signs of slowing growth after 2001, the Southern Baptist Convention gained more than 7 million members to become the nation's largest Protestant denomination. Between 1960 and 2003, the Southern Baptists gained more members than the Methodists, Presbyterians, Episcopalians, and the United Church of Christ together lost. In 1960, there were almost 2 million more Methodists than Southern Baptists in the United States; by 2003, there were more Southern Baptists than Methodists, Presbyterians, Episcopalians, and members of the United Church of Christ combined.

The impact of these trends on national politics has not been hard to find. Self-identified evangelicals provided roughly 40 percent of George W. Bush's total vote in 2004. Among white evangelicals, Bush received 68 percent of the national vote in 2000 and 78 percent in 2004. (The majority of African American evangelicals continue to vote Democratic. Among Hispanics, Bush ran much stronger among the growing Protestant minority than among Catholics; however, both Hispanic Protestants and Hispanic Catholics were more likely to support Bush if they were religiously observant.) Evangelicals have been playing a major role in congressional and Senate elections as well, and the number of self-identified evangelicals in Congress has increased from around 10 percent of the membership in both houses in 1970 to more than 25 percent in 2004.

Fundamentalists, despite some increase in their numbers and political visibility, remain less influential. This is partly because the pervasive optimism of the United States continues to limit the appeal of ultra-Calvinist theology. Moreover, religious politics in the United States remains a coalition sport—one that a fundamentalist theology, which continues to view Catholicism as an evil cult, is ill equipped to play. To make matters more complicated, fundamentalists themselves are torn between two incompatible political positions: a sullen withdrawal from a damned world and an ambitious attempt to build a new Puritan commonwealth.

Finally, many evangelicals remain resistant to fundamentalist attitudes. "I believe the Word of God, I'm just not mad about it," explained the Reverend Frank Page, the new president of the Southern Baptist Convention, after his election in June 2006.

Out in the World

The growing influence of evangelicals has affected U.S. foreign policy in several ways; two issues in particular illustrate the resultant changes. On the question of humanitarian and human rights policies, evangelical leadership is altering priorities and methods while increasing overall support for both foreign aid and the defense of human rights. And on the question of Israel, rising evangelical power has deepened U.S. support for the Jewish state, even as the liberal Christian establishment has distanced itself from Jerusalem.

In these cases as in others, evangelical political power today is not leading the United States in a completely new direction. We have seen at least parts of this film before: evangelicals were the dominant force in U.S. culture during much of the nineteenth century and the early years of the twentieth. But the country's change in orientation in recent years has nonetheless been pronounced.

Evangelicals in the Anglo-American world have long supported humanitarian and human rights policies on a global basis. The British antislavery movement, for example, was led by an evangelical, William Wilberforce. Evangelicals were consistent supporters of nineteenth-century national liberation movements—often Christian minorities seeking to break from Ottoman rule. And evangelicals led a number of reform campaigns, often with feminist overtones: against suttee (the immolation of widows) in India, against foot binding in China, in support of female education throughout the developing world, and against human sexual trafficking (the "white slave trade") everywhere. Evangelicals have also long been concerned with issues relating to Africa.

As evangelicals have recently returned to a position of power in U.S. politics, they have supported similar causes and given new energy and support to U.S. humanitarian efforts. Under President Bush, with the strong support of

Michael Gerson (an evangelical who was Bush's senior policy adviser and speechwriter), U.S. aid to Africa has risen by 67 percent, including $15 billion in new spending for programs to combat HIV and AIDS. African politicians, such as Nigeria's Olusegun Obasanjo and Uganda's Yoweri Museveni, have stressed their own evangelical credentials to build support in Washington, much as China's Sun Yat-sen and Madame Chiang Kai-shek once did. Thanks to evangelical pressure, efforts to suppress human trafficking and the sexual enslavement of women and children have become a much higher priority in U.S. policy, and the country has led the fight to end Sudan's wars. Rick Warren, pastor of an evangelical megachurch in Southern California and the author of The Purpose Driven Life (the single best-selling volume in the history of U.S. publishing), has mobilized his 22,000 congregants to help combat AIDS worldwide (by hosting a conference on the subject and training volunteers) and to form relationships with churches in Rwanda.

Evangelicals have not, however, simply followed the human rights and humanitarian agendas crafted by liberal and secular leaders. They have made religious freedom—including the freedom to proselytize and to convert—a central focus of their efforts. Thanks largely to evangelical support (although some Catholics and Jews also played a role), Congress passed the International Religious Freedom Act in 1998, establishing an Office of International Religious Freedom in a somewhat skeptical State Department.

Despite these government initiatives, evangelicals, for cultural as well as theological reasons, are often suspicious of state-to-state aid and multilateral institutions. They prefer grass-roots and faith-based organizations. Generally speaking, evangelicals are quick to support efforts to address specific problems, but they are skeptical about grand designs and large-scale development efforts. Evangelicals will often react strongly to particular instances of human suffering or injustice, but they are more interested in problem solving than in institution building. (Liberal Christians often bewail this trait as evidence of the anti-intellectualism of evangelical culture.)

U.S. policy toward Israel is another area where the increased influence of evangelicals has been evident. This relationship has also had a long history. In fact, American Protestant Zionism is significantly older than the modern Jewish version; in the nineteenth century, evangelicals repeatedly petitioned U.S. officials to establish a refuge in the Holy Land for persecuted Jews from Europe and the Ottoman Empire.

U.S. evangelical theology takes a unique view of the role of the Jewish people in the modern world. On the one hand, evangelicals share the widespread Christian view that Christians represent the new and true children of Israel, inheritors of God's promises to the ancient Hebrews. Yet unlike many other Christians, evangelicals also believe that the Jewish people have a continuing role in God's plan. In the seventeenth and eighteenth centuries, close study of biblical prophecies convinced evangelical scholars and believers that the Jews would return to the Holy Land before the triumphant return of Christ. Moreover, while the tumultuous years before Jesus' return are expected to bring many Jews to Christ, many evangelicals believe that until that time, most Jews will continue to reject him. This belief significantly reduces potential tensions between evangelicals and Jews, since evangelicals do not, as Martin Luther did, expect that once exposed to the true faith, Jews will convert in large numbers. Luther's fury when his expectation was not met led to a more anti-Semitic approach on his part; that is unlikely to happen with contemporary evangelicals.

Evangelicals also find the continued existence of the Jewish people to be a strong argument both for the existence of God and for his power in history. The book of Genesis relates that God told Abraham, "And I will make of thee a great nation, and I will bless thee.... And I will bless them that bless thee, and curse him that curseth thee: and in thee all families of the earth be blessed." For evangelicals, the fact that the Jewish people have survived through the millennia and that they have returned to their ancient home is proof that God is real, that the Bible is inspired, and that the Christian religion is true. Many believe that the promise of Genesis still stands and that the God of Abraham will literally bless the United States if the United States blesses Israel. They see in the weakness, defeats, and poverty of the Arab world ample evidence that God curses those who curse Israel.

Criticism of Israel and of the United States for supporting it leaves evangelicals unmoved. If anything, it only strengthens their conviction that the world hates Israel because "fallen man" naturally hates God and his "chosen people." In standing by Israel, evangelicals feel that they are standing by God—something they are ready to do against the whole world. Thus John Hagee—senior pastor of an 18,000-member evangelical megachurch in San Antonio, Texas, and author of several New York Times bestsellers—writes that if Iran moves to attack Israel, Americans must be prepared "to stop this evil enemy in its tracks." "God's policy toward the Jewish people," Hagee writes, "is found in Genesis 12:3," and he goes on to quote the passage about blessings and curses. "America is at the crossroads!" Hagee warns. "Will we believe and obey the Word of God concerning Israel, or will we continue to equivocate and sympathize with Israel's enemies?"

The return of the Jews to the Holy Land, their extraordinary victories over larger Arab armies, and even the rising tide of hatred that threatens Jews in Israel and abroad strengthen not only the evangelical commitment to Israel but also the position of evangelical religion in American life. The story of modern Jewry reads like a book in the Bible. The Holocaust is reminiscent of the genocidal efforts of Pharaoh in the book of Exodus and of Haman in the book of Esther; the subsequent establishment of a Jewish state reminds one of many similar victories and deliverances of the Jews in the Hebrew Scriptures. The extraordinary events of modern Jewish history are held up by evangelicals as proof that God exists and acts in history. Add to this the psychological consequences of nuclear weapons, and many evangelicals begin to feel that they are living in a world like the world of the Bible. That U.S. foreign policy now centers on defending the country against the threat of mass terrorism involving, potentially, weapons of apocalyptic horror wielded by anti-Christian fanatics waging a religious war motivated by hatred of Israel only reinforces the claims of evangelical religion.

Liberal Christians in the United States (like liberal secularists) have also traditionally supported Zionism, but from a different perspective. For liberal Christians, the Jews are a people like any other, and so liberal Christians have supported Zionism in the same way that they have supported the national movements of other oppressed groups. In recent decades, however, liberal Christians have increasingly come to sympathize with the Palestinian national movement on the same basis. In 2004, the Presbyterian Church passed a resolution calling for limited divestment from companies doing business with Israel (the resolution was essentially rescinded in 2006 after a bitter battle). One study found that 37 percent of the statements made by mainline Protestant churches on human rights abuses between 2000 and 2004 focused on Israel. No other country came in for such frequent criticism.

Conspiracy theorists and secular scholars and journalists in the United States and abroad have looked to a Jewish conspiracy or, more euphemistically, to a "Jewish lobby" to explain how U.S. support for Israel can grow while sympathy for Israel wanes among what was once the religious and intellectual establishment. A better answer lies in the dynamics of U.S. religion. Evangelicals have been gaining social and political power, while liberal Christians and secular intellectuals have been losing it. This should not be blamed on the Jews.

The New Great Awakening

The current evangelical moment in the United States has not yet run its course. For secularists and liberals in the United States and abroad, this is a disquieting prospect. Measured optimism, however, would be a better response than horror and panic. Religion in the United States is too pluralistic for any single current to dominate. The growing presence and influence of non-Christian communities in the country—of Jews, Muslims, Buddhists, Hindus, and, above all, secularists—will continue to limit the ability of any religious group to impose its values across the board.

Liberals, whether religious or not, may want to oppose the evangelical agenda in domestic politics. For the most part, however, these quarrels can cease at the water's edge. As the rising evangelical establishment gains experience in foreign policy, it is likely to prove a valuable—if not always easy—partner for the mostly secular or liberal Christian establishment. Some fears about the evangelical influence in foreign policy are simply overblown. After the attacks of September 11, for example, fears that evangelical Christians would demand a holy war against Islam were widespread. A few prominent religious leaders (generally fundamentalists, not evangelicals) made intemperate remarks; Jerry Falwell, for one, referred to the Prophet Muhammad as "a terrorist." But he was widely rebuked by his colleagues.

U.S. evangelicals generally seek to hold on to their strong personal faith and Protestant Christian identity while engaging with people across confessional lines. Evangelicals have worked with Catholics against abortion and with both religious and secular Jews to support Israel; they could now reach out to Muslims as well. After all, missionary hospitals and schools were the primary contact that most Middle Easterners had with the United States up until the end of World War II; evangelicals managed more than a century of close and generally cooperative relations with Muslims throughout the Arab world. Muslims and evangelicals are both concerned about global poverty and Africa. Both groups oppose the domination of public and international discourse by secular ideas. Both believe that religious figures and values should be treated with respect in the media; neither like the glorification of casual sex in popular entertainment. Both Islam and evangelicalism are democratic religions without a priesthood or hierarchy. Muslims and evangelicals will never agree about everything, and secular people may not like some of the agreements they reach. But fostering Muslim-evangelical dialogue may be one of the best ways to forestall the threat of civilizational warfare.

Nervous observers, moreover, should remember that evangelical theology does not automatically produce Jacksonian or populist foreign policy. A process of discussion and mutual accommodation can in many cases narrow the gap between evangelicals and others on a wide range of issues. Worrying that evangelical politics will help lock the United States into inflexible and extreme positions is a waste of time; working with thoughtful evangelical leaders to develop a theologically grounded approach to Palestinian rights, for example, will broaden the base for thoughtful—though never anti-Israel—U.S. policies.

Similarly, engaging evangelicals in broader foreign policy discussions can lead to surprising and (for some) heartening developments. A group of leading conservative evangelicals recently signed a statement on climate change that stated that the problem is real, that human activity is an important contributing cause, that the costs of inaction will be high and disproportionately affect the poor, and that Christians have a moral duty to help deal with it. Meanwhile, evangelicals who began by opposing Sudanese violence and slave raids against Christians in southern Sudan have gone on to broaden the coalition working to protect Muslims in Darfur.

Evangelicals are likely to focus more on U.S. exceptionalism than liberals would like, and they are likely to care more about the morality of U.S. foreign policy than most realists prefer. But evangelical power is here to stay for the foreseeable future, and those concerned about U.S. foreign policy would do well to reach out. As more evangelical leaders acquire firsthand experience in foreign policy, they are likely to provide something now sadly lacking in the world of U.S. foreign policy: a trusted group of experts, well versed in the nuances and dilemmas of the international situation, who are able to persuade large numbers of Americans to support the complex and counterintuitive policies that are sometimes necessary in this wicked and frustrating—or, dare one say it, fallen—world.

Fundamentalism

At least within the twentieth century, and especially since the Second World War, American fundamentalism has commonly been strongly aligned with extreme political conservatism. Christianity is, in these circles of the far right, understood to give complete sanction to the capitalist system and to a *laissez-faire* approach to society, and government intervention in social arrangements, the welfare state, mildly reformist attitudes, liberalism and socialism are all alike seen as forms of communism masquerading under another name. In such a milieu, though accusations of communism may be common coin (and even Billy Graham is said to have been called a communist by such extremists, or at least to have been accused of being "soft on communism"), an actual socialist Christian, even a mild one, is as inconceivable among conservative evangelicals as a man with two heads.

—James Barr, *Fundamentalism* (1978)

Political Activism and Strategy

Rooted in the past, connected to the political context of its times, the Christian right has demonstrated a distinctive approach to politics characterized by alternating strains of accommodation, activism, and alienation, continuing tensions between movement members, and a paradoxical synthesis of piety and protest. Far from short-lived, its redemptive approach to politics is cyclical and recurrent.

—Michael Lienesch, *Redeeming America: Piety and Politics in the New Christian Right* (1993)

The handful of losses suffered by its candidates in the November 1998 federal elections hasn't changed the Right's state-by-state plan to impose its agenda on local communities: first, infiltrate school boards where the line between church and state can be obliterated with the most impact and least resistance; second, work stealthily to win control of state and local Republican parties and then, in turn, local elective offices and state legislative seats. Indeed, Radical Right leaders now claim to have taken control of up to 31 state Republican parties—to say nothing of the Impeachment-obsessed Republican leadership in Congress.

—Carole Shields, President, People for the American Way (June 1999)

The phenomenon has been dubbed the "religion gap." The gap is basically between weekly worshippers and the Democratic Party. The most frequent churchgoers have been voting Republican in recent presidential contests. However, the statistical picture of religious voters is as complex as America's spiritual landscape. For one thing, the religion gap disappears, even reverses, when pollsters look at the voting habits of people who go to church a tad less frequently than every week. In addition, there is barely a gap when researchers apply other measures of religiosity, like belief, prayer and Bible reading.

—William Bole, *Baptist Standard* (February 9, 2004)

Clearly, claims that evangelicals have hijacked the nation's politics are greatly exaggerated. In fact, polling data show that President Bush's real base is not religious but economic, the group he jokingly referred to as "the haves and the have mores."

—Father Andrew M. Greeley and Michael Hout, quoted in the *Houston Chronicle* (September 4, 2004)

In a subtle yet tectonic shift, a slightly younger and less reflexively Republican generation of conservative leaders is bidding to dislodge familiar faces such as Pat Robertson, Jerry Falwell, Focus on the Family's James Dobson and the Southern Baptist Convention's Richard Land, who have held a virtual monopoly on the role of movement spokesmen [for the religious right] for more than a decade.

—Mark I. Pinsky, *Houston Chronicle* (September 23, 2006)

I hope Kuo's book [*Tempting Faith*] promotes serious discussion in religious study groups around the country about whether the evangelicals' alliance with political conservatism has actually made the world, well, more Godly from their own point of view. What are the evangelicals actually getting out of this partnership? Are they mostly being used by a coalition that, when the deals are cut, cares far more about protecting the interests of its wealthy and corporate supporters than its church-going foot soldiers?

—E. J. Dionne, Jr., *Houston Chronicle* (October 17, 2006)

BUSH CAMPAIGN SEEKING HELP FROM CONGREGATIONS

By David D. Kirkpatrick

The Bush campaign is seeking to enlist thousands of religious congregations around the country in distributing campaign information and registering voters, according to an e-mail message sent to many members of the clergy and others in Pennsylvania.

Liberal groups charged that the effort invited violations of the separation of church and state and jeopardized the tax-exempt status of churches that co-operated. Some socially conservative church leaders also said they would advise pastors against participating in such a partisan effort.

But Steve Schmidt, a spokesman for the Bush administration, said "people of faith have as much right to participate in the political process as any other community" and that the e-mail message was about "building the most sophisticated grass-roots presidential campaign in the country's history."

In the message, dated early Tuesday afternoon, Luke Bernstein, coalitions coordinator for the Bush campaign in Pennsylvania, wrote: "The Bush-Cheney '04 national headquarters in Virginia has asked us to identify 1,600 'Friendly Congregations' in Pennsylvania where voters friendly to President Bush might gather on a regular basis."

In each targeted "place of worship," Mr. Bernstein continued, without mentioning a specific religion or denomination, "we'd like to identify a volunteer who can help distribute general information to other supporters." He explained: "We plan to undertake activities such as distributing general information/updates or voter registration materials in a place accessible to the congregation."

The e-mail message was provided to The New York Times by a group critical of President Bush.

The campaign's effort is the latest indication of its heavy bet on churchgoers in its bid for re-election. Mr. Bush's top political adviser, Karl Rove, and officials of Mr. Bush's campaign have often said people who attended church regularly voted for him disproportionately in the last election, and the campaign has made turning out that group a top priority this year. But advisers to Mr. Bush also acknowledge privately that appearing to court socially conservative Christians too aggressively risks turning off more moderate voters.

What was striking about the Pennsylvania e-mail message was its directness. Both political parties rely on church leaders—African-American pastors for the Democrats, for example, and white evangelical Protestants for the Republicans—to urge congregants to go the polls. And in the 1990's, the Christian Coalition developed a reputation as a political powerhouse by distributing voting guides in churches that alerted conservative believers to can-

---

David D. Kirkpatrick, a national correspondent, writes on the *New York Times* conservative beat.

This article first appeared in the *New York Times*, June 3, 2004. It is reprinted with permission. Copyright © by the *New York Times* Co.

didates' positions on social issues like abortion and school prayer. But the group was organized as a nonpartisan, issue-oriented lobbying and voter-education organization, and in 1999 it ran afoul of federal tax laws for too much Republican partisanship.

The Bush campaign, in contrast, appeared to be reaching out directly to churches and church members to distribute campaign information as well as ostensibly nonpartisan material, like registration forms.

Trevor Potter, a Washington lawyer and former chairman of the Federal Election Commission, said the campaign's solicitation raised delicate legal issues for congregations.

> "If the church is doing it, it is a legal problem for the church," Mr. Potter said. "In the past, the I.R.S. has sought to revoke and has succeeded in revoking the tax-exempt status of churches for political activity."

If a member of the congregation is disseminating the information, however, the issue is more complicated. If the congregation had a table where anyone could make available any information whatsoever without any institutional responsibility or oversight, then a member might be able to distribute campaign literature without violating tax laws. But very few churches have such open forums, Mr. Potter said. "The I.R.S. would ask, did the church encourage this? Did the church permit this but not other literature? Did the church in any way support this?"

Mr. Bernstein, the e-mail message's author, declined to comment. Mr. Schmidt, the campaign spokesman, said the e-mail message sought only individual volunteers from among the "friendly congregations," not the endorsements of the any religious organizations or groups.

"The e-mail is targeted to individuals, asking individuals to become involved in the campaign and to share information about the campaign with other people in their faith community," Mr. Schmidt said. "Yesterday, a liberal judge from San Francisco overturned a partial-birth abortion ban which banned that abhorrent procedure. That is an example of an issue that people of faith from across the United States care about."

He said that the Pennsylvania e-mail message was part of a larger national effort. The number of congregations mentioned—1,600 in just one state—suggests an operation on a vast scale.

But even some officials of some conservative religious groups said they were troubled by the notion that a parishioner might distribute campaign information within a church or at a church service. "If I were a pastor, I would not be comfortable doing that," said Richard Land, president of the Ethics and Religious Liberty Commission of the Southern Baptist Convention. "I would say to my church members, we are going to talk about the issues, and we are going to take information from the platforms of the two parties about where they stand on the issues. I would tell them to vote and to vote their conscience, and the Lord alone is the Lord of the conscience."

The Rev. Barry Lynn, executive director of Americans United for Separation of Church and State, a liberal group, argued that any form of distributing campaign literature through a church would compromise its tax-exempt status. He called the effort "an absolutely breathtakingly large undertaking," saying, "I never thought anyone could attempt to so completely meld a political party with a network of religious organizations."

In a statement, the Rev. Dr. C. Welton Gaddy, president of the Interfaith Alliance, another liberal group, called the effort "an astonishing abuse of religion" and "the rawest form of manipulation of religion for partisan gain." He urged the president to repudiate the effort.

In a statement, Mara Vanderslice, director of religious outreach for the Kerry campaign, said the effort "shows nothing but disrespect for the religious community." Ms. Vanderslice continued: "Although the Kerry campaign actively welcomes the participation of religious voices in our campaign, we will never court religious voters in a way that would jeopardize the sanctity of their very houses of worship."

How many congregations or worshipers will choose to cooperate remains to be seen. In an interview yesterday, Ronald Fowlkes, pastor of the Victoria Baptist Church in Springfield, Pa., said he had not seen the message but did not think much of the idea. "We encourage people to get out and vote," Mr. Fowlkes said, but as far as distributing information through church, "If it were focused on one party or person, that would be too much."

ON GOD AND DEMOCRATS

By Richard Parker

Shortly before the 2000 presidential race started, Gertrude Himmelfarb, the aging Athena of neoconservatism, found herself struggling to express what she felt were the core values differences between Democrats and Republicans, liberals and conservatives. What she came up with was that America had become "one nation, two cultures." "One is religious, puritanical, family-centered, and somewhat conformist," wrote *The Economist* in describing her vision. "The other is tolerant, hedonistic, secular, predominantly single, and celebrates multiculturalism. These value judgments are the best predictor of political affiliation, far better than wealth or income."

By the time the 2000 election was over, however—even though Himmelfarb's candidate eventually won, with a little jurisprudential help—her "two cultures" idea looked pretty poor as a description of what divides her friends from ours. True, just as she said, 91 percent of George W. Bush's voters had freely identified themselves as "religious" to pollsters—but so had 81 percent of Al Gore's. And while Himmelfarb's reviled "seculars" did make up a fifth of Gore's support, they'd also been one in 10 of Bush's—hardly the signs of a black-and-white divide. But when it comes to faith-and-politics issues, unfortunately for the talking classes, polarity has always been far too simple a frame.

This year, religion is back in the news, and, not surprisingly, so are a lot of the same tired arguments—on both sides of the political fence. Himmelfarb herself has been missing, but absent her presence, and facing a president who drives liberals insane by invoking the Almighty every chance he gets, many of those same liberals have been worriedly wondering what's going on as the Democratic candidates stumble over themselves and one another in what seems at times a hell-bent rush to assure voters that they've "got religion," too. What, some ask, has come of separation of church and state? Is this the end of tolerance? Is there a spiritual inquisition ahead? Salem witch trials, anyone?

Just what sort of faith, and how much of it—and how good that is for the Democrats and the country—has not been an uncontroversial topic this season. Shortly after Christmas, *The New York Times*, for example, ran an op-ed by liberal evangelical preacher Jim Wallis, who chided that the Democrats running for president still weren't getting the issue right. He cited Howard Dean's admission, for one, that the former governor had quit being an Episcopalian to become a Congregationalist after the Episcopal diocese of Vermont refused to

---

Richard Parker, a writer, and co-founder of *Mother Jones Magazine*, is a senior fellow at the Shorenstein Center on the Press, Politics and Public Policy and lecturer at Harvard University's Kennedy School of Government. His books include *The Myth of the Middle Class* and *Mixed Signals: The Future of Global Television News*. His articles have appeared in the *New York Times*, *Washington Post*, *Los Angeles Times*, *New Republic*, *Nation*, *Harper's*, *Le Monde*, *Atlantic Monthly*, and *International Economy*, among others.

sell land for a lakeshore bike path. This struck Wallis as just the sort of "faith-lite" story that too many Americans associate with Democrats and God—and a key reason why Democrats come off as so irreligious to many voters.

Wallis' editorial provoked a rash of letters to the *Times*—and must have prompted a conversation among the editors, because, less than two weeks later, they published an op-ed rejoinder of sorts, headlined "One Nation, Under Secularism." In it, former journalist Susan Jacoby warned darkly that "[i]n Campaign 2004, secularism has become a dirty word." Avoiding mention of Wallis by name, she, too, took aim at Dean—not for his bike-path-provoked conversion but for telling Iowa voters that he prayed daily. Jacoby called the admission "comically opportunistic." The Democrats, it seems, can't catch a break on this issue from anyone this year.

Bush, of course, shows no confusion of any kind about *his* God. It's the Democrats who take the beating—from conservatives, naturally, but as the Wallis and Jacoby pieces (and hundred of others in the past several months) indicate, from a surprising array of liberals with very different agendas. In a year when Iraq and the economy top the list of matters most important to voters, type the words "religion and Democratic presidential candidates" into Google; the bounty retrieved seems to run the highway all the way to heaven itself. Go search Lexis-Nexis and the same thing happens. Little of it is complimentary.

It should come as no surprise to anyone that religion is at play in American politics. Yet exactly which aspect of that vast subject is supposed to be up for grabs this year, why it's important, and what the Democratic candidates should be thinking or doing or saying about it (if anything) remains devilishly elusive.

But there's a bottom line here that some might find surprising: Yes, the right wing will carry on about the Democrats being the party of the godless, and the media will serve as its amplifier. But at the end of day, a sizeable percentage of religious Americans—the ones who tend not to make much noise or hanker for public demonstrations of devotion—will vote Democratic anyway.

This is not to say that Democrats still shouldn't think hard about what they're up against. Obviously the Iraq War and September 11 have played their unsettling roles here. As this unilateralist administration has charged headlong into not one but two wars—wars it's insisted aren't about Islam but about terrorism—it has convinced almost no one that's what it really means. After initial post-9-11 talk about the "crusade" America would lead against its satanic enemies, Bush backtracked, and, ever since, he and his administration have meticulously sworn that they see a huge difference between "Islamic fundamentalists" (always bad, it seems—unlike, say, "Christian fundamentalists") and "Islam" (good, especially when it's the faith of key U.S. allies in the Middle East and Asia, not to mention a billion people on the planet and several hundred thousand Michigan voters). But that need to show tolerance and discernment after 9-11 eventually clashed with a new conflicting need: to stoke war fever over Iraq. And convincing Americans that invading Iraq was necessary has fed darker fears—44 percent, according to Pew polls, now think

Islam itself promotes violence. Left alone, that sort of bias would constitute its own potential weapon of mass destruction in the days and years ahead.

Foreign policy isn't the only source of political God talk nowadays. Bush's almost daily invocation of the deity—brought up in relation to the war on terrorism, prison reform, the future of the family, gay marriage, or drug problems among pro athletes—has been the other visible force driving religion to the top of the news this season. Stealing a page from Ronald Reagan (though notably not from Bush *père*), Bush *fils* has, rhetorically at least, made front-and-center faith a rallying cry in the GOP's ongoing home-front holy war against the Democrats, as well as its guarantor of ultimate victory in the terrorism wars abroad.

Keenly aware that Republicans were once again grabbing the "faith thing" away from them, Democratic Party strategists this year, desperate to hold on to at least a competitive position on any issue they can, have urged their candidates to fight back, to make sure that voters know there's more than a letter's worth of difference between "G-O-D" and "G-O-P." Yet as the criticisms of Dean from sacred and secular Democrats alike suggest, and as the failed campaign of Joe Lieberman only underscores, knowing what voters who practice a faith that isn't hard-right evangelical want to hear about the faith issue is no easy trick.

It's hard to start any discussion on religion and politics these days without someone pulling out the now familiar Gallup Poll data showing that for over half a century, more than 90 percent of Americans have said they believe in God. Somewhat more disquieting to some, America is also a "Christian" country—in Gallup's terms, that is, of citizens' professed religious identity (practice remains another matter), because that's what more than 80 percent of Americans say they are. Yet given those astonishing levels of apparent homogeneity, after that, anything remotely approaching religious majoritarianism in America disappears—and is why these two majoritarian facts about faith have long mattered far less than one might think.

But then what *does* matter about religion in politics this presidential year? Here, as a starting place, are a few suggested themes worth thinking about:

1. The religious landscape does relate to voting behavior. There are three big denominational blocs in America, each representing roughly a quarter of the population: Roman Catholics, mainline Protestants, and evangelical (or fundamentalist or Pentecostal) Protestants. When it comes to politics, the first bloc leans Democratic, the second leans Republican, and the third is, simply, Republican—and proud of it. African-American Protestants are another 10 percent of the landscape, and while theologically evangelical, they're clearly far more Democratic than white evangelicals are Republican. Seculars make up more or less another tenth, and vote 2 to 1 Democratic, while among the remaining 5 percent to 8 percent of Americans, Mormons vote GOP, but Jews, other Christians, and other non-Christians all go Democratic.

In 2000, Protestants made up 48 percent of Gore's vote; Catholics, 23 percent; seculars, 19 percent; and Jews and others, 10 percent. Bush's vote was 41 percent evangelical, 22 percent mainline Protestant, 21 percent Catholic, 11 percent secular, and 5 percent Jewish and others.

2. The geography of religion matters, but is not just about religion. Evangelicals have historically concentrated in the South, with smaller populations in the Midwest, and their location—no surprise—tracks remarkably closely nowadays to the states where the GOP has won heavily in recent years. In the Northeast, the Southwest, and parts of the Great Lakes Midwest, Roman Catholics are the biggest bloc in most places—and it's been these states that Democratic presidential candidates most often win, especially when African-American Protestant turnout has also been strong and mainline Protestants have been persuaded to tilt Democratic along with them.

3. Where is the Christian right? For 20 years, first Jerry Falwell and his Moral Majority and then Pat Robertson and the Christian Coalition seemed everywhere, the scourge of liberals and liberal values, the embodiment of what the preachers bemoaned as "secular humanism." Yet the fact (not always noticed at dinner parties when secular or religious liberals gather) is that the Moral Majority has been nonexistent for 15 years (after going bankrupt), and that the Christian Coalition is almost gone now. Robertson resigned as its leader three years ago, Ralph Reed (its Machiavelli or Richelieu, depending on your taste) left well before that, and 90 percent of what was once the coalition's $26 million budget has gone with them. Robertson and Falwell, of course, still show up regularly on cable TV with their fire-breathing attacks on gays, feminists, and the general overall satanic perfidy of those whom they merely dislike. But it's not clear just who's paying serious attention to them. The Christian right exists now as a voting bloc within the Republican Party, but not as a successful separate group of extra-party organizations the two preachers can claim is still leading disillusioned southern Democrats to the promised conservative land.

4. The "compassionate conservative" conundrum of the GOP. All of Bush's warm-and-fuzzy "faith-based" talk was designed to pull moderates toward him in 2000. But then and since, it has also served double duty as a way to manage the religious-right bloc that's so essential to the GOP's future (that is, where the media hear the "compassionate" part, other ears delight at the second word). Yet the new "compassionate conservatism" also represents an admission of a core set of intermingled paradoxes facing the GOP this year and beyond.

By the late 1990s, after the collapse of both the Moral Majority and Christian Coalition, a surprising number of conservative evangelicals began openly questioning the full-bore politicization of their faith. They weren't less conservative, nor were they ready to jump the Republican ship. But as former Moral Majority Vice President Cal Thomas made clear in *Blinded by Might*, they felt badly used by Falwell, Robertson, and the GOP, which had never really delivered on the social issues that mattered most. Abortion was still legal, and twice as many were being performed as had been when *Roe v. Wade* was decided. Creationism wasn't making headway either, for all the ruckus they'd raised over it. After hundreds of school-board battles across the country, Kansas—the only state willing to put it in the curriculum—had reversed itself 18 months later. The school-prayer amendment drive, vigorous a decade earlier, was dead. And their ongoing, passionate campaign against gay rights—the latest in a long list of ultimately failed evangelical enterprises—was doing poorly, as legal, political, and social discrimination against homosexuals kept declining, even in the South.

Candidate Bush in 2000 had promised to reverse all that, even as he packaged himself for the rest of America in the language of compassion. But look what's happened: The White House's much-heralded effort in 2001 to launch a new faith-based social-welfare system has been long on heat and low on light. It quickly turned out that most evangelical congregations weren't really interested in taking government grants—and that their leaders were more concerned that competitors like the Nation of Islam or liberal Protestant groups never see a dime from the initiative.

The result? The original bill has been bottled up in Congress for nearly three years. And in the White House itself, Bush's whole faith-based initiative has gotten little save rhetorical attention ever since John DiIulio, the president's first appointee to run the program, resigned his post and ripped into the backroom deals and blatant cynicism he found among the "Mayberry Machiavellis" inside the White House. Meanwhile, Bush's unwillingness to make his much-touted (but still unfunded) $15 billion global AIDS initiative contingent on teaching abstinence has further enraged supporters.

Does this mean that the religious right inside the GOP is ready to bolt the party? Hardly—in part because they've nowhere else to go. Bush adviser Karl Rove swears he's doing a massive voter-turnout drive among Christian rightists, and of course their enmity toward all things Democratic and liberal will drive some of them to the polls to stop Satan's march.

But it does mean that there might yet be a "Dixiecan" revolt one day, akin to the 1948 "Dixiecrat" uprising led by Strom Thurmond that almost sank Harry Truman's re-election. And what about those Republican seculars who made up a crucial 10 percent of Bush's vote in 2000? How long will they choose to keep company with the demands that the religious right keeps placing on their shared party? Rove has no doubt been poring over the data on that critical question.

5. So where's the religious left to match the religious right?It's a good question, with far from simple answers. To begin with, the fact that four out of five Gore voters in 2000 identified themselves as religious answers it—they're voting for the Democratic candidate. But that's not quite the whole story, obviously. In 1960, John F. Kennedy was a Catholic candidate in a Protestant country that had a 300 year history of distrust for "rum, Romanism, and rebellion." So to overcome his "Al Smith problem," he set out the modern marker for what it means to be a liberal politician. Before a doubtful audience of ministers in Houston, Kennedy declared that faith was a private matter, and that if elected he would not let his religion determine his presidential decisions.

It was a moment of triumph for secularism, it seemed, and for ecumenism—and it led to the election of the first non-Protestant president in U.S.

history. But the aftereffects were more complex. While his election convinced most American elites that the country had entered what the great Yale historian of religion Sydney Ahlstrom called "the post-Protestant era," American voters didn't quite get the message. Kennedy won because more than 80 percent of Catholics voted for him, while a majority of Protestants opted for Richard Nixon. Twenty years later, by the time Ronald Reagan sought the same office, the conservative southern wing of America's evangelical Protestants had had enough of the Democrats who succeeded Kennedy and of claims that faith was "private"—and so began their now completed exodus to the GOP.

Still, for liberal candidates, there is an immense audience of "faithful" Democrats (and many independents) who aren't looking for a religious left to match the religious right. Unlike evangelicals, they don't feel compelled to use religious tests to guide their voting: Only a quarter of mainliners and a third of Catholics say they frequently or occasionally use faith to determine how to vote (compared with nearly 70 percent of white evangelicals).

The reasons for this are hardly new, unlike the triumph of private-faith or multicultural teaching. Well before the Civil War, the nation's largest Protestant denominations—the Baptists, Methodists, and Presbyterians—split over two issues: slavery and whether to read the Bible literally. The northerners opted to move toward a "civic religion" that rejected slavery and embraced science, industrial progress, and modernism; their southern colleagues went the other way. That freed the northerners to gradually restructure their faith from a purely denominational construct to one that maintained denominational identity while promoting a civic, governmental ideal in which the state was meant to help achieve John Winthrop's "City upon a Hill." The Social Gospel movement in the 1880s and '90s laid the groundwork for not only the Progressive Era but, soon enough, the New Deal as well. Tolerance, ecumenism, and multiculturalism (though a word of recent invention) were all foreseen then, more than a century ago. (Crucial to real ecumenism, American Catholics were embracing this view in the years just before Kennedy ran, and they accelerated their participation in light-year terms while Pope John XXIII was alive.)

Today, just as there always has been, a religious left is alive in America—easily seen in Martin Luther King Jr.'s legacy, in the Catholic bishops' remarkable critiques of nuclear arms and economic injustice at the height of the Reagan era, in the ongoing battles over domestic issues such as the "living wage" campaigns being fought across the country today (often led by religious coalitions), and most recently in the Episcopal Church's willingness to ordain an openly gay bishop.

But religious-left opposition is also divided within itself. For example, the U.S. Conference of Catholic Bishops, which speaks for 60 million American Catholics, may find itself working alongside the National Council of Churches, which tries to speak for an almost equal number of more fractious progressive white and black Protestants (and Orthodox) on issues of economic justice or global security. Yet they part ways when it comes to the controversial God-

and-body issues of abortion, homosexuality, birth control, and the like. No one has yet figured out how to heal those very real divisions.

Even so, innumerable Washington-based organizations defend and promote religious tolerance, and many speak from a clearly religious commitment. Secular groups such as People For the American Way and the American Civil Liberties Union actively cooperate with multidenominational religious allies like The Interfaith Alliance and Americans United for Separation of Church and State, which, supported by hundreds of thousands of members, maintain a prominent profile in the nation's capital. At the same time, the Catholic bishops and the National Council of Churches—and its member denominations—use their own well-staffed Capitol Hill offices to keep watchful eyes on issues from the impact of Bush's tax cuts on the poor to the size of the defense budget to promoting alternatives to the administration's unilateralist foreign policy.

The problem the religious left faces today, however, lies, ironically, in the crisis of modern Judaism, once the steadfast ally of these progressive Christians. Long distrustful of evangelical Christianity, a notable minority of American Jews—thanks to evangelicals' rereading of the Book of Revelation, a New Testament portion that most liberal Christians simply ignore—have begun flirting with an incongruous new alliance that's eating away at the heart of the nation's religious left. Stunningly, there's been a transformation from evangelicals' once commonplace anti-Semitism to a Semitophilicism of an extraordinary sort. In their reading of Revelation, for example, evangelical "premillenarians" have taken the creation of modern Israel as a sign from God that Christ's Second Coming—and with it, the Final Judgment—are now imminent. When that chiliastic moment arrives, though, Jews—like all nonbelievers in Christ's redemptive role—don't fare well in Revelation's vision. But no matter. What this has produced is an unholy alliance of convenience, in which Ariel Sharon and Benjamin Netanyahu have embraced the likes of Pat Robertson and Jerry Falwell as a means to win support for their policies, while for conservative evangelicals, a strong Israel is crucial to Revelation-inspired dreams. And for GOP strategists such as Ralph Reed and Karl Rove, it has meant the opportunity to coax Jewish support away from the Democrats—or at least toward support for a much more conservative Democratic Party less resistant to the GOP's agenda.

As this complicated, fractious, and always messy landscape suggests, American religion can't ever be fitted into boxes as neat as Himmelfarb's "two cultures." Alexis de Tocqueville, the old warhorse on religion and politics, gets trotted out often these days by conservatives who want to use him to support their version of American religiosity's ongoing importance. But Tocqueville never claimed to see any such thing; far from it, he saw the same complicated, fractious, messy landscape we see today. "I even doubt whether religious opinions have as much influence as one at first thinks," he wrote in a letter to a French friend. "The religious state of this people is perhaps the most curious thing ... it's evident that here, generally speaking, religion does not profoundly stir the souls."

What Tocqueville did see was that "the immense majority have faith in the wisdom and good sense of human kind, *faith* in the doctrine of human perfectibility. ... They honestly believe in the excellence of the government which rules them; they believe in the wisdom of the masses provided they are enlightened. ... Will Deism ever be able to satisfy all classes, especially those which most need the rein of religion? I can't persuade myself of that. ... It's obvious there still remains here a greater foundation of Christianity than in any other country of the world to my knowledge, and I don't doubt but that this disposition still influences the political regime...."

Still, Tocqueville warned in conclusion, too much could be made of the whole topic. "That's enough on this subject," he ended his letter, "toward which my imagination draws me continuously and which would end by making me mad if I plumbed it often...." It's advice still worth listening to today.

IS BUSH THE ANTICHRIST?

By Tim Appelo

When President George W. Bush was appointed by five Supreme Court justices in 2000, right-wing Christians sang hosannas for the triumph of God's will over the electorate's. "President Bush is God's man at this hour," said Tim Goeglein, Bush's liaison to evangelicals. Though the Methodist president dishonestly conceals the whole truth about his apocalyptic religious beliefs, he has acted as an evangelist in office. As Esther Kaplan demonstrates in *With God on Their Side: How Christian Fundamentalists Trampled Science, Policy, and Democracy in George W. Bush's White House,* he's doled out millions to far-right Christian groups, systematically crushed secular left and nonright mainstream organizations from Head Start to the Audubon Society, and replaced policy and scientific experts with comically ignorant yet politically cunning fanatic provocateurs. Out with the American Medical Association, in with the American Family Association. Before Bush, the Internal Revenue Service hounded the Christian Coalition; now that Bush is, in extremist Gary Bauer's opinion, the de facto leader of the Christian Coalition, the government selectively harasses non-Christian groups, and a rightist apparatchik tried to sneak through Congress a bill legitimizing the kinds of politically targeted IRS abuses that would have made Richard M. Nixon proud.

Televangelist and onetime presidential candidate Pat Robertson once rallied millions to lobby God for the deaths of liberal Supreme Court justices, recommending prayers for coronaries and cancer. "We ask for miracles!" preached Robertson. Today, the judiciary's Clinton-era moderates haven't even a prayer against the Reagan/Bush rightists. Author Tim LaHaye, whose *Left Behind* thrillers based on the Bible's "end times" stories are America's best-selling books for adults, once helped destroy the Jack Kemp presidential campaign he co-chaired by demanding 25 percent of government jobs for the Christian right's 25 percent of the population. Today, no way does Bush's "Evange taliban"—which claims responsibility for winning Bush a second term in 2004—intend to settle for less than 100 percent.

But not every follower of the Prince of Peace is shouting amen to Bush/Robertson/Falwell's Killer Christians. Granted, the fastest-growing churches are either evangelical—Bible believers out to win your soul—or fundamentalists, out to bend your soul to their bluenose will and so literal when it comes to the Bible that some insist Christ's parables refer to actual people and events. Fundies also incline to the authoritarianism of Oswald Chambers, the 19th-century Christian whose harsh sermonettes against rational analysis and for a gut response to God Bush reads each morning (perhaps on this Web site: www.gospelcom.net/rbc/utmost).

Tim Appelo, former video critic of *Entertainment Weekly,* has written cultural criticism for the *Los Angeles Times,* the *Washington Post,* and the *New York Times.*

This article first appeared in the *Seattle Weekly,* December 8, 2004. Reprinted with permission from the *Seattle Weekly.* Copyright © 2004.

Yet the more love-thy-neighbor-advocating mainstream church is not dead. In *The American Prospect* magazine, Baptist Sunday school teacher Jimmy Carter charges the fundamentalists with "the abandonment of some of the basic principles of Christianity." And in his brilliant 1997 book, *Stealing Jesus: How Fundamentalism Betrays Christianity*, author Bruce Bawer accuses fundamentalism of replacing Christ's Church of Love with a Church of Law, lamenting "the horrible monster that 20th-century legalistic Christians have made out of their God and Savior and the hateful institution that they have made out of his church." He notes acidly that the movement got its biggest boost in reaction not to the Supreme Court's 1963 school-prayer ban but to the Carter-era IRS crackdown on segregated Christian schools. "The Religious Right didn't grow out of a love of God and one's neighbor—it grew out of racism, pure and simple."

"Kids growing up in Church of Law families nowadays think that the only two sins, or at least the only two really, really important ones, are having an abortion and having gay sex," Bawer told *Seattle Weekly*. "The notion that love, tolerance, and inclusiveness are moral values has been dropped down the memory hole."

A soldier in the U.S. Army e-mailed *Seattle Weekly*, "I'm just a citizen who was raised in a Christian community and is tired of having my values hijacked by a conservative movement that only applies them selectively at home and hardly at all overseas." The soldier asks to remain anonymous.

Perversion of Christian Faith?

"Bush is one of the key figures leading the church away from Jesus," says Christian author Don Miller, who wrote the nonbluenose Christian best seller *Blue Like Jazz*. Miller is no pantywaist—he had the balls to run a ministry at Reed College in Portland, Ore., which is so godless that its soccer team is said in campus legend to have once staged a halftime crucifixion in a game against a Christian school. But he couldn't stomach it when, for instance, Texas Gov. Bush not only allowed the execution of his fellow born-again Christian, the penitent ax murderer Karla Faye Tucker, but made vicious fun of her ("Please don't kill me!" Bush said, mocking her prayerful plea for God's mercy). Miller classifies Bush Christians as modern Pharisees—the allegedly proud, rigid, legalistic hypocrites John the Baptist called "a generation of vipers." "The worst condemnation that Jesus has for anybody, I mean the worst, is for Pharisees," says Miller. "If you asked Jerry Falwell who the Pharisees are in our society, they can't point anybody out." There are no mirrors in Bush's church.

"People of faith—especially those whose moral values differ from the values exploited this time around—need to figure out a way to be figured into the political landscape," Philadelphia Presbyterian minister Cynthia Jarvis editorialized in *The New York Times*. "Maybe four years from now, when the number one issue cited by voters in exit polls is again 'moral values,' those values will have something to do with economic justice, racial equality and the peaceable kingdom for which we all were made."

But few have preached harder against the Christian right's wrongs than the Rev. Rich Lang of Seattle's Trinity United Methodist Church in Ballard. "This administration is a culture of death, and so is the religious right," says Lang. In his *Open Letter to George Bush*, published in *Real Change*, Lang thunders, "You claim Christ but act like Caesar. There is blood all over your hands with the promise of even more blood to come. You sit atop the nations like the Biblical Whore of Babylon openly fornicating with the military men of might." His sermon "George Bush and the Rise of Christian Fascism" (posted like Luther's theses on the church Web site, www.tumseattle.org) rails that "the power and seduction of this administration emerges from its diabolical manipulation of Christian rhetoric ... the mirror opposite of what Jesus embodied. It is, indeed, the materialization of the spirit of Antichrist: a perversion of Christian faith and practice."

Lang is not using "Antichrist" in a tone of bitter sarcasm, as many do. Google "George Bush is the Antichrist," and you'll get a startling list of Web sites that argue the case, but with sardonic intent and whimsical 666-numerological riffs. Unwhimsical pundit Robert Wright, who attended Calvary Baptist in Bush's Midland, Texas, hometown, uses modern science to puzzle out what may be God's plan in his bold book *Nonzero: The Logic of Human Destiny*. When he notes in Slate magazine that he supported John Kerry because "He's a long way from being the Messiah, but at least he's not the anti-Christ," Wright says not to take this as gospel. "Obviously, I was kidding—Bush isn't literally the Antichrist. But I do think he could conceivably do some pretty cataclysmic damage to the world...." Even Christian Bush-basher Miller urgently distances himself from the Bush-as-Antichrist meme that's sweeping the Web: "The last thing I want is for someone to say, 'Don Miller thinks Bush is the Antichrist!'"

"He's not the Antichrist, he's just a cynical, callous politician," objects *Stealing Jesus* author Bawer. "I gather some liberal Christians have gone off the rails." He refers to Lang's identification of Bush with the "spirit of Antichrist" warned against in the Bible's 1 John 4:3. "This kind of inane proof texting is the province of the Church of Law types, the right-wing Darbyites," believers in *Left Behind*-style apocalyptic prophecy. "It's depressing to see it practiced by liberal Christians, too." Bawer is appalled by Bush's attempt, "in the name of Christianity, to add to the Constitution what would be far and away its most un-Christian amendment. But I'm also unsettled by the extreme way in which he's been personally characterized by many people."

Granted, Bawer says the right "worships evil," and has "warped Christianity into something ugly and hateful that has little or nothing to do with love and everything to do with suspicion, superstition, and sadism [and] denies the name of Christianity to followers of Jesus who reject its barbaric theology." But "when people start calling somebody the Antichrist, we're in right-wing fundamentalist, Church of Law territory, and I don't like it one bit.... Demonizing (literally) individuals in this way is ugly, scary...."

Lang, though, stands his ground against his famous accuser, and insists that he's missing some crucial distinctions. "This is not about George Bush, this is about this whole administration. It's about Karl Rove, it's about the neocons, some of whom are Christian, some who aren't, but who are using Christian rhetoric. James Dobson [of Focus on the Family] has direct access to the highest echelons of American government. And Robertson and Falwell."

Still, Lang means what he says about Bush. "He has the spirit of the Antichrist. Literally, break the word apart. It is a spirituality that is anti-Christ."

Meet the Beast

So what's an Antichrist, anyhow? The concept has evolved bewilderingly throughout biblical history. As definitively explained in Bernard McGinn's *Antichrist: 2,000 Years of the Human Fascination With Evil* and Robert Fuller's *Naming the Antichrist: The History of an American Obsession*, the character can be traced to Old Testament authors' horrified response to the oppression of ancient colonizers. When Alexander the Great's conquests led to a statue of Zeus in the Temple in Jerusalem, Jews envisioned a final conflict story wherein the Syrian Greek tyrant Antiochus, reimagined as a beast, got burned in God's "fiery stream" on Judgment Day.

Early Christians grafted the Roman Emperor Nero onto the tradition as the Beast from the Abyss in the Apocalypse, known to current Christians as the book of Revelation, the Bible's astonishing finale about the final days. Nero dressed in animal skins to ravage men's and women's genitals, burned Christians in ghastly dramas, demanded to be worshiped as a god, and was rumored to have disappeared to the East, threatening to return one day to rule the world from Rome, or Jerusalem. Actually, he killed himself, but he lives on in beastly legend. To this day, the word for Antichrist in Armenian is "Nero."

Though the story of the Beast and various other biblical verses are associated with the Antichrist, the word itself, "Antichrist," only appears four times in the Bible, in the letters of John. Christians have eternally argued about the Antichrist. Revelation was nearly banned from the Bible, and permitted strictly on condition it should never be used as it is by fundies today. Church father Augustine ordered Christians to quit reading apocalyptic *Left Behind*-style scenarios into scripture and think of the Antichrist as anyone who denies Christ—and he said the first place to hunt for him is in your own heart.

In my evangelical Lutheran childhood I often feared the Rapture had left me behind, even though my church was liberal with Christ's love. But now I'm with Augustine—and also with Robert Wright, who finds in his book *The Moral Animal* a biological basis for original sin. For a Darwinist Christian, the Beast is within: the lizard brain fighting the higher mind for control of one's soul. As Darwin cried out to heaven in his notebook: "The Devil under form of Baboon is our grandfather!"

But people crave apocalyptic stories and an easy answer to spiritual struggle. As the narrator says of a character in *Left Behind*, "He wanted to believe something that tied everything together and made it make sense." The most popular story today was concocted by an English law-student-turned-self-taught-theologian named John Nelson Darby in the 1840s, and popularized by a Kansas City lawyer named C.I. Scofield with his best-selling 1909

Scofield Reference Bible. The *Scofield Bible* cross-referenced Old and New Testament verses to illuminate the hidden figure in the bewildering carpet of scripture, weaving the phantasmagoria of apocalyptic visions into a single system—a magic carpet of narrative to whisk them safely out of time and into heaven. Its systematic beauty was designed as a kind of counterscience to rebuke and refute Darwinism and historical biblical scholarship.

And man, is it a great story. It's not a literal interpretation, but an imaginative deduction as breathtaking as Charles Kinbote's commentary on John Shade in Nabokov's *Pale Fire*, or Charles Manson's prophetic interpretation of the Beatles' *White Album*. The Bible describes Christ's Second Coming and the Rapture of the Saints—the whooshing of Christians bodily into heaven. Anybody reading it for the first time would think these are supposed to happen at the same time, at the end of time. But Darby hawked the notion that the Rapture happens first. Exeunt Christians. Enter the Beast/Antichrist, who perpetrates a hellish seven-year Great Tribulation. Then Christ returns, kicks Beast butt, and reigns for 1,000 years—the Millennium. Fifty-one percent of Americans voted for Bush; 59 percent believe Revelation will come true. Without one scrap of scriptural evidence, almost one-quarter of Americans believe Revelation predicted 9/11.

The Independent newspaper called Revelation "that earliest of airport novels." LaHaye and Jerry Jenkins' *Left Behind* dazzlingly turns it into one. Planes and cars crash, deprived of pilots by the Rapture. Even fetuses get Raptured, deflating their mamas' bellies. The Antichrist becomes Nicolae Carpathia, *People* magazine's Sexiest Man Alive, seizing control of the U.N. to impose one world government! The faithful get saved! The secular humanists get what they deserve! Since latter-day Darbyites believe end times scripture predicts and mandates Israel's resurgence to usher in Christ's return and the Antichrist's smackdown, they help drive Bush's rubber-stamp policy for Israel. The real Middle East road map may be the *Scofield Reference Bible.*

"That's a completely foolish and erroneous interpretation of the scriptures," snaps Jimmy Carter. "But this administration, maybe extremely influenced by ill-advised theologians of the extreme religious right, has pretty well abandoned any real effort that could lead to a resolution of the problems between Israel and the Palestinians."

"It's deeply dismaying that millions of Americans who call themselves Christians are believers in something that has virtually nothing to do with the gospel message," mourns Bawer. "Darby, Scofield, and company have been a disaster for Christianity in America. Millions of people think they are adherents of 'traditional Christianity' when, in fact, they have been roped into a newfangled religion based on bizarre theological propositions that Jesus would never recognize."

"It's so ludicrous!" laments Lang. "Such a twisting of scripture. That history is scripted is something that it seems to me Christians ought to have an instinct to be repulsed against. You follow a code, there's magical meanings in the text."

But Lang knows why people cling to millennial dreams—like Dubya's, his life was saved by a fundamentalist church. "It attracted me because I came out of chaos. Alcohol and drugs; 19 years old and I was dyin'. I needed a strong fence around my life and people who cared for me, and I got both. But after about a year of reading what they taught me, I started to raise questions."

Further study convinced him that Augustine was on the right track, after all, in reading apocalyptic literature as spiritual advice, not a sneak preview of tomorrow's headlines. "Revelation is written to the churches in its time, not to the churches in the 21st century. It's written to seven churches in Turkey." As for the Antichrist warnings in John, he reads them not as a literal prediction of Bush but as a warning against the eternal danger of his hypocritical, Mammon-worshiping, proudly elitist, heartless, narrowly legalistic spirit. "1 John seems to be obsessed with language like this: 'How can you say you love God, who you have not seen, if you do not love your brother and sister, who you have seen?' Who are in need of food, clothing, shelter? The implication of the doctrine of the Antichrist is that there is an economic disparity in the community, and people are using their religion, not practicing it."

Bush policy is based on what he told his Harvard Business School professor—"Poor people are poor because they're lazy." Responds Lang, "Again, anti-Christ. It's just the opposite [of Christ's teaching]. The thrust of right-wing Christianity—their solution to poverty is to discipline the poor. Now, there's a lot to be said for that. I mean, if people would clean up their negative habits. There's some common ground where we can meet. But the right never addresses what Jesus called 'that fox Herod'—the systematic problem that has given rise to homelessness and poverty."

Bringing Back Heresy

Lang argues that followers of Jesus, not Bush, should call an Antichrist an Antichrist—or rather, its spirit. "The progressive church should bring back—and this sounds so crazy—the word 'heresy.' The end times theology and this other thing called Dominionism or Christian Reconstruction—those are heresies." Lang says not to believe Christian Coalition leader-turned-Whore of Enron-turned Bush/Cheney campaign lieutenant Ralph Reed when he claims the Christian right has no plans to upend the Constitution and impose its religion on civic life. "He's a liar," says Lang. "Dominionism is the notion that God has given the dominion, the governance of the world, to the church. And so Christians literally are born to rule, by force if necessary, to bring the Kingdom of God on Earth. I believe that the theology that drives the Bush administration affirms this." When Falwell preached, "We must take back what is rightfully ours," his ambitions did not stop at U.S. borders. This is a Church of a Law Unto Itself.

In the Greek, the word "anti" doesn't just mean "against." It also contains the meanings "equivalent to" or "a substitute for." Nero was anti-Christ because he falsely claimed to be God. The idea of deception is crucial. The Antichrist isn't the devil, the opposite of God. He's an evil human masquerading as a golden god. The Antichrist appears to humanity not as the hideous Beast but as handsome Nicolae Carpathia, who resembles Robert Redford without the facial erosion. "That could be our next Republican president," quips Lang.

In this sense, the Bush church is Antichristlike indeed. It is institutionalized deception, anti-American ugliness with a beguiling face, a neocon job. Only when necessary does it employ the perilous bald-faced lie, the outrageously transparent duplicity—the political equivalent of Robertson arguing that "Do unto others" indicates Christ's support of capitalist selfishness. More often, a smoothly dissembling surface is preferred. Rove notoriously emulates Machiavelli; the Christian right is a stealth movement, infiltrating school boards and mainstream churches and every institution of democracy like a thief in the night—in order to undermine, overthrow, and replace democracy with theocracy. Bush is the father of lies. The Union of Concerned Scientists proclaims Bush's lies about science "unprecedented." In *With God on Their Side*, Kaplan concludes, on mountainous evidence, "The goal is not to engage your opponents in the public square, but to kneecap them, or send them into exile."

"It is a conspiracy in the sense that they have not been public and accountable to their ideology," says Lang. "Follow the money! The same filthy-rich foundations that have funded the rise of neocons are funding the rise of the religious right." He suggests that you check out the expos" Web site www.yuricareport.com for the terrifying particulars.

But—to cop a line from the late Christian-right author Francis Schaeffer, how then should we live? Should we turn the other cheek to the Antichrist? Forgive LaHaye for saying that "Old Testament capital punishment" was less cruel to gays than modern acceptance is? Or counter Robertson's prayers for a divine Supreme Court *fatwa* with our own? As a self-scrutinizing Christian, isn't Lang in danger of succumbing to hate?

"Yeah, I'm there. I have a physical, visceral reaction to Bush, to his image, to when he speaks. I mean, I think the guy is evil. They are willfully deceptive people, and I'm very angry. But . . . hatred is not a very useful strategy of resistance, nor is it very useful to create an alternative."

Bawer preaches that the alternative must not employ the church as a weapon. "For liberals to join in the right-wing game of bashing one's opponents with the Bible only further erodes the wall between religion and government. This, to me, is a major concern—and Bush's reckless contribution to this erosion is, for me, a major offense. It's especially offensive in light of 9/11, which was the work of people who hate the West because it is secular, tolerant, inclusive, and democratic. What distinguishes America and the West from most of the Muslim world is those values. I wish we had a president who recognized this fact and helped Americans recognize it, too."

So does Lang. But he thinks the secular left has to inspire its own flock—with better ministers than dull, brainy Parson Kerry of the Church of God's Frozen People. "Even though I don't like him, Bush is probably a funner person," Lang admits. He insists that the Christian left has its own work to do in saving what he calls "the nation with the soul of a church." "The right has won. I mean, they've seized the language of the church. So against Bruce, I would say, no, the progressive wing of the church has got to reclaim its language and redefine those words. Turning the other cheek wasn't passive, oh, hit me, it hurts so good—it was a form of resistance. You're turning your cheek to strengthen your backbone."

Lang is convinced that secular efforts alone can't reverse the Antichrist tide. "Evangelical churches have a sense of urgency about the doing of 'good' in the world that the mainline church has lost. If the church can't show a positive, enticing, seductive vision of the future, where people fall in love with God and fall in love with this community, then it really doesn't have anything to say." Revelation teaches us what happens to lukewarm Christians.

It won't be easy. The political and religious left are not organized. "And part of the reason it cannot organize is that the people in the pews benefit from the system as it is," says Lang. "They can't work up any kind of passion to change it. As those benefits stop, we'll see the left arise. But it might be too late."

Ultimately, despite his despair, Lang is a man of faith. "I really do believe that we're in for several decades of a very dark time. But that's not the end of the world."

6

Directory of Organizations

The organizations listed here vary considerably in basic ideology and political influence. They differ politically from extreme right stances to more traditional conservative positions, and they vary in terms of specific substantive issues that motivate their membership. Members of some organizations would undoubtedly object strongly to being categorized with other groups that appear here. Many of these groups presently engage actively and successfully in politics; others, influential at one time, have lost their prominence, and several never did gain wide public attention. Several organizations are included that were significant in the evolution of the contemporary religious right but that no longer exist. For instance, the World's Christian Fundamentals Association, established in 1919 by William Bell Riley, articulated the basic beliefs of fundamentalist Christians that informed the movement throughout the twentieth century and that still distinguish conservative Christian groups from mainline denominations. More recently Jerry Falwell's Moral Majority, formed in 1979, gained significant influence in the political arena of the 1980s before the organization, which had become unpopular with the American public, ceased operations in 1989. Present organizations, including the American Family Association, Concerned Women for America, and the Family Research Council, have built on previous successes as well as lessons learned from past failures.

Despite the wide variation, organizations in this section—**In Favor of the Religious Right**—share a family resemblance. They all profess a more traditional Christian faith and advocate minimal government interference in people's lives, except, of course, with regard to specific objectives of their own, such as restricting abortion and pornography, limiting marriage to a union between one man and one woman, and encouraging public displays of religious belief such as tributes to the Ten Commandments.

Unsurprisingly in a pluralist society, the activities of organized interests tend to encourage the development of opposition groups. Therefore, in order to provide a more complete landscape, we have included **Organizations Critical of the Religious Right** beginning on page 308 whose principles and objectives collide with those of the religious right. Certain organizations, such as the American Humanist Association and the Freedom from Religion Foundation, reject any value that Christians claim for religious belief in the public sphere, arguing instead that religion represents a negative force in American society. Other groups, such as Americans United for Separation of Church and State, whose executive director, Barry Lynn, is a minister in the United Church of Christ, wish to keep religion and government in their respective legitimate spheres. These groups tend to oppose the policy agendas of religious right groups, for instance, objecting to further limitations on abortion rights and officially sanctioned religious exercises in the public schools, and supporting gay rights.

Publications are listed for each organization, if any. Such publications allow the groups to communicate with their members and the wider public, informing them of group activities, presenting arguments in favor of the organization's positions on political issues, providing updates of public policy changes, motivating supporters to political action, and soliciting monetary assistance for the organization itself. With the much wider use of the Internet, most organizations listed here display many publications electronically on their Web sites.

Organizations in Favor of the Religious Right

Alliance Defense Fund (ADF)
15333 North Pima Road, Suite 165
Scottsdale, AZ 85260
(800) 835-5233
http://www.alliancedefensefund.org
Alan E. Sears, President

The Alliance Defense Fund was established in 1994 with the support of the evangelical Christian leaders Bill Bright, Larry Burkett, James Dobson, D. James Kennedy, Marlin Maddoux, and Donald Wildmon. Intended to counter the influence of the American Civil Liberties Union, the ADF provides financial and legal assistance to those involved in lawsuits that have the potential for establishing legal precedents in the areas of the free exercise of religion, family values, and opposition to abortion. The organization claims credit for obtaining a favorable Supreme Court decision in *Rosenberg v. Rector and Visitors of the University of Virginia* (1995), in which a Christian, student-run publication won the right to receive student activity funds. The ADF claims to have had a hand in nearly 130 lower court victories involving what the organization calls Christian values, including opposition to legal recognition of homosexual marriages.

PUBLICATIONS: *ADF News Alerts*, monthly newsletters that report on ADF legal activities, pending legal cases, and prayer requests.

American Association of Christian Schools (AACS)
119 C Street, NE
Washington, DC 20003
(202) 547-2991

(202) 547-2992 (fax)
http://www.aacs.org
Keith Wiebe, President

Founded in 1972, this organization focuses on two major goals. First, AACS assists in the maintenance and improvement of the quality, both academic and spiritual, of Protestant Christian schools. It offers a number of services, including teacher placement and teacher certification programs, and acts as a source for instructional materials. Second, AACS provides interest-group representation in protecting the integrity of Christian schools against government interference at both the state and national levels.

PUBLICATIONS: *AACS Capitol Comments*, a monthly newsletter; *Journal of Christian Educators*, quarterly; *Administrative Leadership*, twice each year; *Legal Report*, twice each year.

American Center for Law and Justice (ACLJ)

P.O. Box 90555
Washington, DC 20090-0555
(757) 226-2489
(757) 226-2836 (fax)
http://www.aclj.org
Jay Sekulow, Executive Counsel

1990 Pat Robertson formed the ACLJ, a public-interest law firm concerned with defending traditional family values and the religious and civil liberties of Americans. Believing secularism in America has led to attempts to restrict the preaching of the Gospel in public places, the organization offers legal advice and supports attorneys in cases in which the rights of Christians are challenged. The ACLJ objects to legalized abortion and what it sees as the harmful effects of social welfare agencies on the traditional family unit. Sekulow has argued cases before the U.S. Supreme Court on such issues as the free-speech rights of antiabortion demonstrators, equal access of religious groups to public facilities, and the right of public school students to form and participate in religious groups.

PUBLICATIONS: *Law & Justice Journal*, quarterly.

American Christian Action Council

See Council of Bible Believing Churches

American Coalition of Unregistered Churches (ACUC)

P.O. Box 11
2711 South East Street
Indianapolis, IN 46206
(317) 7783-6753 Note: There is an extra digit in this number.
http://home.inreach.com/dov/unregchs.htm Note: This site was not found.
Greg Dixon, National Chair

Founded in 1983 in Chicago by a group of fundamentalist ministers, the ACUC represents a group of fundamentalist pastors and nondenominational and unincorporated churches that oppose government interference in the activities of pastors, churches, and Christians generally. The organization follows a strict policy of separation of church and state, including resistance to government regulation in such areas as building codes and permits, legally required registration or incorporation of churches, licensing of pastors, and Social Security tax payments for church employees. The ACUC provides churches with educational materials explaining biblical principles and constitutional rights.

PUBLICATIONS: *The Trumpet,* a bimonthly newspaper.

American Council of Christian Churches (ACCC)

P.O. Box 5455
Bethlehem, PA 18015
(610) 865-3009
(610) 865-3003 (fax)
http://www.amcouncilcc.org
Ralph G. Colas, Executive Secretary

Carl McIntire established this organization in 1941 in reaction to the National (then Federal) Council of Churches (NCC), which McIntire considered too liberal. The ACCC requires its members to maintain complete separation from the NCC, the World Council of Churches, and the National Association of Evangelicals. The ACCC has opposed communism and other beliefs that it considers a threat to American religious, economic, and political freedom. Because of dissension between McIntire and other leaders of the ACCC, in 1969 the organization dropped McIntire from the executive council. In 1970 it left the International Council of Christian Churches, another organization created by McIntire. The ACCC holds to a fundamentalist doctrine, advocates the inerrancy of the Bible, supports dissemination of the "historic Christian faith" in America and around the world, and opposes liberal, socialist, and communist doctrines. The organization, which claims a membership of 1.5 million, is affiliated with the Council of Bible Believing Churches.

PUBLICATIONS: *Fundamental News Service,* a bimonthly newsletter that discusses social and political issues of concern to Christians.

American Family Association (AFA)

P.O. Box 2440
Tupelo, MS 38803
(601) 844-5036
(601) 842-6791 (fax)
http://www.afa.net
Donald E. Wildmon, Executive Director

Founded by Donald Wildmon in 1977, this organization promotes what it terms the "biblical ethic of decency in American society" and focuses its attention on the perceived immorality, profanity, and violence on television and in the other mass media. The organization encourages the television networks to broadcast family-oriented entertainment. The AFA compiles data on televised programming it deems objectionable and encourages boycotts of the offending networks and their sponsors. The AFA also employs petition campaigns. Prior to 1988 the AFA was known as the National Federation for Decency.

PUBLICATIONS: *AFA Journal,* which is published monthly, and pamphlets dealing with the organization's opposition to pornography and sex education in the public schools.

American Freemen Association
See Christian Patriot Association

American Life League (ALL)
P.O. Box 1350
Stafford, VA 22555
(540) 659-4171
(540) 659-2586 (fax)
http://www.all.org
Julie Brown, President

Begun in 1982 by five families as the American Life Education and Research Trust, the American Life League considers the pro-life movement a moral crusade to protect human life. In addition to abortion, the ALL focuses on euthanasia, organ transplantation, and other population issues. The organization objects to attempts at political conciliation. To the ALL, life is a gift from God, and so there can be "no exceptions and no compromises" on the question of abortion. The group contends that the survival of the United States depends upon "securing for the preborn the guarantee of being born as honored citizens of a country that practices, under God, liberty and justice for all." The ALL sponsors national pro-life seminars and training conferences.

PUBLICATIONS: *Celebrate Life,* a bimonthly magazine; *Reality Check,* a monthly newsletter.

American Society for the Defense of Tradition, Family and Property (TFP)
P.O. Box 341
Hanover, PA 17331
(717) 225-7147
(717) 225-7382 (fax)
http://www.tfp.org
Raymond E. Drake, President

A civic organization founded in 1973 and based largely on Roman Catholic doctrine, the TFP defends traditional values, the family, Christian cultural heritage, and the right to property, and opposes what are considered socialist and Marxist positions on these subjects. The Society is concerned with what it perceives as a crisis in morality, politics, and religion and works toward educating Americans in ways to defend traditional values and free enterprise. The group sponsors youth programs, holds regional seminars, and offers grants and scholarships to promote research.

PUBLICATIONS: *Crusade Magazine,* bimonthly; *TFP in Action,* a monthly newsletter.

Americans United for God and Country (AUGC)

P.O. Box 183
Merion Station, PA 19066
(215) 224-9235
Leslie Harris, Executive Director

Begun in 1977, this organization, claiming a membership of 10,400, supports tuition tax credits and grants for private schools as a means of furthering the Judeo-Christian tradition. According to the organization, because religious citizens provide tax funds to operate public school systems, their principles deserve attention in the curriculum. These principles include patriotism and the basic governing concepts listed in the Constitution and the Bill of Rights. The AUGC holds an annual conference on July 4.

PUBLICATIONS: None.

Associates for Biblical Research (ABR)

P.O. Box 144
Akron, PA 17501
(717) 859-3443
http://abr.christiananswers.net
Gary Byers, Executive Director

Founded in 1969, this association conducts research on biblical archaeology and promotes creationism as a scientifically legitimate approach to the origins of human life. The organization conducts an educational program and sponsors an annual archaeological excavation in Israel. The organization distributes a catalog of books, videos, and curriculum materials, and also sponsors a weekly radio program, *Stones Cry Out,* that provides archaeological evidence in support of the historical veracity of the Bible.

PUBLICATIONS: *Bible and Spade,* a quarterly journal; *ABR Newsletter,* bimonthly.

Campus Crusade for Christ International (CCC)

100 Lake Hart Drive
Orlando, FL 32832
(407) 826-2000
http://www.ccci.org
Bill Thomas, Director

Bill Bright began the CCC in 1951 on the University of California–Los Angeles campus. In addition to college and university ministries, including Bible study groups, faculty groups, and student, family, and pastoral conferences, Campus Crusade has programs to reach high school students, military personnel, and prisoners. The organization is active in 152 countries around the world "to help fulfill the Great Commission of Christ ... and to work with other members of the Body of Christ."

PUBLICATIONS: *Worldwide Challenge*, a bimonthly magazine; *Departmental Newsletter*, periodic.

Center for Christian Statesmanship

214 Massachusetts Avenue, NE, Suite 220
Washington, DC 20002
(202) 547-3052
(202) 547-3287 (fax)
http://www.statesman.org
George Roller, Executive Director

Established by D. James Kennedy, pastor of Coral Ridge Presbyterian Church in Fort Lauderdale, Florida, the Center for Christian Statesmanship has three goals: "to minister the Gospel of Jesus Christ to leaders in our nation's capital," "to equip our nation's leaders for ministry and service," and "to reestablish the principles and practices of Christian statesmanship." The Center conducts Bible studies on Capitol Hill for elected officials and government workers, and holds Politics and Principle luncheons at which members of Congress and others present views about the relationship between personal faith and public service. Each year the Center presents the Distinguished Christian Statesman award to a public official. Past winners include Senators John Ashcroft (1996) and Sam Brownback (2000) and House Majority Leader Dick Armey (1999). Representative Tom DeLay, the 2002 winner, resigned from Congress in 2006 over allegations of campaign finance irregularities.

PUBLICATIONS: None.

Center for Reclaiming America

P.O. Box 632
Fort Lauderdale, FL 33302
(877) 725-8872
http://www.reclaimamerica.org
Gary Case, Executive Director

Claiming that the United States has fallen away from its appropriate place as a Christian nation, the Center for Reclaiming America works to "inform the American public and motivate people of faith to defend and implement the biblical principles on which our country was founded." Among the concerns about which the organization has campaigned are abortion, the selection of federal judges, pornography, and displays of the Ten Commandments.

PUBLICATIONS: The organization offers books, videos, and audiotapes for sale.

Chalcedon Foundation (CF)

P.O. Box 158

Vallecito, CA 95251
(209) 736-4365
http://chalcedon.edu
Mark R. Rushdoony, President

Founded in 1965, this organization seeks to reconstruct government and society according to biblical principles. The CF issues grants to scholars conducting research into the relevance of biblical law and faith to contemporary life and thought.

PUBLICATIONS: *The Chalcedon Report*, a monthly magazine; *Chalcedon e-Letter*, a monthly newsletter.

Christian Anti-Communism Crusade (CACC)

P.O. Box 129
Manitou Springs, CO 80829
(719) 685-9043
(719) 685-9330 (fax)
http://www.schwarzreport.org
David Noebel, President

Founded in 1953 by Frederick C. Schwarz, originally an Australian physician, this anticommunist religious and educational group has a long history of providing information regarding the evils of communism. Lectures and forums coordinated by the organization for citizen groups, college students, and churches stress communist strategy and philosophy in order to prepare individuals to resist more effectively the communist threat. In explaining its objective, the organization employs a medical analogy, with communism as the disease, the Crusade the pathologist, and politicians, educators, and voters the physicians. The CACC has been active not only in the United States, but also in several foreign nations, including India, the Philippines, Korea, Taiwan, Malaysia, El Salvador, and Chile. In 1998 Schwarz retired as president, but the organization continues under Noebel's leadership.

PUBLICATIONS: *The Schwarz Report*, a monthly newsletter; Fred Schwarz's books and booklets, including *You Can Trust the Communists (To Be Communists) (1960), Why Communism Kills* (1984), *Beating the Unbeatable Foe* (1996), and David Noebel's *Understanding the Times: The Religious Worldviews of Our Day and the Search for Truth* (1995).

Christian Coalition of America (CCA)

499 South Capitol Street, SW, Suite 615
P.O. Box 37030
Washington, DC 20003-7030
(202) 479-6900
(202) 479-4260 (fax)
http://www.cc.org
Roberta Combs, President

The Christian Coalition of America, which was founded in 1989 by Pat Robertson as the Christian Coalition, is a grassroots political organization concerned with an alleged lack of morality in government. The Christian Coalition was reorganized in 1999 into two separate organizations: the Christian Coalition of America, which is involved in "voter education," and the Christian Coalition International, a political action committee. The organization seeks the election of legislators who have high moral values and supports legislation of concern to the Christian right, especially pro-family measures. The CCA has opposed homosexuals in the military, taxpayer-funded "abortion-on-demand," condom distribution in the public schools, "socialized medicine," legal recognition of homosexual marriages, and increased government spending and taxation. Although it does not support specific candidates, the organization distributes Congressional Scorecards, revealing candidates' positions on issues and voting records on measures considered important to Christian voters. In 1993 and 1994 the CCA claimed to have distributed 29 million Congressional Scorecards and 40 million voter guides (candidates' stands on key issues) in an effort to affect election outcomes and government policy.

PUBLICATIONS: *Christian American*, a bimonthly newsletter; *Washington Weekly Review*, a newsletter.

Christian Crusade

P O Box 21228
Tulsa, OK 74121-1228
(918) 665-2345
(918) 438-4235 (fax)

Founded in 1948, the Christian Crusade has had a long history of opposition to communist and socialist ideologies, as well as to what the organization believes were attempts by supporters of such ideologies to infiltrate American government and society. The Christian Crusade (formerly Christian Echoes National Ministry) has worked to preserve the conservative Christian ideals upon which it believes America was founded. In addition to opposing communism, the organization has objected to American participation in the United Nations, government interference in the economy, and federal involvement in areas such as education that it believes are constitutionally reserved to the states. After the 1994 congressional elections, Christian Crusade strongly supported the Republican policy agenda in Congress. The organization strongly criticized Bill Clinton during his presidency. With the death of Billy James Hargis, the Christian Crusade founder and president, in November 2004, the organization faced an uncertain future.

PUBLICATIONS: *Christian Crusade Newspaper*, a monthly publication with a circulation of 15,000 that treats current events from a conservative Christian standpoint. Before his death, Billy James Hargis authored many of the front-page items.

Christian Defense League (CDL)

P.O. Box 449

Arabi, LA 70032
(504) 279-8583
http://home.inreach.com/dov/cdl.htm Note: Bad link
James K. Warner, Executive Officer

Launched in 1964, the CDL supports the perpetuation of traditional Christian values and fosters the development of Christian leaders in the public realm. The organization offers research and educational programs and conducts a speakers bureau.

PUBLICATIONS: Two monthly magazines, *CDL Report* and *Christian Vanguard.*

Christian Echoes National Ministry

See Christian Crusade

Christian Family Renewal (CFR)

P.O. Box 73
Clovis, CA 93613
(559) 347-9324
Dr. Michael Norris, President

Established in 1970, this organization focuses on problems related to the contemporary family. The CFR attempts to offer Christians ways to resolve social problems in politics, business, and education. Among the issues of concern to the organization are abortion, homosexuality, and pornography.

PUBLICATIONS: *Jesus and Mary Are Calling You,* an annual newsletter; a report on pornography, homosexuality, Satanism, and abortion.

Christian Heritage Center (CHC)

10 Croyden Lane
Stanton, VA 24401
(540) 885-7333
http://christianheritageworks.com
Dr. N. Burnett Magruder, Executive Director

A Christian patriotic organization founded in 1964, the CHC advocates a return to the basic faith and liberties of the American founding. The organization supports the introduction of prayer, Bible reading, and the teaching of the Ten Commandments in the public schools, and assesses the influence of atheism, humanism, and communism in American government and society. The organization produces the daily radio broadcast *Liberty Radio Program.*

PUBLICATIONS: *Awake and Alert,* a monthly bulletin.

Christian Law Association (CLA)

P.O. Box 4010
Seminole, FL 33775
(727) 399-8300
(727) 398-3907 (fax)

http://www.christianlaw.org
David C. Gibbs Jr., President

The CLA began in 1977 with David Gibbs's successful defense of a couple who had been arrested and jailed for refusing to send their children to public school, preferring instead home schooling in a religious atmosphere. Attached to the Gibbs and Craze law firm, the CLA uses litigation to defend members' religious rights. The organization receives monthly dues from churches and individuals who, if they require legal assistance regarding their religious rights, will receive representation at no additional cost. The organization provides updates on First Amendment issues and conducts seminars to help laypersons avoid litigation.

PUBLICATIONS: *Teacher's Forum*, monthly.

Christian Legal Society (CLS)
8001 Braddock Road
Springfield, VA 22151
(703) 642-1070
(703) 642-1075 (fax)
http://www.clsnet.org
Samuel B. Casey, Executive Director

Established in 1961, the Christian Legal Society attempts to provide fellowship for Christian lawyers, elucidates the idea of a Christian lawyer, provides the opportunity to discuss the relationship between Christian ministry and the practice of law, and works with bar associations and others in ensuring the ethical standards of the profession. The Society's Center for Law and Religious Freedom (CLRF) files amicus curiae briefs in religious freedom preservation-of-life cases. The Center has supported passage of a marriage protection amendment to the U.S. Constitution. The organization has pursued litigation against universities over the question of freedom for religious student groups. The CLS also has expressed concern for removing the causes of poverty. The organization provides legal services, including biblically based conflict reconciliation to the needy, through forty-six projects in twenty-three states.

PUBLICATIONS: *The Christian Lawyer*, biannual.

Christian Patriot Association (CPA)
P.O. Box 596
Boring, OR 97009
(503) 668-4941
(503) 668-8614 (fax)
Richard G. Flowers, Founder

Founded in 1982 as the American Freeman Association, this patriotic Christian organization apparently is no longer in operation. In June 2002 a federal jury convicted Flowers, his wife, and four others associated with the group of conspiracy for engaging in an illegal banking operation that hid more than $180 million from the Internal Revenue Service. The CPA concerned itself with what members believed to be unconstitutional abuses of government power. The organization's objective was to restore to American citizens the sovereignty that members claimed government abuses had threatened. Information relevant to such abuses was gathered from mass media reports and compiled for distribution.

Christian Research (CR)
P.O. Box 385
Eureka Springs, AR 72632-0385
(479) 253-7185
http://www.christianresearch.info
Daniel Gentry, Director

This organization, founded in 1958, offers itself as an alternative to the secular media and the American educational system. Although the CR calls for upholding the American Constitution, as the organization interprets its original meaning, and encourages patriotism and nationalism, major emphasis is placed on obeying God's commands over any human law. The CR informs Christian Americans of their biblical heritage and responsibilities and warns them of threats to "our theocratic republic." The organization supports a revisionist history of the Holocaust and opposes communism, the United Nations, and the income tax. Christian Research, formerly known as Pro-American Books, distributes Christian literature and fosters Bible study.

PUBLICATIONS: *Facts for Action*, a quarterly newsletter.

Christian Research Institute (CRI)
P.O. Box 8500
Charlotte, NC 28271-8500
(704) 887-8200
(704) 887-8299 (fax)
http://www.equip.org
Hendrik (Hank) Hanegraaff, President

The CRI, established in 1960, opposes perceived threats to the Christian faith. It provides information about the direction of events in the secular world relevant to Christianity. The institute advocates "orthodox" Christianity and critically evaluates groups it considers to be heretical cults, such as the Jehovah's Witnesses and Mormons. The CRI has focused critical attention on such popular televangelists in the so-called faith movement as Benny Hinn, Kenneth and Gloria Copeland, Oral Roberts, and Trinity Broadcasting Network founder Paul Crouch and his wife Jan. Former president Walter Martin was noted for engaging in debates with religious leaders having opposing views. The CRI sponsors the *Bible Answer Man*, a syndicated radio program hosted by Hanegraaff.
PUBLICATIONS: *Christian Research Journal*, quarterly magazine that examines various religious cults, the occult, and doctrinal controversies within Chris-

tianity; *Christian Research Newsletter*, a quarterly that reports on the activities of cults.

Christian School Action
See National Christian Action Coalition

Christian Voice (CV)
This Christian right organization, founded in 1978, became virtually nonexistent after the formation of the American Freedom Coalition in 1987. The CV grew out of the movement opposing civil rights for gays and lesbians in California and was expanded through direct-mail appeals. In 1980 the organization created an associated group, Christians for Reagan, which concentrated on voter registration. The CV focused on such issues as abortion, gay rights, pornography, a school prayer amendment, and the Equal Rights Amendment. It gained publicity through the controversial use of "moral report cards" for members of Congress. In the 1980s, when the religious right concentrated its efforts on influencing the national legislative process, Gary Jarmin served as the major congressional lobbyist for the organization.

Church League of America
George Washington Robnett, an advertising executive, formed the Church League in 1937 to combat the perceived communist threat in America. The organization sought to advance "Christian Americanism" and to oppose centralization of political authority. It opposed President Franklin Roosevelt's "court packing" plan in 1937 and campaigned against his bid for reelection in 1940. In 1956 Edgar C. Bundy succeeded Robnett as the organization's leader. The Church League collected data on individuals and organizations suspected of having communist affiliations and maintained a library of publications the organization considered subversive. One section of the library focuses on John Dewey, whose works were believed to be sympathetic to communism. The organization distributed literature to ministers, informing them of the dangers of communism and socialism, and published a monthly newsletter, *News and Views*, that alerted readers to the activities of leftist organizations. The Church League never attracted a large following and by the mid-1960s had declined into obscurity.

Committee for Religious Freedom
See International Coalition for Religious Freedom

Concerned Women for America (CWA)
1015 15th Street, NW, Suite 1100
Washington, DC 20005
(202) 488-7000
(202) 488-0806 (fax)
http://www.cwfa.org
Beverly LaHaye, Chairperson

Beginning in the late 1970s with just nine members, the CWA currently claims a membership of over a half million women. It reports an annual budget of $8 million. The organization conducts educational programs that emphasize the theme of traditional American values and lobbies the national and state legislatures on issues of concern to members. The organization has backed a number of religious right positions, including support for religious freedom, antiabortion legislation, required AIDS testing for marriage license applicants, and a strong national defense. The group has opposed an equal rights amendment to the U.S. Constitution, pornography, sex and violence in the mass media, condom advertising on television, unisex insurance rates, violence in families, and communism in the Western Hemisphere. The CWA supported President Reagan's efforts to aid the Nicaraguan contras. The CWA, along with Phyllis Schlafly's Eagle Forum, received credit in 1986 for defeating a Vermont equal rights amendment. The CWA has had success as a legal defense foundation, providing legal representation to Christian parents who have challenged local public school policy. The organization has attempted to increase religious right influence at the local level by organizing its members in congressional districts to campaign for favored candidates and to maintain contact with public officials. Members can receive training on how to run for political office, organize a campaign for the board of education, and influence public school policy.
PUBLICATIONS: *Family Voice*, a bimonthly newsletter.

Council of Bible Believing Churches in the U.S.A. (CBBC)
8442 Cook Way
Thornton, CO 80229-4222
Ovid M. Hepler, President

Founded in 1968 as the American Christian Action Council and later known as the National Council of Bible Believing Churches, this organization was established to assist the International Council of Christian Churches in promoting fundamentalist Christian beliefs based on the Bible and the traditional Christian faith. Although the CBBC shows few signs of activity, Hepler, pastor of the Haven Baptist Church in Denver, CO, continues to distribute the organization's newsletter.

PUBLICATIONS: *The Servant*, a monthly newsletter containing items of interest to conservative Christians.

Council on Biblical Manhood and Womanhood (CBMW)
2825 Lexington Road, Box 926
Louisville, KY 40280
(502) 897-4065
(502) 897-4061 (fax)
http://www.cbmw.org
Randy Stinson, Executive Director

The core beliefs of the Council on Biblical Manhood and Womanhood are presented in the Danvers Statement, which organization members prepared at a meeting in Danvers, Massachusetts, in December 1987. Instead of "feminist egalitarianism," which the group opposes, the CBMW emphasizes the leadership position of "redeemed husbands" and the support given to that leadership by "redeemed wives." Group members also object to the unbiblical roles that men and women are assuming in the church and the accommodation that some church members are making to "the spirit of the age." The organization upholds the biblical perspective on the relationship between men and women and publishes materials presenting that view. The CBMW offers books, booklets, brochures, audio and video materials, and curricula that express the organization's views.

PUBLICATIONS: *Journal for Biblical Manhood and Womanhood*, biannual.

Creation Research Society (CRS)
P.O. Box 8263
St. Joseph, MO 64508-8263
http://www.creationresearch.org
Donald B. DeYoung, President

The CRS was founded in 1963 by ten scientists who were unable to publish their research in scientific journals because it was conducted from a creationist perspective. Members of the organization are required to hold the following beliefs: "The Bible is the written word of God"; "All basic types of living things, including humans, were made by direct creative acts of God during the Creation Week described in Genesis"; "The great flood described in Genesis . . . was an historic event worldwide in its extent and effect"; and "We are an organization of Christian men and women of science who accept Jesus Christ as our Lord and Savior." The purpose of the organization is to encourage research and publication that recognizes creation as a valid explanation of the origin of the universe and humankind. The CRS supports a research facility in Arizona.

PUBLICATIONS: *Creation Research Society Quarterly*, a peer-reviewed journal of original research within the creationist framework; *Creation Matters*, a bimonthly newsletter.

Eagle Forum (EF)
P.O. Box 618
Alton, IL 62002
(618) 462-5415
(618) 462-8909 (fax)
http://www.eagleforum.org
Phyllis Schlafly, President

Founded in 1975 by Phyllis Schlafly, in part as a reaction to the Supreme Court abortion decision in *Roe v. Wade*, Eagle Forum is a conservative, pro-family organization that is active at the local, state, and national governmental levels on issues concerning the family, education, and national defense. The EF supports "traditional morality," private enterprise, and a strong national defense, and opposes an equal rights amendment and sex education in public schools. The Forum focuses on tax policy, advocating an increase in tax exemptions for children and the elimination of what it considers discriminatory tax policy against the traditional family.

PUBLICATIONS: *Phyllis Schlafly Report*, a monthly newsletter containing information on such subjects as education, economics, social policy, and national defense and foreign policy.

Evangelicals for Social Action (ESA)
10 East Lancaster Avenue
Wynnewood, PA 19096-3495
(610) 645-9390
(610) 649-8090
http://www.esa-online.org
Ron Sider, President

Evangelicals for Social Action differs from most of the other organizations discussed here because it takes stands on such issues as poverty, disarmament, penal reform, and the environment. The idea of the organization originated in 1973 when a group of approximately forty evangelical leaders met to write and sign the Chicago Declaration of Evangelical Concern, which emphasized the failure of evangelicals to deal with such issues as injustice, racism, and gender discrimination. Five years later ESA was formally established. The group supported what it called a consistently pro-life position: it opposed abortion but also worked to achieve justice for the poor and to end the nuclear arms race. More recently, ESA has focused on environmental issues, providing support for the Evangelical Environmental Network (EEN). Organization members hold that God has entrusted human beings with the care of creation for the benefit of all people.

PUBLICATIONS: *Prism*, a quarterly magazine; *Creation Care*, a quarterly magazine published with the Evangelical Environmental Network and under the editorship of Jim Ball, the executive director of the EEN.

Exodus International (EI)
P.O. Box 540119
Orlando, FL 32854
(407) 599-6872
(407) 599-0011 (fax)
http://www.exodus.to
Alan Chambers, President

A coalition of Christian ministries established in 1976, Exodus International promotes a traditional conception of marriage as a union between one man and one woman. The organization claims that heterosexuality represents God's intent for humankind and calls homosexuality one of the infirmities resulting from the fall of humanity. Therefore, EI considers homosexual behavior detrimental to God's true intention. Although the organization does not consider homosexuality a valid life-style, neither does it project a fearful negative response to homosexuality. Instead, the organization claims to offer a way for homosexuals to adopt a heterosexual life-style. EI has supported an amendment to the U.S. Constitution limiting marriage to heterosexual couples and has advocated similar measures as amendments to state constitutions. The organization has produced media ads to publicize its position on homosexuality.

PUBLICATIONS: *Exodus Update*, a monthly newsletter that includes testimonials of "healings," prayer requests, and announcements of upcoming events.

Family Research Council (FRC)
801 G Street, NW
Washington, DC 20001
(202) 393-2100
(202) 393-2134 (fax)
http://www.frc.org
Tony Perkins, President

Established in 1981 as the Family Research Group, this organization acquired its present name in 1988. The FRC is an affiliate of James Dobson's radio ministry, Focus on the Family. As a research-oriented group with a budget of $11.5 million per year and a claimed membership of 450,000, the organization provides information to government agencies and members of Congress on issues such as parental autonomy, the problems of single parents, tax breaks for parents with preschool children, teen pregnancy, abortion, alternatives to public schools, welfare programs, and housing. The FRC staunchly opposes efforts to legalize same-sex marriage. Gary Bauer, who headed the organization until 2000, served as an aide to Education Secretary William Bennett and as a policy adviser to President Reagan.
PUBLICATIONS: *Washington Watch*, a monthly newsletter.

Family Research Group
See Family Research Council

Focus on the Family (FF)
8605 Explorer Drive
Colorado Springs, CO 80920
(719) 531-3400
(719) 548-4525 (fax)
http://www.family.org NOTE :This Web site is temporarily unavailable.
Jim Daly, President and CEO

Focus on the Family was founded in 1977 as the support organization for James Dobson's radio program of the same name that provides Christian guidance to troubled families. The organization encourages the development and maintenance of the family unit in unison with Christian values. Among its many activities, the FF provides information on such family-related topics as marriage and parenting, conducts educational and charitable programs, and provides child-related programs.

PUBLICATIONS: Several monthly magazines, including *Focus on the Family Citizen*, which evaluates legislative activities at all levels; *Teachers in Focus*, for educators in public and private schools; and *Parental Guidance*, a newsletter examining the media and popular culture; various magazines for youth, including *Breakaway* (for teenage boys), *Brio* (for teenage girls), *Clubhouse* (for children), and *Clubhouse Jr.* (for preschoolers).

Free Congress Research and Education Foundation (FCREF)
717 Second Street, NE
Washington, DC 20002
(202) 546-3000
(202) 543-8425 (fax)
http://www.freecongress.org
Thomas Lee Jipping, Vice President

Founded in 1977, the Free Congress Research and Education Foundation, although not an explicitly religious organization, emphasizes cultural conservatism and the need to maintain traditional Judeo-Christian values. Claiming that multiculturalism and "political correctness" are major threats to the American culture, the organization has concluded that "activist" judges are a main enemy. During President Bill Clinton's administration, the FCREF established the Judicial Selection Monitoring Project to oppose judicial appointments of liberal candidates. The organization also expresses concern about alleged attempts of the national government to eavesdrop on private telephone and e-mail communication. The views of the FCREF have been disseminated on such television programs as *Next Revolution, Endangered Liberties, Legal Notebook, and Taking Back Our Constitution*, which appear via America's Voice, a satellite network.

PUBLICATIONS: *Essays on Our Times* and *Policy Insights*, monthly series treating cultural and political issues; *Weyrich Insider*, a monthly newsletter; occasional books, special reports, and monographs, including *The Judicial Selection Monitor*, an examination of the federal judge selection process.

Freedom Council (FC)
Pat Robertson began the Freedom Council in 1981 and terminated it in 1986. It was headquartered in Virginia Beach, Virginia. Focusing on freedom of religion, the FC attempted to educate Christians on religious and civil liberties. The organization supported litigation on such issues as school prayer and freedom of religion in the workplace. As a grassroots organization, the FC encouraged citizens to write to their representatives on issues related to freedom of religion. Before its termination, charges of financial irregularities

arose involving the use of donations to the Freedom Council for Robertson's political activities. The organization was succeeded by the Christian Coalition.

Institute for Creation Research (ICR)

10946 Woodside Avenue North
Santee, CA 92071
(619) 596-6011
http://www.icr.org
John D. Morris, President

Established in 1972, the Institute for Creation Research is based on a belief in creationism and biblical inerrancy. Although originally the research arm of Christian Heritage College, the ICR became a separate entity in 1981. The Institute asserts that creation science should be taught along with the theory of evolution in the public schools and that scientific as well as biblical creationism should be a part of the curriculum at Christian schools. According to the ICR, among the postulates of scientific creationism are the following: each major kind of plant and animal was created functionally complete and did not develop from some other kind of organism; the first humans were originally created in their present form; scientific evidence exists that supports the biblical account of a relatively recent creation of Earth; and there is always the possibility of divine intervention in natural laws.

PUBLICATIONS: *Acts and Facts*, a monthly newsletter.

International Coalition for Religious Freedom (ICRF)

7777 Leesburg Pike, Suite 404 N-A
Falls Church, VA 22043
(703) 790-1500
(703) 790-5562 (fax)
http://www.religiousfreedom.com
Dan Tefferman, Executive Director

Founded in 1984, reportedly with assistance from Sun Myung Moon's Unification Church, this nondenominational organization, formerly the Committee for Religious Freedom, assists religious groups in dealing with the various levels of government on questions involving freedom of religion. Many of the top religious figures of the 1980s, including Tim LaHaye, Jerry Falwell, Ben Armstrong, Pat Robertson, Rex Humbard, D. James Kennedy, and Jimmy Swaggart, served on the original executive board. The ICRF offers advice and information to churches regarding the activities of all branches and levels of government that have an impact on religious institutions. The organization has dealt with such issues as the licensing of ministries, tax laws as applied to religious groups, government enforcement of health and safety codes and zoning restrictions for private religious schools, and accreditation controversies.

PUBLICATIONS: *Religious Freedom Alert* (approximately ten issues per year), a tabloid that provides information and commentary on church-state relations.

International Council of Christian Churches (ICCC)
10977 E. 23rd Street
Tulsa, OK 74129
(915) 234-0462
(915) 234-0474 (fax)
http://www.iccc.org.sg
John Borela, President

The ICCC was formed in 1948 under the leadership of Carl McIntire as the international version of his American Council of Christian Churches (ACCC). The organization was established as a direct response to the initiation of the World Council of Churches (WCC). McIntire objected to that organization's emphasis upon ecumenism among Protestant churches and its willingness to converse with Roman Catholics and Jews. In the 1950s leaders of the ICCC, along with the ACCC, cooperated with Senator Joseph McCarthy and the House Un-American Activities Committee in identifying possible communist influences in the clergy. The ICCC serves as a gathering point for fundamentalist churches worldwide and encourages a fundamentalist Christianity uncompromisingly opposed to all forms of modernism and unbelief.

PUBLICATIONS: Regional papers.

John Birch Society (JBS)
P.O. Box 8040
Appleton, WI 54912
(920) 749-3780
(920) 749-5062 (fax)
http://www.jbs.org
G. Vance Smith, President

Founded by Robert Welch in 1958, the John Birch Society, although best known for what it opposes—communism, socialism, totalitarian government, the United Nations, and federal regulatory agencies—claims that the U.S. governing system is superior to any other and maintains a positive, though vague, image of a future world made better through the help of God. The organization professes a belief in the traditional moral values as found in the Judeo-Christian heritage and considers the family to be the most important element in society. Local chapters conduct letter-writing campaigns to public officials and distribute the society's literature. The organization supports a speakers' bureau and a seminar program.

PUBLICATIONS: *John Birch Society Bulletin*, a monthly publication; *The New American*, a biweekly newsmagazine.

Kingdom Identity Ministries (KIM)
P.O. Box 1021
Harrison, AR 72602
(870) 741-1119
http://www.kingidentity.com

Kingdom Identity Ministries is an extreme religious right organization that describes itself as "a politically incorrect Christian Identity outreach ministry to God's chosen (true Israel, the White, European peoples)." In 1998 the KIM assumed control of Your Heritage Ministry, which had been established in the 1950s by Bertrand Comparet, whom the organization describes as "the greatest Bible scholar of the twentieth century."

PUBLICATIONS: Several of Bertrand Comparet's writings as well as other books and tracts on such subjects as racial identity, biblical law, "God's Enemies," and the "Anti-Christ Conspiracy" are offered for sale.

Liberty Federation (LF)
P.O. Box 2000
Lynchburg, VA 24506
(804) 582-7310
P. Gilsman, President

Founded in 1979 as the Moral Majority Foundation by Jerry Falwell and given its present name in 1986, the organization never reached the prominence of its forerunner. The Liberty Federation has not been active since the Moral Majority was terminated in 1989. It still maintains an address and telephone number in Lynchburg, Virginia, claims a membership of 72,000 ministers and four million laypersons, and reports active engagement in persuading conservatives to register and vote for candidates that support traditional values as a way of responding to moral decline in America. The organization points to legalized abortion, pornography, and advocacy of homosexual rights as evidence of that moral decline.

PUBLICATIONS: None.

Moral Majority (MM)
Established in 1979 and finally terminated in 1989, three years after its activities had been shifted to the newly formed Liberty Federation, Moral Majority was the best known of the religious right organizations of the 1980s. It was established in order to activate the religious right politically. Moral Majority concentrated on the major religious right issues, including opposition to homosexuality, abortion, pornography, and the Equal Rights Amendment, and support for school prayer. The organization consisted of the Moral Majority Foundation, which claimed tax exemption; Moral Majority, Inc., which served as the political lobbying branch; and the Moral Majority Political Action Committee, the part of the organization responsible for raising campaign funds to support candidates for public office. The organization published the periodical *Moral Majority Report*. Although Moral Majority gained influence over the national political agenda during the early 1980s, it acquired a negative public image due in part to the aggressive lobbying activities of the organization and its leader, Jerry Falwell. Falwell resigned as president in November 1987.

National Association of Evangelicals (NAE)
P.O. Box 23269
Washington, DC 20026
(202) 789-1011
http://www.nae.net
Bill Hamel, Chairman

This interdenominational organization was founded in 1942 to provide an alternative to the National (then Federal) Council of Churches and to serve as a medium of cooperation among evangelical churches and organizations. The NAE includes 45,000 churches representing 30 million people. Such groups as Assemblies of God, Baptists, and evangelical wings of the Lutheran, Methodist, and Presbyterian denominations are represented in the membership. The organization sponsors various events, such as the Washington Insight Briefing and the Washington Student Seminar. The NAE has demonstrated explicitly conservative political preferences. For instance, in 1983 President Ronald Reagan chose an NAE meeting to make his well-publicized speech in which he referred to the former Soviet Union as the "evil empire." President Reagan spoke before the organization again in 1984, calling for a school prayer amendment to the Constitution. The NAE is associated with the Christian Scholarship Association, the Evangelical Fellowship of Mission Agencies, and National Religious Broadcasters.

PUBLICATIONS: *NAE Washington Insight*, a monthly newsletter reporting on national government activities of concern to evangelical leaders; *National Association of Evangelicals—Dateline*, a quarterly newsletter providing a preview of events and meetings and information on state organizations; *National Evangelical Directory*, a biennial publication listing various evangelical organizations; and *United Evangelical Action: A Call to Action from the NAE*, a bimonthly reporting on organization activities and providing a calendar of future events.

National Christian Action Coalition (NCAC)

No longer in existence, this organization was established by Robert Billings in 1978. Billings left the organization after one year to become the first executive director of Moral Majority. He was succeeded at the NCAC by his son, William Billings. The NCAC was preceded by Christian School Action, an organization that Robert Billings formed in 1977. Billings initiated the NCAC in reaction to the Internal Revenue Service's attempts to withdraw the tax-exempt status of private schools that were judged racially discriminatory. The organization included the Christian Voter's Victory Fund (a political action committee), the Christian Education and Research Foundation, and the New Century Foundation (a publishing enterprise). Support declined during the early 1980s, and William Billings finally terminated the organization in 1985.

National Coalition for the Protection of Children and Families (NCPCF)
800 Compton Road, Suite 9224
Cincinnati, OH 45231

(513) 521-6227
(513) 521-6337 (fax)
http://www.nationalcoalition.org
Rick Schatz, President

In 1983 Reverend Jerry Kirk, concerned about the spread of pornography in the United States, established the National Consultation on Pornography and Obscenity, subsequently renamed National Coalition Against Pornography and now known as the National Coalition for the Protection of Children and Families (NCPCF), an ecumenical organization devoted to assisting religious, civic, and legal groups opposed to obscenity and child pornography. The organization calls for strict enforcement of obscenity and child protection laws and participates in efforts to strengthen those laws. The organization plays an educational role by distributing written materials and video- and audiotapes that give advice on how to combat pornography, and holds the annual National City Leaders Conference.

PUBLICATIONS: *NCPCF in Action,* a quarterly newsletter.

National Legal Foundation (NLF)
P.O. Box 64427
Virginia Beach, VA 23467-4427
(757) 463-6133
(757) 463-6055 (fax)
http://www.nlf.net
Steven W. Fitschen, President

This public-interest law firm, founded in 1985 by Pat Robertson and originally financed by the Christian Broadcasting Network, offers legal services to defend constitutional liberties, especially religious freedom. The organization prepares legal briefs and educational materials dealing with church state issues. Attorneys associated with the foundation choose to become involved in cases that are potentially precedent setting and that have national application. The organization conducts seminars for lawyers on First Amendment questions. In the Supreme Court case *Westside Community Schools v. Mergens* (1990), Foundation attorneys successfully argued for the right of students to form a campus Bible club under the 1984 Equal Access Act.

PUBLICATIONS: *The Minuteman,* a quarterly newsletter; *Foundations of Freedom,* a booklet.

National Religious Broadcasters (NRB)
9510 Tech. Drive
Manassas, VA 20110
(703) 330-7000
(703) 330-7100 (fax)
http://www.nrb.org
Frank Wright, President

The membership of this organization includes religious radio and television producers, owners, and operators in the United States and worldwide. Founded in 1944, the NRB is a major data source about Christian broadcasting. The organization protects religious broadcasters' access to the airwaves and conducts meetings at which fundraising techniques and new technology can be shared among members. The NRB provides religious programming to its members and operates religious radio and television stations. In 1988 the organization adopted a new financial code of ethics as a result of scandals involving television evangelists. The new code requires member organizations to provide annual income and expenditure statements to the NRB's executive committee. The organization's leaders have shown a preference for conservative political candidates. For instance, in 1988 all major Republican presidential hopefuls spoke at the NRB convention, while no Democratic candidates were invited. The NRB is associated with the National Association of Evangelicals.

PUBLICATIONS: *Directory of Religious Media*, an annual listing of those engaged in religious broadcasting, including radio and television stations and programmers; *NRB Magazine*, monthly.

National Right to Life Committee (NRLC)
512 Tenth Street, NW
Washington, DC 20004
(202) 626-8800
(202) 347-3668 (fax)
http://www.nrlc.org
David N. O'Steen, Executive Director
Formed in 1973 in reaction to the Supreme Court's *Roe v. Wade* abortion decision, this organization employs a wide variety of strategies, including testifying at congressional hearings, writing legislation, and litigating to protect "all innocent human life" threatened by abortion, euthanasia, and infanticide. The organization supports an amendment to the Constitution that would prohibit abortions. Due to the NRLC's willingness to consider compromise and its opposition to civil disobedience, this antiabortion organization is considered more moderate than other groups. The NRLC responds in the mass media to political and medical events and lobbies Congress in support of further limitations on abortion.

PUBLICATIONS: *National Right to Life News*, eighteen issues per year; books and pamphlets.

Operation Save America (OSA)
P.O. Box 740066
Dallas, TX 75374
(972) 494-5316
(972) 240-9789 (fax)
http://www.operationsaveamerica.org
Philip L. ("Flip") Benham, National Director

Operation Save America, which calls Americans to "repentance" for more than 30 million abortions since 1973, was originally founded as Operation Rescue in 1987 by Randall Terry and his wife, who attempted to dissuade women from entering abortion clinics. The organization began the more confrontational tactic of blocking entrances to abortion clinics and conducting large demonstrations and sit-ins in order to "rescue" innocent children. Demonstrators often refused to leave, thus forcing police to arrest and carry them away. OSA claims that over 50,000 arrests have resulted from such demonstrations and that more than 900 abortions have been prevented. The organization has attempted to discourage doctors who perform abortions by publicizing their names and confronting them in public places, and has threatened similar treatment for physicians prescribing the abortion pill RU-486.

PUBLICATIONS: A monthly newsletter.

Order of the Cross Society (OCS)
P.O. Box 7638
Fort Lauderdale, FL 33338-7638
(954) 564-5588
Reverend K. Chandler, Steward

Initiated in 1975, the OCS advocates the introduction of biblical principles into governmental organization and operation. Strong family ties and honest business practices are the organization's basic goals. The OCS encourages citizens not to accept government actions inconsistent with Christian principles. Unacceptable government policies include legalized abortion, government subsidies, and Social Security.

PUBLICATIONS: *Envoy*, an occasional publication. The group has been inactive since 2003.

Plymouth Rock Foundation (PRF)
1120 Long Pond Road
Plymouth, MA 02360-2626
(508) 833-1189
(508) 833-2481 (fax)
http://www.plymrock.org
Charles Wolfe, Executive Director

This organization, founded in 1970 and claiming a membership of 20,000, wants to base American society and government on biblical principles. The foundation wishes to "restore" America as a Christian republic through the activities of Christians on an individual basis. Christian committees of correspondence have been established to promote action at the local level. The organization holds workshops and seminars for Christian leaders and educators focusing on biblical understandings of government and education and the nation's Christian history.

PUBLICATIONS: *American Christian Heritage Series and the American Christian Statesmen Series,* books; *The Correspondent,* a monthly newsletter that provides information about local committee activities.

Pro-American Books
See Christian Research

Reasons To Believe (RTB)
P.O. Box 5978
Pasadena, CA 91117
(626) 335-1480
(626) 852-0178 (fax)
http://www.reasons.org
Hugh Ross, President

This organization, founded in 1986, strives for an explanation of creation that is compatible with the Bible and at the same time scientifically sound. President Hugh Ross adheres to an "old Earth" version of creationism. Reasons To Believe is affiliated with Campus Crusade for Christ International, Inter-Varsity Christian Fellowship, and the National Association of Evangelicals. RTB seeks to answer skeptics and to offer Christians a stronger foundation for their faith. The organization conducts an annual conference titled Who Is the Designer?

PUBLICATIONS: *Connections,* a quarterly newsletter, deals with scientific issues relevant to the Bible; various books and audio- and videotapes.

Religious Freedom Coalition (RFC)
P.O. Box 77511
Washington, DC 20013
(540) 370-4200
(202) 543-8447 (fax)
http://www.rfcnet.org
William J. Murray, Chairman

William Murray, the son of renowned atheist Madalyn Murray O'Hair who converted to Christianity in 1980, serves as the leader of this organization. The RFC was established in Fredericksburg, Virginia, in 1982. In 1998 the RFC organized religious leaders and conservative voters to support congressional passage of the Religious Freedom Amendment. Although the proposed amendment failed, the organization continues to lobby Congress to pass legislation supporting traditional family values and affirming religious freedom. The RFC has supported a bill to allow the posting of the Ten Commandments in public places. The organization has supported various measures to place limitations on the right to an abortion and fetal tissue research. Murray and other members of the RFC go to atheist conventions, attempting to convert members to Christianity, and run advertisements in local newspapers.

PUBLICATIONS: *William J. Murray Report,* a monthly newsletter.

Religious Heritage of America (RHA)

1750 South Brentwood Boulevard, Suite 502
St. Louis, MO 63144
(314) 962-0001
Barbara J. Eichhorst, Executive Director

Religious Heritage of America, founded in 1951 as Washington Pilgrimage, seeks to preserve traditional American values and attempts to provide individuals with a clearer definition of those values. In 1954 the organization lobbied successfully for the inclusion of "under God" in the Pledge of Allegiance. Each year the RHA sponsors trips to religious, cultural, and historical sites. The organization has been inactive since 2001.

PUBLICATIONS: *Religious Heritage of America,* a quarterly newsletter.

Religious Roundtable (RR)

P.O. Box 11467
Memphis, TN 38111
(901) 458-3795
Edward E. McAteer, President

Founded in 1979 by Ed McAteer to involve fundamentalist ministers and their congregations in politics, Religious Roundtable is concerned with the moral conditions of America, which the organization associates with the very survival of the Judeo-Christian tradition and Western civilization. James Robison was initially the organization's vice president. The Roundtable became active in the 1980 presidential campaign, organizing ministers in support of Ronald Reagan. After McAteer failed to win a U.S. Senate seat in 1984, the Roundtable became less prominent. The Religious Roundtable has emphasized such issues as child abuse, homosexuality, and pornography, and has lobbied to preserve a strong national defense through its affiliate, Roundtable Issues and Answers. In recent years the organization has not been active.

PUBLICATIONS: None.

Rutherford Institute (RI)

P.O. Box 7482
1445 East Rio Road
Charlottesville, VA 22906-7482
(434) 978-3888
(434) 978-1789 (fax)
http://www.rutherford.org
John W. Whitehead, President

John Whitehead began the Institute in 1982, naming it after Samuel Rutherford, a seventeenth-century Scottish minister who argued that all persons, including royalty, must abide by the civil law. The Institute has experienced success using litigation and the threat of litigation to support individuals believed to have been denied their right to religious liberty. The Institute concentrates its efforts on such issues as freedom of speech, parental rights, family values, school prayer, home schooling, abortion, and religious persecution in other countries.

PUBLICATIONS: *Rutherford Newsletter*, quarterly; *oldSpeak Magazine*, an online publication.

Traditional Values Coalition (TVC)

100 South Anaheim Boulevard
Anaheim, CA 92805
(714) 520-0300
(714) 520-9602 (fax)
http://www.traditionalvalues.org
Reverend Louis P. Sheldon, Chairman

Formed in 1982 as the California chapter of Tim LaHaye's American Coalition for Traditional Values, the TVC is concerned with educating Christians about contemporary issues, with the intention that they will become politically active in support of traditional Christian and pro-family values. The coalition focuses on such issues as public school prayer, abortion, sex education in the public schools, and gay rights legislation. It opposes any proposal to allow professed homosexuals in the military and has supported prohibiting them from taking part in the Boy Scouts. The TVC has reportedly succeeded in soliciting the support of African-American conservative Christians, especially in California, on issues such as gay rights and condom distribution in public schools. Louis Sheldon's daughter, Andrea Sheldon Lafferty, serves as the TVC's executive director of lobbying activities in Washington, DC.

PUBLICATIONS: *Traditional Values Report*, an occasional newsletter.

Trinity Broadcasting Network (TBN)

P.O. Box A
Santa Ana, CA 92711
(714) 832-2950
http://www.tbn.org
Paul Crouch, President
Since Paul Crouch established the Trinity Broadcasting Network in 1973, it has become the largest Christian television network, broadcasting on more than 530 stations worldwide. The network has been successful at providing a wide range of programming as an alternative to the secular media, emphasizing "faith in God, love of family, and patriotic pride." Among the televangelists whose programs appear on TBN are Kenneth Copeland, Creflo Dollar, John Hagee, Marilyn Hickey, Benny Hinn, T. D. Jakes, Rod Parsley, Fred Price, James Robison, and Jack Van Impe. On TBN's "flagship production," *Praise the Lord,* Crouch, his wife Jan, and others interview guests on a lavishly furnished set. Striving to provide entertainment for Christians, TBN has opened Trinity Music City in Nashville, Tennessee, offering concerts, dramas, seminars, and other special events. Various movies intended for theater release have been

produced, including *The Omega Code* (1999), a fictional treatment of the end-time events prophesied in Revelation.

PUBLICATIONS: None.

Wake Up America, Inc. (WUA)
P.O. Box 1187
Fuquay-Varnia, NC 27526
(877) 733-5446
(919) 552-1611 (fax)
http://www.wakeupamerica.org
Mike Macon, Acting Executive Director

Concerned about what it calls the nation's steady abandonment of what he considered the American Christian heritage, North Carolina developer Horace Tart formed Wake Up America, Inc. Quoting Matthew 5:16 ("Let your light shine before men that they may see your good works, and glorify your Father which is in heaven"), the organization encourages conservative Christians to become politically active by remaining informed on the issues, supporting appropriate political candidates, contacting public officials, and becoming involved in civic organizations. WUA hopes to "reclaim America" by disseminating biblical principles in order to reestablish moral character and behavior.

PUBLICATIONS: *Nineveh News*, a bimonthly newsletter.

Woman's Christian Temperance Union (WCTU)
1730 Chicago Avenue
Evanston, IL 60201-4584
(847) 864-1397
(847) 864-9497 (fax)
http://www.wctu.org
Sarah Frances Ward, President

The oldest continuing women's organization in the United States, the WCTU was established in 1874 by a group of women who expressed concern about the dangers that alcohol posed for families and society. The WCTU claims a membership of 5,000 in 500 local groups. The organization advocates temperance, which it defines as "moderation in all things healthful" and "total abstinence from all things harmful." Membership involves signing a pledge of total abstinence. The WCTU achieved its greatest success in 1919 with ratification of the Eighteenth Amendment prohibiting the manufacture, sale, or transportation of alcoholic beverages in the United States. However, the obvious failure of this policy to control the use of alcohol resulted in ratification in 1933 of the Twenty-first Amendment repealing Prohibition. Nonetheless, the WCTU continued the campaign against the use of alcoholic beverages as well as drugs and tobacco. At times it issues statements on other issues. For instance, in 2000 the organization distributed a pamphlet disapproving of homosexuality. The WCTU distributes literature on temperance to schools and churches.

PUBLICATIONS: *The Union Signal*, a quarterly journal; *Promoter*, a quarterly newsletter.

World's Christian Fundamentals Association (WCFA)

The WCFA, founded in 1919 under the leadership of William Bell Riley and other noted conservative leaders such as J. Frank Norris and John Roach Straton, played a major role in forming the tenets of fundamentalist Christian belief. At its inaugural meeting in Philadelphia, the association adopted a nine-point Confession of Faith that included belief in the verbal inerrancy of the Bible, the premillennial return of Christ, the trinity, the deity of Jesus, the sinfulness of humanity, "substitutionary atonement," the bodily resurrection of Jesus, justification by faith, and bodily resurrection of the just and the unjust. During the 1920s the association became embroiled in the question of evolution, supporting anti-evolution legislation in twenty states. The WCFA selected William Jennings Bryan to serve as its attorney at the famous Scopes trial in 1925. Riley resigned the presidency in 1929 and the organizational effectiveness of the association declined thereafter. A number of factors led to the WCFA's decline, including the extreme individualism of its leaders, the coming of the Depression that diverted attention away from the concerns of the organization, and the ill-fated struggle over evolution. The association lingered on into the early 1950s.

Organizations Critical of the Religious Right

Atheist Alliance International (AAI)

4773 Hollywood Boulevard
Los Angeles, CA 90026
(800) 437-3842
http://www.atheistalliance.org
Marie Castle, President

This organization, established in 1992, advocates government neutrality toward religion and opposes any legal requirement either mandating or prohibiting personal religious observance. The AAI supports government protection of human rights. Members deny any belief in God, reject any claims of miracles, and criticize supernatural explanations for natural phenomena, such as intelligent design and scientific creationism. According to AAI, the atheist perspective should receive greater recognition in public policy discussions. The organization expresses concern that religious enthusiasm represents a threat to society. The group opposes what it considers the religious bigotry of such organizations as the Boy Scouts of America for requiring its members to believe in God.

PUBLICATIONS: *Secular Nation,* a quarterly magazine.

American Atheists (AA)

P.O. Box 5733

Parsippany, NJ 07053-6733
(908) 276-7300
(908) 276-7402 (fax)
http://www.atheists.org
Ellen Johnson, President

Established by Madalyn Murray O'Hair in 1963, the AA works to achieve the civil liberties of atheists and a strict separation of government and religion. Formation of the organization resulted from the legal efforts of O'Hair to challenge instances of government support of organized religion. In 1995 she disappeared, and subsequently an associate was charged with her murder. When O'Hair disappeared, Ellen Johnson became head of the AA. The AA opposes religious right groups on several issues, including prayer in the public schools, religious accounts of creation, religious ceremony in government, and the claimed status of the Bible as the revealed word of God. In addition to regarding prayer in public institutions as unconstitutional, the AA insists that people cannot receive help through prayer but must rely instead on their own self-understanding and abilities.

PUBLICATIONS: *American Atheist*, a quarterly magazine; *American Atheist Newsletter*, ten times per year.

American Humanist Association (AHA)

1777 T Street, NW
Washington, DC 20009
(202) 238-9088
(202) 238-9003 (fax)
http://www.americanhumanist.org
Tony Hileman, Executive Director

The religious right finds many of the principles of this organization to be antithetical to its beliefs. The AHA holds that human beings are dependent on natural and social foundations alone and denies the relevance of any supernatural being. The organization encourages education in ethics as a substitute for religious training. Humanist counselors are certified with the same legal status as pastors or priests. Among the awards the AHA makes is the annual John Dewey Humanist Award.

PUBLICATIONS: *The Humanist*, a bimonthly magazine; *Free Mind*, a quarterly newsletter. The organization also has a list of publications and audio- and videotapes critical of the religious right.

Americans United for Separation of Church and State (AUSCS)

518 C Street, NE
Washington, DC 20002
(202) 466-3234
(202) 466-2587 (fax)
http://www.au.org
Barry W. Lynn, Executive Director

Founded in 1947, Americans United for Separation of Church and State monitors religious involvement in the public realm, takes part in lawsuits challenging such involvement, and investigates proposed legislation for possible violations of the principle of separation of church and state. The organization has opposed efforts to introduce voluntary prayer in the public schools, establish school voucher programs, and post the Ten Commandments in public places. In election years the organization is especially concerned about religious groups intervening in partisan politics. For instance, in 2000 the organization mailed over 280,000 letters to churches across the nation, warning church leaders about the legal pitfalls of distributing Christian Coalition voter guides to their congregations. Americans United has asked the Internal Revenue Service to investigate the partisan political activities of churches.

PUBLICATIONS: *Church and State*, a magazine published eleven times each year.

Anti-Defamation League (ADL)
823 United Nations Plaza
New York, NY 10017
(212) 490-2525
(212) 867-0779 (fax)
http://www.adl.org
Abraham H. Foxman, Director

Founded in 1913, the ADL, also known as the Anti-Defamation League of B'nai B'rith, states as its goals the elimination of antisemitism and the achievement of justice for all individuals. The organization encourages better relations among differing religious faiths. The ADL supports democratic values and opposes extremist groups it considers threats to democracy. In recent years the organization has published materials, such as its 1994 report, *The Religious Right: The Assault on Tolerance and Pluralism in America*, that are critical of religious right groups and leaders.

PUBLICATIONS: *ADL on the Frontline*, a bimonthly newsletter; *Dimensions*, a semiannual journal; various monographs and teaching materials.

Council for Secular Humanism (CSH)
P.O. Box 664
Amherst, NY 14226-0664
(716) 636-7571
(716) 636-1733 (fax)
http://www.secularhumanism.org
David R. Koepsell, Executive Director

The Council for Secular Humanism rejects any dependence on a transcendent being, emphasizing instead the force of reason and scientific inquiry, individual responsibility, human values and compassion, and the need for cooperation and tolerance. The organization accepts naturalism, the view that physical laws are not superseded by nonmaterial or supernatural entities. Claims about the occurrence of miracles are viewed with great skepticism. The Council conducts campaigns on ethical issues, holds conferences, offers educational courses, and distributes literature on secular humanism. The organization is often critical of the activities of religious right organizations, including their pro-family stance, position on homosexuality, and attempts to proselytize.

PUBLICATIONS: *Free Inquiry*, a quarterly journal; *Secular Humanist Bulletin*, a quarterly newsletter; *Philo*, a semiannual journal.

Feminist Majority Foundation (FMF)

1600 Wilson Boulevard, Suite 801
Arlington, VA 22209
(703) 522-2214
(703) 522-2219 (fax)
http://www.feminist.org
Eleanor Smeal, President

Established in 1987 by five women, the Feminist Majority Foundation strives to improve the status of women and their role in making public policy by supporting research, education, and political action. It defines feminism as "the policy, practice, or advocacy of political, economic, and social equality for women." The organization seeks to eliminate illegitimate forms of discrimination associated with sex, race, sexual orientation, age, religion, national origin, disability, and marital status. The FMF has come into conflict with the religious right particularly over issues relating to the role and status of women in society. The group supported the introduction of the abortion pill RU-486 and backs the right of abortion clinics to operate unhindered by pro-life groups. It criticized the Southern Baptist Convention's boycott of the Walt Disney Company for "gay-friendly" policies.

PUBLICATIONS: *Feminist Majority*, a quarterly newsletter.

Freedom From Religion Foundation (FFRF)

P.O. Box 750
Madison, WI 53701
(608) 256-8900
(608) 256-1116 (fax)
http://www.ffrf.org
Anne Nicol Gaylor, President

Founded in 1978, this organization of atheists, agnostics, secularists, and humanists campaigns against fundamentalist religious beliefs, supports the separation of church and state, and opposes fundamentalist religious attacks on the rights of women and homosexuals. The organization has worked to end prayer in the public schools and at public events and investigates charges of sexual abuse made against the clergy. The organization successfully challenged a policy in Wisconsin that established Good Friday as a state holiday. The FFRF has produced films and public service announcements for television.

PUBLICATIONS: *Freethought Today*, a newspaper published ten times per year.

Institute for First Amendment Studies (IFAS)

P.O. Box 589
Great Barrington, MA 01230
(413) 528-3800
http://naawpflch.org/index/studies.html
Skipp Porteous, National Director

Established in 1984 by former fundamentalist minister Skipp Porteous and attorney Barbara Simon, the IFAS attempts to counter the political activities of religious right groups largely through the dissemination of information. The organization gathers data and prepares reports about individuals and groups it considers a threat to First Amendment freedoms. The institute has a collection of hundreds of religious right publications. IFAS activities have included attending religious right conferences and interviewing leaders. The organization has been inactive since 2001.

PUBLICATIONS: *The Freedom Writer*, a bimonthly newsletter.

National Coalition Against Censorship (NCAC)

275 Seventh Avenue
New York, NY 10001
(212) 807-6222
(212) 807-6245
http://www.ncac.org
Joan E. Bertin, Executive Director

Founded in 1974, the NCAC is an alliance of fifty literary, artistic, religious, educational, professional, labor, and civil liberties organizations striving to defend the First Amendment values of freedom of speech and the press by opposing censorship and restraints on open communication. The coalition attempts to counter the activities of religious right organizations that are considered a danger to free speech. For instance, the NCAC has come to the defense of the *Harry Potter* series of children's books and opposed any outside censorship of Hollywood films, although it has called for movie executives to provide high-quality entertainment.

PUBLICATIONS: *Censorship News*, a quarterly newsletter; various booklets, brochures, and videos.

People for the American Way (PFAW)

2000 M Street, NW, Suite 400
Washington, DC 20036
(202) 467-4999
(202) 293-2672 (fax)
http://www.pfaw.org
Ralph G. Neas, President

Television producer Norman Lear established the PFAW in 1980 to counter the alleged antidemocratic and discordant effects on the American political process of religious right leaders and organizations such as Jerry Falwell and the Moral Majority. The religious right is seen as using religion to further its own political ambitions. According to the PFAW, true traditional American values include cultural diversity, pluralism, the continuing importance of the individual, and freedom of expression. The organization works for tolerance and respect for diversity by monitoring religious right activities, opposing censorship, and supporting such rights as reproductive choice. The group conducts media campaigns to encourage tolerance of diversity in people, religion, and values.

7

Suggested Readings

This chapter is divided into three sections: **1: Works About the Religious Right; 2: Works from the Religious Right;** and **3: Periodicals from Religious Right Organizations**. Section 1 is further divided into three categories: *Biographies; Religious Studies;* and *The Religious Right and Politics.*

Biographies includes such noted conservative Christian figures as Jim Bakker, Jerry Falwell, Billy Graham, and Pat Robertson. Persons in the religious right often have colorful personalities and their lives can reveal much about the nature of the movement's religious beliefs and political strategies. Also included in the *Biographies* category are accounts of the religious beliefs of early Americans, differing interpretations of which have led to conflicting claims about the religious foundations of the nation.

Religious Studies includes works dealing with religious studies in general, focusing on such topics as the history of Christianity in the United States, the origins and nature of evangelicalism and fundamentalism, the influences of millennial thought on contemporary religious beliefs, the religious character of different regions of the nation, and polemical treatments of conservative Christianity.

The Religious Right and Politics includes analyses of the current political positions and activities of those in the religious right, including school prayer and education generally, abortion, separation of church and state, homosexuality, foreign policy, electoral politics, partisan loyalties, same-gender marriage, the use of the mass media, lobbying activity, faith based funding, and the development and use of political strategies. Several of the works involve polemical treatments of religious right positions and activities.

Section 1: Works About the Religious Right

The works listed in this section are divided into three categories. The biographical section presents a sampling of studies dealing with important figures in the development of the religious right. The section on general religious studies includes works that investigate more generally the relationship between religion and the social and political environment. The last section contains sources on the religious right and its activities in American society and politics.

Biographies

Albert, James A. *Jim Bakker: Miscarriage of Justice?* Chicago: Open Court, 1997.

The scandal that forced Jim Bakker's resignation as head of the PTL organization and conviction on fraud charges shook the public's confidence in televangelism. Albert details Bakker's rise and fall as a nationally known televangelist and reports on the trial that resulted in his imprisonment. The author concludes that although Bakker may have used PTL funds carelessly, he likely did not intentionally defraud contributors.

Boston, Robert. *The Most Dangerous Man in America?* Amherst, NY: Prometheus, 1996.

Robert Boston, assistant director of communication for Americans United for the Separation of Church and State, examines the objectives of Pat Robertson, the Christian Coalition, and the Coalition's American Center for Law and Justice. He criticizes Robertson's extremist politics, which, according to the author, involve an attempt to override the constitutional separation of church and state in order to establish a theocratic system. Boston accuses Robertson of attempting to manipulate the public through his media outlets, hypocritically changing political positions, and distorting the evidence on political issues.

Frady, Marshall. *Billy Graham: A Parable of American Righteousness*. Boston: Little, Brown, 1979.

Well-researched and based on extensive interviews, this biography provides a largely sympathetic portrait of the famous evangelist. The author emphasizes Graham's basic innocence, which led to his failure to deal adequately with political events, especially during the turbulent 1960s.

Harding, Susan Friend. *The Book of Jerry Falwell: Fundamentalist Language and Politics*. Princeton, NJ: Princeton University Press, 2000.

Harding, an anthropologist, investigates the rise of religious right leader Jerry Falwell during the 1980s and the ways in which he altered the nature of fundamentalism in the United States. The author focuses on fundamentalists' use of language, shedding light on the continued success of religious right leaders such as Falwell in such areas as fundraising.

Harrell, David Edwin, Jr. *Pat Robertson: A Personal, Religious, and Political Portrait*. San Francisco: Harper and Row, 1987.

A political biography written shortly before Robertson's 1988 presidential bid, this book is a balanced and useful study of the Virginia televangelist. Divided into three parts, the work presents a biographical overview, a survey of Robertson's religious views, and a brief review of his political thinking on a variety of issues. Harrell also discusses Robertson's success in establishing the Christian Broadcasting Network.

Ingersoll, Julie. *Evangelical Christian Women: War Stories in the Gender Battles*. New York: New York University Press, 2003.

Ingersoll investigates the gender difficulties that women face in the evangelical Christian community, particularly when they assume leadership positions contrary to traditional notions of the place women should assume in the community. The author focuses on women who have remained within the evangelical religious tradition while challenging traditional gender roles.

Lippy, Charles H., ed. *Twentieth-Century Shapers of Popular Religion*. Westport, CT: Greenwood Press, 1989.

This biographical volume includes entries on over sixty people who have played important roles in the development of popular religious movements in the United States. Many of the biographical sketches are of religious right leaders.

Martin, William. *A Prophet with Honor: The Billy Graham Story*. New York: William Morrow, 1991.

This biography of Billy Graham offers insights into the well-known and respected evangelist, describing his youth, early adult years, and preparation for the ministry. Martin presents interesting details about Graham's early years, including his job as a successful Fuller Brush salesman before he entered the Florida Bible Institute. Graham first gained national attention when the media widely reported a meeting with President Harry Truman. Graham's association with Presidents Dwight Eisenhower and Richard Nixon kept him in the national limelight during the 1950s and 1960s. Martin explains the successful marketing techniques used by the Billy Graham Evangelistic Association and recounts Graham's evangelistic activities in various parts of the world.

Russell, Charles Allyn. *Voices of American Fundamentalism: Seven Biographical Studies*. Philadelphia: Westminster Press, 1976.

This exceptionally good study illustrates the diversity and complexity of fundamentalism through the careers of seven prominent fundamentalists—J. Frank Norris, John Roach Straton, William Bell Riley, Jasper C. Massee, J. Gresham Machen, William J. Bryan, and Clarence E. Macartney. Although a varied and colorful group, they were unified in their opposition to "modernism."

Simon, Merill. *Jerry Falwell and the Jews*. Middle Village, NY: Jonathan David, 1999.

This reissue of Simon's book on Jerry Falwell and his public pronouncements regarding Judaism and Israel provide insights into the religious right leader's political stances, which mirror those of many conservative Christians. Simon, who died in 1997, was a political adviser in Israel and a research associate at the Tel Aviv University Center for Strategic Studies.

Straub, Gerard Thomas. *Salvation for Sale: An Insider's View of Pat Robertson's Ministry*. New York: Prometheus, 1986.

Straub, former producer for Pat Robertson's *The 700 Club* television program, writes of his increasing doubts about Robertson and television evangelism in general. Writing prior to Robertson's 1988 presidential bid, the author questions Robertson's media strategies.

Religious Studies

Ahlstrom, Sydney E. *A Religious History of the American People*. New Haven, CT: Yale University Press, 1972.

An extensive analysis of America's religious history, this book examines the moral development of Americans through the evaluation of varied religious movements, especially in the nineteenth and twentieth centuries. Ahlstrom examines such topics as regional beliefs, separation of church and state, and the relationship between religion and scientific progress. The book provides an excellent context for studying the Christian right.

Allen, Leslie H., ed. *Bryan and Darrow at Dayton*. New York: Russell and Russell, 1925.

Allen offers an account of the famous trial of John T. Scopes, who was prosecuted for violating a state law that forbade teaching evolution in the public schools of Tennessee. Published soon after the trial, the book provides portions of the official court record. In an attempt to be impartial, the editor includes an appendix in which appear excerpts from Genesis and a biology textbook of the times.

Ammerman, Nancy Tatom. *Bible Believers: Fundamentalists in the Modern World*. New Brunswick, NJ: Rutgers University Press, 1987.

A noted sociologist examines the conflict between "moderates" and "fundamentalists" within the Southern Baptist Convention, a conflict which by 1989 had been resolved in favor of the fundamentalists. According to Ammerman, a "gentlemanly consensus" among Southern Baptists of varying degrees of theological conservatism eroded as the South became more urban. Frightened by the changes inherent in urbanization, fundamentalists not only sought security in the "inerrant Word," but also outmaneuvered moderates for control of the convention.

Balch, David L. *Homosexuality, Science, and the "Plain Sense" of Scripture*. Grand Rapids, MI: Eerdmans, 2000.

These twelve essays written by biblical scholars, theologians, and psychologists present different interpretations of biblical statements (in Genesis, Leviticus, Romans, and I Corinthians) about the morality of homosexuality and evaluate scientific research on the subject. The book clarifies the viewpoints taken on the issue of homosexuality.

Balmer, Randall. *Mine Eyes Have Seen the Glory: A Journey into the Evangelical Subculture in America*. New York: Oxford University Press, 1993.

This highly readable religious travelogue through America's heartland focuses on fundamentalists, charismatics, and Pentecostals. Balmer illuminates the diversity of America's evangelical subculture. His journey took him from a holiness meeting in Florida to an Indian reservation in the Dakotas to a fundamentalist Bible camp in New York. This work is a must for anyone prone to easy generalization about evangelicalism.

————. *Grant Us Courage: Travels Along the Mainline of American Protestantism*. New York: Oxford University Press, 1996.

In this sequel to *Mine Eyes Have Seen the Glory*, Balmer portrays his visits to twelve mainline Protestant churches which were originally the subjects of a series of articles published in *Christian Century*. Although the highly individualized treatments are not conducive to drawing generalizations, they do suggest possible explanations for the losses that such churches have suffered at the hands of more fundamentalist and evangelical movements.

Balmer, Randall, and Mark Silk, eds. *Religion and Public Life in the Middle Atlantic Region: The Fount of Diversity*. Lanham, MD: AltaMira, 2006.

The editors note that from the seventeenth century, this region, composed of New York, Pennsylvania, New Jersey, Maryland, Delaware, and the District of Columbia, has experienced religious diversity. Rather than shifts from one denomination or religion to another, the diversity originates in many established religious groups. In the concluding chapter, Randall Balmer observes that the only U.S. senator from the region associated with the religious right is Rick Santorum of Pennsylvania, who is from the western section of the region, which is generally considered more conservative.

Barlow, Philip, and Mark Silk. *Religion and Public Life in the Midwest: America's Common Denominator?* Lanham, MD: AltaMira Press, 2004.

The editors observe that the Midwest closely reflects the nation in religious beliefs, with virtually every religious group and issue being represented, with Lutherans especially plentiful west of the Mississippi. In the concluding chapter, Peter W. Williams notes that the rise of the religious right in the 1970s has become a major challenge to mainline Protestantism in the region.

Barr, James. *Fundamentalism*. Philadelphia: Westminster Press, 1978.

A British scholar, Barr has spent considerable time in America. This insightful study calls attention to links between British and American fundamentalism. According to Barr, fundamentalism has been more denominational in America than in Britain, resulting in bitter intradenominational splits in the United States. By contrast, fundamentalism in Britain has been non-denominational.

Baumgartner, Frederic J. *Longing for the End: A History of Millennialism in Western Civilization*. New York: Palgrave, 2001.

Baumgartner explores the history of various cults and sects which were established on the belief that the end of the world was imminent. Many of the groups, including some of recent origin, such as the Branch Davidians and Heaven's Gate, have led to violence, either against themselves or others.

Bawer, Bruce. *Stealing Jesus: How Fundamentalism Betrays Christianity*. New York: Crown, 1997.

Bawer argues that fundamentalist Christian movements, far too legalistic and lacking in compassion and a mission of loving service, fail to meet the requirements of Christianity. He investigates the rise of fundamentalism from the nineteenth century, focusing on John Nelson Darby, C.I. Scofield, and the rise of dispensational premillennialism, the belief that Christ will return to reign for a thousand years. Bawer investigates the work of more contemporary religious right figures such as Pat Robertson, Ralph Reed, Hal Lindsey, and James Dobson.

Bloom, Harold. *The American Religion: The Emergence of the Post-Christian Nation*. Hyattsville, MD: Daedalus, 1992.

Although he claims that America is not a Christian nation but rather is dominated by a form of Gnosticism, Bloom nonetheless observes that the nation is "religion-soaked." Americans tend to believe in a personal and loving God. The author examines a number of Christian organizations, including Pentecostalism, Jehovah's Witnesses, Seventh-day Adventism, and the New Age movement, and gives special attention to Mormons and Southern Baptists.

Boone, Kathleen C. *The Bible Tells Them So: The Discourse of Protestant Fundamentalism*. Albany: State University of New York Press, 1989.

Boone focuses on biblical inerrancy, a principle of utmost importance to fundamentalism and the doctrine of dispensational premillennialism. The author argues against the plausibility of inerrancy, referring to the lack of original texts and to the fact that interpreters tend to disagree over the meaning of biblical texts. Even inerrantists, Boone argues, have difficulty with words like "day" and "hour," resulting in questionable interpretations.

Boyer, Paul. *When Time Shall Be No More: Prophecy Belief in Modern American Culture*. Cambridge, MA: Belknap Press, 1992.

This is the best available study about the influence on contemporary American society of apocalyptic literature, a genre that reached fruition among the ancient Hebrews between the eighth and sixth centuries B.C.E. The post-World War II threat of nuclear destruction bred an intense concern about the end of time. According to Boyer, American foreign policy since the 1940s cannot be fully understood without some understanding of dispensational premillennialism. Such religious thinking helps explain President Ronald Reagan's reference to the Soviet Union as an "evil empire."

Braden, Bruce, ed. *"Ye Will Say I Am No Christian": The Thomas Jefferson/John Adams Correspondence on Religion, Morals, and Values*. Amherst, NY: Prometheus, 2005.

Braden attempts to clarify much of the controversy over the religious beliefs of early Americans, especially arising from the writings of such religious right figures as Don Barton, by focusing on the correspondence between Thomas Jefferson and John Adams that they conducted from 1812 until 1826, when both died on July 4. Although Braden states that both men considered themselves Christians, he notes that each had his own definition of what that meant.

Bull, Malcolm, ed. *Apocalypse Theory and the Ends of the World*. Oxford: Blackwell, 1995.

The scholarly essays contained in this work provide a broad overview of apocalyptic thought, covering the history of millenarianism from the ancient Greeks to the present. The authors examine the idea, persistent throughout recorded history, that the world must have a definite end. The essays provide an excellent basis for evaluating the many popular publications on the millennium that appeared at the close of the twentieth century.

Burgess, Stanley, and Gary McGee, eds. *Dictionary of Pentecostal and Charismatic Movements*. Grand Rapids, MI: Zondervan, 1989.

This reference work includes more than 800 entries on Pentecostal and charismatic movements primarily in the United States, but also in Europe. Individual entries focus on denominations, specific individuals within the movements, and varied topics such as the Healing Movement and Christian Perfection. The book includes entries on Jim Bakker and Jimmy Swaggart, detailing their fall from grace.

Caplan, Lionel, ed. *Studies in Religious Fundamentalism*. Albany: State University of New York Press, 1987.

The contributors to this volume examine Islamic, Jewish, Sikh, Hindu, West African, and American Protestant fundamentalism in an effort to discover cross-cultural similarities. Although aware that fundamentalism in different parts of the world cannot be understood apart from its specific cultural context, the authors cautiously suggest several parallels. Interestingly, fundamentalists in many parts of the world tend to identify the erosion of male authority and the growing assertiveness of women with spiritual and national decline.

Carter, Stephen L. *The Culture of Disbelief: How American Law and Politics Trivialize Religious Devotion*. New York: Basic Books, 1993.

Carter deals with the dilemmas of religious involvement in the public arena that arise from an American society that is basically secular, despite the widespread expressions of religious belief. Though critical of the religious right, the author is concerned with establishing an appropriate balance in the principle of separation of church and state, recognizing that religion can strengthen those values Americans esteem.

Chaves, Mark. *Congregations in America*. Cambridge, MA: Harvard University Press, 2004.

Employing data from the 1998 National Congregations Study, Chaves observes that the media focus on the political and social activities of religious groups notwithstanding, local congregations tend to focus their attention on worship activities, religious education, and the arts. White conservative and Evangelical Protestant congregations, although less politically active than Catholic or black Protestant congregations, are more likely to engage in distributing voter guides. Seventy percent of voter guides distributed in conservative Protestant congregations originated with Christian right organizations.

Conkin, Paul K. *When All the Gods Trembled: Darwinism, Scopes, and American Intellectuals*. Lanham, MD: Rowman and Littlefield, 1998.

In a series of essays, Conkin discusses the controversy between fundamentalism and modernism over the status of religion and science in American society. The author focuses on the influence of modern scientific and philosophical naturalism, including Darwinist evolutionary theory, on American religious perspectives during the 1920s.

Cotton, Ian. *The Hallelujah Revolution: The Rise of the New Christians*. Amherst, NY: Prometheus, 1996.

Cotton, a British journalist, investigates the rise of evangelical and charismatic Christian movements during the twentieth century, predicting that such beliefs may become far more widespread in the twenty-first century. He associates such movements worldwide with a combination of irrationalist beliefs involving miracles, healings, and modern communications technology. He examines the political dimensions of the movement, which are not always conservative, and the possible psychological and neurological bases of religious experience.

Davis, Edward B., ed. *The Antievolution Pamphlets of Harry Rimmer*. Hamden, CT: Garland, 1995.

Volume six in the *Creationism in Twentieth-Century America* series (Ronald L. Numbers, general editor) contains sixteen of Harry Rimmer's works criticizing the theory of evolution. Rimmer, the most noted anti-evolutionist until his death in 1952, was a Presbyterian minister. Among the works included are "Modern Science, Noah's Ark, and the Deluge" (1925), "Modern Science and the First Fundamental" (1928), and "It's the Crisis Hour in Schools and Colleges" (no date).

Dayton, Donald. *Theological Roots of Pentecostalism*. Metuchen, NJ: Scarecrow, 1987.

This volume examines the history of Pentecostalism, tracing its Wesleyan roots to Great Britain. Dayton identifies four basic elements of this Christian belief:

Christ as savior, Christ as baptizer in the Holy Spirit, Christ as healer, and Christ as the future king.

Dunn, Charles W., ed. *Religion in American Politics*. Washington, DC: CQ Press, 1989.

The contributors to this volume examine the conflicts that have arisen in the relationship between religion and politics in America. Individual articles deal with such topics as the First Amendment, the role of religion in maintaining community, religious right involvement in party politics, and religious lobbying efforts.

———. *American Political Theology: Historical Perspective and Theoretical Analysis*. New York: Praeger, 1984.

This book provides an excellent selection of religious documents from the Mayflower Compact in 1620 to the Resolutions of the World Congress of Fundamentalists in 1980 and 1983. Dunn concludes with chapters on the theology of American presidents and theoretical propositions regarding American political theology.

Edel, Wilbur. *Defenders of the Faith: Religion and Politics from the Pilgrim Fathers to Ronald Reagan*. Westport, CT: Praeger, 1987.

Edel's purpose is to expose the myths and misunderstandings about America's religious heritage—myths some groups and individuals exploit in order to gain political office. He explores the role of religion in public life throughout American history and observes that religious organizations have recently become significantly more involved in varied public policy issues. Edel notes with concern the desire of some political leaders to return to a relationship between church and state that existed in colonial times.

Fuller, Robert C. *Naming the Antichrist: The History of an American Obsession*. New York: Oxford University Press, 1995.

Fuller provides a detailed history of the use of the Antichrist theme in American religion and culture from the colonial period to the contemporary writings of such religious figures as Pat Robertson and Hal Lindsey. Various people and institutions have been identified as the "Antichrist," a term that appears only four times in the Bible. Among those suggested for the label included Native Americans, French Catholics, and the British king. More recently, many individuals and innovations have been associated with the Antichrist, including Pope John Paul II, the European Economic Community, the National Council of Churches, supermarket barcodes, and fiber optics. Fuller claims that Americans' tendency to speak of conflicts in terms of the battle of absolute good versus absolute evil has led to the preoccupation with identifying the Antichrist.

Gamwell, Franklin I. *The Meaning of Religious Freedom: Modern Politics and the Democratic Revolution*. Albany: State University of New York Press, 1994.

This religious-philosophical-political work examines religious freedom in the context of First Amendment protections, over which there has been much disagreement. Gamwell argues that religious pluralism can lead to political agreement only through free discussion among the varying religious commitments.

Gasper, Louis. *The Fundamentalist Movement*. The Hague: Mouton, 1963.

This book is a historical treatment of fundamentalism, primarily from 1930 to the early 1960s. It contrasts two groups that developed during this time period: the militant American Council of Christian Churches and the more moderate National Association of Evangelicals. The author records the development of youth organizations and Bible institutes, the move toward nationalism, and the rise of evangelist Billy Graham.

Gatewood, Willard B., ed. *Controversy in the Twenties: Fundamentalism, Modernism, and Evolution*. Nashville, TN: Vanderbilt University Press, 1969.

Through this useful collection of documents, Gatewood shows that the modernist-fundamentalist conflict originated long before the 1920s and that its impact was more pervasive and enduring than other scholars suggest. The struggle within the churches was a reaction to processes, such as industrialization, urbanization, and scientific advancement, that had gradually undermined orthodox Protestantism and had raised moral issues for which orthodox Protestants had few relevant answers.

Hart, D. G. *That Old-time Religion in Modern America: Evangelical Protestantism in the Twentieth Century*. Ivan R. Dee, 2002.

Hart traces the development of evangelicalism in the United States during the twentieth century. The author chronicles the resurgence of the evangelical movement and its re-entrance into politics beginning in the 1960s after forty years on the margins following the fundamental controversies of the 1920s, including the trial of John T. Scopes for teaching evolution in the public schools.

Hatch, Nathan O. *The Democratization of American Christianity*. New Haven, CT: Yale University Press, 1989.

This book is a good background for the study of contemporary conservative Christianity. The author examines the development of eighteenth- and nineteenth-century Protestant denominations, focusing on the emergence of the Baptist and Methodist denominations, as well as the Mormon church.

Hunter, James Davison. *Evangelicalism: The Coming Generation*. Chicago: University of Chicago Press, 1987.

Hunter bases this study on a survey of faculty and students at sixteen evangelical colleges and seminaries. The major focus is the encounter between religious beliefs and the modern secular world. The book is a good presentation of contemporary evangelical thought and culture.

———. *American Evangelicalism: Conservative Religion and the Quandary of Modernity*. New Brunswick, NJ: Rutgers University Press, 1983.

Hunter investigates the tensions in the twentieth century between conservative American Protestantism and modern secularism. The book analyzes evangelicalism from a sociological and demographic perspective. Aspects of the evangelical view of the world, Hunter claims, have in fact been adjusted to modernity. Hunter employs survey data and the analysis of evangelical documents.

Hutchison, William R. *The Modernist Impulse in American Protestantism*. Oxford: Oxford University Press, 1976.

Hutchison provides one of the better accounts of the development of liberalism, the intellectual foundation of the modernist impulse, within American Protestantism from the early 1800s through the 1920s. Like fundamentalism, modernism can be defined in varying ways. But as used by Hutchison, the term involves three ideas: the conscious adaptation of religious ideas to modern culture, the immanence of God in human cultural development, and the movement of human society toward the Kingdom of God.

Katloff, Mark A., ed. *Creation and Evolution in the Early American Scientific Affiliation*. Hamden, CT: Garland, 1995.

The tenth volume in the *Creationism in Twentieth-Century America* series contains 46 articles written by various authors associated with the American Scientific Affiliation Society, a group founded in 1941 by evangelical scientists. Among the articles are "Biology and Christian Fundamentals" (R. L. Mixter, 1950), "Why God Called His Creation Good" (William J. Tinkle, 1950), and "The Origin of Man and the Bible" (J. Frank Cassel, 1960).

Killen, Patricia O'Connell, and Mark Silk, eds. *Religion and Public Life in the Pacific Northwest: The None Zone*. Lanham, MD: AltaMira Press, 2004.

The editors note that the Pacific Northwest, composed of the states of Oregon, Washington, and Alaska, is unique in that most of the population is considered "unchurched." James K. Wellman Jr., in "The Churching of the Pacific Northwest: The Rise of Sectarian Entrepreneurs," notes that in this region, the older forms of evangelicalism have experienced little growth, but evangelical groups having greater success are those willing to employ modern communication methods to convey the traditional message.

Krannawitter, Thomas L., and Daniel C. Palm. *A Nation Under God? The ACLU and Religion in American Politics*. Lanham, MD: Rowman and Little-field, 2005.

Krannawitter and Palm question the claim of the American Civil Liberties Union and other organizations that the U.S. Constitution's First Amendment requires a total separation of religious expression from the public realm. Examining the principles that informed the American founding, the authors conclude that these principles allow for at least limited public religious expression without violating the First Amendment protection of religious liberty.

Kurtz, Paul. *In Defense of Secular Humanism*. Buffalo, NY: Prometheus, 1983.

In this collection of papers written over a thirty-year period, Kurtz attempts to defend secular humanism, while acknowledging that most attention given to the idea today originates with the religious right. Kurtz argues that much improvement can occur in morals and politics without religion.

Larson, Edward, and Jesse Fox Mayshark. *The Scopes Trial: A Photographic History*. Knoxville: University of Tennessee Press, 2000.

This fascinating book includes many photographs of the key figures taken during the twelve-day trial of John T. Scopes, who was indicted for teaching Darwin's theory of evolution in the public schools of Dayton, Tennessee, in violation of state law. Mayshark provides a perspective on the trial in the Afterword.

Lawrence, Bruce B. *Defenders of God: The Fundamentalist Revolt Against the Modern Age*. New York: Harper & Row, 1989.

This is an effort to place Islamic, Judaic, and Christian fundamentalism within a global context. Lawrence portrays fundamentalists as "moderns" who use science, technology, and the mass media to challenge the "heresies" of the modern age—rationalism, relativism, pluralism, and secularism. These "defenders of God" use modern means to uphold age-old transcendent values.

Lindsey, William, and Mark Silk. *Religion and Public Life in the Southern Crossroads: Showdown States*. Lanham, MD: AltaMira Press, 2005.

This entry in the *Religion by Region* series focuses on the states of Texas, Oklahoma, Louisiana, Arkansas, and Missouri. In his contribution to the volume, Andrew Manis ("Protestants: From Denominational Controversialists to Culture Warriors") argues that these Southern Crossroads states have traditionally been an area of religious controversy and presently are the central focus of the country's "culture wars."

Marsden, George M. *Fundamentalism and American Culture: The Shaping of Twentieth-Century Evangelicalism, 1870–1925*. Second edition. New York: Oxford University Press, 2006.

Marsden offers insights into the fundamentalist Christian movement as it altered its relationship to changing American culture and responded to scientific developments from the late nineteenth century through the 1920s. This revised edition of a work originally published in 1980 includes a new chapter comparing fundamentalism since the 1970s with the fundamentalist movement of the 1920s.

————. *Reforming Fundamentalism: Fuller Seminary and the New Evangelicalism*. Grand Rapids, MI: Eerdmans, 1987.

This is an account of Fuller Theological Seminary in Pasadena, California. Founded in 1947, this seminary soon became a focal point of sorts for an intellectual tug-of-war within fundamentalism itself. The Fuller fundamentalists, such as Charles Fuller, Harold Ockenga, Wilbur Smith, and Carl F. H. Henry, were determined to defend the supernatural aspects of Christianity, but they could not fully embrace the rigid separatism and dispensational premillennialism of the more intractable voices of the religious right, such as Carl McIntire. By the early 1950s the Fuller fundamentalists had begun to call themselves "evangelicals."

————, ed. *Evangelicalism and Modern America*. Grand Rapids, MI: William B. Eerdmans Publishing Company, 1984.

Containing essays by thirteen scholars, this collection probes the diversity and unity of fundamentalism. Arranged in two parts, the essays first treat the rise of fundamentalism since World War II more or less chronologically, then move on to topics such as women, science, the arts, modernity, and biblical authority. The book is an excellent guide for anyone interested in the emergence and recent prominence of fundamentalism.

————. *Understanding Fundamentalism and Evangelicalism*. Grand Rapids, MI: Eerdmans, 1991.

Marsden examines the historical roots of fundamentalism and evangelicalism in the United States. Although diverse groups, such as holiness churches, Pentecostals, traditional Methodists, Baptists, Presbyterians, and Churches of Christ, compose the fundamentalist movement, the author identifies similarities. They have to some extent separated themselves from modern culture, but in recent years have experienced revitalization. Marsden focuses on fundamentalist views of science and politics. A final chapter examines the fundamentalist legacy of J. Gresham Machen.

Martin, William. *With God on Our Side: The Rise of the Religious Right in America*. New York: Broadway Books, 1996.

Martin describes the development of the religious right in seventeenth-century Massachusetts, and against that background presents a detailed account of the present positions of conservative Christians. The author believes conservative fundamentalists wish to impose their religious beliefs, including an insistence on biblical inerrancy, on all Americans, and therefore pose a threat to the constitutional doctrine of separation of church and state. However, religious right leaders are weakened by their unwillingness to compromise with those with whom they disagree.

Marty, Martin. *Religion and Republic: The American Circumstance*. Boston: Beacon, 1987.

This series of articles by Marty looks to the achievement of consensus in a pluralistic society by discovering a common framework for diverse religious communities. The author examines what he considers the major characteristics of religion in America, such as the notion of civil religion and the perceived status of the Bible in Christian belief.

————. *Modern American Religion, Volume I, 1893–1919: The Irony of It All*. Chicago: University of Chicago Press, 1986.

This broad examination of American religion, including treatment of mainline churches as well as evangelical and fundamentalist movements, emphasizes the difficulties Christians face when attempting to respond to change and modernization. Marty identifies the theological and political consequences of the resulting tension.

————. *Righteous Empire: The Protestant Experience in America*. New York: Dial, 1970.

This treatment of Protestantism in America can be contrasted with the later narratives that religious right authors have developed. Marty emphasizes the unfortunate results, including racism and slavery, of the assumption of early settlers that they were superior, God-chosen people with a special destiny. The author analyzes more recent changes in religious movements.

Marty, Martin E., and R. Scott Appleby. *Fundamentalisms Observed*. Chicago: University of Chicago Press, 1991.

This book is an excellent study of international movements of religious reaction in the twentieth century. Following a thematic approach, it examines the political, social, cultural, and religious context within which each movement emerges; its distinguishing beliefs; and the way in which each has responded to the modern world. This work demonstrates that American fundamentalism was part of a global phenomenon.

———. *The Glory and the Power: The Fundamentalist Challenge to the Modern World*. Boston, MA: Beacon, 1992.

Co-directors of the Fundamentalism Project at the University of Chicago, Marty and Appleby focus on three religious movements in different countries. They examine Protestant fundamentalism in the United States; Israel's Gush Emunim, a small right-wing Jewish activist group, and Islamic fundamentalism especially as it exists in Egypt. According to the authors, fundamentalist groups see history as a confrontation between good and evil, reject rationalism, and seek to maintain tradition.

Mead, Frank S., Samuel S. Hill, and Craig D. Atwood. *Handbook of Denominations in the United States*. Twelfth edition. Nashville, TN: Abington, 2005.

The authors have provided a wealth of information—including historical development, organizational and governing structure, and membership trends—on most denominations in the United States, including mainline, evangelical, and fundamentalist churches.

Moen, Matthew C., and Lowell S. Gustafson, eds. *The Religious Challenge to the State*. Philadelphia: Temple University Press, 1992.

These essays provide a comparative view of the relationships between religion and politics. Individual essays treat topics such as religion in revolutionary Cuba, religion and politics in Israel, Islamic fundamentalism in Africa, and church-state relations in Mexico and Argentina.

Moore, R. Laurence. *Selling God: American Religion in the Marketplace of Culture*. New York: Oxford University Press, 1994.

This social history of religion in America investigates the use of commercial methods by religious leaders to advance religious causes. Moore also looks at business leaders who have employed religion to promote commercial interests. This book provides insightful background information for the study of the religious right and contemporary religion generally.

Nash, Robert J. *Faith, Hype, and Clarity: Teaching About Religion in American Schools and Colleges*. New York: Teachers College Press of Columbia University, 1998.

Nash presents four basic approaches (fundamentalist, prophetic, alternative spiritualities, and post-theist) to teaching religion. He defines and presents a brief history of fundamentalism (within Christianity as well as other religious traditions) and examines the fundamentalist worldview and the challenge of modernism. Referring to "the failure of the fundamentalist narrative," Nash describes the tendency of fundamentalists to claim their beliefs and employ unimpeachable sacred texts to explain every aspect of life.

Neuhaus, Richard John. *The Naked Public Square: Religion and Democracy in America*. Grand Rapids, MI: Eerdmans, 1984.

This is a general treatment of the role of religion in American government and politics. The author's major theme is that politics and the Judeo-Christian faith are compatible. There, religion can play an important role in the American political process by helping to keep the public sphere viable.

Nelson, Paul, ed. *The Creationist Writings of Byron C. Nelson*. Hamden, CT: Garland, 1995.

The fifth volume in the *Creationism in Twentieth-Century America* series (Ronald L. Numbers, general editor) includes four works by Byron C. Nelson, a Lutheran supporter of creationism and a founder of the Religion and Science Association in 1935. Among the works are "Before Abraham: Prehistoric Man in Biblical Light" (1948) and "A Catechism on Evolution" (1937).

Neuhaus, Richard John, ed. *Unsecular America*. Grand Rapids, MI: Eerdmans, 1986.

This group of essays is drawn from a 1985 conference on the relationship between religion and society conducted by the Rockford Institute Center on Religion and Society. Among the topics discussed are the interdependence of capitalism, democracy, and religion; the ability of religion and modernization to coexist; secular humanism as a religion; and the American commitment to evangelicalism. Results of surveys of religious opinion are also included.

Noll, Mark A. *A History of Christianity in the United States and Canada*. Grand Rapids, MI: Eerdmans, 1992.

This book focuses on the rise and more recent decline of Protestantism in the United States. The author traces the development of a uniquely American brand of Christianity through the "great awakening" and the American Revolution. He associates the decline of evangelicalism with the emergence of modernism and the social gospel. Noll suggests that pluralism represents the future for religion in America.

Noll, Mark A., Nathan O. Hatch, and George M. Marsden. *The Search for Christian America*. Westchester, IL: Crossway, 1983.

This book contributes to the debate over the religious status of the Founding Fathers, which is an important issue for the religious right. Unlike many on the religious right who claim that the Founding Fathers based the nation on Christian principles, the authors, who are evangelical historians, argue that the notion of a Christian America is complex and difficult to demonstrate.

Numbers, Ronald L., ed. *Antievolution Before World War I*. Hamden, CT: Garland, 1995.

This first volume in the *Creationism in Twentieth-Century America* series (Ronald L. Numbers, general editor) includes four important critiques of evolution that were written prior to the anti-evolution movement of the 1920s. Authors are Alexander Patterson, Eberhard Denhert, Luther Tracy Townsend, and G. Frederick Wright.

———. *Creation-Evolution Debates*. Hamden, CT: Garland, 1995.

The second volume in the *Creationism in Twentieth-Century America* series (Ronald L. Numbers, general editor) contains seven debates between creationists and evolutionists during the 1920s and 1930s. One such debate between William Jennings Bryan and Henry Fairchild Osborn appeared in *The New York Times* in 1922.

———. *The Antievolution Works of Arthur I. Brown*. Hamden, CT: Garland, 1995.

This third volume in the *Creationism in Twentieth-Century America* series (Ronald L. Numbers, general editor) is composed of seven anti-evolution pamphlets by Arthur I. Brown, a surgeon whom fundamentalists in the 1920s regarded as a great scientist. Among the pamphlets are "Evolution and the Bible" (1920s) and "Men, Monkeys and the Missing Link" (1923).

———. *Selected Works of George McCready Price*. Hamden, CT: Garland, 1995.

Volume seven in the *Creationism in Twentieth-Century America* series (Ronald L. Numbers, general editor) includes four of George Price's works on creationism. Price is given credit for establishing a geology of the flood, which ultimately came to be known as scientific creationism. Among the works are "Q.E.D. or New Light on the Doctrine of Creation" (1917) and "Theories of Satanic Origin" (no date).

———. *The Early Writings of Harold W. Clark and Frank Lewis Marsh*. Hamden, CT: Garland, 1995.

This eighth volume in the *Creationism in Twentieth-Century America* series (Ronald L. Numbers, general editor) includes two works by Clark ("Back to Creation" [1929] and "The New Diluvialism" [1946]) and one by Marsh ("Fundamental Biology" [1941]). The authors, all students of creationist George McCready Price, were educated as biologists.

———. *Early Creationist Journals*. Hamden, CT: Garland, 1995.

The ninth volume in the *Creationism in Twentieth-Century America* series (Ronald L. Numbers, general editor) presents issues from three early creationist journals: *Creationist* (1937–38), *Bulletin of Deluge Geology* (1941–45), and its continuation, *Forum for the Correlation of Science and the Bible* (1946–48).

Packer, J. I. *"Fundamentalism" and the Word of God*. Grand Rapids, MI: Eerdmans, 1958.

Written from a sympathetic viewpoint, this work is a good introduction to fundamentalism. With wit and humor, the author covers the usual territory of biblical authority and inerrancy and takes exception to the view of fundamentalists as obscurantists and unthinking biblical literalists. The tendency to use fundamentalism and evangelicalism synonymously is a major flaw in Packer's treatment.

Perry, Michael J. *Love and Power: The Role of Religion and Morality in American Politics*. New York: Oxford University Press, 1991.

This excellent, scholarly work examines the appropriate relationship between religious morality and politics in a morally pluralistic society. The author suggests that more "ecumenical politics" might allow moral positions, especially about what is good for human beings, to contribute to political arguments.

Reichley, A. James. *Religion in American Public Life*. Washington, DC: Brookings, 1985.

This general treatment of religion and politics deals with historical interpretations of the First Amendment protection of religion and religious influence on policy making. Reichley examines topics such as the intentions of the constitutional framers and the positions denominations took on public issues during the Vietnam War era.

Robbins, Thomas, and Susan J. Palmer, eds. *Millennium, Messiahs, and Mayhem: Contemporary Apocalyptic Movements*. New York: Routledge, 1997.

Published as the interest in the "millennial myth" rose prior to the year 2000, this group of sixteen essays deals with variations on millennial movements, including economic, racist, environmental, and feminist groups, as well as organizations in more traditional churches. The authors investigate the tendency toward violence and confrontation with the established order. Individual essays deal with such topics as the more secular millennial movements of the survivalists and militias, technologically oriented groups, American Catholic apocalypticism, Mormon millenarianism, and Christian reconstructionism.

Roof, Wade Clark, and Mark Silk. *Religion and Public Life in the Pacific Region: Fluid Identities*. Lanham, MD: AltaMira Press, 2005.

The editors of this volume categorize the states of California, Nevada, and Hawaii as the Pacific Region, an area where no religious tradition dominates and a secular perspective tends to hold sway. However, as Douglas Firth Anderson notes in "Toward an Established Mysticism: Judeo-Christian Traditions in Post-World War II California and Nevada," evangelical entrepreneurs have experienced success. For instance, Tim LaHaye, author along with Jerry Jenkins of the popular *Left Behind* series, worked primarily in California from the 1960s to the mid-1980s.

Sandeen, Ernest Robert. *The Roots of Fundamentalism: British and American Millenarianism, 1800–1930*. Chicago: University of Chicago Press, 1970.

The author contends that fundamentalism may best be understood in the context of the history of millenarianism. The book traces the development of fundamentalism during the nineteenth and early twentieth centuries, discussing the importation of millenarianism from Great Britain to the United States and the development of dispensationalism. Whereas some scholars see publication of *The Fundamentals* and creation of the World Christian Fundamentals Association as the beginning of the fundamentalist movement, one that climaxed in the 1920s, Sandeen argues instead that the unity of fundamentalism was already dissolving by about 1910. From that point on, divisive factionalism plagued the fundamentalists.

Schultz, Jeffery D., John G. West, Jr., and Iain Maclean, eds. *Encyclopedia of Religion in American Politics*. Phoenix, AZ: Oryx, 1998.

This compendium of nearly 700 entries explores such topics as legal decisions, organizations, persons, and major events related to religion and politics. One essay presents a summary of religion and politics in the United States. Of major concern are the influences that religious considerations have had on politicians and the decisions they have made and the possible interaction between religion and politics in the future, especially over the issue of religious freedom.

Schultze, Quentin J., ed. *American Evangelicals and the Mass Media*. Grand Rapids, MI: Zondervan, 1991.

This collection of essays deals with how various aspects of the evangelical movement have been treated in the secular media. Individual essays focus on televangelism and the response to it by the secular media. Additional essays cover other examples of the media, including books, magazines, and music.

Schultze, Quentin J. *Televangelism and American Culture: The Business of Popular Religion*. Grand Rapids, MI: Baker Book House, 1991.

Schultze argues that mass-media evangelism has strong ties to secular commercial broadcasting. Televangelists are portrayed as encouraging a religious belief related to a society of affluence and individualism, but the author moderates his conclusions by claiming that there are likely very few "charlatans" engaged in the enterprise.

Shipps, Jan, and Mark Silk, eds. *Religion and Public Life in the Mountain West: Sacred Landscapes in Transition*. Lanham, MD: AltaMira Press, 2004.

The editors note that this region can be divided into three subregions: in Arizona and New Mexico, the Catholic Church dominates public life; in Utah and Idaho, Mormon influence tends to prevail; and in Colorado, Wyoming, and Montana, no denomination dominates. Ferenc Morton Szasz, in "How Religion Created an Infrastructure for the Mountain West," observes that beginning in the 1960s, the mainline denominations began to decline and a large conservative evangelical growth began.

Simmons, Paul D., ed. *Freedom of Conscience: A Baptist/Humanist Dialogue*. Amherst, NY: Prometheus, 2000.

The essays in this volume resulted from a conference at the University of Richmond in Virginia attended by liberal Baptist scholars and advocates of secular humanism. Among the issues discussed were academic freedom; social, political, and religious tolerance; separation of church and state; and the participants' mutual disapproval of the religious right and the conservative direction taken by the Southern Baptist Convention.

Smith, Christian. *American Evangelicalism: Embattled and Thriving*. Chicago: University of Chicago Press, 1998.

Basing his analysis on survey results, Smith takes exception to the common view of evangelicals as less educated, less affluent, and more fearful of contemporary culture than other Americans. He claims evangelicals are better educated than most of those who could be labeled religious liberals and tend not to feel threatened by modern life. Yet, Smith concludes that evangelicals find themselves in a potentially stressful situation, perched between opposition to and integration into mainstream society.

Spong, John Shelby. *Rescuing the Bible from Fundamentalism: A Bishop Rethinks the Meaning of Scripture*. New York: Harper, 1992.

John Shelby Spong, the controversial Episcopal bishop of Newark, New Jersey, challenges the fundamentalist belief in the Bible as the inerrant word of God. He offers examples of claimed inconsistencies and contradictions. Spong argues that biblical literalism has been used to justify slavery and war, deny rights to minorities, and subordinate women.

———. *Here I Stand: My Struggle for a Christianity of Integrity, Love, and Equality*. San Francisco: Harper, 2000.

In this autobiography, Spong outlines his efforts to offer American Christians an alternative to fundamentalism, discussing his opposition to the conservative views of such religious right leaders as Jerry Falwell and Pat Robertson and struggles within the hierarchy of the Episcopalian church. He describes his defense of the rights of African Americans, women, and homosexuals within the church and argues for the need to make Christianity relevant to the realities of contemporary society.

Stone, Jon R. *On the Boundaries of American Evangelicalism: The Postwar Evangelical Coalition*. New York: Palgrave, 1999.

Stone traces the rise of a coalition of moderate Protestants in the 1940s and 1950s from the amorphous coalition called American Evangelicalism. This moderate coalition distinguished itself from both conservative fundamentalist and liberal factions. The author searches for reasons for the decline of this moderate group from the 1960s to the 1990s.

Thomas, R. Murray. *Religion in Schools: Controversies Around the World.* Westport, CT: Praeger, 2006.

Thomas focuses on controversies in twelve countries regarding the place of religion in the public schools. In the United States, the author examines such issues as the permissibility of prayer, the Pledge of Allegiance, and the display of the Ten Commandments.

Trollinges, William Vance, and Edwin Grant Conklin, Jr., eds. *The Antievolution Pamphlets of William Bell Riley.* Hamden, CT: Garland, 1995.

The fourth volume in the *Creationism in Twentieth-Century America* series (Ronald L. Numbers, general editor) includes ten pamphlets by William Bell Riley, pastor of the First Baptist Church in Minneapolis, Minnesota. Riley was founder of the World Christian Fundamentals Association, a major anti-evolution group in the 1920s. Among the pamphlets are "Are the Scriptures Scientific?" (no date), "Darwin's Philosophy and the Flood" (no date), and "The Scientific Accuracy of the Sacred Scriptures" (no date).

Tuveson, Ernest Lee. *Redeemer Nation: The Idea of America's Millennial Role.* New Haven, CT: Yale University Press, 1977.

This book provides an interesting and enlightening treatment of the background and consequences of millennial thought. Of particular interest is Tuveson's examination of the belief that America has been chosen as the instrument to achieve God's purposes in the final days.

Walsh, Andrew, and Mark Silk, eds. *Religion and Public Life in New England: Steady Habits, Changing Slowly.* Lanham, MD: AltaMira Press, 2004.

This volume in the *Religion by Region* series focuses primarily on the traditional mainline Protestant churches as well as the Catholic Church. However, Andrew Walsh ("Conservative Protestants: Prospering on the Margins") recounts the revival of conservative Protestantism in the region since the 1950s, noting that although less that 40 percent of Protestant congregations are evangelical, that proportion represents a significant increase. In addition, the mainline churches have solid proportions of their membership who are evangelical and who have organized renewal movements within these traditional denominations.

Watt, David Harrington. *A Transforming Faith: Explorations of Twentieth-Century American Evangelicalism.* New Brunswick, NJ: Rutgers University Press, 1991.

This brief treatment of evangelism covers the period from 1925 to 1976. The author focuses on recent cultural changes in politics, the status of the public and private realms, the role of women in society, and contributions in psychology. This approach illuminates the interaction of evangelicalism with the larger culture.

Weber, Timothy P. *Living in the Shadow of the Second Coming: American Premillennialism, 1875–1925*. New York: Oxford University Press, 1979.

This book is a good treatment of the rise of the premillennialist movement in America in the late nineteenth and early twentieth centuries. The author, a Baptist church historian, focuses on the social consequences of premillennialism, a doctrine that attempted to preserve orthodox beliefs against modernism and faith in social progress.

White, Ronald C., Jr., and Albright G. Zimmerman, eds. *An Unsettled Arena: Religion and the Bill of Rights*. Grand Rapids, MI: Eerdmans, 1991.

Written by a group of distinguished scholars, these essays confront the problem of maintaining a religious heritage in a pluralistic society. Such issues as prayer in public schools, public aid to parochial schools, the teaching of creationism, and the inclusion of religious ceremony in public events have led to nationwide debates about the meaning of the First Amendment and its applicability to contemporary America.

Wilcox, Clyde. *The Latest American Revolution? The 1994 Elections and Their Implications for Governance*. New York: St. Martin's, 1995.

This brief work discusses the importance of the religious right to the outcome of the 1994 elections. An appendix includes The House Republican "Contract With America," which discloses the influence of the religious right on that party's agenda. Among the promised measures are a "personal responsibility act" to discourage illegitimacy and teen pregnancy; a "family reinforcement act" that includes more stringent enforcement of child support, parents' rights in the education of their children, and stronger child pornography laws; and a stronger anti-crime act.

Wills, Gary. *Under God: Religion and American Politics*. New York: Simon and Schuster, 1990.

With his usual grace, Wills explores American history from Roger Williams to Pat Robertson, focusing on those points of collision between religion and politics. Separation of church and state to the contrary notwithstanding, religion has always been a vital force in American society, and its influence has often been positive. As Wills writes, the abolitionist, women's, and civil rights movements derived considerable strength from the churches.

Wilson, Charles Reagan, and Mark Silk, eds. *Religion and Public Life in the South: In the Evangelical Mode*. Lanham, MD: AltaMira Press, 2005.

The nine essays contained in this volume, which is part of the *Religion by Region* series, cover the history and development of religion in the ten southern states. Although the contributors discuss various denominations in the South, they recognize that the white evangelicals, who come closest to composing a religious establishment, have greatly influenced southern politics and culture, from the Civil War to the Scopes Trial to the more recent Moral Majority.

Witham, Larry A. *Where Darwin Meets the Bible: Creationists and Evolutionists in America*. New York: Oxford University Press, 2005.

Witham, a senior writer with *The Washington Times*, investigates the conflict between evolution and creation views of the origins of human life, examining such events as the 1925 John T. Scopes trial and the 1999 anti-evolution vote of the Kansas state board of education. The author conducted interviews with individuals on both sides of the controversy.

————. *By Design: Science and the Search for God*. New York: Encounter Books, 2002.

Witham recounts developments in the sciences that led at least some to consider the possibility that an intelligent force designed the laws of nature in order to make possible the start of life. The author focuses on two basic themes: the dialogue between science and religion, and the intelligent design movement tied primarily to the Seattle, Washington-based Discovery Institute, an organization that suggests that material laws do not sufficiently explain the development of complex organisms and human consciousness.

The Religious Right and Politics

Abraham, Ken. *Who Are the Promise Keepers? Understanding the Christian Men's Movement*. New York: Doubleday, 1997.

Abraham takes a sympathetic look at the Promise Keepers movement, an organization that schedules rallies for Christian men. The author examines the establishment of the Promise Keepers, its objectives, and many of the questions and criticisms that have been raised about the group, such as its relationship to women, minorities, the Republican party, and other Christian groups.

Alexander-Moegerle, Gil. *James Dobson's War on America*. Amherst, NY: Prometheus, 1997.

Alexander-Moegerle, co-founder and former executive in James Dobson's Focus on the Family, presents a highly critical examination of Dobson and his organization. The author co-hosted Focus on the Family's radio program and served on the organization's board of directors as a fundraising consultant. He contrasts the "public" Dobson with the "private" individual who allegedly is motivated by competition, a desire for political power, and materialism. To the author, Dobson's conservative views could be a threat to civil liberties.

Alley, Robert S. *School Prayer: The Court, the Congress, and the First Amendment*. Amherst, NY: Prometheus, 1994.

Focusing on prayer in public schools, Alley investigates the historical background to the writing of the First Amendment's religion clauses, the courts' interpretations of these clauses for the past 200 years, and congressional debates over their application. The author makes a balanced presentation of views on both sides of the school prayer issue.

————. *Without a Prayer: Religious Expression in Public Schools*. Amherst, NY: Prometheus, 1996.

The U.S. Supreme Court, in *Engel v. Vitale* (1962) and *Abington v. Schempp* (1963), ruled that prayer and Bible reading in the public schools is unconstitutional. Alley explores subsequent court cases dealing with the First Amendment guarantee of separation of church and state. He interviewed many of those engaged in such cases who objected to the continuing introduction of religious ceremony in the public schools. The author elaborates on the justifications that communities have used to reintroduce school prayer, including "nonpreferentialism," "toleration," and "accommodation."

Balmer, Randall Herbert. *Thy Kingdom Come: How the Religious Right Distorts the Faith and Threatens America*. New York: Perseus, 2006.

Although the history of American evangelicalism includes many progressive causes, such as the abolition of slavery, universal suffrage, and public education, Balmer contends that current evangelical leaders have abandoned this tradition, forming an alliance with the Republican party in advancing a conservative political agenda. The author offers explanations for the political success of the religious right.

Barkun, Michael. *Religion and the Racist Right: The Origins of the Christian Identity Movement*. Annapolis, MD: University of North Carolina Press, 1996.

Barkun analyzes white supremacist groups on the religious right, groups which hold beliefs referred to as Christian Identity. He examines the basic ideology and organizational development of the Christian Identity movement and traces the roles individuals in the movement played in activities such as the bombing of the federal building in Oklahoma City and the rise of militia movements across the country.

Bernstein, Richard. *The Abuse of Evil*. Malden, MA: Blackwell, 2005.

Bernstein argues that many today employ the concept of evil as a tool of politics that limits discussion of complex issues and degrades democratic politics and religion. The author indicates that there is a division of perspectives between those who emphasize absolutes and a strict division between good and evil, and those who oppose any simple dichotomies.

Blanchard, Dallas A. *The Anti-Abortion Movement and the Rise of the Religious Right: From Polite to Fiery Protest*. Old Tappan, NJ: Twayne, 1994.

Blanchard describes the history of the antiabortion movement in the United States, including the initial efforts primarily by Roman Catholic priests and laypersons in the 1960s; the court decisions, such as *Roe v. Wade*, that liberalized abortion policy; and the more extreme and sometimes violent antiabortion protests of the 1990s. An important trend in the antiabortion movement, the author concludes, has been its merging with a conservative political and cultural ideology and fundamentalist religious beliefs.

Boston, Robert. *Why the Religious Right Is Wrong About Separation of Church and State*. Amherst, NY: Prometheus, 1993.

Boston, assistant director of communications for Americans United for the Separation of Church and State, argues that the religious right poses a danger to the principle of separation of church and state. He believes that those on the religious right intend to create a theocratic system in the United States. Countering the arguments leaders in the religious right have made about the First Amendment guarantee of religious freedom, Boston examines the history of church-state relations and reviews court decisions on the issue.

————. *Close Encounter With the Religious Right: Journeys into the Twilight Zone of Religion and Politics*. Amherst, NY: Prometheus, 2000.

Boston has attended religious right conventions, listened to speeches of the movement's leaders, and read their many mailings to gather information for this book about the conservative Christian political agenda. Subjects covered include the Christian Coalition, the Promise Keepers, the Rutherford Institute, Focus on the Family, and religious right leaders Pat Robertson, D. James Kennedy, Jerry Falwell, James Dobson, and Gary Bauer. Boston argues that although the religious right has suffered recent setbacks, it still remains a potent force in American politics.

Brasher, Brenda E. *Godly Women: Fundamentalism and Female Power*. Piscataway, NJ: Rutgers University Press, 1998.

Basing her findings on in-depth interviews with women in fundamentalist churches, Brasher identifies an interesting paradox: while fundamentalist women adhere to the traditional conservative view of the place of women in the family and church, they nonetheless often play active and influential roles in church and community affairs. Noting that the interaction between conservative religious beliefs and the contemporary society and culture are often complex, the author claims that women who hold fundamentalist beliefs hold a wide variety of positions regarding the role of women in church and society.

Bruce, Stephen. *The Rise and Fall of the Christian Right*. New York: Oxford University Press, 1988.

Employing a sociological perspective, Bruce examines the efforts of the Christian right in the 1970s and 1980s to organize politically and influence election outcomes. Although predictions of the religious right's downfall have proven premature, the problems involved in attempting to establish political coalitions are still relevant to the fortunes of the movement.

———. *Conservative Protestant Politics*. New York: Oxford University Press, 1998.

Bruce compares conservative Protestant political activity in the United Kingdom, the United States, South Africa, Australia, New Zealand, and Canada. The author emphasizes the limitations to success that those promoting a religiously motivated political agenda face in culturally diverse societies.

Bruce, Stephen, Peter Kivisto, and William H Swatos, Jr., eds. *The Rapture of Politics: The Christian Right as the United States Approaches the Year 2000*. New Brunswick, NJ: Transaction, 1994.

These essays examine the current influence of the religious right on American politics. The authors provide differing perspectives, from highly critical to sympathetic, on the efforts of this movement to combine religious and political concerns in the public arena.

Bull, Christopher, and John Gallagher. *Perfect Enemies: The Religious Right, the Gay Movement, and the Politics of the 1990s*. New York: Crown Publishing Group, 1996.

Bull and Gallagher trace the history of the religious right and the gay movement from the late 1960s, portraying them as groups bound to collide. The authors examine instances of the struggle, including state elections, the 1992 presidential election, and the congressional hearings on gays in the military. The authors appeal to both sides to jettison fierce rhetoric and accept greater civility.

Cantor, David. *The Religious Right: The Assault on Tolerance and Pluralism in America*. New York: Anti-Defamation League, 1993.

Cantor, senior research analyst at the Anti-Defamation League, provides a highly critical overview of the religious right in the early 1990s. He examines the major individuals and organizations on the religious right, their objectives and tactics, and their strengths and weaknesses. Cantor believes the religious right poses a major threat to American democracy and therefore warns the reader of the danger he perceives emanating from a radical religious movement.

Capps, Walter H. *The New Religious Right: Piety, Patriotism, and Politics.* Columbia: University of South Carolina Press, 1990.

This is an excellent account of the better-known Christian right personalities of the 1980s. The author deals in depth with Jerry Falwell, interviewing him at the Thomas Road Baptist Church; Bob Jones, Jr., and Bob Jones III and their court battle over Bob Jones University; Francis A. Schaeffer, the famous theologian of the religious right; the rise and fall of Jim and Tammy Bakker; and Pat Robertson's failed bid for the Republican presidential nomination.

Carpenter, Joel A. *Revive Us Again: The Reawakening of American Fundamentalism.* New York: Oxford University Press, 1999.

Offering insights into the origins of the contemporary influence of the religious right in American politics, Carpenter traces the history of Christian fundamentalism from the Scopes trial in 1925 to the beginning of Billy Graham's crusades in 1949. Following the Scopes trial, which Carpenter considers an embarrassing debacle, fundamentalists continued to build a strong subculture through Bible schools, seminaries, small publishing houses, and usage of the new technology of radio to spread their message across the country.

Carter, Jimmy. *Our Endangered Values: America's Moral Crisis.* New York: Simon and Schuster, 2005.

Offering an alternative to the religious right agenda, former President Jimmy Carter defends the separation of church and state, women's rights, and civil liberties. Carter covers such topics as preemptive war, homosexuality, abortion, the death penalty, the relationship between science and religion, nuclear weapons, fundamentalism, and the environment.

Clarkson, Frederick. *Eternal Hostility: The Struggle Between Theocracy and Democracy.* Monroe, ME: Common Courage Press, 1997.

Focusing on such groups as The Christian Coalition, the Unification Church, and the Promise Keepers, Clark claims that the religious right is subverting democracy in the United States. As proof, the author cites the Christian Coalition's attempts to dominate the Republican party, violence at abortion clinics committed by more radical antiabortion groups, and attacks on homosexuals.

Cord, John. *Christian Right—or Wrong? An Exhaustive Study Exposing the False, Outrageous, and Deceptive Teachings Propagated by Today's Foremost Media Evangelists.* Nevada City, CA: Blue Dolphin, 2004.

Cord claims to expose the false teachings of forty Christian leaders, primarily televangelists such as Jerry Falwell, Pat Robertson, Robert Schuller, and Jimmy Swaggart, on such issues as abortion, homosexuality, and religious terrorism. The author viewed over 700 hours of religious television programs and talk shows in documenting his claims.

Crier, Catherine. *Contempt: How the Right Is Wronging American Justice*. New York: Rugged Land, 2005.

Conservatives and those in the religious right consider too many U.S. judges to be "activist," deciding cases by making law rather than interpreting it. Crier claims that conservative politicians, backed by religious fundamentalists, are attempting to remold the judiciary into a supporter of their policy agenda.

Eisenberg, Jon B. *Using Terri: The Religious Right's Conspiracy To Take Away Our Rights*. San Francisco: Harper, 2005.

Eisenberg, one of the attorneys representing Michael Schiavo, Terri Schiavo's husband, recounts the court battle to have Terri's feeding tube removed. The author focuses on the funding of lawyers for Terri's parents, who opposed having the tube removed. Eisenberg suggests ways he believes the religious right will use the Schiavo case to attack judges and change laws dealing with the right to die.

Cromartie, Michael, ed. *Disciples and Democracy: Religious Conservatives and the Future of American Politics*. Washington, DC: Ethics and Public Policy Center, 1994.

This volume of essays, originally presented at an Ethics and Public Policy Center Conference, examines the current status of the religious right mostly from a sympathetic perspective. Individual essays deal with such topics as the religious right's impact on the 1992 presidential election, media treatment of the movement, and its relationship to the Republican party.

———. *No Longer Exiles: The Religious New Right in American Politics*. Washington, DC: Ethics and Public Policy Center, 1993.

This volume, drawn from a conference on the religious right, features four major chapters on the history of the religious right, future prospects for the movement, past failures, and evangelical voting patterns from 1976 to 1988.

———. *Evangelicals and Foreign Policy: Four Perspectives*. Washington, DC: Ethics and Public Policy Center, 1989.

These essays examine the applicability of evangelical Christian beliefs to American foreign policy and international relations. The Bible is seen as establishing possible tenets for foreign policy makers, including positions on terrorism and tyranny. Those on the political left are criticized for failing to separate political systems that are flawed from those that are fundamentally evil.

D'Antonio, Michael. *Fall from Grace: The Failed Crusade of the Christian Right*. New York: Farrar, Straus, and Giroux, 1989.

This book examines the Christian right through a series of interesting personal profiles of individuals committed to the movement. The book also deals with the fall of major television evangelists, such as Jim Bakker and Jimmy Swaggart, in the late 1980s, and recounts Pat Robertson's failed campaign for the presidency.

Diamond, Sara. *Spiritual Warfare: The Politics of the Christian Right*. Boston: South End Press, 1989.

In her highly critical account of the religious right, Diamond examines the various aspects of the movement, including religious broadcasting networks, extremist political activity such as bombing abortion clinics, and activities in foreign nations in support of a conservative American foreign policy.

———. *Roads to Dominion: Right-Wing Movements and Political Power in the United States*. New York: Guilford, 1995.

In this sequel to *Spiritual Warfare: The Politics of the Christian Right*, Diamond presents a more scholarly treatment of right-wing politics in the United States. The author analyzes the differences among the political right, the racist right, and the religious right, and suggests connections among these groups. The book contains detailed information about the rise of right-wing political groups since World War II and speculates about their possible future rise to power.

———. *Facing the Wrath: Confronting the Right in Dangerous Times*. Monroe, ME: Common Courage Press, 1996.

Diamond presents a comprehensive view of the religious right's involvement in the political realm. Topics include organizations such as the Christian Coalition, conservative attacks on the Public Broadcasting System, the radio ministry of James Dobson's Focus on the Family, and "dominion theology." The author concludes that the religious right threatens secular education, has an anti-gay agenda, participates in aggressive antiabortion politics, and ultimately wishes to replace secular law with biblical law.

———. *Not By Politics Alone: The Enduring Influence of the Christian Right*. New York: Guilford, 1998.

In her continuing examination of the religious right, Diamond explores its cultural underpinnings and its deep roots within evangelical Christianity in order to shed light on the persistence of the movement as a force in American politics. Diamond claims that the major objective of the Christian right is to influence moral attitudes through cultural and political means, including a complex alliance with the Republican party. The author details the proliferation of talk radio shows, publishing companies, law firms, and music studios, all a part of the continuing cultural influence of the religious right.

Durham, James R. *Secular Darkness: Religious Right Involvement in Texas Public Education, 1963–1989*. New York: Peter Lang, 1995.

Durham describes the increasing influence of conservative Christian individuals and organization on public school policy in Texas during the period from the 1960s through the 1980s. Especially interesting is the rise of Norma and Mel Gabler as self-proclaimed experts on textbook selection who developed significant influence over the policies of the state board of education. In 1974 the Gablers pressured the board to issue a "proclamation" stating that "Textbooks that treat the theory of evolution shall identify it as only one of several explanations of the origins of humankind and avoid limiting young people in their search for meanings of their human existence."

Dwyer, James G. *Religious Schools v. Children's Rights*. Ithaca, NY: Cornell University Press, 1998.

Dwyer takes a critical look at religious schooling, a sensitive area for fundamentalist Christians and Roman Catholics. He claims religious schools are almost completely unregulated and may not serve the best interests of children. Therefore, public policy should focus not so much on the right of families and religious communities to raise children as they deem appropriate, but rather on what is best for the affected children from a secular perspective.

Edwards, Lee. *The Conservative Revolution: The Movement That Remade America*. New York: Free Press, 1999.

Edwards discusses those events and individuals, including those in the religious right, who contributed to the growth of conservatism as a major force in American society and politics.

Feder, Don. *Who's Afraid of the Religious Right?* Ottawa, IL: Jameson, 1998.

Feder examines the membership of the religious right and explores the movement's political and social agenda. The author analyzes the positions of the religious right on such topics as gays in the military, abortion, and prayer in the schools.

Feldman, Noah. *Divided by God: America's Church-State Problem—and What We Should Do About It*. New York: Farrar, Straus and Giroux, 2005.

Noting the increasing religious diversity of the United States, Feldman identifies a conflict between those he calls "legal secularists," who seek to achieve total separation of church and state, and "values evangelicals," who advocate public policy that supports their religious principles. Feldman proposes a middle ground between these extremes, combining greater allowance for religious expression in the public realm with less government support for religious institutions.

Foege, Alec. *The Empire God Built: Inside Pat Robertson's Media Machine*. New York: Wiley, 1996.

Foege, a contributing editor to *Rolling Stone* magazine, investigates the media empire behind Pat Robertson's political activity. The author describes the corporate structure of Robertson's empire, investigates the inner workings of the organization, and explains how it achieves its economic and political goals.

According to Foege, Robertson has lessons for those who support as well as those who oppose him, especially regarding the effective use of mass media technology.

Garrison, Becky. *Red and Blue God, Black and Blue Church: Eyewitness Accounts of How American Churches Are Highjacking Jesus, Bagging the Beatitudes, and Worshiping the Almighty Dollar*. Hoboken, NJ: John Wiley and Sons, 2006.

Garrison, senior contributing editor of the *Wittenburg Door*, a religious satire magazine, focuses on the deficiencies of both the religious right and the more liberal denominations, criticizing any approach claiming to be the one appropriate Christian response to social and political issues. Garrison supports a reinvigorated separation of church and state.

Green, John C., Mark J. Rozell, and Clyde Wilcox, eds. *Prayers in the Precincts: The Christian Right in the 1998 Elections*. Baltimore, MD: Georgetown University Press, 2000.

This book contains essays analyzing the role of the Christian right in the 1998 campaigns and elections in fourteen states. Although the authors generally conclude that the Christian right was not especially effective in recruiting like-minded candidates and raising campaign funds, they predict this religious coalition will continue to have significant influence on American politics.

Griffith, R. Marie. *God's Daughters: Evangelical Women and the Power of Submission*. Berkeley, CA: University of California Press, 1997.

This examination of Women's Aglow Fellowship, the largest women's international evangelical association, provides insights into the complex interaction of Christian women with contemporary culture. Griffith challenges the generally accepted view of evangelical Christian women, noting important connections between them and feminist causes they are often considered to oppose.

Guth, James L., and John C. Green, eds. *The Bible and the Ballot Box: Religion and Politics in the 1988 Election*. Boulder, CO: Westview, 1991.

The authors examine the wide variety of religious influences on the 1988 presidential campaign in which two Baptist ministers—Jesse Jackson, a liberal Democrat, and Pat Robertson, a conservative Republican—vied in their respective parties for the nomination. One suggestion is that the United States may be moving toward a party system similar to those in Europe, with a conservative religious party competing against a liberal secular one.

Hacker, Hans J. *The Culture of Conservative Christian Litigation*. Lanham, MD: Rowman and Littlefield, 2005.

With the increased activity of conservative Christian groups in litigation, the author examines the work of three conservative Christian law firms and attempts to explain why they employ differing agendas and approaches. Hacker investigates the internal workings of the law firms to determine what influences their court behavior.

Hadden, Jeffrey K. and Anson Shupe, eds.*Secularization and Fundamentalism Reconsidered*. New York: Paragon House, 1989.

In the wake of renewed religious right activity in the 1980s, the contributors to this volume, who are sociologists of religion, examine the relationship between religion and politics in the United States and other nations. Of primary concern is the status of secularization theory in light of recent developments. Other topics include the role of the mass media in religious right successes, religious attitudes toward the capitalist system, and religious right involvement in presidential elections.

Hart, Gary. *God and Caesar in America: An Essay on Religion and Politics*. Golden, CO: Fulcrum, 2005.

Hart, who was raised in the Church of the Nazarene (as was religious right leader James Dobson) and graduated from Bethany College and Yale Divinity School, criticizes the Republican party for a too-close relationship with evangelical Protestant interests. Criticizing various conservative Christian issue positions, he argues, for instance, that the religious right defines the value of life too narrowly, being unwilling to take a stand against the death penalty. Hart also criticizes Democrats for failing to take part in the values debate.

Heineman, Kenneth J. *God Is a Conservative: Religion, Politics, and Morality in Contemporary America*. New York: New York University Press, 1998.

Examining conservative religious and political leaders such as Patrick Buchanan, Jerry Falwell, Michael Novak, and Pat Robertson, Heineman discusses the influence of religion on contemporary conservatism. The author investigates the influence of the religious right on the 2004 presidential campaign.

Herman, Didi. *The Antigay Agenda: Orthodox Vision and the Christian Right*. Chicago: University of Chicago Press, 1997.

Herman criticizes the positions of conservative Protestants on the issue of gay rights from the 1950s to the present. He relies heavily on the periodical *Christianity Today* to discern religious right attitudes on this issue, describing how conservative Christians have used anti-homosexual language in politics and journalism.

Hertzke, Allen. *Representing God in Washington: The Role of Religious Lobbies in the American Polity*. Nashville, TN: University of Tennessee Press, 1988.

The empirical research for this study includes interviews with policy makers and lobbyists. The analysis of lobbying activities of religious groups involves not only fundamentalist and evangelical organizations, but also Catholic and

Jewish groups. Lobbyists' concerns vary from abortion to peace and world hunger.

Hofrenning, Daniel J.B. *In Washington But Not Of It: The Prophetic Politics of Religious Lobbyists*. Philadelphia, PA: Temple University Press, 1995.

Hofrenning provides a detailed examination of the activities of religious lobbyists at the national level. The author concludes that religious lobbyists, regardless of their ideological positions, are similar in that they all hold an anti-elitist position while pursuing their individual efforts to alter national policy.

Jelen, Ted G. *The Political Mobilization of Religious Beliefs*. New York: Praeger, 1991.

This book, based on an attitude survey Jelen conducted in fifteen churches in Greencastle, Indiana, contains a wealth of data on the political attitudes of those who support the Christian right. Of great interest is Jelen's discussion of the relation between the political activities of the religious right and opposition to other groups in society, including feminists, homosexuals, and atheists.

Jorstad, Erling. *The New Christian Right, 1981–1988: Prospects for the Post-Reagan Era*. Leiston, NY: Edwin Mellen, 1987.

Jorstad discusses the relationship between the Reagan administration and the new Christian right in the 1980s, focusing on such figures as Jerry Falwell, Pat Robertson, and Tim LaHaye, and their assistance in Reagan's 1984 re-election campaign. The book also deals with the religious right's efforts leading up to the 1988 election, and adjustments in its agenda.

Judges, Donald P. *Hard Choices, Lost Voices: How the Abortion Conflict Has Divided America, Distorted Constitutional Rights, and Damaged the Courts*. Chicago: Ivan R. Dee, 1993.

The religious right has consistently employed the abortion issue to distinguish itself from what the movement considers secularizing influences in contemporary society. Treating pro-choice and pro-life movements equally, Judges criticizes both sides for misstating the nature of the conflict and demonstrating lack of knowledge and understanding of the choices women face. According to the author, the nature of the debate, characterized by distortion on both sides, has contributed to the polarization of American society.

Kaplan, Esther. *With God on Their Side: George W. Bush and the Christian Right*. New York: New Press, 2005.

Kaplan alleges that many of the policies President George W. Bush implemented during his first term were intended to win the continued support of Christian fundamentalists. She mentions budget cuts for family planning groups and AIDS organizations and increased funding for church-sponsored programs to promote sexual abstinence and marriage, appointments to the federal courts agreeable to the religious right, Bush's limitations on stem cell research, and his support for intelligent design as an alternative to the theory of evolution.

Kintz, Linda. *Between Jesus and the Market: The Emotions That Matter in Right-Wing America*. Durham, NC: Duke University Press, 1997.

Although analysts often identify men as the major force within the religious right, Kintz notes the unique contribution women have made to the movement. The author observes that conservative Christian women have cultivated a unique power. They often stay home, where they can participate in furthering the political agenda of the religious right through phone calls, distribution of petitions, and usage of e-mail. A source of the movement's strength is found in what Kintz calls "resonance," which the author identifies as appeal to the emotions.

Kintz, Linda, and Julia Lesage, eds. *Media, Culture, and the Religious Right*. University of Minnesota Press, 1998.

Scholars from various academic fields, including media studies, sociology, religious studies, and political science examine the increased significance of contemporary conservative Christian media, which coincides with attempts by those on the religious right to increase their social and political influence.

Kramnick, Isaac, and R. Laurence Moore. *The Godless Constitution: The Case Against Religious Correctness*. New York: Norton, 1996.

The authors take issue with claims that the United States was founded as a Christian nation. They note that the founders, hoping to avoid the severe religious conflicts of European nations, intentionally made no mention of God in the Constitution. The intellectual background and constitutional history of separation of church and state are examined, as well as contemporary attempts by religious groups to destroy the wall of separation between church and state by introducing a standard of "religious correctness" into American politics.

Larson, Edward J. *Summer for the Gods: The Scopes Trial and America's Continuing Debate over Science and Religion*. Cambridge, MA: Harvard University Press, 1998.

Larson presents a detailed account of the 1925 Scopes trial, held in Dayton, Tennessee, in which John T. Scopes was found guilty of teaching evolution to his pupils. The trial showcased the tug-of-war between evolutionists and creationists of the time. The author recounts the legal maneuverings of the prosecution, led by William Jennings Bryan, and the defense, led by Clarence Darrow, and investigates the event's broader religious, cultural, educational, and political consequences.

Lerner, Michael. *The Left Hand of God: Taking Back Our Country from the Religious Right*. New York: Harper Collins, 2006.

Criticizing the religious right's perspective on government, Lerner distinguishes between the "right hand of God," advocated by those who believe in an avenging God and who view the world as controlled by evil, and the "left hand of God," supported by those who believe in a merciful and compassionate God. In contrast to the religious right, the author recommends policies based on the search for peace, social justice, and ethical behavior informed by kindness and generosity both domestically and in international relations.

Lienesch, Michael. *Redeeming America: Piety and Politics in the New Christian Right*. Chapel Hill: University of North Carolina Press, 1993.

This excellent work provides an in-depth view of social and political positions crucial to the religious right. Lienesch presents an intricate and fascinating analysis of conservative Christian writings. Among the topics included are the perceived social roles of men and women, defenses of capitalism, attitudes toward the political system, and the role of the United States as a redeemer nation.

Lugg, Catherine A. *For God and Country: Conservatism and American School Policy*. New York: Peter Lang, 1996.

Lugg offers a policy analysis of the influences that conservative groups, including the Christian right, had on federal school policies during President Ronald Reagan's first administration from 1981 to 1984. She focuses on the conservative social agenda which received renewed support following the 1980 Reagan election victory.

Menendez, Albert J. *Visions of Reality: What Fundamentalist Schools Teach*. Amherst, NY: Prometheus, 1993.

Even though a majority of those polled has consistently registered opposition to public support for non-public schools, Menendez notes that fundamentalist religious leaders have been pressuring Congress and state legislatures to initiate aid programs to those schools through such programs as "vouchers" and "tuition tax credits." The author claims that history, English, and science textbooks used in fundamentalist private schools distort history, demonstrate prejudice against other religious faiths, question mainstream science, and generally indoctrinate children with "visions of reality" that should not be supported with public funds.

Meyers, Robin. *Why the Christian Right Is Wrong: A Minister's Manifesto for Taking Back Your Faith, Your Flag, Your Future*. Hoboken, NJ: John Wiley and Sons, 2006.

Expanding on an antiwar speech delivered at a peace rally at the University of Oklahoma in November 2004, Meyers, a United Church of Christ minister, faults the religious right for neglecting Jesus' condemnation of the sin of religious hypocrisy. The author claims that the values of the religious right and the George W. Bush administration conflict with the gospel of Christ for failing to address what he considers the religious concerns of peace, poverty, and the environment.

Moen, Matthew C. *The Transformation of the Christian Right*. Tuscaloosa: University of Alabama Press, 1992.

This examination of changes in the religious right during the 1980s is crucial to understanding the present status of the movement. Moen documents the religious right's shift away from uncompromising positions on the national level to a more politically sophisticated strategy that includes a greater regional and local emphasis.

———. *The Christian Right and Congress*. Tuscaloosa: University of Alabama Press, 1989.

This well-done empirical study examines the influence of the religious right in Congress, focusing on the years 1981 through 1984. Moen investigates the major legislative efforts (antiabortion legislation, a school prayer amendment, and tuition tax credits for parents with children in private schools) and the religious right's failure to achieve their objectives. The author notes the lesser successes of the movement.

Neuhaus, Richard John, and Michael Cromartie, eds. *Piety and Politics: Evangelicals and Fundamentalists Confront the World*. Lanham, MD: University Press of America, 1987.

This edited work provides a variety of views about, and from, the religious right. Articles feature the origins of evangelicalism and fundamentalism and the contemporary political significance of Christian conservatives. Articles by individuals within the movement provide assessments of the United States and the problems it faces.

Numbers, Ronald. *The Creationists: The Evolution of Scientific Creationism*. Ewing, NJ: California Princeton Fulfillment Services, 1993.

After conducting many interviews and investigating various manuscripts, Numbers describes the formation of the creationist movement. The author investigates the origins of the debates between creationists and evolutionists, focusing on events in courtrooms, legislatures, and school boards.

Oldfield, Duane M. *The Right and the Righteous: The Christian Right Confronts the Republican Party*. Lanham, MD: Rowman and Littlefield, 1996.

Oldfield discusses the relationship between the Christian right and the Republican party, analyzing the history and objectives of each organization. The author probes the significant influence the religious right has had on the Republican national platform and on the conservative political agenda, and examines the potential dilemmas this poses for the Republican party in forging broader coalitions with other groups.

Peck, Janice. *The Gods of Televangelism: The Crisis of Meaning and the Appeal of Religious Television*. Cresskill, NJ: Hampton, 1993.

While cautioning against exaggerating the media influence of the Christian right, Peck notes that the activist evangelicals, who compose one-fifth of the population, can be an influential force in American politics. The author focused her research on two televangelists: Jimmy Swaggart, who, prior to his fall due to personal indiscretions, employed a revivalist version of religious broadcasting, and Pat Robertson whose *700 Club* follows a talk show/news program format. Each represents a distinct way of combining conservative religious belief with contemporary media technology.

Phillips, Kevin. *American Theocracy: The Peril of Radical Religion, Oil and Borrowed Money in the 21st Century*. New York: Viking, 2006.

Phillips, a long-time observer of U.S. politics, argues that the Republican party has become increasingly theocratic, allying itself with the religious right. Phillips presents a highly critical analysis of Republicans' promotion of a consumer society increasingly in debt, radical religion, and dependence on foreign energy supplies, and focuses on such issues as the Terry Schiavo case and federal government intervention in science education.

Pinello, Daniel R. *America's Struggle for Same-Sex Marriage*. New York: Cambridge University Press, 2006.

Pinello investigates the major events in the push for same-sex marriage, beginning with the 2003 Massachusetts Supreme Judicial Court decision that the state's prohibition on same-sex marriages violated the state's constitutional guarantee of equality under the law. He examines subsequent events, including the debates in the Massachusetts legislature and same-sex marriage controversies in California, Oregon, and New York.

Porteous, Skipp. *Jesus Doesn't Live Here Anymore*. Amherst, NY: Prometheus, 1991.

Porteous, president and national director of the Institute for First Amendment Studies, recounts his personal experience with Christian fundamentalism. He became a "born again" Christian at the age of eleven and came to believe the Bible could provide the answer to any problem. The author spent many years in the Pentecostal ministry before finally deciding to leave. Why and how he left the ministry, which he describes as a liberating experience, and why he decided to fight against the fundamentalist movement, comprise much of this study.

Press, Bill. *How Republicans Stole Christmas: The Republican Party's Declared Monopoly on Religion and What Democrats Can Do to Take It Back*. New York: Doubleday, 2005.

Press claims that conservative Christians such as Jerry Falwell and Pat Robertson, along with Catholic bishops, have narrowed the criteria for being a Christian to such an extent that Democrats and liberals have been excluded. The author states that the religious right has transformed a loving Jesus who cared for the poor into a supporter of the rich and powerful, and offers suggestions to the Democratic party for reclaiming religion from the religious right.

Rapp, Sandy. *God's Country: A Case Against Theocracy*. Binghamton, NY: Haworth, 1991.

Rapp focuses on the religious right's role in sexual politics, describing that movement's emotional attacks on homosexuals and the right to privacy. She encourages readers to become politically active in opposition to the religious right and recommends effective strategies.

Ribuffo, Leo P. *The Old Christian Right: The Protestant Far Right from the Great Depression to the Cold War*. Philadelphia: Temple University Press, 1983.

The author places the new resurgence of the Christian right in the context of twentieth-century America from the 1930s to the 1950s. Ribuffo presents historical examples of religious right activity that are intended to trouble the reader.

Risen, James, and Judy L. Thomas. *Wrath of Angels: The American Abortion War*. Boulder, CO: Basic Books, 1999.

Risen and Thomas trace the history of the antiabortion movement as it expanded from a largely Catholic cause into a fundamentalist Protestant one. Although the antiabortion movement has not achieved the objective of banning abortion, the authors argue it contributed to the rise of the religious right in American politics.

Rozell, Mark J., and Clyde Wilcox. *Second Coming: The New Christian Right in Virginia Politics*. Johns Hopkins University Press, 1996.

The authors investigate the influence of the religious right in Virginia politics since 1978 and analyze competition within the Republic party between the centrists and the religious right activists. The book focuses on two candidates strongly supported by the religious right who gained Republican party nominations: Michael Farris, who ran for lieutenant governor in 1993, and Oliver North, who ran for a seat in the U.S. Senate in 1994. Although neither was elected, their defeats by narrow margins may indicate further influence of the religious right in Virginia politics.

Rudin, James. *The Baptizing of America: The Religious Right's Plans for the Rest of Us*. Emeryville, CA: Avalon Publishing Group, 2006.

A retired U.S. Air Force chaplain, Rudin warns against what he considers the plan of Christian fundamentalists to gain influence in every aspect of American life, from the schoolroom to the hospital room to the courtroom. The author refers to Christian conservatives as "Christocrats" who jeopardize basic American rights and freedoms in their campaign to fulfill what they consider God's plan for the nation.

Shields, Carole. *Change the Hostile Climate*. Washington, DC: People for the American Way, 1999.

This publication, issued by People for the American Way, is an annual report on what the organization considers anti-gay discrimination by government, businesses, elected officials, and conservative religious groups across the nation. The 1999 edition reports on 300 such incidents.

Smidt, Corwin, ed. *Contemporary Evangelical Political Involvement: An Analysis and Assessment*. New York: University Press of America, 1989.

This edited volume contains both analytic and evaluative articles on the religious right. Contributors to the volume discuss such topics as the party identification of evangelicals, possible commonalities between evangelicals and secular humanists, the need for political sophistication among evangelicals, and possible limitations on the goals of a religious movement in a secular society.

Smith, Christian. *Christian America? What Evangelicals Really Want*. Berkeley, CA: University of California Press, 2000.

Continuing his analysis of evangelical Christians, Smith concludes from empirical studies that evangelicals are typically not extremists and do not believe in imposing their religious views of the world on the rest of society. The author indicates that evangelicals share with the rest of American society the same values of tolerance and individualism.

Snowball, David. *Continuity and Change in the Rhetoric of the Moral Majority*. Westport, CT: Praeger, 1991.

This study of the Moral Majority examines the history of the organization from 1979 to 1985, focusing on the rhetorical style its leaders employed to convey messages on such issues as abortion and pornography. The author investigates the interesting use of metaphor in organization statements and concludes with an evaluation of the Moral Majority, suggesting possible reasons for its termination.

Stacey, Judith. *In the Name of the Family: Rethinking Family Values in the Postmodern Age*. Boston, MA: Beacon, 1997.

Contrary to conservative and religious right positions regarding family breakdown and the consequent need to restore family values, including male authority, Stacey argues that alternative forms of family organization, including homosexual marriage, represent viable social groupings.

Stanton, Elizabeth Cady. *The Woman's Bible*. Northeastern University Press, 1993.

Originally published in the 1890s, this reworking of the Bible by one of the more noted figures of the women's movement challenges the commonly expressed conservative Christian view, still expressed in the religious right, that women should remain subservient to men. Focusing on scriptural passages involving women, Stanton claimed that the Bible was a major cause of the suppression of women.

Wald, Kenneth D. *Religion and Politics in the United States*. Fourth edition. Lanham, MD: Rowman and Littlefield, 2003.

Wald's overview of religion and politics in the United States extends beyond evangelical religious activity to include other religious influences. Although the author notes the secular nature of American society, he recognizes the importance of traditional interactions between religion and politics. Wald discusses the incentives for religious intervention in politics as well as the limitations on religious influence in that sphere.

Wallis, Jim. *God's Politics: Why the Right Gets It Wrong and the Left Doesn't Get It*. New York: Harper San Francisco, 2005.

Wallis, an evangelical and founder of Sojourners, an organization of progressive Christians working for peace and justice, claims that while the political right has taken possession of the language of faith in order to further the conservative agenda, the political left has generally separated moral discussions from public policy. Highly critical of the Republican party's association with the conservative Christian movement, Wallis calls on public officials and the religious community to emphasize such values as justice, peace, equality, and an inclusive understanding of the family.

———. *The Soul of Politics: Beyond "Religious Right" and "Secular Left"*. Orlando, FL: Harcourt, 1995.

Relying on personal experiences with the problems of ghettos in Washington, DC, Wallis contends that liberal and conservative emphases on social justice or individual values do not provide solutions. He calls for a reintegration of politics and spirituality.

Watson, Justin. *The Christian Coalition: Dreams of Restoration, Demands for Recognition*. New York: St. Martin's, 1997.

Basing much of his analysis on the writings of Pat Robertson and Ralph Reed, leaders of the Christian Coalition, Watson traces the conservative Christian organization from its founding in 1989 through its political successes, often based on accommodations with political allies. The author discusses the organization's objectives and offers explanations for its popularity among many Americans and its political influence. Although the vast majority of Americans profess to believe in a Christian God, the Coalition perceives itself as representing a minority beleaguered by a socially and politically liberal society.

Weber, Paul J., and W. Landis Jones. *U.S. Religious Interest Groups*. Westport, CT: Greenwood Press, 1994.

The authors present information on 120 national religious organizations in the United States. Although not limited to conservative groups, the volume includes a number of organizations on the religious right. The book contains a chapter on the history of religious interest groups in America.

Welch, Robert.*The Blue Book of the John Birch Society*. Appleton, WI: Western Islands, 1959, 1961, 1992.

This book is a transcript of the two-day presentation Robert Welch made at a meeting with eleven other men in 1958 that began the organization named for a fundamentalist Baptist missionary. Welch observes the loss of faith among fundamentalists of all religions and warns that this faith is being replaced by opportunism and hedonism. Communists are taking advantage of this loss. Though believing that fundamentalist faith cannot be restored, Welch suggests a broader faith that will be acceptable to "the most fundamentalist Christian or the most rationalistic idealist."

White, Mel. *Religion Gone Bad: Hidden Dangers of the Christian Right*. New York: Penguin, 2006.

White, a gay man who formerly served in the Christian right movement, claims that the leaders of the religious right are attempting to destroy the wall of separation between church and state, have the U.S. Constitution interpreted in terms of their Christian values, and replace democracy with a theocracy. The author perceives that the religious right leadership is conducting a war against gays and lesbians and will ultimately become a threat to anyone who disagrees with it.

———. *Stranger at the Gates: To Be Gay and Christian*. New York: Penguin, 1995.

White recounts his experiences as a ghostwriter for major figures in the religious right such as Jerry Falwell and Pat Robertson even though he was gay. The author tried various "cures," but ultimately accepted his homosexuality. White claims that the religious right has distorted the Bible to find condemnations of homosexuality and notes that gays have become a target of conservative Christians as a fundraising technique. He went on to become dean of Dallas Cathedral of Hope, a church that maintains an outreach to the gay and lesbian community.

Wilcox, Clyde. *God's Warriors: The Christian Right in Twentieth-Century America*. Baltimore: Johns Hopkins University Press, 1992.

This study of religion and conservative politics provides a historical survey of the religious right through the twentieth century and examines previous efforts that used statistical analysis to explain religious activism. The book explores not only the Christian right and anticommunist movement of the 1950s, but also the more current fundamentalist and Pentecostal movements led by individuals such as Jerry Falwell and Pat Robertson.

Wilcox, Clyde, and Carin Larson. *Onward Christian Soldiers? The Religious Right in American Politics*. Third edition. Nashville, TN: Westview, 2006.

In this revised third edition, Wilcox and Larson update the history of the religious right movement, detailing its increasing influence in American society and politics. The authors claim that although religious right mobilization played a significant role in George W. Bush's re-election in 2004 and in the passage of state constitutional amendments banning same-sex marriage, in most cases, the movement's policy agenda still has not been fulfilled.

Willis, Clint, and Nate Hardcastle, eds. *Jesus Is Not a Republican: The Religious Right's War on America*. Emeryville, CA: Avalon, 2005.

The authors in this edited work argue that the religious right uses the name of Jesus to further policies leading to injustice and war and that benefit the rich and powerful. Jim Wallis, founder of Sojourners, argues that the Bible calls for people to work for social justice. The editors claim that members of the Republican party, who invoke strong religious beliefs, pursue policies that Jesus would reject.

Section 2: Works From the Religious Right

This second section includes works on a wide variety of subjects relevant to the religious right. There is, of course, unavoidable overlap among the various categories, as the writers range from personal accounts of the development of their beliefs to explorations of how those beliefs relate to the contemporary world. The categories in this section are *The Religious Right Worldview; Political and Economic Issues; Personal and Family Topics;* and *Millenarianism*.

In order to understand the political motivations and actions of those in the religious right, it is necessary to grasp the way in which conservative Christians view the world and their place in it. In *The Religious Right Worldview*, authors treat such topics as popular culture and cultural relativism, the compatibility of faith and scientific naturalism, the nation's Christian heritage, patriotism, and biblical prophecy and scriptural inerrancy.

The second category, *Political and Economic Issues*, focuses on the stances that representatives of the religious right have taken on specific political and economic issues as well as their perceptions of political engagement in general. Among the various topics covered are abortion, prayer in the public schools, economics, taxation, welfare, homosexuality, judicial decision making, euthanasia, capital punishment, and foreign policy.

Personal and Family Topics is of special interest given the great importance conservative Christians place on the role the family plays in maintaining religious values and moral behavior that provide the foundation for a Christian nation.

A final category, *Millenarianism*, includes several examples of the "end-times" literature that flooded book stores as the new millennium approached. Conservative Christian writers have continued to publish such literature for a receptive audience. Some have suggested that the belief among many conservative Christians, especially premillennialists, that true believers will be raptured from the earth in the final days prior to the "great tribulation" has resulted in a lack of major concern among many evangelical and fundamentalist Christians for such contemporary problems as pollution and global warming.

The Religious Right Worldview

Abanes, Richard. *The Truth Behind the Da Vinci Code: A Challenging Response to the Bestselling Novel*. Eugene, OR: Harvest House, 2004.

Abanes's book is representative of the large number of publications that conservative Christian apologists have written in response to Dan Brown's fictional work, *The Da Vinci Code*. Abanes deals with such claims as the marriage of Jesus and Mary magdalene, the church's suppression of other Gospels, and the true nature of the Holy Grail.

Ackerman, Paul D. *In God's Image After All: How Psychology Supports Biblical Creationism*. Grand Rapids, MI: Baker Books, 1990.

Ackerman relates psychological notions such as personality, self-will, perception, and self-image to biblical accounts. The author concludes that psychological data support the truth of scripture and the creation story.

Anderson, Leith. *Winning the Values War in a Changing Culture: Thirteen Distinct Values That Mark a Follower of Jesus Christ*. Minneapolis, MN: Bethany House, 1994.

Pointing to such phenomena as high rates of divorce and illegitimate births as signs of cultural collapse, Anderson argues that those in the Christian community too often act like the rest of society. To overcome what he considers the dangers of relativism, the author recommends that Christians adhere to thirteen biblically based values in order to win what he calls the values war.

Ankerberg, John, and John Weldon. *Darwin's Leap of Faith: Exposing the False Religion of Evolution*. Eugene, OR: Harvest House, 1998.

Ankerberg and Weldon examine the evolution versus creation controversy, arguing that the Darwinian theory of evolution resembles a religion more than a scientific theory. The authors accuse Americans who adhere to the theory of evolution of persecuting those who do not.

Bakker, Jim. *Prosperity and the Coming Apocalypse*. Nashville, TN: Nelson, 1998.

Bakker, former head of the PTL ministry who was imprisoned for the misuse of donated funds, explains his beliefs about the end of the world. Bakker, who revealed in *I Was Wrong* his changed position on the place of wealth in a Christian's life, claims that contemporary Christians have developed a dependency on money, material things, and all the conveniences of modern society that have often become substitutes for God. Regarding eschatology, Bakker believes Christians will undergo at least part of the Great Tribulation prophesied in the book of Revelation.

Ball, William B., ed. *In Search of a National Morality: A Manifesto for Catholics and Evangelicals*. Grand Rapids, MI: Baker Books, 1992.

These articles by Catholic and evangelical Protestant scholars present moderate religious right positions on issues with which it is hoped many Catholics and Protestants can agree. Among the topics covered are government and politics, secularization, abortion, education, family values, and morality.

Barton, David. *The Bulletproof George Washington: An Account of God's Providential Care*. Aledo, TX: Wallbuilders, 1990.

In this brief book Barton, believing God has granted special protection to the United States, focuses on God's alleged protection of George Washington during the French and Indian War. According to the author, Washington expressed appreciation for God's intervention in his life.

Behe, Michael J. Tenth edition. *Darwin's Black Box: The Biochemical Challenge to Evolution*. New York: Simon and Schuster, 2006.

Behe, a biochemist and Roman Catholic, offers a scientific argument for the existence of God. Originally published in 1996, this book contributed to the popularity of intelligent design as an alternative to the Darwinian theory of evolution. Examining such examples as blood clotting and vision, the author observes an irreducible complexity at the micro level that science cannot explain. Arguing that Charles Darwin's gradualistic theory of evolution is inadequate in explaining elaborate life processes, Behe posits an intelligent designer.

Blamires, Harry. *The Post-Christian Mind: How Should a Christian Think?* Ann Arbor, MI: Vine, 1997.

Taking a broad brush, Blamires criticizes contemporary society, claiming it is dominated by a "new paganism." Examining contemporary directions in such areas as human rights, morality, health, and politics, the author identifies secularism as a major threat to civilization and Christianity. He calls Christians to oppose what he considers cultural decadence encouraged by bad laws and a morally indifferent mass media.

Bock, Darrell L. *Breaking the Da Vinci Code: Answering the Questions Everybody's Asking*. Nashville, TN: Thomas Nelson, 2004.

Bock adds to the large number of responses to Dan Brown's fictional work, *The Da Vinci Code*, a book that raises doubts about some of the basic beliefs of Christians. Meant to assure Christians of their faith, Bock's book deals with such claims as the existence of secret organizations that have hidden centuries-old secrets that could reveal the true nature of Jesus, including the possibility that he was married to Mary magdalene, who was one of the disciples.

Boys, Don. *Pilgrims, Puritans, and Patriots: Our Christian Heritage*. Maitland, FL: Freedom University/Freedom Seminary/Freedom Institute Press, 1983.

Boys examines the history and beliefs of the early settlers to the North American continent in order to trace the nation's Christian heritage. He discusses the religious beliefs of Columbus and the Puritans and the motivations of the colonists in coming to the New World. An additional topic is the meaning of the First Amendment and the role Christians have played in defending personal and religious freedom.

Bright, Bill, and Ron Jenson. *Kingdoms at War: Tactics for Victory in Nine Spiritual War Zones*. San Bernadino, CA: Here's Life Publishers, 1986.

To Bright and Jenson Christians are engaged in a war for the minds of Americans. The enemy is humanism. It is a war that requires commitment and sacrifice and does not allow for neutrality. This war entered a new phase when the Supreme Court in 1963 restricted Bible reading in public schools. The authors blame this decision for a series of evils, including political assassinations.

Brown, Walter T. *In the Beginning: Compelling Evidence for Creation and the Flood*. Phoenix, AZ: Center for Scientific Creation, 1995.

Brown defends creationism, employing geological, fossil, and biological data. The author employs traditional discussions of the worldwide flood recorded in the book of Genesis and the purported resulting geological evidence to support creationsim and to debunk evolution.

Colson, Chuck. *How Now Shall We Live?* Wheaton, IL: Tyndale House, 1999.

Colson, a White House official during the Richard Nixon administration who became a born-again Christian while serving time in prison for misdeeds committed during the Watergate scandal, diagnoses the flaws he sees in American culture and offers a religious-based solution. The author describes a culture characterized by disintegrating civility, violence, and moral indifference. He claims that although the culture presently dismisses and ridicules Christianity, only adherence to biblical principles can save the nation.

Crismier, Charles. *Preserve Us a Nation: Returning to Our Historical and Biblical Roots*. Sisters, OR: Multnomah, 1995.

Crismier views such problems as gangs, family dissolution, and unorthodox sexual practices as symptoms of a loss of moral character. He wants to return to a past time when biblical principles were practiced so that religious faith might be rekindled and moral character reestablished.

Davis, Percival, and Dean H. Kenyon. *Of Pandas and People: The Central Question of Biological Origins*. Dallas, TX: Haughton, 1989.

Davis and Kenyon present an argument for intelligent design as an alternative to Darwinian evolution theory. The work is made more attractive through the inclusion of seventy-five color photographs.

DeMar, Gary. *America's Christian Heritage*. Nashville, TN: Broadman and Holman, 2003.

Using historical sources, DeMar argues that the United States was established on Christian principles. The author presents quotations indicating that earlier Americans recognized the importance of Christianity to the founding of the nation.

DeMar, Gary. *America's Christian History: The Untold Story*. 2nd rev. ed. Powder Springs, GA: American Vision, 1993.

DeMar continues his argument, begun in earlier works, that the United States is, and always has been, fundamentally a Christian nation. The author examines events in American history, providing what he considers proof that Christianity shaped the basic character of the nation.

Dembski, William A. *Intelligent Design: The Bridge Between Science and Theology*. Downers Grove, IL: InterVarsity, 1999.

Dembski, a supporter of the view that creation was the result of an intelligent force, deals with such topics as the perception of divine activity in nature, the importance of miracles, and criticisms of evolutionary theories.

Dembski, William A., ed. *Mere Creation: Science, Faith, and Intelligent Design*. Downers Grove, IL: InterVarsity, 1999.

The essays included in this work, written by nineteen scholars in the fields of mathematics, physics, astrophysics, biology, philosophy, and theology, explore possible weaknesses in, and question the foundations of, Darwinian theory.

Denton, Michael. *Evolution: A Theory in Crisis*. Portland, OR: Alder and Alder, 1997.

Denton, a self-proclaimed agnostic, challenges traditional theories of biological evolution. After an analysis of fossil records and biochemical data, he concludes that exclusively natural evolution cannot explain the biological diversity existing on earth.

DeParrie, Paul. *Dark Cures: Have Doctors Lost Their Ethics?* Lafayette, LA: Vital Issue, 1999.

De Parrie argues that since traditional ethical standards have been replaced by "pagan ethics," people can no longer assume that doctors and medical institutions hold in high regard the health and well-being of patients. The author laments the development of a medical profession that disregards human life, harvesting body parts of people considered less valuable, and using aborted fetuses for profit.

Devos, Dick. *Rediscovering American Values: The Foundations of Our Freedom for the 21st Century*. East Rutherford, NJ: Dutton, 1997.

Devos outlines twenty-four values, including honesty, compassion, initiative, self-discipline, and leadership, which he claims are the basis of liberty and will guide the country into the next century. The author believes these values provide the foundation for American power and prosperity.

Drosnin, Michael. *The Bible Code*. New York: Simon and Schuster, 1998.

This book has the same popular appeal that Hal Lindsey's *The Late Great Planet Earth* had three decades ago. Both books foreshadow coming disasters for humankind. Drosnin's account is based on the claim that the Old Testament contains a secret code that, once deciphered through computer programs, reveals many past wars, famines, floods, assassinations, and wars as well as possible future catastrophes. Some argue that the appeal of this book and others like it is associated with a desire to believe in a divine order behind the apparent chaos of events.

Federer, William J. *America's God and Country: Encyclopedia of Quotations*. Coppell, TX: Fame, 1996.

This lengthy work (over 800 pages) presents inspirational quotes from prominent early Americans, presidents, statesmen, court decisions, military heroes, scientists and inventors, religious leaders, educators, and artists. Federer attempts to demonstrate that national leaders have relied on God for their inspiration and that they built the nation on biblical principles.

Guiness, Os, and John Seel, eds. *No God But God: Breaking with the Idols of Our Age*. Chicago: Moody Press, 1992.

This group of essays deals with the perceived problems of contemporary evangelicalism. An over-reliance on marketing and management techniques, psychology, and politics has created idols that threaten the true Christian mission. The authors ask American evangelicals to recall their long past, confront modern idolatry, and campaign for religious freedom for all.

Hagee, John C. *The Revelation of Truth: A Mosaic of God's Plan for Man*. Nashville, TN: Nelson, 2000.

Taking a dispensational perspective popularized by C.I. Scofield, Hagee outlines the seven time periods from creation to the end time and the creation of a new heaven and a new earth. He argues that the time of Jesus's return is drawing near.

Ham, Kenneth. *The Lie: Evolution*. Green Forest, AR: Master Books, 1996.

Ham seeks to discredit Charles Darwin's theory of evolution, challenging the veracity of evolution theorists. Referring to scripture, the author employs arguments developed earlier in the twentieth century, contending that the theory of evolution is a serious threat to moral values. Ham associates biological evolution with the social philosophy of Social Darwinism developed by Herbert Spencer.

Ham, Kenneth, Andrew Snelling, and Carl Wieland. *The Answers Book*. Colorado Springs, CO: Master Books, 1991.

The authors attempt to answer questions of concern to supporters of the biblical creation thesis. They tackle such topics as dinosaurs and their extinction, the ice ages, the origin of different races, and the origin of animals in Australia.

Hanegraaff, Hank. *Christianity in Crisis*. Eugene, OR: Harvest House, 1993.

Hanegraaff, president of Christian Research Institute, offers an evangelical warning against the 'faith movement' and its leaders, among whom are Kenneth Copeland, Charles Capps, and Paul Crouch. Those in the faith movement, by emphasizing such things as physical healing and financial prosperity, stray from the orthodox Christian understanding of God. The book demonstrates the sort of disagreements that arise within conservative Christianity.

Hanegraaff, Hank. *The Face That Demonstrates the Farce of Evolution*. Nashville, TN: Word, 1998.

Hanegraaff, president of the Christian Research Institute, argues that the evolutionary theory of human existence cannot be correct. Citing racistt quotes from Charles Darwin, the author attempts to associate evolution with racism. Contending that the theory of evolution depends on the working of random chance, Hanegraaff asserts that the probability is extremely small that complex biological systems could have developed randomly.

Hayward, Alan. *Creation and Evolution*. Minneapolis, MN: Bethany House, 1995.

Using biblical references regarding creation, scientific data about evolution, and an investigation of the age of the universe, Hayward concludes that, statistically, the Darwinian theory of evolution is defective.

Hittinger, Russell. *First Grace: Rediscovering the Natural Law in a Post-Christian World*. Wilmington, DE: ISI Books, 2002.

First defining natural law and its relationship to positive law, Hittinger discusses the guidance that natural law can and should provide for judicial decision making. The author objects to the tendency of liberals in the legal establishment to emphasize privacy to such an extent that the individual reaches sovereign status. Hittinger approaches several contemporary issues from the perspective of natural law.

Howse, Brannon. *One Nation Under Man? The Worldview War Between Christians and the Secular Left*. Nashville, TN: Broadman and Holman, 2005.

Howse claims that contemporary liberalism, based on a religious belief in humanism, is anti-American. The author argues that liberals use intimidation to advance their agenda of defeating conservative political candidates, legalizing same-gender marriage, and passing right-to-die laws. In contrast to the liberal perspective, the sources of U.S. civil laws, Howse argues, are the moral laws of the Bible and the Ten Commandments.

Hunter, Cornelius G. *Darwin's Proof: The Triumph of Religion Over Science*. Grand Rapids, MI: Brazos, 2003.

Contrary to the claims of supporters of Darwin's theory of evolution, Hunter argues that the Darwinian theory makes basic assumptions about the character of God, and that the creator that Darwin rejected is more closely associated with Deism and nineteenth-century natural theology than with traditional Christianity. Hunter tends to support the position of conservative Christians on the question of evolution.

Huse, Scott M. *The Collapse of Evolution*. Grand Rapids, MI: Baker, 1998.

Examining the evidence for the theory of evolution and using the Bible as a source of information, Huse contends that evolution and creationism are incompatible. Noting examples of design in the natural world, the author concludes that evolution is fatally flawed. An appendix titled "Scientific Facts that Prove Evolution" is left blank.

Jakes, T.D. *The Great Investment: Faith, Family and Finance*. New York: Putnam, 2000.

T.D. Jakes, the popular television minister, discusses the relevance of the Christian faith to the maintenance of the family and achieving economic prosperity. Jakes states that God calls Christians to prosper so that their wealth can be used to spread the Gospel. He advises people to act wisely in financial matters, distinguishing between needs and wants and avoiding gambling and lotteries.

Johnson, Phillip. *Darwin On Trial*. Washington, DC: Regnery, 1991.

This book offers an interesting analysis of Darwin's theory of evolution conducted by a legal expert. Johnson charges that scientists inappropriately accept Darwin's theory and have unsuccessfully attempted to establish supporting evidence. The author examines the problem of fossils and other topics relevant to a creationist response to evolution.

———— . *Defeating Darwinism By Opening Minds*. Downers Grove, IL: InterVarsity, 1997.

Attempting to turn the tables on pro-evolution arguments, Johnson claims that clear thinking about the issues involved in the creation-evolution debate will result in greater skepticism about the validity of Darwinian theory.

———— . *Reason in the Balance: The Case Against Naturalism in Science, Law and Education*. Downers Grove, IL: InterVarsity, 1998.

Johnson challenges naturalism, the belief dominating the contemporary worldview which holds that the material world is all that has existed or ever will exist. According to the author, this belief has had adverse moral consequences for science, law, and education.

———— . *Objections Sustained: Subversive Essays on Evolution, Law and Culture*. Downers Grove, IL: InterVarsity, 1998.

In this volume of collected essays, Johnson criticizes what he calls the "idolatry of Darwin." Topics include American pragmatism, postmodernism, "pop" science, and religious freedom.

———— . *The Wedge of Truth: Splitting the Foundations of Naturalism*. Downers Grove, IL: InterVarsity, 2000.

Johnson argues that naturalism, which he states has been the dominant perspective of contemporary science, will no longer hold its preeminent place. The author believes the message of Christianity offers a new beginning for consideration not only of science and religion but of all meaningful human activity.

Kennedy, D. James, ed. *The Gates of Hell Shall Not Prevail: The Attack on Christianity and What You Need to Know to Combat It*. Nashville, TN: Nelson, 1997.

Noting that Christianity has often been the subject of attack throughout its history and presently is the subject of a culture war, the authors insist the church always has, and always will, prevail. They contend the church continues to grow despite such attacks and that opponents are historically destined to lose.

Klicka, Christopher J., and Gregg Harris. *The Right Choice: The Incredible Failure of Public Education and the Rising Hope of Home Schooling*. Rev. ed. Gresham, OR: Noble Books, 1994.

Klicka sets forth for parents considering home schooling the cultural beliefs supposedly being inculcated in the public schools. D. James Kennedy, a major religious leader, has written the foreward, and Gregg Harris of Christian Life Workshops offers practical advice about how to begin home schooling.

Knight, Robert H. *The Age of Consent: The Rise of Relativism and the Corruption of Popular Culture*. Dallas, TX: Spence, 1998.

With a foreward by 2000 religious right presidential candidate Gary Bauer, this book focuses on the dangers of philosophical relativism. Knight investigates what he considers the indications of cultural decline in such areas as film, television, popular music, architecture, and even religion.

LaHaye, Tim. *The Race for the 21st Century*. Nashville, TN: Thomas Nelson, 1986.

The race referred to in the title is the competition between Christians and humanists for control of American culture into the twenty-first century. The Christian must not only guard his family against humanist pressures, but also work to defeat the humanistic forces that are distorting society. Although LaHaye accepts political pluralism among religious groups, he rejects any legitimate political role for secular humanists.

———. *Faith of Our Founding Fathers*. Brentwood, TN: Wolgemuth and Hyatt, 1987.

A leading figure in the Christian right provides his perceptions of the constitutional framers' religious beliefs. LaHaye stresses, in some cases beyond credibility, what he considers the Christian beliefs of the framers, concluding the nation was founded on a general agreement regarding Christian principles.

LaHaye, Tim, and David Noebel. *Mind Siege: The Battle for Truth in the New Millenium*. Nashville, TN: Word, 2001.

LaHaye, coauthor of the popular *Left Behind* series, and Noebel, president of the Christian Anti-Communism Crusade, expose the alleged dangers of secular humanism. They claim that mainline churches have accepted many of the tenets of humanism, including evolution, socialism, higher criticism of the Bible, moral relativism, liberation theology, and world government.

Lightner, Robert P. *The Last Days Handbook: A Comprehensive Guide to Understanding the Different Views of Prophecy*. Nashville, TN: Thomas Nelson, 1990.

This is a good source for understanding an issue important to many on the religious right. Lightner discusses the premillennial, amillennial, and postmillennial approaches to biblical prophecy, acknowledging that sharp disagreements sometimes emerge over these various positions. The author encourages evangelical Christians to recognize basic agreements over biblical prophecy.

Lindsey, Hal. *Planet Earth–2000 A.D.* Palos Verdes, CA: Western Front, 1994.

Lindsey discounts any inherent significance to the year 2000 but does suggest that the 'seven-year countdown' to Christ's return could begin before that date. Lindsey refers to a variety of occurrences, including political events in Asia and the Middle East, the formation of the European Community, the increased popularity of occultism, an increasing crime rate, the spread of AIDS, and more severe natural disasters such as earthquakes and floods to support his argument that the end times are near.

MacArthur, John. *Reckless Faith: When the Church Loses Its Will To Discern.* Wheaton, IL: Crossway, 1994.

MacArthur expresses a common concern among more fundamentalist Christians about the moral health of American churches. He believes modern secular society, in which no limits on behavior seem to exist, has had too great an influence on the church. Using biblical prescriptions, MacArthur suggests ways in which Christians can discern the authentic from the inauthentic in the church.

Machen, J. Gresham. *Christianity and Liberalism*. Grand Rapids, MI: Eerdmans, 1997.

Originally published in 1923, this book presents an "orthodox" Christian response to a more liberal theology that became popular in the early twentieth century. Machen deals with distinctions between liberalism and orthodoxy in such areas as the relationship between God and man, the authority of the Bible, the person of Christ, the meaning of salvation, and the institution of the church. Machen's views influenced the development of more recent positions taken by the religious right.

Marshall, Peter, and David Manuel. *Sounding Forth the Trumpet*. Grand Rapids, MI: Baker, 1998.

In this third volume examining American history from a conservative Christian perspective, the authors investigate the events preceding the Civil War. The book begins with John Quincy Adams's administration and closes with the 1860 election, focusing on those people the authors believe were used by God to shape the history of the nation.

Matrisciana, Carly, and Roger Oakland. *The Evolution Conspiracy*. Eugene, OR: Harvest House, 1991.

Defending the Christian fundamentalist position on creationisn, the authors portray the conflict between creationism and evolution theory as one between two religions. The authors emphasize what they consider the moral consequences of a complete victory for evolution theory.

McDowell, Josh, and Bob Hostetler. *The New Tolerance: How a Cultural Movement Threatens to Destroy You, Your Faith, and Your Children*. Wheaton, IL: Tyndale, 1998.

The authors argue that tolerance, often considered a positive virtue, in fact threatens the maintenance of a Christian society. They object to a permissive attitude toward what they consider threats to Christian beliefs, such as homosexuality, feminism, and alternative religious beliefs.

Moreland, J. P., ed. *The Creation Hypothesis: Scientific Evidence for an Intelligent Designer*. Downersgrove, IL: InterVarsity, 1994.

The authors of these essays argue that explanations for the existence of the universe and of life must include God. Contributors deal with the beginnings of life, the source of organic groupings, explanations of language, and the origins of the universe, with emphasis placed on the "Big Bang" theory.

Moreland, J.P., and Scott B. Rae. *Body and Soul: Human Nature and the Crisis in Ethics*. Downers Grove, IL: InterVarsity Press, 2000.

Holding the traditional doctrine of Christian dualism, Moreland and Rae argue that ethical questions of abortion, fetal research, cloning, and euthanasia must be informed by the religious view that human beings possess a soul.

Noebel, David A. *Understanding the Times: The Religious Worldviews of Our Day and the Search for Truth*. Eugene, OR: Harvest House, 1994.

Noebel, president of Summit Ministries and an associate of the Christian Anticommunism Crusade, compares and contrasts four major contemporary world views: Christianity, Marxism/Leninism, Secular Humanism, and the New Age Movement. According to the author, a world view includes beliefs about theology, philosophy, ethics, biology, psychology, sociology, law, politics, economics, and history. Noebel, who asserts the superiority of Christianity over the other world views, has been criticized for failing to consider other religious faiths.

North, Gary. *Is the World Running Down?: Crisis in the Christian Worldview*. Tyler, TX: Institute for Christian Economics, 1988.

North urges the religious right to accept pluralism. Those on the religious right should be willing to strive within the existing governmental structure, a strategy which has already brought some success. Nonetheless, North does not lose sight of conservative Christian values that are ultimately hostile to a pluralist perspective.

Novak, Michael, and Jana Novak. *Washington's God: Religion, Liberty, and the Father of Our Country*. New York: Basic Books, 2006.

Michael Novak and his daughter Jana attempt to refute assumptions that historians have made about George Washington's religious beliefs, such as that he was a deist and had no strong religious convictions. Examining Washington's public and private speeches and correspondence, the authors conclude that the first president expressed deep religious feelings.

Oakland, Roger, with Dan Wooding. *Let There Be Light*. Santa Ana, CA: Oakland Communications, 1993.

This work contrasts the moral and religious effects of evolution and creation theories. The authors contend the teaching of evolution has been deceitful and has taken God out of people's lives, while creationism, restores humankind's relationship with God.

Oden, Thomas C. *Turning Around the Mainline: How Renewal Movements Are Changing the Church*. Grand Rapids, MI: Baker, 2006.

Oden, an executive editor of the evangelical magazine *Christianity Today*, discusses the rise of renewal movements in the mainline denominations, including the United Methodist Church, the Episcopal Church, the Presbyterian Church (U.S.A.), and the United Church of Christ. Members of these movements adhere to evangelical beliefs and attempt to move their denominations in a more conservative direction.

O'Hear, Anthony. *Beyond Evolution: Human Nature and the Limits of Evolutionary Explanation*. New York: Oxford University Press, 1999.

While not writing from a Christian perspective, O'Hear contends the Darwinian theory fails to account for crucial aspects of human existence, including human consciousness, the search for knowledge, a sense of morality, and the perception of beauty.

Parks, Jerald. *False Security: Has the New Age Given Us a False Hope?* Lafayette, LA: Huntington House, 1992.

Parks examines the New Age claim that humankind is being transformed into a higher level of civilization and compares it to biblical notions of the last days and the collapse of civilization. Humanity may be faced with a time of darkness not seen since the fall of the Roman Empire and the beginning of the Middle Ages.

Pearcy, Nancy. *Total Truth: Liberating Christianity from Its Cultural Captivity*. Wheaton, IL: Crossway, 2006.

Pearcy discusses the public/private division regarding religion, arguing that such a split limits the possibility of personal and cultural advance. She provides advice to Christians who wish to free Christianity from its captivity to current culture.

Pearcy, Nancy, and Charles B. Thaxton. *The Soul of Science: Christian Faith and Natural Philosophy*. Wheaton, IL: Crossway, 1994.

Pearcy and Thaxton distinguish between a period when scientists and people generally accepted Christianity publicly and more recent times in which science has become hostile to Christian belief. The authors relate the accomplishments of scientists such as Robert Boyle, Isaac Newton, and Carl Linnaeus, whose scientific achievements occurred in the context of the Christian faith.

Peretti, Frank E. *The Oath*. Nashville, TN: Word, 1996.

This best-selling fictional account of a small town's struggle with sinister forces is relevant to the cultural views of the religious right, portraying a battle between forces of good and forces of evil in this world.

Pierce, Alfred R. *It Is Finished*. Rev. ed. Camden, N J: Radiant Publications, 1993.

A lawyer, former mayor of Camden, New Jersey, former chairman of the Delaware River Port Authority, and student of the Bible, Pierce claims the United States is the Babylon of the Book of Revelation and will be destroyed. He argues that Satan is now in control of the world.

Pitts, F. E. *The U.S.A. in Bible Prophecy: Two Sermons Preached to the U.S. Congress in 1857*. Baltimore: J.W. Bull, 1862.

These two sermons, 'The United States of America Foretold in the Holy Scriptures' and 'The Battle of Armageddon,' delivered prior to the Civil War, are notable for their inclusion of the United States in biblical prophecy. Pitts identifies the United States and Russia as those powers described in Ezekiel 38 that will be involved in the final battle of Armageddon.

Quayle, Dan. *Worth Fighting For*. Nashville, TN: Word, 2000.

Former Vice President Dan Quayle argues that scandal in government and unwise policies have led the United States in the wrong direction. To set the country on the right track, Quayle believes, will require a return to faith in God and a willingness to take responsibility for one's own actions. The author offers his position on such subjects as social security, abortion, and gay marriage.

Richards, Jay W., and Guillermo Gonzalez. *The Privileged Planet: How Our Place in the Cosmos Is Designed for Discovery*. Washington, DC: Regnery, 2004.

Richards, who earned a Ph.D. in philosophy and theology from Princeton Theological Seminary, and Gonzalez, assistant professor of astronomy at Iowa State University, argue for the unique condition of the earth in the universe. For instance, the claim that the way the earth is positioned in the Milky Way provides for conditions favorable to life as well as for making scientific discoveries about the mysteries of the universe. The implication of the authors' argument is that the earth is the result of an intelligent creator.

Robertson, Pat. *The New Millennium*. Dallas, TX: Word, 1990.

Robertson examines the history of Christianity, its present situation in the world, and its prospects for the twenty-first century. He claims the United States is the strongest Christian nation since the fall of the Roman Empire and the 'last great expression' of Christianity's victory.

Ross, Hugh. *Creation and Time: A Biblical and Scientific Perspective on the Creation-Date Controversy*. Colorado Springs, CO: NavPress, 1994

Ross attempts to resolve the apparent conflict between Christian and scientific views about the age of the earth and the beginning of the universe. He explores biblical texts and early church beliefs as well as scientific findings regarding these topics.

_____ . *The Genesis Question: Scientific Advances and the Accuracy of Genesis*. Colorado Springs, CO: NavPress, 1998.

Ross, a physicist and head of the organization Reasons To Believe, investigates the view that the biblical account of creation amounts to pre-scientific myth and attempts to demonstrate that the book of Genesis coincides with scientific evidence supporting divine intervention in the natural world.

Russo, Steve. *Halloween: What's a Christian To Do?* Eugene, OR: Harvest House, 1998.

Russo expresses the discomfort that evangelical Christian parents feel when faced with the traditions of the larger secular culture. He offers advice to parents who wish to protect their children against what are perceived to be pagan observances.

Schaeffer, Francis A. *A Christian Manifesto*. Westchester, IL: Crossway Books, 1981.

Written by perhaps the foremost conservative Christian political thinker, this work refutes socialism and humanism and calls Christians to organize against the trend toward immorality in our society. Schaeffer bases his argument on the notion of a 'form-free balance,' an equilibrium between social responsibility and individual rights. With the antiabortion movement in mind, the author justifies civil disobedience when the government demonstrates its tyrannical nature by disobeying the law of God.

_____ . *How Should We Then Live? The Rise and Decline of Western Thought and Culture*. Old Tappan, NJ: Fleming H. Revell, 1976.

Schaeffer did not mint the term 'secular humanism,' but in this sweeping assessment of western culture he certainly makes it the bete noire of conservative Christians in much of the English-speaking world. From the Greeks and Romans to the Renaissance and Enlightenment he contrasts the 'strengths' of Christianity, rooted in God's absolute truth, to the 'weaknesses' of human-centered cultures whose moral relativism inevitably led to a cheapening of human life. Schaeffer admires the Reformation, for it represented the restoration of divine absolutes.

_____ . *No Final Conflict: The Bible Without Error in All That It Affirms*. Downers Grove, IL: InterVarsity, 1975.

This is a vigorous defense of biblical literalism based upon a rather traditional fundamentalist position. That is, Schaeffer argues that if one questions the historicity of Genesis, such as the actual existence of Adam and Eve, for instance, there is no reason to trust any factual statement in the Bible, including the resurrection of Jesus.

_____ . *The God Who Is There*. Downer Groves, IL: InterVarsity, 1968.

Schaeffer emphasizes the nature of human despair in modern times. He investigates the origins of this condition of hopelessness and its evil consequences. Christianity is offered as the only means of combating despair.

_____ . *Escape From Reason*. Madison, WI: InterVarsity, 1968.

In this brief volume, Schaeffer investigates contemporary thought, tracing its development from Aquinas to the present. The author is highly critical of the present age, especially the 'God is dead' movement, the rejection of rationality, and the turn toward nonrational experience. Evangelical Christians are urged not to separate Jesus from the content of scripture.

Schlossberg, Herbert. *A Fragrance of Oppression: The Church and Its Persecutors*. Wheaton, IL: Crossways, 1991.

Beginning with the supposition that American culture is in crisis and that humanism has become the dominant perspective, Schlossberg provides biblical guidance for Christian believers who want to have an impact on American cultural institutions by voicing their preference for a Christian worldview.

Scofield, C.I. *Scofield Study Bible*. New York: Oxford University Press, 1917, 2004.

This King James version of the Bible contains extensive notes that present a fundamentalist perspective on such topics as dispensational premillennialism, scriptural inerrancy, and the distinction between Jews and Christians. This Bible became a major statement of belief for many conservative fundamentalist Christians. Oxford offers several versions of this still-popular Bible. The 2004 reader's edition includes the New King James Version (NKJV) translation of the Bible.

Shiflett, David. *Exodus: Why Americans Are Fleeing Liberal Churches for Conservative Christianity*. Frenchtown, NJ: Sentinel, 2005.

According to Shiflett, a conservative journalist, millions of members of mainline denominations are shifting to Catholic, evangelical, and Orthodox churches, which emphasize more traditional Christian beliefs. The author discusses the trend in mainline churches to emphasize inclusion more than sin and redemption, a course that more conservative members have been unable to prevent. Shiflett discusses the election of Gene Robinson, an openly gay priest, as a bishop in the Episcopal Church.

Spencer, James R. *Bleeding Hearts and Propaganda: The Fall of Reason in the Church*. Lafayette, LA: Huntington House, 1995.

Spencer criticizes popular church leaders for failing to maintain what he considers sound truth and principles of reason based on scripture. He faults some religious leaders for failing to maintain the tradition of biblical truth, compromising with contemporary secular beliefs, and participating in a general moral decline. He uses contemporary attitudes of some Christians toward homosexuality as an example of inappropriate compassion for what he considers a biblically unacceptable practice.

Stanley, Lynn. *The Blame Game: Why Society Persecutes Christians*. Lafayette, LA: Huntington House, 1996.

Stanley argues for absolute moral values, claiming the United States was built on Christian principles. She attacks the mass media for alleged attempts to repress Judeo-Christian values, and she targets the National Education Association for using public funds and public classrooms to establish humanism as the national religion of the United States. According to Stanley, New Age religions and occultism are being disseminated in school classrooms. To combat such tendencies, the author urges members of Christian churches to maintain a biblically sound way of life.

Strobel, Lee. *The Case for a Creator: A Journalist Investigates Scientific Evidence That Points Toward God*. Grand Rapids, MI: Zondervan, 2004.

Strobel attempts to demonstrate the compatibility of Christian beliefs and scientific theories. He investigates such topics as cellular biology, DNA research, astronomy, and physics, arguing that scientific discoveries present evidence for a creator.

Terrel, Steve. *The 90's, Decade of the Apocalypse: The European Common Markett–The End Has Begun*. South Plainfield, NJ: Bridge Publishing, 1992.

This premillennialist treatment of biblical prophecy shifts attention away from the United States and Russia to the formation of the European Community as a sign of the end times. The Antichrist will be the first president of the United States of Europe, and this person supposedly will become the emperor of a new Holy Roman Empire and will begin wars of conquest.

Thompson, Bert. *Creation Compromises*. Montgomery, AL: Apologetics Press, 1995.

Thompson surveys the 200-year development of geology, paying particular attention to the belief that geological discoveries are incompatible with biblical claims of a recent creation and a worldwide flood. Some scientists and theologians, attempting to discover evidence of a much older earth in scripture, are considered to be parties to a compromise.

Torrey, Reuben A., A. C. Dixon, et al. *The Fundamentals: A Testimony to the Truth*. 4 vols. Los Angeles, CA: Bible Institute of Los Angeles, 1917.

A set of twelve pamphlets each about 125 pages in length, these booklets not only assail modernism but also enunciate what came to be, and in essence still are, the key tenets of fundamentalism: the inerrancy of the Bible and the virgin birth, substitutionary atonement, bodily resurrection, and the second coming of Jesus. Along with these most frequently cited five fundamentals, the pamphlets emphasize the deity of Jesus, the sinful nature of humanity, salvation by faith, and the bodily resurrection of believers; they refute evolution and higher criticism; and they denounce Catholicism, Mormonism, Jehovah's Witnesses, Christian Scientists, and Spiritualism.

Van Bebber, Mark, and Paul Taylor. *Creation and Time: A Report on the Progressive Creationist Book by Hugh Ross*. Mesa, AZ: Eden Publications, 1994.

The authors criticize Hugh Ross, president of Reasons to Believe, for his advocacy of a 'progressive creation' position. While agreeing with Ross that life could not have arisen through natural processes, they point to his alleged erroneous biblical interpretations, such as the claim that the earth is billions of years old, that there was death before Adam's fall, and that the biblical flood was not worldwide.

Veith, Gene Edward, Jr. *Postmodern Times: A Christian Guide to Contemporary Thought and Culture*. Wheaton, IL: Crossway, 1994.

Veith associates postmodernism with a rejection of firm notions of truth, meaning, individual identity, and the value of human life. He argues that postmodernist ideas have proliferated among judges, writers, journalists, and teachers, and have had deep influences on film, television, art, film, literature, and politics. The author calls for a proclamation of the gospel in order to counteract the cultural consequences of postmodernist thought.

Walvoord, John F. *Armageddon, Oil and the Middle East Crisis: What the Bible Says about the Future of the Middle East and the End of Western Civilization*. Rev. ed. Grand Rapids, MI: Zondervan, 1990.

This contribution to apocalyptic literature explains why the presence of oil in the Middle East makes that region the focus of biblical prophecies about the final battle of Armageddon. Walvoord establishes a chronology of events he claims will lead to the rapture and Christ's return.

Walton, Rus. *FACS!: Fundamentals for American Christians*. Nyack, NY: Parson, 1979.

Walton portrays an America based on fundamental biblical principles. The American revolution was influenced by the political thought of John Locke, who is described as a Christian thinker. The conservative Christian objective is to return the United States to its Christian roots, and to reject any attempt to combine Christianity with humanism.

Watt, David Harrington. *Bible-Carrying Christians: Conservative Protestants and Social Power*. New York: Oxford University Press, 2002.

Watt identifies "Bible-carrying Christians" with evangelical and fundamentalist churches, which he claims have played an important role in determining the nature of contemporary American society. The author presents a view of conservative evangelicals Christians that he claims corrects the common misunderstandings of non-evangelical Americans.

Whitehead, John W. *The End of Man*. Westchester, IL: Crossway Books, 1986.

Although America still publicly expresses religious faith, Whitehead argues that the dissemination of humanist doctrines has become so extensive that discussion of what is right and wrong can no longer occur. The author advises Christians to maintain their values, avoid accommodation, and actively confront humanist beliefs.

Winnick, Pamela R. *A Jealous God: Science's Crusade Against Religion*. Nashville, TN: Thomas Nelson, 2005.

Claiming that science has itself become a religion, the author notes that the scientific community has imposed its worldview on the rest of society. Countering the arguments of others who claim that conservative Christians are meddling in science, Winnick contends that science is conducting a crusade against religion, promulgating atheism in textbooks, the classroom, and the mass media. According to the author, stem cell research has become a greedy race for grant dollars.

Zacharias, Ravi K.. *A Shattered Visage: The Real Face of Atheism*. Grand Rapids, Michigan: Baker Books, 1993.

The author contends America has proceeded toward atheism, both personally and institutionally. Christian civilization has been decimated by this atheism and citizens suffer the consequences of alienation, loneliness, and guilt. Zacharias claims that violence is a logical result of atheism.

_____ . *Deliver Us from Evil: Restoring the Soul in a Disintegrating Culture*. Nashville, TN: Word, 1998.

Zacharias argues that many contemporary popular ideas represent a threat to the traditional culture based on Christianity. Although humans have attempted to create an earthly utopia, the author contends they have ignored truth and the problem of evil and therefore have brought themselves close to social disintegration.

Political and Economic Issues

Alcorn, Randy C. *Is Rescuing Right?* Breaking the Law to Save the Unborn. Downers Grove, IL: InterVarsity, 1990.

Admitting that the rescuing strategy has been controversial within the Christian community, Alcorn nonetheless claims that the willingness of some to 'make sacrifices' means 'the lives of babies are being saved.' Christians should do all they can to prevent abortions, the author concludes, even taking part in civil disobedience if necessary.

Bahnsen, Greg L. *By This Standard: The Authority of God's Law Today*. Tyler, TX: Institute for Christian Economics, 1991.

Instead of the moral relativism which dominates contemporary society, Bahnsen argues that individual Christians and society as a whole should be guided by both Old and New Testament laws and precepts.

Barton, Charles D. *Myth of Separation*. Rev. ed. Aledo, TX: Wallbuilders, 1991.

Taking quotes from the writings of the constitutional founders and from Supreme Court decisions in the period 1795 to 1952, Barton argues the separation of church and state is more myth than historical fact. In Barton's view, American history supports a close union between church and state.

————— . *America: To Pray or Not To Pray*. Rev. ed. Aledo, Texas: Wallbuilders, 1989.

This work provides statistical evidence of an American decline ever since 1962, when the Supreme Court instituted the ban on school prayer and, according to the author, began to disallow religious principles generally in public affairs.

Benne, Robert. *Reasonable Ethics: A Chrisian Approach To Social, Economic, and Political Concerns*. St. Louis, MO: Concordia, 2006.

Identifying basic conservative Lutheran theological and ethical beliefs, Benne demonstrates how those beliefs provide appropriate perspectives on political, cultural, and economic issues as well as church concerns.

Bolton, Richard, ed. *Culture Wars: Documents from the Recent Controversies in the Arts*. New York: New Press, 1992.

This volume contains documents dealing with the controversy over funding the National Endowment for the Arts (NEA), including congressional testimony, scholarly articles, opinion pieces, and personal correspondence. Individuals on the religious right, including Jerry Falwell, were major critics of the NEA.

Borst, W. A. *Liberalism: Fatal Consequences*. Lafayette, LA: Vital Issue, 1998.

Recounting the history of the liberal ideology in the United States, Borst exposes what he claims is the hypocrisy of liberalism. The author wants to empower the reader to resist cultural changes he attributes to liberal thinking.

Carson, D. A. *The Gagging of God: Christianity Confronts Pluralism*. Grand Rapids, MI: Zondervan, 1996.

Carson, professor of the New Testament at Trinity Evangelical Divinity School, critically examines pluralism and pluralistic attitudes that he sees capturing American culture. The author rejects pluralistic perspectives, opting instead for what he considers the unique truth found in the New Testament account of Jesus.

Colson, Chuck, and Jack Eckerd. *Why America Doesn't Work: How the Decline of the Work Ethic Is Hurting Your Family and Future–and What You Can Do*. Dallas, TX: Word, 1991.

Colson, chairman of Prison Fellowship, and Eckerd, former head of the Eckerd drugstore chain, believe the spiritual foundation of the work ethic has eroded, thus causing many of the problems now facing the United States, including the decline of American competition in the world market, the deterioration of American schools, and the millions of unproductive people in prison and on welfare. The churches are given a major role in restoring the work ethic.

Colson, Chuck, with Ellen Santilli Vaughn. *Kingdoms in Conflict*. Grand Rapids, MI: William Morrow/Zondervan, 1987.

Colson, a former member of Richard Nixon's administration, was 'born again' while serving time in prison because of Watergate misdeeds. This volume presents his views on the relationship between the Christian church and politics.

Coulter, Ann H. *Godless: The Church of Liberalism*. New York: Crown Publishing Group, 2006.

In this controversial book, Coulter posits liberalism as a religion. She compares abortion to a sacrament, public school teachers to the clergy, public schools (where prayer is prohibited and, she claims, condoms are free), to the churches, and the 1973 U.S. Supreme Court abortion decision in *Roe v. Wade* to holy writ.

Dennehy, Raymond. *Anti-Abortionist at Large: How To Argue Intelligently About Abortion and Live To Tell About It*. For Collins, CO: Ignatius, 2002.

Dennehy, a professor of philosophy at the University of San Francisco, discusses his long experience of debating with those who support the right of abortion, providing advice to those who oppose abortion. He has appeared on radio and television and on university campuses around the nation.

Dobson, Ed, and Ed Hindson. *The Seduction of Power*. Old Tappan, NJ: H. Revell, 1988.

The authors, each of whom formerly worked with Jerry Falwell, reflect on the flurry of religious right activity in the 1980s. The authors appear less optimistic about the results of this political activity, but recognize the need for continued, but possibly more subdued, involvement.

Domingo, Roger. *Orphans in Babylon: Abortion in America. Where Are We Now? How Did We Get Here? Where Should We Go?* Sun City, CA: Turnstyle, 1998.

Presenting an overview of the pro-life movement, Domingo's purpose is to prepare readers for a ministry of saving "orphans" in what he considers the hostile world of American culture, which he refers to as "Babylon."

Doner, Colonel V. *The Samaritan Strategy: A New Agenda for Christian Activism*. Brentwood, TN: Wolgemuth and Hyatt, 1988.

Doner, a lobbyist for Christian Voice in the 1980s, evaluates religious right strategies in retrospect and concludes the movement was far too negative in its objectives. The religious right was concerned primarily with blocking the objectives of more liberal groups. He suggests an overall change in tactics that includes the positive goal of helping the deserving poor as an alternative to the welfare state.

Eakman, B.K. *Cloning of the American Mind: Eradicating Morality Through Education*. Lafayette, LA: Huntington House, 1998.

Recommended by Billy James Hargis's Christian Crusade, this book accuses those running the present public education system of employing psychological manipulation that is having devastating effects on children. The widespread usage of psychological assessments, Eakman contends, have troubling implications for the maintenance of individual privacy.

Eidsmoe, John. *Christianity and the Constitution*. Grand Rapids, MI: Baker, 1995.

Countering the position that the United States Constitution is neutral with regard to religious belief, Eidsmoe argues that the constitutional framers favored Christianity and wanted that religion to be sanctioned by the nation's governing document. The author summarizes the religious beliefs of some noted early Americans.

_____ . *Columbus and Cortez: Conquerors for Christ*. Green Forest, AR: New Leaf, 1992.

Admitting that Indians suffered abuses at the hands of Columbus and other explorers, Eidsmoe nonetheless defends Christian intervention in the New World by arguing that many native Americans who endured oppression under native American traditions joined the explorers as liberators.

_____ . *Gays and Guns: The Case Against Homosexuals in the Military*. Lafayette, LA: Huntington House, 1991.

Eidsmoe, proponent of a strong relationship between Christianity and the American political system, argues that admitting homosexuals openly into the military weakens combat effectiveness, creates risks to national security, and ends the traditional notion of the military as a rite of passage for young men.

_____ . *God and Ceasar: Biblical Faith and Political Action*. Westchester, IL: Crossways Books, 1984.

The author focuses on a conservative economic interpretation of the Bible. He identifies the existence of private property in scripture extending from pre-Mosaic times to the millennium of Revelation. Eidsmoe highlights examples of private enterprise in several of Jesus's parables. Aspects of the Constitution, such as separation of powers, are viewed as rooted in the Christian tradition.

Feder, Don. *A Jewish Conservative Looks At Pagan America*. Lafayette, LA: Huntington House, 1993.

Feder claims abortion is not a right because it lacks any moral foundation. He traces America's problems to a lack of sexual inhibitions that leads to the excessive display of other human passions. Suggestions for remedying the situation are offered.

Ferris, Michael. *Anonymous Tip*. Nashville, TN: Broadman and Holman, 1996.

Ferris, president of the Home School Legal Defense Association, wrote this novel to highlight his belief that government is attempting to prevent people of faith from caring for their own children. An anonymous and vindictive call to Child Protective Services, falsely charging mistreatment of a child, leads to a struggle between the government bureaucracy and a parent trying to exercise her parental rights.

Folger, Janet L. *The Criminalization of Christianity: Read This Before It Becomes Illegal!* Sister, OR: Multnomah, 2005.

Referring to such policies as the prohibition on officially sanctioned prayer in the public schools and the elimination of Ten Commandments displays, Folger concludes that public policy will ultimately lead to the criminalization of opposition and the imprisonment of Christians who oppose such policies.

Foreman, Joseph L. *Shattering the Darkness: The Crisis of the Cross in the Church Today*. Montreat, NC: Cooling Spring, 1992.

Foreman gives a biblical defense for Christians conducting 'abortion rescues.' The book includes a letter written from prison by antiabortion leader Randall Terry in which he justifies his actions.

Fries, Michael, and C. Holland Taylor. *A Christian Guide to Prosperity*. Oakland, CA: Communications Research, 1984.

This work offers investment and savings advice for Christians. The authors criticize the present system which allows people to prosper without working. To rectify this situation, they recommend a return to the gold standard and suggest keeping assets in gold and Swiss francs.

Fuhrman, Mark. *Silent Witness: The Untold Story of Terri Schiavo's Death*. Fort Collins, CO: Ignatius, 2005.

Fuhrman presents an account of the legal and political battles surrounding the life and death of Terri Schiavo, the Florida woman who for many years was in a vegetative state. The author consulted with Schiavo's parents, other family members, and others close to the case, and examined the legal case files and police records.

Gentry, Kenneth L., Jr. *God's Law in the Modern World*. Phillipsburg, NJ: Presbyterian and Reformed Publishing, 1993.

Focusing on 'theonomy,' the claim that Old Testament moral and civil law remain applicable for Christians and society generally, the author discusses the role of law not only in preaching the gospel and personal Christian conduct, but also in the formation of national public policy.

Gills, James P., and Ronald H. Nash. *A Biblical Economics Manifesto: Economics and the Christian Worldview*. Lake Mary, FL: Creation House, 2002.

In this brief treatment of economic theory, the authors present a biblical interpretation of the best economic system. According to Gills and Nash, biblical exegesis leads to the conclusion that capitalism is the most appropriate economic structure because it respects human freedom and responsibility.

Grant, George. *Bringing in the Sheaves: Transforming Poverty into Productivity*. Brentwood, TN: Wolgemuth and Hyatt, 1988.

In this treatment of poverty, Grant contends the objective of assistance to the poor is the return to productivity and independence. The author claims the poor are often responsible for their own poverty, especially because of lack of faith in God and the resulting sinfulness.

———. *The Changing of the Guard: Biblical Blueprints for Political Action*. Fort Worth, TX: Dominion Press, 1987.

Grant argues that Christian right successes result from a refusal to compromise religious principles. To return America to the theocratic status the Founders intended, he recommends a strategy of local, grass-roots politics that includes activities beyond conventional participation. Churches should offer political education as well as opportunities for worship.

_____ . *In the Shadow of Plenty: The Biblical Blueprint for Welfare*. Fort Worth, TX: Dominion, 1986.

Grant describes government welfare programs as wicked, biblically heretical, and administered by sinful people who have no genuine concern for the poor. Although the church has responsibility for charity, Grant argues this is a limited role. The ultimate purpose of charity should be to make the poor more responsible and productive.

_____ . *The Dispossessed: Homelessness in America*. Fort Worth, TX: Dominion, 1986.

Grant analizes poverty from a conservative Christian perspective. Poverty and homelessness result from the sinfulness of Adam and Eve and therefore can be thought of as punishment. Christians can, through diligence, obedience to God, and the inspiration of the Holy Spirit, achieve prosperity. The responsibility for helping the poor and homeless falls not on government, but the church, a responsibility that includes the need to admonish the idle.

Hagee, John C. *Final Dawn Over Jerusalem: Why Israel's Future Is So Important to Christians*. Nashville, TN: Nelson, 1999.

Hagee claims that Israel remains the chosen nation of God and discusses the history of Jerusalem and the Jewish people and nation. Attacking anti-Semitism, the author argues from biblical references that the Jewish people are the favored people of God and that anyone who attacks Israel will suffer God's wrath. The book coincides with a Christian right perspective that favors United States support for the state of Israel. Hagee believes Israel is the key to the end times prophesied in the Bible.

Hall, Verna M.., and Rosalie J. Slater, eds. *The Bible and the Constitution of the United States of America*. Chesapeake, VA: Foundation for American Christian Education, 1983.

The authors have compiled a large number of historical documents, including sermons and public proclamations, they claim demonstrate the Bible was a fundamental influence in the American founding.

Hargis, Billy James. *The Federal Reserve Scandal*. Tulsa, OK: Christian Crusade Books, 1995.

Hargis, leader of the Christian Crusade, argues that 'liberals' are the cause of inflation, that the American economy is out of control, and that the value of money continues to fall. The author suggests ways for Christians to oppose these trends.

_____ . *Day of Deception*. Tulsa, OK: Christian Crusade Books, 1991.

Hargis focuses on the many ways in which Christians can be deceived. Marxists, 'one-worlders,' the New Age movement, religious liberals, supporters of theological heresies, and 'enemies of the Christian home' such as the entertainment industry and amoral schools, are targeted for attack.

Heath, Charles C. *The Blessings of Liberty: Restoring the City on the Hill*. Lafayette, LA: Huntington House, 1991.

Heath reviews 200 years of American history during which he believes God has blessed Americans with liberty. Now we are in danger of losing this liberty, so Heath encourages the reader to return to Christianity and choose honest national leaders who will follow a conservative policy agenda that includes providing work for those on welfare, cutting federal government spending, and instituting term limits. The author considers this agenda the way to reestablish 'God's city on the hill.'

Hirsen, James L. *The Coming Collision: Global Law Versus U.S. Liberties*. Lafayette, LA: Huntington House, 1998.

Distributed by Billy James Hargis's Christian Crusade, this book attacks "global activists" who are claimed to support everything from environmental extremism and radical feminism to New Age mysticism. Hirsen argues that international law is being used to spread this radical philosophy.

Hunter, Paul. *The Many Faces of Babylon: The Babylonian Influences Upon Our Churches*. New York: Revelation Books, 1994.

Contrasting human and biblical systems of organization, Hunter claims God's plan as presented in the Bible must be followed. The New Age movement comes under attack, as do television, motion pictures, the recording industry, and the government, each of which is charged with deceiving and manipulating Christians.

Hynes, Patrick. *In Defense of the Religious Right: Why Conservative Christians Are the Lifeblood of the Republican Party and Why That Terrifies the Democrats*. Nashville, TN: Thomas Nelson, 2006.

Hynes, a political commentator and consultant, attempts to clarify the claimed misunderstandings of the general public regarding conservative Christians and their status in American society. The author delimits the meaning of the religious right, presents the beliefs of its members, and defends those beliefs.

Kah, Gary. *En Route to Global Occupation*. Lafayette, LA: Huntington House, 1991.

Kah, a trade representative for the state of Indiana, claims to have exposed a frightening secret plan to unite the nations of the planet into a godless New World Order.

Kincaid, Cliff. *Global Taxes for World Government*. Lafayette, LA: Vital Issue, 1997.

Expressing the fear many conservatives, including those on the religious right, have of the potential power of the United Nations, Kincaid claims the international organization intends to tax American citizens and businesses trillions of dollars to support a host of spending programs around the world.

Luksik, Peg, and Pamela Hobbs Hoffecker. *Outcome-Based Education: The State's Assault on Our Children's Values*. Lafayette, LA: Huntington House, 1995.

This is an indictment of outcome-based education (OBE), which the authors define as "education based on outcomes instead of time spent in class in specific disciplines." OBE focuses on skills that a student demonstrates rather than a body of knowledge that a student learns." The authors fear that students will be made to achieve academic as well as non-academic outcomes, thus allowing the state to determine what are acceptable behaviors and beliefs. OBE is seen as a dangerous intervention by the state and national governments in the family's role in the determination of children's values.

Marshall, Peter, and David Manuel. *From Sea to Shining Sea*. Old Tappan, NJ: Fleming H. Revell, 1986.

The authors offer a history of the United States from the writing of the Constitution to the Civil War from a conservative Christian perspective. Although many non-Christians took part in developing America, God is seen as guiding the entire nation according to His own plan.

————. *The Light and the Glory*. Old Tappan, NJ: Fleming H. Revell, 1977.

This survey of American historical events from Christopher Columbus's landing to the writing of the Constitution depicts God's benevolent intervention. The Puritans are given much of the credit for establishing a Christian nation. Ultimately, however, God's divine guidance is responsible for the successful Revolutionary War and the Constitution. The authors argue that America is now suffering the consequences of straying from the spiritual path.

McGuire, Paul. *Who Will Rule the Future?* A Resistance to the New World Order. Lafayette, LA: Huntington House, 1991.

McGuire argues that Christians must be willing to take a political stand in order to combat the political and spiritual forces confronting the United States. Christians must oppose the 'New Age conspiracy,' the move toward socialism, and the globalism of the United Nations.

McIlhenny, Chuck, Donna McIlhenny, and Frank York. *When the Wicked Seize a City: A Grim Look at the Future and a Warning to the Church*. Lafayette, LA: Huntington House, 1993.

When a father takes a biblical stand against homosexual rights, he and his family face a violent reaction. According to the authors, homosexuality is a threat to children, schools, and the Christian way of life.

Moore, Roy, with John Perry. *So Help Me God: The Ten Commandments, Judicial Tyranny, and the Battle for Religious Freedom*. Nashville, TN: Broadman and Holman, 2005.

Moore, the former chief justice of the Alabama Supreme Court, explains why he refused to remove the Ten Commandments memorial from the state judicial building, even though his refusal led to his removal from office. Moore claims that his oath of office required him to recognize publicly the Judeo-Christian God who, he argues, provided the foundation of the nation's judicial system through the Ten Commandments. He asserts that those who ordered him to remove the memorial were the ones who truly violated the law.

Noll, Mark A. *Adding Cross to Crown: The Political Significance of Christ's Passion*. Grand Rapids, MI: Baker, 1996.

Noll originally presented these thoughts on the proper relationship between Christianity and politics as the inaugural Kuyper Lecture, an annual forum on religion and public life sponsored by the Center for Public Justice. James Bratt, Max Stackhouse, and James Skillen provide responses to the lecture. Noll urges Christians to concentrate on Christ when they think about, or engage in, political activity, asking them not to "forget the cross" and to take a "godlike stance" toward the world.

North, Gary. *Inherit the Earth: Biblical Blueprints for Economics*. Fort Worth, Texas: Dominion Press, 1987.

North recommends a religious right emphasis on local politics. Opting for a more long-term strategy, the author sees the importance of political struggles not at the national but at the local governmental levels.

———. *Honest Money: The Biblical Blueprint for Money and Banking*. Forth Worth, TX: Dominion Press, 1986.

North observes that the reconstruction of an economy based on capitalism and Christian values may first require a total collapse of the economy. The author recommends that Christians prepare for hard times by purchasing gold and silver and storing up basic supplies.

———. *The Sinai Strategy: Economics and the Ten Commandments*. Tyler, TX: Institute for Christian Economics, 1986.

North argues for the compatibility of Christianity and capitalism, finding a basis for a free enterprise system beginning in Old Testament references. The

Ten Commandments provide the religious, legal, and economic preconditions for the development of a free market.

North, Gary, and Gary Demar. *Christian Reconstruction: What It Is, What It Isn't*. Tyler, TX: Institute for Christian Economics, 1994.

North and Demar explain what is meant by Christian reconstruction. It is a theological movement the goal of which is to transform, or reconstruct, the world according to biblical principles. The authors argue that Christians have surrendered the public realm to the secular world, limiting themselves to the private world of the family and the church. Christians must enter public life and act to reform the world before Christ's second coming.

Olasky, Marvin. *The American Leadership Tradition: Moral Vision from Washington to Clinton*. Free Press, 1999.

Olasky, advisor to George W. Bush during the 2000 presidential campaign, investigates the lives of 13 prominent Americans, including ten presidents. Arguing that personal morality plays a significant role in political behavior, the author concludes that devotion to God and faithfulness in marriage are closely related to wise political decision making. Olasky concludes that the actions of presidents influence the behavior of future presidents and affect the public's trust in political leaders.

_____ . *Compassionate Conservatism: What It Is, What It Does, and How It Can Transform America*. Free Press, 2000.

Olasky argues that government and religious groups–so-called "faith-based" organizations–should cooperate more closely in providing assistance to the poor. This can be done by government partially funding the social welfare activities of private religious organizations. Olasky believes such organizations can not only provide assistance for physical deficiencies but also minister to spiritual needs. President George W. Bush, who made "compassionate conservatism" a major theme in his 2000 campaign, wrote the introduction.

O'Leary, Dale. *The Gender Agenda: Redefining Equality*. Lafayette, LA: Vital Issue, 1997.

O'Leary examines the feminist movement, tracing its activities since the early 1970s. The author focuses on what he considers the destructiveness of the movement, claiming it threatens the ideals of family, marriage, and motherhood. According to O'Leary, the feminist movement opposes the right of women to follow their traditional roles, seeking to alter the position of women in society through government adoption of a radical feminist ideology and spreading their doctrines worldwide through the United Nations.

Opitz, Edmund A. *Religion and Capitalism: Allies, Not Enemies*. Irvington-on-Hudson, NY: Foundation for Economic Education, 1992.

This book, originally published in 1970, examines differing forms of governing. Opitz concludes that a liberal ideology is conducive to strong government, whereas Christianity and capitalism mutually support one another.

Peters, Peter J. *America the Conquered*. LaPorte, CO: Scriptures of America Ministries, 1991.

Pastor Pete Peters argues that anti-Christian elements in society have conquered America. Evidence that the United States has been subdued are found in the Supreme Court's decisions on flag burning, the decline of sexual morality, the harassment of churches, an extensive increase in police powers, the secularization of schools, and the legalization of abortion. Peters advises Americans to turn to God in order to regain their freedom.

Rae, Debra. *The ABCs of Globalism: A Vigilant Christian's Glossary*. Lafayette, LA: Huntington House, 1999.

Rae presents definitions and discussions of terms related to a Christian interpretation of current economic and political trends, including what is considered a move toward a global social, economic, and political system.

————— . *After the Revolution: How the Christian Coalition Is Impacting America*. Nashville, TN: Word, 1996.

Reed supports Christian involvement in the movement to improve American society, which he contends is in crisis. Christians must become aware of the nature of political and cultural problems, resist being placed by the secular world at the margins of public life, and cast ballots according to their Christian values.

————— . *Politically Incorrect: The Emerging Faith Factor in American Politics*. Nashville, TN: Word, 1996.

Reed discusses the declining presence of religion in politics during the twentieth century and calls Christians to increase their participation at all levels, particularly local politics. He asks people to make their opinions known to government representatives. While Reed admits that at times Christian involvement in politics has been detrimental, as with white resistance of integration and civil rights, he believes that organizations such as the Christian Coalition can have a beneficial impact on American society and politics.

————— . *Active Faith: How Christians Are Changing the Face of American Politics*. New York: Free Press, 1996.

Reed, discusses his experience as head of the Christian Coalition, presents his own story of religious commitment, describes the importance of religious belief in the history of the United States, and analyzes the status of the Democratic and Republican parties. The author outlines for religious conservatives a strategy of political activism.

Richardson, Stephen. *The Eagle's Claw: Christians and the IRS*. Lafayette, LA: Vital Issue, 1998.

Basing the discussion on his experience as a certified public accountant who represented Christians and Christian organizations before the Internal Revenue Service, Richardson describes what he considers the IRS's politically motivated intimidation of churches and how Christians can defend themselves against such attacks.

Remnant Resolves. LaPorte, CO: Scriptures for America Ministries, 1988.

The series of resolutions agreed to by 'a remnant of God's people,' meeting at the Rocky Mountain Family Bible Camp in Cederedge, Colorado, July 1988, calls for self-government under God both in the family and the nation. The resolves promote the God-given right to defend life, liberty, property, and the family, and condemn abortion as murder and homosexuality as a sin against God.

Robertson, Pat. *The Turning Tide: The Fall of Liberalism and the Rise of Common Sense*. Nashville, TN: Word, 1993.

Robertson discusses the end of liberalism dominance in America. He claims President Clinton and his wife Hillary are committed to an unacceptable radical and unbiblical political agenda.

———. *America's Dates with Destiny*. Nashville, TN: Thomas Nelson, 1986.

Robertson presents various episodes in American history, emphasizing the importance of religious belief. The author attributes the nation's contemporary problems to acceptance of liberalism at the beginning of the twentieth century. A return to conservatism and evangelical Christianity represents the hope of reestablishing traditional values.

Robertson, Pat, with Bob Slosser. *The Plan*. Nashville, TN: Thomas Nelson, 1989.

This book, published after Robertson's unsuccessful bid for the Republican presidential nomination, deals with the campaign and the reasons for Robertson's failure. God has a plan for everyone, and Robertson claims that despite his lack of success, the plan for him was to involve more Christians in politics and to spread the conservative Christian message.

Rushdoony, Rousas John. *Institutes of Biblical Law*. Nutley, NJ: Craig Press, 1972.

This book examines the Ten Commandments and other biblical laws. Rushdoony believes these laws provide a course for action when Christians follow the biblical command to achieve dominion over this world.

Satinover, Jeffrey. *Homosexuality and the Politics of Truth*. Grand Rapids, MI: Baker, 1996.

Coinciding with the religious right position, Satinover argues that behavioral studies are flawed and that an individual's homosexuality, a pattern of sexual behavior resulting from an interaction of psychological, biological, and habitual factors, is ultimately alterable. The author considers homosexuality a form of "soul sickness" that is inherent in the human race's "fallen nature."

Scheidler, Joseph M. *Closed: 99 Ways to Stop Abortion*. Westchester, IL: Crossway, 1988.

Scheidler, who heads the Pro-Life Action League, presents practical advice about stopping abortions, including fund raising techniques, ways of coping with police during demonstrations, finding alternatives to abortion for women, and strategies for debate. The author advocates nonviolence.

Schenck, Paul, with Robert L. Schenck. *The Extermination of Christianity: A Tyranny of Consensus*. Lafayette, LA: Huntington House, 1993.

The authors contend that radical liberals are attempting to eliminate Christianity in America. American Christians are being subjected to slander and ridicule that represents the prelude to oppression rivaled only by the persecution of early Christians. To back their claim, the authors refer to what they consider the unfavorable depiction of the clergy in movies, on television, and in popular music, and to the perceived bias against Christians in the public schools.

Schweizer, Peter. *Disney, the Mouse Betrayed: Greed, Corruption, and Children at Risk*. Washington, DC: Regnery, 1998.

Schweizer echoes the criticisms of conservative Christian groups who charge that the Walt Disney company, widely known as an organization providing family entertainment, has made too many compromises in order to increase profits. The author takes the Walt Disney company to task for what he considers a betrayal of American values.

Sekulow, Jay Alan. *From Intimidation to Victory: Regaining the Christian Right to Speak*. Lake Mary, FL: Creation House, 1990.

Sekulow, chief counsel for the American Center for Law and Justice, argues that Christians are winning against those forces the he believes are attempting to restrict the right of religious expression. The author deals with such issues as the separation of church and state, the rights of parents, abortion, censorship, and civil disobedience.

Sekulow, Jay Alan. *Witnessing Their Faith: Religious Influences on Supreme Court Justices and Their Opinions*. Lanham, MD: Rowman and Littlefield, 2005.

Focusing on such legal issues as prayer in the public schools, government sid to parocial schools, the Pledge of Allegiance, and public displays of the Ten

Commandments, Sekulow examines court eases and their historical contexts and investigates the influence of Supreme Court justices' religious beliefs on their decisions regarding the two religion clauses of the first amendment to the Constitution.

Sekulow, Jay Alan, and Keith Fournier. *And Nothing But the Truth: Real-life Stories of American Defending Their Faith and Protecting Their Families.* Nashville, TN: Thomas Nelson, 1996.

Sekulow and Fournier discuss the First Amendment freedoms as applied to Christians, focusing on such issues as the right to display the Bible in the workplace or discuss religion with co-workers, the rights of churches under local zoning laws to be protected from such establishments as bars, and the right to show Christian-produced films in public buildings.

Sileven, Everett. *The Christian and the Income Tax.* Louisville, NE: Council for Religious Education, 1986.

Sileven holds that the Constitution limits public officials, not the people, who are subject only to God's law. Rules and regulations over the people, particularly the income tax, are unconstitutional, unscriptual, and contrary to the intentions of the founding fathers. Americans should refuse to go into debt, avoid credit cards, refuse to use FDIC banks, and, when on a jury, vote 'not guilty' in cases concerning taxes. Sileven claims that anyone who supports such government programs as mass transit, public highways, and the public school system is a 'practicing Communist.'

Sproul, R. C. *Money Matters: Making Sense of Economic Issues that Affect You.* Wheaton, IL: Tyndale House, 1985.

This conservative evangelical look at economics praises the value of labor, claiming that God expected even Adam and Eve to work in the Garden of Eden. God has called us to be constructive managers of his creation, to subdue the earth and to make it fruitful.

Terry, Randall A. *Operation Rescue.* Springdale, PA: Whitaker House, 1988.

Terry, organizer of sit-ins at abortion clinics, advocates the coerced closing of these clinics as a means of creating sufficient unrest to force government to outlaw abortion through passage of a Human Rights Amendment.

Thoburn, Robert L. *The Christian and Politics.* Tyler, TX: Thoburn Press, 1984.

Thoburn notes that as Christians retreated from the political realm, secular humanists captured the playing field, to the disadvantage of Christians. The author develops a biblical view of government, analyzes a number of issues–including education, welfare, taxation, and foreign policy–from a biblical stance, and discusses how Christians can involve themselves in politics more effectively.

Thomas, Cal, and Ed Dobson. *Blinded by Might: Can the Religious Right Save America?* Grand Rapids, MI: Zondervan, 1999.

Thomas, a former spokesperson for the Moral Majority, and Dobson, co-drafter of the Moral Majority platform and former assistant to Jerry Falwell, express their apprehension about the participation of the Christian right in politics. Although adhering to many of the values advocated by the religious right, the authors argue that America cannot be made virtuous through political activity, but instead must depend for its salvation on individual Christians living moral lives and caring for the poor and the oppressed. Noting that politics inherently involves compromise, Thomas and Dobson indicate their concern for past cases of untruthfulness and violations of trust attributed to leaders in the religious right.

Turek, Frank S., and Norman L. Geisler. *Legislating Morality: Is It Wise? Is It Legal? Is It Possible?* Minneapolis, MN: Bethany House, 1999.

Turek and Geisler argue that a society cannot avoid legislating morality in order to support good and oppose evil. Such legislating can occur within a society characterized by religious diversity. The authors reject the standard position that law should not legislate against victimless crimes such as gambling and the useage of drugs, contending that such action do have adverse effects on others.

Vernon, Robert. *L.A. Justice: Lessons from the Firestorm*. Colorado Springs, CO: Focus on the Family, 1993.

The author, a former assistant police chief in Los Angeles, discusses satanic influences in southern California that are responsible for such things as mob violence, racial conflict, and earthquakes. Vernon explains how the present situation developed and discusses whether there is a way to 'save' Los Angeles.

Walton, Rus. *Biblical Solutions to Contemporary Problems: A Handbook*. Brentwood, TN: Wolgemuth and Hyatt, 1988.

Walton looks to the Bible for solutions to a wide variety of political questions, including taxation, welfare, and economic growth. The author advocates a strong national defense as crucial to maintaining a Christian nation and cautions that the United Nations is a major humanist institution. Major aspects of the American constitutional order are claimed to be found in Old Testament accounts of the Hebrew people.

————. *One Nation Under God*. Nashville, TN: Thomas Nelson, 1987.

This work advocates an active political role for Christians, especially at the local level, in order to reestablish God's place in American government. Socialism and humanism are seen as destructive of biblical principles regarding government, economics, and education. The author supports a strong national defense, including nuclear deterrence. He expresses opposition to the United

Nations, pointing to that organization's anti-American position and support of communism.

West, Jonathan. *Good-Bye America?* Bethesda, MD: Prescott, 1999.

Appalled by all the he finds wrong with the United States, including the failure of Congress to act effectively, the objectionable behavior of the president, the inadequacies of the judicial system, and an arbitrary bureaucracy, West calls for a rebirth of the nation as it enters the twenty-first century.

Whitehead, John W. *An American Dream*. Westchester, IL: Crossway Books, 1987.

Whitehead, a legal scholar, is wary of the connection between religion and the state, noting that, except for Massachusetts, theocratic systems were rejected in colonial times. However, the author recognizes the importance of the clergy historically in establishing those rights and liberties so important to the 'American dream.' According to the author, it was through John Locke that Reformation thought was transmitted to America during the revolutionary era.

————. *The Stealing of America*. Westchester, IL: Crossway Books, 1983.

Whitehead portrays the historical development of freedom and individualism in conjunction with responsibility that he claims originated in Martin Luther's writings during the Reformation. This individualism, Whitehead argues, has been increasingly threatened in recent years by a growing governmental structure. The spread of collectivist influences originating in European thinkers is given some of the blame for the contemporary trend of limiting religious freedoms.

Whitemarsh, Darylann, and Bill Reisman. *Subtle Serpent: New Age in the Classroom*. Lafayette, LA: Huntington House, 1993.

The authors argue that the public school systems have allowed such evils as suicide, rape, drug use, violence, teen pregnancy, and a general disregard for authority. They identify the cause of these evils in attempts to introduce new moral codes without the permission or knowledge of parents.

Woods, Dennis. *Disciplining the Nations: The Government Upon His Shoulder*. Phoenix, AZ: Vantage Group, 1998.

Woods, a political pollster, argues that in order to counter what he considers threats to the moral status of the nation, Christians must realize that scripture and the dissemination of the gospel concerns all aspects of life, including government and social affairs.

Zorea, Aharon W. *In the Image of God: A Christian Response to Capital Punishment*. Lanham, MD: University Press of America, 2000.

Zorea, a conservative Catholic and a graduate student in history at the University of St. Louis, argues that conservative Christians should adopt a consistent position on the ethics of life regarding capital punishment, asking them to end their support for the death penalty. The author claims that support for capital punishment threatens the commitment to end abortion and to prevent euthanasia and assisted suicide.

Personal and Family Topics

Bakker, Jim. *I Was Wrong*. Nashville, TN: Nelson, 1996.

Jim Bakker, former host of the popular *PTL* television show and head of Heritage USA and the Inspirational Network, recounts his personal fall from grace for misusing donated funds, a fall that shook the televangelism community. In 1989 Bakker, then 49 years old, received a forty-five-year prison sentence for misusing donated funds. While in prison Bakker claims that he had a change of heart, discovering fellowship among those in suffering. He now criticizes the "health and wealth gospel" he previously touted to his audience.

Dobson, James C. *The New Dare to Discipline*. Wheaton, IL: Tyndale, 1996.

Dobson, head of Focus on the Family, has revised his popular book about establishing parental authority through appropriate discipline. The author wrote the first edition, released in 1970, to counter what he believed were permissive child-rearing practices which fail to provide children with sufficient guidance for adulthood.

Falwell, Jerry. *Strength for the Journey: An Autobiography*. New York: Simon and Schuster, 1987.

Falwell begins with an account of family heritage and ends in the late 1980s after his stormy experience in the public sphere as leader of the Moral Majority. Of special note are accounts of his alcoholic father, his conversion experience in his mother's kitchen, subsequent preparation for the ministry, and his early days at Thomas Road Baptist Church.

————. *Falwell: An Autobiography*. Lynchburg, VA: Liberty House, 1997.

Jerry Falwell, the controversial religious right leader headquartered in Lynchburg, Virginia, offers insights into his life and the development of his conservative religious beliefs. He touches on such topics as sin, forgiveness, the importance of prayer, and the significance of the Bible to contemporary Christians.

LaHaye, Beverly, and Terri Blackstock. *Seasons Under Heaven*. Grand Rapids, MI: Zondervan, 1999.

Beverly LaHaye followed her husband Tim into the field of fiction writing with this novel about love and Christian faith. This story about four women in different stages of life is intended to instruct women readers about issues of concern to conservative Christians, such as sex education in the public schools and the willingness to be a stay-at-home mother.

————. *Showers in Season*. Grand Rapids, MI: Zondervan, 2000.

A sequel to *Seasons Under Heaven*, this novel continues the portrayal of the lives of families in a small town. Religious right issues are raised as the families face such difficulties as marital infidelity and the birth of a Down's syndrome baby.

LaHaye, Beverly, and Tim F. LaHaye. *The Act of Marriage: The Beauty of Sexual Love*. Grand Rapids, MI: Zondervan, 1998.

This revised edition of the LaHayes' best-selling book on sex and love in marriage add reports on medical and social research findings gleaned since the book's original publication in 1976. The authors contend that married Christians can experience greater sexual satisfaction than non-Christians.

LaHaye, Tim. *If Ministers Fall, Can They Be Restored?* Grand Rapids, MI: Zondervan, 1991.

Christian right leader LaHaye approaches the contemporary problem of ministers who have strayed sexually. He offers a formula for evading temptation and gives advice to churches that must deal with a minister who has fallen so that the minister might be returned to his position.

————. *Sex Education Is for the Family*. Grand Rapids, MI: Zondervan, 1985.

This is a conservative Christian view of sexuality. LaHaye identifies basic God-determined, biological differences between men and women, claiming men are more capable of leadership while women are more passive. LaHaye denies any biological origin to homosexuality, attributing its development to the faults in child rearing of one or both parents. Advice is given to parents regarding the control of children, especially as they approach puberty.

Robison, James. *Thank God, I'm Free: The James Robison Story*. Nashville, TN: Thomas Nelson, 1988.

Christian right leader Robison tells of his turn to Christianity after a difficult early life. Robison's mother, a single woman who was a victim of rape, took Robison from a foster home when he was five years old to live a fatherless and impoverished childhood. It was his foster mother, however, who was with him when he committed his life to God.

Schaeffer, Francis A. *Letters of Francis Schaeffer*. Westchester, IL: Crossway, 1985.

Schaeffer, the noted evangelical theologian, deals with a number of topics in this volume, including homosexuality, divorce, spirituality, sinfulness, and the role of the Holy Spirit in a Christian's life.

Santorum, Rick. *It Takes a Family: Conservatism and the Common Good*. Wilmington, DE: ISI Books, 2005.

Santorum, U.S. senator from Pennsylvania who has bee a faithful supporter of social and religious conservatism, presents his vision of just public policy, focusing on the importance of the family in achieving the common good rather than government action. The book's title distinguishes Santorum's emphasis from that of Senator Hillary Rodham Clinton, who wrote *It Takes a Village*.

Schaffer, James, and Colleen Todd. *Christian Wives: Women Behind the Evangelists Reveal Their Faith in Modern Marriage*. Garden City, NY: Doubleday, 1987.

Schaffer and Todd portray the wives of the following television evangelists: Jim Bakker, Jerry Falwell, Billy Graham, Rex Humbard, Oral Roberts, Robert Schuller, and Jimmy Swaggart. The authors relate how each couple deals with the pressures of the evangelist's profession.

Schwarz, Frederick. *Beating the Unbeatable Foe: The Story of the Christian Anti-Communist Crusade*. Washington, DC: Regnery, 1996.

Schwarz, now retired from his leadership position in the Christian Anti-Communism Crusade (CACC), recounts his own Christian beliefs and the CACC's four-decade-long campaign to educate Americans about the dangers of communism. The author focuses on the communist goal of eliminating religious belief and reveals that evangelist Billy Graham urged him to form his anti communist organization. A physician, Schwarz approached communism as a pathologist, portraying it as a spreading disease.

Sproul, R. C., Jr. *Bound for Glory: God's Promise for Your Family*. Wheaton, IL: Crossway, 2003.

Claiming that a culture war is damaging the institution of the family, Sproul urges Christians to consult the Bible for guidance in understanding the covenant of marriage. Sproul identifies men as the leaders of the family and encourages them to nurture and safeguard wives and children for a godly life.

Millenarianism

Boys, Don. *Y2K*. Lafayette, LA: Huntington House, 1999.

Religious right organizations like Christian Crusade have hailed books that predicted devastation resulting from computers not recognizing the year 2000. Boys speculated about the possible effects of this computer problem on water supplies, the operation of automobiles, the rail system, and medical equipment. Such problems coincided with the fundamentalist Christian expectation of the Great Tribulation.

Byers, Marvin. *The Final Victory: The Year 2000*. 2nd ed. Shippensburg, PA: Destiny Image, 1994.

This attempt to predict the end times based on biblical interpretation was published prior to much of the Y2K publicity. Using calculations based on the works of Isaac Newton, Byers argued that Christ would return in 2000.

Capps, Charles. *End Time Events: Journey to the End of the Age*. Lawrenceville, GA: Dake, 1999.

Capps explores what the Bible has to say about the possibility that the new millennium will bring the end of the world. He suggests how such biblical events as Solomon's temple, Elijah's method of exiting the earth, and the transfiguration of Christ foreshadow the end times.

Coppes, Charles H. *Millennium Time Bomb: How To Prepare For and Survive the Coming Technological Disaster*. Lafayette, LA: Huntington House, 1998.

Sold by Billy James Hargis's Christian Crusade, this book deals with several possible catastrophes anticipated by many millennial thinkers. Coppes explores the possibility of martial law, global famine, and world government.

Crouch, Paul. *The Omega Code: Another Has Risen From the Dead*. Torrance, CA: Western Front, 1999.

Crouch, head of the Trinity Broadcasting Network, presents a fictional account, based on the book of Revelation, of how the world might end. The novel, which became the popular movie of the same name, examines the possible political implications of end times events.

Gentry, Kenneth L., Jr. *He Shall Have Dominion: A Postmillennial Eschatology*. Tyler, TX: Institute for Christian Economics, 1992.

In opposition to the belief of many contemporary Christians of a premillennial persuasion, Gentry contends postmillennialism is the true biblical position: Christians will rule on earth for a thousand years, enforcing the laws of the Old Testament, before Christ returns.

Goetz, William. *The Economy to Come in Prophetic Context*. Camp Hill, PA: Christian Publications, 1999.

Goetz adds to the Y2K question with this treatment of the possible global consequences of the American economy failing as a result of the computer crisis. Examining biblical prophecy, the author conjectures that a worldwide economic crisis could result in a global dictator coming to power, someone who looks suspiciously like the Antichrist.

Hagee, John C. *Beginning of the End: The Assassination of Yitzhak Rabin and the Coming Antichrist*. Nashville, TN: Nelson, 1996.

Hagee's book is an example of the attempt to interpret contemporary political events in the context of biblical prophecy. The author argues that the assassination of Israeli Prime Minister Yitzhak Rabin will lead Israel to agree to a peace process with Syria that will result in surrendering control of the Golan Heights to the United Nations. This is seen as the prelude to the war described in the Old Testament book of Ezekiel, chapters 38-39, and the rise of the Antichrist.

_____ . *Day of Deception: Separating Truth From the Falsehoods That Threaten Our Society*. Nashville, TN: Nelson, 1997.

Continuing his theme that the end of the world is near, Hagee notes that Jesus, in Matthew 24, prophesied that deception would be the major indicator of the last generation. The author discovers deception in the U.S. government that is meant to destroy democracy. He identifies evil forces that are attempting to destroy the traditional family and the separate roles appropriate for men and women, property rights, patriotism, and individualism.

_____ . *From Daniel to Doomsday*. Nashville, TN: Nelson, 1999.

Hagee continues his examination of biblical prophecy, focusing on the Old Testament book of Daniel. He attempts to place such contemporary events as the anticipated computer crisis after January 1, 2000, the Chinese theft of American military secrets, Saddam Hussein's aggressive intentions in the Middle East, and Israeli electoral politics into the anticipated end of the world.

Hart, Frank. *Revelation and the Rapture Unveiled! Ancient Hebrew Prophecies for the Year 2000 and Beyond*. Lafayette, LA: Prescott, 1999.

Hart presents his understanding of biblical prophecy, attempting to unravel the mysteries found in the books of Revelation and Daniel. As have so many authors at the end of the twentieth century, Hart offers what he believes is the relevance of biblical prophecy to the new millennium.

Hayford, Jack. *E Quake*. Nashville, TN: Nelson, 1999.

Television minister Jack Hayford interprets the last days prophesied in the Bible, contending an appropriate understanding of the mysteries cloaked in scripture can be found in events involving the series of earthquakes predicted in the book of Revelation. The author suggests how Christians should set their priorities and live their lives in anticipation of the last days.

Hunt, Dave. **A** *Cup of Trembling: Jerusalem and Bible Prophecy*. Eugene, OR: Harvest, 1995.

In the context of Bible prophecy, Hunt examines the significance of Jerusalem, the capital of Israel. He investigates the origins of the Middle East conflict between Jews, Muslims, and Christians and speculates about the potential world consequences of the Israelis rebuilding the Jewish temple in Jerusalem, an event which supposedly will signal the beginning of the end times.

———— . *Y2K: A Reasoned Response to Mass Hysteria*. Eugene, OR: Harvest, 1999.

Bible teacher Dave Hunt joins other students of biblical prophecy, presenting his own interpretation of the significance of the feared computer crisis. He advises Christians to rely on God's provision and to take steps to prepare for the inconveniences that might occur, warning them not to submit to the panic atmosphere alarmists have been generating.

Jeffrey, Grant R. *The Signature of God: Astonishing Biblical Discoveries*. Wheaton, IL: Tyndale House, 1997.

Jeffrey relies on historical, archaeological, and scientific documents to argue that the Bible was inspired by God. The author claims to have discovered Hebrew codes within scripture which prophesy events in the contemporary world.

———— . *Millennium Meltdown: The Year 2000 Computer Crisis*. Belleville, MI: Spring Arbor Distributors, 1998.

Jeffrey provides a conservative Christian perspective on the Y2K frenzy that engulfed the nation prior to the turn of the century, thus combining worries about computers and biblical eschatology. While giving advice on dealing individually with the possible problems associated with computers, the author speculates about the potential political consequences related to biblical prophecy, such as the formation of a world government and a cashless society.

Jeremiah, David. *Escape the Coming Night*. Nashville, TN: Word, 1999.

With the end of the twentieth imminent, Jeremiah examines the book of Revelation, indicating that predictions made in that book of prophecy are relevant to the contemporary world. The author urges readers to be prepared for the events he claims could soon be fulfilled.

Joyner, Rick. *A Prophetic Vision for the 21st Century: A Spiritual Map to Help You Navigate into the Future*. Nashville, TN: Nelson, 1999.

Joyner focuses on the prophesied reign of Christ on earth and provides practical advice to Christians for what he considers the uncertainties of the early twenty-first century.

LaHaye, Tim F. *Revelation Unveiled*. Grand Rapids, MI: Zondervan, 1999.

In this work, LaHaye explains his interpretation of biblical prophecy which undergirds the popular novel series, *Left Behind*, which he has been coauthoring with Jerry Jenkins. The author employs charts and diagrams in a simplified explanation of the book of Revelation.

LaHaye, Tim F., and Jerry B. Jenkins. *Left Behind: A Novel of the Earth's Last Days*. Wheaton, IL: Tyndale, 1996.

In the first of a series of novels, LaHaye and Jenkins have created a fictional account of what might happen after the rapture they believe is prophesied in the book of Revelation. The authors alert readers to be prepared spiritually for the rapture, an event fundamentalist Christians believe will shortly occur. In the novel, people all over the world have disappeared, and various explanations are offered, from terrorists to extraterrestrial aliens. When Nicolae Carpathia, a popular Romanian politician, begins to establish a world government, those who are penitent establish the Tribulation Force to resist the Antichrist.

————— . *Tribulation Force*. Wheaton, IL: Tyndale, 1997.

This sequel to *Left Behind* finds the main characters left behind after the rapture, struggling to resist the evil intentions of Nicolae Carpathia, the Antichrist who is becoming more powerful. Airline pilot Rayford Steele, his daughter Chloe, journalist Buck Williams, and Pastor Bruce Barnes join hands to study the Bible and resist the intentions of the Antichrist. Although Rayford and Buck become employees of Carpathia, they keep their faith a secret so that they can fight on the side of the Tribulation Force.

————— . *Nicolae: The Rise of the Antichrist*. Wheaton, IL: Tyndale, 1997.

In this third novel of the *Left Behind* series, LaHaye and Jenkins focus on their fictional Antichrist, Nicolae Carpathia. In terms suggestive of the "New World Order" so feared by conservatives, Nicolae unifies nations into a "Global Community," consolidates the mass media into the "Global Community Network" and "Global Weekly," and establishes one religion, "Enigma Babylon One World Faith," with a spiritual leader appointed by Nicolae. The heroes, Rayford Steele and Buck Williams, come to a full realization of Nicolae's evil purposes. The sixth seal of the book of Revelation is opened, bringing a huge earthquake, with the moon turning red, the sun becoming black, and the stars falling from the sky.

————— . *Soul Harvest: The World Takes Sides*. Wheaton, IL: Tyndale, 1999.

In the fourth novel of the *Left Behind* series, LaHaye and Jenkins continue their fictional rendition of the events prophesied in the book of Revelation. Having survived the devastation of the great earthquake, or the "wrath of the Lamb," portrayed in *Nicolae*, members of the Tribulation Force, including reporter Buck Williams, pilot Rayford Steele, and his daughter Chloe, continue their efforts to resist the evil intentions of the Antichrist, Nicolae Carpathia.

————— . *Apollyon: The Destroyer Is Unleashed*. Wheaton, IL: Tyndale, 1999.

This fifth novel in the best-selling series on the tribulation prophesied in the book of Revelation portrays the actions of Apollyon, the chief demon of the abyss, who leads a plague against the survivors of the tribulation. The drama of Nicolae Carpathia, the Antichrist, continues, as believers continue to resist his political maneuvering. A divine plague of locusts is unleashed against those without the seal of God on their foreheads. The authors maintain the reader's interest with the characters' personal crises, including marital infidelity and pregnancies.

———. *Assassins*. Wheaton, IL: Tyndale, 1999.

LaHaye and Jenkins continue in this sixth volume their fictional account of the tribulation and the rise of the antichrist. The authors describe the last half of the tribulation prophesied in the book of Revelation.

———. *Are We Living in the End Times?* Wheaton, IL: Tyndale, 1999.

LaHaye and Jenkins, authors of the popular fiction series, *Left Behind*, offer what they consider scriptural confirmation of their belief that the world is approaching the final days. They offer twenty reasons why they believe people now living will see the rapture, the event some Christians believe will signal the beginning of the end times when the true believers will be taken into heaven.

———. *The Indwelling: The Beast Possession*. Wheaton, IL: Tyndale, 2000.

This seventh book in the *Left Behind* series, continues the end times scenario, taking characters past the half-way point of the seven-year tribulation foretold in the book of *Revelation*.

———. *The Mark: The Beast Rules the World*. Wheaton, IL: Tyndale, 2000.

In the eighth installment of the *Left Behind* series, Nicolae returns from the dead and plans to place the mark of the beast on all human beings. The Tribulation Force, evading the global security contingent, continues to preach the gospel in a disintegrating world.

———. *Desecration: Antichrist Takes the Throne*. Wheaton, IL: Tyndale, 2002.

In the ninth novel in the *Left Behind* series, the world reaches the brink of Armageddon as the evil figure Nicolae Carpathia, the antichrist, enters the Jerusalem temple and declares himself to be God.

———. *The Remnant: On the Brink of Armageddon*. Wheaton, IL: Tyndale, 2003.

In the tenth volume of the *Left* Behind series, the earth continues to suffer under divine judgments and the remaining Christians prepare to defend themselves against the antichrist, Nicolae Carpathia, and his forces of evil.

———. *Armageddon: The Cosmic Battle of the Ages*. Wheaton, IL: Tyndale, 2003.

As the battle of Armageddon finally approaches in this eleventh installment of the *Left Behind* series, the forces of the antichrist and the Christians who compose the Tribulation Force move toward the Middle East for the final show-down.

_____ . *Glorious Appearing: The End of Days*. Wheaton, IL: Tyndale, 2004.

In the twelfth book in the *Left Behind* series, the action takes place just over seven years after the Rapture as the forces of evil and the Tribulation Force have gathered in the Valley of Megiddo for the final battle of Armageddon.

Lindsey, Hal. *Apocalypse Code*. Torrance, CA: Western Front, 1997.

In a continuing effort to provide interpretations of Bible prophecy, Lindsey focuses on the books of Daniel and Revelation, contending that biblical secrets about the final days have been revealed. The author claims he has deciphered Old Testament prophecies regarding what he considers the near future of the earth's present generation.

Lindsey, Hal, and Cliff Ford. *Facing Millennial Midnight: The Y2K Crisis Confronting America and the World*. Torrance, CA: Western Front, 1999.

Popular Bible prophet Hal Lindsey enlists the assistance of economist Cliff Ford to speculate about the potential effects on such structures as government, the monetary system, and utilities of the feared computer crisis. Lindsey is cautious in attempting to relate the anticipated crisis to biblical prophecy.

_____ . *The Late Great 20ᵗʰ Century: Prelude to Catastrophe*. Torrance, CA: Western Front, 1999.

Lindsey and Ford focus on what they consider the disintegration of the moral culture of the United States, examining events of the twentieth century that contributed to the precarious condition of the nation. The authors make recommendations for returning the United States to its former greatness.

Lockyer, Herbert. *All About the Second Coming*. Peabody, MA: Hendrickson, 1998.

Bible teacher Herbert Lockyer presents a detailed exposition of the book of Revelation. The author treats such controversial eschatological issues among Christians as the battle of Armageddon, the tribulation and rapture, the return of Christ, and the millennium.

McGuire, Paul. *Countdown to Armageddon*. Lake Mary, FL: Creation House, 1999.

McGuire examines biblical prophecy of the end times, referring to such contemporary events as wars, famine, disease, and earthquakes to confirm his conclusion. The author looks to the establishment of Israel following World War II as a crucial sign of the final days.

Miller, Harland W. *Make Yourself Ready: Preparing to Meet the King*. Lafayette, LA: Vital Issue, 1998.

At the time of publication, interest in the millennium still raged in religious literature and film. Miller describes the signs of the end times–plagues, disasters, and wars–that the Bible predicts and places biblical prophecy in the context of events of the twentieth century.

Parsley, Rod. *On the Brink: Breaking Through Every Obstacle into the Glory of God*. Nashville, TN: Nelson, 2000.

Parsley argues that the world is in a "fullness of time" period when "demon power" is leading humankind to devastation. The author provides advice about resisting the coming evil and the consequences of disaster.

Rawles, James Wesley. *Patriots: Surviving the Coming Collapse*. Lafayette, LA: Huntington House, 1998.

Sold by Billy James Hargis's Christian Crusade, this novel describes the collapse of modern civilization, exemplified by riots, looting, and the general breakdown of the technological infrastructure. Through this fictional account the author claims to be providing information about how to survive the predicted devastation.

Robertson, Pat. *The End of the Age*. Nashville, TN: Word, 1996.

Robertson, popular television evangelist and erstwhile presidential candidate, weighs in with his own fictional rendition of the end times as prophesied in the book of Revelation. A series of natural disasters, including an asteroid that smashes into the sea between California and Hawaii, and a series of social and political upheavals, such as U.S. presidents who commit suicide and are murdered, lead to Antichrist Mark Beaulieu's world rule. Robertson takes the faithful through the hard times to the ultimate return of Jesus Christ, interspersing his conservative political commentary throughout.

Swindoll, Charles R., John F. Walvoord, and J Dwight Pentecost, eds. *The Road to Armageddon*. Nashville, TN: Word, 1999.

Six Bible prophecy scholars–Charles Swindoll, John Walvoord, Dwight Pentecost, Charles Dryer, Ronald Allen, and Mark Bailey–discuss biblical prophecies regarding the return of Christ, intending to provide the reader with hope and confidence about the future.

Van Impe, Jack. *2001: On the Edge of Eternity*. Nashville, TN: Word, 1996.

For many years Van Impe has engaged in speculation about biblical prophecy in his published works as well as on a television program which he hosts with his wife. Here he discusses contemporary world events, claiming that they have significance in light of Bible passages prophesying the end of the world and the return of Jesus.

Van Kampen, Robert D. *The Rapture Question Answered: Plain and Simple*. Ada, MI: Fleming H. Revell, 1997.

Believing that the end times are near, Van Kampen offers his own biblical interpretation of the rapture of the church, when believers are to be taken into heaven. Not willing to accept the standard positions on the question, which include the pre-, mid-, and post-tribulation interpretations, the author develops a "pre-wrath" position, arguing that believers will endure the tribulation, or suffering, prophesied in the book of Revelation, but will escape the "Day of the Lord," or the "Wrath of God," described in Daniel 12 and Matthew 24.

Walvoord, John F. *Every Prophecy of the Bible*. Colorado Springs, CO: Chariot Victor, 1999.

Walvoord, who previously has written about the importance of oil and the Middle East to the fulfillment of biblical prophecy, offers in this book guidelines for interpreting scriptural prophecy, from Genesis to Revelation. The author reviews predictions he believes have already been fulfilled and considers those yet to occur.

Section 3: Periodicals From Religious Right Organizations

The following periodicals and journals present the varied positions of, and examine questions relevant to, the religious right. Some of the periodicals, such as the *Traditional Values Report* and the *Phyllis Schlafly Report*, are geared to activate readers to political action. Many of these publications are not available through libraries or the more popular distribution channels, but must be acquired directly from the organization. In recent years several organizations have de-emphasized print periodicals, relying instead on Internet communication. Therefore, many of the following periodicals can be found on the Internet. Consult Chapter 8, Multimedia Resources, for appropriate Web sites.

The ACCC Report
American Council of Christian Churches
P.O. Box 5455
Bethlehem, PA 18015
Monthly. Free on request.
This newsletter reports on issues relevant to contemporary fundamentalist churches and comments critically on the National Council of Churches and the National Association of Evangelicals for their alleged compromising attitude toward the faith. The publication also treats social and political issues of interest to conservative Christians.

American Family Association Journal
American Family Association
P.O. Drawer 2440

Tupelo, MS 38803
Monthly. Contribution suggested.

This monthly publication reports on cultural issues of concern to the religious right, including homosexuality and same-sex marriage, pornography and obscenity on television, and preservation of the traditional family.

Biblical Worldview
American Vision
P.O. Box 720515
Atlanta, GA 30328
Monthly. $20.

This newsletter holds that the Bible should be applied to all aspects of Christian life and provides instruction in the nature of government and the Christian's role in politics. A biblical view is provided for many current issues, such as secular humanism, the New Age movement, homosexuality, and government intervention in people's lives.

Chalcedon Report
Chalcedon Foundation
P.O. Box 158
Vallecito, CA 95251-0158
Monthly. Donation requested.

This newsletter deals with issues involving the Christian reconstruction movement and includes articles dealing with the application of Christian principles to contemporary society and culture.

Christian Book Distributors Catalog
P.O. Box 7000
Peabody, MA 01961-7000
Bimonthly. Free on request.

This catalog of Christian reading, listening, and viewing resources often contains materials with themes that are of concern to the religious right.

Christian Century
Christian Century Foundation
407 South Dearborn Street
Chicago, IL 60605
Biweekly. $49.

This moderate Christian publication comments extensively on religious right activities and activities.

Christian Reconstruction
Institute for Christian Economics
P.O. Box 6116
Tyler, TX 75711
Bimonthly. Free on request.

This newsletter, published in alternate months with *Biblical Economics Today*, provides scriptural discussions relevant to advancing the biblical reconstruction viewpoint.

Christian Research Book and Tape Catalog

Christian Research
P.O. Box 385
Eureka Springs, Arkansas 72632
Yearly. Free on request.

This catalog lists a variety of books relevant to the religious right that can be ordered from Christian Research. In addition to Bibles and Bible reference works, many other categories of books are included, such as economics and money, evolution vs. creationism, government, history, law and constitution, and taxes and taxation.

Christian Research Journal

Christian Research Institute
P.O. Box 8500
Charlotte, NC 28271-8500
Six issues. $30.

This journal contains biblically based articles that deal with such current topics as cults, false doctrine, the New Age movement, and secular humanism. Techniques of evangelizing are presented and current literature on defending the faith is reviewed.

Christian Research Newsletter

Christian Research Institute
P.O. Box 8500
Charlotte, NC 28271-8500
Bimonthly. Free on request.

This newsletter presents brief updated accounts of false doctrines and cults, recent events considered relevant to Christian belief, and new publications distributed by the organization.

Christian Standard

Standard Publishing Company
8121 Hamilton Avenue
Cincinnati, OH 45231-2396
Weekly. $20.

This magazine includes news, commentary, and essays dealing with the revival of the doctrines and rules of Christianity as set out in the New Testament.

Christianity Today

Christianity Today, Inc.
465 Gunderson Drive

Carol Stream, IL 60188
Eighteen issues per year. $24.95.

This relatively moderate evangelical publication offers commentary on all aspects of the evangelical movement and news from around the world.

Chronicles

The Rockford Institute
P.O. Box 800
Mount Morris, IL 61054
Monthly. $39.99.

This magazine provides conservative commentary on issues of concern to social and religious conservatives. Recent issues have included articles about gay marriage, education, foreign policy, and conflicts within mainline denominations, including the controversy over the election of a gay bishop in the Episcopal Church.

Church & State

Americans United for Separation of Church and State
518 C Street, N.E.
Washington, DC 20002
Monthly. $24 (including membership).

This magazine reports on the current relations between religious groups and government, including the political activities of religious right organizations and leaders.

Connections

Reasons To Believe
P.O. Box 5978
Pasadena, CA 91117
Quarterly. Free with contribution.

This newsletter includes articles on scientific subjects, arguing that scientific discoveries offer demonstrations of the existence of an intelligent creator. Also included are reports of the activities of Reasons to Believe, promotions of the organization's publications, and announcements of coming events.

The Correspondent

Plymouth Rock Foundation
1120 Long Pond Road
Plymouth, MA 02360
Monthly. $25 (included in membership dues).

This newsletter provides information about local PRF committee activities and reprints articles from these organizations. The prime concern is promoting biblical principles in local government.

Facts & Faith

Reasons to Believe
P.O. Box 5978

Pasadena, CA 91117
Quarterly. $24 donation.

This interdenominational newsletter reports on scientific discoveries that are believed to substantiate the biblical account of creation. The newsletter supports the view that science and religious faith are compatible.

Facts for Action

Christian Research
P.O. Box 385
Eureka Springs, AR 72632
Quarterly. $8.

This newsletter presents a fundamentalist Christian, highly patriotic, and conservative view of current events in American society and politics, and focuses on new from Israel of relevance to conservative Christians. The national government and its agencies are the focus of opposition and deep suspicion (for instance, the Internal Revenue Service is referred to as the 'Gestapo' and the 'Beast').

First Things

Institute on Religion and Public Life
156 Fifth Avenue, Suite 400
New York, NY 10010
Ten issues per year. $39.

Edited by Richard John Neuhaus, this monthly journal of religion and public life includes articles that investigate public policy questions that stem from the intersection of religion and the political realm.

Focus on the Family Citizen

Focus on the Family, Inc.
8605 Explorer Drive
Colorado Springs, CO 80920
Monthly. $24.

This publication from James Dobson's organization focuses on public policy and issues related to traditional family values. Articles are intended to strengthen families and to support conservative Christian objectives such as limiting abortion and obscenity.

The Humanist

American Humanist Association
7 Hardwood Drive
P.O. Box 1188
Amherst, NY 14226-7188
Bimonthly. $24.95.

This magazine promotes the principles of humanism (the belief that human beings are interdependent and mutually responsible without any help from an acknowledged supreme being) so often considered by the religious right to be in direct opposition to Christian belief.

Letter from Plymouth Rock
Plymouth Rock Foundation
1120 Long Pond Road
Plymouth, MA 02360
Four times per year. $25 (minimum membership fee).

This newsletter contains articles on law, economics, education, and the history of the United States relevant to the nation's religious heritage.

Midnight Call Magazine
Midnight Call Ministries
P.O. Box 280008
Columbia, SC 29228
Monthly. $24.50.

This magazine deals with biblical prophecy and the end times, arguing that contemporary events have been predicted in the Bible. Articles focus on such topics as conflict between Israel and Arab nations, the New Age movement, the Antichrist, and the possibility of nuclear war.

NAE Washington Insight
National Association of Evangelicals
P.O. Box 23269
Washington, DC 20026
Monthly. $14.95.

This newsletter reports on the various activities of the federal government and political issues at the national level that are of concern to the evangelical leadership.

National Evangelical Directory
National Association of Evangelicals
P.O. Box 23269
Washington, DC 20026
Biennial. $20.

This directory contains listings of evangelical organizations, schools, camps, counselors, and media people.

The New American
John Birch Society
P.O. Box 8040
Appleton, WI 54912
Bimonthly. $39.

This John Birch Society publication stands for traditional values, patriotism, independence, and the United States Constitution. The magazine's stated goal is 'to educate and to activate Americans in support of God, family, and country.' Articles focus on political science, social opinion, and economic theory and hold to a conspiracy theory regarding the influences on American culture and politics.

Phyllis Schlafly Report
Eagle Forum
P.O. Box 618
Alton, IL 62002
Monthly. $20.

This newsletter provides reports and commentary in areas of interest to conservative Christians, including education, foreign policy and national defense, feminism and the family, economics, and social policy.

Reason and Revelation
Apologetics Press
230 Landmark Drive
Montgomery, AL 36117-2752
Monthly. $10.

Founded in 1981, this journal includes articles on the existence of God, biblical inspiration, creation and evolution, and the deity of Christ, offering defenses of Christianity and evidence for its truth..

The Religion and Society Report
The Howard Center
934 North Main Street
Rockford, IL 61103-7061
Monthly. $24.

Founded in 1984, this newsletter of religious opinion presents conservative views on such topics as homosexuality, school prayer, and church-state relations. Articles have taken an especially strong stand against abortion.

The Rock
Plymouth Rock Foundation
6 McKinley Circle
P.O. Box 425
Marlborough, NH 03455
Quarterly.

This journal focuses on the responses that the Bible provides to secular humanism and to the perceived socialist-inspired alternatives in public policy.

The Schwarz Report
Christian Anti-Communism Crusade
P.O. Box 129
Manitou Springs, CO 80829
Monthly. Free on request.

Named for Fred Schwarz, the former head of the Christian Anti-Communism Crusade, this publication presents information about continuing communist activities around the world (referring to 'lively communist corpses') and the efforts of the Christian Anti-Communism Crusade to counteract those activities. The newsletter includes commentary on such topics as abortion, homosexuality, AIDS, the history of the fight against communism, and current opponents of Christianity in the culture war.

The Servant
Haven Baptist Church
P.O. Box 9562
Denver, CO 80209-0562
Monthly. Free on request.

This newsletter of the Council of Bible Believing Churches (United States affiliate of the International Council of Christian Churches) presents a conservative Christian perspective on current events in the United States and around the world. The publication opposes what are seen as liberal trends within the Christian church.

Tabletalk
Ligonier Ministries
P.O. Box 547500
Orlando, FL 32854
Monthly. $30.

A publication of R.C. Sproul's Ligonier Ministries, the devotional magazine includes daily Bible studies. Each month this conservative Christian periodical includes a theme such as adultery, homosexuality, and the "spiritual adultery" of liberal churches. A 2006 issue focused criticism on the *The Da Vinci Code* book and film.

Touchstone
The Fellowship of St. James
P.O. Box 410788
Chicago, IL 60641
Ten issue per year. $29.95.

This conservative Christian journal includes articles from Protestant, Catholic, and Orthodox contributors. In addition to the fundamental doctrines of the Christian faith, the journal contains commentary on social and political trends.

Traditional Values Report
Traditional Values Coalition
139 C Street, SE
Washington, DC 20003
Occasional. Individual issues provided on request.

This newsletter from the Traditional Values Coalition reports on current issues, such as perceived inroads of homosexuality in the educational system, sex education in the schools, and the relationship between church and state.

Traditional family values are supported, and readers are encouraged to promote a constitutional amendment to protect the rights of religious persons.

World
P.O. Box 20002
Asheville, NC 28802
Weekly (48 issues). $49.95.

This weekly news magazine, edited by Marvin Olasky, reports on national and international news stories and analyzes current events from a biblical perspective. The magazine accepts the Bible as the inerrant word of God.

8

Selected Multimedia Resources

This chapter contains a variety of multimedia resources from and about the religious right. The number of listings are nearly double the previous edition, for obvious reasons. As cable and satellite television access expanded, many organizations developed programs to reach sympathetic viewers. Religious groups and leaders have taken advantage of the new formats to distribute their message to the general public. Previously relying primarily on mailed newsletters, groups now disseminate information on web sites and offer videotapes and video disks on a wide variety of topics. For instance, John Hagee, who broadcasts from Cornerstone Church in San Antonio, Texas, makes available many video presentations on current political and cultural topics several samples of which are included here.

Resources in this chapter are arranged in eight categories: Multiple Formats; DVDs; Videotapes; Audiotapes; Audio CDs; CD Roms; Radio and Television Programs; and Internet Sources. Within each category, listings are arranged in alphabetical order, by title.

The subject of these resources include issues of major concern to the religious right, and span politics, culture and religion. Topics include abortion, God's perceived role in American history and the founding of the Republic, creationism, evolution, intelligent design, end times and the expected millennium, electoral politics, education policy, environment issues, secular humanism, homosexuality, biblical inerrance, American support for the state of Israel, patriotism, anticommunism, and encouraging political activism among conservative Christians.

In addition to societal issues, these resources include descriptions of religion and the religious right, analyses of the issues that have activated conservative Christians, and critical evaluation of religious right positions, objectives and activities. The authors have included sources that present fairly objective, as well as polemical, accounts.

Multiple Formats

7 Secrets of Financial Freedom
Type: DVD, VHS
Length: 180 min.
Date: Not available
Cost: $55
Source: John Hagee Ministries
          P.O. Box 1400
          San Antonio, TX 78295
          (210) 494-3900
          http://www.jhm.org

John Hagee claims that the Bible can serve as an excellent financial manual. Declaring that prosperity is the result of wisdom and choice, not chance, Hagee develops seven biblical truths that can show Christians the way to wealth.

Abortion: A Rational Look at an Emotional Issue VHS, CD, MP3, audiocassette
Length: 180 min.
Date: 1994
Cost: $30 VHS; $24 CD; $12 MP3; $14 audiocassette
Source: Ligonier Ministries
P.O. Box 863595
Orlando, FL 32886
(800) 435-4343
http://www.ligonier.org

R. C. Sproul, head of the Ligonier teaching ministry, discusses what he considers the deepest moral problem in our society. He argues that abortion is against God's law, against the laws of nature, and against reason.

Abortion: The Moral Dilemma
Type: DVD, VHS
Length: 28 min.
Date: 1995
Cost: $89.95 DVD; $99.95 VHS
Source: Films for the Humanities and Sciences
P.O. Box 2053
Princeton, NJ 08543-2053
(800) 257-5126
http://www.films.com

This program discusses the troubling dilemmas underlying the pro- and antiabortion positions. The Christian parents of one healthy child, having already lost two babies to a fatal inherited disease, but still wanting another child, must face the abortion option.

America in Prophecy
Type: DVD, VHS
Length: 150 min.
Date: 2005
Cost: $24.95
Source: Armageddon Books
P.O. Box 230
West Jefferson, NC 28694
(336) 246-2628
http://www.armageddonbooks.com

Stan Johnson focuses on the eighteenth chapter of the Book of Revelation, chapters 50 and 51 of Jeremiah, and chapter 13 of Isaiah, contending that the prophecies appearing in these biblical references refer to the United States.

America: One Nation Under God?

Type: DVD, VHS
Length: 53 min.
Date: 2002
Cost: $16.99
Source: Christian Book Distributors
P.O. Box 7000
Peabody, MA 01961-7000
(978) 977-5000
http://www.christianbook.com

This video claims that the United States must return to the beliefs of the founders if the nation is to survive. An honest and ethical social and economic system requires that the people recognize the sovereignty of God.

America's Godly Heritage

Type: DVD, VHS
Length: 59 min.
Date: 1993
Cost: $19.95
Source: Wallbuilders
P.O. Box 397
Aledo, TX 76008
(817) 441-6044
http://www.wallbuilders.com

David Barton discusses the Christian beliefs and ideals he claims have guided America since the founding. Barton cites early Supreme Court decisions that affirmed the role of Christian principles in the public realm and criticizes more recent decisions that he considers to be ill conceived because they ignore the intentions of the Christian Founders.

Battle for Our Minds: Worldviews in Collision

Type: VHS, CD, audiocassette
Length: 90 min.
Date: 1994
Cost: $17 CD; $15 VHS; $10 audiocassette
Source: Ligonier Ministries
P.O. Box 863595
Orlando, FL 32886
(800) 435-4343
http://www.ligonier.org

R. C. Sproul examines three worldviews in Western culture: the classical/biblical perspective, the Enlightenment viewpoint, and post-Christian secularism. Sproul claims that secularism is now dominant and offers Christians advice for an effective defense of the Christian worldview.

The Battle for the Bible

Type: DVD, VHS
Length: 60 min.
Date: 1992
Cost: $89.95 DVD; $99.95 VHS
Source: Films for the Humanities and Sciences
P.O. Box 2053
Princeton, NJ 08543-2053
(800) 257-5126
http://www.films.com

This second video in the Bill Moyers series *God and Politics* deals with the liberal-conservative conflict within the Southern Baptist Convention. Fundamentalists have wrested control of the Convention from moderates and ultimately want to affect American politics.

Beyond Iraq: The End of the Age

Type: DVD, VHS, CD, audiocassette
Length: 180 min.
Date: 2005
Cost: $55 DVD, VHS; $24 CD; $18 audiocassette
Source: John Hagee Ministries
P.O. Box 1400
San Antonio, TX 78295
800-854-9899
http://www.jhm.org

John Hagee explores the continuing instability in the Middle East, including Iran's apparent development of nuclear weapons. Hagee refers to Bible prophecies in the books of Jeremiah and Revelation to present an interpretation of contemporary events.

The Bible in Translation: God's Word vs. Man's Words

Type: DVD, VHS
Length: 47 min.
Date: 1998
Cost: $149.95 DVD; &159.95 VHS
Source: Films for the Humanities and Sciences
P.O. Box 2053
Princeton, NJ 08543-2053
(800) 257-5126
http://www.films.com

Fundamentalists, who often hold to a doctrine of biblical inerrancy, are sensitive to differing scriptural translations. In this video Elizabeth Castelli, Paige Patterson, Rabbi Burton Visotzky, and others debate such issues as the influence of the Greco-Roman world on the Bible, the use of gender-neutral language in more recent translations, the accuracy of more recent Bibles compared with the King James version (the only acceptable translation for many fundamentalists), and the use of the Bible in the pre–Civil War United States both to defend and denounce slavery.

Bible Positions on Political Issues

Type: Three DVDs, VHS, CD
Length: 180 min.
Date: Not available
Cost: $55 DVD/VHS; $24 CD
Source: John Hagee Ministries
P.O. Box 1400
San Antonio, TX 78295
(210) 494-3900
http://www.jhm.org

Claiming that Americans have failed to uphold biblical principles that guide the nation, John Hagee urges Christians to register to vote and to make vote choices according to their beliefs. Hagee presents what he claims to be the biblical positions on such issues as abortion and homosexuality.

Billy Graham: God's Ambassador

Type: DVD, VHS
Length: 122 min.
Date: 2006
Cost: $15.99
Source: Christian Book Distributors
P.O. Box 7000
Peabody, MA 01961-7000
(978) 977-5000
http://www.christianbook.com

This video contains scenes from Billy Graham's early life and his ministry and revival events. Included are interviews with President George W. Bush, former president George H. W. Bush, NBC news reporter Brian Williams, and various family members and friends.

City of Man

Type: CD, audiocassette
Length: 115 min.
Date: 2006
Cost: $17 CD; $14 audiocassette

Source: Ligonier Ministries
P.O. Box 863595
Orlando, FL 32886
https://www.ligonier.org

R. C. Sproul discusses the "City of Man," expressing the view that all human empires will fail. Therefore, human beings must focus their efforts on becoming citizens of the City of God.

Countdown to Eternity
Type: DVD, VHS
Length: 75 min.
Date: 1997
Cost: $17.95 DVD; $8.95 VHS
Source: Christian Reality Videos
P.O. Box 115
Hamlin, NY 14464
888-437-7558
http://www.christianreality.com

Bill Gallatin examines scripture, arguing that biblical prophecies are now being fulfilled. He points to such things as the advancement of technology, deterioration in moral standards, and the history of modern Israel as signs that the end is near.

Creation or Evolution?
Type: DVD, VHS
Length: 58 min.
Date: Not available
Cost: $15.99 DVD; $4.99 VHS
Source: Gateway Films/Vision Video
P.O. Box 540
Worcester, PA 19490-0540
(800) 523-0226
http://www.visionvideo.com

This video provides a Christian perspective on the controversy between creationism and evolution, asking whether the biblical account of creation is consistent with scientific findings. Such topics as the existence of differing life-forms and the geological record are treated.

The Design Revolution
Type: MP3 CD
Length: Not available
Date: 2004
Cost: $24.95

Source: Christian Research Institute
P.O. Box 8500
Charlotte, NC 28271-8500
(800) 228-1563
http://www.equip.org

William A. Dembski, associate professor at Baylor University, senior fellow with the Discovery Institute, and supporter of intelligent design as an alternative to the theory of evolution, responds to questions about, and challenges to, the intelligent design approach to explaining the origins of life and human beings. Dembski contends that there is no rational reason for excluding the hypothesis of intelligence and purpose from scientific investigation.

End-Times Video Collection
Type: DVD, VHS
Length: 6 hrs.
Date: Not available
Cost: $9.99 DVD; $3.49 VHS
Source: Christian Book Distributors
P.O. Box 7000
Peabody, MA 01961-7000
(978) 977 5000
http://www.christianbook.com

This three-video collection of fictionalized biblical prophecy begins with a young woman awaking one morning to discover that her husband and millions of others have been raptured and that she now faces the coming great tribulation.

Ezekiel's View on the Middle East Crisis
Type: CD; audiocassette
Length: Not available
Date: 2003
Cost: $14.99 CD; $12.99 audiocassette
Source: Christian Book Distributors
P.O. Box 7000
Peabody, MA 01961-7000
(978) 977-5000
http://www.christianbook.com

Relying on the Old Testament book of Ezekiel to interpret contemporary events, Hal Lindsey discusses the enemies of Israel, contrasts between the Bible and the Koran, the history of Israel, the role of Russia in the end times, and the place of the United States in biblical prophecy.

The Feud Between Two Families: WW III Has Begun

Type: Three DVDs, VHS, CD, audiocassette
Length: 180 min.
Date: 2004
Cost: $55 DVD/VHS; $24 CD; $18 audiocassette
Source: John Hagee Ministries
   P.O. Box 1400
   San Antonio, TX 78295
   (210) 494-3900
   http://www.jhm.org

John Hagee claims that World War III has already begun, and the enemy is trying to destroy Christians and anyone who supports freedom. Hagee refers to the Old Testament Book of Ezekiel and the war depicted there as a prophecy of the current world situation.

Fossil Evidence of Creation

Type: DVD, VHS
Length: 27 min.
Date: Not available
Cost: $24.95 DVD; $19.95 VHS
Source: American Portrait Films
   P.O. Box 809
   Brunswick, OH 44212
   (800) 736-4567
   http://www.amport.com

Arguing for a "young earth," this video presents fossil evidence of creation, including the rapid development of coal, petrified forests, and the discovery of unfossilized dinosaur bones, suggesting that dinosaurs became extinct more recently.

Foundations of American Government

Type: DVD, VHS
Length: 60 min.
Date: 1993
Cost: $9.95
Source: Wallbuilders
   P.O. Box 397
   Aledo, TX 76008
   (817) 441-6044
   http://www.wallbuilders.com

David Barton discusses the biblical principles that once influenced American government and points to contemporary religious right and conservative political leaders who are striving to reintroduce those principles.

Four Centuries of American Education

Type: DVD, VHS
Length: 120 min.
Date: 2004
Cost: $19.95
Source: Wallbuilders
P.O. Box 397
Aledo, TX 76008
(817) 441-6044
http://www.wallbuilders.com

Although noting that for four centuries the American educational system combined the acquisition of knowledge with religious and moral training, this video claims that more recently education has become secularized. The program focuses on the relative effects of secularization in contrast to the more traditional form of education.

God and the Constitution

Type: DVD, VHS
Length: 60 min.
Date: 1987
Cost: $69.95 DVD; $79.95 VHS
Source: Films for the Humanities and Sciences
P.O. Box 2053
Princeton, NJ 08543-2053
(800) 257-5126
http://www.films.com

Bill Moyers hosts a discussion about the legality of school prayer with Martin Marty, professor of the history of modern Christianity at the University of Chicago, and Leonard Levy, editor of *The Encyclopedia of the American Constitution*. The participants also discuss the issues of tax exemption for religious institutions and religious symbols on public property.

The Gospel of Liberty

Type: DVD, VHS
Length: 37 min.
Date: 1997
Cost: $15.99 DVD; $7.99 VHS

Source: Gateway Films/Vision Video
P.O. Box 540
Worcester, PA 19490-0540
(800) 523-0226
http://www.visionvideo.com

This video explores the possible influence that religious leaders such as George Whitefield and Samuel Davies, who were involved in the religious revival known as the Great Awakening during the early eighteenth century, had on the subsequent development of the United States.

Intelligent Design vs. Evolution

Type: DVD, VHS, Digital On-Demand
Length: 22 min.
Date: 2005
Cost: $89.95 (DVD, VHS); $44.98 (Digital On-Demand)
Source: Films Media Group
P.O. Box 2053
Princeton, NJ 08543-2053
(800) 257-5126
http://www.films.com

This ABC News program investigates the push to teach intelligent design in the public schools as an alternative to the theory of evolution in the science curriculum. Conservative news commentators George Will and Cal Thomas debate whether intelligent design would involve the inclusion of religious belief in biology courses.

Interviews with Israel

Type: CD, audiocassette
Length: 300 min.
Date: Not available
Cost: $29 CD; $24 audiocassette
Source: John Hagee Ministries
P.O. Box 1400
San Antonio, TX 78295
(210) 494-3900
http://www.jhm.org

John Hagee, who strongly believes that God gave the land of Israel to Abraham, Isaac, and Jacob in a still-binding covenant, interviews such Jewish figures as Rabbi Arnold Scheinberg, Natan Sharansky, Micah Halpern, and Yoram Etinger.

It's Not Gay

Type: DVD, VHS
Length: 30 min.

Date: 2006
Cost: $15
Source: American Family Association
P.O. Drawer 2440
Tupelo, MS 38803
(662) 844-5036
https://www2.afastore.net

Individuals claiming to be former homosexuals present their stories, warning against the view of homosexuality presented in the popular media. Medical and mental health experts also take part in the discussion.

Keys to Good Government

Type: DVD, VHS
Length: 59 min.
Date: 1994
Cost: $19.95
Source: Wallbuilders
P.O. Box 397
Aledo, TX 76008
(817) 441-6044
http://www.wallbuilders.com

David Barton examines the advice for good government given by such early Americans as William Penn, Benjamin Rush, John Adams, and George Washington. Barton concludes that morality remains the key characteristic of good government.

The Kingdom Divided

Type: DVD, VHS
Length: 90 min.
Date: 1992
Cost: $129.95: $139.95 VHS
Source: Films for the Humanities and Sciences
P.O. Box 2053
Princeton, NJ 08543-2053
(800) 257-5126
http://www.films.com

This program, the first in the Bill Moyers series *God and Politics*, focuses on the effect that a conflict between two different interpretations of Christianity (liberation theology and evangelicalism) is having on American foreign policy in Central America.

Left Behind: The Movie

Type: DVD, VHS
Length: 120 min.

Date: 2000
Cost: $8.99 DVD; VHS $.99
Source: Christian Book Distributors
P.O. Box 7000
Peabody, MA 01961-7000
(978) 977-5000
http://www.christianbook.com

This movie is a film adaptation of the Tim LaHaye and Jerry Jenkins novel about the prophesied end times. Millions of people around the world disappear in the "rapture," and those remaining on earth are left to contend with the resulting chaos and the tribulation that some Bible interpreters claim is predicted in scripture.

Liberal Protestantism in the '90s: Forrester Church

Type: DVD, VHS
Length: 30 min.
Date: 1988
Cost: $89.95 DVD; $99.95 VHS
Source: Films for the Humanities and Sciences
P.O. Box 2053
Princeton, NJ 08543-2053
(800) 257-5126
http://www.films.com

Bill Moyers, program host, and Forrester Church, pastor of All Souls Unitarian Church in New York City and son of the late Senator Frank Church, discuss the state of religion in America from a liberal Protestant perspective. Church deals with the ambiguities of his ministry and what can be learned from the variety of religious positions, including the religious right.

The Life and Legacy of Bob Jones Jr.

Type: DVD, VHS
Length: 25 min.
Date: 2001
Cost: $12.95
Source: Bob Jones University Press
Customer Services
Greenville, SC 29614
(800) 845-5731
http://www.bjupress.com

Host Erin Jones presents significant events in the life of Bob Jones Jr., former president of Bob Jones University. The video focuses on Jones's contributions through the university's museum and gallery.

On Earth As It Is in Heaven

Type: DVD, VHS
Length: 60 min.
Date: 1992
Cost: $89.95 DVD; $99.95 VHS
Source: Films for the Humanities and Sciences
      P.O. Box 2053
      Princeton, NJ 08543-2053
      (800) 257-5126
      http://www.films.com

Bill Moyers, in this third program in the *God and Politics* series, examines Christian Reconstructionism, a radical religious movement that advocates political activity to achieve a government that adheres to strict biblical standards. Moyers concludes that this movement may prove to be more significant than the religious right of the 1980s.

The Passion of the Christ

Type: DVD, VHS
Length: 126 min.
Date: 2004
Cost: $9.99 DVD; $17.99 VHS
Source: Christian Book Distributors
      P.O. Box 7000
      Peabody, MA 01961-7000
      (978) 977-5000
      http://www.christianbook.com

Mel Gibson produced this portrayal of the last twelve hours in Jesus's life. The dialogue is in ancient Aramaic, Latin, and Hebrew, with English subtitles. Although many devout Christians praised the film, others were repelled by the graphic violence and perceived anti-Semitic overtones in the film.

Portrait of America: 1776-2005

Type   DVD, VHS
Length: 120 min.
Date: 2005
Cost: $20
Source: John Hagee Ministries
      P.O. Box 1400
      San Antonio, TX 78295
      (210) 494-3900
      http://www.jhm.org

In this sermon, John Hagee presents an interpretation of the United States from its founding in 1776 to the present. Hagee focuses on the values of the Founders as stated in the Declaration of Independence.

The Religious Right
Type: DVD, VHS, Digital-on-Demand
Length: 37 min.
Date: 1992
Cost: $89.95 DVD; $99.95 VHS; $44.98 Digital
Source: Films for the Humanities and Sciences
        P.O. Box 2053
        Princeton, NJ 08543-2053
        (800) 257-5126
        http://www.films.com

Bill Moyers reports on the "National Affairs Briefing" of religious right members after the 1992 Republican National Convention. Conservative leaders such as Pat Buchanan, Oliver North, Donald Wildmon, and Phyllis Schlafly state positions on homosexuality, feminism, abortion, and the media.

The Role of Pastors and Christians in Civil Government
Type: DVD, VHS
Length: 59 min.
Date: 2003
Cost: $19.95
Source: Wallbuilders
        P.O. Box 397
        Aledo, TX 76008
        (817) 441-6044
        http://www.wallbuilders.com

This video recounts the contributions of laypersons such as Roger Sherman and Charles Thomson and pastors such as Samuel Cooper and Jonathan Mayhew to America's struggle for independence. The video encourages today's Christians to become engaged in the public realm, using these historical figures as models.

A Spiritual Heritage Tour of the United States Capitol
Type: DVD, VHS
Length: 120 min.
Date: 1999
Cost: $19.95
Source: Wallbuilders
        P.O. Box 397
        Aledo, TX 76008
        (817) 441-6044
        http://www.wallbuilders.com

David Barton tours the United States Capitol building, presenting it as a symbol of liberty and an expression of the nation's spiritual heritage. The video includes reenactments of historical events. A tour guidebook is included.

Total Truth: Liberating Christianity From Its Cultural Captivity

Type: MP3 CD
Length: Not available
Date: 2005
Cost: $24.98
Source: Christian Research Institute
          P.O. Box 8500
          Charlotte, NC 28271-8500
          (800) 228-1563
          http://www.equip.org

Author Nancy Randolph Pearcey presents an analysis of the division between the public and private realms and of how this separation tends to limit Christian involvement in public matters. Pearcey recommends ways in which Christians can become more completely involved and gain influence in the larger culture.

A War on Science: Intelligent Design in the Classroom

Type: DVD, VHS
Length: 50 min.
Date: 2006
Cost: $149.95 DVD; $159.95 VHS
Source: Films Media Group
          P.O. Box 2053
          Princeton, NJ 08543-2053
          (800) 257-5126
          http://www.films.com

This program investigates the development of intelligent design theory and documents the legal battles that have arisen over the attempt to include this theory in the public school curriculum. Also included are an overview of the clash between creationism versus evolution and the conflict over separation of church and state in the twentieth century.

What Is True?: An Introduction to Secular Humanism

Type: DVD, VHS
Length: 40 min.
Date: 2006
Cost: $129.95 DVD; $139.95 VHS

Source: Films Media Group
P.O. Box 2053
Princeton, NJ 08543-2053
(800) 257-5126
http://www.films.com

This video investigates such topics as the development of religion, the possibility of morality without religious belief, and the creation of rational public policy. Prominent humanists, including Paul Kurtz, founder of the Council for Secular Humanism; Toni Van Pelt, women's rights activist; and Ronald Bailey correspondent for *Reason* magazine, take part in the discussion.

Where Is America in Prophecy?
Type: DVD, VHS
Length: 55 min.
Date: 2001
Cost: $23.95 DVD; $21.95 VHS
Source: Armageddon Books
P.O. Box 230
West Jefferson, NC 28694
(336) 246-2628
http://www.armageddonbooks.com

Hal Lindsey, noted for his contention that the world is approaching the end times, discusses the role that the United States supposedly will play in the last days prophesied in the Bible.

Who Is John Birch?
Type: DVD, VHS
Length: 55 min.
Date: 2004
Cost: $18.95
Source: American Opinion Book Services
P.O. Box 8040
Appleton, WI 54912
(920) 749-3780
http://aobs-store.com

This video explores the life of John Birch, after whom Robert Welch named the John Birch Society. Birch, a Baptist missionary in China, was killed by Chinese communists at the end of World War II.

With God On Our Side: George W. Bush and the Rise of the Religious Right
Type: VHS, DVD
Length: 100 min.
Date: 2004
Cost: $298

Source: First Run Icarus Films
32 Court Street, 21st Floor
Brooklyn, NY 11201
(800) 876-1710
http://www.frif.com

This film is divided into two parts. The first describes the rise of the religious right as a force in U.S. politics and the movement's relationship with past presidents. The second investigates the life of George W. Bush from his religious conversion through his first term as president. The film focuses on the role that Bush's religious beliefs play in presidential decision making.

The Young Age of the Earth
Type: DVD, VHS
Length: 80 min.
Date: Not available
Cost: $20.95
Source: Creation Moments
P.O. Box 839
Foley, MN 56329
(800) 422-4253
http://www.creationmoments.net

Robert Gentry and host Lonnie Melashenko provide arguments that the earth was created fairly recently and in accord with the literal six days of the Genesis account. For instance, Gentry contends that coal and oil can develop quickly and that the Grand Canyon resulted from a fast erosion process.

DVDs

AIDS: What You Haven't Been Told
Type: DVD
Length: 60 min.
Date: 1989
Cost: $21.95
Source: Jeremiah Films
P.O. Box 1710
Hemet, CA 92546
(714) 652-1006
http://www.jeremiahfilms.com

Fundamentalists provide their perspective on AIDS, assess blame for its spread, and discuss possible protection against the disease.

The Awesome Forces of God's Creation
Type: DVD

Length: 135 min.
Date: 1995
Cost: $32.95
Source: Christian Reality Videos
P.O. Box 115
Hamlin, NY 14464
(888) 437-7558
http://www.christianreality.com

This video presents stunning views of the forces of nature and interprets them as evidence of creation and the intelligent design of the world.

The Bible Answer Video
Type: DVD
Length: 45 min.
Date: 2005
Cost: Donation $7.50
Source: Christian Research Institute
P.O. Box 8500
Charlotte, NC 28271-8500
888-700-0274
http://equip.org

Hank Hanegraaff, president of the Christian Research Institute and host of the "Bible Answer Man" radio program, answers questions about biblical guidance regarding such topics as embryonic stem-cell research and the Darwinian theory of evolution. The video was recorded live at First Family Church in Overland Park, Kansas.

The Case for a Creator
Type: DVD
Length: 100 min.
Date: 2006
Cost: $17.95
Source: Christian Reality Videos
P.O. Box 115
Hamlin, NY 14464
(888) 437-7558
http://www.christianreality.com

This video traces journalist Lee Strobel's shift from religious skepticism to faith in God and the conviction that science should include more than materialistic assumptions. Interviewing several scientists, Strobel explores the possibility that scientific evidence supports a belief in a supernatural creator.

Christian Life and Today's World/Christian Life and Work
Type: DVD

Length: 299 min.
Date: 2000, 2002
Cost: $31.99
Source: Gateway Films/Vision Video
P.O. Box 540
Worcester, PA 19490-0540
(800) 523-0226
http://www.visionvideo.com

This two-video package first explores how the contemporary culture influences the Christian and suggests how the Christian should respond to the secular world. Five 30-minute programs investigate such topics as personal identity, pluralism, and the consumer culture. The second video applies biblical teaching to the issues that Christians face each day in the workplace and suggests how they can make their faith known.

The Da Vinci Code
Type: DVD (2 discs)
Length: 149 min.
Date: 2006
Cost: $20.99
Source: Movies Unlimited
3015 Darnell Road
Philadelphia, PA 19154
(215) 637-4444
http://www.moviesunlimited.com

This movie, based on the popular novel by Dan Brown, resulted in strong negative responses from Catholics and Protestant conservative Christians in various books and videos. The book and movie raised doubts about the biblical account of Jesus and portrayed the Catholic organization Opus Dei as a sinister group of individuals committed to maintaining the 2,000-year-old secrets of the Christian religion.

Evolution: Fact or Fairy Tale?
Type: DVD
Length: 66 min.
Date: Not available
Cost: $17.49
Source: Christian Book Distributors
P.O. Box 7000
Peabody, MA 01961-7000
(978) 977-5000
http:// www.christianbook.com

Ralph Stewart, who worked for fifteen years on nuclear weapons development at Sanida National Laboratories, claims that the theory of evolution amounts to the equivalent of a fairy tale. He compares the evidence for creation versus evolution and attempts to answer such questions as the fate of dinosaurs and the age of the earth

Gay Rights/Special Rights

Type: DVD
Length: 45 min.
Date: 1994
Cost: $21.95
Source: Jeremiah Films
          P.O. Box 1710
          Hemet, CA 92546
          (800) 828-2290
          http://www.jeremiahfilms.com

This program provides a conservative Christian view of what is considered the "homosexual agenda." The observation is made that homosexuals wish to amend the 1964 Civil Rights Act to make sexual preference a right guaranteed under the Constitution.

George W. Bush: Faith in the White House

Type: DVD
Length: 70 min.
Date: 2004
Cost: $12.95
Source: Christian Reality Videos
          P.O. Box 115
          Hamlin, NY 14464
          (888) 437-7558
          http://www.christianreality.com

This video focuses on President George W. Bush's Christian faith and his emphasis on prayer and attempt to apply biblical lessons to his life and role as president. Bush's religious beliefs are viewed as significant ingredients in the war on terror.

The Great Debate on Science and the Bible

Type: Three DVDs
Length: 90, 95, and 47 min.
Date: 2006
Cost: $39.95

Source: Reasons To Believe
P.O. Box 5978
Pasadena, CA 91117
(800) 482-7836
http://www.reasons.org

Ken Ham and Jason Lisle (representing the "young Earth" view) and Hugh Ross and Walter Kaiser (representing the "day-age" view), all supporters of creationism, debate such issues as the age of the universe, the accuracy of radiometric dating methods, the death of plants and animals prior to Adam's sin, the extinction of dinosaurs, and the effectiveness of science in exploring the past.

How Should We Then Live?
Type: DVD
Length: 360 min.
Date: 1978
Cost: $49.99
Source: Christian Book Distributors
P.O. Box 7000
Peabody, MA 01961-7000
(978) 977-5000
http://www.christianbook.com

This series features the conservative Christian thinker Francis Schaeffer. Each of twelve half-hour programs treats a historical era and offers biblical answers to contemporary problems. A study guide accompanies the videotapes.

Icons of Evolution
Type: DVD
Length: 51 min., 60 min.
Date: 2002
Cost: $19.95 DVD
Source: Reasons To Believe
P.O. Box 5978
Pasadena, CA 91117
(800) 482-7836
http://www.reasons.org

This critique of the theory of evolution revolves around the experience of high school biology teacher Roger DeHart, who adds to the curriculum subject matter critical of the "icons of evolution." The video suggests questions that students should ask their biology teacher.

Inherit the Wind
Type: DVD
Length: 127 min.

Date: 1960
Cost: $14.99
Source: Movies Unlimited
3015 Darnell Road
Philadelphia, PA 19154
(800) 668-4344
http://www.moviesunlimited.com

This fictionalization of the 1925 Scopes trial in Dayton, Tennessee, stars Spencer Tracy and Frederick March, who play roles corresponding respectively to Clarence Darrow and William Jennings Bryan. Fundamentalism is treated in a far from favorable light.

Journey Toward Creation

Type: DVD
Length: 60 min.
Date: 1998
Cost: $19.95
Source: Reasons To Believe
P.O. Box 5978
Pasadena, CA 91117
(800) 482-7836
http://www.reasons.org

Hugh Ross, astronomer and president of Reasons To Believe, conducts a journey back in time to examine such phenomena as nebulae, black holes, and quasars. Ross does not accept the more fundamentalist belief in a six-day creation, but concludes that God created the universe and human beings.

The Late Great Planet Earth

Type: DVD
Length: 91 min.
Date: 1987
Cost: $8.99
Source: Christian Book Distributors
P.O. Box 7000
Peabody, MA 01961-7000
(978) 977-5000
http://www.christianbook.com

Orson Welles narrates this video based on Hal Lindsey's best-seller by the same name. Biblical prophecy is interpreted from a premillennial perspective in predicting future disasters for the planet.

Let My Children Go

Type: DVD
Length: Not available

Date: Not available
Cost: $21.95
Source: Jeremiah Films
P.O. Box 1710
Hemet, CA 92546
(800) 828-2290
http://www.jeremiahfilms.com

This video, noting that Christians allow their children to be influenced by the secular public school system, urges Christian parents and churches to take control of the education of their children according to the biblical mandate.

A Night to Honor Israel Goes to Israel 2005
Type: Three DVDs
Length: 180 min.
Date: 2005
Cost: $59
Source: John Hagee Ministries
P.O. Box 1400
San Antonio, TX 78295-1400
(210) 494-3900
http://www.jhm.org

John Hagee continues to publicize his support for Israel in this video based on Hagee's nine-day trip to that country. Included are an event at the Jerusalem Convention Center honoring the state of Israel, Hagee speaking at the Knesset, and a sermon given by Hagee at Mount Scopus.

Obsession: Radical Islam's War Against the West
Type: DVD
Length: 120 min.
Date: 2006
Cost: $20
Source: John Hagee Ministries
P.O. Box 1400
San Antonio, TX 78295
(210) 494-3900
http://www.jhm.org

Using footage from Arab television and first-hand accounts given by a former terrorist and others, John Hagee identifies radical Islam as the new enemy confronting Western civilization. Hagee compares the seriousness of this enemy to Adolf Hitler and the Nazis during World War II.

The Omega Code
Type: DVD
Length: 100 min.

Date: 2000
Cost: $8.99
Source: Christian Book Distributors
P.O. Box 7000
Peabody, MA 01961-7000
(978) 977-5000
http://www.christianbook.com

This film, produced by the Trinity Broadcasting Network, proved to be a commercial success at theaters, likely due to the interest of evangelical Christians. Some of the events described in the Book of Revelation are placed in dramatic form. The plot revolves around the attempt to understand a biblical code that supposedly foretells the events of the last days. The Antichrist proves to be the "European Union Chairman."

One World: Striving for Unity in the Last Days
Type: DVD
Length: 52 min.
Date: 2001
Cost: $21.95
Source: Jeremiah Films
P.O. Box 1710
Hemet, CA 92546
800-828-2290
http://www.jeremiahfilms.com

Authors Hal Lindsay, Tim LaHaye, Marlin Maddoux, and Chuck Missler discuss biblical prophecy in the context of the post-September 11, 2001, world. They speculate about the possible future events that they claim have been prophesied in the Bible.

Revelation
Type: DVD
Length: 97 min.
Date: 2000
Cost: $8.99
Source: Christian Book Distributors
P.O. Box 7000
Peabody, MA 01961-7000
(978) 977-5000
http://www.christianbook.com

This fictionalized account of the end times deals with the Antichrist coming to power and establishing a worldwide government. Government representatives are distributing virtual reality headsets that all are to wear on a "Day of Wonders." The Christian underground attempts to foil the evil plan

Searching for the Truth on Origins
Type: DVD
Length: 200 min. (4 discs)
Date: Not available
Cost: $45
Source: Creation Moments
           P.O. Box 809
           Foley, MN 56329
           (800) 422-4253
           http://www.creationmoments.net

Roger Oakland makes fourteen presentations on various aspects of the contrasting creation and evolution accounts of the origin of human beings. Oakland speculates about the potential effects of evolution theory on human morality and spirituality as expressed in the Bible.

The Signature of God
Type: DVD
Length: 160 min.
Date: 1997
Cost: $11.99
Source: Christian Book Distributors
           P.O. Box 7000
           Peabody, MA 01961-7000
           (978) 977-5000
           http://www.christianbook.com

Grant R. Jeffrey argues that Hebrew codes in the Bible reveal highly accurate biblical prophecies. Jeffrey claims to have developed a mathematical formula to prove that the Bible is the revealed word of God.

Terrorism: The New War on Freedom
Type: DVD
Length: 60 min.
Date: 2004
Cost: $7.99
Source: Christian Book Distributors
           P.O. Box 7000
           Peabody, MA 01961-7000
           (978) 977-5000
           http://www.christianbook.com

This program asks whether Islam encourages terrorism and explores possible explanations for Islamic jihad, or "holy war." The video examines the threat that terrorism poses to freedom and suggests how Americans can preserve that freedom.

A Thief in the Night Collector's Series

Type: Four DVDs
Length: Not available
Date: Not available
Cost: $99.95
Source: Russ Doughten Films, Inc.
          5907 Meredith Drive
          Des Moines, IA 50322
          (800) 247-3456
          http://www.rdfilms.com

The four videos in this series—A Thief in the Night, A Distant Thunder, Image of the Beast, and The Prodigal Planet—portray the events prophesied in the Book of Revelation, beginning with the rapture of the righteous and ending with God's seven bowls of wrath described in the sixteenth chapter.

Unholy War: Christian Genocide in Sudan

Type: DVD
Length: 40 min.
Date: 2002
Cost: $24.95
Source: Jeremiah Films
          P.O. Box 1710
          Hemet, CA 92546
          800-828-2290
          http://www.jeremiahfilms.com

Calling the conflict in Sudan the longest war of the twentieth century, this video claims that since 1955 the Muslim-controlled government has been conducting a terrorist campaign against Christians in southern Sudan.

Weapon of Mass Destruction: The Murderous Reign of Saddam Hussein

Type: DVD
Length: 95 min.
Date: 2004
Cost: $21.95
Source: Jeremiah Films
          P.O. Box 1710
          Hemet, CA 92546
          800-828-2290
          http://www.jeremiahfilms.com

Responding to the "liberal bias" against the war in Iraq, this video attempts to justify U.S. military intervention by providing accounts of the atrocities that Saddam Hussein allegedly committed against the Iraqi people.

Why Not Gay Marriage?
Type: DVD
Length: 60 min.
Date: Not available
Cost: $15
Source: American Family Association
P.O. Drawer 2440
Tupelo, MS 38803
(662) 844-5036
https://www2.afastore.net

Glenn T. Stanton, senior analyst for Focus on the Family, presents arguments against gay marriage that he learned from engaging in debates on the subject on several college campuses

The Wonders of God's Creation
Type: DVD
Length: 189 min., 3 DVDs
Date: 2004
Cost: $32.99
Source: Christian Book Distributors
P.O. Box 7000
Peabody, MA 01961-7000
(978) 977-5000
http://www.christianbook.com

The three video disks in this series ("Planet Earth," "Animal Kingdom," and "Human Life") present the wonders of nature and attribute them to a creator. Biblical references are frequently provided during each presentation.

Videotapes

All Rapped Up
Type: VHS
Length: 130 min.
Date: 1991
Cost: $39.95
Source: American Portrait Films
P.O. Box 809
Brunswick, OH 44212
(800) 736-4567
http://www.amport.com

A continuation of the *Hell's Bells* video, this program examines recent rock music and claims to reveal the true nature of developments such as rap and hip-hop, and exposing what are considered the harmful effects of such music.

The American Covenant

Type: VHS
Length: 52 min.
Date: 1994
Cost: $19.95
Source: American Portrait Films
P.O. Box 809
Brunswick, OH 44212
(800) 736-4567
http://www.amport.com

Filmed at various historical sites around the nation, this tape examines the formation of the American Republic. Marshall Foster, a Christian historian, narrates ten events in the history of the nation, including the Pilgrims' *Mayflower* voyage and Patrick Henry's "Give me liberty or give me death" oration.

Apocalypse!

Type: VHS
Length: 120 min.
Date: 1999
Cost: $19.98
Source: PBS Video Customer Service
PO Box 279
Melbourne, FL 32902
(800) 344-3337
http://www.shoppbs.org

The notion of an apocalypse, the end time of devastation for the sinful and deliverance for the faithful, has influenced human thought for over two millennia. This video explores the ways in which the meaning of the idea has changed in more recent times.

Billy Graham: Great Preachers Video Series

Type: VHS
Length: 25 min.
Date: 1997
Cost: $11.99
Source: Christian Book Distributors
P.O. Box 7000
Peabody, MA 01961-7000
(978) 977-5000
http://www.christianbook.com

Host Bill Turpie interviews Billy Graham to explore Graham's religious journey. Also included is one of Graham's sermons.

The Biological Evidence for Design

Type: VHS
Length: 55 min.
Date: 1998
Cost: $8
Source: Reasons To Believe
P.O. Box 5978
Pasadena, CA 91117
(800) 482-7836
http://www.reasons.org

Michael Behe uses examples from biochemistry in an attempt to discredit the neo-Darwinian theory of evolution and examines evidence he believes indicates that human life resulted from intelligent design.

The Biological Evidence of Creation

Type: VHS
Length: 28 min.
Date: 1998
Cost: $19.95
Source: American Portrait Films
P.O. Box 809
Brunswick, OH 44212
(800) 736-4567
http://www.amport.com

Challenging the view that human beings evolved from amphibians, Werner Gift, an information scientist, and Don Batten, a biologist, argue that biological change has definite limits. They conclude that the origins of life can be found in the creative activities of a deity.

The Brutal Truth

Type: VHS
Length: 29 min.
Date: 1990
Cost: $19.95
Source: American Portrait Films
P.O. Box 809
Brunswick, OH 44212
(800) 736-4567
http://www.amport.com

This video focuses on the struggle of abortion protestors who have undergone arrest and imprisonment in their attempts to stop abortion. The claim is made that the constitutional rights of protestors have been violated and that the national news media have ignored such violations.

The Case for Creation
Type: VHS
Length: 45 min.
Date: Not available
Cost: $19.95
Source: Creation Moments
P.O. Box 839
Foley, MN 56329
(800) 422-4253
http://www.creationmoments.net

This video presents scientific evidence for a creation approach to the origin of human beings as opposed to the theory of evolution and examines the historical and legal aspects of the conflict between creationism and evolution.

Dawn's Early Light
Type: VHS
Length: 28 min.
Date: 1994
Cost: $19.95
Source: American Portrait Films
P.O. Box 809
Brunswick, OH 44212
(800) 736-4567
http://amport.com

This tape provides a history of the development of liberty in the United States and examines the major events leading to the founding of America. The purpose is to rediscover the heritage of the nation.

Dr. Bob Jones, Sr. (1883–1968): A Film Tribute
Type: VHS
Length: 48 min.
Date: 2000
Cost: $14.95
Source: Unusual Films
Bob Jones University Press
Customer Services
Greenville, SC 29614
(800) 845-5731
http://www.bjupress.com

This video includes two segments: the first provides an overview of the life of Bob Jones, Sr., founder and first president of Bob Jones University; and the second is a sermon that Jones preached on Luke 23, entitled "Calvary."

The Evidence for Creation: Examining the Origin of Planet Earth

Type: VHS
Length: 60 min.
Date: 1994
Cost: $7.95
Source: Creation Moments
P.O. Box 839
Foley, MN 56329
(800) 422-4253
http://www.creationmoments.net

Roger Oakland asserts the logic of creationism, maintaining that evidence derived from observations of the galaxy as well as rock formations on earth support the creationist theory of the origin of the earth.

Foundations of Freedom

Type: VHS (two tapes)
Length: 100 min.
Date: 1998
Cost: $23.99
Source: Gateway Films/Vision Video
P.O. Box 540
Worcester, PA 19490-0540
(800) 523-0226
http://www.visionvideo.com

This video, which includes interviews with contemporary historians, presents an account of the values and principles said to be most important to early American leaders. Religious beliefs are said to have played a major role in the development of the nation.

God's Providence in History

Type: VHS
Length: 59 min.
Date: 1986
Cost: $19.95
Source: Bob Jones University Press
Customer Services
Greenville, SC 29614
(800) 845-5731
http://www.bjupress.com

Old Testament history is examined in the context of contemporary events. The tape makes the case for the Bible's relevance to modern times.

Hard Truth

Type: VHS

Length: 9.5 min.

Date: 1991

Cost: $14.95

Source: American Portrait Films

P.O. Box 809

Brunswick, OH 44212

(800) 736-4567

http://www.amport.com

This video is a graphic presentation of arguments against abortion. It is presented as a useful tool against pro-choice advocates, portraying abortion as murder. A study guide accompanies the video.

Hell's Bells: The Dangers of Rock and Roll

Type: VHS (two tapes)

Length: 185 min.

Date: 1990

Cost: $49.95

Source: American Portrait Films

P.O. Box 809

Brunswick, OH 44212

(800) 736-4567

http://www.amport.com

Through film clips and interviews with performers, this video explores the effects of popular music, claiming that America's youth are being seduced by the medium.

I Do Exist

Type: VHS

Length: 48 min.

Date: 2004

Cost: $23

Source: American Family Association

P.O. Drawer 2440

Tupelo, MS 38803

(662) 844-5036

https://www2.afastore.net

Five individuals claiming to be former homosexuals describe the process through which they reoriented their sexual preference. Psychiatrist Robert Spitzer and psychologists Mark Yarhouse and Warren Throckmorton present their perspectives on the subject.

In the Image of God

Type: VHS
Length: 28 min.
Date: 1998
Cost: $19.95
Source: American Portrait Films
      P.O. Box 809
      Brunswick, OH 44212
      (800) 736-4567
      http://www.amport.com

This video provides "compelling new evidence" about the creation of human beings through an act of divine will rather than evolution. It provides arguments against the evolution of human beings from ape creatures such as *Homo habilis* and Piltdown Man.

The Massacre of Innocence

Type: VHS
Length: 85 min.
Date: 1988
Cost: $19.95
Source: American Portrait Films
      P.O. Box 809
      Brunswick, OH 44212
      (800) 736-4567
      http://www.amport.com

This video explores the sociological and medical history of abortion. The claim is made that "spiritual forces" are behind the continuation of the practice, including such rituals as child sacrifice and feminist goddess worship.

Mine Eyes Have Seen the Glory

Type: VHS
Length: 165 min.
Date: 1991
Cost: $23.99
Source: Gateway Films/Vision Video
      P.O. Box 540
      Worcester, PA 19490
      (800) 523-0226
      http://www.visionvideo.com

Randall Balmer, who traveled to various denominations and churches around the United States, presents a view of Evangelicals: who they are, what they believe, and how their beliefs influence the way they live. Balmer describes how Evangelicals are attempting to protect themselves and their children from the influences of secular society and how they are striving to change society.

MTV Examined
Type: VHS
Length: 30 min.
Date: 1994
Cost: $19.95
Source: American Portrait Films
P.O. Box 809
Brunswick, OH 44212
(800) 736-4567
http://www.amport.com

Based on an examination of the content of the cable television station MTV, this video charges that the music station must take responsibility for increased violence, sexual activity, rebellion, and moral relativism among young people.

A Nation Adrift: A Chronicle of America's Providential Heritage
Type: VHS
Length: 93 min.
Date: Not available
Cost: $19.95
Source: New Liberty Videos
P.O. Box 664
Oak Grove, MO 64075
(800) 771-2147
http://www.theorderline.net

This video provides an overview of American history, claiming that God has guided the development of the nation, and presents a warning that Americans must withstand the danger that humanism poses to the nation's spiritual infrastructure.

Raging Waters
Type: VHS
Length: 28 min.
Date: 1997
Cost: $19.95
Source: American Portrait Films
P.O. Box 809
Brunswick, OH 44212
(800) 736-4567
http://www.amport.com

Examination of such physical phenomena as ripple marks, marine fossils in mountain ranges, and the rapid development of coal deposits in Australia are presented as evidence for a Genesis flood. The video also refers to the legends of Australian Aborigines that describe a general flood.

The Religion of Secular Humanism

Type: VHS
Length: 40 min.
Date: 1998
Cost: $15.99
Source: Gateway Films/Vision Video
P.O. Box 540
Worcester, PA 19490-0540
(800) 523-0226
http://www.visionvideo.com

The video considers secular humanism to be an identifiable worldview accepted by many influential people in the United States. The claim is made that the viewpoint of secular humanism is the dominant position presented in contemporary public education.

Revelation Illustrated

Type: VHS
Length: 46 min.
Date: 1992
Cost: $15.99
Source: Christian Book Distributors
P.O. Box 7000
Peabody, MA 01961-7000
(978) 977-5000
http://www.christianbook.com

This retelling of the prophetic Book of Revelation includes narration from the original text, the artwork of Pat Marvenko Smith, and music by the Back Choir of Pittsburgh.

Science, Creation, and the Bible

Type: VHS
Length: 49 min.
Date: 1993
Cost: $19.95
Source: Creation Moments
P.O. Box 839
Foley, MN 56329
(800) 422-4253
http://www.creationmoments.net

Dr. Walter Brown, a former evolutionist, explains how evolutionary theory challenges the Christian faith and conflicts with science. Brown presents evidence from fossil records.

A Scientist Looks at Creation

Type: VHS
Length: 80 min.
Date: 1994
Cost: $19.95
Source: American Portrait Films
           P.O. Box 809
           Brunswick, OH 44212
           (800) 736-4567
           http://www.amport.com

This two-part program explaining creationism claims to show why many physicists, engineers, and astronomers have changed their minds on the debate between evolution and creation.

The Seven Days of Creation

Type: VHS
Length: 30 min.
Date: Not available
Cost: $19.95
Source: Creation Moments
           P.O. Box 839
           Foley, MN 56329
           (800) 422-4253
           http://www.creationmoments.net

The video includes footage of animals in their natural surroundings and scenes of the world from outer space combined with the account of creation as found in the King James version of the Bible.

The Silent Scream

Type: VHS
Length: 28 min.
Date: 1984
Cost: $18.95
Source: American Portrait Films
           P.O. Box 809
           Brunswick, OH 44212
           (800) 736-4567
           http://www.amport.com

In this early antiabortion video, Dr. Bernard N. Nathanson, who formerly ran an abortion clinic but now opposes abortion, explains the abortion procedure in graphic terms.

Sound and Fury: An Examination of the Power of Music
Type: VHS
Length: 45 min.
Date: 1999
Cost: $15.99
Source: Christian Book Distributors
P.O. Box 7000
Peabody, MA 01961-7000
(978) 977-5000
http://www.christianbook.com

Host Eric Holmberg examines the popular music culture, referring to popular music as an addition that has serious pernicious consequences for society. For instance, the program associates popular music with sexual immorality.

The Story of America's Liberty
Type: VHS
Length: 65 min.
Date: 1994
Cost: $19.95
Source: American Portrait Films
P.O. Box 809
Brunswick, OH 44212
(800) 736-4567
http://www.amport.com

This treatment of America's Christian heritage focuses on the alleged miracles that God performed in assisting the American birth.

Suffer the Children
Type: VHS
Length: 60 min.
Date: 1999
Cost: $25
Source: American Family Association
P.O. Drawer 2440
Tupelo, MS 38803
(662) 844-5036

In order to counter a pro-homosexual video titled "It's Elementary: Talking about Gay Issues in School," the American Family Association produced this video, based on what the organization considers a biblically correct view of the issue.

Test of Faith
Type: VHS
Length: 55 min.
Date: 1989
Cost: $17.95
Source: ChristianCinema.com, Inc.
P.O. Box 6430
Visalia, CA 93290
(888) 527-2388
http://www.christiancinema.com

A physics professor, claiming that faith is an enemy of science, pressures a young college student to abandon his belief in biblical creation and to concentrate instead on scientific thinking. The tape ultimately points to the errors in the professor's position.

The Triumph of Design and the Demise of Darwin
Type: VHS
Length: 55 min.
Date: 1999
Cost: $19.95
Source: American Portrait Films
P.O. Box 809
Brunswick, OH 44212
(800) 736-4567
http://www.amport.com

Host Woody Cozad presents Phillip Johnson, author of *Darwin On Trial*, who discusses the claimed deficiencies in the Darwinian theory of evolution. The video contends that persuasive evidence exists for the alternative theory of intelligent design as an explanation of the origin of human beings.

Winning the Sexual Revolution
Type: VHS
Length: 35 min.
Date: Not available
Cost: $19.95
Source: American Portrait Films
P.O. Box 809
Brunswick, OH 44212
(800) 736-4567
http://www.amport.com

James Dobson, head of Focus on the Family, actor Ricardo Montalban, and movie critic Michael Medved emphasize the importance of family values and how to defend them against the humanistic influences of the public schools and the mass media.

With a Vengeance: The Fight for Reproductive Freedom
Type: VHS
Length: 40 min.
Date: 1989
Cost: $225 purchase; $75 rental
Source: Women Make Movies
           462 Broadway, Suite 500
           New York, NY 10013
           (212) 925-0606
           http://www.wmm.com

This video is a reaction to the religious right's opposition to abortion, focusing on the reproductive rights of women. The struggles over abortion rights in the 1960s and 1980s are compared.

The World That Perished: Evidence for the Global Flood of Genesis
Type: VHS
Length: 35 min.
Date: 1988
Cost: $19.99
Source: Creation Moments
           P.O. Box 839
           Foley, MN 56329
           (800) 422-4253
           http://www.creationmoments.net

This video presents flood legends from various cultures around the world and examines geological evidence of the effects of a claimed worldwide flood.

Audiotapes

The Challenge of Religious Pluralism
Type: Audiocassette
Length: 155 min.
Date: 2003
Cost: $7.17
Source: Reasons To Believe
           P.O. Box 5978
           Pasadena, CA 91117
           (800) 482-7836
           http://www.reasons.org

Philosopher and theologian Kenneth Samples presents the biblical basis for the position that Christianity has a unique claim to religious truth.

Creation and the Supreme Court
Type: Two audiocassettes
Length: 120 min.
Date: 1997
Cost: $3.58
Source: Reasons To Believe
P.O. Box 5978
Pasadena, CA 91117
(800) 482-7836
http://www.reasons.org

Dr. Hugh Ross discusses the 1987 U.S. Supreme Court decision on teaching creationism in public schools (*Edwards v. Aguillard*), explores the history of creation science, and suggests a way to present creationism appropriately in the classroom.

Education and the Founding Fathers
Type: Audiocassette
Length: 60 min.
Date: 1993
Cost: $4.95
Source: Wallbuilders
P.O. Box 397
Aledo, TX 76008
(817) 441-6044
http://www.wallbuilders.com

Arguing against the "revisionists" who deny the importance of the Christian religion to education, David Barton emphasizes the educational works of Founders such as George Washington, Gouverneur Morris, and Fisher Ames, who upheld biblical teaching. Barton refers to the original texts and writings of the Founders to support his claim. Various historians have criticized Barton for what they consider his misuse of historical evidence.

Explaining Inerrancy
Type: Audiocassette
Length: 5 hrs.
Date: 1989
Cost: $22
Source: Ligonier Ministries
P.O. Box 863595
Orlando, FL 32886
(800) 435-4343
http://www.ligonier.org

R.C. Sproul presents an extended examination of the doctrine that the Bible is without error, arguing that Christians should submit to the authority of scripture.

God and Science
Type: Audiocassette
Length: 120 min.
Date: 1998
Cost: $13.96
Source: Reasons To Believe
          P.O. Box 5978
          Pasadena, CA 91117
          (800) 482-7836
          http://www.reasons.org

Noted conservative columnist and talk show host William F. Buckley moderates this debate between atheist Peter Atkins, an Oxford professor, and William Lane Craig, who received a doctor of theology degree from the University of Munich. The participants consider whether Christian theism or atheistic naturalism best explains the preconditions to science and what science might have to say about the existence of God.

Putting Creation to the Test
Type: Audiocassette
Length: 6 hrs.
Date: 2000
Cost: $20.78
Source: Reasons To Believe
          P.O. Box 5978
          Pasadena, CA 91117
          800-482-7836
          http://www.reasons.org

Astronomer Hugh Ross, biochemist Fazale Rana, philosopher Kenneth Samples, and others examine what they consider a testable creation model. They claim that a theory of creation has been developed that satisfies scientific requirements while remaining faithful to the biblical account.

The Scopes Trial Revisited
Type: Audiocassette
Length: 120 min.
Date: Not available
Cost: $3.58

Source: Reasons To Believe
             P.O. Box 5978
             Pasadena, CA 91117
             (800) 482-7836
             http://www.reasons.org

Hugh Ross, president of Reasons To Believe, testifies at a reenactment of the famous 1925 Scopes "monkey" trial. Ross defends a creation model of the origins of human beings, arguing that such an account is scientifically testable and therefore should be granted a place in the public school curriculum.

Audio CDs

Beyond Irreducible Complexity

Type: CD
Length: 60 min.
Date: 2003
Cost: $7
Source: Reasons To Believe
             P.O. Box 5978
             Pasadena, CA 91117
             (800) 482-7836
             http://www.reasons.org

Fazale Rana extends the claim for an intelligent design alternative to a theory of evolution beyond the argument from irreducible complexity in an attempt to construct a more convincing case for biochemical design.

Christian Worldview

Type: CD
Length: 360 min.
Date: 2006
Cost: $45
Source: Ligonier Ministries
             P.O. Box 863595
             Orlando, FL 32886
             (800) 435-4343
             https://www.ligonier.org

R. C. Sproul examines various worldviews, including secularism, existentialism, humanism, pragmatism, positivism, and hedonism and their influence on science, economics, government, art, and literature. Sproul argues that only the Christian worldview is capable of answering life's more important questions.

The Spirit of the American Revolution

Type: CD

Length: 55 min.
Date: 1993
Cost: $11.95
Source: Wallbuilders
P.O. Box 397
Aledo, TX 76008
(817) 441-6044
http://www.wallbuilders.com

David Barton discusses the importance of the Christian faith to the colonists during the American Revolution. Barton refers to the faith of prominent Americans at the time, such as John Adams, George Washington, Samuel Adams, and Patrick Henry, and focuses on the role they saw God playing in the course of the Revolution. God is portrayed as an unqualified supporter of the American revolutionaries.

Tribulation Force
Type: CD
Length: 5 hrs.
Date: 1999
Cost: $16.99
Source: Christian Book Distributors
P.O. Box 7000
Peabody, MA 01961-7000
(978) 977-5000
http://www.christianbook.com

In a sequel to Jerry Jenkins's and Tim LaHaye's fictional depiction of the end times as prophesied in the Book of Revelation, this audio presentation continues the story of the last days.

CD-ROMs

The Bible and Spade
Publisher: Associates for Biblical Research
Distributor: Associates for Biblical Research
P.O. Box 144
Akron, PA 17501
(800) 430-0008
http://abr.christiananswers.net/bascdrom.html
Price: $79.95

This resource includes all issues of the quarterly magazine *The Bible and Spade* from 1972 to 2005. Articles, written from a conservative perspective, affirm the inerrancy of the Bible.

International Bulletin of Missionary Research

Publisher: Overseas Ministries Study Center
490 Prospect Street
New Haven, CT 06511
http://www.OMSC.org
Price: $23.00
(203) 624-6672

This CD-ROM, containing the "Best of IBMR," includes a collection of fifty articles from the ecumenical International Bulletin that deal with the history and current problems of Christian missionary work. Among the articles are "Repositioning Mission Agencies for the Twenty-first Century" (Ted Ward, 1999) and "Terrorism, Islam, and Mission: Reflections of a Guest in Muslim Lands" (J. Dudley Woodberry, 2002).

Left Behind: Eternal Forces

Distributor: Left Behind Games
25060 Hancock Avenue, Suite 103-110
Murrieta, CA 92562
http://www.leftbehindgames.com
Price: $39.95

When this video game, based on the popular Tim LaHaye and Jerry Jenkins book series *Left Behind*, liberal Christian groups objected to the game's violence, which they considered contrary to the Gospel message, and asked Wal Mart stores not to sell the product. The game story begins after the rapture, when most Christians have been taken to heaven. Remaining Christians must battle the forces of evil, represented by an organization supporting one-world government called Global Community Peacekeepers.

Original Intent: The Courts, the Constitution, and Religion

Distributor: Wallbuilders
P.O. Box 397
Aledo, TX 76008
(817) 441-6044
http://www.wallbuilders.com
Price: $9.95

This resource provides information about the tendency of the U.S. Supreme Court to reinterpret the Constitution in ways that minimize the claimed biblical foundations of the nation. Included are hundreds of quotes from early Americans on the role of religion in the public realm and the appropriate functions of the courts.

R. C. Sproul Digital Library on CD-ROM
Distributor: Ligonier Ministries
        P.O. Box 863595
        Orlando, FL 32886
        (800) 435-4343
        http://www.ligonier.org
        Price: $99.95

This source includes five books by Ligonier Ministries head R. C. Sproul: *Grace Unknown, The Last Days According to Jesus, The Holiness of God, Chosen by God, and Essential Truths of the Christian Faith.* In these books, Sproul presents his understanding of the reformed faith, the end times, and the basic beliefs of historical Christianity.

Radio and Television Programs

Conservative religious organizations broadcast a wide variety of programs that touch on political and social issues in some way. We include a selection of such programs here. Usually these programs do not appear at a uniform time nationwide but are syndicated. Readers should check local station and cable listings to determine if individual programs appear in their area. Program hosts, often called televangelists, solicit donations in order to acquire the funds necessary to pay the high costs of broadcasting. Critics of conservative Christian broadcasters often criticize aggressive fundraising campaigns, charging that noted religious figures are profiting at the expense of the less well-to-do.

See article *"TV Evangelists Call Signals from the Same Playbook"* by Bill Smith and Carolyn Tuft, following this listing of programs.

ACLJ This Week
Jay Sekulow, chief counsel for the American Center for Law and Justice, hosts this weekly thirty-minute television program. The topics for discussion have included abortion, secondary and higher education curricula, national security, and the war on terror. Viewers may call with questions for Sekulow.

Beverly LaHaye Today
Beverly LaHaye, president of Concerned Women for America, interviews various activists in the religious right on this daily radio program. LaHaye focuses on cultural issues such as education, the moral upbringing of children, marriage tax relief, and decency in the entertainment industry. Segments of

the program can be heard via the Internet:
http://www.oneplace.com/ministries/Beverly_LaHaye_Today.

Bible Answer Man

This radio program, hosted by Hank Hanegraaff of the Christian Research Institute. Hanegraaff takes phone calls from listeners who submit questions on biblical subjects. Hanegraaff provides traditional interpretations of scripture and has been a vocal critic of the theory of evolution.

Breakthrough

Rod Parsley telecasts this program from his 12,000-member World Harvest Church in Columbus, Ohio, which is seen on the Trinity Broadcasting Network and various other television networks. Parsley proclaims a conservative Christian message on social issues and encourages viewers to contribute to the church with the expectation of receiving health and wealth in return.

Coral Ridge Hour

On this weekly television broadcast, D. James Kennedy, pastor at Coral Ridge Presbyterian Church in Fort Lauderdale, Florida, deals with current social issues, urging the establishment of Christian values in the United States.

Cornerstone with John Hagee

This fundamentalist program is telecast from John Hagee's Cornerstone Church in San Antonio, Texas, and can be seen on Trinity Broadcasting Network at 8 a.m. EST on Sunday mornings. Although not as explicitly political as other broadcasts, such as Billy James Hargis's television program and Jerry Falwell's *Old-Time Gospel Hour,* Hagee often offers, with passion and without apology, the religious right position on such social issues as homosexual rights, abortion, and the women's movement. He is highly critical of the Clinton administration and the "atheists in Washington." Hagee often presents evidence from scientific authorities for his positions on social issues, but the Bible is his ultimate authority.

Creation Moments

This two-minute daily radio program, produced by Creation Moments, Inc., is heard on 700 radio outlets in the United States and around the world. The program presents a creationist understanding of science, offering facts about nature and demonstrating their connection to a creator. The program's Web site (http://creationmoments.com/radio/station_finder.php) provides a list of all stations that carry the presentations.

Creation Update

Hugh Ross, president of Reasons To Believe, and four associates take questions from the listening audience on this weekly radio broadcast. Ross attempts to demonstrate the compatibility of Christian beliefs and the Bible with scientific findings.

Enjoying Everyday Life

Joyce Meyers provides advice for a satisfying daily life on this television program broadcast on cable and satellite networks and via podcasts.

Focus on the Family

This daily radio program hosted by Dr. James Dobson is broadcast over 1,450 stations across the country as well as on Satellite Radio Family Talk Channel 170 and Sirius Satellite Radio Family Net Channel 159. Although not an explicitly religious program, Dobson and his guests deal with topics related to Christian family values.

Hal Lindsey Report

Hal Lindsey, popular author of books dealing with biblical prophecy, discusses current events in the context of Bible prophecy on this weekly television program broadcast available on the Daystar satellite network.

Issues, Etc.

Todd Wilken, former pastor in the Lutheran Church Missouri Synod (LCMS), hosts this daily radio talk show, which originates from the LCMS's St. Louis, Missouri, Jubilee Network. Approximately 100 radio stations nationwide broadcast the program. The program's stated purpose is "to call the Church back to the proclamation of Law and Gospel, Sin and Grace." Wilken interviews various religious figures, many of whom are from the religious right. Former Lutheran pastor Don Matzat hosts a three-hour Sunday evening edition of the program.

Jay Sekulow Live

On this daily radio program, Jay Sekulow, chief counsel for the American Center for Law and Justice, discusses current issues relevant to religious liberty and answers listeners' questions about specific cases regarding religious observance in such contexts as the public schools and the workplace.

John Ankerberg Show

Headquartered in Chattanooga, Tennessee, this syndicated evangelical Christian television program, hosted by John Ankerberg, presents defenses of orthodox evangelical Christianity against various cults and perceived heresies. Representatives of "heretical" groups are invited to take part in debate. The program presents conservative Christian positions on such issues as abortion and pornography. Since the September 11, 2001, terrorist attach, the program has aired segments on terrorism and Islam.

Life Today

This television program features James Robison and his wife Betty who discuss current the current missionary activities of the Life Outreach International organization, which provides assistance in countries around the world. The organization encourages adoption from other countries, although it does not participate directly in the adoption process. Various guests appear with James and Betty, and they take calls from the viewing audience.

Old-Time Gospel Hour

This program, which is seen on nearly 400 television stations and heard on 500 radio stations, features former leader of the Moral Majority Jerry Falwell. Falwell presents his fundamentalist beliefs and offers his views in opposition to abortion, homosexual rights, pornography, and crime. He often expresses strong criticism of liberals in government.

Renewing Your Mind

On this thirty-minute radio and television program (National Religious Broadcasters' Direct TV Channel 378), broadcast six days each week, R. C. Sproul, founder and head of Ligonier Ministries, offers Bible study from a conservative perspective and discusses such topics as systematic theology, ethics, and church history.

The 700 Club

Produced and syndicated by the Christian Broadcasting Network and hosted by Pat Robertson, this television program follows a talk- and variety-show format and offers news analysis from a conservative Christian perspective. Viewers are invited to call for counseling and prayer.

Stones Cry Out

This fifteen-minute weekly radio program, sponsored by Associates for Biblical Research, is heard on more than 200 stations in the United States. Host Clifford Wilson presents archaeological evidence supporting the historical reliability of the Bible.

Truths That Transform

On this daily radio program, D. James Kennedy, pastor of Coral Ridge Presbyterian Church in Fort Lauderdale, Florida, discusses issues of concern to conservative Christians, including such topics as abortion, Christian apologetics, creationism, personal spirituality, and Christian activism.

TV EVANGELISTS CALL SIGNALS FROM THE SAME PLAYBOOK:
TV PREACHERS SUPPORT, PROMOTE EACH OTHER

By Bill Smith and *Carolyn Tuft*

* Fifteen years after the scandals of the '80s, Joyce Meyer and a new breed of TV preachers are part of an evangelical renaissance. The end of the 1980s was a bad time for TV preachers. One moment, men like the PTL Club's Jim Bakker and television's Jimmy Swaggart seemed bigger than life, supermen who had been blessed with an uncanny ability to attract followers and money. The next, they were only men—fragile, flawed, and the butt of barroom jokes and newspaper cartoons. In many ways, it seemed like the beginning of the end for big-time TV religion. Look, the critics said, the emperors really have no clothes.

But Americans, at least many of them, seem to have forgotten and forgiven. TV's salvation shows are still here, bigger and flashier than ever, thanks to the proliferation of the Internet and the continued spread of satellite and cable TV. The names may have changed—Juanita Bynum, Kenneth and Gloria Copeland, Creflo Dollar, Benny Hinn, T.D. Jakes and St. Louis' Joyce Meyer have replaced Bakker, Swaggart and Oral Roberts at the top of the evangelical mountain—but the message remains virtually identical. Believe with all your heart and soul, they tell the faithful. And give, give, give until you can't give any more. God, they say, loves a cheerful giver.

In the late 1980s, when the sex and fraud scandals boiled over into America's living rooms, Joyce Meyer's little radio ministry was scarcely a blip on the evangelical radar screen. Today, Meyer heads a ministry with an annual income fast approaching $100 million a year, and she is among a dozen or so evangelical superstars headlining a revived, and very healthy, industry.

Wild and Wacky Theology

The word-faith, or prosperity, gospel has been dubbed by some critics the "name it and claim it" religion. God wants His people to prosper, evangelists like Meyer maintain. The proof, they say, is in the Bible. Give and you shall receive; sow and you shall reap.

But critics, from Bible-quoting theologians to groups devoted to preserving the separation of church and state, argue that the theology is simply wrong. At best, they argue, it is an excuse to take advantage of their followers to accrue power and wealth.

Michael Scott Horton, who teaches historical theology at the Westminster Theological Seminary in Escondido, Calif., calls the word-faith, or "seed-faith," message a twisted interpretation of the Bible—a "wild and wacky theology." "Some of these people are charlatans," Horton said. "Others are honestly dedicated to one of the most abhorrent errors in religious theology." "I often think of these folks as the religious equivalent to a combination of a National En-

---

Bill Smith and Carolyn Tuft are reporters for the *St. Louis Post-Dispatch*.

quirer ad and professional wrestling. It's part entertainment and very large part scam."

Sociologist William Martin of Rice University said that most people who follow TV religious leaders put so much trust in them that they want them to thrive. Martin is a professor of sociology at the university, specializing in theology. The preachers' wealth is "confirmation of what they are preaching," Martin said.

Ole Anthony's Dallas-based Trinity Foundation, best-known for working with the national media to uncover questionable activities involving TV evangelists, often resorts to digging through preachers' trash to find incriminating evidence. Anthony said that most of the preachers begin with a "sincere desire to spread the faith. But the pressure of fund raising slowly moves all of them in the direction of a greed-based theology."

Even J. Lee Grady, editor of Charisma & Christian Life magazine, has become alarmed at what he sees as the excesses of some TV preachers in their constant trolling for money. He is most concerned about preachers who guarantee that God will reward followers with new homes, cars or better jobs in exchange for their donations. Grady's concern is remarkable because his magazine gets most of its advertising from TV preachers. In the magazine's August issue, Grady wrote a column headlined "Fair Warning," in which he said: "Some charismatic churches in this country are headed for serious trouble."

Grady said he still believes in the principle that Christians who are generous with their money will be blessed, while those who are stingy will want. "But that doesn't mean you can treat God like a slot machine," Grady said in an interview. "It's not fair for a minister to get up and say, 'If you give tonight, you'll be rich.' ... What if you are living immorally and give an offering? That's not a guarantee that you will be blessed."

"Let's cut out the craziness and manipulation and the shenanigans and the pressure that is rampant right now." Even Bakker, who spent five years in prison for defrauding Heritage USA investors, says he has had a change of heart about the prosperity gospel. The same man who once told his PTL coworkers that "God wants you to be rich" now says he made a tragic mistake. "For years, I helped propagate an impostor, not a true gospel, but another gospel," Bakker said in his 1996 book, "I Was Wrong." "The prosperity message did not line up with the tenor of the Scripture. My heart was crushed to think that I led so many people astray."

I am Here. It Worked

While Bakker may have changed his beliefs—he now uses the same Bible passages to criticize the prosperity theology that he once used to defend it—many more TV preachers are adamant that the more a Christian gives, the more he will receive.

Meyer spends much of her three-day conferences emphasizing the importance of giving. Her critics, she says, are simply wrong. "Why would He (God) want all of his people poverty stricken while all of the people that aren't living for God have everything?" Meyer said. "I think it's old religious thinking, and I believe the devil uses it to keep people from wanting to serve God."

In Tampa, TV preacher Rodney Howard-Browne went so far as to tell his flock that if they gave to the building fund for his River at Tampa Bay church, they could expect God to give them a house in return. "For whatever he sows, it is what he will reap," Howard-Browne said. "People stop reaping because they quit sowing."

Randy White, a TV preacher from the other end of Tampa at the Without Walls International church, told his followers in September that if they were broke, they should still give to his church. "If you don't have anything to give, ask the person beside you to borrow $100," White said. "If they don't have it, ask them to give you a blank check. I'm asking everyone to give."

Those who support the ministries say they have seen first-hand the miracles of seed-faith giving. Rallies and church services are filled with people who say they are living proof of the seed-faith message.

At a recent Sunday morning service in Meyer's Dream Center, Luchae Manning of St. Louis said she was jobless and homeless when she began volunteering at the center. Almost from the moment she began donating 10 percent of her state aid check to the ministry, her life began to change. She says she now has a GED and her own apartment. "I have a car," she told those who had crowded into the sanctuary. "And it's not an old, raggedy car." "I am here. It worked."

Preachers Teach Each Other

Fifteen years have passed since Bakker's Praise the Lord empire turned to dust, the victim of a motel tryst with Jessica Hahn and a criminal conviction of defrauding thousands of investors in his Heritage USA theme park. Swaggart, too, fell fast and hard, after a rival minister caught him meeting with a prostitute. His guilt-ridden, tear-streaked face still graces mocking Internet Web sites.

Even Roberts, dubbed the father of television evangelism, took fire for claiming that God would "call me home" unless his viewers sent him $8 million, a statement seen by some as a form of evangelical blackmail. Since then, cooperation among televangelists seems to be growing. They regularly contribute money to each other's ministries and often come together for rallies and conferences.

When one comes up with a new idea for making more money, the others seem to follow. In September, Meyer stood on stage before 3,000 worshippers in Randy and Paula White's church in Tampa. Meyer, clearly the biggest name of the three, told the flock that they had to start copying each others' successes. She told them how Paula White, an up-and-coming preacher with a TV show of her own, wanted to pick Meyer's brain to find out how Meyer had become one of the most successful women evangelists.

She said White wanted to ask her: " 'How did you do this? How did you do that? What about this? What about that?'... She wants to know how I got where I am, because she has a dream and a vision." Paula White, sitting in a chair on the side of the stage, smiled and nodded. Days later the Whites hosted a five-day "Fall Campmeeting" session, a kind of classroom for new preachers. Creflo Dollar, Jesse Duplantis and Robert Kayanja appeared to share their knowledge.

Start-up ministers begin by organizing with the IRS as a tax-exempt religious organization. That allows them to accept tax-free donations, buy and sell products like books and videotapes—mostly free of sales taxes—and keep their financial books closed to the public and the government. Most set up boards made up of themselves, friends and family members. Some board members are also employees of the ministries.

Next, an upwardly mobile TV evangelist needs to find a way to get on cable television. The cost can be relatively inexpensive, depending on the station. The more and bigger the stations, the bigger the audience. The bigger the audience, the bigger the gifts to support the ministry and the ministers.

Paul and Jan Crouch's Trinity Broadcast Network, home to some of the biggest names in TV evangelism, is considered the top of the Christian TV ladder's rung and a kingmaker, or queenmaker, for television preachers.

The Internet

The ministers now have added another medium: the Internet. An Internet check turns up a seemingly endless number of preachers asking for prayers and money. Many of the sites point to their ministry's support of a variety of outreach programs, such as programs for hungry or abandoned children. The sites often show the preacher's TV program 24 hours a day.

Most televangelists release dozens of self-help and religious books and tapes that are available to their followers who send them a set donation.

The newest tool to assure a continuous pipeline of funding allows supporters to make direct monthly deductions from their bank accounts. Ministries tout it as a "more convenient" method of monthly giving.

Many also make use of marketing companies to saturate a certain demographic group with requests for money. Using target lists, the preachers send out mailers and catalogs. Some send out "free gifts"—small booklets with inspirational messages, blessed cornflower and bottles of holy water—through the mail to woo the recipients to send money to them.

Last month, Meyer began using her Web site to ask followers to send the ministry money for $7 million worth of new TV equipment to help her improve the quality of her show, saying she needs to compete with sports shows and movies on television. In return, she promised to send out free crystal globes—small, medium and large—depending on whether the follower's gift was $100, $500 or $1,000.

As a result, many of the ministries have enjoyed astonishing success. Of the 17 ministries researched by the Post-Dispatch, six surpass the $100 million-a-year mark.

Attempts to Police the Industry

Even before the televangelist scandals of the 1980s, many in the business had begun quietly looking for ways to recover their credibility. A watchdog group called the Evangelical Council for Financial Accountability was set up in 1979. In 1989, after the scandals, the group began random on-site checks to verify that cooperating ministries were following their standards. The group's goal: to help "Christ-centered organizations earn the public's trust through developing and maintaining standards of accountability that convey God-honoring ethical practices."

The council monitors how much money a preacher raises and how the money is used. The group then provides the financial information free on the Internet. The problem: Most TV preachers don't participate. Of the 17, including Meyer, surveyed by the Post-Dispatch, only the Rev. Billy Graham's ministry is a member of the group. The council has said it has received no financial information from any of the rest.

Because internal policing has fallen short, an external watchdog group is trying to fill in. The group—Wall Watchers Ministries—sends out questionnaires to 400 of the largest Christian ministries in the United States. Wall Watchers asks for full financial disclosure of revenue and expenses for each group. Wall Watchers then grades the religious group for its willingness to share its financial information with the world. Wall Watchers gave Meyer an F, or failing, grade. That's because Meyer's ministry refused to disclose how she raises or spends the $95 million a year her ministry is taking in.

Of the rest of the ministries researched by the Post-Dispatch, five more—Dollar, Hinn, the Copelands, TBN Christian network owners Paul and Jan Crouch, and Kenneth Hagin - got an F grade from Wall Watchers. The 11 others were not listed as ministries researched by Wall Watchers.

Last month, Wall Watchers called on the IRS and Congress to investigate the finances of Meyer and other TV preachers, specifically mentioning the ones who got failing grades. "Such a high level of profitability is appalling for a ministry," said Wall Watchers founder Rusty Leonard. "However you slice it, what they're doing is wrong." "If a ministry or person is going to solicit money by invoking the name of Jesus Christ, they should certainly be completely open with their finances." Tom Winters, Meyer's lawyer from Tulsa, Okla., said that everything Meyer's ministry has done is legal. Meyer herself says only that the ministry has no obligation to release specific financial information.

Graham is the only TV evangelists to get an A grade from Wall Watchers. Graham's ministry, in fact, helped form the Evangelical Council for Financial Accountability. His records, available on the groups' Web sites, show that Graham took in $117.8 million in 2001, the latest year for which the information is available. In 2000, Graham got $197,911 in salary, benefits and an expense account for his work as chairman of the ministry, according to the latest figures available from the organization.

Nearly every TV preacher talks about aspiring to be like Graham. Yet, most evangelists operate differently. The most obvious difference: Graham has an independent board that votes on what his ministry can do. To theologian Horton, the difference is that most TV preachers today have only one goal in mind: to personally prosper. "With the exception of Billy Graham, it is hard to see any of the televangelists who are not personally flourishing today," Horton said.

Sociologist William Martin at Rice University sees little changing in the way that television evangelists do business, at least in the near future. TV preachers will continue to prosper, he said, and journalists will continue to report their excesses. And their supporters, Martin said, will continue to "chalk it up to a liberal media controlled by Satan."

Internet Resources

Like many interest groups in the United States, conservative Christian organizations have taken advantage of the Internet to convey their message to the general public. As commonly happens, the presence of one viewpoint encourages the expression of opposing perspectives. Therefore, included in this category are websites that represent the positions of the religious right as well as those that present critical views of conservative Christianity. In addition to such sites as D. James Kennedy's Center for Reclaiming America and the Liberty Council are opposing sources such as People for the American Way and the Anti-Defamation League's Religion in the Public Schools.

The Advocate

http://www.advocate.com

The Advocate, a national gay and lesbian newsmagazine Internet site, contains segments critical of those organizations and individuals on the religious right, such as the Christian Action Network, that oppose attempts by homosexuals to gain recognition of various rights.

American Reformation Project

http://www.americanreformation.org

This site, dedicated to reforming American politics and churches, contains commentary on such topics as abortion, crime, national defense, gun control, drug abuse, education, and election reform. Links are provided to recent news stories.

The American Religious Right

http://www.webpan.com/dsinclair/rright.html

This site, which is critical of conservative Christian political activity, provides links to many other sites related to the religious right. The site includes quotes from religious right organizations and leaders.

American Theological Library Association

http://www.atla.com

The American Theological Library Association offers for purchase a religion database that includes 366,000 journal articles, 14,500 edited works containing 192,000 articles, 357,000 book reviews, and 1,461 journal titles (600 of which are currently indexed).

Antigay Propaganda of the Religious Right

http://www.qrd.org/grd/www/RRR/propag.html

This site offers evaluations of the religious right position on homosexuality and includes sources on such topics as gays in the military, attacks against gays, and civil liberties for homosexuals.

Attacks on the Freedom to Learn Online

http://www.pfaw.org

This website newsletter, maintained by People for the American Way, reports on school censorship and what the organization considers an assault on public education by religious right groups, including attempts to introduce school prayer, the teaching of creationism in science courses, and passage of "parental rights" legislation.

The Barna Group

http://www.barna.org

The Barna Group, directed by George Barna, provides various resources for individuals, churches, and ministers. The site includes regular updates on such religious topics as American attitudes toward religious belief, religious behavior, and popular culture. The Group provides information on many subjects, including religious beliefs, the Bible, evangelism, the mass media, economics, and parenting.

Beliefnet

http://www.beliefnet.com

This site offers information on various religious topics, links to other sites, and blogs presenting opinion on issues relevant to religious belief.

Bibleinfo.com

http://en.bibleinfo.com

This site contains resources for those wishing to study the Bible. Over 340 Bible topics are available. Individuals may ask Bible questions and make prayer requests. A page gives answers to frequently asked questions.

Biblical Conservatism: Toward a Definition of a Political Philosophy

http://www.natreformassn.org/statesman/96/polphil.html

James L. Sauer discusses conservatism and Christianity, stating that "there is a sense in which all Christians, at least all consistent, orthodox and Biblical ones, are conservative."

Center for Reclaiming America for Christ

http://reclaimamerica.org

This website, maintained by D. James Kennedy's Coral Ridge Ministries, asserts that it "provides nonpartisan, interdenominational information, training, and support to all those interested in positively affecting the culture and renewing the vision of our Founding Fathers." Topics covered include the homosexual rights movement, abortion, and the importance of morality in law.

Christian Broadcasting Network

http://www.cbn.com

The Christian Broadcasting Network (CBN), founded by religious right leader Pat Robertson in 1960, offers information about the network's history, its present organization, and individuals involved in its management. CBN requests donations from those visiting the site.

Christian Reconstructionism
http://www.qrd.org/QRD/www/RRR/recon.html

This site contains several sources on Christian reconstructionism, a postmillennial view that Christians have the obligation to establish moral government here on earth prior to Christ's return.

Christian Reconstructionism, Dominion Theology and Theonomy
http://www.religioustolerance.org/reconstr.htm

This site contains information about Christian reconstructionism, a belief that contemporary society, which is morally degenerate, must be reformed according to biblical principles.

Christians on the Net
http://www.christiansnet.com

The site contains over thirty-five Christian e-mail discussion lists, including those engaged in Bible study, conservative Christian discussion, and the history of evangelical Christianity.

Creation Research Society
http://www.creationresearch.org

The Creation Research Society adheres to a creationist view of the origins of the universe, which it calls "scientific special creation." The Society sells books and videotapes and publishes the *CRS Quarterly*.

CultureWatch
http://www.damaris.org/cw

This site offers articles on various media subjects, including books, films, music, and television, from a Christian perspective.

Eleven Things You Can Do to Fight the Religious Right
http://www.galah.org/11things.html

The organization Gay and Lesbian Atheists and Humanists suggests methods that those sympathetic to their cause can employ to oppose the religious right.

Ethics and Religious Liberty Commission
http://www.erlc.com

Associated with the Southern Baptist Convention (SBC), this site contains information about current political and social issues. For instance, the site includes the 1997 SBC Resolution on Moral Stewardship and the Disney Company, which charges that Disney promotes "immoral ideologies such as homosexuality, infidelity, and adultery." The resolution urges Southern Baptists not to purchase Disney products.

Fight the Right Action Kit
http://www.qrd.org/qrd/www/FTR/tblcntnt.html

This site includes information on various topics, including religious right views of homosexuality and race and religious right organizations such as the Christian Coalition and Concerned Women for America. Strategies are suggested for competing with religious right organizations in the political arena.

Freedom of Religion and Belief

http://www.aclu.org/religion/index.html

The American Civil Liberties Union advocates strict separation of religion from the public realm.

Gospel Communications Network Online Christian Resources

http://www.gospelcom.net

Gospel Communications Network, an association of organizations committed to traditional Christian beliefs, is dedicated to disseminating information about the gospel on the World Wide Web.

Hal Lindsey Oracle

http://www.hallindseyoracle.com

Hal Lindsey, popular author of works dealing with the relevance of Bible prophecy to current events, presents news items from the United States and around the world, interpreting them in the context of a premillennial view of Christian doctrine.

Institute for the Study of Religion in Politics (ISRP)

http://www.isrp.org

Although this organization holds many of the same beliefs espoused by those on the religious right—including labeling "secular humanism" a major threat to humankind—it opposes the intrusion of religion into politics.

Interfaith Alliance

http://www.interfaithalliance.org

The Alliance dedicates itself to protecting the basic freedoms of speech, press, and religion from the restrictive tendencies of groups that wish to exercise political power. The group intends to assist in building a mainstream religious movement active in civic participation.

Kingdom Identity Ministries

http://www.kingidentity.com

This site contains a doctrinal statement of Kingdom Identity Ministries, an organization contending that God has chosen a select group of people for salvation. Also included are a directory of radio broadcasts and a catalog of books, audiotapes, and videocassettes that may be purchased.

Liberty Counsel

http://www.lc.org

This website is maintained by the Liberty Counsel, which describes itself as a religious civil liberties education and legal defense organization. The site includes news accounts of issues of importance to the religious right, including advocacy of prayer in the public schools.

People for the American Way
http://www.pfaw.org

Claiming to be "the largest resource of religious right materials," People for the American Way presents information critical of conservative Christian political activities. The organization claims to be a watchdog, monitoring and countering information that religious right organizations submit to the mass media.

Promise Keepers Online
http://promisekeepers.org

This site contains information about future conferences sponsored by the Promise Keepers, described as "a Christ-centered ministry dedicated to uniting men through vital relationships to become godly influences in their world."

Promise Keepers: A Real Challenge from the Right
http://www.now.org/nnt/05-97/pk.html

On this site the National Organization for Women offers information about the Promise Keepers and its founder, Bill McCartney. This male-only self-improvement organization is said to advance "an ultra-conservative social and political agenda."

Purpose Driven Life
http://www.purposedrivenlife.com

This web site revolves around Rick Warren, pastor of Saddleback Church in Lake Forest, California, and author of the best-selling book *The Purpose Driven Life* (2002). The site presents information and advice about living a better life. Unlike many evangelical leaders, Warren focuses on social and economic conditions, calling these problems the five "Global Goliaths"—"spiritual emptiness," "egocentric leadership," poverty, disease, and illiteracy.

The Quarterly Journal
http://www.pfo.org/resources2.htm

Maintained by Personal Freedom Outreach, this site contains articles from back issues of *The Quarterly Journal* that offer critical analyses of Christian right evangelists and other religious personalities.

The Radical Religious Right
http://www.qrd.org/qrd/www/RRR/rrrpage.html

Supportive of gay rights, this site provides links to various resources on the religious right as well as sites critical of conservative Christian organizations and issue positions.

Religion in the Public Schools

http://www.adl.org/religion_ps_2004/

The Anti-Defamation League (ADL) presents information about the issue of prayer in schools, including religion in the curriculum, the evolution versus creationism controversy, student religious clubs, dress codes, teachers' religious expression, and teaching about religious holidays.

Religious Freedom

http://www.religious-freedom.org

This website provides information about laws that protect religious freedom as a fundamental right, and informs individuals about the right to worship as they wish. A key concern is the Religious Freedom Restoration Act, which was intended to protect free exercise of religion.

The Rise of the Religious Right in the Republican Party

http://www.theocracywatch.org

This site traces the development of political ties between religious right organizations and the Republican party. Advice is given for responding to the influence of the religious right.

The Secular Web

http://www.infidels.org

This Web site contains sources on various topics critical of religion, including videos, books, periodicals, and organizations around the world.

Toward Tradition

http://towardtradition.org

Toward Tradition is an educational group of Jews and Christians dedicated to limited government, representative democracy, the free market system, a strong military, and morality in the political realm. Rabbi Daniel Lapin, the organization's president, has conducted a series of lectures that are available for purchase.

Turning Point

http://www.gnnradio.org/framedj.htm

This website presents an online version of David Jeremiah's radio program of the same name. The site states that "Turning Point stands for the supreme authority of the Word of God."

Wallbuilder Report

http://www.wallbuilders.com/resources

This online newsletter issued three times each year covers such topics as the contemporary culture war, current political issues, patriotism, and the religious history of the United States.

Glossary

Antichrist   The Antichrist is a beguiling, satanic figure who supposedly will wreak havoc on Earth, particularly upon Israel and the Jews, until his ultimate destruction by Jesus at the battle of Armageddon. At various times the Antichrist has been identified with everyone from the Catholic popes, Charles I, and George III to Hitler, Ronald Reagan, and Saddam Hussein.

Apocalypse   Of Greek derivation, apocalypse means to uncover or reveal the future, specifically regarding the Second Coming of Christ. Couched in bizarre symbolism intelligible only to believers, apocalyptic literature not only points toward the deliverance of God's people from earthly travail, but also looks beyond the end of time. For examples of such writing, see Mark 13:3–31, II Thessalonians 2:3–12, Revelation, and Daniel.

Armageddon   This is the site of the climactic battle between the forces of good and evil, between Jesus and Satan. As foretold in Revelation, a warrior Jesus will descend from heaven garbed in battle armor and mounted on a white steed to defeat the followers of the Beast (Satan). This is a strongly held view among many conservative Christians who subscribe to a literal interpretation of Revelation, an interpretation at the heart of the *Left Behind* novels by Tim LaHaye and Jerry Jenkins.

Baptism of the Holy Spirit   See Pentecostalism.

Born Again   In John 3:3–7 Jesus tells Nicodemus that he "must be born over again" in order to "see the kingdom of God." Accordingly, in contemporary parlance, a "born again Christian" is one who allegedly has had a personal, emotional encounter with God through Jesus.

Cane Ridge Revival   This was an enormous camp meeting near Lexington, Kentucky, in August 1801. Noted for its emotional excesses, such as the "jerks" and the "barks," this revival fueled the Second Awakening in the American West and gave momentum to such evangelicals as Methodists, Baptists, Cumberland Presbyterians, and, later, Disciples and Christians.

Charismatic Movement   Characterized by emotional, ecstatic forms of worship in which speaking in tongues and faith healing are encouraged, this is a twentieth-century phenomenon. Protestants and Catholics, especially since the 1960s, have been influenced by this movement.

Charitable Choice   This term refers to the practice of allowing faith-based organizations to bid on federal contracts for various social services, such as housing, job training, and drug and prison rehabilitation. The welfare reform legislation passed in 1996 permits this, and many religious and social conservatives applaud it, convinced religious institutions do a better job than secular ones at providing certain services for the needy. A concern of many critics is that charitable choice, aside from the fundamental issue of church-state separation, neither proscribes faith-based organizations from proselytizing nor ensures compliance with federal laws regarding such things as gender and racial discrimination.

Chiliasm   See Millennialism.

Christian Reconstructionism   Drawing primarily upon Genesis 1:26–28 and Matthew 28:16–20, this movement, which apparently evolved from teachings at J. Gresham Machen's Westminster Theological Seminary, attempts to reconstruct society in accordance with God's law. Guided by the example of the seventeenth-century Puritans, who had sought to build the Massachusetts Commonwealth on biblical principles, Christian reconstructionists want to subordinate all aspects of life to God's authority. Accordingly, they encourage Christian schooling, certain that public education has been corrupted by secular humanism, condemn the modern state, convinced it has usurped the authority of God, and embrace an optimistic eschatology, persuaded of the possibility of constructive change. In pursuit of their objectives, however, Christian reconstructionists do not advocate civil disobedience.

Civil Religion   Broadly, this refers to the usage of transcendent religious symbols to explain national purpose and destiny. On one hand, civil religion provides a unifying set of values for Americans of all persuasions, values which inspire the pursuit of justice and equality of treatment for all people; on the other hand, when suffused with an intense nationalism where God and country become one, civil religion easily gives support to aggression abroad and intolerance at home.

Compassionate Conservatism   Derived in large part from Marvin Olasky's *The Tragedy of American Compassion* (1992), compassionate conservatism nourishes both the soul and the body, in contrast to the "false compassion" of the existing welfare state which allegedly doles out material aid without imposing discipline on the poor or providing spiritual guidance. Based on the assumption that religion and government have in America's past worked closely together, compassionate conservatism today looks to "faith-based" institutions to administer various programs to help the needy. And for doing this, faith-based institutions would receive tax support.

Creationism (Scientific Creationism)   First enunciated in *What Is Darwinism?* (1874) by Charles Hodge, a noted Presbyterian theologian at Princeton Theological Seminary, creationism is the belief that the Genesis account of the world's origin is historically true and accurate. Promoted today primarily by conservative Christians, creationism is an alternative explanation to Darwinian evolution for human origins. Although all creationists attribute creation to God, as described in the early chapters of Genesis, they differ among themselves on critical points. Those who tend to be biblical literalists insist that God created the various species, each of which reproduces its own kind, in a short span of time. Those who interpret Genesis allegorically are inclined to agree with conventional geologists regarding Earth's ancient origins. While divided over geology, creationists are usually united in their opposition to Darwinian biology.

Death of God Theology   Based upon *The Death of God* by Gabriel Vahanian, this movement gained attention in the 1960s. Arguing that many educated Americans no longer relied on God to explain phenomena once attributed to the divine, such as natural disasters and sickness, Vahanian labored to recast Christian theology without a doctrine of God. Many conservative Christians saw this movement as just another indication of the nation's growing godlessness.

Dispensational Premillennialism   This theory was popularized by C. I. Scofield of Dallas, Texas, in 1909. Scofield divided history into seven dispensations, or eras, each beginning with a divine covenant and ending with God's judgment. He believed humanity was nearing the end of the sixth dispensation, which would culminate in the Second Coming of Jesus, who then would preside over the world for a millennium.

Dominion (Kingdom) Theology   Used by politically involved evangelicals, this term lends biblical sanction to efforts to Christianize the nation's political, economic, legal, educational, military, and communications institutions. Dominion theology undergirds much of Christian reconstructionism.

Election (Predestination)   The belief that certain people and groups have been foreordained to fulfill God's divine purposes, this view undergirds Israel's position as God's chosen people, as well as the New Testament belief of humanity's underserved. Given the influence of such conservative Presbyterians as Charles Hodge, Benjamin Warfield, J. Gresham Machen, and Carl McIntire, this sentiment runs deep among many American fundamentalists.

Eschatology   Derived from two Greek words, eschatology means "end" or "final." Central to eschatology, therefore, are beliefs about death, resurrection, the Second Coming, judgment, and the Kingdom of God. In both the Old and New Testaments, eschatological writers were concerned with the ultimate triumph of God over evil.

Evangelical   Derived from a Greek word meaning "good news," evangelical refers to those Christians who emphasize a personal relationship to Jesus ("born again"), biblical authority in matters of faith and practice, and the necessity of sharing the Gospel with others (witnessing). Since the late 1940s many conservative Christians, such as Billy Graham, have preferred to be known as evangelicals rather than fundamentalists because of the negative image many Americans have of fundamentalism.

Faith-Based Institutions   See Charitable Choice and Compassionate Conservatism.

Fundamentalism   By the 1920s the terms "fundamentalist," "evangelical," and "conservative Christian" were more or less synonymous, each referring broadly to those Christians who subscribed to the five or six basic fundamentals set forth at the Niagara Bible Conference of 1895 and in *The Fundamentals: A Testimony to the Truth* (1910–1915). But the term "fundamentalism," coined in 1920, increasingly became identified with an aggressively strident and exclusionist variety of conservative Christianity, and critics increasingly applied the term pejoratively and indiscriminately to all conservative Christians. As a result, conservative Christians such as those who founded the National Association of Evangelicals in 1942 preferred the term evangelical to fundamentalist. As this suggests, the difference today between a fundamentalist and an evangelical is more a matter of temperament than theology.

Glossolalia (Speaking In Tongues)   Apparently coined in the nineteenth century, glossolalia refers to the New Testament practice of "speaking in tongues." Acts 2:4 reports that on the day of Pentecost the Apostles "were all filled with the Holy Ghost and began to speak with other tongues as the Spirit gave them utterance." Christians have never been of one mind regarding this practice. Today, for instance, Pentecostal bodies, such as the Assemblies of God, encourage tongues, but the Baptist fundamentalist Jerry Falwell disapproves.

Gog, Magog   Various biblical passages—Daniel 11:15, Jeremiah 1:14, Ezekiel 38, and Revelation 20:8—allude to an evil ruler, Gog, from the northern land of Magog. In the Cold War aftermath of World War II, many American fundamentalists identified Russia as Magog and interpreted conflicting American and Russian interests in Israel and the Middle East in light of biblical prophecy. Such views influenced even former President Ronald Reagan.

Great Tribulation   See Rapture.

Heterodoxy (Heresy)   This term is used for a departure from established beliefs and traditions. For fundamentalists, for instance, the denial of such things as the virgin birth and resurrection of Jesus would be heterodoxy.

Higher Criticism   This is a scientific examination of biblical texts, attempting to determine authorship, date of composition, and place of origin. Higher critics study such questions as, Did Moses write all of the Pentateuch? and Was there a second Isaiah? To many conservative Christians from the nineteenth century to the present, this kind of scrutiny undermines the veracity of the scriptures.

Identity Christianity   Based upon the belief that white Anglo-Saxons are God's chosen people and that Jews and all other non-whites are a subspecies of humanity, Identity Christianity unites such white supremacist groups as the Ku Klux Klan and Aryan Nations.

Imminency   This is the belief that the Second Coming could occur at any moment. This idea fuels much of the millennial speculation regarding the end of time and has contributed to the enormous popularity of the *Left Behind* series of novels by Tim LaHaye and Jerry Jenkins.

Inerrancy   This refers to a belief common among many Protestants since the later nineteenth century that the Bible is without error in its "original autographs" with regard to history, science, and accounts of its literary origins. A remarkable similarity exists between Presbyterian inerrantists Charles Hodge and Benjamin Warfield of the 1880s and Southern Baptist inerrantists of the 1980s. For both, the Bible would be an unreliable guide on matters of salvation and humanity's relationship to God if it were known to be in error on matters of history and science. Inerrantists, of course, concede that scribal errors have over time slipped into existing biblical texts.

Lower Criticism   A scientific examination of biblical texts, lower criticism seeks to ascertain the actual words of a manuscript as it was originally written by the author; or, slightly differently, to determine how accurately existing translations reflect what was said or written. This kind of study poses no serious problem for conservative Christians, for they too are concerned about the accuracy of existing biblical texts and translations. While insisting that the Bible is inerrant in its "original autographs," conservative Christians concede that scribal errors and discrepancies have slipped into the texts over time.

Mark of the Beast (666)   Quite similar to Daniel 7:2–8, Revelation 13:1–18 describes a Beast, or an Antichrist that rivals Jesus in the final days, and ascribes to it the number "666," the presumed numerical equivalent of the Beast's name. The followers of the Beast were to be branded on either the right hand or the forehead with the triple six.

Millennialism   This refers to a thousand-year period in which the kingdom of God will prevail. Christians are usually divided over whether the Second Coming of Jesus will occur before (premillennialists) or after (postmillennialists) the thousand-year reign. Millennial expectations are fueled by the apocalyptic portion of the Bible, especially Revelation, and groups such as the Seventh Day Adventists and Jehovah's Witnesses reflect the influence of millennial ideas.

Modernism   Although many conservative Christians by the 1920s used modernism loosely to cover a multitude of alleged "sins," scholars usually use the term more precisely to mean (1) the adjustment of religious ideas to contemporary culture, (2) the immanence of God in human development, and (3) the belief that history is evolving toward the Kingdom of God. As this suggests, modernism is an optimistic view, one at sharp odds with the conservative Christian emphasis upon original sin and human depravity.

Natural Theology   Broadly, this is the belief that God can be fathomed by reason alone without the need of scripture or revelation. For instance, subscribers to this view would argue that the order of nature, as well as purposeful human existence, affords rational evidence of an intelligent Creator. This attempt at human self-sufficiency disturbs many Christian thinkers who believe that God is more than can be grasped by reason alone. To many Christians, the God of natural theology is little more than a projected image of humanity, a God limited by the human senses.

New Age Movement   Drawing upon both Eastern and Western religious traditions, this phenomenon gained momentum in the 1980s. Its adherents subscribe to an eclectic assortment of beliefs and practices, such as reincarnation, astral projection, astrology, extraterrestrial life, astrology, immortality of the soul, miracles, angels, and yoga.

Original Autographs   This refers to the original biblical manuscripts which were untainted by scribal errors. Although these texts do not exist, inerrantists in the tradition of Charles Hodge, Benjamin Warfield, and J. Gresham Machen contend the Bible cannot be proven to be in error unless the discrepancy exists in the original autographs, which, of course, are unavailable for scrutiny.

Original Sin   Based primarily upon the creation story and the fall of Adam and Eve from grace in the opening chapters of Genesis, this is the Christian doctrine of flawed humanity.

Orthodoxy   Derived from the Greek words "*orthos*" (correct) and "*doxa*" (opinion), orthodoxy refers to "correct" or "right" beliefs.

Pentecostalism   Drawing upon Acts 1:1–5 and 2:4–21, modern pentecostalism stresses those gifts resulting from "baptism in the Holy Spirit," such as glossolalia, prophecy, healing, and exorcism. Historically, contemporary pentecostalism emerged from the Holiness tradition within Methodism and the Asuza Street revival in Los Angeles, California, in 1906. While its early adherents were largely poor and disinherited, Pentecostals have become increasingly middle class. The predominantly African-American denomination, Churches of God in Christ, is the largest Pentecostal body in the United States today, followed by the white-dominated Assemblies of God.

Postmillennialism   This is the belief that steadily improving world conditions will culminate in the Second Coming. By this interpretation, Jesus will return *after* a millennium of human progress. This optimistic viewpoint not only reinforced the reform efforts of liberal social gospel ministers in the late nineteenth and early twentieth centuries, but also undergirds the labors of contemporary Christian reconstructionists.

Premillennialism   This refers to the belief that steadily deteriorating world conditions (wars and rumors of wars) will precede the Second Coming, at which time Jesus will establish a thousand-year reign. Thus, Jesus will return *before* the millennium. This viewpoint is generally more harmonious with a conservative, pessimistic assessment of contemporary world conditions, and is the backdrop for the popular *Left Behind* series by Tim LaHaye and Jerry Jenkins.

Pro-Life (Right-to-Life) Movement   Originating among Roman Catholics, this movement today embraces Catholics, Protestants, and others opposed to abortion. The Supreme Court's decision in *Roe v. Wade* (1973), which legalized abortion during the first two trimesters of pregnancy, gave impetus to the movement.

Prophecy   Derived from a Greek word meaning one who speaks for another, prophecy supposedly is an expression of divine will. Unlike apocalyptic literature, however, which forecasts the end of time, prophetic literature is present-minded, predicting dire consequences in this life if "God's people" persist in their wicked ways. Examples of the prophetic tradition among the ancient Hebrews are Amos, Joel, Isaiah, Jeremiah, Ezekiel, and Elijah.

Rapture   This refers to that moment when Christ supposedly will come to resurrect the righteous who have already died and to remove, or harvest, the righteous who are still alive, and they will all rise to meet Christ in the sky. This will leave the forces of evil in complete control of the earth for seven years, the period of the "Great Tribulation." In both literature and art, many contemporary Christians portray a world in chaos after the Rapture. Contrary to popular thought, this was not a significant aspect of Christian thought until the 1840s or so, when it was popularized by John Nelson Darby, a former member of the Church of Ireland who emerged as the leader of the Plymouth Brethren. Darby's idea of dispensational premillennialism was subsequently popularized in America by C. I. Scofield.

Revivalism   This word refers to a reawakening or quickening of the divine spirit, an awakening sometimes accompanied by emotional fervor. Scholars usually trace the phenomenon from Solomon Stoddard, Jonathan Edwards, and George Whitefield to James McGready, Barton Stone, and Charles G. Finney. The Great Awakening (1720s-1740s) swept the eastern seaboard, while the Second Awakening (1790s-1830s) carried the Gospel via emotional camp meetings across the western frontier. Methodists, Baptists, Cumberland Presbyterians, and Disciples prospered during this second wave of revivalism. Of particular interest to scholars have been the techniques of revivalism, with debate sometimes centering on whether revivals were "sent down" by God or "worked up" by more human methods.

Schism   This term means a factious division, or split, of a religious body. Although sometimes used synonymously, schism and heresy are not the same. Heresy always involves doctrinal matters, whereas schism results primarily from disputes over authority and organizational structure.

Scofield Reference Bible   Published in 1909 by Oxford University Press, this perhaps has been the most influential source of John Nelson Darby's dispensational premillennial teachings for American Protestants. Annotated by Cyrus I. Scofield, a lawyer-turned-Congregational preacher, it was originally meant to be a portable reference for missionaries. Since Scofield's commentaries appeared on the same page as the biblical text, it was easy for readers to forget whether a particular idea came from Scofield or the Bible. By 1967, when a revision was released, at least five million copies had been sold.

Secular Humanism   This is the belief that humans, relying upon reason and acting independently of God, are sufficient unto themselves. Some intellectual spokesmen for the religious right, such as Francis Schaeffer, trace this human-centered view from the Greeks through the Renaissance to the Enlightenment. An alleged consequence of this outlook is the replacement of God-centered absolutes with moral relativism. Much like "modernism" in the 1920s, secular humanism since the 1970s has become for the religious right a popular catchall for practically all social ills.

Situation Ethics   Coined in 1959 by Joseph Fletcher, situation ethics was a pragmatic and relativistic method for making moral judgments. It aroused the ire of many conservative Christians, implying as it did an abandonment of absolute standards of morality.

Social Gospel   This movement emerged among more liberal Protestants in the late nineteenth century and reached its peak in the optimistic years preceding World War I. Convinced that the Gospel message was social as well as personal, ministers such as Washington Gladden and Walter Rauschenbusch sought to focus the attention of the churches on social ills spawned by industrialization and urbanization. Many conservative Christians objected to the social gospel, believing its social emphasis detracted from the primary responsibility to individuals.

Theonomy   Coined by Cornelius Van Til of Westminster Theological Seminary, theonomy, derived from two Greek words, "*theos*" (God) and "*nomos*" law), is submission to God's law. As such, it is an argument for Christian reconstructionism, one steeped in Calvinistic influences. To Van Til, God's elect could grasp divine laws and live accordingly, while those who relied on human judgment, or autonomy, lived in darkness. Broadly, theonomy holds that Old Testament Law differentiates between right and wrong and, therefore, should be the basis for modern society.

Index

Photographs are indicated with *italic* page numbers and tables are indicated with page number and a (t).